Encyclopedia of Western Colonialism since 1450

FIRST EDITION

Encyclopedia of Western Colonialism since 1450

FIRST EDITION

VOLUME 3
P-Z

Thomas Benjamin
EDITOR IN CHIEF

MACMILLAN REFERENCE USA
An imprint of Thomson Gale, a part of The Thomson Corporation

THOMSON
GALE

Detroit • New York • San Francisco • San Diego • New Haven, Conn. • Waterville, Maine • London • Munich

Encyclopedia of Western Colonialism since 1450

Thomas Benjamin, Editor in Chief

© 2007 Thomson Gale, a part of The Thomson Corporation.

Thomson, Star Logo and Macmillan Reference USA are trademarks and Gale is a registered trademark used herein under license.

For more information, contact
Macmillan Reference USA
An imprint of Thomson Gale
27500 Drake Rd.
Farmington, Hills, MI 48331-3535
Or you can visit our Internet site at
http://www.gale.com

Since this page cannot legibly accommodate all copyright notices, the acknowledgments constitute an extension of the copyright notice.

While every effort has been made to ensure the reliability of the information presented in this publication, Thomson Gale does not guarantee the accuracy of the data contained herein. Thomson Gale accepts no payment for listing; and inclusion in the publication of any organization, agency, institution, publication, service, or individual does not imply endorsement of the editors or publisher. Errors brought to the attention of the publisher and verified to the satisfaction of the publisher will be corrected in future editions.

LIBRARY OF CONGRESS CATALOGING-IN-PUBLICATION DATA

Encyclopedia of Western colonialism since 1450 / Thomas Benjamin, editor in chief.
    p. cm.
  Includes bibliographical references and index.
  ISBN 0-02-865843-4 (set hardcover : alk. paper) – ISBN 0-02-865844-2 (vol 1 : alk. paper) – ISBN 0-02-865845-0 (vol 2 : alk. paper) – ISBN 0-02-865846-9 (vol 3 : alk. paper)
  1. Colonies–History–Encyclopedias. 2. Imperialism–History–Encyclopedias. 3. Postcolonialism–Encyclopedias. 4. Europe–Territorial expansion–Encyclopedias. I. Benjamin, Thomas, 1952-
    JV22.E535 2007
    325'.303–dc22
                        2006010042

This title is also available as an e-book.
ISBN 0-02-866085-4
Contact your Thomson Gale representative for ordering information.

Printed in the United States of America
10 9 8 7 6 5 4 3 2 1

Editorial Board

Editorial and Production Staff

PROJECT EDITOR

Jenai Mynatt

CONTRIBUTING EDITORS

Mark Drouillard
Rachel J. Kain
Christine Slovey

EDITORIAL TECHNICAL SUPPORT

Mark Springer

MANUSCRIPT EDITORS

Anthony C. Coulter
Judith Culligan
Gina Renee Misiroglu

ADDITIONAL EDITORIAL SUPPORT

Judith Clinebell

PROOFREADERS

Laura Patchkofsky

Diane Sawinski
Julie Van Pelt

TRANSLATOR

Loes Nas

INDEXER

Laurie Andriot

PRODUCT DESIGN

Kate Scheible
Tracey Rowens

IMAGING

Dean Dauphinais
Lezlie Light
Michael Logusz
Christine O'Bryan

GRAPHIC ART

XNR Productions

RIGHTS ACQUISITION AND MANAGEMENT

Ronald Montgomery
Shalice Shah-Caldwell
Andrew Specht

COMPOSITION

Evi Seoud
Mary Beth Trimper

MANUFACTURING

Wendy Blurton

DIRECTOR, NEW PRODUCT DEVELOPMENT

Hélène Potter

PUBLISHER

Jay Flynn

Contents

P

PACIFIC, AMERICAN PRESENCE IN

Two nineteenth-century novels of New Englander Herman Melville (1819–1891), *Typee* (1846) and *Omoo* (1847), based on his adventures as a whaling sailor in the Pacific Islands, set fire to the imagination of the West to Polynesia as a literary landscape, where missionaries and seamen exploited the decline of Polynesians. This Western view of a paradise in decline has been developed by artists and writers as diverse as French painter Paul Gauguin (1848–1903) and American author Paul Theroux (b. 1941). The vision of Polynesia as a declining paradise has not changed much since Melville, except in the writings of authors of Pacific Island ancestry, such as Hawaiian Haunani-Kay Trask (b. 1949) and Epeli Hau'ofa (b. 1939), who was born in Papua New Guinea to Tongan parents. Hau'ofa wrote in his influential essay "Our Sea of Islands," "There are no more suitable people on earth to be guardians of the world's largest ocean than those for whom it has been home for generations" (1993, p. 14).

Such early nineteenth-century industries as whaling and sandalwood quickly led Western countries to exploit the resources of the Pacific. The West also exploited the region for slave labor. South American and Australian slavers kidnapped entire island populations. The British enslaved the people of Tasmania, Australia, and the Torres Strait Islands, and the Americans enslaved native Puerto Ricans and Hawaiians. Slave trade was also conducted between Peru and the Pacific Islands.

Eighteenth-century European writers saw Polynesia as a paradise, while nineteenth-century Victorians, especially representatives of the missionary movements of New England and the London Missionary Society, saw Polynesia as a paradise lost. Pandemics of European diseases depleted generations of Pacific Islanders. The missionaries spread a monotheism that they claimed would protect the islanders from the diseases that the Europeans themselves had brought to the Pacific. The missionaries exploited the much-weakened condition of the islanders by claiming lands and eventually inciting takeovers by the United States and other Western nations.

The advent of missionaries in the Pacific led to the formation of plantations using Asian migrant and Pacific Islander slave labor. The missionaries also precipitated a search for shipping routes to Asia. It was this search for Pacific routes to Asia and Australia that set the eye of the United States on the great natural harbors of the Pearl River in the kingdom of Hawaii, as well as Pago Pago Bay in Samoa. Both harbors were mapped and explored by a U.S. naval expedition of six ships, led by Charles Wilkes (1798–1877) from 1838 to 1842. The expedition included such scientists as geologist James Dwight Dana (1813–1895) at a time when the Pacific region was still largely unknown in the West.

In 1876, with the help of the U.S. government, several former American missionaries forced Hawaii's leaders to agree to a reciprocity treaty in the sugar trade. The treaty limited the kingdom's economic dealings to trade with the United States, although Hawaiian King David Kalakaua (1836–1891) refused to cede Pearl Harbor. Kalakaua traveled to Washington, D.C., where a compromise was worked out. Hawaii would allow no other foreign countries to use its lands and ports. In return, Hawaiian sugar would be exported to the United States duty-free. By this time, sugar was the center of Hawaii's economy, and white Americans controlled the sugar plantations and such related businesses as shipping and banking. Kalakaua was deeply concerned about his people and their culture, but eventually the now wealthy and powerful Americans in Hawaii incited the U.S. military takeover of the Hawaiian kingdom in the 1890s.

U.S. naval strategists were inspired by Admiral Alfred Thayer Mahan's (1840–1914) theory of sea power as the key to world power. Mahan argued in *The Influence of Sea Power Upon History, 1660–1783* (1890), that there were three keys to sea power: "production, with the necessity of exchanging products, shipping, whereby the exchange is carried on, and colonies, which facilitate and enlarge the operations of shipping and tend to protect it by multiplying points of safety" (chap. 1).

Mahan's analysis coincided with important trends in domestic and international affairs, and it provided a timely rationale for both the emerging navalism and the expanding global role of the United States in the late nineteenth century. His 1890 book made him internationally known. His views would greatly influence the thinking of such political leaders as U.S. President Theodore Roosevelt (1858–1919) and Congressman Henry Cabot Lodge (1850–1924) and would help shape America's destiny at the turn of the century. By the twenty-first century, part of the U.S. Pacific Fleet was based in Hawaii, and most transpacific sea-lanes passed through the Hawaiian Islands.

Since the 1950s, many of the South Pacific islands have become tourist centers. In French Polynesia, Tahitian soldiers returning from fighting for France after World War II (1939–1945) questioned the oppression of Tahitians within their own nation by the French government. The independence movement they started, however, was suppressed and its leaders were imprisoned when producers arrived from Hollywood to film *Mutiny on the Bounty* with Marlon Brando in 1962. With the film, the French government saw an opportunity for a rise in tourism in Tahiti. At this time France was also conducting nuclear tests on other islands of French Polynesia. It was not until the 1980s and the rise of the antinuclear movement in Tahiti that the Tahitian independence movement regained strength. Tourism, more than any other industry, creates a false international perception of the value and meaning of Pacific Islands nationality.

The term *postcolonial*, often used in contemporary discussions of colonialism, may not apply to many of the Pacific Islands, which remain colonies of the United States and France. Perhaps the greatest example of colonialism in Oceania lies in the way many economically

powerful countries, both in the West and in Asia, have ignored or subverted the political sovereignty of Pacific Islanders.

The socioeconomic concept of a "Pacific Rim" exploits the region's sea-lanes and sea resources, including fishing rights. Pacific Rim is a term used to describe the nations bordering the Pacific Ocean, but not always the island countries situated in it. In the post–World War II era, the Pacific Rim became an increasingly important and interconnected economic region. Twenty-one Pacific Rim nations, including the United States and Canada, are members of Asia-Pacific Economic Cooperation (APEC), established in 1989 to provide a forum for discussion on a broad range of economic issues of concern to the Pacific region.

Except for the larger countries of Papua New Guinea, Australia, and New Zealand, APEC does not include any Pacific Islands nations. The Pacific Island nations themselves are members of the Pacific Islands Forum, which promotes intergovernmental economic, cultural, and humanitarian cooperation in the region. The members of the forum are the Cook Islands, the Federated States of Micronesia, Fiji, Kiribati, Nauru, Niue, Palau, Papua New Guinea, the Republic of the Marshall Islands, Samoa, the Solomon Islands, Tonga, Tuvalu, Vanuatu, New Zealand, and Australia. Nonmember colonial states that are gaining some autonomy, such as Tahiti (French Polynesia) and New Caledonia, have been allowed to send observers to Pacific Islands Forum meetings.

The United States maintains a strong military presence in the Pacific Islands, as well as strong relations with its former and present colonial territories, and is attempting to organize the governments of U.S. territories in the region according to an "organic act" passed by the U.S. Congress. The legislation provides for a bill of rights and an American-style tripartite government and system of law that preempts whatever native law exists. Historically, the organization of a territory in this manner is a prelude to statehood.

Some American Pacific territories are considered *commonwealths*, which are organized but unincorporated. *Incorporation* is a permanent condition under the jurisdiction of the U.S. Constitution. Palmyra Atoll, which was once part of the kingdom of Hawaii, is an example of an incorporated territory. Unincorporated, organized territories include Guam and the Commonwealth of the Northern Mariana Islands. Unincorporated, unorganized territories include American Samoa (technically unorganized but self-governing under a 1967 constitution) and several islands and atolls uninhabited by indigenous peoples.

United Nations Committee on Decolonization includes Guam and American Samoa on the United Nations list of Non-Self-Governing Territories, along with the Pacific Islands nations of Pitcairn (New Zealand), Tokelau (New Zealand) and New Caledonia (France). In the 1950s Hawai'i and French Polynesia were removed from the list by the United States and France, which led to Hawaii's statehood.

Most of the Micronesian islands that came under United Nations trusteeship with the United States after World War II have since gained greater autonomy or sovereignty. In 1946 the United States began relocating the native people of the remote Marshall Islands for the purpose of conducting nuclear tests. In the 1970s and 1980s the people of Bikini Atoll in the Marshall Islands were awarded monetary reparations along with a settlement to be used to clean Bikini Atoll. Many Bikini residents were also resettled on other islands because of lingering unsafe radiation levels.

SEE ALSO *American Samoa; Federated States of Micronesia; Indigenous Responses, the Pacific; Marshall Islands; Occupations, the Pacific; Pacific, European Presence in.*

BIBLIOGRAPHY

Epeli Hau'ofa, ed. *A New Oceania: Rediscovering Our Sea of Islands.* Suva, Fiji: School of Social and Economic Development, University of the South Pacific, 1993.

Kame'eleihiwa, Lilikala. *Native Land and Foreign Desires: Pehea la e pono ai? How Shall We Live in Harmony?* Honolulu, HI: Bishop Museum Press, 1992.

Mahan, Alfred Thayer. *The Influence of Sea Power Upon History, 1660–1783.* Boston: Little, Brown, 1890. Available from Project Gutenberg at http://www.gutenberg.org/files/13529/13529.txt.

Vaai, Saleimoa. *Samoa Faamatai and the Rule of Law.* Le Papa-I-Galagala: National University of Samoa, 1999.

Dan Taulapapa McMullin

PACIFIC, EUROPEAN PRESENCE IN

Although the Pacific can be defined to include all the countries that lie along the littoral of the Pacific Ocean, and all the islands that lie in its waters, a more restricted perspective limits the Pacific to islands, and generally excludes such Asian archipelagos as Japan, the Philippines, and Indonesia. Conventionally the islands are divided into Polynesia, largely in the central and eastern part of the South Pacific, Melanesia, in the southwestern Pacific, and Micronesia, primarily in the northwestern Pacific. Anthropologists contest this categorization—

"many-island," "dark-island," and "small-island" groups—for constructing arbitrary boundaries between geographical zones and cultures. The continent of Australia is often included in the "Pacific," but sometimes joined with New Zealand as Australasia. The nomenclature and definitions underline the role of the Pacific basin as a crossroads of migration, trade, and cultures, as well as a terrain of European discovery and fantasy.

HISTORY

Portuguese and Dutch ships ventured past the western Pacific islands in voyages to the East Indies and East Asia from the 1500s, and Spanish galleons sailed past other islands going from Mexico to Manila. These early explorations left few traces other than long-lasting names: the Marquesas, Espirito Santo, Easter Island, and the Solomons islands; only in Micronesia did the Spanish undertake efforts at evangelization. With the voyages of James Cook and Louis-Antoine de Bougainville, and their British and French successors, joined by other navigators, Oceania entered the European worldview in the late 1700s.

As the Age of Enlightenment discovered these distant and exotic islands and their flora, fauna, and people, commentators embroidered legends around paradises lost or found. Tahiti was proclaimed the "New Cythera," Denis Diderot published a treatise inspired by Bougainville's travels, and Jean-Jacques Rousseau articulated the myth of the *bon sauvage* ("noble savage"). A contrary image, more popular among priests and pastors than philosophers, portrayed islands of cannibals and head-hunters, human sacrifices and violent warfare (including the murder of Cook in Hawaii). Both images have bedevilled the islands to the present. Pierre Loti, Paul Gauguin, and Victor Segalen, to use French examples, perpetuated the myth of Tahiti still visible in tourist brochures and popular representations; popular culture indulged in caricatures of stone-age primitive peoples.

Scientists, particularly naturalists, navigators, and cartographers, promoted European expeditions, but others had different reasons for establishing European outposts. Politicians saw potential sites for settlement—as occurred at Botany Bay in 1788—and viewed the Pacific as a new theater of geopolitical rivalries. Islands, they argued, with claims that the center of the world's economic and political gravity would eventually shift from the Atlantic to the Pacific, provided vital provisioning and garrisoning ports on the long voyage between the Americas, Asia, and Australasia.

With the nineteenth-century upsurge in missionary fervor, Catholics and Protestants (of various denominations) vied to convert the native peoples. Traders were interested in commercial opportunities. Whaling and sealing dominated early nineteenth-century economic activities, while merchants exploited supplies of sandalwood and *bêche-de-mer* valuable for exchange in China. As these resources became depleted, there was hope for establishment of plantation economies in tropical islands, and for discovery of mineral resources. Meanwhile, beachcombers and adventurers drifted onto the islands, establishing European toeholds. These various interests combined to promote a "scramble" for Oceania.

In the early modern age, the Spanish had advanced a nominal claim to Micronesian islands, and the Dutch retained a somewhat vague claim to the western half of New Guinea. The British extended their colonial imperium in Australia from Botany Bay and Van Dieman's Land (Tasmania) to the whole of the continent by the 1820s. In 1840, they narrowly beat the French in a race to claim New Zealand; two years later, the French took over the Marquesas and Society islands, gaining control of Tahiti. A perceived slight to a Catholic missionary precipitated the move—Protestant missionaries had worked in Tahiti since 1797 and gained influence over the local chieftain—that allowed France to get a stake in Oceania. In 1853, France annexed New Caledonia to create a penal colony. Believing that they could imitate and perfect the British system of transportation, the French sent convicts and political prisoners (including Communards in 1871) to the islands from the 1860s to the 1890s. The British riposted by taking over the Fiji islands in 1874.

In the 1880s, other imperial powers entered the scramble. Germany took over northeastern New Guinea and neighboring islands, as well as the western Samoan islands, while the United States raised the flag over the eastern Samoan islands. Washington increased its holdings in 1898 when victory in the Spanish-American War allowed it to acquire the Philippines and Guam, and in 1900 the United States formally took over the Hawaiian Islands. Britain had by now taken over southeastern New Guinea, the Solomon islands, and the Gilbert and Ellis islands; France had claimed Wallis and Futuna; and Chile incorporated Easter Island. By the end of the century, only Tonga had not been formally integrated into a colonial empire. The New Hebrides, contested between Britain and France, became a "condominium" with two flags, two currencies, and two colonial administrators, a situation that endured as one of the most peculiar colonial arrangements until Vanuatu became independent in 1980.

As claims were made (and very often before), missionaries, traders, and planters arrived. Sugar became the major export of Fiji, and tropical fruits gained profits for planters in Hawaii. In the western Pacific, planters concentrated on copra, the dried meat of coconuts that European factories transformed into soap and other oil-based products. An attempt to create cotton plantations in Tahiti enjoyed only temporary success during the American Civil War. The French discovered huge reserves of nickel in New Caledonia, the world's major producer by the late 1800s; settlers also developed pastoralism. The British mined phosphate in the Gilbert islands and Nauru, as did the French on Makatea. Prospectors later found a wealth of minerals in New Guinea.

Economic initiatives created a demand for labor. "Kanakas" (Melanesians) were recruited, sometimes under duress, for plantations around the islands and in Queensland. The British imported Indian indentured laborers to Fiji, where they came to outnumber indigenous islanders. In New Caledonia, the French employed Japanese, East Indians, and Indochinese; Chinese, Japanese, Europeans, and Americans migrated to Hawaii. Others Europeans settled in New Zealand and New Caledonia, though their presence elsewhere was relatively small.

Culture contact had a dramatic effect on islanders, though without the "fatal impact" that some writers postulated. Infrastructural development, paid employment, and imported goods changed material life. Evangelists succeeded in converting most islanders to Christianity (and establishing virtual theocracies in some islands), though with syncretism of Christian and local beliefs. Law codes regulated behavior, and secular and ecclesiastical authorities tried to stamp out what they termed immoral behavior: semi-nudity, dancing, and promiscuity. Diseases brought by Europeans, as well as intensive labor and even cultural *anomie*, caused a steep demographic decline in some islands. Health care and education nevertheless became more widely available. Sexual liaisons between Europeans or Asians and islanders created a *métis* population in Tahiti and Hawaii, while in some other islands virtual segregation prevailed. Colonial rule eroded the authority of traditional chiefs, and everywhere islanders remained politically disenfranchised.

THE TWENTIETH AND TWENTY-FIRST CENTURIES

The islands stayed sleepy if picturesque outposts of empires, as described by Robert Louis Stevenson and Somerset Maugham, despite international changes. World War I (1914–1918) saw a few shots fired between German and French warships off Tahiti, and contingents of islanders were sent as soldiers to fight on European battlefields. Defeated Germany was ejected from the Pacific, its possessions divided between Japan (Micronesian islands),

BORSUMIJ

USIR BELANDA DARI IRIAN-BARAT

Anticolonial Slogans on an Office Building in Jakarta. When the Indonesian government took control of Dutch-owned commercial properties in the 1950s, Indonesian nationalists celebrated by painting anti-Dutch slogans on the buildings. The text on this wall, photographed in December 1957, reads Usir Belanda Dari Irian-Barat *(Expel the Dutch from West New Guinea).* © **BETTMANN/ CORBIS. REPRODUCED BY PERMISSION.**

Australia (New Guinea), and New Zealand (western Samoa). World War II (1941–1945) had an even greater impact, as Japan pushed forward to create a Greater Co-Prosperity Sphere, and islands, notably Hawaii (with the Pearl Harbor attack), Guadalcanal, and New Guinea, witnessed intense fighting. The Kokoda Trail in New Guinea remains an iconic Australian war experience. The United States stationed troops on such islands as Bora Bora and New Caledonia, and thousands of GIs, dollars, and the "American way of life" sent shock waves through Oceania. With war's end, Japan's possessions became a U.S. trust territory under United Nations aegis.

Most observers thought that many decades, and probably generations, would pass before Pacific islands gained independence. Indeed, campaigns for independence were notable by their absence, though political movements (especially in Tahiti) demanded greater political rights and indigenous cultural recognition. In 1958 French Polynesia and New Caledonia chose to remain "overseas territories" of France, and the following year Hawaii became the fiftieth state of the United States. The

Netherlands withdrew from West Papua, the remainder of its East Indian empire, in the 1960s, and Indonesia annexed the territory, which was substitution, in the eyes of local people, of one imperialism for another.

In 1962 New Zealand withdrew from Western Samoa, the first independent Oceanic state. Fiji followed in 1970, despite opposition from traditional chiefs concerned that parliamentary government would give power to Indians. In 1975 an Australian Labor government rushed Papua New Guinea to independence. The British, also eager to disengage, granted independence to the Solomon islands, the Gilbert islands (Kiribati) and the Ellis islands (Tuvalu) by the end of the decade, and persuaded France to join in releasing Vanuatu. Decolonization in the island Pacific thus occurred later than in other parts of the world, and generally without the militant nationalist struggles or violence that characterized separation of some other colonies.

New Zealand, Britain, and Australia nevertheless retained vestiges of old empires. New Zealand kept Niue and Tokelau; the Cook islands, nominally independent, signed a treaty of "free association" with Wellington. Norfolk Island, populated partly by descendants of the *Bounty*, remained an Australian territory, and Britain reluctantly held on to Pitcairn, home to several dozen people (also *Bounty* descendants). The United States and France showed no inclination to leave the Pacific. In the midst of the cold war and military involvement in Asia, the United States judged its outposts vital strategic bases, and on Bikini atoll it tested nuclear weapons. American Samoa and Guam remain unincorporated territories whose residents are nationals with right of entry and abode in the United States, but with limited representation in Congress. Under pressure from the United Nations to wind up the Trust Territory in Micronesia, the United States made the Northern Marianas a commonwealth and preserved close links with independent Belau and the Federated States of Micronesia.

The French were concerned about the "Caldoche" settler population in New Caledonia, but also considered retention of its islands as a guarantee of a political and military presence in the Pacific. The French, too, carried out nuclear testing of atmospheric and underwater devices at Mururoa from the early 1960s until the mid-1990s, much to the consternation of neighbors in Oceania and Australasia. Paris also faced nationalist opposition in French Polynesia and especially in New Caledonia, where the Front de Libération Nationale Kanak et Socialiste coalition led a struggle for independence in the 1980s. This placed the largely Melanesian movement in direct conflict with Europeans and migrant Polynesians who allied with them. The French government proposed several new constitutional arrangements—opinion about relinquishing New Caledonia was hotly divided in France—while violence escalated until agreement on a twenty-five-year moratorium on independence was reached in 1988.

The islands of postcolonial Oceania face problems of economic underdevelopment, ethnic divisiveness, international marginalization, and cultural globalization. Gang violence and elite corruption are rife in Papua New Guinea, ethnically motivated coups overturned governments in Fiji in the 1980s and again in the 1990s, the Solomon islands in the early 2000s verged on civil war, Vanuatu has seen continued political instability, Nauru is bankrupt, and the Cook islands host dubious financial institutions. Considerable emigration is a response to limited economic opportunities. Many islands rely on aid, and the European Union is one of the largest donors, while tourists from Europe represent an economic resource, evidence of a continued, if reduced, European presence in a region where the French and British flags still fly.

SEE ALSO *American Samoa; Anticolonialism; Assimilation, East Asia and the Pacific; Australia; Bismarck Archipelago; Fiji; French Polynesia; Hawaii; Missions, Civilizing; Missions, in the Pacific; New Caledonia; New Zealand; Pacific, American Presence in; Self-Strengthening Movements, East Asia and the Pacific.*

BIBLIOGRAPHY

Aldrich, Robert. "The Decolonization of the Pacific Islands." *Itinerario* 24 (3–4) (2000): 173–191.

Campbell, I. C. *Worlds Apart: A History of the Pacific Islands.* Christchurch, New Zealand: Canterbury University Press, 2003.

Fisher, Stephen Roger. *A History of the Pacific Islands.* London: Macmillan, 2004.

Lal, Brij, ed. *Pacific Islands: An Encyclopedia.* Honolulu: University of Hawaii Press, 2000.8

Robert Aldrich

PAHLAVI DYNASTY

On December 12, 1925, Iran's parliament amended Iran's constitution of 1906–1907 to replace the Qajar dynasty (1797–1925) with the Pahlavi dynasty as the legitimate sovereigns of Iran. On April 25, 1926, Rezā Pahlavi was formerly crowned Rezā Shāh. Rezā Shāh ascended the throne after four years of political intrigue that began when he, as commander of the Persian Cossack Brigade, committed those troops in support of a coup on February 21, 1921. Though his military rank was never higher than colonel during his career in the Persian Cossack Brigade, he rose through the ranks of government from minister of war to prime minister (in 1923) and finally king. Along the way he destroyed political allies, outmaneuvered or coopted the Qajar aristocracy, and crushed provincial and tribal challenges to central government control. With a unified military that was fed by an efficient tax-collection policy (organized in part by Arthur C. Millspaugh, an American financial advisor to Iran from 1922 to 1927) and the Conscription Law (1924), Rezā Shāh wielded the state as his personal tool for Iran's modernization.

Rezā Shāh built on some of the late achievements of the Qajar period: he coopted his generation's "best and brightest" for the development and execution of modernization policy, continued the legacy of "constitutional monarchy," and followed a modernization scheme that owed some of its ambitions to failed or partially realized Qajar policies. There was an expansion in education, the creation of a national railway funded without foreign capital (1927–1938), an expansion of state control over

The Shah of Iran. *Reza Pahlavi (1919–1980), the shah of Iran, crowned himself emperor on October 26, 1967, causing opposition from many segments of Iranian society.* © **APIS/SYGMA/ CORBIS. REPRODUCED BY PERMISSION.**

the religious establishment and the judiciary, and the realization of monumental projects that emphasized the theme of Iranian revival (e.g., the thousandth anniversary celebrations of the poet Ferdowsi in 1934 and the creation of a modern administrative and cultural center in Tehran with Sassanian and Acheamenid architectural motifs). His legacy to the institutional and social life of Iran was cemented in revisions to the legal code (some strands of which have survived to Islamic Republican times) and through his "state feminism" projects, which began with minor revisions to the Marriage Law in 1931 and ended with forced unveiling and the expansion of educational and professional opportunities for women under the auspices of the Women's Awakening Project of 1936 to 1943 (the project survived Rezā Shāh's deposition *de jure* for two years).

Rezā Shāh's anticolonial credentials were mixed. He enjoyed success in abolishing most extraterritorial

privileges for foreigners in 1927, but foundered when he attempted to renegotiate the D'Arcy Concession with the British in 1932 and 1933. His increasingly repressive tactics directed against all potential opposition in the 1930s eroded the support he enjoyed in 1925. Furthermore, his effort to secure Iran's borders through regional diplomacy (for example, the Sa dabad Pact of 1937, or the marriage of Crown Prince Mohammad Rezā Pahlavi to the Egyptian princess Fawzia in 1939) proved of no avail in the face of Allied demands in 1941 that Iran expel all German agents and permit military supplies to flow to Soviet Russia from the Persian Gulf. Soviet and British troops occupied Iran in August of 1941 and forced the abdication of Rezā Shāh in favor of his son Mohammad on September 16 of that year.

In what was to be a pivotal moment for U.S.–Iranian relations, some 30,000 American personnel joined the occupation of Iran after America's entrance into the war. Until World War II, Americans had enjoyed a reputation as being a largely disinterested foreign presence—missionary activity and governmental advisors notwithstanding. With the ending of World War II, it became clear that America and not Great Britain would be the main counterweight to Soviet Russia. The United States took the lead in the newly formed United Nations in protesting delays in Soviet withdrawals from Iran and in giving support to separatist Kurdish and Azeri republics in the northwest in Iran in 1946.

America's reputation as an imperialist presence was born in the Anglo-American-sponsored coup against Prime Minister Mohammad Mosaddeq, which occurred on August 22, 1953. Mosaddeq had become prime minister in 1951, elected on the strength of his championing of oil nationalization in Iran. Mosaddeq's confrontation with the Anglo-Iranian Oil Company over nationalization would be the ultimate source of his undoing, but he also challenged the Pahlavi dynasty. As Mohammad Rezā Shāh looked on, Mosaddeq also used his popularity to further dismantle the control of the Pahlavi court over government institutions, especially the military. The 1953 coup did not reverse the dismantlement of the Anglo-Iranian Oil Company (through which the British government had dominated the Iranian oil industry), but replaced it with an international oil consortium that now included American oil companies. With American support, Mohammad Rezā Shāh began a program of modernization and political consolidation that culminated in two grand projects. The first was the White Revolution of 1960 to 1963, which, in turn, evolved into the Great Civilization program by the end of the decade. Designed to steal the thunder of leftist opposition to the Pahlavis, the program expanded the welfare state, granted women the right to vote, improved compensation for industrial workers, and distributed land to peasants from the major holdings of the old aristocracy. The second grand project was the creation of a one-party state in 1975. The way to the creation of the Rastākhiz (Resurgence) Party was paved by the Shāh's military and secret police, SAVAK (formed in 1958 with American help). The Shāh's government destroyed or disrupted radical Islamist and Communist opposition in the 1950s and suppressed liberal and clerical opposition in the 1960s. Nonetheless, there was evidence by the early 1970s that the Shāh's twin policies of modernization and political suppression had begun to backfire. Ayatollāh Ruhollāh Khomeini, banished from Iran in 1964 for his opposition to the White Revolution, organized a new generation of clerical opposition from exile in Iraq. Students sent abroad for undergraduate and graduate degrees were politicized by Islamist and leftist opposition to the Shāh. In Iran itself, militant Islamic-Marxist groups had begun a sustained campaign against the regime.

As with his father, Mohammad Rezā Shāh found that foreign policy and royal spectacle added very little to his regime's legitimacy. An elaborate coronation ceremony in 1967 and even more extravagant celebrations of monarchy in 1971 and 1975 earned him little credit in the courts of world or Iranian public opinion. Growing international criticism of Iran's human rights record and state visits of Western leaders (most notably that of Jimmy Carter in late 1977) seemed to confirm his status as a tyrant and Western puppet. As the oil boom of the late 1960s and early 1970s gave way to rampant inflation and unemployment, Mohammad Rezā Shāh found his worst nightmares realized when all sectors of Iranian society rallied in opposition to the regime under the leadership of Ayatollah Khomeini. Cycles of protest and repression escalated from the spring of 1977 until, finally, on January 4, 1979, the Shāh agreed to appoint Shahpur Bakhtiar (d. 1991) as prime minister and leave the country. Mohammad Rezā Shāh fled Iran for a second time on January 16, 1979. On February 1, 1979, Khomeini returned to Iran. The government of Bakhtiar fell and he became one of many members of Iran's social and political elite that fled in the face of the new order. While Khomeini consolidated power in Iran, the Shāh languished in exile. When President Carter allowed the Shāh to visit America for cancer treatment in October 1979, nervous radicals, fearing a repeat of 1953, seized the American embassy on November 4. This escalated into the hostage crisis of 1979 to 1981 that, along with America's economic woes, cost Carter his bid for reelection in 1980. The Pahlavi dynasty effectively died with Mohammad Rezā on July 27, 1980; he was buried with state honors in Egypt. His son, Rezā Pahlavi II (b. 1960), still styles himself as a political leader in exile (not surprisingly, he lives in the United States) and is the head of the Constitutionalist Party of Iran.

SEE ALSO *Iran; Khomeini, Ayatollah Ruhollah.*

BIBLIOGRAPHY

Abrahamian, Ervand. *Iran Between Two Revolutions.* Princeton, NJ: Princeton University Press, 1982.

Cronin, Stephanie, ed. *The Making of Modern Iran: State and Society Under Riza Shāh, 1921–1941.* New York: Routledge, 2003.

Elm, Mostafa. *Oil, Power ,and Principle: Iran's Oil Nationalization and Its Aftermath.* Syracuse, NY: Syracuse University Press, 1992.

Ghani, Sirus. *Iran and the Rise of Rezā Shāh: From Qajar Collapse to Pahlavi Rule.* London: I. B. Taurus, 1998.

Keddie, Nikki R. and Richard Yann, eds. *Roots of Revolution: An Interpretive History of Modern Iran.* New Haven, CT: Yale University Press, 1981.

Camron Michael Amin

PAN-AFRICAN CONGRESS

The Pan-African Congress helped identify and shape African nationalism in the first half of the twentieth century. Its origins lie first in a developing sense of nationalism among a mission-educated and increasingly university-educated elite who began challenging the notion of European dominance in the African colonies. Second, African Americans advanced the sense of racial unity capable of surpassing state borders. W. E. B. Du Bois, whose efforts in Pan-Africanism propelled it forward in the twentieth century, urged blacks to look to Africa for inspiration. Africa was to be central to the movement's expanding theories of black nationalism.

HENRY SYLVESTER WILLIAMS AND THE PAA

Although the post–World War I (1914–1918) congressional meetings are more well known, they were the fruit of the late-nineteenth-century efforts of African nationalists from the British Empire and the United States. Henry Sylvester Williams, a Trinidadian teacher and lawyer, formed the African Association in 1897 (changed to the Pan-African Association [PAA] in 1898). The group worked to establish contact with leading black intellectuals throughout the African diaspora. From the irregularities in native rights across Britain's African colonies, to the Black Codes in the American South, the organization sought to stress the common nature of black existence.

The black press was crucial to the development of the PAA's message, and as the rhetoric matured, leaders planned a conference to be held in London. The Pan-African Conference transpired in July 1900, attracting delegates from Africa, Canada, the West Indies, and the

United States. One American representative was Du Bois, who continued to promote the Association's interests upon his return home.

Williams was not a socialist, but the goals of civil rights and sovereignty meshed well with the interests of the political Left. While these similarities certainly worked in the interest of the PAA, the differences that remained had the potential to undermine the organization's overall effectiveness. Following the 1900 conference, the movement suffered from ideological factionalism, and with its disbandment in 1902, and Williams's death in 1911, Pan-Africanism appeared to falter.

SOCIALISM AND REBIRTH

It was socialism, however, that helped reinvigorate Pan-Africanism, especially after the successful Soviet Revolution in 1917. European socialists preached racial equality and the themes that united those who were oppressed. As the small African elite began to access socialist publications, there developed a sense of a continent united across ethnic lines.

African and African-American soldiers in World War I had various expectations of national service, especially with regard to the touted principle of democracy. American troops saw combat with French forces that commonly employed their colonial troops at the front. Those African Americans who served under their own commanders performed manual labor, leaving the fighting to their white colleagues. While colonial African troops did see combat, they, like their American allies, did not receive the respect they believed was owed them. Upon returning from the war, both black American and colonial soldiers discovered that the war victory had served to protect the status quo in their respective societies.

Socialist organizations had been active in providing literature to black soldiers moving through the large cities toward the front, a fact African-American troops discovered in London. It was a common socialist theme that colonial powers waged the war to defend their principles of Bourgeois dominance. Black troops were simply the tools with which the imperial powers maintained control. Du Bois easily tapped into this rhetoric when he organized a meeting among African nationalists to discuss the commonality of the African experience, both in Africa and in the United States.

The Pan-African Congress met in Paris in 1919, with Du Bois and other delegates from fifteen nations debating proposals to present to the Peace Conference. Primarily, the delegates would demand that Africans play a role in administering their states. This platform, promoted chiefly by the National Association for the Advancement of Colored People (NAACP), held that, at a future date, Africans would assume control in a home-rule status. Their approach was quite reasonable in light of the lessons learned about the violence in the Soviet Revolution. Delegates appreciated the limit of their political abilities in 1919, and so sought to move forward cautiously.

The Pan-African Congress met again in 1921, holding several sessions in London, Paris, and Brussels. Perhaps as a result of the ineffectiveness of the 1919 demands, the delegates assumed a more radical posture, publishing their demands in the "London Manifesto." The British government, argued the Congress, had developed a spirit of ignorance and neglect among Africans. Regardless of is pro-democracy rhetoric, Britain's African colonies had been and continued to be victimized. Du Bois's goal was to animate African Americans to lead the Pan-African struggle, as they had benefited from America's position as a leading international state. This was a well-established theme by 1921, one that also stressed the connection between black success in the United States and in Africa. The race as a whole had to advance in order for anyone to advance.

A third summit followed in 1923 and spoke more to the problems faced by the African diaspora, including the ongoing efforts of the colonial powers to exploit African resources. This exploitation was aided by the advancement of settler colonialists, white minorities that had achieved political control at the expense of the black majority. Racial policies came to define these societies, most notably in Rhodesia and South Africa. Yet, while the delegates now had still stronger evidence of the inequalities of the white/black relationship in both the United States and Africa, it appeared as if they were making little headway in the fight for civil rights and international black political identity.

The 1923 session lacked the momentum of the first and second meetings. Poorly planned and attended, there appeared to be fissures in the foundation of Pan-Africanism. The organization's socialist tendencies augmented these divisions, as the differences between liberalism and socialism were difficult to reconcile. Moreover, nationalist organizations in the different African states were still coming to terms with their own issues of concern. It was becoming evident that organizing an international movement was impossible without first coordinating state and local initiatives.

NATIONALISM AND INDEPENDENCE

A fourth summit in 1927 varied little from 1923, giving credence to the idea that Pan-Africanism had lost its way after the optimism of 1919. Not until 1945 did another Pan-African Congress meet, this time in Manchester,

England. Du Bois was in attendance, along with delegates from all over Africa and nationalist organizations. In the eighteen years that had passed since the last conference, a new spirit had come to animate the nationalists. In the intervening years the African national organizations had matured, honing their skills and redefining their goals. A new, younger generation of leaders also began to appear, thus reinvigorating the struggle. Socialism continued to be the ideology of choice, with delegates tying racial discrimination to capitalism and the onslaught of the white, industrial West.

More importantly, however, is the direction in which the Manchester meeting was pointing. By 1945 it had become quite apparent to the imperial powers that change was on the horizon. The British had even begun to make some preliminary plans to turn over the colonies to sovereign, African rulers. The optimism that Manchester represented would be obvious in the coming decade, but even in 1945 a feeling of change was in the air. It was due to the efforts of Pan-Africanists such as Williams and Du Bois that the ideas of African independence and black liberty would not die. While the struggle continued as the second half of the twentieth century began, great strides already had been made. Where the Pan-Africanist movement failed, however, was in its efforts to create an African solidarity. The newly independent African states, and their leaders, proved just as effective as the former colonial masters at exploiting resources for the advancement of their own ethnic communities. African cohesiveness continued to be checked by the very dynamic nature of the African diaspora.

SEE ALSO *Pan-Africanism.*

BIBLIOGRAPHY

Bandele, Ramla. "Henry Sylvester Williams: Progenitor of Pan-Africanism Movement." Available from http://diaspora.northwestern.edu/mbin/WebObjects/DiasporaX.woa.

Bandele, Ramla. "Pan-African Conference in 1900: Origins of the Movement for Global Black Unity." Available from http://diaspora.northwestern.edu/mbin/WebObjects/DiasporaX.woa.

Berry, Mary Frances, and John W. Blassinghame. *Long Memory: The Black Experience in America.* New York: Oxford University Press, 1982.

Du Bois, W. E. B. *Darkwater: Voices from Within the Veil.* Mineola, NY: Dover Publications, 1999.

Lewis, David Levering. *W. E. B. Du Bois: The Fight for Equality and the American Century 1919–1963.* New York: Henry Holt & Company, 2000.

Marable, Manning. *W. E. B. Du Bois: Black Radical Democrat.* Boulder, CO: Paradigm, 2005.

Mathurin, Owen Charles. *Henry Sylvester Williams and the Origins of the Pan-African Movement, 1869–1911.* Westport, CT: Greenwood Press, 1976.

Sherwood, Marika, and Hakim Adi. *Pan-African History: Political Figures from Africa and the Diaspora since 1787.* New York: Routledge, 2003.

Jeffrey Lee Meriwether

PAN-AFRICANISM

Pan-Africanism is an internationalist philosophy that is based on the idea that Africans and people of African descent share a common bond. Pan Africanism, therefore seeks the unity and autonomy of African peoples and peoples of African descent; it is also a vision dedicated to fulfilling their right to self-determination. African diasporas—the global dispersion of people of African descent from their original homelands—emerged through slave trading, labor migration, commerce, and war. Imagining home, through a collective identity and cultural identification with Africa, Pan-Africanists mobilize for the continent's restoration, prosperity, and safety. Pan-Africanism allows African and African Diaspora communities to transcend the status of ethnic minority or oppressed nationality by replacing it with the consciousness of being "a nation within a nation."

Colonial degradation took many forms in the African world, depending on the varying policies of Britain, Portugal, France, Germany, Holland, Belgium, or the United States. These policies included direct military occupation, economic subordination through labor exploitation and the regulation of trade relations, cultural imperialism, indirect rule using traditional or even manufactured tribal leaders, promises of citizenship for select Africans, and seemingly benevolent development programs.

The attitudes of imperial officials were far from monolithic. Some insisted Africans were racially inferior and needed to be controlled through corporal punishment, including rape and the chopping off of limbs; others saw African peoples as primitive yet noble, even potential equals someday with proper mentoring over time.

An idea of Africa as "the dark continent" was created over time, by both official intellectual and government institutions and popular culture. Africa came to be seen as suffering from dependency complexes and as unfit for self-government. Importantly, racist viewpoints did not always preclude recognition of African elites, who could function on many levels as modern "credits to their race" or, alternatively, as keepers of ethnic wisdom and traditions. Close engagement with such elites was inherent to the civilizing mission and a crucial component of "enlightened" imperial government.

The efforts of African peoples to achieve independence and emancipation were distinguished by collectivist economic planning, defense against discrimination and brutality, a people-to-people foreign policy across national borders, community control of education, and a rethinking of religious and ethnic practices. Uncritical attitudes toward the nation-state often thwarted the full democratic potential of anticolonial movements.

The Pan-African movement has contributed significantly to the development of African nationalism, anticolonial revolt, and the postcolonial governmental strategies of African nation-states. The major torchbearers of the modern Pan-African movement were the African American W. E. B. Du Bois and Marcus Garvey, a native of Jamaica. Strong foundational pillars include George Padmore, Kwame Nkrumah, Julius Nyerere, C. L. R. James, and Walter Rodney.

W. E. B. DU BOIS

As a scholar and advocate, W. E. B. Du Bois (1868–1963) endeavored to make Africa central to world civilization. Among the foremost historians, sociologists, literary figures, and politicians of his generation, he foreshadowed in his many publications the future significance of Africa in an era distinguished by unapologetic subordination of the continent. Believing that the enslavement and colonization of African peoples was not only an indignity, but a burden to Western civilization, Du Bois understood what few ministers of foreign affairs, travelers, and journalists of the early twentieth century could: the necessity of involving peoples of African descent in politics and government.

Du Bois, with the Trinidadian attorney Henry Sylvester Williams, organized the first Pan-African Conference of 1900 in London. Subsequently, he chaired four Pan-African Congresses in 1919, 1921, 1923, and 1927, which gathered in London, Paris, Brussels, Lisbon, and New York City (one congress having sessions in two cities). Du Bois played a leading role in shaping protest against colonial land theft and global racial discrimination; he drafted letters to European and American rulers, calling on them to fight racism and promote self-government in their colonies, and to demand political rights for blacks in the United States. Arguing that land and mineral wealth in African colonies must be reserved for Africans, whose poor labor conditions must be ameliorated by law, Du Bois argued that Africans had the right to participate in government, to the extent their development permitted. Basing his claims on the human rights standards of both the United States and Soviet Union, Du Bois confidently predicted—though without ever quite overcoming

the elitist perspective embodied in his notion of a Talented Tenth—that Africa would be governed by Africans in due time.

MARCUS GARVEY

Whereas W. E. B. Du Bois focused on the production of professional scholarly literature and petitioning racist and imperial regimes, Marcus Garvey (1887–1940) took up the task of building a Pan-African movement of everyday people and propagated for the first time a global vision of black autonomy. Through mass-oriented journalism, uplift programs promoting health, alternative education, entrepreneurship, and the trappings of military regalia, Garvey's Universal Negro Improvement Association (UNIA) invented notions of provisional government for African peoples. Garvey's doctrine created an image of the continent as a homeland for disenfranchised African Diaspora communities, restoring pride in an African past and confidence in a vibrant destiny, and inspiring art, music, and literary representations.

At its height, from 1917 to 1934, UNIA functioned in the United States, the Caribbean, and Latin America, and had an inspirational influence on the anticolonial struggle in Africa. Garvey's ideas found a mixed reception in Africa. The Harry Thuku revolt in Kenya has been partially attributed to Garvey's inspiration. In contrast, Kobina Sekyi of Ghana resented the notion that Garvey was Africa's provisional president. Garvey also saw some of his notions of Africa challenged. He became a critic of Liberia's ruling elite, and his "Back to Africa" scheme was partially undermined by growing awareness of African slavery and feudal class relations.

Garvey, an autodidact, was at times unpolished, romantic, or bombastic in his intellectual claims. His claims about the various African personalities and civilizations he wished to defend were not always factually accurate. Nonetheless, without a professional or scholarly pedigree, and possessing limited resources, Garvey inspired political ambitions and a desire for independence in multitudes of ordinary people of African descent.

GEORGE PADMORE

George Padmore (1903–1959), a native of Trinidad, produced books, journalism, and strategic guides—backed between 1928 and 1935 by the authority of Moscow and the Communist International—that helped create a global network of black workers and fomented labor strikes and anticolonial revolts. Early in his career, Padmore was hostile to both Garvey and Du Bois, for what he saw as their insufficient resistance to the empire of capital; later, out of necessity, he modified his stance toward their legacies, while continuing to defend his own uncompromising positions.

During World War II, the Soviet Union subverted socialist ideals by, among other means, forging an alliance with Britain, France, and the United States against Italy, Germany, and Japan. When the Soviets ended their policy of promoting national liberation struggles in the African and Caribbean colonies, Padmore was asked to encourage friendship with "the democratic imperialists." He refused this absurdity. Surfacing in London, he formed the International African Service Bureau with C. L. R. James; he defended Ethiopia from Italian invasion, and continued advocating the destruction of all colonial regimes worldwide.

Working with future African independence leaders—Sierra Leone's Isaac Wallace-Johnson, Kenya's Jomo Kenyatta, and Ghana's Kwame Nkrumah—Padmore maintained and extended his vast network. These efforts culminated in the Fifth Pan-African Congress of 1945, held in Manchester, England. A watershed event, this assembly gathered for the first time vast numbers of African activists, many of whom were trade unionists or students. This time few proposed merely lobbying colonial authorities. Rather, a commitment was made to mass politics and armed struggle, if necessary, as the means to establish self-government on the African continent. Padmore ended his career as Nkrumah's advisor on African affairs upon Ghana's independence in 1957.

KWAME NKRUMAH

Kwame Nkrumah (1909–1972) was one of the two greatest Pan-African statesmen, along with Tanzania's Julius Nyerere. As with Nyerere, Nkrumah's vision of federation and cooperation for the liberation of the entire African continent transcends the mixed legacy of his domestic governance.

Nkrumah employed "positive action"—strikes and other forms of nonviolent civil disobedience—as a means to overthrow British colonialism. He confronted tribal and customary authorities in Ghana and initiated modern development projects. Promoting the idea of the African personality and seeking to incorporate and unify Islamic, Christian, and African theologies and ethnic traditions, Nkrumah made Ghana a center for African American expatriates. Nkrumah linked Ghana with Sekou Toure's Guinea and Modibo Keita's Mali in a three-nation federation. He also sponsored the All African Peoples Conference of 1958, which was attended by various luminaries of the national liberation struggle, such as Congo's Patrice Lumumba, Kenya's Tom Mboya, and Algeria's Frantz Fanon. At the conference, anticolonial trade union movements were organized, and further federations of nation-states were conceived.

The idea of Pan Africanism took a new turn with the formation of the Organization of African Unity (OAU) in

Kwame Nkrumah and W. E. B. Du Bois, Ghana, 1962.
Kwame Nkrumah (second from right), president of Ghana, converses with the American scholar and exponent of Pan-Africanism W. E. B. Du Bois shortly before the opening of the World Peace Conference in Accra, Ghana, on June 21, 1962.
AP/WIDE WORLD PHOTOS. REPRODUCED BY PERMISSION.

1963. The OAU was founded to promote unity and cooperation among all African states and to bring an end to colonialism in all parts of the continent. Haile Selassie's Ethiopia, brokered an uneasy compromise between Nkrumah's call for the total unification of Africa and the desire for autonomous nation-states. A collective commitment was made to liberate southern Africa from colonialism in the future. Yet colonial nation-state boundaries were to be respected in the post-colonial era, thus creating a country club of ruling elites whose governments rarely interfered in each other's affairs on behalf of ordinary people waging democratic struggles. The fall of Nkrumah's regime in 1966 came through military coup and imperial intervention. His rule was increasingly an undemocratic populist dictatorship, even as he began to articulate the neocolonial dilemma—the continuing dependency of seemingly sovereign African nation-states. Nkrumah lived out his last years in exile in Sekou Toure's Guinea.

JULIUS NYERERE

The Tanzanian leader Julius Nyerere (1909–1972) developed his Pan-African perspective slowly, but grew into a remarkable politician. After foiling several early coup attempts, and operating under the shadow of Cold War intrigue, he cautiously united mainland Tanganyika with the Zanzibari islands off the Swahili coast. He attempted but failed at the creation of an East African federation with Kenya and Uganda. Nyerere then developed a vision of self-reliance rooted in the values of the African peasantry. Terming this vision Ujamaa Socialism, he introduced resolutions that aimed at excluding capitalists and major property owners from political power. He spoke and wrote eloquently in Swahili, which he made widespread as a national and Pan-African language. In the same spirit of unity, he sought to reduce ethnic conflict and permitted intellectual autonomy at Dar es Salaam's university, where professors and students were often critical of him.

Nyerere welcomed a global expatriate African community, continuing the legacy of Nkrumah's Ghana, and sponsored guerilla forces fighting for the liberation of Mozambique, Angola, Zimbabwe, and South Africa. He stood up to the aggressive impulses of Uganda's Idi Amin, whose overthrow he later sponsored, following a war between Tanzania and Uganda. Yet, Nyerere too eventually became a populist autocrat of a one-party state. His compulsory state plans for rural development according to the principles of Ujamaa proved to be a failure. Even his internationalism had its limits.

C. L. R. JAMES

When Tanzania sponsored the Sixth Pan-African Congress in 1974, the Call was drafted by former SNCC and Black Panther activists under the guidance of C. L. R. James (1901–1989). A native of Trinidad, James had a long career as a mentor and colleague of postcolonial statesmen that cannot be reconciled easily with his life as an insurgent socialist political philosopher advocating the overthrow of states and ruling elites. Indeed, James's life and work embodied the contradictions of the Pan-African movement in the postcolonial era.

The 1974 Congress, which was supposed to unify grassroots activists from across the globe under the sponsorship of a progressive state, imploded before it began. Nyerere collaborated with postcolonial Caribbean governments to exclude Caribbean insurgents, such as Maurice Bishop of Grenada's New Jewel Movement. Furthermore, prior to the Congress, Nyerere had jailed radical democrats in Tanzania, such as A. M. Babu, and in so doing had revealed the limits of the Pan-African vision and the necessity of what has come to be called "a second liberation of Africa." In the end, in a decision that perhaps suggests his unique political legacy, James boycotted the Sixth Pan-African Congress, even though he had traveled globally to organize it.

WALTER RODNEY

Walter Rodney (1942–1980), a native of Guyana, perhaps best imagined the Pan-African philosophy and practice necessary for a second liberation. As a scholar and activist, Rodney sought to reconcile the secular modernist tradition of class struggle–based Pan-Africanism with the prophetic cultural, nationalist, and theological visions of ordinary African and Caribbean peoples. He did not work in the service of populist state power, but rather organized everyday people against state power. Rodney's charismatic teaching inspired great democratic rebellions, against the postcolonial regime in Jamaica in 1968 and during the late 1970s in Guyana, for which he was assassinated. As a professor of history in Julius Nyerere's Tanzania, he taught, among other lessons, how Europe historically had underdeveloped Africa through its colonial policies. Yet it is Rodney's famous conference paper at the Sixth Pan-African Congress that most clearly suggests what are perhaps the most instructive perennial questions concerning African struggles for liberation. Rodney stressed—and this brief survey suggests he is correct—that an examination of which classes led the national liberation struggle, focusing especially on conflicting desires at the start of the postcolonial phase, is crucial to evaluating the legacy of Pan-African freedom struggles.

PAN-AFRICANISM IN THE TWENTY-FIRST CENTURY

The new millennium witnessed the OAU's transformation into the African Common Market, devoted to seeking the continental integration of financial markets and the facilitation of labor exploitation, with the blessings of American empire. Globally, progressives can only lament that the United States does not offer enough financial aid to Africans nor sufficiently forgive their governments' debts—in short, many defenders of the continent believe the imperialists are not involved in Africa enough! The contemporary moment is for many a time in which African peoples' struggle to delink from empire amounts to a dream, and subordinate African nation-states and ruling classes have given up even the pretext of such a possibility. A rethinking of the Pan-African community-organizing tradition may hold out some hope of finding new pathways and refashioning ideas about the future of self-government.

SEE ALSO *Nkrumah, Kwame; Nyerere, Julius; Organization of African Unity (OAU); Pan-African Congress.*

BIBLIOGRAPHY

Abdul-Raheem, Tajudeen, ed. *Pan-Africanism: Politics, Economy, and Social Change in the Twenty-First Century*. New York: New York University Press, 1996.

Esedebe, P. Olisanwuche. *Pan-Africanism: The Idea and Movement, 1776–1991*. 2nd ed. Washington, DC: Howard University Press, 1994.

James, C. L. R. *A History of Pan-African Revolt*. Rev. ed. Chicago: C. H. Kerr, 1969; reprint, 1995. (Originally published in 1938 as *A History of Negro Revolt*)

Langley, J. Ayodele. *Pan-Africanism and Nationalism in West Africa, 1900–1945*. Oxford: Clarendon, 1973.

Padmore, George. *Pan-Africanism or Communism*. New York: Roy, 1956; reprint, New York: Anchor, 1972.

Walters, Ronald W. *Pan-Africanism in the African Diaspora: An Analysis of Modern Afrocentric Political Movements*. Detroit, MI: Wayne State University Press, 1993.

Matthew Quest

PAPAL DONATIONS AND COLONIZATION

The Roman Catholic popes influenced European expansion into Africa, the Atlantic, and the world at large. One of the key ways they did so was through decrees and church policy. The religious influence was especially great before the Protestant Reformation of the sixteenth century fractured Christendom in western Europe. This, then, is the period most under consideration in this entry, and the texts and wider contexts for papal donations or bulls in regard to colonization will be the main focus. Bulls are papal letters or edicts, the name of which derives from the Latin *bulla*, or leaden seal, which most often sealed the documents. These letters gathered more weight as the Middle Ages progressed. Donations were gifts or endowment of lands. The most famous was the *Donation of Constantine*, which stated that the Roman Emperor gave Italian lands to Sylvester, bishop of Rome (pope), in order to give papal territorial claims longer and more sturdy and lofty origins, but Lorenzo Valla (ca. 1407–57), an Italian humanist, showed this to be a forgery of the eighth century. This donation was a prototype to the donations made by the Holy Roman Emperor and the popes. Bulls of donation were, then, edicts setting out a gift of lands.

PAPAL LANGUAGE, LAW, AND AUTHORITY

The language of the church, of canon law, and of papal authority became an instrument of European expansion and the subjugation of other regions and peoples. A legal framework was developed as the Iberian powers expanded.

Until the fifteenth century, relations with Islam had been a significant political and juridical consideration. In Iberia (a peninsula now occupied by Spain and Portugal), also known as Hispania, the Moors were thought to inhabit *terra irredenta*, lands that needed to be restored to legitimate Christian rulers, whereas pagan lands in Africa were considered *terra nullius*, uninhabited lands in the sense that these people lived without civility or a polis. Earlier writings, like those of Hortensius (Cardinal Henry of Susa, d. 1271), were used to justify Portuguese claims in Africa: Christ embodied temporal and spiritual lordship over the world, and this dominion was passed on to his representatives, the pontiffs or bishops of Rome, who could also delegate lordship over non-Christian lands.

PAPAL BULLS OR DONATIONS TO COLUMBUS'S LANDFALL IN 1492

The rediscovery of the Canary Islands off northwest Africa led to a conflict between Portugal and Castile. Pope Clement VI's (1291–1352) bull of 1344 gave Don Luis de la Cerda (d. 1348), uncle of King Alfonso XI, king of Castile (1312–1350), the authority to Christianize the islands, but when he failed to take possession, Portugal and Castile, which had supported his claim, continued their disagreement. Later bulls of donation alternately favored the two sides. Not until 1479 was the question of ownership settled: by the Treaty of Alcaçovas, Portugal ceded the Canaries to Castile.

Africa was the ground for the second controversy between Portugal and Castile. After the conquest of Ceuta in Morocco in 1415, Portugal made its claim in Africa by carrying out military expeditions in Morocco and voyages to Guinea. In the language of papal bulls, treaties and travel narratives attempted to establish the authority of the Europeans over various local or native populations. Slavery, trade, religion, and possession all were expressed in these documents. The Moors and Portuguese took slaves from each other. After the capture of Ceuta, slaves were more abundant and the papacy sanctioned the Portuguese practice.

On April 4, 1418, Pope Martin V (1368–1431) issued the bull *Sane Charissumus*, in which he appealed to Christian kings and princes to support João I (John I, 1357–1433) of Portugal in his fight against the Saracen Muslims from the Middle East and other enemies of Christ. Duarte Pacheco Pereira (ca. 1450–ca. 1526) noted the "holy revelation" that Prince Henry (1394–1460) of Portugal experienced when he learned of the "discovery" and "when the first negroes were brought to these realms," so that "he wrote to all the kings of Christendom inviting them to assist him in this discovery and conquest in the service of Our Lord, each of them to have an equal share of the profits, but they, considering it to be of no account, refused and renounced their rights" (63–64). Pereira observed that Prince Henry, under the authority of his brother, Afonso V (1432–1481), then presented, as part of his case for the right of conquest, the renunciation of the other European kings.

On September 8, 1436, Pope Eugene IV (1383–1447) published the bull *Rex regum*, which said that all newly conquered lands would belong to Portugal. This language was part of a conflict of expansion between Christian and Muslim states, but would set a precedence for western Europe in its expansion into sub-Saharan Africa, Asia, and the New World. The route of Vasco da Gama (ca. 1469–1524) to India was a great event. Language, trade, and empire traveled the same routes. In 1434 the Portuguese navigator Gil Eanes helped to lead the way to the upper Niger, Guinea, and Senegal, where in the 1440s and 1450s slaves and gold made for a lucrative trade.

In Africa, as in the Canaries, the kings of Castile based their claim to conquest on its possession by their ancestors, the Visigoths. The doctrine of dominion over non-Christians imbued the language of a papal bull in 1452, which donated to the crown of Portugal sovereignty over subjects in the lands that had been discovered, and another in 1454 over peoples in territories that the Portuguese might discover in Africa as they proceeded south. By 1454, the two countries were embroiled in this African controversy. The crown was obliged to convert these peoples, who could be conquered if they resisted trade with, the dominion of, and evangelization by Christians.

In these bulls the pope gave Portugal a monopoly in the expansion south of Morocco on the Atlantic coast of Africa. Pope Nicholas V (1397–1455) issued the bull *Romanus pontifex* on January 8, 1455, giving exclusive rights to King Alfonso of Portugal in this African exploration and trade and thus extending the bull *Dum diversas* (June 18, 1452), in which Nicholas had given Alfonso the right to conquer pagans, enslave them, and take their lands and goods. The language of these bulls attempted to extend the pope's authority and to rule on how Europe would expand. This linguistic framework had consequences for the European powers and the peoples with whom they came into contact. In the bull *Rex regum* (January 5, 1443), Pope Eugenius IV (1383–1447), Nicholas's predecessor, had taken a neutral stance between Castile and Portugal regarding Africa.

The Europeans themselves did not accept these papal documents, but used them to establish authority over other cultures. The Castilians would not recognize the authority of the papal letters and continued to claim Guinea until 1479, when, after the War of Succession (in which Alfonso invaded Castile in an attempt to annex it), Portugal ceded the Canaries and Castile acknowledged Portugal's claim to Guinea, the Azores, Madeira, and the Cape Verde Islands. This language of church authority had, but did not have, the power of enforcement.

The bulls of donation, or papal bulls, were not permanent laws. The parties involved in the disputes did not always accept them as remedies. Even though Portugal and Spain did not always admit the authority of these papal bulls or donations, these states insisted—from the late fifteenth century onward—that other nations, like France and England, abide by the papal bulls dividing the "undiscovered" world between the Iberian powers. Religious, legal, economic, and political aspects of language blend in the story of European expansion.

Portugal worked hard to differentiate itself: its quest for a Christian and "national" identity involved defeating the Moors and expanding effectively into Africa earlier than Spain. In the early 1450s, Muslim armies attacked Constantinople (now Istanbul, Turkey) and laid siege to Cyprus, Rhodes (in Greece), and Hungary. With expectations that this offensive would counter the attacks on Europe, Nicholas V was hopeful that the people of India would help Christians fight against Islam.

On February 16, 1456, Pope Callistus III (1378–1458) published the bull *Etsi cuncti*, in which he no longer addressed the other rulers of Europe, but instead appealed directly to Portugal to maintain monasteries in Ceuta. On August 31, 1471, Afonso published a law that forbade, under pain of death and the confiscation of ships, trade in and about Guinea. The Treaty of Toledo (March 6, 1480) confirmed Africa as Portugal's sphere and the Canary Islands as Spain's. A month later, Afonso ordered Portuguese captains that found foreigners in the seas in and about Guinea to seize their ships and throw those on board into the ocean.

During the fifteenth century, Portugal was cautious about expansion, looking after national self-interest and control. The Portuguese court had turned down the proposal of Paolo Toscanelli (1397–1482) for a westward voyage in 1474 and dismissed Christopher Columbus (1451–1506) ten years later. During the fourteenth and fifteenth centuries, the French, Portuguese, and Spanish attempted to make territorial claims and seek remedies through papal bulls, even though the bulls were not permanent laws. The Portuguese had their own plans for southern and eastern expansion but also reacted to Columbus's voyages by dividing the world unknown to Europeans with the Spanish by way of papal bulls.

Legal and political differences marked the Iberian expansion. One way of addressing controversies between Spain and Portugal was canon law, a mixing of legal

to the story of western European, and particularly Iberian, expansion into Africa, the Atlantic, and beyond. To some, the donations might seem distant and strange to the modern world, perhaps not even immediate enough to display in collections, as in 1893, but they were key to the shaping of the modern world well beyond the Catholic domain.

SEE ALSO *Catholic Church in Iberian America; Religion, Roman Catholic Church.*

BIBLIOGRAPHY

Curtis, William Eleroy. *Papers. Four Volumes on the World's Fair: Vols. 104–105 of the Scrapbooks.* Princeton, NJ: Seeley G. Mudd Library, Princeton University.

Davenport, Frances Gardiner, ed. *European Treaties bearing on the History of the United States and its Dependencies.* 4 vols. Washington, DC: Carnegie Institution of Washington, 1917–1937.

d'Avity, Pierre. *Les estats, empires, et principavtez de monde.* Paris: Chez Olivier de Varennes, 1613. Translated by Edward Grimestone as *The Estates, Empires, and Principalities of the World.* London, 1615.

Duviols, Jean-Paul. *L'Amérique espagnol vue et rêvée: Les livres de voyages de Christophe Colomb à Bougainville.* Paris: Promodis, 1985.

Eden, Richard. *The Decades of the Newe Worlde or West India.* London: G. Powell, 1555.

Fernández-Armesto, Felipe. *Before Columbus: Exploration and Colonisation from the Mediterranean to the Atlantic, 1229–1402.* Philadelphia: University of Pennsylvania Press, 1987.

Gibson, Charles, ed. *The Black Legend: Anti-Spanish Attitudes in the Old World and the New.* New York: Knopf, 1971.

Hakluyt, Richard, the Younger. *Discourse on Western Planting.* Edited by David B. Quinn and Alison M. Quinn. London: Hakluyt Society, 1993.

Hart, Jonathan. *Representing the New World: The English and French Uses of the Example of Spain.* New York and London: Palgrave, 2001.

Johnson, Robert. *Nova Britannia.* London: S. Macham, 1609.

Las Casas, Bartolomé de. *A Short Account of the Destruction of the Indies.* Translated and edited by Nigel Griffin. London and New York: Penguin, 1992.

Léry, Jean de. *History of a Voyage to the Land of Brazil, Otherwise Called America.* Translated by Janet Whatley. Berkeley: University of California Press, 1990.

McAlister, Lyle N. *Spain and Portugal in the New World, 1492–1700.* Minneapolis: University of Minnesota Press, 1984.

Pereira, Duarte Pacheco. *Esmeraldo de situ orbis.* Translated and edited by George H. T. Kimble. London: Hakluyt Society, 1937.

Rego, António da Silva. *Portuguese Colonization in the Sixteenth Century: A Study of the Royal Ordinances (Regimentos).* Johannesburg, South Africa: Witwatersrand University Press, 1965.

Savelle, Max. *The Origins of American Diplomacy: The International History of Angloamerica, 1492–1763.* New York: Macmillan, 1967.

Strachey, William. *The Historie of Travell into Virginia Britania* (1612). London: Hakluyt Society, 1953.

Jonathan Hart

PAPUA NEW GUINEA

Western influence was slow to reach the interior of the massive island of New Guinea. Traders and missionaries began to arrive in the mid-nineteenth century but their numbers remained small: malaria and the hostility of some Papua New Guinea (PNG) communities deterred more widespread settlement. The earliest traders were primarily British, or colonial Australian, and they traded in people as well as tropical products. Inexpensive labor was needed on the expanding plantations of Australia and Fiji during the last half of the nineteenth century, although concerns about slavery, along with developing a White Australian policy, put an end to the Western Pacific labor trade by the early twentieth century.

By this time, the Australian colony of Queensland maneuvered Britain into declaring Papua New Guinea a colony in 1884. The Netherlands and Germany eventually claimed the remaining parts of the island. These imperial rivalries were largely symbolic; New Guinea was not particularly important economically.

In Papua New Guinea the British operated largely by indirect rule, interfering as little as possible with village government, and allowing missionaries a large role in education. PNG islanders had responded enthusiastically to Anglicanism (as well as other Christian denominations), and by 1906 Britain handed control of the colony over to the new Commonwealth of Australia. Australia also took over the administration of German New Guinea and other areas after 1918.

By the interwar period, Papua New Guinea's small settler community, mainly plantation owners, pressured the colonial government into regulating village life and enforcing increasingly draconian penalties for offenses committed by islanders. This process peaked in 1926 with the passage of the White Women's Protection Ordinance; this new law made the death penalty mandatory for the *attempted* rape of a white woman by a PNG man.

World War II saw Papua New Guinea suddenly become strategically and politically important. Large numbers of troops poured into the region, and the contributions of PNG islanders to the Allied war effort were substantial. Calls for decolonization grew louder after 1945. Australia increased its spending on colonial infrastructure, and in 1962 the western part of New Guinea (formerly a Dutch colony) became the Indonesian province of Irian Jaya. PNG islanders pressed for rapid constitutional reform, and the country became independent in 1975.

Papua New Guinea had not had substantial preparation for self-rule, and this, combined with strong regional identities, created many intractable problems. The island of Bougainville attempted to secede almost immediately after independence. Political compromises broke down in the 1990s, and the PNG armed forces intervened several times on Bougainville. Papua New Guinea's fractured polity, and its ongoing reliance on Australian economic and military assistance, raises the question of whether technical independence brought about actual decolonization or not.

SEE ALSO *Missions, in the Pacific; Pacific, American Presence in; Pacific, European presence in.*

BIBLIOGRAPHY

Griffin, James, Hank Nelson, and Stewart Firth. *Papua New Guinea:. A Political History.* Richmond, Australia: Heinemann, 1979.

Siers, James. *Papua New Guinea.* Wellington, New Zealand: Millwood, 1981. Reprint, New York: St. Martins Press, 1984.

Waiko, John Dademo. *A Short History of Papua New Guinea.* Melbourne, Australia: Oxford University Press, 1995.

Jane Samson

PERRY, MATTHEW CALBRAITH
1794–1858

Matthew Calbraith Perry was born on April 10, 1794, in South Kingston, Rhode Island. His older brother, Oliver Hazard Perry, won a great victory over the British in the War of 1812 on Lake Erie. Matthew also enlisted in the U.S. Navy, being commissioned in 1809 and initially serving on the USS *Revenge*, which his older brother commanded.

For the next thirty years, Perry held a typical series of assignments. He saw little action in the War of 1812, for the Royal Navy trapped his main ship, the USS *United States,* at New London, Connecticut. After the war, he served on ships mostly assigned to suppress trade in West African slaves. Perry commanded the *Shark*, rotated to shore duty in Charleston, South Carolina, and in 1830 gained command of the USS *Concord*.

Perry became a noted advocate for naval education and for naval modernization. He helped design the curriculum for the U.S. Naval Academy and an education/apprentice system for new sailors. He was a leader in moving to steam propulsion from sail, and oversaw construction of the USS *Fulton,* the U.S. Navy's second stream frigate, organized the first corps of naval engineers, and conducted the first navy gunnery school near Sandy Hook, New Jersey, while commanding the *Fulton.* During the Mexican War, he led the squadron that took Frontera, Tabasco, and Laguna in 1846 and that helped General Winfield Scott in besieging Vera Cruz in 1847.

Perry, however, is best known for his trips to Japan. In 1852, Perry led four ships from Norfolk, Virginia, to Japan, a useful coaling stop on the route to China. On arriving near Edo, modern Tokyo, on July 8, 1853, he refused to move to Nagasaki and the Dutch concession in far southwest Japan, and marching with some four hundred armed sailors and marines insisted on delivering a letter from President Millard Fillmore to the Emperor. The Tokugawa Shogunate accepted the letter and Perry promised to return for a reply after a stop in China. Perry returned in February 1854 with eight steam ships—one-third of the U.S. Navy— belching their black smoke and once again impressing the Japanese (who called the men "barbarians . . . in floating volcanoes").

The United States and the Japanese soon signed an agreement, the Treaty of Kanagawa, on March 31, 1854, that reflected President Fillmore's demands, which included humane treatment for shipwrecked sailors, permission for U.S. ships to purchase coal and supplies, and the opening of two distant ports, Shimoda and Hakodate, to U.S. trade. Perry did not understand the structure of Japanese politics, and he never reached the emperor, dealing strictly with officials of the ruling Tokugawa shogunate. On his return to the United States, Perry received an award of $20,000 voted by a grateful Congress.

Perry's visit accelerated trends already present in Japan. The Tokugawa shogunate was tottering. Great lords (known as *daimyos*) in the southwest were aware of increasing Western encroachments on China, and feared for Japan. Perry's visit and his demand to open relations called into question the two-centuries-old Tokugawa policy of isolation. Perry's visit and the threat of European imperialism eventually caused the Tokugawa to ask the daimyos for advice, and the daimyos wanted to strengthen the emperor and the nation. The result was the end of 250 years of Tokugawa rule, and the onset of the Meiji Restoration. Within forty years, Japan cast off its past, modernized the nation, and bested a European power, Russia, at war in 1904–1905, and seemingly became a significant regional power. Perry died on March 4, 1858, in New York City.

SEE ALSO *Empire, United States; Japan, Colonized; Japan, Opening of.*

BIBLIOGRAPHY

Blumberg, Rhoda. *Commodore Perry in the Land of the Shogun.* New York: Lothrop, Lee & Shepard Books, 1985.

Neumann, William L. *America Encounters Japan: From Perry to MacArthur.* New York: Harper and Row, 1965.

Reischauer, Edwin O. *The United States and Japan.* Cambridge, MA: Harvard University Press, 1965.

Wiley, Peter B. *Yankees in the Land of the Gods: Commodore Perry and the Opening of Japan.* New York: Viking, 1990.

Charles M. Dobbs

PERU UNDER SPANISH RULE

Spanish rule in Peru was consolidated in 1533 with the execution of Atahualpa, the reigning Inca monarch, and the conquistadors' military occupation of the Inca capital of Cuzco. And in that same year Spanish rule was solidified by the installation of Manco Inca Capac, a nephew of Atahualpa, as a puppet king in alliance with the Spaniards. The leader of the conquistadors, Francisco Pizarro (ca. 1475–1541), established a Spanish municipal government in Cuzco in 1534 that was modeled on Spanish cities. But in order to further establish Spanish hegemony, Pizarro moved the capital in 1535 to the newly established Spanish city of Lima on the Pacific coast, where there had been no prior Inca city.

Other Spaniards established municipalities at key points throughout the interior in order to facilitate trade and communication with other Spanish territories. These towns and cities became the building blocks of colonization in Peru, from which the Spanish implemented a policy of "pacification and colonization" (*pacificación y población*) that enabled Spanish military rule in the Andean regions, underpinned by a steady influx of Spaniards in search of land, wealth, and new opportunities. The new city of Lima would become the capital of the viceroyalty of Peru and, when the discovery of Peruvian silver stimulated the development of a rich commerce with Europe, the largest and most important trading center in South America. Internal rivalries amongst Pizarro and his associates, however, would lead to civil wars among the Spaniards—and finally to the assassination of Pizarro in 1541.

Hence, the rapid collapse of the Inca kingdom did not ensure the immediate stability of Spanish rule in Peru. Although consolidation of Spanish rule continued apace, Peru remained wracked by tensions and conflicts between Spaniards and the indigenous population for most of the sixteenth century. Manco Inca Capac broke his alliance with the Spaniards and led a great rebellion that almost overturned Spanish rule in Cuzco. Manco then withdrew to the mountains, where in 1536 at Vilcambamba he established a small Inca kingdom. Though Manco's kingdom never constituted a serious threat to Spanish rule, it remained independent until finally destroyed in 1572. Yet the revived Inca kingdom provided further impetus for a reinforced Spanish military presence and stronger colonial administrative apparatus.

At Cuzco, the Spaniards reestablished peace with the Incas by crowning Paullu (ca. 1510–1550) as Inca king, but they quickly entered into violent conflicts among themselves. While factions led by Francisco Pizarro and Diego de Almagro (ca. 1474–1538) fought over the spoils of conquest during the late 1530s, they also resisted efforts by the Spanish Crown to impose its authority by sending a viceroy to Peru—which finally transpired with the appointment of Blasco Nuñez Vela (d. 1546) to the office in 1544.

Faced with the near decimation of the indigenous population by the end of the sixteenth century—some estimates suggest up to 90 percent of the indigenous population was lost to war, disease, and forced labor—the Spaniards were caught between their need for labor, mounting pressures from the Spanish monarchs for laws protecting the rights of the Indians, and the interests of the colonizers to maintain control over their newly acquired property in Peru. As in New Spain, a system of royal land grants (*encomiendas*) to Spanish colonists was the primary mode of colonization—controversial grants that also included rights to indigenous labor and taxation over the Indians, although outright slavery was forbidden. These grants also included the obligation to provide for the conversion to Christianity and continued religious education of the indigenous charges, the failure of which was a source of continued tension between landowners and religious communities.

Following vociferous complaints from the religious communities in New Spain, the Spanish monarchs implemented the "New Laws" in 1542, which, among other things, required these grants, or *encomiendas,* be returned to the crown's jurisdiction upon the death of the original *encomendero* (grant holder). The uproar in Peru over the denial of heredity value to their newly acquired land led Gonzalo Pizarro (ca. 1506–1548), the brother of Francisco, to lead a rebellion against and finally execute Viceroy Nuñez Vela, who demanded that Spaniards comply with the New Laws. Gonzalo Pizarro was defeated in 1548, but conflict with the crown did not end there. In 1553 Francisco Hernández Girón (1510–1554) lead another rebellion of other *encomenderos* who rejected royal attempts to curb their exploitation of the Indians. Using Indians as auxiliary troops, Hernández Girón fought until he was defeated the following year.

Pizarro and the Inca. *An undated woodcut depicts a meeting between Francisco Pizarro and the leader of the Incas. Spanish rule in Peru was consolidated in 1533 with the execution of the reigning Inca monarch.* © BETTMANN/CORBIS. REPRODUCED BY PERMISSION.

The consolidation of the Spanish presence and the transformation of Peru into a prosperous and stable Spanish colony were most closely linked not to agriculture but to the development of silver mining. The discovery of the vast silver mines of Potosí in 1545 heralded a new era that transformed the social and economic landscape of Peru and led to its conversion into Spain's wealthiest colony.

The millions of tons of silver extracted from the mines of Cerro Rico at Potosí—at the expense of as many as eight million of the coerced indigenous workers and imported African slaves—made Potosí among the most populous cities in the world before the eighteenth century. At over 200,000 inhabitants, and with more churches than any other city in the Spanish world, Potosí rapidly became a key economic center of the Spanish Empire, financing rich flows of transatlantic trade, stimulating agriculture and industry throughout the Andean region, and providing Spanish kings with the fiscal revenues that underpinned their exercise of power in Europe and beyond.

Potosí further funded the extravagant lives of many European monarchs, and financed continued global exploration for more than two hundred years. Although the decline of silver production in the seventeenth century did much to precipitate the declining power of the Spanish Empire, the recovery of Peruvian mining during the later eighteenth century ensured that Peru remained an important colony with close ties to Spain.

The long-term modes of colonial administration in Peru were consolidated by the end of the sixteenth century. The viceroyalty of Peru became the administrative arm of the Spanish monarchy in South America, and the person of the viceroy presided over a society stratified by class and ethnicity, and almost wholly dependent upon forced indigenous labor. Second in geographical expanse only to the viceroyalty of New Spain, the authority of Lima covered the entire South American continent save Portuguese-controlled Brazil and part of Venezuela. The viceroy implemented laws, collected taxes, settled disputes among the local colonists, and managed the delicate and tenacious relations between the Spaniards and the indigenous population.

The new capital of Lima also became the center for the royal *audiencia*, a supreme court and administrative body that acted as a support for and check upon the viceroy, and which oversaw relations between the colonists and the crown. Governance of the indigenous population throughout Peru was brought under the office of the *corregidor*, an office implemented to provide royal supervision over local indigenous leaders who were installed in certain areas to govern, albeit in a limited way, their own territories. The *corregidor* also oversaw disputes between the indigenous and Spanish populations.

The stabilization of Spanish rule in Peru owed much to Viceroy Francisco de Toledo (1520–1583), the most influential of the Spanish viceroys. Toledo attempted during his long viceregency between 1569 and 1581 to reaffirm royal authority and to bring an end to the tumultuous period following the conquests of Pizarro. In taking steps to implement systematic control over the Spanish and indigenous population, Toledo combined repression with reform. He ordered the end of the Inca kingdom at Vilcambamba in 1572 and finally executed Túpac Amaru, the last remaining Inca king—bringing about a sharp rebuke from the Spanish monarch in Madrid, but not a reduction of the viceroy's power.

Toledo established indigenous communities *(reducciones)* under the supervision of Catholic priests. The *reducciones* isolated the Indians from contact with Spaniards save for religious education and required labor. Toledo also worked to end abuses of indigenous labor and promoted limited local rule in indigenous communities based on pre-extant Inca laws. It was also under Toledo's leadership that intensive investigations into indigenous religious life were conducted; this information was used in the "extirpation of idolatry" campaigns of the late sixteenth and early seventeenth centuries, which attempted to end altogether pre-Columbian religious practices. But, perhaps most importantly from the Spanish perspective, Toledo provided a system of coerced native labor for the silver mines through the infamous *mita* system, which forced indigenous communities to supply a steady labor force for the mines at Potosí and elsewhere.

Under Toledo's leadership Lima also became the center for religious control over Peru, especially as the archbishopric of Lima quickly became among the most highly paid and powerful positions in colonial society. The archdiocese controlled the religious education of colonial elites through the newly founded University of San Marcos, and oversaw the rapid growth of convents and monasteries under its expansive jurisdiction. New

authority was granted to the archdiocese with the arrival of the Inquisition in 1569. Three major councils of the church met between 1570 and 1583, the third and most famous of which required priests and missionaries to learn indigenous languages and formally adopted catechisms in the Aymara and Quechua languages.

In 1700 the Bourbon dynasty replaced Hapsburg rule in Spain, and the new Bourbon rulers promoted economic development and reform in the colonies. However, Peru was weakened in the eighteenth century by the creation of two other new viceroyalties—New Granada (1717) and Río de la Plata (1776). These new jurisdictions ended the domination of Lima in continental affairs and its monopoly over trade relations, and further meant the loss of Peru's lucrative silver mines at Potosí.

Bourbon rule was further complicated by a series of indigenous revolts that shook Peru in the eighteenth century. After more than a dozen large-scale uprisings, a Jesuit-educated *mestizo* named José Condorcanqui (ca. 1742–1781) took on the name of his executed ancestor, Túpac Amaru, and executed the Spanish *corregidor* in Cuzco on charges of cruelty. Appealing both to Inca traditions and to Christian traditions, Túpac Amaru launched a revolt against the excesses of the colonial government that began in the Cuzco region, but quickly spread throughout the southern Andes, only ending with his capture and execution in 1781.

Spanish rule survived this great threat from the indigenous population, and during the emerging years of the independence movements in Latin America, Peru tended to side with the Spanish monarchs. Weary of their treatment by the same Spanish Creoles who fought Spain for liberty, much of the indigenous population sided with royalist forces even during the wars of independence. Suspicious of Argentine and Chilean ambitions, and with a sizable number of elites still protective of their institutional and economic privileges with the crown, Peru was only liberated from Spanish rule by the successful occupation of Lima by the Argentine general José de San Martín (1778–1850) in 1821.

A failed alliance between San Martín and General Simón Bolívar (1783–1830) resulted in Bolívar finally establishing the Republic of Peru after the battles of Ayacucho and Junín in 1824. With these military victories, Bolívar not only established a new republic, but opened the way to the subsequent declaration of independence in 1825 of Upper Peru into the new Republic of Bolivia. Hence Peru's silver mines at Potosí, which had determined so much of its history, were permanently liberated from Peruvian rule by an independent Bolivia.

SEE ALSO *Inca Empire; Lima; Mining, the Americas; Pizarro, Francisco; Túpac Amaru, Rebellion of.*

BIBLIOGRAPHY

Andrien, Kenneth J. *Crisis and Decline: The Viceroyalty of Peru in the Seventeenth Century.* Albuquerque: University of New Mexico Press, 1985.

Arzáns de Orsúa y Vela, Bartolomé. *Tales of Potosí.* Edited by R. C. Padden. Providence, RI: Brown University Press, 1975.

Bethell, Leslie, ed. *The Cambridge History of Latin America.* Cambridge, U.K.: Cambridge University Press, 1984.

Bowser, Frederick P. *The African Slave in Colonial Peru: 1524–1650.* Stanford, CA: Stanford University Press, 1974.

Cameron, Ian. *The Kingdom of the Sun God: A History of the Andes and Their People.* New York: Facts on File, 1990.

Cook, Noble David. *Demographic Collapse: Indian Peru, 1520–1620.* Cambridge, U.K.: Cambridge University Press, 1981.

de la Vega, Garcilasco. *Royal Commentaries of the Incas and General History of Peru.* Translated by Harold V. Livermore. Austin: University of Texas Press, 1987.

Fisher, John R. *Silver Mines and Silver Miners in Colonial Peru, 1776–1824.* Liverpool, U.K.: University of Liverpool, 1977.

Flores Galindo, Alberto. *Túpac Amaru II–1780: Sociedad colonial y sublevaciones populares.* Lima, Peru: Retablo de Papel Ediciones, 1976.

Guamán Poma de Ayala, Felipe. *Letter to a King: A Peruvian Chief's Account of Life Under the Incas and Under Spanish Rule.* New York: Dutton, 1978.

Lockhart, James. *Spanish Peru, 1532–1560: A Colonial Society.* Madison: University of Wisconsin Press, 1968.

MacCormack, Sabine. *Religion in the Andes: Vision and Imagination in Early Colonial Peru.* Princeton, NJ: Princeton University Press, 1991.

Mejía Baca, Juan, ed. *Historia del Perú.* 12 vols. Lima, Peru: Editorial Mejía Baca, 1980.

Mills, Kenneth. *Idolatry and its Enemies: Colonial Andean Religion and Extirpation, 1640–1750.* Princeton, NJ: Princeton University Press, 1997.

O'Phelan Godoy, Scarlett. *Rebellions and Revolts in Eighteenth-Century Peru and Upper Peru.* Cologne, Germany: Bohlau, 1985.

Prescott, William H. *History of the Conquest of Peru.* New York: Modern Library, 1936.

Stern, Steve J. *Peru's Indian Peoples and the Challenge of Spanish Conquest: Huamanga to 1640.* Madison: University of Wisconsin Press, 1982; 2nd ed., 1993.

Wachtel, Nathan. *The Vision of the Vanquished: The Spanish Conquest of Peru Through Indian Eyes, 1530–1570.* Translated by Ben and Sian Reynolds. New York: Barnes and Noble, 1977.

Patrick Provost-Smith

PIZARRO, FRANCISCO
1475–1541

Born in Trujillo, Spain, the product of an illegitimate liaison between Captain Gonzalo Pizarro and Francesca Gonzales, a peasant girl, there was nothing to indicate that great things could be expected from Francisco Pizarro. In fact, the first years of his life seemed to have been spent tending the pigs at the home of his grandparents. However, if his father had given him anything, it was apparently his love for adventure and the soldier's life. His appetite for both was whetted first at home, where he participated in conflicts between prominent landed families for control of the Spanish countryside, and later in Italy, where he soldiered under the command of Gonzalo Fernández de Córdoba (1453–1515).

In 1502, at age twenty-seven, Pizarro left Europe, bound for Hispaniola, known today as Haiti and the Dominican Republic, to assist the governor in running the new colonies created by the discoveries of Christopher Columbus (1451–1506). But he soon tired of the daily grind of the administrator's world in favor of the adventurer's life, and in 1510 joined Alonso de Ojeda's (ca. 1468–1515) expedition to Colombia. Three years later he accompanied Vasco Núñez de Balboa (1475–1519) as Balboa laid claim to the Pacific Ocean. That expedition won Pizarro the post of mayor of Panama from 1519 until 1523. But his ambition remained unsatisfied, and in 1523 Pizarro began the work that would help bring him fame, fortune, and would eventually claim his life.

It started with a partnership, formed with a fellow soldier, Diego de Almagro (ca. 1474–1538), and a priest, Hernando de Luque (d. 1532). Between 1523 and 1528 they conducted two expeditions along the Colombian coast. The journeys were both difficult and dangerous, and on the second trip Pizarro and most of his crew were forced to stop and rest, while a smaller team led by Bartolomé Ruiz (d. 1534) continued on, passing the equator. It was there that Ruiz intercepted a trading craft headed north from what its known today as Peru, loaded with fabrics and precious metals. Ruiz returned to Pizarro's camp, reported the news, and then led the entire expedition southward, stopping while Diego del Almagro returned to Panama for more men and supplies.

Almagro's reception by Spanish authorities in Panama proved to be a hostile one. The new governor, afraid of sacrificing more men and money, refused Pizarro's request, and ordered Almagro to tell Pizarro and his men to come home. Not interested in abandoning the expedition in light of the treasures already found, and convinced there were more to be had, Pizarro went to Spain in 1528 to plead his case directly to King Charles I (1500–1558). By 1530, he had won not only royal approval, but also the rank of governor and captain-general with control of territory stretching more that 960 kilometers (about 600 miles) south of Panama to be called New Castile. He was also given enough money to outfit three ships and provision 180 men.

In January 1530, Pizarro left Spain with everything he needed to conquer Peru. In April of that year, he and his two partners, de Almagro and Hernando de Luque, made contact with Atahualpa (ca. 1502–1533), emperor of the Incas, the dominant indigenous force in Peru. Atahualpa was engaged in a civil war to maintain control of the Inca empire. A meeting was arranged in November in the town of Cajamarca. Pizarro's objective was to have Atahualpa embrace Christianity and the rule of King Charles. Atahualpa arrived in Cajamarca with an escort of several thousand soldiers, and after listening to Pizarro's representatives, rejected both demands. The meeting then turned into an ambush, as Pizarro's men opened fire with muskets, crossbows, and cannons. Most of Atahualpa's men were killed. Atahualpa himself was captured by the Spanish and held until 1533, when Pizarro had him executed. Upon hearing news of Atahualpa's death, most armed resistance to Spain collapsed, and Pizarro occupied Cuzco, the Inca capital without incident in November 1533.

Pizarro sought to take control of highland Peru by distributing *encomiendas* among his trusted followers, while also using puppet Inca kings enthroned in Cuzco. But his ascendancy was marked by deep and growing conflict. Manco Inca (d. 1545) rejected his role as a puppet king in 1535 and led a great rebellion against the Spaniards before retreating to the countryside. After surviving the Inca rebellion, the Spaniards fought among themselves in recurrent civil wars, driven by a fight for the spoils of conquest and the rivalries of the Pizarro and Almagro factions.

The last eight years of Francisco Pizarro's life were spent in Lima, the new capital of Peru, where he consolidated Spain's control over the country, making sure he and his family members reaped the benefits of their efforts. This was a unique combination of a new business enterprise coupled with traditional colonial administration. But the distribution of the spoils apparently did not extend far enough beyond Pizarro's family to satisfy his original partners, Diego de Almagro and Hernando de Luque. In fact, Almagro went so far as to occupy Cuzco in a bid for power. He was persuaded to leave the city and head south to Chile, which King Charles had awarded him. But the riches of Chile were nothing in comparison to Peru's, and Almagro returned to fight for his share, only to be captured and executed by Pizarro's forces. King Charles made Pizarro a marquis, but his triumph did not last long. Almagro's supporters, including his son, plotted revenge, and on June 26, 1541, they attacked Pizarro's stronghold in Lima. Pizarro died in the attack.

SEE ALSO *Conquests and Colonization; Peru Under Spanish Rule.*

BIBLIOGRAPHY

Hemming, John. *The Conquest of the Incas.* New York: Harcourt, 1970. Rev. ed., New York: Penguin, 1983.

Syme, Ronald. *Francisco Pizarro: Finder of Peru.* New York: Morrow, 1963.

Varón Gabai, Rafael. *Francisco Pizarro and His Brothers: The Illusion of Power in Sixteenth-Century Peru.* Translated by Javier Flores Espinoza. Norman: University of Oklahoma Press, 1997.

John Morello

PLANTATIONS, THE AMERICAS

The plantation developed in the Americas as part of the region's incorporation into the European world economy. Plantation agriculture was at once linked to the emergence of world markets for tropical staples, and to the control of an abundant, cheap, and disciplined labor force secured by direct or indirect compulsion. Slavery, indentured or contract labor, sharecropping, and tenancy concentrated laborers in commercial crop production, reduced their bargaining power, subjected them to lowered standards of living, and imposed a strict labor discipline enforced by a hierarchical staff of supervisors. A clear distinction existed between powerful owners, who generally claimed European descent, and a subordinate, and racially and culturally distinct, labor force. The planters' coercive control over labor, guaranteed by the colonial state, established the conditions for profitable, large-scale commodity production in the American plantation zone. Over the course of its evolution, plantation agriculture transformed tobacco, coffee, bananas, cacao, cotton, and, above all, sugar cane from luxury items into articles of mass consumption.

THE EMERGENCE OF THE PLANTATION

Specialized production of plantation staples depended upon overseas markets for the sale of the crops, while capital, technology, consumer goods, and labor were imported from abroad. The development of the plantation was shaped by colonial rivalries between European powers, the expansion and diversification of markets, growing productive capacities, and changing sources of labor supply and forms of labor control throughout this international socioeconomically complex world.

Plantation production developed along the coastal lowlands from Brazil to Chesapeake Bay and throughout the Caribbean islands where soil, climate, and ease of transport facilitated large-scale production. The sparse indigenous populations in these regions, unaccustomed to settled agriculture and European diseases, provided

Plantation Slaves in Brazil. *Household slaves working on a Brazilian plantation are engaged in domestic chores in this mid-nineteenth-century engraving.* **THE GRANGER COLLECTION, NEW YORK. REPRODUCED BY PERMISSION.**

insufficient labor and were replaced by imported workers. Later, with changes in transportation, production technologies, and market patterns, plantation production spread along the coastal lowlands of Peru, Ecuador, and Central America and to inland regions of Brazil, the United States South, Mexico, Colombia, and Argentina. Throughout these zones, the plantation degraded environments, disrupted preexisting cultural norms, and eliminated competing forms of economic and social organization.

SUGAR AND TOBACCO PRODUCTION

Plantation regimes were at once shaped by the material conditions required to produce specific staples and by their dependence on world markets. Historically, sugar was perhaps the most important plantation crop and the one that developed this productive form to the fullest. Beginning in the eleventh century, growing European demand stimulated the spread of sugar production westward across the Mediterranean to the Atlantic. By 1470, refineries in Venice, Bologna, and Antwerp established a colonial relationship between producing regions and dominant importers.

The adoption of Arab production techniques, especially irrigation, transformed cultivation and allowed intensification of land use. In the fifteenth century sugar

mills in southern Spain and Portugal turned to African slaves as a source of labor. Nonetheless, the sugar industry in the European Mediterranean was characterized by small-scale production and diverse ways of organizing land and labor. This pattern of sugar cultivation was extended to Madeira, and the Canary Islands in the Atlantic. Sugar remained a costly luxury product.

During the sixteenth century, the emergence in Spanish Hispaniola and, above all, in the Portuguese colony of São Tomé of large plantations using African slaves to produce cheap, low-quality sugar for metropolitan refiners signaled the transition from Mediterranean polyculture to American sugar monoculture. The decisive break with the Mediterranean pattern came in Brazil. Ideal climate, together with unlimited supplies of fuel, land, and at first indigenous and then imported African servile labor, established the characteristic pattern of American plantation agriculture.

The growing demand for slave labor in Brazil increased the volume of the slave trade and consolidated the plantation's fateful association with African slavery. Powerful *senhores de engenho* (the masters of the mill) monopolized access to river courses in order to grind their own cane and that of dependent cane farmers who themselves often employed large numbers of slaves in a complex division of labor that combined sugar cultivation and manufacture. African slavery, fertile soil, and improved milling techniques promoted large-scale production. Brazil dominated world production as sugar reached growing numbers of European consumers and became a significant source of colonial wealth. In contrast, tobacco was an indigenous American crop. It required no large investment to start up, and it could be cultivated successfully on a small scale. Nonetheless, by the 1620s rising European demand for tobacco stimulated concentration of land and labor in the Chesapeake Tidewater region as wealthy planters achieved economies of scale at the expense of native peoples and European smallholders. Initially indentured Europeans provided labor, but after the 1640s changing patterns of migration in combination with local conditions resulted in a shift to African slave labor.

Tobacco was grown on small scattered plots and required skilled labor working under close supervision. Its labor force was smaller than that for other plantation staples. Nonetheless, ownership of land and slaves was the key to success. Recurrent depressions in the tobacco market drove out smallholders while big planters were better able to survive hard times and reaped disproportionate benefits from upswings. The slave-owning gentry dominated the Chesapeake tobacco region until the 1780s when the War for Independence (1775–1781) disrupted access to markets, and tobacco was no longer profitable. Planters turned to general farming as better and cheaper tobacco was produced on the western frontier.

With the expulsion of the Dutch from Brazil in 1654, the Caribbean emerged as the center of sugar production. Rather than directly organizing production, the Dutch offered slaves, technology, credit, and access to Dutch markets to British and French planters. By the 1720s the consolidation of large estates and massive importation of slaves eliminated the European yeomanry and indentured labor. The West Indies were transformed into "sugar islands," with majority populations of African descent. They became the cornerstone of imperial politics and were at the heart of the transatlantic commercial complex linking the African slave trade, European manufactures, and livestock, lumber, fish, and grain from North America.

Almost one-third of the slaves transported during the course of the entire African slave trade were imported to the British and French Caribbean between 1701 and 1810. In Saint Domingue, the richest colony in the world, nearly half a million slaves produced more wealth than all of British West Indies and allowed France to compete with Britain in international politics and trade.

EMERGENCE OF MODERN PLANTATION AGRICULTURE

By the nineteenth century, industrialization and urbanization in Europe and North America and slave emancipation

throughout the hemisphere led to the decline of the old sugar colonies and the emergence of modern plantation agriculture. World demand for sugar, coffee, cotton, cacao, and later bananas resulted in the extension and diversification of plantation production. The railroad and steamship opened new areas to cultivation and linked them more firmly to international trade.

Paradoxically, growing world demand for key agricultural commodities expanded plantation slavery in certain regions even as the international slave trade was being suppressed. Cuba, with a slave population of up to 400,000 in the mid-nineteenth century, emerged as the world's leading sugar producer. The first railroad in Latin America and the introduction of modern milling and refining technologies in Cuba increased the scale of production and transformed the relation between land, labor, and capital. The expansion of the slave cotton plantation allowed the United States South to dominate world production and fueled the Industrial Revolution.

With the emergence in the 1830s of the *fazenda* (a large-scale agro-industrial unit that both cultivated and processed coffee) worked by African slaves in the Valley of Paraíba and the west of São Paulo state, Brazil became the world's foremost coffee producer. In Cuba, slave labor was obtained legally and illegally through the transatlantic slave trade while American and Brazilian planters obtained the majority of their labor though internal slave trades. Cuba, Brazil, and the United States were the last countries in the hemisphere to abolish slavery, the United States being engaged in the civil war.

By the second half of the nineteenth century, plantation agriculture spread beyond the Americas. Java, India, Ceylon, the Philippines, Australia, and South Africa, among others, emerged as important centers of plantation production. In the Americas, the cultivation of sugar as a plantation crop spread to Peru, Colombia, Puerto Rico, the Dominican Republic, and Louisiana. Coffee was also grown as a plantation crop in Colombia, Puerto Rico, Cuba, Guatemala, and El Salvador. With the introduction of the refrigerator ship, bananas became an important plantation crop in Central America, Columbia, and Ecuador. At the same time, coffee, cotton, bananas, and other plantation crops began to be produced on a significant scale in a variety of nonplantation arrangements of land, labor, and capital for an expanding and increasingly integrated world market.

Slave emancipation and growing demand for plantation products initiated a search for new sources of labor. In many places, state-sponsored immigration provided an alternative source of labor. Contract laborers from India, China, Indochina, Japan, Africa, Madeira, and the Canary Islands were variously distributed to British Guiana, Trinidad, Jamaica, Cuba, Peru, and Brazil. Italian *colonos* replaced African slaves in the Brazilian coffee zone. In the lowlands of the Andes and Central America labor was recruited from highland peasant communities.

The demand for labor sharpened conflicts between plantations and smallholders and shaped racial, ethnic, and cultural diversity throughout the plantation zones. By the 1920s large-scale international migration ended. A variety of forms of sharecropping, tenancy, contract labor, and wage labor prevailed. The plantation monopolized resources and eliminated alternative economic activities. Workers were exposed to seasonal employment, and, where labor was insufficient, regional inequalities created local sources of migrant labor.

Conversely, technical innovation, the growing scale of production, and capital investment transformed plantation ownership and financing. Local planter classes were increasingly subordinated to or eliminated by corporate capital as plantations were integrated into production, marketing, and financial networks dominated by transnational enterprises. The plantation lost its distinctive character and came to resemble other forms of large-scale capitalist agriculture.

SEE ALSO *African Slavery in the Americas; Cacao; Caribbean; Coffee Cultivation; Coffee in the Americas; Cotton; Haciendas in Spanish America; Sugar Cultivation and Trade; Tobacco Cultivation and Trade; Virginia Company.*

BIBLIOGRAPHY

Beckford, George. *Persistent Poverty: Underdevelopment and the Plantation Economies of the Third World.* New York: Oxford University Press, 1972.

Bergad, Laird W. *Cuban Rural Society in the Nineteenth Century: The Social and Economic History of Monoculture in Matanzas.* Princeton, NJ: Princeton University Press, 1990.

Curtin, Philip D. *The Rise and Fall of the Plantation Complex: Essays in Atlantic History.* Cambridge, U.K.: Cambridge University Press, 1990.

Dunn, Richard. *Sugar and Slaves: The Rise of the Planter Class in the English West Indies, 1624–1713.* New York: W.W. Norton, 1973.

Gonzales, Michael J. *Plantation Agriculture and Social Control in Northern Peru, 1875–1933.* Austin: University of Texas Press, 1985.

Kulikoff, Allan. *Tobacco and Slaves: The Development of the Southern Cultures in the Chesapeake, 1680–1800.* Chapel Hill: University of North Carolina Press, 1986.

Mintz, Sidney W. *Sweetness and Power: The Place of Sugar in Modern History.* New York: Penguin Books, 1985.

Moreno Fraginals, Manuel Moya, Frank Pons, and Stanley L. Engerman. *Between Slavery and Free Labor: The Spanish Speaking Caribbean in the Nineteenth Century.* Baltimore: Johns Hopkins University Press, 1985.

Morgan, Philip. *Slave Counterpoint: Black Culture in the Eighteenth-Century Chesapeake and Lowcountry.* Chapel Hill: University of North Carolina Press, 1998.

Schwartz, Stuart B. *Sugar Plantations in the Formation of Brazilian Society: Bahia, 1550–1835.* Cambridge, U.K.: Cambridge University Press, 1985.

Scott, Rebecca J. *Slave Emancipation in Cuba: The Transition to Free Labor, 1860–1899.* Princeton, NJ: Princeton University Press, 1985.

Sheridan, Richard. *Sugar and Slavery: An Economic History of the British West Indies, 1623-1775.* Bridgetown, Barbados: Caribbean Universities Press, 1974.

Stein, Stanley J. *Vassouras: A Brazilian Coffee County, 1850–1900: The Roles of Planter and Slave in a Plantation Society.* Princeton, NJ: Princeton University Press, 1985.

Stolcke, Verena. *Coffee Planters Workers and Wives: Class Conflict and Gender Relations on São Paulo Plantations, 1850–1980.* London: Macmillan, 1988.

Wright, Gavin. *The Political Economy of the Cotton South: Households, Markets, and Wealth in the Nineteenth Century.* New York: W.W. Norton, 1973.

Dale W. Tomich

POLYNESIA

Polynesia is a region of the Pacific Ocean and forms, together with Melanesia and Micronesia, one of the three cultural areas of Oceania. Polynesia extends from the Hawaiian Islands in the north to New Zealand in the south, and from Tuvalu in the west to Rapanui (Easter Island) in the east. The region includes Samoa, Tonga, Tahiti, and the Cook and Marquesas Islands. The name Polynesia derives from Greek words meaning *many islands* and refers to the numerous islands of the region.

Human beings began settling in western Polynesia over 3,000 years ago but did not reach its fringes until between 1,000 and 2,000 years ago. Polynesians are excellent sailors and discovered and settled nearly every island in the region. Traditional Polynesian society was based on a hierarchical system of hereditary chiefs with individuals divided into nobility and commoners. Polynesian kings extended their control over entire archipelagos, forming kingdoms such as those in Tonga and Hawai'i.

The first European to visit Polynesia was the Spaniard Álvaro de Mendaña (1541–1595), who reached Tuvalu in 1568. Dutch explorers followed in the 1600s, with the English and French beginning their own expeditions in the 1700s. The English explorer Samuel Wallis (1728–1795) reached Tahiti in 1767 and Captain James Cook (1728–1779) reached the Cook Islands (later named after him) in 1773 and Hawai'i in 1778.

As in other parts of Oceania, European colonialism really began in the nineteenth century. Britain claimed

For the next four decades, the Portuguese conducted an ongoing military campaign to subjugate the native African populations of its colonies in southern Africa. By the beginning of the twentieth century, they had subdued the populous Ovimbundu states in central Angola. The large kingdom of the Kwanhana in southern Angola was not vanquished, however, until after World War I (1914–1918). Indeed, although the Portuguese formally declared in 1922 that Angola had been "pacified," armed resistance to Portuguese rule continued throughout the colony, especially among the Bakongo and Mbundi people of northern Angola. In the process of "pacification," the native Africans were displaced, and through a decree that made it a crime to be unemployed, most were forced to labor on the extensive coffee plantations that were established by the colonials.

The mixed-race Creoles who were descended from the earliest Portuguese traders and settlers and who were centered in the Luanda area in Angola initially prospered under the more formal colonial regime, but they gradually lost influence as resistance to Portuguese rule became more entrenched in the farther reaches of the colony. In Mozambique, Portugal had hoped to subdue the interior through the establishment of strong colonial agricultural communities. But when it became clear that Portugal lacked the resources to succeed in this effort, the Portuguese government sold economic concessions within regions of the colony to three international consortia. Commercial mercenaries, these consortia could exploit the resources and native labor in the undeveloped interior in exchange for developing a rail system and other transportation and communication infrastructure that would accelerate European settlement.

In both Angola and Mozambique, the rise of the dictatorial regime of António Salazar (1889–1970) in Portugal meant an increasingly repressive reaction to African demands for just treatment and political and economic rights. Especially in Angola, the Portuguese became expert at exploiting longstanding tensions among the dominant ethnic groups, and in both Angola and Mozambique, the native insurgencies became proxy conflicts in which the Cold War competition between the United States and the Soviet Union was played out. Through direct military and economic aid and covert operations, the United States supported the Salazar regime's campaigns against the largely Soviet-supported insurgencies. In Angola, three independence movements developed—the MPLA (the Popular Movement for the Liberation of Angola), the FNLA (the National Front for the Liberation of Angola), and UNITA (the National Union for the Total Independence of Angola). In Mozambique, the insurgency was dominated by Frelimo (the Mozambican Liberation Front), whose leadership had been trained in Algeria and Egypt.

The African discoveries of Portugal	
THE FIFTEENTH CENTURY	
1433–1434	Cape Bojador
1444	Senegal River
1446	Gambia River
1456	Cape Verde Islands
1460	Cape Palmas
1471	Fernando Po
1482	Construction of Elmina Castle
1483	Congo River
1488	Cape of Good Hope

THE GALE GROUP.

After Salazar's regime collapsed in 1974 and the new Portuguese government committed itself to a quick transition to independence in the colonies, the United States and Soviet Union supported contending African factions in the now-independent states—factions that they supported through, respectively, South African and Cuban surrogate forces. For the next decade and a half, both Angola and Mozambique were devastated by these ongoing and often very anarchic conflicts. By 2006, their economies had still not become self-sustaining, and large portions of their populations remained in refugee camps where large commitments of foreign aid provided basic foodstuffs and rudimentary medical care as a stopgap against mass starvation and epidemics.

After the end of the international slave trade in the 1830s, Portugal's small West African colonies decreased in importance and became increasingly impoverished. The Portuguese attempted to establish a plantation economy, but the fields in the Cape Verde Islands, in particular, were devastated by cyclic droughts. The Portuguese lacked the resources to compensate for the crop failures, and in at least seven periods between the 1770s and the late 1940s, between 15 percent and 40 percent of the islands' population starved to death as a consequence. After 18 percent perished from 1948 to 1949, the Portuguese government responded to international pressure and in 1951 designated the Cape Verde Islands as a province of Portugal. Educational and economic opportunities within Portugal were opened to Cape Verdeans. Some of those educated in Portugal then returned to Cape Verde and went to Guinea-Bissau and São Tomé in order to provide the nucleus of an independence movement. In 1963 an active insurgency began in Guinea-Bissau, but it would take just over a decade for the ongoing insurgencies in all of Portugal's African colonies to cause the collapse of the Salazar regime and to achieve independence.

SEE ALSO *Berlin Conference; Empire, Portuguese; Scramble for Africa.*

BIBLIOGRAPHY

Abshire, David M., and Michael A. Samuels, eds. *Portuguese Africa: A Handbook.* New York: Praeger, 1969.

Cann, John P. *Counterinsurgency in Africa: The Portuguese Way of War, 1961–1974.* Westport, CT: Greenwood, 1997.

Chilcote, Ronald H. *Emerging Nationalism in Portuguese Africa: A Bibliography of Documentary Ephemera Through 1965.* Stanford, CA: Hoover Institutions on War, Revolution, and Peace, Stanford University, 1969.

Chilcote, Ronald H. *Portuguese Africa.* Englewood Cliffs, NJ: Prentice-Hall, 1967.

de Bragança, Aquino, and Immanuel Wallerstein. *The African Liberation Reader.* 3 vols. London: Zed, 1982.

Duffy, James. *Portugal in Africa.* Cambridge, MA: Harvard University Press, 1962.

Ferreira, Eduardo de Sousa. *Portuguese Colonialism in Africa, the End of an Era: The Effects of Portuguese Colonialism on Education, Science, Culture, and Information.* Paris: UNESCO Press, 1974.

Hammond, Richard James. *Portugal and Africa, 1815–1910: A Study in Uneconomic Imperialism.* Stanford, CA: Stanford University Press, 1966.

Humbaraci, Arslan, and Nicole Muchnik. *Portugal's African Wars: Angola, Guinea Bissao, Mozambique.* New York: Third Press, 1974.

Lyall, Archibald. *Black and White Make Brown: An Account of a Journey to the Cape Verde Islands and Portuguese Guinea.* London: Heinemann, 1938.

Marcum, John A. *Portugal and Africa, the Politics of Indifference: A Case Study in American Foreign Policy.* Syracuse, NY: Program of Eastern African Studies, Syracuse University, 1972.

Minter, William. *Portuguese Africa and the West.* Harmondsworth, UK: Penguin, 1972.

Moreira, Adriano. *Portugal's Stand in Africa.* Translated by William Davis et al. New York: University Publishers, 1962.

Schneidman, Witney. *Engaging Africa: Washington and the Fall of Portugal's Colonial Empire.* Lanham, MD: University Press of America, 2004.

Sykes, John. *Portugal and Africa: The People and the War.* London: Hutchinson, 1971.

Martin Kich

POSTCOLONIALISM

There is remarkably little agreement among the practitioners of postcolonial criticism, theory, and history regarding exactly what postcolonialism is other than radical intellectual opposition to all forms of Western colonialism, past and present, and an unshakable belief in colonialism's irreparable disfigurement of the modern world. The term *postcolonial* is quite pliant and a source of vigorous debate. Definitions of postcolonialism as a theory and a field of academic study are abundant and diverse. Not unlike disagreements among religious and revolutionary schismatics, the disputes among postcolonialists are bitter battles about fine points of ideology.

Academic interest in the postcolonial—that is, post-independence—literature of the Middle East, Africa, and the Caribbean, a literature that represented the interactions between the colonizers and the colonized (and often described the psychological and cultural damage caused by colonization), developed in Great Britain and the United States in the 1970s and the 1980s. Postcolonial academic critics discovered, as Indian-born British novelist Salman Rushdie put it, that "the Empire writes back to the Centre." Classic postcolonial novels include *Things Fall Apart* (1958) by Nigeria's Chinua Achebe, *The Mimic Men* (1967) by Trinidad's V. S. Naipaul, and *Another Life* (1972) by Saint Lucia's Derek Walcott.

At first, postcolonial studies examined the process by which language and literature was reclaimed by former colonials. Postcolonial literature, like everything Creole, was discovered to be hybrid, meaning a mixture of European and non-European. Postcolonialists argued that imperial rule had created the binary categories of the imperial "self" in opposition to the colonized "other," but hybridity subverted this rigid construction of ruler versus ruled.

Postcolonial literature, and the study of colonial and postcolonial literature, became more ideological in the 1980s and 1990s. In the Caribbean, supposedly, the teaching of William Shakespeare (1564–1616) brought indoctrination not enlightenment. West Indian novelist Merle Hodge writes: "From the colonial era to the present time, one of the weapons used to subjugate us has been fiction."

Antiguan-American writer Jamaica Kincaid in *Annie John* (1985) uses literature and literacy to discipline the title character when she "is forced to copy out Books I and II of *Paradise Lost* as punishment for her rebelliousness." English is transmogrified into an alien—even if internalized—imperial language, a burden to bear. To the Canadian poet Dennis Lee: "The language [is] drenched with our non-belonging . . . words had become the enemy."

Edward W. Said (1935–2003) published *Orientalism*, one of the fundamental texts of postcolonialism, in 1978. Said argued that Eurocentric writing about the Arab Middle East exoticized, eroticized, romanticized, and essentialized the "Orient" and "licensed pillage of other cultures in the name of disinterested scholarship." With Said, the study of colonialism increasingly became the study of colonial discourse. The production of "knowledge" about others not only justified the exploitation and domination of non-Europeans, supposedly, but also facilitated colonial rule. Although Said's *Orientalism* was the subject of potent scholarly criticism at the time and since, his attack on Western writers opened the door to multitudinous literary critics, anthropologists, and historians who have unpacked colonial discourses from the chronicles of the Spanish conquest of the Aztecs and Incas to the British histories of South Asia. "The conquest of India," wrote anthropologist Bernard Cohn (1928–2003), "was a conquest of knowledge. . . . The vast social world that was India had to be classified, categorized and bounded before it could be hierarchalized."

One of the most famous subjects of colonial discourse analysis in recent decades has been Shakespeare's drama *The Tempest* (1611). This virtually plotless play is about the ruler of Milan, Prospero, a scholar and magus, shipwrecked with others on what cannot otherwise be a Mediterranean island with the half-human creature Caliban. In numerous scholarly articles and books, not to mention many stage and film versions, postcolonialists have interpreted *The Tempest* as a discourse on early English colonialism, primarily American colonialism. In these readings Prospero represents the colonial planter and white male oppressor. Caliban has become a New World cannibal slave or an Afro-Caribbean freedom fighter. *The Tempest*, in this view, not only displays racial prejudice but also "enacts" colonialism by justifying Prospero's power over Caliban.

Even Shakespeare, it would seem, created colonial "knowledge." The play, however, is more complex than any colonial reading can give it. Two other characters, Sycorax and Ariel, reveal some of the problems of this brave new postcolonialist perspective. Ariel, an airy spirit, was on the island before Sycorax, a witch who gives birth to Caliban, thus making Ariel the island's first true reigning lord. When Sycorax arrived, however, she enslaved Ariel and became the first colonialist (one could say) before Prospero even arrived on the island. Caliban, half-human, is also only a half-native of the island.

Shakespeare's text about an island and its last ruler, Prospero, if it is about anything other than certain universal values, concerns Britain as an island nation. There is no external evidence that seventeenth-century English audiences thought the play referred to the New World. *The Tempest* has been twisted to fit a preconceived picture of the evils of Western colonialism.

The study of colonial discourse has become an important element in the historical study of colonialism and imperialism. The great histories, chronicles, and "relations" of the early Spanish New World have been retranslated, republished, and analyzed in a myriad of volumes and studies. The "letter" narrative of Felipe Guaman Poma de Ayala, the polemics of Bartolomé de Las Casas (1474–1566), the castaway narrative of Álvar Núñez Cabeza de Vaca (ca. 1490–1560), the history of the Incas by Juan de Betanzos (fl. mid-1500s), and the "natural history of the Indies" by José de Acosta (1539–1600), to mention only a few, have been expertly studied and interpreted in the larger context of colonial discourse.

Peter Hulme explores the invention of the Caribs in early colonial discourse and the uses of tales of cannibalism. Jorge Cañizares-Esguerra, who explicitly follows the key insights of postcolonial scholarship, shows how eighteenth-century Spanish American writers challenged European colonial knowledge based on reinterpretation of noble Indian testimony. The Spanish Empire fell, postcolonialists argue, when Creoles destabilized the categories of colonizers and colonized. Warships are afterthoughts when words are recognized as effective weapons. Critics of discourse analysis, however, maintain that postcolonialists give too much power to words and too little significance to the common activities of colonial realities, that is, planting, working, trading, fishing, constructing, fighting, training, loving, and much more.

It is salutary to recall that what is today referred to as colonial discourse theory was not invented by Edward Said or postcolonialists. In 1949 the Spanish philosopher Edmundo O'Gorman (1906–1995) argued that America did not emerge "full-blown as the result of the chance discovery" but "developed from a complex, living process of exploration and interpretation." O'Gorman's book was entitled *La invención de América* (The Invention of America). O'Gorman was a scholar of philosophy and history.

A few years later, the psychiatrist Frantz Fanon (1925–1961), born in Martinique but committed to anticolonialism in Africa, critiqued colonialism in *White Skin, Black Masks* (1952) and *The Wretched of the Earth* (1961). Fanon's books, like *Discourse on Colonialism* (1955) by fellow Martiniquan author Aimé Césaire (b. 1913), unveiled the racism and corrosive effects of colonialism and colonial discourse. Fanon was a revolutionary as well as a critic. He joined the Algerian National Liberation Front (FLN) and in his writing he supported the option of armed struggle. Since Fanon, postcolonialists have maintained their radical, even revolutionary, ideological stance and sensibility.

Postcolonialist discourse analysis has dissolved all distinctions between the periods or categories called "colonial" and "modern." Fernando Coronil describes the Western mythology of portraying Europe as a civilization, culturally distinct, which had evolved ("progressed") over centuries, as Occidentalism. Thus, with all the differences and even nuances between colonialism and modernity, or between the Spanish Inquisition and Auschwitz, ended, scholarship and political activism intertwine. "Today I am looking at coloniality at large, and at the coloniality of power and the colonial difference in a modern/colonial world in which we are still living and struggle," writes Walter D. Mignolo. "Globalization and neoliberalism are new names, new forms of rearticulating the colonial difference. The colonial period may have ended, but the coloniality of power continues to order planetary relations."

Historians, political scientists, and anthropologists of India (and also Britain) began their shaping of postcolonial studies through the journal *Subaltern Studies*, which was published in Delhi beginning in 1982. The term *subaltern* was taken from Italian political theorist Antonio Gramsci's (1891–1937) concept of a dominated group without class consciousness. Subalternity became a general category for the objects of economic, social, cultural, gender, and linguistic domination. Indian scholars not only sought to take the focus away from the elite in Indian society, the British colonials and the privileged princes, but to reveal the subaltern as actors and agents in history. Their aim has been to rescue the neglected and repressed, the "people without history," from the silence and condescension of the grand master narrative of imperial history.

To do this, scholars have attempted to discover the radical consciousness of the underprivileged in colonial India, particularly in times of rebellion. Since the early 1980s Indian historians have led the field of postcolonial studies. Very quickly, however, historians and anthropologists of Latin America, Africa, the Middle East, and other regions adopted the model and the politics. Staying within a vaguely Marxist tradition, scholars of the subaltern have shifted from social to cultural history, and they seek "fragments" of alternative histories that lie buried in colonial discourse. Historians also explore the issue of Creole, hybrid cultures and identities. Subalternists seek to break down the colonial dichotomies of colonizer/colonized, master/slave, ruler/ruled, white/black, metropolis/colony, and so on. "The goal," according to Arif Dirlik, "indeed, is no less than to abolish all distinctions between center and periphery as well as other 'binarisms' that are allegedly a legacy of colonial(ist) ways of thinking."

Subalternity has been extended to women, the subaltern of the subaltern according to Gayatri Chakravorty Spivak, an original member of the subaltern studies historians. Feminist and postcolonialist historians have discovered that while gender and imperialism may have been ignored by scholars in the past, the subjects are inextricably intertwined. Gender is a question of imperial plunder, subdued labor, political alliance, cultural identity, missionary evangelization, and much more. "The vast, fissured architecture of imperialism was gendered throughout by the fact that it was white men who made and enforced laws in their own interests," writes the historian Anne McClintock.

In the 1990s Dipesh Chakrabarty argued that Indian history itself, the academic discourse of history, was in a position of subalternity. History, whether it is "Indian," "Egyptian," or "French," is an academic discourse, a knowledge system, that has developed to justify the capitalist mode of production and the bourgeois order in the West. In the nineteenth and twentieth centuries, according to Chakrabarty, European imperialism and third world nationalism universalized the discourse of history. His solution is to "provincialize Europe," that is, imagine the world as radically heterogeneous. Chakrabarty, of course, is not the only postcolonialist to want to put "history on trial."

Chakrabarty in his antihistoricism, along with subalternists, anti-Orientalists, and "poco" literature critics, all share opposition to what postcolonists generally refer to as "coercive knowledge systems" and the universalizing knowledge claims of Western civilization. Postcolonialism as a theoretical position stands against the "imperial ideas" of linear time, hypermasculinity, progress, narcissism, and aggressivity, and the omnipotent colonizing "self" and the marginal colonized "other." It seeks a decentering in multidimensional time, ambivalence, syncreticism, and hybridity. Postcolonialists assert the validity of other, non-Western cultures and often adopt a stance of political advocacy and commitment for those oppressed, subaltern, underprivileged, or in some way disadvantaged people whom they study and write about in Latin America, Africa, the Middle East, South Asia, or East Asia.

Criticism of postcolonialism comes from all directions. Radical critics like Arif Dirlik suggest that postcoloniality's emphasis on discourse, categories, and historicism ignores real-world problems of military and police power, economic development, income inequality, and globalization. Postcoloniality developed, Dirlik notes, because of the increased visibility of academic intellectuals of third world origins as pacesetters in cultural criticism. They have made a career out of "marginality" in the intellectual centers of the Western world.

Other critics have questioned the potency of literary practices. Postcolonialist discourse theorists proclaim that knowledge (or misknowledge) about another culture translates into the exercise of power over the subject culture, but rarely do they try to explain how this colonial discourse of power works in practice. Other, more conservative critics argue that outrage from the West should be focused on loci of mass murder and terrorism rather than the faux colonialism of the banana republic.

Pragmatic colonial historians have pointed out that postcolonialist insights regarding the role of the colonized and exploited in history, the artificiality of colonial dichotomies, the value and reality of hybridity, and so on, are not exactly original or even profound except, perhaps, in the inscrutable theoretical manner and language in which they are expressed. Similarly, many critics have often noted the inaccessibility of the language of postcolonialist writers, pointing to its dense, clotted, and evasive style. One of the most notable aspects of postcolonialist writing is the pervasiveness of jargon, the specialized and often invented vocabulary and idiom of what is seen as an academic fashion. This type of writing reflects a self-important posturing within the academy and a radicalism that only appeals to other cultists who know the special code and how to qualify a term like "discovery" as politically charged through the use of inverted commas or quotation marks. Academic postcolonialism, like colonialism, has become a discourse that critics and cronies can analyze and endlessly argue about.

In the early twenty-first century, postcolonial studies has become an important part of the academic and intellectual world. There are postcolonial studies institutes, departments, programs, journals, book series, conferences, and internet websites around the globe. Postcolonial studies in pursuit of radical politics are established within the most exalted academic institutions of Western Europe and the United States, as well as in the postcolonial nations. Postcolonial studies institutes, programs, and professors are also distributed thickly and widely throughout academia. North Carolina State University, for example, supports and hosts *Jouvert: A Journal of Postcolonial Studies*, a multidisciplinary journal published on the World Wide Web. The National University of Singapore has brought together scholars from various disciplines from across the world to sustain *The Postcolonial Web*, a site with terms, theories, definitions, historical contexts, debates, opinion pieces, critical essays, and bibliographical materials.

Other recent specialized journals include such titles as *Interventions: International Journal of Postcolonial Studies*; *Postcolonial Studies: Culture, Politics, Economy*; *Identities: Global Studies in Power and Culture*; *Post Identity*; *Social Identity*; and *Inscriptions*. Congenial publications such as *Representations, Critical Text, October, Critical Inquiry, Cultural Critique, Ariel, Third Text, Public Culture, New Formations,* and others publish postcolonialist studies and essays. Princeton University Press has published the series Princeton Studies in Culture/Power/History. The entire Duke University Press catalogue in one way or another is postcolonialist, but to look at just one part of the world, the Duke University Press has created the series Latin American Otherwise: Languages, Empires, Nations. Today one cannot read about or study Western colonialism or anticolonialism without the influence, to some degree or another, of postcolonialism.

SEE ALSO *Imperialism, Liberal Theories of; Imperialism, Marxist Theories of; Neocolonialism.*

BIBLIOGRAPHY

Ashcroft, Bill, Gareth Griffiths, and Helen Tiffin. *The Empire Writes Back: Theory and Practice in Post-colonial Literatures,* 2nd ed. London: Routledge, 2002.

Ashcroft, Bill, Gareth Griffiths, and Helen Tiffin, eds. *The Post-Colonial Studies Reader,* 2nd ed. London: Routledge, 2005.

Bhabha, Homi K. *The Location of Culture.* London: Routledge, 1994.

Chakrabarty, Dipesh. *Provincializing Europe: Postcolonial Thought and Historical Difference.* Princeton, NJ: Princeton University Press, 2000.

Chatterjee, Partha. *The Nation and its Fragment: Colonial and Postcolonial Histories.* Princeton, NJ: Princeton University Press, 1993.

Dirlik, Arif. *The Postcolonial Aura: Third World Criticism in the Age of Global Capitalism.* Boulder, CO: Westview Press, 1997.

Fanon, Frantz. *Les damnés de la terre.* Paris: F. Maspero, 1961. Translated by Haakon Chevalier as *The Wretched of the Earth.* New York: Monthly Review Press, 1967.

Gruzinski, Serge. *La colonisation de l'imaginaire: Sociétés indigènes et occidentalisation dans le Mexique espagnol, XVIe–XVIIIe siècle.* Paris: Gallimard, 1988.

Hulme, Peter. *Colonial Encounters: Europe and the Native Caribbean, 1492–1797.* London: Methuen, 1986.

Jouvert: A Journal of Postcolonial Studies. Available from http://social.chass.ncsu.edu/jouvert/.

Loomba, Ania. *Colonialism/Postcolonialism.* London: Routledge, 1998.

Mallon, Florencia E. *Peasant and Nation: The Making of Postcolonial Mexico And Peru.* Berkeley: University of California Press, 1995.

McClintock, Anne. *Imperial Leather: Race, Gender, and Sexuality in the Colonial Context.* London: Routledge, 1995.

Mignolo, Walter D. *The Darker Side of the Renaissance: Literacy, Territoriality, and Colonization.* Ann Arbor: University of Michigan Press, 1995; 2nd ed., 2003.

Moore-Gilbert, Bart. *Postcolonial Theory: Contexts, Practices, Politics.* London: Verso, 1997.

Porterfield, Todd. *The Allure of Empire: Art in the Service of French Imperialism, 1798–1836.* Princeton, NJ: Princeton University Press, 1998.

The Postcolonial Web: Contemporary Postcolonial and Postimperial Literature in English. Available from http://www.postcolonialweb.org.

Prakash, Gyan, ed. *After Colonialism: Imperial Histories and Postcolonial Displacements*. Princeton, NJ: Princeton University Press, 1995.

Said, Edward W. *Orientalism*. New York: Pantheon, 1978.

Silverblatt, Irene. *Modern Inquisitions: Peru and the Colonial Origins of the Civilized World*. Durham, NC: Duke University Press, 2004.

St. George, Robert Blair, ed. *Possible Pasts: Becoming Colonial in Early America*. Ithaca, NY: Cornell University Press, 2000.

Thurner, Mark, and Andrés Guerrero, eds. *After Spanish Rule: Postcolonial Predicaments of the Americas*. Durham, NC: Duke University Press, 2003.

Todorov, Tzvetan. *La conquête de l'Amérique: La question de l'autre*. Paris: Seuil, 1982. Translated by Richard Howard as *The Conquest of America: The Question of the Other*. New York: Harper, 1984.

Young, Robert J. C. *Postcolonialism: An Historical Introduction*. Oxford: Blackwell, 2001.

Thomas Benjamin

POTOSÍ

Founded in 1547 at a height of over 4,000 meters (13,123 feet) in Upper Peru (modern Bolivia) and, until 1776, one of the Spanish kingdoms in the viceroyalty of Peru, the rich and imperial town of Potosí (a title granted by Philip II [1527–1598] in 1561) was the world's premier silver producer for two centuries. Its population grew to 100,000 by 1600 as it drew in prospectors, adventurers, laborers (free and coerced), functionaries, artisans, merchants, and many others attracted by the wealth generated by the abundant silver deposits of the Rich Hill above the town.

In its peak period, 1550–1630, registered production totalled 372 million pesos or ounces (compared with 90 million at its nearest rival, Zacatecas, Mexico's principal producer). These figures understate real production because an unquantifiable, but vast amount of contraband avoided registration and, thereby, payment of taxes, of which the most significant was the quint (20 percent). Potosí's preeminence was made possible by three factors: the abundance of rich ores, a guaranteed supply from nearby Huancavelica (in Central Peru) of mercury, essential for the refining process, and up to 14,000 a year native conscripts from surrounding provinces, following the implementation of the mita system by viceroy Francisco de Toledo (1515–1582) in 1573. Depopulation in the contributing provinces was one factor leading to a gradual fall in output after 1700 (when total viceregal production, including that from other centers, was 4 million pesos). The reduction in 1736 of the quint to 10 percent stimulated growth and eventually annual output stabilized at about 3 million pesos.

After the middle of the seventeenth century (when Dutch, French, and British ships began to penetrate the Pacific with increasing impunity, both to attack settlements and to trade, despite Spain's attempts to maintain a commercial monopoly) the Crown's share of this silver was used increasingly to meet the rising costs of defense and administration within the viceroyalty. However, the bulk of the private silver produced at Potosí continued to be remitted to Spain—until the early eighteenth century via the Isthmus of Panama, thereafter via Cape Horn—in exchange for manufactured goods (many of them of non-Spanish origin) and the traditional viticultural and agricultural products of the mother country.

Even in the late eighteenth century, when Spain was making strenuous efforts to promote the more systematic exploitation of South America's potential as a supplier of agricultural and pastoral products to international markets, silver represented almost 90 percent of the value of Peru's registered exports, much of which continued to flow to Lima from Potosí despite the fact that in 1776 Upper Peru was transferred to the newly-created viceroyalty of the Río de la Plata, governed from Buenos Aires. In exchange, Peru continued to supply Potosí with imported manufactures (including Chinese silks and porcelain that reached Lima via Manila-Acapulco), and a wide range of locally produced commodities, including sugar, brandy, coca, and coarse textiles. Potosí also acted as a magnet, whose silver drew in supplies from a wide range of networks of regional and intercolonial trade: for example, mules and hides from Tucumán and Córdoba (in modern Argentina), wheat from Chile, tea from Paraguay, and black slaves imported through Buenos Aires.

The formal opening of the new viceregal capital to direct trade with Spain in 1778 diverted some of the registered silver production of Potosí from Pacific to Atlantic trade routes. However, the cultural and economic ties between Upper Peru and the rump viceroyalty of Peru remained strong, and the region as a whole resisted the repeated attempts of Buenos Aires to retain political control there after the overthrow of the viceregal regime in Buenos Aires in 1810. Although the eventual solution to more than a decade of fighting would be the creation of an independent Bolivia in 1825, the struggle to achieve this led to a total collapse in activity at Potosí from 1813 to 1815 as a result of the flight of labor, destruction of equipment, and flooding. Recovery from 1816 to 1820 was only partial, with annual production averaging 1.5 million pesos. This level was sustained until the late nineteenth century when silver gave way to tin as the mainstay of Potosí's economy.

SEE ALSO *Empire in the Americas, Spanish; Peru Under Spanish Rule.*

range of goods—such as tea, silk, and porcelain—that were attractive to Britain, whereas British merchants could not find any British manufactured products that could sell well in the China market. In 1773 the English East India Company was granted a monopoly over the opium trade in Bengal, and marketed the illegal drug in China. In 1793, received by Emperor Qianlong, British emissary Sir George Macartney (1737–1806) requested greater freedom of trade and the establishment of diplomatic relations, but was rejected because Qianlong did not feel the need for foreign goods.

In 1833 the breakup of the English East India Company trade monopoly by the British government and the lowering of the opium price vastly increased the Chinese demand for opium. A significant number of Chinese became addicted, prompting Qing Emperor Daoguang (r. 1821–1850) to halt opium smuggling. British merchants and the British government responded by attacking Guangzhou and starting the Opium War with China in 1840.

Unprepared to deal with unprecedented military threats from the sea, the Qing lost the Opium War and was forced to accept the Treaty of Nanjing on August 29, 1842. The treaty, along with its supplementary pact, temporarily satisfied British needs: four more Chinese ports—Fuzhou, Ningbo, Shanghai, and Xiamen—were opened to trade; the tariff rate was regulated; the island of Hong Kong was ceded to Britain; and foreign immunity from Chinese law was granted. The Treaty of Nanjing—the first of the "Unequal Treaties"—inaugurated the "Treaty Century" (1842–1943) in China, during which the legal, diplomatic, political, economic, religious, and military aspects of Sino–foreign encounters were regulated in various treaties signed between China and foreign powers.

China fought the Second Opium War with France and Britain from 1856 to 1860. The war ended with China's defeat. In consequence, China had to sign the Treaty of Tianjin of 1858 and the Convention of Beijing of 1860, which specified foreign diplomatic residence and representation in Beijing, as well as the formation of the Zongli Yamen (Office of General Management) to handle foreign affairs.

The Qing regime was further weakened by a series of internal rebellions, the most damaging being the Taiping Rebellion (1851–1864). The Taiping Rebellion broke out in the Guangxi Province under the leadership of Christian-influenced Hong Xiuquan (1813–1864). At their height, the Taipings controlled most of South China and founded their capital in the important city Nanjing on the Yangzi River.

In the 1860s some high-ranking court officials came to realize the importance of modernizing China's military forces by initiating the self-strengthening movement. In the following decades the Qing suffered further defeat in the Sino-Japanese War (1894–1895), which prodded some open-minded Chinese reformers, including Kang Youwei (1858–1927) and Liang Qichao (1873–1929), to persuade Emperor Guangxü (r. 1875–1908) to launch the short-lived "One Hundred Days Reform" in 1898.

In 1899, the antiforeign Boxer Uprising erupted in the Shangdong Province, and the Boxers, under tacit encouragement from the Qing court, rapidly moved up north to Beijing, attacking foreigners and besieging foreign quarters. Joint international forces quelled the Boxer Uprising and punished the Qing authority with the Boxer Protocol of 1901, in which the Qing was forced to pay large sums of indemnities.

The Manchu's domestic and external failures since the early nineteenth century culminated in a final blow set off by the Wuchang Uprising of October 10, 1911. On January 1, 1912, the Republic of China was proclaimed. One month later, Puyi (1906–1967), the last emperor of the Qing, abdicated, putting an end to imperial rule in China.

The study of Qing history in North America has developed further since 1980. In the early 1980s, Paul A. Cohen suggested going beyond the impact–response paradigm (i.e., the West exerted influence upon an inert China, and China responded passively), which had been laid out by Sinologists represented by John K. Fairbank. Cohen's China-centered approach aimed at a better understanding of the inner dynamics of development during the Qing period. Since the 1990s topics including civil society, the public sphere, marginalized social forces, globalization, and nationalism have prompted further debates about late imperial China and its relevance to contemporary Chinese modernization and democratization.

SEE ALSO *Boxer Uprising; China, to the First Opium War; Chinese Revolutions; Li Hongzhang; Opium; Opium Wars; Taiping Rebellion; Zongli Yamen (Tsungli Yamen).*

BIBLIOGRAPHY

Cohen, Paul A. *Discovering History in China: American Historical Writing on the Recent Chinese Past.* New York: Columbia University Press, 1984.

Fairbank, John King, and Merle Goldman. *China: A New History,* enl. ed. Cambridge, MA: Harvard University Press, 1999.

Gamer, Robert E, ed. *Understanding Contemporary China,* 2nd ed. Boulder, CO: Lynne Rienner, 2003.

Spence, Jonathan D. *The Search for Modern China,* 2nd ed. New York: Norton, 1999.

Wang, Gungwu. *Anglo-Chinese Encounters Since 1800: War, Trade, Science, and Governance.* Cambridge, U.K.: Cambridge University Press, 2003.

Dong Wang

QUEBEC CITY

Founded by Samuel de Champlain in 1608 at the point where the broad St. Lawrence narrows enough to form a strong position capable of commanding maritime traffic, Quebec began as a small fur-trading post. Over the century and a half of French rule it grew into a substantial city, modest in population but combining all the functions of a colonial metropolis. As the capital of New France, it housed the civil and ecclesiastical administration, in addition to its role as military strongpoint, seaport, and commercial center of the colony.

Along the river at the foot of Cap Diamant lay "Lower Town," an area of shipyards, warehouses, wharfs, and taverns. Because of Quebec's severe winter climate, shipping was mostly limited to a few busy months in the summer. From Lower Town, a sinuous road led up a cleft in the cliffs to the plateau above. Upper Town's landscape was dominated by the palaces of the governor, the intendant, and the bishop, as well as the cathedral, the seminary, the hospital, and a number of convents. One of the peculiarities of Canada under the French regime was the complete absence of municipal institutions; colonial officials appointed by Versailles established market days and laid down fire regulations.

Improvised fortifications begun in the seventeenth century were gradually improved, so that by the 1750s Quebec could boast reasonably complete city walls. A British siege was repelled in 1690, but when the enemy returned with an overwhelming invasion force in 1759, the city finally fell. For two months prior to the decisive battle of September 13, Major-General James Wolfe's army had subjected the civilian population, already weakened by hunger, to a ferocious bombardment. And yet, although the British regime began amidst ruin and devastation, the city rose from the ashes to resume its position as the capital city of Canada, only to yield its economic and demographic supremacy to upstart Montreal in the nineteenth century.

SEE ALSO *Empire in the Americas, French; Fur and Skin Trades in the Americas; New France.*

BIBLIOGRAPHY

Charbonneau, André, Yvon Desloges, and Marc Lafrance. *Québec: The Fortified City: From the 17th to the 19th Century.* Ottawa: Parks Canada, 1982.

Hare, John, Marc Lafrance, and David-Thiery Ruddel. *Histoire de la ville de Québec, 1608–1871.* Montreal: Boréal, 1987.

Harris, R. Cole, ed. *Historical Atlas of Canada,* Vol. 1: *From the Beginning to 1800.* Toronto: University of Toronto Press, 1986.

Havard, Gilles, and Cécile Vidal. *Histoire de l'Amérique française.* Paris: Flammarion, 2003.

Lachance, André. *La vie urbaine en Nouvelle-France.* Montreal: Boréal, 1987.

Allan Greer

R

RACE AND COLONIALISM IN THE AMERICAS

In the period immediately preceding New World exploration and conquest, the two major powers in that enterprise—Portugal and Spain—were involved in a process that would shape the European conception of people with dark skin; whether African or Native American, this conception would be applied to the advantage of Europeans.

After the centuries-long presence of the Moors, or Muslim North Africans, in Iberia (the peninsula occupied by Spain and Portugal), the Christian Iberians adopted the Muslim view of sub-Saharan Africans. As the Portuguese and Spanish transitioned from warring with the Moors to colonizing the New World, they transferred this Muslim-influenced conception of blackness to the Americas. Most importantly, the connection between having black skin and being a slave became more common not only in Iberia but throughout Europe.

The development of this idea accelerated as the Portuguese, in an effort to find an all-water route to India, established trade relations with peoples along the west coast of Africa. Informed by their interaction with the Moors, the Portuguese saw the West Africans' religion and appearance as reasons for their inferiority. Though it would take decades for slavery and the slave trade to emerge, the Portuguese became the main purveyors of the racial ideology upon which both New World colonization and slavery were based.

Prior to the arrival of Christopher Columbus (1451–1506) in the New World, notions of differences among groups of people—and their implications for who could be enslaved—were based on a combination of religion, law, and historical examples. First and foremost, the Bible was filled with references to slaves and slavery. The entire Old Testament, in fact, granted tacit justification for the legality of human bondage, provided it conformed to certain religious precepts. As the Portuguese sailed around the west coast of Africa, encountering more and more people with black skin, Europeans turned to the biblical passage involving the curse of Ham, the son of Noah (*Gen.* 9:20–27). They argued that black Africans were descended from the accursed Ham and thereby subject to eternal slavery. Europeans also melded the story of Ham with the tradition that blacks were descendents of Cain, who had been cursed by God.

Similarly, the New Testament, particularly the letters of Paul, reveals a certain recognition of slavery as a legitimate human institution. By echoing what the ancient Greek philosopher Aristotle (384–322 B.C.E.) called "natural slavery"—or the belief that some people were actually meant to be slaves by their nature—the Bible became a commonly cited justification for enslaving both Native Americans and Africans during the colonization of the Americas. Nevertheless, although the Spaniards used the concept of natural slavery as a means of justifying the subordination of Indians, they did not conceive the Indians as "natural slaves" before they developed a need for their labor, and views of Indians were far from uniform at the time.

Though the Spanish would have to determine how the indigenous peoples of the Americas fit within this system of whiteness and blackness, they and the Portuguese were not strangers to Africans. In fact, both nations enslaved Africans on the Iberian Peninsula throughout the sixteenth century, producing African populations of 5 to 10 percent in the major Iberian cities. As a result of this familiarity with dark-skinned people, both the Spanish and Portuguese would turn to Africans as potential slaves during their colonization enterprise in the New World.

Northern Europeans were also familiar with slavery. Although England, France, and the Netherlands were beginning to enhance personal freedoms and celebrate political liberty as a national characteristic that set them apart from the Portuguese and Spanish, they still condoned forms of bondage akin to slavery in the early modern era. Customary forms of servitude fit this mold, particularly in the authority that masters were accorded to circumscribe their servants' lives. Combined with the growing sentiment across the continent that blackness equaled slavery, Europeans began arguing that slavery actually ameliorated the inferior natural status of Africans and other dark-skinned peoples. The combination of various strands of such ideology provided a potent force in the conquest and eventual colonial reordering of the Americas.

THE ROLE OF RACE IN COLONIAL LABOR SYSTEMS

From almost the instant Columbus encountered the Tainos in the Caribbean, Europeans saw Native Americans as an invaluable source of labor. During the decades that followed the planting of Spanish, Portuguese, French, and English colonies, Indians were systematically preyed upon and regularly reduced to a state of slavery. The prevailing belief among Europeans that Native Americans were the lost tribes of Israel produced sufficient justification that enslavement by Christians would bring them back into God's kingdom. However, this was not a justification for enslaving Indians that was widely used by Spaniards. The Spanish monarchy allowed enslavement of Indians only in special conditions such as resistance to evangelization, cannibalism, and sodomy. Their brown skin—deemed problematic by those Europeans well versed in issues related to blackness—suggested that at one time these people had been white, but had become sunburned through many years of hard work. By reorganizing native populations according to what they believed was their God-favored social organization, Europeans rationalized the enslavement of Indians.

The enslavement of Indians, however, did not come without controversy, even among Europeans. The issue was particularly complicated within the Spanish Empire. The Spanish monarchs, Ferdinand (1452–1516) and Isabella (1451–1504), for example, evidenced their

concern with the legality of Indian slavery when they drafted a letter to Pedro de Torres in Seville in 1500 ordering the release of the Indians in his custody and their return to the Americas. Even so, Indians continued to be enslaved during the first half-century of the Spanish conquest, especially in peripheral zones, where the practice was justified as a natural outgrowth of an ongoing "just war." Between 1515 and 1542, historians estimate that as many as 200,000 Indians were captured in what is now Nicaragua and sold into slavery in the West Indies.

In 1542, however, the Council of the Indies issued the famous New Laws, which were designed to end indigenous slavery. The New Laws provided several imperial protections to Indians, but they did not signify a departure from the idea that Indians were, and should be, bound laborers. In Peru, Indian labor was extracted through the *mita*, a compulsory, forced rotational labor draft that was used primarily in silver mines. To the north, Spanish authorities continued to countenance the *encomienda* system, which had been formalized in the Laws of Burgos (1512–1513). An *encomienda* was a grant to an individual (the *encomendero*) of the right to the labor of a group of Indians in exchange for the promise to protect the Indians and see to their conversion to Christianity.

Abuses in the *encomienda* system had been evident from the beginning, and famous defenders of native rights, such as the Spanish Dominican missionary Bartolomé de las Casas (1474–1566), attacked the system vigorously. The New Laws attempted to rein in the prerogative power of *encomenderos* as part of their effort to address the catastrophic demographic losses being suffered by Indians. Labor demands, however, continued to be placed on Indians through the *repartimiento*, a tribute system that funneled labor to private individuals through government mechanisms. This system, too, was abolished in 1635. Nonetheless, because the system of slavery—itself key in the development of colonies—was predicated on an inflexible belief in the inferiority of Indians, the plight of the indigenous Americans did not improve.

Indian slavery was not confined to the Spanish-American world alone. Virtually every European nation participated in the practice. Almost as quickly as the Portuguese began to establish coastal outposts in Brazil, for example, they began to deal in Indian slaves. As early as April 1503, a fleet returned to Portugal with a cargo of brazilwood and Indian slaves. Since the Portuguese waited several decades to establish permanent settlements, however, it was not until the middle of the sixteenth century that they began to enslave Indians in larger numbers, locally either knocking down brazilwood trees or, increasingly, as laborers on the developing sugar plantations.

Regardless of medieval legacies and flexible notions of human bondage, the enslavement and transportation of African peoples was already commonplace during the sixteenth century among northern and southern Europeans alike. Yet, while every European colonizing nation in America was familiar with racial slavery from the outset, each nation initially relied on either Native Americans or other Europeans as their primary labor force. Every European nation, however, would eventually turn to enslaved Africans as their primary labor force.

By the eighteenth century, although indentured servitude and Indian labor systems continued to operate, racial slavery and labor—especially in the cultivation and production of cash crops and the mining of precious metals—became virtually inseparable notions. How, when, and to what degree this transformation occurred, however, depended upon a number of factors, including European politics, mortality rates among indigenous peoples, the evolution of the transatlantic slave trade, European labor concerns, and even choice.

FROM INDIAN TO AFRICAN

The transition to a labor force predominantly made up of enslaved Africans occurred first in the Iberian-American colonies. This shift represents further evidence of the centrality of servile labor—whether of Indians or of Africans—to the colonizing project of Europeans.

Before 1580, African slaves were rare in the Americas, though they were common in the Atlantic islands—where many were already laboring on sugar plantations—and in Iberian port cities like Lisbon and Seville. During the last third of the sixteenth century, however, there were two important developments that increased the potential supply of African slaves for American markets: a more readily available supply of Africans, and the unification of Spain and Portugal under Philip II (1527–1598) in 1580, which gave Spain access to the Portuguese monopoly of the Atlantic slave trade.

Between 1595 and 1640, more than 268,000 Africans were imported into Spanish colonies, and another 150,000 slaves arrived in Portuguese Brazil. Thus, even the demographic collapse of the indigenous population did not arrest the economic growth of the Americas, as Europeans' racial ideologies could readily justify replacements for the declining numbers of Indian slaves.

The transition to black slavery in Latin America, then, represented a transition from exploiting the labor of Indians to exploiting the labor of Africans. Nonetheless, while enslaved Africans numerically dominated in places like Brazil, Spanish colonists continued to expropriate the labor of Indians in both Mexico and Peru. Mexico's Indian population was particularly large

and even began to recover from the devastation wrought during the first 150 years of colonization.

Furthermore, the transition to enslaved Africans represented more than a demographic shift at the beginning of the seventeenth century—it was a cultural transformation as well. During the early part of the sixteenth century, most of the Africans who were transported to Spain's American colonies were actually *ladinos*, or Africans who were already assimilated into European society and culture by pre-residence on the Iberian Peninsula. By the middle of the sixteenth century, however, *bozales*, or Africans who have been exposed to neither European culture nor Christianity, were increasingly being shipped to America directly from Africa. In that regard, the nature of the colonial population was significantly transformed once the transatlantic slave trade intensified.

By the middle of the seventeenth century, then, Brazil and several parts of Spanish America were fully committed to the slave labor of Africans. The colonial possessions of other European nations, however, continued to rely on their own distinctive labor systems, primarily indentured servitude. Neither Spain nor Portugal relied on their fellow countrymen as laborers during the colonial period, mainly because of the availability of Indians who could be coerced into work and the possibility of importing African slaves.

After the initial conquest of the indigenous peoples in Spanish and Portuguese America, birth became an increasingly significant factor in determining a person's social status. *Limpieza de sangre*, or blood purity, had been a crucial issue in fifteenth-century Spain; in particular, not having any Jewish or Muslim ancestors was essential to advancing in Spanish society. Like their concepts of race and slavery, the Spanish transferred their construct of pure blood when they settled the Americas. For example, children of two Spanish parents were infinitely more advantaged than peers who were not so endowed. *Mestizos*, or children born out of Spanish-Indian relationships, discovered a rigid social stratification that ranked them lower than *peninsulares* (people born in Spain) and Creoles (people born in the New World, but of "pure" Spanish blood). The corresponding groups in Portuguese America—*mamelucos, mestiços*, and *caboclos*—all found themselves limited in their opportunities for social advancement. The dramatic growth in the population of these mixed-raced peoples—as well as those with African heritage—made the *sistema de castas* (caste system) all the more complex, and yet, even more important for those at the top.

BRITISH NORTH AMERICA

The English, unlike the Spanish, had a profound overpopulation problem. From the late sixteenth century,

A West India Sportsman. Europe's imperial powers built their colonies on a racial hierarchy that exploited the indigenous population and imported Africans as slaves. This cartoon, published in England in 1807, satirizes the situation as it developed in colonial Jamaica. © BOJAN BRECELJ/CORBIS. REPRODUCED BY PERMISSION.

English colonizers imagined the colonial enterprise as one that would not only enrich the nation and advance the cause of Protestant Christianity, but would also help rid the land of the idle, underfed, and unemployed masses. England also had little choice but to use European laborers because the West Indies and North America did not possess the high concentrations of native peoples encountered by the Iberians.

The transition to racial slavery for northern Europeans, particularly the English, therefore, amounted to the gradual replacement of European indentured servants with enslaved Africans, especially in plantation agricultural zones, during the second half of the seventeenth century. There were several factors related to supply and demand that coincided to make this possible. North American Indians experienced a dramatic population decline as a consequence of their encounter with Europeans. Although northern Europeans never relied on Indian labor like the Spanish and Portuguese, Indian slaves were nonetheless exploited in small numbers, particularly in the southwestern frontier region.

Indian slavery, however, proved to be an unattractive option in the long run because Indians were relatively scarce in North America even before the English and French arrived. There were probably fewer than two million native inhabitants east of the Mississippi River in 1492, and that number decline to roughly 250,000 in subsequent centuries. Additionally, the people most likely to profit from Indian slavery quickly developed the idea that Indians were poor workers. Thus, the English enslaved indigenous Americans, but only as a secondary or tertiary enterprise and usually as slave traders rather than slave drivers.

The need for labor, enslaved or otherwise, intensified in English North America and the West Indies with the shift to tobacco and sugar cultivation during the seventeenth century. In the West Indies, economic prosperity hinged on sugar agriculture, which began in the 1640s when Barbados experienced an agricultural boom. Tobacco and sugar cultivation subsequently developed in virtually every English, French, and Dutch West Indian colony, bringing African slavery in its wake.

Initially, the northern European colonies in the West Indies were hardscrabble settlements where small planters and their indentured servants cleared the land, cultivated tobacco, and raised livestock for export. In the 1640s, however, with the technological and financial assistance of Dutch traders who had been chased out of Brazil, English planters began to develop sugar plantations. Almost immediately, the sugar economy transformed the island into a profitable enterprise, and within two decades Barbados would be more profitable than all other English colonies combined. Visions of potential riches also attracted immigrants. Between 1640 and 1660 the English West Indies were the most popular destination of English emigrants, free and indentured.

As the European population expanded in the West Indies during the middle decades of the seventeenth century, so too did the enslaved African population. This growth was in part a product of the commercial relationship between primarily English planters and Dutch traders who, in addition to transporting English sugar to European markets, imported African slaves to American plantations. Even more, however, the rise of African slavery in the West Indies was demand driven. Sugar cultivation was dangerous and degrading work that required many more laborers than tobacco. Already by 1660 there were about 25,000 enslaved Africans in Barbados working alongside a roughly equal number of indentured servants and free whites. At the same time, there were probably no more than five thousand additional Africans in all of the other English colonies combined, with Virginians possessing only about one thousand slaves.

Though the English did not develop the same kind of racial stratification system as existed in Iberian America, the presence of a dark-skinned "other" still gave English colonists an economic and social force upon which to grow crops and construct a racially divided society. Even with that and other differences between British and Iberian America, however, one touchstone remained prominent: race informed early colonization, and came to define the very contours of each nation's respective colonies.

By the mid-nineteenth century, both colonialism and slavery were on the wane throughout the Americas. But the oldest tenet of the colonial enterprise—race—remained. Without it, colonialism in the Americas would have been dramatically different.

SEE ALSO *African Slavery in the Americas; Encomienda; Indentured Labor.*

BIBLIOGRAPHY

Davis, David Brion. *The Problem of Slavery in Western Culture.* Ithaca, NY: Cornell University Press, 1966.

Degler, Carl N. *Neither Black Nor White: Slavery and Race Relations in Brazil and the United States.* New York: Macmillan, 1971.

Goldenberg, David M. *The Curse of Ham: Race and Slavery in Early Judaism, Christianity, and Islam.* Princeton, NJ: Princeton University Press, 2003.

Jordan, Winthrop D. *White Over Black: American Attitudes Toward the Negro, 1550–1812.* Chapel Hill: University of North Carolina Press, 1968.

Klein, Herbert S. *Slavery in the Americas: A Comparative Study of Virginia and Cuba.* Chicago: University of Chicago Press, 1967.

Morgan, Edmund S. *American Slavery, American Freedom: The Ordeal of Colonial Virginia.* New York: Norton, 1975.

Palmer, Colin A. *Slaves of the White God: Blacks in Mexico, 1570–1650.* Cambridge, MA: Harvard University Press, 1976.

Rout, Leslie B., Jr. *The African Experience in Spanish America: 1502 to the Present Day.* Cambridge, U.K.: Cambridge University Press, 1976.

Sweet, James H. *Recreating Africa: Culture, Kinship, and Religion in the African-Portuguese World, 1441–1770.* Chapel Hill: University of North Carolina Press, 2003.

Thornton, John K. *Africa and Africans in the Making of the Atlantic World, 1400–1800,* 2nd ed. New York: Cambridge University Press, 1998.

Kevin D. Roberts

RACE AND RACISM

With the expansion of European power outside of the region's own borders in the fifteenth century, and the continuous colonization of territories outside of Europe through the twentieth century, the practice of labeling both the colonizer and the colonized on the basis of cultural differences tied to conceptions of race became widespread. Cultural notions of identity tied to race, which have their origin in the fifteenth century, remain in practice in the twenty-first century. As a result, any understanding of race and racism requires an understanding of the history of Western colonialism, which laid the foundations for current ideas of differences tied to race. For purposes of clarity, it is necessary to distinguish between the terms *xenophobia, bigotry,* and *racism* before providing a brief overview of the history of race and racism in Western colonialism.

DEFINING AND DISTINGUISHING *RACE* AND *RACISM*

Where race, racial classifications, and racism (i.e., the subordination of one racial group by another) have been the defining features of Western societies, they have contained three broad elements. First, in its most restricted sense, racial identity represents an inheritable status that cannot be overcome by change in education, legal status, religious affiliation, or nationality. Europeans came to conceive individuals as born into their race—they did not become their race. Thus, regardless of wealth, religious conversion, or changing legal status, individuals remained primarily identified by race.

Second, while societies throughout history have shown a tendency to view some groups and nations as inferior, and have therefore treated them differently, racism involves the organization of the political and legal apparatus of the state for the exploitation of a subordinated racial group. Such exploitation has primarily involved limited access to political and legal rights because of racial identity. And third, racial classifications have primarily been used to organize and justify the economic exploitation of one group by another, most commonly by coercive labor regimes.

Xenophobia and bigotry also involve extreme antipathy of one group toward another, but unlike racism, they do not represent an inheritable and unchangeable status. For example, while the ancient Greeks and Romans described other groups as "barbarous" and "savage," they believed members of these groups could become "civilized." While not common, it was possible for slaves to become full members of society in the ancient world if they adopted the ideals and beliefs of the dominant group.

Likewise, the religious bigot may have condemned and persecuted others for what they believed, but not for what they intrinsically were. Thus, missionaries may have despised the beliefs of the group they attempted to convert, but they did believe these groups were convertible. If an individual could be redeemed through baptism, or if an ethnic stranger could be assimilated into a culture in such a way that their origins ceased to matter in a significant way, this more accurately represented a situation of ethnocultural discrimination, not necessarily racism.

Unlike xenophobia and bigotry, racism does not allow for individuals the possibility to become members of the dominant society, regardless of cultural changes. In societies structured by racial hierarchies, the subordinated groups are forever shut out of society because of their "inferior" racial condition. It is when differences that might be explained as ethnocultural become regarded as innate, indelible, and unchangeable that a racial order often comes into existence to divide society into separate racial categories. The history of Western colonialism has created two dominant racial orders that are (1) tied to pigmentation, as in white supremacy, and (2) tied to religion, as in anti-Semitism.

By serving as one of the dominant guiding ideologies for Western colonialism since the fifteenth century,

racism has involved the articulation of difference and the exercise of power. Differences between the colonizer and the colonized resulted from a mindset that regarded "them" as different from "us" in ways that were permanent and unbridgeable. The sense of difference between the colonizer and the colonized provided a motive and rational for treating the racial subordinate in ways that the dominant group would regard as cruel or unjust if applied to members of its own society. At their core, societies structured around racism presume that the racializers and the racialized cannot coexist, except on the basis of domination and subordination.

ORIGINS OF THE CONCEPT OF RACE IN FIFTEENTH-CENTURY IBERIA

Race, as a concept that defined an individual's identity as unchangeable and innate, dates to roughly the fifteenth century. The ancient Greeks distinguished between the civilized and the barbarous, but did not regard these states as hereditary. Likewise, while the Roman Empire was built on slavery, Romans held slaves of all colors and nationalities, and these slaves could become citizens.

During the fourteenth and early fifteenth centuries, sub-Saharan African slaves were introduced into Iberia (Spain and Portugal). In the Iberian cities of Seville and Lisbon, witnessing who labored for whom daily solidified the association between blackness and slavery. In the second half of the fifteenth century, as Portuguese slave traders began to trade down the west coast of Africa, they brought back black slaves, and the association between Africans and racial slavery was further solidified. Europeans were ceasing to enslave other Europeans at the time that the African slave trade began to expand, which fueled the purchasing of sub-Saharan slaves and their use throughout Europe.

Further evidence of how slavery became identified with the black race in the minds of Iberians was that Africans were non-Christians, and thus could be treated as heathens and not like Christians. Hence the temptation to acquire them and treat them as unfree did not raise any major religious dilemma. Initially, it was less skin color and more availability and existing trading patterns that explain the presence of sub-Saharan African slaves in Europe. There is very little evidence of an explicitly racial nature that justifies or even explains the enslavement of sub-Saharan Africans. The significance of this early trade was that it set an initial pattern and a means of easily identifying by pigmentation a group of individuals to be exploited for racial slavery.

Occurring at roughly the same time as the introduction of sub-Saharan Africans into Iberia, the concept of "purity of blood" and ancestry became increasingly important to Europeans. Dating back to the thirteenth century, an increase in anti-Semitic thought based in folk mythology resulted in Europeans associating the region's Jewish population with the devil and black magic. At the time of the Black Death (a plague pandemic) in the mid-fourteenth century, thousands of Jews were massacred because of the widespread belief that they had poisoned the wells. In fifteenth-century Iberia, a wave of pogroms and discriminatory legislation against Jews resulted in coerced conversion to Christianity. These actions culminated in 1492 with the expulsion or forceful conversion of Spain's Jewish population. As a result, as many as half a million Jews became "New Christians" or *conversos*. Previous forced conversions across Europe involved small towns or regions that could be relatively easily assimilated into the larger society.

Spain faced a unique set of circumstances—the question of how to deal with a substantial ethnic group that, despite its official change of religious beliefs, retained distinct cultural elements. As a result, for legal, political, bureaucratic, and religious offices, Spain began to emphasize family ancestry as a prerequisite for employment. Certificates of pure blood were required for many positions, and Jewish ancestry took on negative connotations that followed individuals beyond their conversion and from one generation to the next. Spanish legal culture permitted individuals to purchase purity-of-blood certificates for a fee, which allowed for flexibility against rigid racial categories. The emphasis on purity of blood, however, resulted in the stigmatization of an entire ethnic group on the basis of deficiencies that could not be eradicated by conversion or assimilation.

Taken together, the importation of sub-Saharan African slaves into Europe and the legal, political, and cultural actions against the Jewish population provided Iberians with a unique historical experience compared to the rest of Europe. They were accustomed to dealing with large groups of individuals who were considered outsiders. They developed a legal system that served to incorporate these groups by providing them a legal identity in codes such as the Siete Partidas (Seven Parts) and by recognizing them as part of society, but at the same time they made sure to separate and stigmatize them from society as whole. The concept of racial difference tied to skin color, the idea of labor associated with African slaves, and the notion of purity of blood in dealing with the Jewish population provided Spain a cultural and historical framework that it would draw upon when it set up colonies in the New World in the sixteenth century.

CONQUEST AND COLONIZATION OF THE NEW WORLD

Although the voyages of Christopher Columbus (1451–1506) and subsequent explorers ushered in the beginning of European colonization of the New World at the end of the fifteenth century, it was interactions with Africans and the indigenous populations on the Atlantic islands during the 1400s that provided the initial racial framework. When Columbus first wrote about the indigenous peoples of the Caribbean, he described them as being similar in color to the Canary Islanders, which Spain had colonized in the early part of the fourteenth century. The Iberians, and in particular the Portuguese, had already created racial categories for the sub-Saharan African population and the indigenous populations that inhabited the islands just off the West African coast. The Iberians drew upon this experience and knowledge in their interactions with the indigenous populations of the New World. Consequently, indigenous Americans were quickly classified as a different group that required its own set of laws to govern interactions, subjugation, and conversion.

In the Spanish Caribbean and later on the Spanish mainland of Latin America, the legal, geographic, and political concept of the "two republics"—the Spanish republic and the Indian republic—generated a different set of laws for each group. While these laws were rarely followed, their historical importance is that they indicate how the colonized subjects were being racially classified by the juridical and political institutions of the Spanish state. In brief, they were being placed outside of the colonizer's society and racialized as the subordinated colonized. As a result, various indigenous groups with their own history, culture, and language became collapsed together under the racial category of the "Indian."

The Portuguese followed a similar pattern in their colonization of Brazil. They did not recognize ethnic differences among the indigenous population, at least in terms of legal identity. They also applied the term *Indian* to the various Native American groups they encountered. Unlike the Spanish, the Portuguese made a more direct connection between the indigenous population of Brazil and slave labor. Stemming from their familiarity with sub-Saharan African slaves in the West African regions of Angola and the Congo, whom they classified as *negros* (the Portuguese term for black slaves), they referred to the indigenous population of Brazil as *negros da terra*, literally, "blacks of the earth." They did this not because of the skin color and physical appearance of the indigenous population, but because of their enslavement for hard labor. In the Portuguese colonizing mind of the sixteenth century, the black race and slavery were synonymous. Consequently, they applied the term *negro* to those who labored as slaves, even when they were not black in skin color. Unlike the Spanish, who had a philosophical debate over whether the indigenous American population should be enslaved, which in the end had little effect on

The Treatment of African Slaves in the New World. *This engraving was included in Theodor de Bry's 1594–1596 edition of* La historia del Mondo Nuovo (History of the New World) *by Girolamo Benzoni, originally published in 1565. It depicts Spaniards overseeing slaves from Guinea as they labor in the Americas.* © **CORBIS. REPRODUCED BY PERMISSION.**

everyday colonial policy, the Portuguese voiced no significant reservations at all.

The British, French, and Dutch all followed in the Iberians' wake to the New World during the sixteenth and seventeenth centuries. Like the Spanish and Portuguese, they would build their colonies on a racial hierarchy that exploited the indigenous population and imported Africans as slaves. By 1700 all of the European countries had devised legal codes that extended different legal rights to the indigenous and African population. For example, the French developed the Code Noir (Black Code) at the end of the seventeenth century to specify the treatment of its enslaved African subjects. Significantly, it defined slavery in terms of race and as an inheritable status that passed from mother to child. Collectively, these different legal codes served to fully distinguish the European, indigenous, and African populations from each other. Buttressed by a distinct legal code and reinforced by everyday policy, the various populations now represented separate and distinct races in colonial policies.

As a result of colonial encounters and the defining of colonized subjects as "others," it is during this period that the term *race* began to be used in European languages to refer to a people and nation. Just as they identified subordinate groups by the collective racial categories of black or Indian, Europeans defined themselves in contrast to these groups. The French and the English began to refer to themselves as a "race" of people unified as much by who they were as by who they were not. By the end of the seventeenth century, the term *race* increasingly came to be used and was understood as an inherent and unchangeable characteristic.

RACE IN THE ENLIGHTENMENT AND THE AGE OF REVOLUTION

When two hundred years of colonial history, constructed in part by the process of racially subordinating colonized subjects, combined with the Enlightenment-era fascination for establishing order over the natural world through classifying and defining organisms, *scientific racism* emerged in European intellectual thought. The scientific thought of the Enlightenment served as a precondition for the growth of modern racism based on physical appearance. Such well-known Enlightenment scientists as the Swedish botanist Carl Linnaeus (1707–1778), the German physiologist Johann Friedrich Blumenbach (1752–1840), and others began to classify humans into distinct races that were not based on political or legal status such as nationality, but on somatic appearance and phenotype.

Although many Enlightenment scientists were not interested in creating a racial hierarchy of intelligence and superiority, once science classified human beings as part of the animal kingdom rather than viewing all people as children of God, the way was open for a scientific explanation for racial differences rather than a cultural one. To the French naturalist Georges-Louis Leclerc, Comte de Buffon (1707–1788), for example, it was obvious that differences between black and white pigmentation were the result mainly of the differing effects of sun and temperature. These geographic and racial differences then influenced intelligence, he dubiously reasoned, because Africans could easily provision themselves from their lush environment, whereas European survival required greater ingenuity due to the need to raise food on barren soil.

The racial typologies that emerged from Enlightenment thought established a framework for specifying racial differences and biological racism, but they did not have an immediate practical application beyond scientific circles. It would take a new discourse over natural rights and who should exercise these rights to spread these views for political purposes.

The "age of the democratic revolution," roughly 1750 to 1850, marked the end of the eighteenth century with the American and French revolutions, followed by the creation of independent countries throughout Latin America from 1808 to 1830 and then the final blows against many European monarchies with the revolutions of 1830 and 1848. These developments brought serious ideological challenges both to racial enslavement and the legalized pariah status of Jews. The idea that people were endowed with natural political rights rather than being accorded those rights by a monarch or sovereign was difficult to reconcile with lifetime enslavement based on race or exclusion based on religion. As a result of

convenience and expediency, scientific racism could be used to describe blacks, mixed-blood peoples, and indigenous populations as less than human, and consequently not entitled to the natural rights exercised by the white European population.

The age of the democratic revolution and the first wars against European colonialism in the Americas were not designed explicitly to strengthen racism, but racism became one of the byproducts of the period with the formation of new independent nations organized along racial hierarchies. The French Revolution of the late 1700s initially extended its emancipatory provisions to the French colonies. In 1794 the French National Assembly liberated more than 400,000 slaves and declared them citizens of the new French Republic. With the rise of Napoléon Bonaparte (1769–1821), however, slavery was reinstated, and it would take complete separation from France for Haitians to defeat their colonial masters. On the nearby French Caribbean islands of Martinique and Guadeloupe, freed men, women, and children were re-enslaved until final abolition came in 1848.

The war for American independence resulted in the expansion of slavery in the South, and slaves were enshrined in the new U.S. constitution as counting only three-fifths of a person when allocating congressional representation according to population. In Latin America, the wars for independence served to weaken forms of human bondage and racial domination as the indigenous population and slaves throughout the region joined the armies that fought against Spanish colonialism to lay claim to political liberty, among other motivations. When new nations drafted constitutions, however, the Creole elite assumed political control and did not equally share political power with those of African, indigenous, and mixed-race ancestry.

The reason pre-Darwinian scientific racism found an eager audience in the United States, France, and various Latin American countries, more than in England, derives ironically from the revolutionary legacies of the nation-states premised on the equality of all citizens. Egalitarian norms required specific reasons for exclusion. Many of the political elite of the nineteenth century adopted the view that biological unfitness as a result of racial ancestry was a reason to deny full citizenship to segments of the population. The emphasis on political virtue in nineteenth-century republican theory did not apply equally to those who were not of a "virtuous," white racial ancestry. The practice of excluding women, children, and the insane from the electorate and denying them political equality could be applied to racial groups deemed by science to be incapable of rationally exercising the rights and privileges of democratic citizenship.

The expansion and reception of Darwinian scientific theory in the late nineteenth century and first half of the twentieth century, during the same period when the United States and Europe scrambled over colonial and imperial control of Africa, Asia, and Latin America, resulted in scientific theory and imperialism combining to justify human domination for racist reasons. Charles Darwin's (1809–1882) notion of "survival of the fittest" and "the struggle for existence" were transformed to explain global racial hierarchies based on colonial relations.

In the United States and Europe, colonial powers came to regard racism as a "natural order" for positive political evolution. Social Darwinism—Darwin's theory of human evolution applied to creating a hierarchy among human societies—was employed to justify the idea that colonialism required a racial hierarchy that "naturally" privileged the population of European ancestry. Darwinian scientific theory served to racialize the colonial relationship between the colonizer and colonized. Moreover, social Darwinism went so far as to blame the colonial subject for "burdening" the colonizer with the duty of colonizing the world in the interest of bettering humanity and racial superiority. The British author Rudyard Kipling (1865–1936) summed up the racial ideology that underpinned late nineteenth- and early twentieth-century colonialism in the poem "The White Man's Burden," which he penned in 1899 in the wake of the Spanish-American War (1898). Kipling's poem served as racist propaganda to encourage Americans to establish colonial rule over the Philippines.

RACE IN THE TWENTIETH CENTURY

Racism and overtly racist regimes of political and colonial domination reached their height during the twentieth century. W. E. B. DuBois (1868–1963), the African-American civil rights leader and advocate for colonial peoples' right to self-determination, accurately predicted in the opening to *The Souls of Black Folk* (1903) that "The problem of the Twentieth Century is the problem of the color line." In the United States, and especially in the southern states, a whole series of racial segregation laws and restrictions on black voting reduced African Americans to lower-class status. Designed for economic exploitation and societal disenfranchisement, the goal of America's Jim Crow segregation was the complete separation of the black and white races from all social interactions from birth to death. Racial domination was maintained and exercised through public lynchings and other forms of brutal and deadly intimidation, often with tacit, and sometimes official, encouragement by the state.

Nazi Germany carried the logic of racial-supremacy ideology to its most deadly conclusion with attempts to exterminate an entire ethnic group on the basis of race. The revulsion and shock expressed by people throughout the world to the Jewish Holocaust during World War II

(1939–1945) served to undermine scientific studies of racial superiority that had been respected and admired in the United States, Europe, and many other parts of the globe before the end of the war.

In South Africa, the apartheid system included laws banning all marriage and sexual relations between people of different races, and establishing separate residential areas for whites, mixed races, and Africans. While other racial regimes emerged across the globe in colonial and national contexts during the twentieth century, South Africa, Nazi Germany, and the United States stand out in the degree of legal and political authority exercised by the state in enforcing racial regimes.

Perhaps the single greatest force contributing to the end of racist regimes in the colonized portions of the world was the movement for independence and the struggle over national sovereignty that spread throughout Africa, Asia, and Latin America. The decolonization movement that ended up bringing political independence to dozens of countries in Africa, Asia, and the Caribbean directly challenged and refuted the racial ideology that underpinned colonialism. The supporters of radical movements for national sovereignty and independence—such as India's in 1947, the Cuban Revolution of 1959, the Algerian war for independence from 1954 to 1962, the independence of the Congo in 1960, the independence of British Caribbean countries in 1962, the Vietnam War from 1955 to 1975, and numerous other such movements—all called into question the colonial order by making claim to their own political future and right to self-determination.

In the United States, the civil rights movement of the 1950s and 1960s both inspired and took inspirations from the liberation of colonized countries, especially in Africa. The movement effectively ended legal segregation in the United States and provided African Americans with political rights. New countries quickly flexed their independence by confronting the economic, political, and racial hierarchies that structured relations between Europe and the United States and the developing world of people of color based in Africa, Asia, and Latin America. New nations had their representatives at the United Nations attack racism and promote decolonization for African and Asian countries in a display of solidarity born out of their common experience of colonialism and racial subordination.

By the end of the twentieth century, none of the European countries or the United States could openly justify their colonial and imperial policies on racist grounds. No longer could colonial subjects be described as childlike and incapable of running their own countries because of racial inferiority, as had been done less than a century earlier.

The cultural and scientific assumptions held by the West that endorsed and informed racial policies that guided colonialism for five hundred years no longer receive the full and explicit support of the state and the law. But racism does not require colonies or the endorsement of the state to thrive. The legacy of the relationship between Western colonialism and racism is that deeply entrenched notions of cultural differences tied to race continue to inform social interactions from personal relationships among individuals to state-to-state relations. The rise in hostility and discrimination against newcomers from the third world in several European countries and the United States at the beginning of the twenty-first century has breathed new life into cultural criteria to explain racial differences that have their origins in past colonial encounters.

Historically, racist regimes have thrived in colonies because racism allows colonizers to treat the colonized in a way they would not treat themselves through such policies as enslavement and the denial of political and legal rights. In the twenty-first century, with millions of formerly colonized peoples and their descendents living in Europe and the United States, the racism that once structured relations between the imperial country and the colony is now often practiced in an altered form inside a single country, albeit without full and open endorsement by the state. Consequently, the ongoing relationship between racism and Western colonialism that began more than five hundred years ago has entered a new stage in Europe and the United States with the battle over what entitles an individual to the benefits of citizenship and political rights. Increasingly, those who are not considered representative of the ethnic and racial heritage that has historically defined the nation have unequal access to the protection of the law and are most vulnerable to economic exploitation.

SEE ALSO *African Slavery in the Americas; Apartheid; Race and Colonialism in the Americas; Social Darwinism.*

BIBLIOGRAPHY

Davis, David Brion. *The Problem of Slavery in Western Culture.* Ithaca, NY: Cornel University Press, 1966.

Davis, David Brion. *The Problem of Slavery in the Age of Revolution, 1770–1823.* Ithaca, NY: Cornell University Press, 1975.

DuBois, W. E. B. *The Souls of Black Folk: Essays and Sketches.* Chicago: McClurg, 1903. Available online from the Avalon Project at Yale Law School at http://www.yale.edu/lawweb/avalon/treatise/dubois/dubois_01.htm.

Fredrickson, George M. *Racism: A Short History.* Princeton, NJ: Princeton University Press, 2002.

Hannaford, Ivan. *Race: The History of an Idea in the West.* Washington, DC: Woodrow Wilson Center Press, 1996.

Holt, Thomas C. *The Problem of Race in the Twenty-First Century.* Cambridge, MA: Harvard University Press, 2000.

Sweet, James H. "The Iberian Roots of American Racist Thought." *William & Mary Quarterly* 54 (1) (1997): 143–166

Winant, Howard. *The New Politics of Race: Globalism, Difference, Justice.* Minneapolis: University of Minnesota Press, 2004.

Matt D. Childs

RACIAL EQUALITY AMENDMENT, JAPAN

Japan participated in the great post–World War I (1914–1918) peace conferences in Paris in 1919 with three goals. Japan had declared war against Germany early in the war, and expected the resulting treaty to recognize Japan's contribution. The Japanese delegation sought to take over German-held islands in the Pacific Ocean, to keep the German concession in Shandong, China that the Japanese army had seized during the war, and to secure approval for an amendment on racial equality among nations in the final Versailles Peace Treaty.

The so-called racial equality amendment challenged the comfortable European, Caucasian-controlled world. It aroused furious opposition from Australian Premier William H. Hughes. Hughes felt it threatened his clearly racist "white" Australia policy, and he worried at this early date about Japanese expansion in the Pacific. Hughes received support from Arthur Balfour and Robert Cecil and Dominion leaders who feared the amendment might threaten their control over native peoples. One reading of the amendment implied it could limit the sovereignty of nations in controlling immigration and rights of aliens. Britain worried about roiling the waters of its expanded Middle Eastern empire; French and British ruling classes in Africa and Asia had similar concerns. And Hughes threatened to lead a campaign to arouse opposition in the British Dominions and the United States.

The amendment and the opposition it aroused threatened the goals of U.S. president Woodrow Wilson. He wanted to contain Japanese expansion and obtain Japanese support for America's Open Door policy in China so that American business could find markets for trade. He believed the racial equality amendment would appease Japanese pride while he worked to return Shandong to China and to have Japan remove its 70,000 troops in eastern Siberia, which Japan initially sent as part of the effort to help keep Russia on the Allied side in the war. But Wilson could not afford the kind of vicious

The Opening of the First Railway in Japan, 1872. *Japan was able to negotiate autonomy in railroad construction, using a loan from Great Britain to build its first railroad. This engraving, published in 1872 in the* Illustrated London News, *depicts the ceremony marking the completion of Japan's first railroad; both European and Japanese dignitaries were in attendance.*
© CORBIS. REPRODUCED BY PERMISSION.

its enduring disparities between expansive, industrialized powers and the underdeveloped third world.

In some regions, railroads served a direct style of imperialism, where virtually enslaved indigenous laborers harvested cash crops or mined valuable commodities, and railroads hauled such goods to port cities for export. More significantly, however, railroads made possible and profitable what historians have come to describe as *informal imperialism*, where an indigenous government was held in place, and the tethers of dominance took the form of high-interest loans by private investors to the indigenous government, special treaty-based privileges, and spheres of influence. As historian Ronald Robinson notes in his introduction to *Railway Imperialism*, "the railroad was not only the servant but also the principal generator of informal empire; in this sense imperialism was a function of the railroad" (Davis et al. 1991, p. 2).

Beholden to foreign banks and financiers, indigenous governments could ensure repayment and continued investment only by harsh labor policies, suppression of anti-imperialist movements, and diversion of revenue away from, for example, education and housing initiatives. Local labor and capital markets, as well as seemingly autonomous indigenous political systems, were ever more pulled into the gravitational orbit of expansive, more developed nations. For indigenous populations, railroads brought a mix of possibilities and exactions. Affording unprecedented geographic mobility, modern conveniences, new areas of employment, and potential profits, railroads also displaced traditional occupations, such as barge workers, and carried ever more foreign settlers into colonial areas, exacerbating tensions with local communities. Although privately funded for the most part, railroad building in colonial areas depended upon home governments and colonial officials to provide the legal and political wherewithal, with financial guarantees, land grants, and a periodic deployment of troops to quash rebellion or teach locals a preemptive object lesson.

Japan was able to negotiate autonomy in railroad construction, using a loan from Great Britain to build its first railroad in 1872, and drawing upon substantial exports of tea and silk to fund other related projects. The first foreign railway initiative in China came in the 1860s with the tiny Woosung Railroad, built by Anglo-American partners with the tacit permission of business-minded local officials in the Shanghai area, but shut down by central authorities in response to local agitation. Dynastic weakness and forced indemnities following defeat in the first Sino-Japanese War in the mid-1890s opened the way to foreign loans and investment, a situation redoubled by the terms imposed by treaty powers after the Boxer Uprising (1900). Much of the noted "scramble for China" at the turn of that century was a scramble for railroad concessions.

According to historian Clarence Davis (1991), Chinese officials were initially successful in playing off imperial rivals with selective railway concessions, but the dynamic set in motion by these railroads once built contributed to the spread of antiforeign insurgence, with "antiforeign" coming to include the Manchu Qing dynasty (1644–1911). By the early twentieth century, a dense network of railroads concentrated in the eastern regions of the country connected up port cities, such as Shanghai and Tianjin, to supplies of coal, cotton, rice, tea, cassia, sugar, and silk. Cities such as Shanghai boomed as entrepôts, receiver and distribution points in an expanding network of trade linked to world markets. This, in turn, led to the proliferation of factories in port cities to process raw materials for export, the emergence of a wealthy Chinese commercial elite, and growing disaffection among urban workers.

In China as in Africa, even while promoting the interests of expansive governments, railroad building paradoxically generated intense conflict among imperialist rivals, with a high-stakes competition over huge swaths of exclusive "railway zones" in Africa and Asia. Russo–Japanese rivalries flared over Manchuria, as Russia sought to extend the trans-Siberian railway through Manchuria, posing a threat to Japan's colonial consolidation of Korea. Franco–British commercial rivalry led to ambitious claims over territorial blocs in China, while Germany established a railroad monopoly in Shantung to expand market possibilities and provide a naval base for its increasingly powerful navy. Japan's seizure of Manchuria in 1931 and eventual push to empire turned upon effective control of regional railroad systems.

SEE ALSO *Railroads, Imperialism.*

BIBLIOGRAPHY
Davis, Clarence B, and Kenneth E. Wilburn Jr., with Ronald E. Robinson, eds. *Railway Imperialism.* New York: Greenwood, 1991.

Duiker, William J., and Jackson J. Spielvogel. *World History*; Vol. 2: *Since 1400*, 4th ed. Belmont, CA: Thompson-Wadsworth, 2004.

Murphey, Rhoads. *A History of Asia*, 5th ed. New York: Longman, 2006.

Jyoti K. Grewal

RAILROADS, IMPERIALISM

As the age of high imperialism began in 1871, British Prime Minister Lord Salisbury (Robert Arthur Talbot Gascoyne-Cecil, 1830–1903) said, "The great organizations and greater means of locomotion of the present day mark out the future to be one of great empires" (Davis, Wilburn, and Robinson 1991, p. 2). Salisbury believed that the railway of industrialized Europe would extend the imperial power of stronger industrial countries over weaker agrarian ones. By 1907, Salisbury's prediction had come to pass. European imperialists, with the capital investment of some £1.5 billion in railway stocks and bonds, brought much of the world under European rule. The effects of the engine of empire on people in the metropoles (centers of imperial power) and in the periphery (the colonies) proved to be profound.

The idea of nineteenth-century railway imperialism seems simple enough—use railways and the industry and money behind them to gain and maintain control of other people's countries and resources for the primary benefit and security of the imperial country. European economies and investors were to be the primary beneficiaries, not local economies or indigenous populations. Imperial incursions were often wrapped in national flags and humanitarian propaganda, including campaigns to end slavery, extend European civilization, spread Christianity, and encourage economic development throughout the empire. Yet critics have seriously challenged the realities and consequences of such alleged benefits.

Just a glance at railway lines throughout the African continent during the age of high imperialism reveals their intent. Trunk lines (the main railway lines that connect commercial centers with seaports and other commercial areas) were constructed to transport extracted resources from the African interior to the coast, where the raw materials were destined for European factories and markets. In South Africa, for example, trunk railway lines were constructed primarily to connect the diamond and gold fields to the ports. Even the inter-African dream of the Cape-to-Cairo railway of Cecil Rhodes (1853–1902) was understood in the context of imperial interests. The locomotive was used similarly to extend European imperialism in Argentina, Canada, China, India, Iran, Mexico, the Ottoman Empire, and Thailand.

Yet imperialism remains complex; as the Australian historian Keith Hancock (1898–1988) once quipped, "Imperialism is 'no word for scholars'" (Porter 1994, p. 6). Nonetheless, scholars have advanced several theories to explain imperial behavior. The German social philosopher Karl Marx (1818–1883) emphasized economic causes related to oppressed workers and greed inherent in inevitable stages of capitalism.

Others have argued that nineteenth-century imperialism contained far more reluctance. To these historians, imperialists were driven less by economic motivations than by long-standing combinations of factors, including culture, religion, nationalism, military bases, ports, European settlers, and economies, which had previously quite satisfactorily bound together collaborators on the colonial periphery to officials in the imperial metropole. Now that these relationships were breaking down, reluctant imperialists had to react or lose much of their empire. Whether intentional or reluctant, imperialists built railways to repair those relationships, extend territory, and promote economic colonial-imperial bonds of European empire worldwide.

Another way to understand railway imperialism is to examine how railways contributed to formal and informal empire. When colonial railways were used primarily to transport soldiers and supplies, and assist the infrastructure of political rule, the locomotive served formal empire. Yet railways also contributed to informal empire, due to the large amounts of capital necessary to purchase European engines, rolling stock (railroad cars), and rails, and then to construct the lines. Europeans who invested in colonial railway stocks and bonds relied on colonial borrowers to guarantee dividends and keep trade flowing. In such informal ways, partnerships of imperial, financial, and commercial interests converged behind the locomotive to create railway imperialism.

Sometimes railway imperialism was opposed by railway republicanism; that is, when a colony sought its independence, it would use railways to weaken imperial control. The South African statesman Paul Kruger (1825–1904), for example, sought to sever the gold-laden Transvaal with its railway hub in the Witwatersrand from the British Empire by using railway ownership, railway rates, customs duties, and alliances with other European powers to oppose British rule and railways in South Africa. To those at the metropole, such anti-imperial policy put at risk not only the investments of thousands of Europeans, but also British rule worldwide. The challenge of Kruger's railway republicanism contributed to the Second Anglo-Boer War (1899–1902).

Whatever their motivations, empire builders needed the support of local populations to carry out their imperial agendas. Ronald Robinson and John Gallagher (1953) have examined the lynchpin of imperialism—the collaborator, often the European settler with ties to Great Britain. The key to maintaining empire was knowing what colonials wanted, then providing them with that perceived need in return for allegiance. Wealth, security, state loans, economic development, power, and railways were often used to forge collaborators in colonies with officials at the metropole. Without collaborators in the colonies, Great Britain could not have controlled such vast expanses of the planet. In that imperial equation, the railway was crucial.

Robinson poignantly stated, "Europe's high age of imperialism, to a great extent, [was effected] because it was the railway age in other continents.... The grand central stations in cathedral style are the monuments" (Davis, Wilburn, and Robinson 1991, pp. 194–195). Former colonies continue to refine their relationships with European metropoles in the aftermath of nineteenth-century railway imperialism. The imperial foundation of the railway, which helped reduce time and space, along with the steamship and telegraphy, supports today's succeeding technologies of flight, nuclear power, and the information age, with all their ties to international capital and markets. Railway imperialism in this foundational sense remains under construction.

SEE ALSO *Empire, British; Imperialism, Cultural; Imperialism, Free Trade; Kruger, Paul.*

BIBLIOGRAPHY

Davis, Clarence, and Kenneth Wilburn, eds., with Ronald Robinson. *Railway Imperialism.* New York: Greenwood, 1991.

Etherington, Norman. *Theories of Imperialism: War, Conquest, and Capital.* London: Croom Helm, 1984.

Falola, Toyin, ed. *The Dark Webs: Perspectives on Colonialism in Africa.* Durham, NC: Carolina Academic Press, 2005.

Fieldhouse, David. K. *Colonialism, 1870–1945: An Introduction.* London: Weidenfeld and Nicolson, 1981.

Gallagher, John, and Ronald Robinson. "The Imperialism of Free Trade." *Economic History Review* 6 (1953): 1–15.

Headrick, Daniel R. *The Tools of Empire: Technology and European Imperialism in the Nineteenth Century.* New York: Oxford University Press, 1981.

Hobson, J. A. *Imperialism: A Study.* London: Nisbet, 1902.

Lenin, V. I. *Imperialism, the Highest Stage of Capitalism: A Popular Outline.* Moscow: Foreign Languages Publishing House, 1917.

Louis, William Roger, ed. *Imperialism: The Robinson and Gallagher Controversy.* New York: New Viewpoints, 1976.

Mommsen, Wolfgang J. *Theories of Imperialism.* Translated by P. S. Falla. New York: Random House, 1980.

Owen, Roger, and Bob Sutcliffe, eds. *Studies in the Theory of Imperialism.* London: Longman, 1972.

Porter, Andrew. *European Imperialism, 1860–1914.* London: Macmillan, 1994.

Robinson, Ronald. "The Excentric Idea of Imperialism, with or without Empire." In *Imperialism and After: Continuities and Discontinuities,* edited by Wolfgang J. Mommsen and Jürgen Osterhammel, 267-289. London: Allen and Unwin, 1986.

Robinson, Ronald. "Non-European Foundations of European Imperialism: Sketch for a Theory of Collaboration." In *Studies in the Theory of Imperialism,* edited by Roger Owen and Bob Sutcliffe, 117–140. London: Longman, 1972.

Wolfe, Martin, ed. *The Economic Causes of Imperialism.* London: John Wiley, 1972.

Kenneth Wilburn

RANGOON

SEE *Colonial Port Cities and Towns, South and Southeast Asia*

RELIGION, ROMAN CATHOLIC CHURCH

The relationship between the Roman Catholic Church and the centuries of European colonial expansion that began to take shape in the fifteenth and sixteenth centuries is complex, and at times enigmatic. The church acted as a legitimating institution for various colonial projects, at times as financier, and profited tremendously from the revenue generated by its increasingly global presence. It often acted to buttress colonial regimes in the face of internal and external criticism and in large part remained antagonistic toward later independence movements. Yet, the church also worked to impose strict laws regulating treatment of indigenous peoples, outlawed certain forms of exploitation and slavery, deeply criticized the violence of European wars of conquest, and purported itself to be the conscience of the European monarchs. The Roman Catholic Church was both a legitimator of the early phases of the colonial enterprise, and a critic of what it perceived to be its excesses.

The Roman Catholic Church, while hierarchical in organization and in control over its own official dogma, was by no means of one mind in its interactions with European colonial projects. Tension between the Vatican, members of the religious orders, and diocesan priests among themselves or with European monarchs and colonial administrators was often palpable. Debates over the legitimacy of European wars of expansion, the

nature of colonial regimes, and the rights of indigenous peoples often created immense conflict.

Although it did occur in the colonial context, no church doctrine actually supported the forced conversion of peoples to Christianity, and there were ample resources for legitimating the use of force to create social, cultural, and political conditions in which conversion by "persuasion" was more likely to be successful. Yet the requirements for those conditions sometimes ran against the interests of the European monarchs, colonial administrators, and colonists themselves, who were at times less interested in the conversion of indigenous peoples than their potential for economic profit. Colonists who exploited indigenous labor for agriculture or mining were constantly reprimanded by the church for failing to see to the religious education and conversion of their laborers to Christianity. Hence, it is precisely the tensions and edges of the colonial experience that shaped the Catholic Church's complex relationship to European colonialism rather than its own dogmatic or ideological positions.

The colonial projects of early modernity were also not homogenous, and the relationship of the Roman Catholic Church to those projects differed according to national context, shifts in the geopolitical realities of Europe, and significant variations in the church's own institutional and moral power vis-à-vis European states and monarchies. The first phase of modern European expansion coalesced around the efforts of the Spanish and Portuguese crowns—with church backing—in the middle of the fifteenth century. Hence the relationship between the Catholic Church and those colonial projects also reflected the political and ideological particularities of the Iberian empires.

By the seventeenth century, however, other European nations joined the race for establishing a global colonial presence. The power of the Spanish and Portuguese empires began to decline and those of England, France, and Holland began to ascend. As the religious experiences of both the English and Dutch colonial enterprises were quite different from those formed by Catholicism, marked shifts in the relationship of the Catholic Church to those colonial projects also followed, inaugurating what may be considered a second phase of European colonial expansion.

Each of those phases, however, witnessed a recurrence of certain themes of Christian thought and practice that marked the structural and cultural aspects of its relationship to European colonial projects. The transformation of the early Christian communities into institutions that wielded almost incomparable political, moral, and economic power was itself a long historical process. That process involved coming to terms with the legacy— political, theological, institutional—of the Roman

Empire and its successors. On the other hand, it may be rightly argued that throughout the Middle Ages and by the end of the seventeenth century the Catholic Church constituted an empire of its own, whose reach spanned from Canada to Patagonia (in southern South America), and from China to Madagascar. The Spanish and English colonial projects both constituted empires on which the sun never set, yet the reach of global Catholicism exceeded them both by constituting forms of colonial relations even where there was no formal colonial jurisdiction.

Thus, the first and foremost of the recurrent themes that emerged by way of defining or shaping colonial relations with the Catholic Church was the relationship between the Christian *evangelium pacis* (literally, "good news of peace") and the political, legal, and ideological superstructure of imperium that underwrote the Roman Empire and later European expansion. As the church acquired instruments of political power by the fourth century, debates emerged over the use of the coercive force of the Roman Empire for specifically Christian ends. As the debate sometimes divided the early Church Fathers, later Christians who were to reread the Fathers and dispute these things anew in the wake of the European colonial enterprises would find support for multiple and conflicting positions. Yet as a consequence of the Christianization of the Roman Empire in the fourth century, these disputes were not merely theological, but had deep ramifications for the institutions of civil and religious laws, patterns of commentary on those laws, and theological reflection over how those institutions and laws reflected upon the political and social shape of the church.

Centuries of Christian thought and practice also produced questions that deeply affected the intellectual culture and identity of the Catholic Church. The experience of missionaries sometimes served to remind Catholics that Christianity was no more natural to Italy than it was to China, and that the Christianization of the old Roman Empire and the remainder of the European continent had been a long, arduous, complex, and even violent process. The identification of Christianity with European cultural norms was therefore itself a historical product of significant cultural transformations in European history and in Christian thought and practice. The necessity of differentiating between what was European and what was Christian became important enough to be codified as instructions to missionaries in Vatican documents by the seventeenth century. Hence Christianity's views of its own history, attitudes toward other religions, and theological reflections on how God orchestrates history and ostensibly uses empires for his own purposes would deeply affect the ways that the church would interact with various colonial projects.

THE *PATRONATO REAL*

The tensions that shaped Catholic thought and practice in relationship to the first phase of European colonialism reflected very deep conflicts within the long history of Christian thought and the particularities of the Spanish and Portuguese imperial projects. These monarchies enjoyed a privileged relationship to the Vatican vis-à-vis other European nations, through direct rivalry over control of southern Italy and other cultural relations as much as through papal nepotism. Portugal established successful outposts in Africa, India, and eventually the coast of China, while Spain conquered the Canary Islands off the coast of Morocco in the late fifteenth century, with the islands becoming a staging ground for the further exploration to the west that covered much of the Americas and ended only with the conquest of the Philippines.

Spanish colonization of the Americas proceeded initially from wars of conquest and the establishment of territorial control and colonial governance, while the Portuguese were less concerned with large-scale colonization and worked rather to monopolize sea routes and established independent garrisons to protect commercial interests. The Catholic Church played a central role in both cases by sending missionaries to work in Spanish territories from California to Paraguay, and in the Portuguese territories from Africa to Japan. The church also granted ideological and institutional legitimacy to those imperial projects, if not always to what it perceived to be the excesses of the conquistadors.

However, the long history of Christian thought on questions of governance that ranged from scholastic theology and jurisprudence to commentary on canon and civil law would see to it that the relationship of the Catholic Church to European colonial projects was shaped in complex ways. First of all, it was commonly held and codified in canon law that neither popes nor Christian rulers had any authority outside their own jurisdictions; this meant that Christian rulers could not impose laws on lands not under their direct rule except in the case of a "just war," and that popes held no authority over nonbelievers and could not compel them to accept Christianity against their will. Yet the extension of Spanish jurisdiction over the New World, accompanied precisely by the use of violence, and ostensibly for the purposes of evangelism, created conditions in which many of the qualifications that accompanied those earlier arguments about the limits of authority were invoked or otherwise found to justify substantive aspects of the colonial projects even while working to check what were thought to be colonial excesses. Hence the church emerged in the sixteenth and seventeenth centuries as both the enabler of and impediment to Spanish and

Portuguese imperial ambitions. It justified their possessions but required them to facilitate the evangelization of their respective domains—a requirement that often clashed with other commercial or colonial interests.

The success of the voyages of Christopher Columbus (1451–1506) and of the Portuguese establishment of commercial colonies in Asia occasioned what was to become the defining structure of Catholic relationships with early modern colonial projects: the so-called *patronato real* ("royal patronage"), which legally obliged missionaries and other church representatives to work under the jurisdiction of the Catholic monarchs of Spain and Portugal. Thus, the dependence of Christian missionary work on commercial interests occasioned by new discoveries and sea travel was furthered by legally obliging the Spanish and Portuguese monarchs to oversee the missionary endeavors of the church in their own jurisdictions.

The occasion for this new arrangement was the "donation" made in 1493 by Pope Alexander VI (1431–1503) of "temporal and spiritual dominion" over newly discovered territories in the east to the Portuguese and in the west to the Spanish monarchs. This papal bull, *Inter caetera* (1493), and related decrees and treaties were known collectively as the Bulls of Donation. They effectively carved the non-European world into two domains. Dispute over how to interpret the boundaries of the donations indeed raged, and the Portuguese eventually laid claim to Brazil in 1532 and the Spanish to the newly conquered Philippine Islands in 1565. Missionaries to the newly discovered Americas or to Asia included Italian, German, English, and Irish priests and members of religious orders, but they remained legally subject to the patronage of the Iberian monarchs.

The Bulls of Donation were not new to Catholic thought and experience, although by the time of Alexander VI's decrees, such donations were in substantial ways dubitable and disreputable. Alexander's own reputation was that of a warlord and nepotist, and the legality of such donations was subject to increasing critique. One Spanish theologian and jurist quipped that for the pope to donate what was not rightfully his was nothing short of theft.

The institutional and ideological cache of the donations was not, however, easily cast aside even by its critics. The Bulls of Donation and their precedents in church history were the vehicle by which claims to the legitimacy of European presence in the New World were carried, and the long history of canon and civil law upon which the donations rested determined much of the jurisprudential vocabulary that sustained property rights in the New World, rights over indigenous labor, rights to use at least indirect coercive force in the service of evangelization, and rights to suppress heresy, idolatry, and "crimes

against nature" wherever they were found to exist under the jurisdiction of a Christian ruler. Other crimes ostensibly against persons, nature, or God that occurred not under the jurisdiction of a Christian ruler may be occasion for a "just war" that sought to vindicate the innocent against harm done to them. Both the proper jurisdiction of Christian rulers over territories granted to them and the occasion for a just war were invoked repeatedly as justifications for the Spanish conquest of the Americas and the Philippines. Although the terms of the Alexandrine donations and the applicability of the just war argument were subject to continuous criticism, rejection, and reinterpretation throughout the Spanish and Portuguese empires, the relationships of patronage and responsibility were established nonetheless.

The ideological weight of the Bulls of Donation rested on a long history within Catholic thought and practice that went back to the fourth century. Legend had it that as a token of gratitude to God for victories over the rival claimant to the imperial title at the Battle of the Milvian Bridge (312) on the Tiber River, the Roman emperor Constantine (ca. 234–337) converted to Christianity and then "donated" jurisdiction over the city of Rome and the Western Empire to Pope Sylvester (d. 335). Constantine then relocated the seat of the empire to the Bosporus and the newly founded city of Constantinople (now Istanbul, Turkey), leaving the jurisdiction of Rome to the pope, who in turn bestowed "temporal" jurisdiction over the empire to a successor to Constantine while retaining "spiritual" jurisdiction to the papacy.

Although the so-called "donation of Constantine" was itself a fiction, papal coronations of Holy Roman emperors for the next several centuries were not. Later Christian theologians would argue that the papacy possessed "two swords" representing both temporal and spiritual power, and that it would grant the exercise of temporal power to secular rulers so that the popes could focus more exclusively on the needs of spiritual governance. The language of proper jurisdiction that remained central to the development of canon and civil law during the Middle Ages also drew extensively from Roman codes and the significant transformations that did occur with the conversion of Constantine to Christianity and the transformation of the Roman Empire from a pagan power to an empire thought to be divinely ordained for the service of Christianity.

Although the story of the so-called donation of Constantine was suspect throughout Christian history—not least by Holy Roman emperors who resented receiving their legitimacy from the popes, with whom they were sometimes at war—the documentary basis for the legend was definitively established as a forgery in the middle of the fifteenth century by the Italian humanist Lorenzo Valla (ca. 1407–1457). The full impact of Valla's arguments was not immediately realized, but the practice of such donations was cast under a shadow from which it did not easily emerge. The donations of Alexander VI, made a half-century after Valla's exposure of that forgery, contain language explicitly reminiscent of the Constantinian donation, and wholly dependent upon it both theologically and institutionally. It was also a contested donation, and the practice of such territorial and jurisdictional donations ended with Alexander VI.

The institutional and ideological power of the Catholic Church to legitimate the new colonial enterprises of the sixteenth and seventeenth centuries did not rest on the theological legitimacy of the Alexandrine donations, but upon the terms of royal patronage made initially possible by the donations. Most importantly, the donations obliged the Catholic monarchs to finance and support the increasingly global Catholic missionary enterprise. Even critics of the Spanish conquests of the Americas, such as Bartolomé de las Casas (1474–1566), accepted the donations of Alexander VI only insofar as they required the monarchs to finance and support the evangelization of the American Indians—and see to it that Spanish greed and avarice was restrained enough to allow missionaries to peacefully persuade indigenous communities to convert of their own accord. Other critics rejected the donations entirely. Augustinian missionaries first to arrive in the Philippines quite routinely denied the Spanish monarchs just title to dominion over the indigenous populations there, but also appealed to the crown for material support and stricter laws against exploitation of indigenous labor.

In 1580 King Philip II of Spain (1527–1598) also claimed succession to the crown of Portugal, offering to unite the Spanish and Portuguese domains into a single global monarchy that effectively undid the division of the world enforced by the terms of the Bulls of Donation. He was heralded by some as a "new Constantine" capable of bringing Christianity even to China, but his claims were fiercely contested by Portuguese and Italian missionaries in Goa in India, Macao in southern China, and Japan, who often used the Bulls of Donation to derail Spanish ambitions in the Pacific after Spain's conquest of the Philippines.

CONQUESTS AND JUST WARS

As the legitimacy of any claims to property rights in the New World rested on often contested and shaky ground, the predominant language of justification that emerged by the middle of the sixteenth century was that of the "just war." If the pope could not donate territory, it was often argued, it could be legally acquired as the legitimate

spoils of a just war. Hence, whether or not the conquests of the Americas or the Philippines constituted just wars became a topic of not inconsiderable dispute among jurists, theologians, and missionaries.

The Spanish wars of conquest in the Caribbean, Mexico, Peru, and the Philippines were thought to be just wars by their protagonists. In fact, they were also *enacted* as just wars—not that they were fought justly, quite the contrary—but in that they imitated the very archaic Roman practices meant to establish just wars. Hernán Cortés (1484–1547), leader of the conquistadors responsible for the conquest of Mexico, established the practice of approaching an indigenous village and reading a formal complaint, followed by demands for restitution and a declaration of a just war should the community fail to comply by a certain time—precisely the formula that any Spanish schoolboy taught his Latin by reading Livy's histories of Rome could easily find.

The just war argument is often thought to be derived from the early Christian theologian Augustine of Hippo's (354–440) reflections over just and unjust wars in his monumental *The City of God*. However, both the ideological framework and the technical vocabulary of the *iustum bellum* (Latin, "just war") emerged a thousand years before Augustine, and remained deeply imbedded in Roman civil theology and legal practice from the time of the second Roman king Numa Pompilius (753–674 B.C.E.). A just war was properly defined, as Augustine affirmed, as the rectification of injuries done to an innocent party. In cases in which there was no formal court of appeal in which to settle the matter, an external authority could step in to act—by force if necessary—in order to rectify the wrong done. A just war had to be properly declared by a legitimate authority, had to have a just cause, and had to be fought justly and in accordance with its object of rectifying wrongs done.

Yet for all its theoretical nicety, the ideology of the just war sustained Roman imperial expansion for centuries, as it later did for the Spanish in the sixteenth and seventeenth centuries. A point not lost on later critics of the Spanish Empire was that Augustine himself ruthlessly criticized Numa Pompilius for the fact that Roman wars became far more frequent after Numa's establishment of religious and legal codes determining just wars.

Centuries of Christian thought and practice found the Roman language of the just war—filtered in part through Augustine—highly adaptable for ostensibly Christian purposes. It was a language of proper jurisdiction, as only a legitimate authority had the right to declare a just war. The language of sovereignty was in some sense thus inseparable from just war arguments. And, especially as Christian thought turned to Augustine and even earlier Christian writers, such as Eusebius (ca. 275–339), the language of the just war provided another account of how God worked in the world and used empires such as Rome both to establish justice and to pave the way for the successful evangelization of the world under the auspices of the Roman Empire. Augustine wrote that God granted dominion to Rome "when He willed and to the extent that He willed," and that Roman wars were generally just wars, thus establishing another language of donation that became immensely useful to later advocates of European empires.

The most vocal apologist for the conquests of the Americas as just wars was the Spanish royal historian Juan Ginés de Sepúlveda (ca. 1490–1573). Sepúlveda was a classicist and highly respected translator and interpreter of the ancient Greek philosopher Aristotle (384–322 B.C.E.). Sepúlveda has become known today almost exclusively for his claim, drawn from an application of the first book of Aristotle's *Politics*, that the American Indians were "natural slaves" and fit to be ruled by "natural masters" like the Europeans. However, his famed dispute with the Dominican priest Bartolomé de las Casas over the humanity and rights of the Indians was primarily an argument about just wars rather than the status of the Indians as human beings or natural slaves—after all, Sepúlveda's book that led to the debate was titled *Democrates Alter, or On the Case for a Just War Against the Indians*.

Critics of Sepúlveda, particularly theologians and jurists at the University of Salamanca in Spain, such as Francisco de Vitoria (ca. 1483–1546) and Domingo de Soto (1494–1560), successfully blocked the publication of Sepúlveda's book while publishing material of their own that sought to define the perimeters of just and unjust wars that they considered more in keeping with the commentaries of the medieval Christian theologian Thomas Aquinas (1225–1274), and Thomas's own use of Aristotle. This so-called School of Salamanca became a formidable critic of the Spanish conquests of the Americas, and of the use of coercive force for the purposes of evangelization—both of which Sepúlveda vigorously defended.

The primary difficulty with the just war argument, whether in the hands of Sepúlveda or Vitoria, was that it simply did not describe the realities of the Spanish conquest nor exhaust the many reasons why the Spanish claimed legitimate title to the Americas—and especially why the Spanish and Portuguese empires continued to receive the support of the Catholic Church quite in spite of their ruthlessness and systematic exploitation of indigenous peoples and expropriation of what one Spanish critic called their "lands, liberty, and property in exchange for their faith in Christ." Cortés most certainly imitated the Roman practices of declaring just wars, but

the massive Spanish colonial enterprise that nearly covered two continents was self-evidently not about saving innocent Aztecs from human sacrifice or cannibalism. José de Acosta (ca. 1540–1600), himself a missionary in Peru and critic of the Spanish conquests who was deeply familiar with Vitoria's thought, was not alone in thinking the language of just wars ill-adapted to the realities of the Indies and something of an ideological distraction from the violent effects of the wars of conquest.

The support of the Catholic Church for the colonization projects of the Spanish and Portuguese empires rested in part on the long-established history of interpretation of the privileged role of Christian governance to establish conditions for successful Christianization. The rights and responsibilities of Christian rulers dominated medieval jurisprudence, just war theory, and political theology in a manner that sought to privilege institutional and political stability, and both strengthen and check the excesses of temporal Christian rulers. And most importantly, those rulers were necessary partners in establishing the conditions for successful evangelization of unbelievers.

The paradox of the preservation of order and the mediation of excess in the name of good governance was the very building block of Augustinian political theology inherited by the early modern church, and the colonial context of the sixteenth and seventeenth centuries provided yet another stage on which to work out that tension. Only then does it become apparent that the same church that brought the Inquisition to Mexico and Peru and violently suppressed what it deemed idolatry by other measures was also the church that worked to stave off the excesses of colonial rapacity and protect indigenous communities with new laws, and which was able to exercise its influence even in places where colonial projects could not reach.

By the early seventeenth century, the church had largely repudiated what it considered the excesses of conquest, but worked diligently to sustain colonial political order. It also reserved, at least in theory, its right to endorse violence in cases where states or communities actively prohibited or impeded the free preaching of the gospel. This was the conclusion of the Spanish theologian Francisco Suarez (1548–1617), and it was institutionalized by 1622 in the founding documents of the new Vatican-sponsored Congregation for the Propagation of the Faith that was established to oversee the new global presence of Catholic missionaries on six continents.

STRUCTURES OF CULTURAL CONFLICT

The questions that shaped the relationship of the Catholic Church to the early modern colonial enterprises were not only political and institutional, but also deeply embedded in the church's own cultural and intellectual history. The questions of how to conceive of non-Christian religions and their place in the "sacred history" of the world from a providential perspective was by no means new to early modern missionaries, as the intellectual topography had been established at least in contour by many of the Church Fathers and Augustine in particular. Hence the process of evangelizing the newly discovered New World sent many missionaries back to Augustine's texts, along with those of Pope Gregory the Great (540–604), the Venerable Bede (673–735), and other exemplary accounts of the conversion of Europe to Christianity in late antiquity. Further, the intellectual and cultural transformations experienced by Europe during the Renaissance—particularly the revival of classical learning—provided the impetus to include Herodotus and Thucydides as well as Livy, Plutarch, Pliny, and Tacitus to the sources within which missionaries sought out exempla for how to think about the new cultures that they encountered from Mexico to Macao.

The tendency to classify indigenous cultures in the Americas or Asia according to models derived from ancient Roman historians was evident in most of the missionary encounters. Hence, "barbarians" were often categorized according to their level of civilization—specifically measured by their customs and practices, the construction of cities, the level of literacy, and the institution or lack thereof of laws and governance recognizable to Europeans. Catholic thinkers did not always consider Europe the most advanced civilization, and sometimes wrote of China and Japan as more culturally sophisticated and advanced, but as lacking the one thing (Christianity) that would perfect them. Nomadic or hunter-gatherer civilizations, like many found in the Americas, were considered the lowest form of civilization. Missionaries amassed a tremendous amount of ethnographic material about other religions from the sixteenth to the eighteenth centuries, although it most often remained simultaneously deeply invested in classical models and interpreted through Christian theological lenses.

As the consolidation of colonial control was most often the means through which the church sought to "civilize" indigenous peoples, cultural conflicts continually erupted in most missionary contexts. In some areas colonial administrators forcibly resettled populations, forced indigenous people to submit to religious indoctrinations and attend mass, and used force to "extirpate idolatry" by destroying indigenous religious sites and prohibiting participation in indigenous religious practices. Although not all of the missions were amenable to colonial control, most of the religious encounters in the sixteenth and seventeenth centuries tended toward religious paternalism and the affirmation of colonial

institutions as the order necessary to both civilize and evangelize indigenous populations. By the nineteenth century, new theories of scientific racism replaced earlier classicizing models of humanity and civilization, creating a perhaps more insidious version of the "white man's burden" to civilize and Christianize under the auspices of empire.

In areas subject to Spanish or Portuguese colonial control, attempts were nevertheless made by mestizo missionaries such as Blas Valera in Peru or others in Mexico to work outside of the structures of colonial cultural chauvinism and with more sympathetic approaches to indigenous religions. In areas not subject to Spanish or Portuguese colonial control, a different kind of encounter with non-Christian religions developed. Italians such as Alessandro Valignano (1539–1606) and Matteo Ricci (1552–1610) sought to enter Japan and China as "wise men from the West," having worked to gain significant fluency in Asian languages and intellectual traditions. In many of those encounters, Catholics were invested in a kind of utopian impulse to rediscover the nature of primitive Christian communities and the missions themselves became experiments in pre-Constantinian Christianity.

COLONIAL CONSOLIDATION AND CONFLICTS

As the Catholic Church worked out its own internal conflicts and troubled history on the stage of the New World, the church was also forced to deal with its declining power in Europe. The Reformation and subsequent wars of religion that only subsided in the mid-seventeenth century permanently altered Catholic self-perception as the institution that acted as both legitimator and moral conscience of the European colonial regimes. The church after the mid-seventeenth century no longer possessed the power to coerce or control the remains of the Roman Empire, and certainly not the newly emerging European states that did not depend on the church for their own legitimation.

This second stage of European colonial expansion also witnessed the decline of the Iberian powers and the rapid ascendance of France and England as the architects of the next two centuries of colonial expansion. Catholic relations with Protestant England were clearly strained and clearly competitive on the colonial stage, and certainly papal bulls and moral injunctions held no force in England or the Netherlands.

Hence the shape of colonial relations during the second phase of European expansion did not and could not have invoked the complex history of the Roman past that so animated Catholic thought in the fifteenth through seventeenth centuries. The collapse of European Christendom precipitated by the Reformation

The Expulsion of the Jesuits from Spain. *In the wake of increasing anticlericalism in Europe, the Jesuits were expelled from Portuguese dominions in 1759, from those under French jurisdiction in 1761, and finally from Spanish territories in 1767. This late eighteenth-century engraving by Charles Maucourt depicts their expulsion from Spain.* **TIME LIFE PICTURES/GETTY IMAGES. REPRODUCED BY PERMISSION.**

and wars of religion left the Catholic Church working less to establish its own political power than to exert its moral influence in both supporting and regulating what were now the apparently permanent realities of a Spanish-American colonial presence, and to regulate its missions in areas not directly subject to the old and now quite antiquated terms of the *patronato real*. After the initial uncertainties and conflicts over the discovery and conquest of the New World subsided in the early seventeenth century, the Catholic Church sought primarily to consolidate its relationship with the colonial enterprises, and worked to augment and expand its institutions, newly founded universities for colonial elites, monasteries and convents, and social services such as poverty relief and hospital work.

The changed conditions that began in the seventeenth century that altered the Catholic Church's relationship to various colonial projects may be exemplified in particular by the fate of the Jesuits' missions to

Paraguay and the so-called Chinese rites controversy. The questions of civilization, language, history, and the urge to rediscover a primitive Christianity all found their way into what became the most famous of the Jesuit missionary enterprises. The new model of mission that was begun in the Peruvian altiplano and most fully implemented in the Río de la Plata region of modern Paraguay, Argentina, Brazil, and Bolivia was immensely successful, and imitated in Canada, California, and the Philippines.

The missions among the Tupi-Guaraní Indians in Paraguay were originally established in the early seventeenth century under the leadership of Antonio Ruíz de Montoya (1585–1652), a Peruvian mestizo and native of Lima. Although the model of a *reducción*—a village or compound set aside for indigenous people and to which Spaniards were denied access—was adapted from colonial practice in Peru, Ruíz de Montoya adopted what missionaries called the "apostolic model" of traveling in pairs, refusing the protection of soldiers, and placing oneself at the mercy of another's hospitality. Spaniards and especially soldiers were denied access to the missions.

The missions were built on improvised classical models, with streets aligned on grids, ordered housing, and a central plaza meant to imitate the Greek agora (marketplace). These "Indian republics" were highly successful in agriculture and livestock husbandry and grew to be potent economic forces in parts of Argentina, Brazil, Paraguay, and Bolivia. However, the missions were also initially established as refuges for Indians from the slave trade, and Ruíz de Montoya traveled to Madrid to successfully lobby for the rights of the Indians to bear arms to defend themselves from Portuguese slave traders and Spanish accomplices.

Although the missions continued until late into the eighteenth century, their economic power and established tensions with the Spanish colonial authorities in the administrative provinces of Brazil, Peru, and the Río de la Plata resulted in accelerating the deterioration of church–state relations in Europe. Under various popes' attempts to improve relationships with European states in the wake of increasing anticlericalism, the Jesuits were expelled from all Portuguese dominions in 1759, from those under French jurisdiction in 1761, and finally from all Spanish territories in 1767. The *reducciones* in Brazilian territories were closed by Portuguese force of arms, and in the Río de la Plata by Spanish soldiers. The Jesuits were disbanded as a religious order and not reestablished until 1814.

Although no European power established a colonial presence in China, conflicts over Christian activity consistently raised questions that directly related to how the church thought of its global missions in colonial terms. Catholic presence in China was established in the late sixteenth century primarily through the work of the Italian Jesuit Matteo Ricci. However, important to Ricci's permission to reside permanently in China was the question of whether or not Chinese converts to Christianity would be subjects of the European monarchs or the pope. Ricci's denial undoubtedly contravened many theological opinions in Europe, and further developments led to strained relationships between Chinese Catholics and the Vatican.

As the Catholic Church could not resort to pressuring colonial administrators into controlling missionary activities in China, the tensions erupted on predominantly theological grounds. Ricci's tactic of aligning Christian thought with the teachings of the ancient Chinese philosophers Confucius (ca. 551–479 B.C.E.) and Mencius (Mengzi, ca. 371–289 B.C.E.) had proven highly controversial, especially when he held that the practice of Confucian rites of honoring ancestors was

not opposed to Christian teaching, and when Ricci chose to use Chinese names for God that were drawn from Confucian resources. The old questions of idolatry and syncretism quickly dominated the controversy, and tensions between the religious orders heightened the stakes. The Chinese rites controversy was settled by papal decree in 1715 when Clement XI (1649–1721) ruled that Chinese Catholics must use the Latin word *deus* to refer to the Christian God, and that the rites of ancestor veneration were forbidden to Chinese Catholics. In 1721 the Chinese Emperor Kangxi (r. 1661–1722) expelled all Catholic missionaries in retaliation and disgust.

The marked tendency of the Catholic Church toward the defense of colonial institutions as the arbiters of order in the New World while simultaneously seeking to restrain their excesses was highly visible both in Catholic attitudes toward the slave trade and eventually the wars of independence that in the early nineteenth century ended colonial control over the Americas. Popes continued to issue bulls condemning the enslavement of Africans from the sixteenth century through the nineteenth, although the tools of ecclesiastical discipline were rarely invoked on the slaves' behalf. Although formally condemned, Catholic ambivalence toward the slave trade remained intact, and Catholic colonists and even missionaries continued to hold African slaves in some areas well into the nineteenth century. Thought to be socially disruptive, antislavery pamphlets that circulated in the Americas also appeared on the Index of Forbidden Books drawn up by the Holy Office of the Inquisition. Negotiation among European colonial powers and the force of the British Empire finally had more to do with ending slavery than Catholic moral injunction.

Many Catholic priests and members of religious orders were engaged in the nineteenth-century wars of independence that ended the colonial projects that began in the sixteenth century, as others were involved in ending the slave trade. But the Roman Catholic Church, especially after the anticlericalism of the French Revolution in the late eighteenth century, again tended toward the reinforcement of colonial regimes as the necessary order under which it sought to act alternatingly as legitimator and as public conscience. The Catholic Church thus entered the nineteenth century seeking to sustain a semblance of its old Augustinian political theology, but increasingly lacking the political and institutional power that earlier allowed the church to sustain—in spite of its internal and external tensions—a position as both institutional advocate and moral critic of the European colonial enterprises.

SEE ALSO *Catholic Church in Iberian America; Justification for Empire, European Concepts; Papal Donations and Colonization.*

BIBLIOGRAPHY

Alden, Dauril. *The Making of an Enterprise: The Society of Jesus in Portugal, its Empire, and Beyond, 1540–1750.* Stanford, CA: Stanford University Press, 1996.

Aragón, J. Gayo. "The Controversy Over Justification of Spanish Rule in the Philippines." In *Studies in Philippine Church History,* edited by Gerald H. Anderson. Ithaca, NY: Cornell University Press, 1969.

Bangert, William. *A History of the Society of Jesus.* Saint Louis, MO: Institute for Jesuit Sources, 1972.

Boxer, Charles R. "Portuguese and Spanish Projects for the Conquest of Southern Asia, 1580–1600." *Journal of Asian History* 3 (2) (1969): 118–136.

Boxer, Charles R. *The Church Militant and Iberian Expansion, 1440–1770.* Baltimore: Johns Hopkins University Press, 1978.

Brading, David A. *The First America: The Spanish Monarchy, Creole Patriots, and the Liberal State, 1492–1867.* Cambridge, U.K.: Cambridge University Press, 1991.

Brett, Stephen F. *Slavery and the Catholic Tradition: Rights in the Balance.* New York: Peter Lang, 1994.

Camporeale, Salvatore I. "Lorenzo Valla's 'Oratio' on the Pseudo-Donation of Constantine: Dissent and Innovation in Early Renaissance Humanism." *Journal of the History of Ideas* 57 (1996): 9–26.

Cummins, J. S. *A Question of Rites: Friar Domingo Navarrete and the Jesuits in China.* Aldershot, U.K.: Scholar's Press, 1993.

d'Elia, Pasquale M., ed. *Fonti Ricciani: Documenti originali concernenti Matteo Ricci e la storia delle prime relazioni tra l'Europa a la Cina, 1579–1615.* Rome: Liberia della Stato, 1949.

Dussel, Enrique. *A History of the Church in Latin America: Colonialism to Liberation (1492–1979).* Translated by Alan Nelly. Grand Rapids, MI: Eerdmans, 1981.

Dussel, Enrique. *The Invention of the Americas: Eclipse of "the Other" and the Myth of Modernity.* Translated by Michael D. Barber. New York: Continuum, 1995.

Goti Ordeñana, Juan. *Del Tratado de Tordesillas a la doctrina de los derechos fundamentales en Francisco de Vitoria.* Valladolid, Spain: Universidad de Valladolid, 1999.

Graham, Cunningham R. B. *A Vanished Arcadia, Being Some Account of the Jesuits in Paraguay, 1607 to 1767.* London: Heinemann, 1901.

Gutiérrez, Gustavo. *Las Casas: In Search of the Poor of Jesus Christ.* Translated by Robert R. Barr. Maryknoll, NY: Orbis, 1993.

Hamilton, Bernice. *Political Thought in Sixteenth-Century Spain.* Oxford: Clarenden, 1963.

Hanke, Lewis. *The First Social Experiments in America: A Study in the Development of Spanish Indian Policy in the Sixteenth Century.* Cambridge, MA: Harvard University Press, 1935.

Hanke, Lewis. *The Spanish Struggle for Justice in the Conquest of America.* Philadelphia: University of Pennsylvania Press, 1949.

Hanke, Lewis. *Aristotle and the American Indians: A Study in Race Prejudice in the Modern World.* Chicago: Regnery, 1959.

Hanke, Lewis. *All Mankind is One: A Study of the Disputation Between Bartolomé de las Casas and Juan Ginés de Sepúlveda in 1550 on the Intellectual and Religious Capacity of the American Indians.* DeKalb: Northern Illinois University Press, 1974.

Headley, John. "Spain's Asian Presence, 1565–1590: Structures and Aspirations." *Hispanic American Historical Review* 75 (1995): 623–646.

Headley, John. *Church, Empire, and World: The Quest for Universal Order, 1520–1640.* Aldershot, U.K.: Ashgate, 1997.

Hyland, Sabine. *The Jesuit and the Incas: The Extraordinary Life of Padre Blas Valera.* Ann Arbor: University of Michigan Press, 2003.

Imbruglia, Girolamo. *L'invenzione del Paraguay: Studio sull'idea di comunità tra Seicento e Settecento.* Naples, Italy: Bibliopolis, 1983.

Johnson, James Turner. *Just War Tradition and the Restraint of War: A Moral and Historical Inquiry.* Princeton, NJ: Princeton University Press, 1981.

Kamen, Henry. *Inquisition and Society in Spain in the Sixteenth and Seventeenth Centuries.* Bloomington: Indiana University Press, 1985.

Klaiber, Jeffrey. *Religion and Revolution in Peru, 1824–1976.* Notre Dame, IN: University of Notre Dame Press, 1977.

MacCormack, Sabine. *Religion in the Andes: Vision and Imagination in Colonial Peru.* Princeton, NJ: Princeton University Press, 1991.

MacCormack, Sabine. "Ubi Ecclesia? Perceptions of Medieval Europe in Spanish America." *Speculum* 69 (1994).

MacKenney, Richard. *Sixteenth-Century Europe: Expansion and Conflict.* New York: St. Martin's Press, 1993.

Mignolo, Walter. *The Darker Side of the Renaissance: Literacy, Territoriality, and Colonization,* 2nd ed. Ann Arbor: University of Michigan Press, 2003.

Moran, Joseph Francis. *The Japanese and the Jesuits: Alessandro Valignano in Sixteenth-Century Japan.* New York: Routledge, 1993.

Muldoon, James M. *Popes, Lawyers, and Infidels: The Church and the Non-Christian World, 1250–1550.* Philadelphia: University of Pennsylvania Press, 1979.

Muldoon, James M. "The Conquest of the Americas: The Spanish Search for Global Order." In *Religion and Global Order,* edited by Roland Robertson and William Garrett, 78–81. New York: Paragon, 1991.

Muldoon, James M. *The Americas in the Spanish World Order: The Justification for Conquest in the Seventeenth Century.* Philadelphia: University of Pennsylvania Press, 1994.

Muldoon, James M. *Empire and Order: The Concept of Empire, 800–1800.* New York: St. Martin's Press, 1999.

Mungello, David. *Curious Land: Jesuit Accommodation and the Origins of Sinology.* Stuttgart, Germany: Verlag Wiesbaden, 1985.

Mungello, David, ed. *The Chinese Rites Controversy: Its History and Meaning.* Nettetal, Germany: Steyler Verlag, 1995.

Murphy, Terence, ed. *A Concise History of Christianity in Canada.* Toronto and New York: Oxford University Press, 1996.

Neill, Stephen. *A History of Christian Missions,* 2nd ed. Harmondsworth, U.K., and New York: Penguin, 1986.

O'Donovan, Oliver, and Joan Lockwood O'Donovan, eds. *From Irenaeus to Grotius: A Sourcebook in Christian Political Thought, 100–1625*. Grand Rapids, MI: Eerdmans, 2000.

O'Malley, John W., ed. *Catholicism in Early Modern History: A Guide to Research*. St. Louis, MO: Center for Reformation Research, 1988.

O'Malley, John W. *The First Jesuits*. Cambridge, MA: Harvard University Press, 1993.

Pagden, Anthony. *The Fall of Natural Man: The American Indian and the Origins of Comparative Ethnology*. New York: Cambridge University Press, 1982.

Pagden, Anthony. "Dispossessing the Barbarian: The Language of Spanish Thomism and the Debate over the Property Rights of the American Indians." In *The Languages of Political Theory in Early-Modern Europe*, edited by Anthony Pagden, 79–98. Cambridge, U.K.: Cambridge University Press, 1987.

Pagden, Anthony. *Spanish Imperialism and the Political Imagination: Studies in European and Spanish-American Social and Political Theory, 1513–1830*. New Haven, CT: Yale University Press, 1990.

Pagden, Anthony. *European Encounters with the New World: From Renaissance to Romanticism*. New Haven, CT: Yale University Press, 1993.

Pagden, Anthony. *Lords of All the World: Ideologies of Empire in Spain, Britian, and France, c. 1500–c. 1800*. New Haven, CT: Yale University Press, 1995.

Parker, Geoffrey, *The Grand Strategy of Philip II*. New Haven, CT: Yale University Press, 1998.

Phelan, John Leddy. *The Hispanization of the Philippines: Spanish Aims and Filipino Responses, 1565–1700*. Madison: University of Wisconsin Press, 1959.

Prosperi, Adriano. "America e apocalisse: Nota sulla 'conquista spirituale' del Nuovo Mondo." *Critica Storica* 13 (1976): 1–61.

Prosperi, Adriano. "Otras Indias." In *Scienze credenze occulte livelli di cultura*. Florence, Italy: Istituto Nazionale di Studi sul Renascimento, 1980.

Ricard, Robert. *The Spiritual Conquest of Mexico: An Essay on the Apostolate and the Evangelizing Methods of the Mendicant Orders of New Spain, 1523–1572*. Translated by Leslie Byrd Simpson. Berkeley: University of California Press, 1966.

Rivera, Luis N. *A Violent Evangelism: The Political and Religious Conquest of the Americas*. Louisville, KY: Westminster/John Knox Press, 1992.

Russell, Frederick H. *The Just War in the Middle Ages*. Cambridge, U.K.: Cambridge University Press, 1975.

Spence, Jonathan. *The Memory Palace of Matteo Ricci*. New York: Viking Penguin, 1984.

Todorov, Tzvetan. *The Conquest of America: The Question of the Other*. Translated by Richard Howard. New York: Harper and Row, 1984.

Tuck, Richard. *The Rights of War and Peace: Political Thought and the International Order from Grotius to Kant*. Oxford and New York: Oxford University Press, 1999.

Valla, Lorenzo. *The Treatise of Lorenzo Valla on the Donation of Constantine*. New Haven, CT: Yale University Press, 1922.

Vitoria, Francisco de. *Political Writings*. Edited by Anthony Pagden and Jeremy Lawrence. Cambridge, U.K.: Cambridge University Press, 1991.

Patrick Provost-Smith

RELIGION, WESTERN PERCEPTIONS OF TRADITIONAL RELIGIONS

The colonization of the Americas, Africa, India, and Southeast Asia brought European Christians in contact with other religious groups never before known to the West. Historians and anthropologists have given considerable attention to the ways this encounter between peoples of different religious traditions unfolded. Western perceptions of traditional religions initially depended upon a Christian framework for understanding variations in religious beliefs and practices, which often resulted in the characterization of non-Christian religions as somehow unfit to be called religions or to be the work of the devil. At other times, Western observers romanticized and incorporated some components of traditional religions into Western philosophical and religious systems. Yet no matter the perception, the imaginative and actual interactions between disparate religious traditions transformed all involved parties.

Christian missionaries, philosophers, and explorers were most responsible for the creation of popular perceptions of traditional religions throughout periods of colonialism, all of which were contingent upon social and cultural changes over time and in particular places. These Western perceptions, however, rarely encapsulated the religious experiences of people in full. What is more, interaction with Westerners or conversion to Christianity rarely generated a total destruction of traditional religious beliefs and practices. Instead, through a process of accommodation and adjustment, many aspects of traditional religions survived the initial period of colonization and continue to demonstrate themselves in the twentieth century, but not without immeasurable changes.

NATIVE AMERICA

In 1492 Christopher Columbus (1451–1506) and his entourage of Spanish sailors landed on the Caribbean island of Guanahani and thus initiated a massive and destructive encounter with non-Western peoples in North America. The Spanish, under the sanction of both the Roman Catholic popes and the Spanish monarchs, arrived with the dual goal to Christianize and civilize the native inhabitants of the New World. Such missionary ideals, however, took well over a half century to become even haphazardly implemented by the Spanish. During the sixteenth century, Bartolome de Las Casas (1474–1566), a Dominican missionary to New Spain, criticized Spaniards for killing, terrorizing, afflicting, torturing, and destroying the native peoples, who he considered to be by nature the most humble, patient, and peaceable of human beings. Indeed, it took the intervention of Pope Paul III (1468–1549) to officially pronounce that Native Americans were human beings worthy of conversion to Christianity. Franciscan missionaries provided the primary impetus for converting native peoples all over New Spain. They established mission settlements in order to indoctrinate native peoples in Christianity and thus purge them of what the missionaries perceived to be satanic and superstitious beliefs and practices. Franciscans also worked hard to repress the liberal sexuality of many native groups and then reorganize their societies based on European and Christian models.

French explorers brought a similar missionary zeal to the North American colonies of Canada. During the 1530s, Jacques Cartier (1491–1557) led an expedition through the waterways of Newfoundland and Prince Edward Island, and there referred to the god of the Stadaconans as a wicked spirit with deceptive powers over native peoples. However, it was not until the founding of Quebec in 1608 that the French Crown effectively supported the advancement of Catholic missions to native inhabitants of the Great Lakes region. Recollects and Jesuits began arriving in New France soon thereafter. Recollect missionaries, also known as Gray Robes, considered all native peoples to be so brutish and savage that it was futile to attempt conversion until they were properly civilized. They tried to transform the Huron people into Frenchmen by forcing them to live in small enclaves known as reductions. Jesuit missionaries, also known as Black Robes, differed from the Recollects in their consideration of all native peoples as innately good and civil. The Jesuits also demonstrated a willingness to convert Hurons without frenchifying them. Instead, they decided to live as traveling itinerants or temporary inhabitants of native communities far removed from French settlements. Such a total immersion brought the religions of the Jesuits and the Hurons in close contact with each other. Yet while Jesuits attempted to adapt Catholicism to native idioms, they also saw such adaptations as a necessary step toward conquering native superstitions and the religious authority of shamans.

English Puritans founded the colonies of Plymouth and Massachusetts Bay during the 1620s and 1630s. These Protestant peoples brought with them the perception of native peoples as suffering from savagery and barbarism. The Protestant settlers associated Native American forms of ritual with those practiced by Roman Catholics, and thus referred to both traditions as idolatrous. Yet they also believed that native peoples were easily susceptible to Christian education and conversion. This impression lasted well into the eighteenth century, and especially the notion that missionaries had to civilize the savages before converting them to Christianity. The English process of civilizing and converting native peoples required that the religious and social habits of native peoples be reduced to the level of false religion. It also required that native peoples leave their customary lifestyles and enter into the strictly ordered confines of praying towns. John Eliot (1604–1690), the leading English missionary of the seventeenth century, popularized this form of civilizing and Christianizing native peoples, a form very similar to that of the Spanish missions. Conversion to Christianity was necessary for the elimination of what was seen as demonism, Satanism, and devil worship in native rituals and beliefs.

By the nineteenth century, the conversion of Native Americans to Christianity was widespread. Many European inhabitants of the Americas, however, continued to question the extent to which native beliefs and practices could be incorporated into Christian systems. Many believed that Native Americans lacked the essential human qualities necessary for religious understanding. Native ceremonial practices received considerable attention from European observers, especially the popularization of the Lakota Ghost Dance in the Great Plains of North America. A Native American prophet and visionary named Wovoka (1858–1932) instructed fellow American Indians to perform a ceremonial dance in preparation for the Second Coming of Christ. Christian missionaries and federal officials became concerned about the native religious movement. In 1890 tension ultimately turned to violence at Wounded Knee, where the United States military killed 250 women and children. The legacy of Lakota religion remained present throughout the twentieth century. Black Elk (1863–1950), an Oglala Sioux holy man, demonstrated how Catholicism and native religious traditions complemented each other, whereas members of the American Indian Movement laid siege to the village of Wounded Knee in 1973 in an effort to raise awareness of their civil rights concerns.

AFRICA

Slave traders and Catholic missionaries from Portugal landed on the west coast of Africa during the fifteenth century. They brought with them very little knowledge of traditional religions on the Dark Continent. Catholic missionaries of the Capuchin order quickly recognized the difficulty in converting Africans without first gaining the support of African monarchs. For this reason, European priests and African kings often acted out of diplomatic and political necessity. As missionaries serving at the pleasure of African kings, Capuchins had to tread more softly than they would have liked when it came to the total conversion of Africans to Christianity. Africans, as a result, largely controlled the commingling of Catholicism and traditional religions, especially in relation to spirit worship, religious specialists and healers, rites of passage, and religious icons. The willingness to adapt Catholicism to traditional African religious systems, however, did not mean that missionaries thought favorably of African religions. In fact, when it was possible to get the support of a strong African-Christian leader, missionaries waged severe assaults on what they considered to be heathenish, pagan, and sinful abominations.

The political and economic alterations of the European Reformation allowed for a Protestant missionary presence in Africa. This new evangelization coincided with the explosive growth in the Atlantic slave trade. The correlation between missions and trade, though not always in complete accord, was evident in both Dutch and British ventures during the eighteenth century. Thomas Thompson (1708–1773), the first Anglican missionary sent to what was known as the Gold Coast, tried and largely failed to convert Africans to Christianity. Many Africans, upon identifying all Europeans as Christians, could not reconcile the ideas espoused by Thompson and other missionaries with the actions of European slave traders. Further south along the coast of Africa, Europeans of all religious backgrounds encountered the people of the Cape, also known as Hottentots, during the seventeenth century. Many observers of these native peoples disputed the legitimacy of the Hottentot religion. In fact, many Europeans refused to even recognize the beliefs and practices of Hottentots as religious, instead choosing to refer to them as beasts and savages devoid of reason. It was not until the establishment of a Dutch settlement at the Cape during the 1650s that Europeans recognized Hottentots as moon worshipers.

The international slave trade altered the traditional religions of Africa to an incalculable degree. Historians and anthropologists, however, have identified survivals of African religious beliefs and practices in both Africa and the Americas. The enslavement of Africans set in motion a series of ruptures in individual lives and communities. Enslaved persons experienced the Middle Passage from Africa to North America, South America, or the Caribbean islands. The British, alone, brought 1.5 million to the Caribbean, and another 500,000 to North America. Upon arrival, enslaved persons were sold to slaveholders without respect for family bonds or ethnic identification. Traditional religious systems, therefore, rarely survived the fragmentation of the slave trade in full. However, once settled into new slave communities

either on plantations or in cities, enslaved Africans generated new religious systems that incorporated many components of African traditional religions, especially herbalism and conjuring.

Enslaved Africans also experienced a new wave of Christian missionary activities in the American colonies. Many Anglicans, Moravians, Baptists, and Methodists attempted to convert the enslaved within the British colonies of North America and the Caribbean, often despite the unwillingness of slaveholders to allow for such attempts. The interaction between European and African religious traditions created new forms of Christianity that incorporated music, dance, and spirit possession. So, too, did Catholic priests convert, or at least baptize, many enslaved persons in French and Spanish colonies. The mixture of French and Spanish Catholicism with African religious traditions produced the religions of Vodou and Santeria.

INDIA AND SOUTHEAST ASIA

In 1498 the explorer Vasco de Gama (1460–1524) led a Portuguese expedition to the port city of Calicut in southern India. The first Catholic missionaries followed soon thereafter. However, they did not immediately refer to the traditional religion of India as Hinduism or Buddhism. It took centuries of Western encounters with the people of India to gather a comprehensive understanding of their many and diverse religious systems. Roberto Nobili (1577–1656), a Catholic missionary, exhibited an uncommon willingness to interact with the people and consume the culture of India. He studied the languages of India, translated the Catholic catechism into Tamil, and transcribed Indian texts, all with an effort to find Christian-like components of Indian religions. Many Catholic missionaries and travelers compared the idea of the Brahman, or the supreme deity, with the Christian godhead, and they compared the Brahmans, or the members of the highest caste in Indian society, with Catholic priests. The Indian texts of the Vedanta and Upanishads also appealed to missionaries because of their similar investment in sacred texts such as the Bible. Protestant missionaries tended to compare Indian religions with Roman Catholicism in derogatory ways.

European philosophers of the eighteenth and nineteenth centuries also contributed to the public perception of Indian religions. Voltaire (1694–1778), the French philosopher of the Enlightenment, viewed India as the cradle of world religion and civilization. Immanuel Kant (1724–1804) described Indian religions as once the purest of religions that was now spoiled by superstitions. Some Romantic philosophers from Germany highlighted the pantheism of Indian religions, or the idea that all things were united in one Supreme Being. The German

Sioux Indians Performing the Ghost Dance. *Native American ceremonial practices, especially the Lakota Sioux Ghost Dance of the late nineteenth-century Great Plains of North America, received considerable attention from European observers.* © **CORBIS. REPRODUCED BY PERMISSION.**

Romantics then used their perception of Indian religions to criticize the science-based philosophy of the Enlightenment in Europe. Some scholars have identified August Wilhelm Schlegel (1767–1845), a leading spokesperson for Romantic philosophy, as the first professional Indologist. Even the most influential of German philosophers, Georg Wilhelm Friedrich Hegel (1770–1831), incorporated his perception of Indian religion and philosophy into his understanding of world history. For Hegel, India was the cradle of civilization, but he saw the progress of civilization as moving from the East in ancient India to the West in contemporary Europe.

Interestingly, the term Hinduism did not enter the common parlance of Europe until the nineteenth century. Friedrich Max Muller (1823–1900), an Oxford professor, translated a six-volume edition of the *Rig Veda*, an important Indian text, whereas another Oxford professor, Sir Monier Monier-Williams (1819–1899), wrote the book *Hinduism* in 1877 for a series entitled *Non-Christian Religious Systems*. Afterward, a large portion of Europeans began to regard Hinduism on par with the other world religions of Buddhism,

Judaism, and Confucianism. Yet, according to Monier-Williams, most Indians did not recognize Hinduism as their religious system. It was not until the creation of Pakistan and the independence of India in the 1940s that Indians started to consider themselves Hindus on a massive scale.

By the 1620s, Antonio de Andrade (1580–1634), a Jesuit priest from Portugal, crossed the Himalayan Mountains north of India and entered into Tibet. Yet instead of recognizing Tibetan religion as a form of Buddhism, Andrade tended to notice similarities between Tibetan religion and Catholicism, such as the idea of the Trinity, the sacraments of baptism and confession, and the performance of exorcisms. He turned his observations into a book, which was soon translated into Spanish, Italian, French, German, Flemish, and Polish. The Italian Jesuit Ippolito Desideri (1684–1733) followed Andrade a century later in what he described as the false sect of the highly curious religion observed in Tibet. He considered it his responsibility to study the religion of Tibet in order to logically refute their claims and convert them to Catholicism. Protestant observers, and particularly the British, also recognized similarities between Roman Catholicism and traditional Tibetan religion. However, whereas Catholics looked with favor on these findings, Protestants meant for such features to prove their illegitimacy. British explorers, in particular, likened the Dalai Lama to the pope, the city of Lhasa to Rome, Tibetan monasteries to Catholic monasteries, and Tibetan rituals to the Catholic mass. Non-Catholic observers, in addition to the negative associations with Catholicism, also perceived of some components of Tibetan religion with favor, including its social organization, diplomatic acumen, and rationality.

The Western attraction to Hindu and Buddhist traditions has resulted in any number of novel manifestations throughout the nineteenth and twentieth centuries. Henry David Thoreau (1817–1862), the famous American transcendentalist, brought the *Bhagavad Gita* with him on his now-famous stay at Walden Pond, which inspired the words, "The pure Walden water is mingled with the sacred water of the Ganges." The public notoriety of Hinduism reached a pinnacle during the 1893 World's Parliament of Religions at Chicago. Swami Vivekananda (1863–1902), a Hindu mystic, became an international celebrity after he spoke on several occasions before the parliament about the commonalities and discrepancies between Christianity and Hinduism. In an illuminating statement, Vivekananda admitted that it was difficult for an Indian representative to request humanitarian assistance from Christians because of the Christian interpretation of Hinduism as heathenism. In a similar fashion, the fourteenth Dalai Lama (b. 1935) of Tibet has captured the attention of many Westerners. The exiled Buddhist leader has redefined the Western perception of Tibetan Buddhism, mixing mysticism and contemplative practices with political interests and nationalism. *Free Tibet* bumper stickers and popular publications such as the *Tibetan Book of the Dead* have contributed to Western perceptions of Buddhism in both North America and Europe.

To the east of India and Tibet, in what is now referred to as Southeast Asia, the religions of Hinduism, Buddhism, and Islam form one of the most religiously diverse regions in the world. In 1511 Portuguese explorers attacked the port of Malacca in an effort to disrupt Muslim traders. Dutch, British, French, and Spanish expeditions followed soon thereafter, making contact with the peoples of Sri Lanka, Myanmar, Thailand, Malaysia, Singapore, Brunei, Indonesia, Laos, Cambodia, Vietnam, and the Philippines. The Spanish capture of Manila in 1571 allowed for an extensive Western assessment of traditional religion and the large-scale conversion of the Filipino population to Roman Catholicism. Countries such as Thailand, Burma, and Cambodia remained Buddhist countries despite the best efforts of British missionaries and colonists. Portuguese Catholics and Dutch protestants encountered the syncretic religious cultures of Java and Bali during the sixteenth and seventeenth centuries. The resilience of Hinduism, Buddhism, Islam, and traditional Indonesian religions made it difficult for Western missionaries intent upon the conversion of the island peoples. And even where Protestant missions were somewhat successful, in places such as the Molucca Islands of the late twentieth century, religious violence often developed between Muslims and Christians.

During the 1950s, over four centuries after the European colonization of Southeast Asia, the anthropologist Clifford Geertz (b. 1926) performed extensive research on the traditional religions of Indonesia, and particularly the religious beliefs and practices of Java and Bali. His perception of traditional religions lacked the missionary zeal of the past, relying instead on an emerging body of work in the sociological, psychological, and anthropological study of religion. Geertz, like his academic predecessors Max Weber (1864–1920), Emile Durkheim (1857–1917), Sigmund Freud (1856–1939), and Bronislaw Malinowski (1884–1942), looked to traditional religions in Africa, India, and Southeast Asia for insight into the origins and patterns of religions worldwide and throughout history. Geertz defined religion as a cultural system based on rituals and symbols that gave meaning to life for its participants. He did not ask questions of value, legitimacy, or truth when examining religious traditions of Southeast Asia. Instead, at least ideally, he attempted to interpret traditional religious systems on their own terms and in their own settings, all the while admitting that the process of interpretation always reveals just as much about the observer as the observed.

SEE ALSO *London Missionary Society; Missionaries, Christian, Africa; Religion, Roman Catholic Church; Religion, Western Perceptions of World Religions; Religion, Western Presence in Africa; Religion, Western Presence in East Asia; Religion, Western Presence in Southeast Asia; Religion, Western Presence in the Pacific.*

BIBLIOGRAPHY

Axtell, James. *The Invasion Within: the Contest of Cultures in Colonial North America.* New York: Oxford University Press, 1985.

Chidester, David. *Savage Systems: Colonialism and Comparative Religion in Southern Africa.* Charlottesville: University Press of Virginia, 1996.

Frey, Sylvia R., and Betty Wood. *Come Shouting to Zion: African American Protestantism in the American South and British Caribbean to 1830.* Chapel Hill: University of North Carolina Press, 1998.

Geertz, Clifford. *The Interpretation of Cultures: Selected Essays.* New York: Basic Books, 1973.

Gutierrez, Ramon A. *When Jesus Came, the Corn Mothers Went Away: Marriage, Sexuality, and Power in New Mexico, 1500–1846.* Stanford, CA: Stanford University Press, 1991.

Halbfass, Wilhelm. *India and Europe: An Essay in Understanding.* Albany: State University of New York Press, 1988.

Holler, Clyde. *Black Elk's Religion: The Sun Dance and Lakota Catholicism.* Syracuse, NY: Syracuse University Press, 1995.

Horton, Robin. *Patterns of Thought in Africa and the West: Essays on Magic, Religion, and Science.* Cambridge, U.K. and New York: Cambridge University Press, 1993.

Inden, Ronald. *Imagining India.* Oxford, U.K. and Cambridge, MA: Basil Blackwell, 1990.

Jenkins, Philip. *The Next Christendom: the Coming of Global Christianity.* Oxford and New York: Oxford University Press, 2002.

Lopez, Donald S. *Curators of the Buddha: The Study of Buddhism under Colonialism.* Chicago: University of Chicago Press, 1995.

Lopez, Donald S. *Prisoners of Shangri-La: Tibetan Buddhism and the West.* Chicago: University of Chicago Press, 1998.

Niezen, Ronald. *Spirit Wars: Native North American Religions in the Age of Nation Building.* Berkeley: University of California Press, 2000.

Raboteau, Albert J. *Slave Religion: The "Invisible Institution" in the Antebellum South.* New York: Oxford University Press, 1978.

Michael Pasquier

RELIGION, WESTERN PERCEPTIONS OF WORLD RELIGIONS

As one names the various religious traditions now grouped under the rubric *World Religions*—Buddhism, Hinduism, Christianity, Judaism, Islam, Jainism, Sikhism, Shinto, Confucianism, Zoroastrianism—it is important to note from the outset two very significant points. First, the category of "world religions" is itself a historical phenomenon, emerging through specific forms of academic and popular discourse in the nineteenth century. Human beings have not always named religions in this way, nor understood in the same way which human practices or beliefs should be described as "religious." Second, such a list of "world religions" by no means names the full range of religions around the globe. Those so named have become, through complex historical and ideological transformations, the "great religions of the world" that were thought to have grown out of more "primitive" religious practices such as shamanism, totemism, ancestor worship, or other practices more commonly associated with "indigenous religions." Yet what makes one religion "great" and another "primitive" is not intrinsic to the religious practices or beliefs themselves. Rather, such designations are a reflection of the intellectual and cultural habits of an emerging "human science" of religious studies, which undertook the ordering and ranking of different religions in the world in a way that met the intellectual and social needs of Europeans preoccupied with managing a rapidly expanding colonial enterprise.

Indeed, the category of "world religions" emerged in part from that colonial experience. Like other intellectual practices developed by Europeans in the nineteenth century that sought to describe "religion" as an essential and qualitatively human experience with many diverse facets, faces, and practices around the globe, the study of World Religions was not itself an explicitly colonialist project, but it nevertheless participated in an ordering of the world that corresponded to rapidly expanding colonial ambitions and the needs of a new elite colonial administration. Certainly, some knowledge of the religious worlds in which colonial peoples lived—and of how their religious beliefs affected and shaped their political and social lives—was important to effectively governing such places as India during the time of the British *raj.* Civil servants faced with the diverse religious contexts found in the Middle East, India, Africa, and Latin America ranked high among those for whom the new science of religions was developed. In recent decades, this interaction between an emergent science of religion and the needs of a new elite colonial administration has become one of the focal points of the postcolonial critique of religious studies.

The emerging science of religious studies, as with other human sciences, required the accumulation of an immense body of knowledge concerning human practices, beliefs, and histories in diverse contexts around the world—but it was not as if the acquisition of this knowledge had to start from scratch. After all, Europeans had long encountered other religions, and it was in part from the history of these encounters that knowledge of non-European societies was made available to nineteenth-century theorists of religion. The data on which the new science of religious studies relied was found in the accumulated accounts of religious practices, beliefs, and histories written primarily by missionaries, adventurers, and later colonial administrators themselves. However, also like the other human sciences, the emergent discipline of religious studies sought to shape and transform such data on the basis of contemporary philosophical, theological, and scientific models. The goal was to make such enquiries into human customs and practices truly "scientific" in ways analogous to the transformation of the study of various natural phenomena into the "natural sciences" of geography, geology, or zoology. But how did one find the "truth of religion" (rather than "the true religion") in such an array of "unscientific" and hardly disinterested accounts?

RELIGION BEFORE "WORLD RELIGIONS"

Postcolonial critics of the disciplinary presumptions of religious studies often argue that the very term *religion* is also a nineteenth-century phenomenon and derived from within the history of Christian thought itself, rendering problematic at best the use of the word to describe other forms of thought, practice, and ritual performance outside the Christian West. Yet it is also the case that religious studies inherited and subsequently transformed terms and models dating from the European Renaissance, which have their roots in a history of European interaction with non-European "others" that stretches back to late antiquity.

Renaissance humanists became outspoken advocates of the study of history, culture, and language (*studia humanitatis*), over and against the modes of theological and philosophical thinking that had dominated the Middle Ages. It was through their influence that Classical vocabularies and models for describing human practices as "religious" were recuperated and applied to contemporary cultures. It was also during those same centuries that both the largest expansion of the Christian missionary enterprise and the largest geographical expansion of European colonial projects took shape, providing ample opportunity to encounter and describe human practices.

The terms invoked to describe these practices were not originally Christian, but derived from Roman usage. The Latin language possessed no single word for "religion" as a set of beliefs, practices, and ritual performances, but it did rely on several terms to describe human practices now collapsed under the term *religion*. The cognate *religio* described not beliefs or practices *per se*, but rather one's orientation toward duties, ritual observances, and public rites—hence a "religious" person performed his or her obligations faithfully and was considered trustworthy. Classical and Renaissance writers contrasted this with the term *superstitio*, literally "in terror of the gods," which was applied to the performance of rites and rituals out of fear and as an attempt to manipulate the gods to do what one needed or wished. Renaissance writers often preferred the term *cultus* to describe the object or form of those rites and rituals themselves, and used the language of *mores* (customs and habits) to describe other aspects of belief and social practice. Therefore, to speak of "true religion," as some Renaissance writers argued, was not to describe a belief system but to speak of properly carrying out one's duties,

cultic practices, and obligations toward the gods. The application of these terms to the non-Christian practices of newly discovered peoples in the Americas, Africa, and Asia became possible in part out of the recognition that the terms were themselves pre-Christian and had already been adapted and put to multiple uses.

Such moments of adaptation and cultural transformation were nothing new to Christianity: as Renaissance writers argued, it was in late antiquity that the "pagan" religions of the Greco-Roman and Persian worlds were directly challenged by the rise of Christianity and Christianity emerged from its own conflicted history with Judaism. Classical understandings of the interaction of human beings with the world of the gods, Classical ritual practices, and debates over the nature of oracles and prophecies were now confronted with new exclusionary categories and the particularity of Christian claims. After the conversion to Christianity of the Roman emperor Constantine in the fourth century, Christians increasingly held positions of political and intellectual privilege, and new forms of imperial authority were instituted to ensure the suppression of pagan religious practices deemed idolatrous or heretical. Furthermore, in the early Middle Ages the combined impacts of the Christianization of the Roman Empire, early missionary movements in places as distant as Britain and Scandinavia, and resistance to Islamic expansion into North Africa and Spain coalesced to create a Europe distinct from the old borders of the Roman Empire. The "reconquest" of Spain that ended in 1492 with the expulsion of Muslims and Jews from the Iberian mainland—and Turkish threats to Christian kingdoms in Austria—furthered the identification of Christendom (as a matrix of religious, political, and social structures) with a new European consciousness. Latin Christianity achieved hegemonic cultural status, and the precepts and norms accompanying it were encoded in civil laws.

Although rich moments of interreligious encounter and dialogue did exist on the frontiers of Christendom in the Middle Ages, the European identity emerging in the fifteenth and sixteenth centuries tended to reinforce the privileged position of Christianity as a constituent of that identity. As a consequence, European approaches to the problem of religion were forcefully shaped by encounters in which "others"—like Jews and Muslims—were considered guilty of *invincible ignorance*; that is, inexcusable, willful, and irreparable rejection of religious truth given their presumed knowledge of Christianity. This orientation toward Jews and Muslims was to be sharply contrasted with the attitude taken toward the indigenous peoples of the Americas or the Chinese, Indians, and Japanese, who were thought to be guilty of *evincible ignorance*—unknowing and hence reparable rejection of Christian truth. The legal distinction between *evincible* and *invincible* ignorance—formed in part to respond to problems posed by the Crusades and the treatment of Jews in parts of Europe—divided the world into Christians, Jews, Muslims, and *evincible* "others." Borrowing from their Greek heritage the term for non–Greek speakers, Europeans named those others *barbarians*. Although the term may have often been pejorative, it was not necessarily so—and it was at times invoked by those who favored better treatment of others, because "barbarians" were nonculpably ignorant and thus not subject to the legal or religious strictures applied to those guilty of willful rejection of Christian truth.

The complex mix of intellectual exchange, polemic, and politics that shaped Christian encounters with Judaism, Islam, and "others" shaped certain categories for understanding religion that would remain remarkably resilient in European thought until the nineteenth century. Among the most potent of early Christian claims was that Christian truths served to "fulfill" the promises or intentions of other religions. Hence, the life of Jesus was said to have "fulfilled" both the promises of God to the people of Israel and the intent of the Mosaic Law as understood by Judaism, thus rendering Jewish understandings to be imperfect in their originary form and now antiquated by the revelation of God in Christ. Christian writers such as St. Augustine of Hippo would extend that framework and write that Roman religious practices were also "shadows" of which Christ was the fulfillment, and were idolatrous by virtue of misdirecting the human drive for worship to "false gods" now that the "one and true God" had been revealed in Christ. Hence modes of thinking emerged that posited "true religion" as the implicit goal of all religions, and that rendered other religious practices outmoded, incomplete, or imperfect expressions of one essential religion. In this way the conception of "sacred history" as the processual narration of God's self-revelation—first in the people of Israel and then in Christ and the Church—often provided the basis for analogous narration of the history of other religions yet to be fulfilled in Christ.

RELIGION AND COLONIALISM IN THE EARLY MODERN PERIOD

The first religions to be described as such by Europeans were thus not conceived of as "World Religions" in the contemporary sense of the term: Judaism and Islam were seen as recalcitrant, and the newly encountered indigenous religions of the Americas were thought of as *evincible*. Furthermore, early modern discourses on religion were shaped by the most expansive phase of the European colonial enterprise that began in the fifteenth century with Spanish and Portuguese exploration in Africa and culminated with the conquest of the Americas by the Spanish Empire. By the end of the sixteenth century, as the rapidly growing Christian missionary enterprise took shape around the globe alongside rapidly expanding European colonial interests, Europeans would begin to describe the religious worlds of Japan, China, and India. Although Christianity arrived in the Americas as part of the Spanish practices of "pacification, evangelization, and colonization," Christian missionaries, particularly in Mexico and Peru, began to learn indigenous languages and produced tomes full of detailed ethnographic descriptions of beliefs and ritual practices. The writings of Bernardino de Sahagun in Mexico and José de Acosta in Peru, deeply shaped by Renaissance humanism, formed the basis for what some contemporary historians refer to as *comparative ethnography*. Acosta's *Natural and Moral History of the Indies* offers a naturalizing and developmentalist account of indigenous American *religio* that would be read by many nineteenth-century scholars of religion. Yet the ways in which Christian orientations informed the very basis of such accounts, and shaped their description of indigenous practices—seen as everything from innocent or benign to idolatrous and even demonic—demonstrate the extent to which the history of Christian thought about the "other" would reflect and shape histories of non-European customs, beliefs, and practices. Christian writers, adopting and shaping the model of "fulfillment" developed by Augustine, would often find indigenous religions to be precursors to Christianity; on other occasions, documentation of the practices of indigenous religions allowed for a more thorough "extirpation of idolatry" from the American religious landscape.

However, in areas not subject to Spanish or Portuguese colonial control, a different kind of encounter with non-Christian religions developed. Jesuit missionaries such as Alessandro Valignano sought to enter Japan as "wise men from the West," albeit, in the case of Valignano, dressed as a Buddhist and speaking Japanese. This strategy would be most successful with another Jesuit, Matteo Ricci, who adopted Confucian dress and customs after entering China from the Portuguese garrison of Macao. Roberto de Nobili lived in India as a Brahmin and learned Sanskrit from gurus, and Alexander de Rhodes lived in what is now modern-day Vietnam conversant with Buddhists. In those contexts, missionaries often studied Hindu, Buddhist, or Confucian doctrines, histories, and rites under the direction of practitioners, sought to introduce Christian teachings as sympathetic to aspects of those religions, and intervened in internal debates. The writings of these missionaries were among the primary vehicles for introducing Europeans to Asian religious thought, as evidenced in particular by the seventeenth-century fascination of European *philosophes* with China. The comparatively positive approach to these other religions evidenced by the Jesuits in Asia may account in part for the early inclusion of Asian religions in the category of World Religions. In contrast, study of the indigenous religions of the Americas continued to be shaped by revulsion at the practices of human sacrifice, and the highly developed Aztec and Inca religious worlds were collapsed within the category of shamanic and natural religions.

WORLD RELIGIONS AND COLONIALISM IN THE NINETEENTH CENTURY

The emergent human science of the study of religion took as its evidentiary base the mass of documentation about human customs, practices, and rituals provided in part by missionaries, travelers, and colonial administrators from previous generations. To this was added the new experiences of missionaries, travelers, and colonial agents in the early nineteenth century. However, what began to shift was not the nature of data, but the mode of interpretation. The problem for Europeans now, after the catastrophic loss of religious authority following the collapse of a unified Christendom in the years of the Reformation and subsequent wars of religion, was not to find in other religions imperfect forms of Christian revelation, but something more ostensibly universal. Religious particularity, Christian or otherwise, appeared to be yet another occasion for war, and dependence upon religious authority was seen—especially by philosophers like Immanuel Kant—as a form of intellectual immaturity that must be cast off with vigor. Kant framed in particularly potent ways the search for a new "cosmopolitan history" of humankind in the wake of the apparently irreconcilable cultural and historical differences among human beings, and argued that it was only the universality of reason that could transcend the differences of human particularity. From this argument flowed his assertion that religion achieved its highest level of development when casting off the culturally embedded history of language, forms of authority, and ritual practices—and that "religion within the limits of reason alone" would be realized only by finding universalizable ethical norms within the teachings of all religions. Theorists of Indian religions, such as the Sanskrit scholar Max Müller, would remain highly indebted to Kant's philosophical framework.

In Kant's philosophical reflections on history and religion, the old genre of "sacred history" began to give way to other forms of universality, and religion itself became something to be "fulfilled" not by universal revelation in Christ, but by universal reason embodied in the ethical life. Sympathetic critics of Kant, wishing to preserve aspects of human religiosity against excessive rationalization, insisted on the primacy of interior religious experience as a transformative moment that fulfilled the intent of external religious practices, and gave the ethical life an added experiential dimension. Hence, rites and rituals no longer were the primary referents for discussing human religiosity, but came to be seen as those things that hindered the realization of a true universal religion. Once there was a decreasing emphasis on rites, rituals, and structures of religious authority—along with increasing rationalization and an emphasis on ethical teaching and private religious experience—it was possible to speak of a common and essential core of all religiosity. These shifts would later allow Emile Durkheim to argue that religion was simply a primitive form of the modern institutions of law, science, and political life.

The search for the ethical teachings of religions and for transcendent religious experience was enabled by the hierarchical classification of religions into "lower" and "higher" forms according to the extent to which they could be freed from "externalities" such as ritual observances and forms of religious authority. Forms of developmental progression were certainly central to the older genre of sacred history, but the fulfillment now represented was to be realized in the ethical teachings of all developed religions and in private religious experience itself rather than in one particular "true religion." That passage from lower to higher religious forms could be expressed in evolutionary terms that were later made analogous to the passing of a species from less-developed to more-developed biological forms. The search for the common source of all religions, not unlike the search for common ancestral life forms that preceded all species differentiation, led to the creation of the elaborate diagrams, charts, and genealogical accounts of religions springing from one another that proved ubiquitous in literature on the newly categorized "great religions of the world." Only when categorized and organized in this way could the various World Religions be presumed to all share the essential defining characteristics of religion: identifiable *traditions*, canons of sacred *texts*, and sets of ethical *teachings*, all of which can be taught comparatively, and in each of which one may find the genuinely universal truth of human religious experience.

THE POSTCOLONIAL CRITIQUE OF WORLD RELIGION

Although the shift from religious particularity to universal ethics and experience has allowed many scholars of religion to remain committed to the idea of World Religions as a genuine celebration of religious plurality, critics writing in the wake of the collapse of the European colonial projects in the twentieth century have taken a dimmer view less amenable to Western culture's celebrations of its own great accomplishments. Rather than seeing the study of World Religions as leading to the triumph of religious diversity, these critics point to the imposition—more insidious than in the past because more hidden from view—of Christian categories of interpretation on the diverse human cultures of the world. In their view, the developmentalist and evolutionary models upon which religious studies was built privileged highly rationalized forms of Protestant Christianity as the model through which other religions were to be interpreted. And, critics charged the discipline of religious studies with providing an indispensable service to colonial regimes—the rationalization of religions, thereby meeting the needs of an increasingly rationalized colonial bureaucracy. In the wake of that critique, many contemporary religious studies scholars remain committed to the "human science" approach, but are seeking new and less universalistic idioms to describe the various cultural and social practices of the world subsumed under the term *religion.*

SEE ALSO *Christianity and Colonial Expansion in the Americas; Religion, Western Perceptions of Traditional Religions.*

BIBLIOGRAPHY

Asad, Talal. *Genealogies of Religion: Discipline and Reasons of Power in Christianity and Islam.* Baltimore: Johns Hopkins University Press, 1993.

Dubuisson, Daniel. *The Western Construction of Religion: Myths, Knowledge, and Ideology.* Translated by William Sayers. Baltimore: Johns Hopkins University Press, 2003.

Durkheim, Emile. *The Elementary Forms of the Religious Life: A Study in Religious Sociology.* Translated by Karen Fields. New York: Free Press, 1995.

Fletcher, Richard. *The Barbarian Conversion: From Paganism to Christianity.* New York: Holt, 1997.

Frazer, James G. *The Golden Bough.* Abridged ed. New York: Touchstone, 1995. (Originally published in two-volume form in 1890, and in 12 volumes in 1911–1915.)

Geertz, Clifford. *The Interpretation of Cultures.* New York: Basic Books, 1973.

Kant, Immanuel. "An Answer to the Question 'What is Enlightenment?'" In *Kant's Political Writings,* 2nd ed., edited by Hans Reiss and translated by H. B. Nisbet. Cambridge, U.K.: Cambridge University Press, 1991.

Kant, Immanuel. "Idea for a Universal History with a Cosmopolitan Purpose." In *Kant's Political Writings,* 2nd ed., edited by Hans Reiss and translated by H. B. Nisbet. Cambridge, U.K.: Cambridge University Press, 1991.

Kant, Immanuel. "What Is Enlightenment?" In *What is Enlightenment? Eighteenth-Century Answers and Twentieth-Century Questions,* edited by James Schmidt. Berkeley: University of California Press, 1996.

Masuzawa, Tomoko. *The Invention of World Religions, or, How European Universalism Was Preserved in the Language of Pluralism.* Chicago: University of Chicago Press, 2005.

Müller, F. Max. *The Essential Max Müller: On Language, Mythology, and Religion.* Edited by Jon R. Stone. New York: Palgrave Macmillan, 2002.

Pagden, Anthony. *The Fall of Natural Man: The American Indian and the Origins of Comparative Ethnography.* New York: Cambridge University Press, 1982.

Pals, Daniel L. *Seven Theories of Religion.* New York: Oxford University Press, 1996.

Said, Edward. *Orientalism.* New York: Pantheon, 1978.

Smart, Ninian. *The Religious Experience of Mankind.* 3rd ed. New York: Scribners, 1984.

Smith, Wilfred Cantwell. *The Meaning and End of Religion: A Revolutionary Approach to the Great Religious Traditions.* San Francisco: Harper and Row, 1978.

Tylor, E. B. *Primitive Culture: Researches into the Development of Mythology, Philosophy, Religion, Language, Art, and Custom.* New York: Gordon, 1974. (Originally published in 1871)

Patrick Provost-Smith

RELIGION, WESTERN PRESENCE IN AFRICA

The earliest contact between Western religious presence and Africa occurred when various European nations, including Punics, Greeks, and Italians, colonized the northern regions, the Maghrib. Africa served as their breadbasket. Cultural and religious flows linked this region to the Roman Empire, whose intellectual centers included Alexandria. Europe was pagan at this time. The nationalist Donatists contested foreign religious domination, while Circumcellions displayed the resentment of indigenous peoples against exploitative agricultural merchants.

HISTORY

Egyptian religions dovetailed with Roman mystery cults to produce a variety of enduring religious traditions. In the seventh century C.E., Islamic bands disrupted the Christian presence and constructed a cultural and religious heritage that overwhelmed the Maghrib. Various Muslim dynasties consolidated Islamic influence and attacked Nubia, Ethiopia, and the Iberian peninsula. Ethiopia survived and Iberians initiated the *reconquista* crusades of the fifteenth century after the military failures of the crusades.

The search for a sea route to circumvent the Muslim monopoly of the spice and gold trades brought Africa into contact with the West. But the Portuguese occupied islands and coastal strips, trading for gold, pepper, and

Livingstone Reads the Bible. *British explorer and missionary David Livingstone, who was sent to Africa in the mid-1800s by the London Missionary Society, reads the Bible to African natives.* © MARY EVANS PICTURE LIBRARY/THE IMAGE WORKS. REPRODUCED BY PERMISSION.

slaves from their *feitoras* (forts) and avoided the full cultural clash. The lucrative trade attracted other European countries into Africa specifically for commerce and the glory of their nations. Mercantalism as a nascent form of capitalism overawed the subterfuge of missionary enterprise. Only in the Kongo-Soyo kingdoms did they penetrate inland to establish an ornamental Christianity based on court alliance. Popular religion represented by Beatrice Vita Kimpa, who claimed to be possessed by St. Anthony, and her *ngunza* (divinatory) cult predominated.

Gold trade declined as the pull of the Atlantic slave trade shifted the pattern of Western presence in the seventeenth century. African middlemen, colluding with Europeans, prosecuted internal wars and increased the appetite for gin and manufactured goods that served as the medium of exchange. In the ensuing rivalry, the Danes, Dutch, French, and English established more than twenty-one forts in West Africa, displaced the Iberians, and enlarged the scale of Western presence by the eighteenth century. Christianity survived mainly in the forts until the nineteenth century when the combination of abolitionism, evangelical revival, and imperialism

reshaped the scale and nature of Western presence: administrative officers, missionaries, commercial companies, educationists—surged with the intention to establish Western administrative and judiciary structures, a new economy, and Western civilization—mediated through Christianity.

Negative attitudes toward African political structures, religions, cultures, and worldview intensified after 1885 when European nationalist rivalry led to the partition of Africa. Armchair theorists provided the intellectual arsenal; enlightenment worldview supported new technologies, values, and ideas. Western presence created fundamental shifts as conquests and colonization destroyed autonomous African development. Colonialism was a process, an ensemble of institutional mechanisms created to protect European interests with violence, and a culture that regulated the material and mental lives of victims. Christianity domesticated colonial values through translation of the Bible into vernacular, education, and charitable institutions.

THE AFRICAN WORLDVIEW

The end of colonialism started in the 1960s but its impact endured, especially the attack on indigenous African worldviews. African cultures vary widely but possess a recognizable structure of a worldview. Africans share a cyclical perception of time and a three-dimensional perception of space. Time is measured as events, *kairos*. Life moves from birth through death to a reincarnation or return. Rites of passage celebrate each phase: naming, puberty, membership in secret societies for youths in age grades, participation in adult roles, membership in adult secret societies, death, first and second burial rites, journey through the ancestral world and back to the human world. The world is divided into the sky inhabited by the Supreme Being and powerful deities (thunder, moon, lightning). The earth is divided into land and water. The Earth Mother controls various spirits: nature (rocks, trees, hills, caves), human, evil, and professional/guardian spirits. In the water, marine spirits rule.

According to the African worldview, the ancestral world is a mirror of the human world; spirits continuously cross the frontiers. Human spirits become ancestral depending on how they lived and died: Those who died with strange diseases, were struck down by lightning, or committed suicide are punished for wickedness and may not reincarnate. They become malevolent spirits that haunt farm roads. Families honor the dead with proper rituals because they are "living-dead" who protect their families. Ancestors are feared because offending them brings bad luck and punishment. It is a charismatic, precarious worldview sustained by religious values,

Christian Mission, French Equatorial Africa, Early 1900s. *Christianity domesticated European colonial values in Africa through education, translation of the Bible into vernacular languages, and charitable institutions such as this mission in French Equatorial Africa.* © 2005 ROGER-VIOLLET/TOPHAM/THE IMAGE WORKS. REPRODUCED BY PERMISSION.

rituals, and sacrifices that afford the powers of the benevolent gods for warding off the malevolent ones and witchcraft.

Festivals follow the agricultural cycle to turn daily human life into sacred activities and renew covenants with the gods of the fathers. Salient environmental ethics emanate from a sacred perception of land and a holistic world. Salvation has immediacy, solid, and material context: people seek for healing, security, protection, fertility, wealth, and harmony with other human beings and world of nature. Religion serves to explain, predict, and control space–time events. Spirits cause events and reshape life trajectories because what is seen is made of things not seen.

Enlightenment worldview essayed to destroy African cultures and their unique worldview and installed new scientific religions like Rosicrucianism, Freemasonry, and Eckanakar. Cultural transplantation ignored the fact that the biblical worldview that shaped Western imagination resonates prominently with African worldviews: Though the biblical worldview perceives time (*kronos*) as linear, measured in the abstract, it recognizes kairotic time and a three-dimensional space. It is charismatic because supernatural forces control and imbue human social and political realities with moral quality. Its rituals, prohibitions, symbols, the power attributed to blood, word, and name (*onomata*), resonate in African worldviews and provide pathways for inculturation.

In culture contact, receivers are hardly passive; they exercise agency, and appropriate through selection and reconstruction. In the twentieth century, Christianity grew massively in Africa by providing answers to questions raised in the indigenous worldviews. Local identities contested global processes because the broken indigenous worldviews had questions that the enlightenment worldview could not answer.

In the twenty-first century indigenous religions remain resilient; but emergent religions proliferate because Africans seek religions that would better perform the functions of the old religions. Africans seek religious structures that are based on a wealth of indigenous knowledge.

SEE ALSO *Missionaries, Christian, Africa; Religion, Western Perceptions of Traditional Religions; Slave Trade, Atlantic.*

BIBLIOGRAPHY

Appiah, Anthony. *In My Father's House.* New York: Oxford University Press, 1992.

Magesa, Laurenti. *African Religion: The Moral Traditions of Abundant Life.* Maryknoll, NY: Orbis Books, 1997.

Roberts, Andrew D., ed. *The Colonial Moment in Africa: Essays on the Movement of Minds and Materials, 1900–1940.* New York: Cambridge University Press, 1990.

Sanneh, Lamin. *Encountering the West: Christianity and the Global Cultural Process.* Maryknoll, NY: Orbis Books, 1993.

Ogbu Kalu

RELIGION, WESTERN PRESENCE IN EAST ASIA

Prior to 1450, Christian missionaries from the west (Nestorians in the seventh century and Franciscans in the thirteenth century) had failed to establish an enduring presence in East Asia. After 1450, the currents of global history generated a continual flow of missionaries to East Asia, where they planted the seeds for a religious presence that has continued to the present day.

The greatest receptivity was initially found in Japan, where Francis Xavier (1506–1552) arrived in 1549 in the wake of Portuguese traders who introduced firearms to Japan. Initially, Christianity was enthusiastically received along with a Japanese craze for Portuguese things; by 1600 there were 300,000 Christians and by 1615 possibly 500,000. However, the victory of the Tokugawa shogunate after a long period of feudal chaos was tenuous and made the Tokugawa fearful of foreigners as a subversive force. This led to a persecution of European missionaries and Japanese converts that intensified until the Portuguese traders and missionaries were expelled in 1639 and replaced by Dutch Calvinist traders who did not engage in proselytizing. The anti-Christian campaign and the Tokugawa's attempt to control foreign trade led to an exclusion policy that lasted until the mid-nineteenth century. Christianity was forced underground and thereafter was reduced to a tiny minority religion in Japanese history.

The Chinese initially were less enthusiastic about Christianity than were the Japanese. The syncretic culture of the Ming dynasty (1368–1644) blended the three dominant religions of China (Buddhism, Confucianism,

and Daoism) into a unified whole that minimized their differences. Just as Buddhism had once been a foreign religion that was assimilated into Chinese culture by initially blending with Daoism, Christianity now underwent a similar process. With the assistance of eminent literati converts, the Jesuits realized that Confucianism was the most likely candidate for synthesis with Christianity. They believed Confucian moral teachings were compatible with Christianity and needed only to be supplemented with the truths of Christian revelation.

Missionaries became divided on the basis of nationalistic rivalries fostered by mercantilism. The early Portuguese monopoly *(padroado)* on shipping routes to the East enabled them to dominate the mission field prior to 1800. The Dutch and French began to make inroads on this monopoly in the seventeenth century.

Judaism also formed part of the Western religious presence in East Asia. In the seventeenth century, Jesuits encountered Chinese Jews whose ancestors had arrived in China during the Tang dynasty (618–1279) as part of the Diaspora, or dispersal of Jews from Jerusalem. In the nineteenth century, Shanghai became a growing magnet for Jews, beginning with the arrival of Iraqi Jews, followed by the arrival of Austrian and German Jews fleeing Nazi persecution during the late 1930s. While many Jews fled Shanghai after World War II, others were absorbed into the Chinese populace such that there are no identifiable Jews in China today.

Protestant missionaries (mainly from Great Britain and the United States) began entering East Asia after 1800 during the high tide of colonialism. Europeans and Americans used gunboat diplomacy to force the Japanese and Chinese to open their gates to trade. In a series of military defeats and unequal treaties beginning in 1842, Christian missionaries gained access to inland China. Both Protestants and Catholics proselytized a religious stew of Christianity and Western culture that most sophisticated Chinese found offensively alien. Consequently, most of the nineteenth-century converts in China were poor "rice bowl Christians" who sought baptism as much for the practical benefits offered by the well-funded missions as for spiritual salvation.

The message of the Protestants stimulated one of the most turbulent events in Chinese history. Gospel pamphlets distributed on the streets of Canton (present-day Guangzhou) evoked a mystical vision in a frustrated, poor examination candidate named Hong Xiuquan (1814–1864), who blended an incomplete knowledge of Christianity with peasant Chinese traditions and millennial Buddhism. Claiming in distinctively Chinese style that he was the younger brother of Jesus, Hong attracted thousands of destitute Chinese who followed their messiah's commands in what became known as the Taiping

French Missionary School in China, 1911. *Chinese children play at a French missionary school in Mukden (Shenyang), the capital of Liaoning Province in northeastern China.* ROGER VIOLLET/GETTY IMAGES. REPRODUCED BY PERMISSION.

Rebellion. Had the Western powers not rejected Hong, he might have succeeded in toppling the Qing dynasty and replacing it with a theocratic "Heavenly Kingdom of Great Peace." By the time he died in 1864, the Taiping movement had caused the death of over twenty million Chinese.

By 1900, Christian missionaries were increasingly viewed in the Chinese countryside as foreign devils who should be driven out of China. This xenophobia blended with one of the indigenous traditions of Chinese peasant secret societies to produce the Boxer Rebellion. The Boxers claimed as part of their arsenal of martial arts the ability to render themselves impervious to bullets. Before this claim was disproved by a multinational military force, the Boxers killed many missionaries and Western businessmen in northern China and laid siege to the diplomatic quarters in Beijing.

The decline of traditional Chinese culture around 1900 fostered a new receptivity to Western religions among the youth of China, particularly in the coastal cities where the colonialist presence was greatest. Enthusiastic young Christians from the West flocked to China in the name of an interdenominational and international movement called the Social Gospel that focused on education and social work rather than saving souls. Capitalism was criticized, and religion was said to be compatible with science. However, World War I demonstrated the superficiality of this movement. The cynical treatment of China in the Versailles peace negotiations in Paris in 1919 provoked disillusionment with the Western democracies among Chinese youth, giving birth to the anti-Christian May Fourth Movement.

China attempted to break free of colonialist forces by reshaping Christianity on more indigenous grounds. The Chinese attempted to free themselves of Western denominational differences by merging sixteen different missionary-fostered Protestant churches in 1927. One of the most creative Chinese movements was an expression of indigenous Chinese evangelicalism led by Ni Duosheng (Watchman Nee, 1902–1972). While Ni was reacting against the Western Social Gospel, he was deeply influenced by Margaret Barber (1866–1930), a missionary associated with the Brethren movement of England, which emphasized adult baptism. Ni believed in the principle of local churches, hence the name by which his movement became known, Little Flock, which represented an indigenous Chinese revivalism.

After the Communists took control of China in 1949, they expelled the foreign missionaries, who were seen as tools of colonialism, and they forced Chinese Christians to break off relations with foreign religious bodies. The government forced all Chinese Protestants into the Three-Self Patriotic Movement (self-management, self-support, and self-propagation), which was postdenominational. Catholics were forced into the Chinese Catholic Patriotic Association. The members of these government-supervised organizations became targets during the anti-Christian campaigns run by the radical leftist government of Mao Zedong (1893–1976). In order to avoid government control and persecution, many Chinese chose to join underground religious organizations. With the Protestants, these took the form of "house churches," which met informally in private homes. With the Catholics, this took the form of an underground hierarchy of priests and bishops who refused to relinquish their apostolic relationship with Rome.

The Western notion of religious liberty has encountered difficulty in Chinese culture because of the lack of a tradition of separation of church and state. One of the major postcolonial legacies in East Asia stems from the fear among China's leaders that international efforts to secure religious freedom in China are disguised attempts to subvert the government of China.

SEE ALSO *Missions, China; Missions, in the Pacific; Religion, Roman Catholic Church; Religion, Western Perceptions of Traditional Religions; Religion, Western Perceptions of World Religions; Religion, Western Presence in the Pacific.*

BIBLIOGRAPHY

Dunch, Ryan. *Fuzhou Protestants and the Making of a Modern China, 1857–1927.* New Haven, CT: Yale University Press, 2001.

Leung, Beatrice. "The Sino-Vatican Negotiations: Old Problems in a New Context." *China Quarterly* 153 (1998): 128–140.

Malek, Roman, ed. *From Kaifeng...to Shanghai: Jews in China.* Nettetal, Germany: Steyler, 2000.

Spence, Jonathan D. *God's Chinese Son: The Taiping Heavenly Kingdom of Hong Xiuquan.* New York: Norton, 1996.

Uhalley, Stephen, Jr., and Xiaoxin Wu, eds. *China and Christianity: Burdened Past, Hopeful Future.* Armonk, NY: Sharpe, 2001.

Whyte, Bob. *Unfinished Encounter: China and Christianity.* Harrisburg, PA: Morehouse, 1988.

D. E. Mungello

RELIGION, WESTERN PRESENCE IN SOUTHEAST ASIA

The religious mosaic of modern Southeast Asia shows a unique pattern; the mainland has been dominated by Theravada Buddhism, the Malay Archipelago by Islam, and the Philippines by Catholicism. The island of Bali has maintained a Hindu identity, and Vietnam a blend of Confucianism and Mahayana Buddhism. The coming of the European colonial powers to Southeast Asia after the sixteenth century paved the way for the spread of Christianity in the region, as can be seen in Table 1.

Some parts of Southeast Asia were referred to in early Western literature as *Chryse*, that is, the Golden Island or the Golden Chersonese. Suggestions have been made that two early Christian sects, the Nestorians and Syriacs, might have established communities in Java and Sumatra (Indonesia) as early as the seventh century. Indeed, Southeast Asian ports became stopping stations for Europeans who were heading to or from the Yuan court (1279–1368) in Beijing, China. But it was only after 1497 that regular communication between the West and Southeast Asia became possible, and the work of evangelization of the region could begin in earnest.

Christianity was first introduced successfully to Southeast Asia by Iberian (Portuguese and Spanish) missionaries and colonists. After having secured their position in Malacca (Malaysia) in 1511, the Portuguese began spreading Catholicism in the region. They and the Spanish contributed significantly to establishing Catholicism in Maluku (the Moluccas) and eastern parts of Nusa Tenggara (Timor and Flores) in Indonesia, the Philippines, and Tonkin and Annam in Vietnam.

The Portuguese mostly directed their missionary activities toward people who had not been brought under Buddhist or Islamic influence. In Maluku, the Portuguese concentration on making Ambon their center resulted in steady conversion and a support base for their trading and political competition with the Muslim rulers of Ternate. Interestingly, after a fifteen-month stay (1546–1547) in Maluku, the Spanish Jesuit missionary Francis Xavier (1506–1552) remained unimpressed by the development of Catholicism in the area, and left for China.

In the second half of the sixteenth century, the Portuguese brought Roman Catholicism beyond Maluku to East Nusa Tenggara, and the extreme north of Maluku was missionized by Spaniards from Manila. In

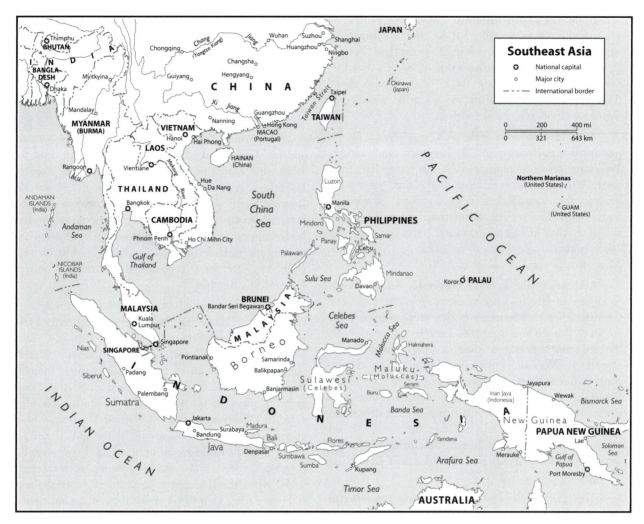

MAP BY XNR PRODUCTIONS. THE GALE GROUP.

East Timor and Flores, the Portuguese successfully maintained themselves and their religion vis-à-vis the Dutch after 1605. Indeed, Catholicism in East Timor survived and even prospered under Portuguese rule. Some argue that the Indonesian occupation of East Timor from 1975 to 1999 made Catholicism in the region even stronger (see Table 1).

A more successful evangelism was led by the Spanish Catholic orders in the Philippines. The Spanish came to Southeast Asia with a concrete and feasible agenda of missionary activities: Manila served as the center for various Catholic orders to evangelize and plant the church in the country and other parts of Asia. By the beginning of the seventeenth century, the entire country at least nominally was in the fold of the Roman Catholic Church, with the exception of the mountainous aborigines and the Muslims of Mindanao and the Sulu Archipelago.

INDONESIA

Christianity has had a long history in the islands of Southeast Asia. When the Dutch took the Portuguese fortress of Ambon in 1605, however, Catholic missionaries were forbidden to come to Maluku. The Calvinist Dutch Reformed Church was the only Christian church in the region during the time of the Dutch United East India Company (Verenigde Oost-Indische Compagnie, or VOC). Under the VOC, founded in 1602, Christianity made some advances in Maluku, northern Sulawesi, and eastern Nusa Tenggara. Protestantism also spread via the VOC-occupied port towns on Java's northern coast beginning in the eighteenth century. Christians were also found on a number of more remote islands as a result of Portuguese or Spanish missionary work or of Protestant activities. But these groups were more or less neglected.

Under the Dutch Reformed Church, the Protestant congregations were formally led by church councils in various towns, such as Ambon, Kupang, and Batavia (now Jakarta). The church council of Batavia acted as the central governing body. By 1795 there were about 55,000 Protestant Christians and a smaller number of Roman Catholics in the archipelago.

After the dissolution of the VOC in 1799, the Dutch permitted proselytizing in the territory, and various Protestant missions capitalized on this evangelical freedom. Active Protestant missions commenced principally among the non-Muslim ethnic groups. Waves of European missionary activity intensified from the beginning of the nineteenth century, especially by the Nederlandsch Zendelingsgenootschap (Netherlands Missionary Society), established in 1797.

Affiliates of the London Missionary Society began to engage in mission work in eastern Java in 1814. The German Rhenish Missionary Society worked from 1836 in South Borneo and from 1861 on Nias and among the Toba Bataks in northern Sumatra, where eventually the largest Indonesian Protestant Church, the Huria Kristen Batak Protestan, emerged. In 1820 Indonesia's various Protestant churches were brought under government supervision and united into a state-sponsored church, the Indies Church (Indische Kerk). From around 1900, this church began substantial missionary activities in Central Sulawesi, Maluku, and East Nusa Tenggara.

The earlier Nederlandsch Zendelingsgenootschap missionaries took care of the neglected Christian parishes in Java, and after 1830 they gradually reached neglected Christians in the outer regions, such as North Sulawesi and the Sangir Archipelago. Moreover, a number of new missionary bodies, informally linked with the Netherlands Reformed Church, were active in the Indies. They started work in West Papua (1855), North Sumatra (1857), the North Moluccas (1866), Central Sulawesi (1892), and South Sulawesi (1852/1913/1930). Southern Central Java and Sumba also became their mission field.

After World War I (1914–1918), the Basel Mission, a mission society founded in 1815 in Switzerland, took over missionary work in Kalimantan from the German Rhenish Missionary Society. These missions stressed the use of tribal languages instead of Malay, and aimed at individual conversion and sufficient Christian maturity. The Salvation Army came to Indonesia in 1894, the Seventh-Day Adventists in 1900, and the American Christian and Missionary Alliance in 1930. The Baptists reentered Indonesia in 1951 after they had abandoned their mission in the late nineteenth century. The Pentecostal movement was brought from Europe and the United States around 1920. In the twentieth century, the government allowed the Protestants to do missionary work in Sulawesi, the South Moluccas, and Timor.

In the second half of the nineteenth century, an independent Javanese Protestant community was founded in Central Java by Kiai Sadrach (d. 1924). Indigenous Protestant churches later conducted services in local languages. Protestantism was strongest in North Sumatra and in Maluku and Minahasa. But it was not until the 1930s that a number of autonomous churches emerged in various parts of Indonesia. Interestingly, it was the Japanese wartime occupation of Southeast Asia that gave local Christians the opportunity to assume prominent leadership positions and manage church affairs while the Europeans were interned or expelled. Most of these churches were later represented in the Indonesian Council of Churches.

The Dutch East India Company banned the promotion of Catholicism, and though formal freedom of religion was allowed with the fall of the company, many practical restrictions remained. The Catholic Church continued to be banned from certain regions, notably the Batak regions of northern Sumatra and the Toraja areas of Sulawesi, but from 1859 the church was allocated to Flores and Timor. Militarized Dominican friars claimed much of the islands of Flores and Timor for Portugal in the mid-sixteenth century, and they were the principal agents of Portuguese domination there until 1834, when the Portuguese government expelled them, following King Pedro IV's enunciation of an anticlerical policy in the same year.

Roman Catholic missions at first remained limited to the pastoral care of European Catholics. However, in time a number of societies were able to resume mission work, especially amongst the surviving congregations in Maluku, northern Sulawesi, Solor, Flores, and western Timor. The Roman Catholics concentrated their work in Flores (1860) and in Central Java (1894), but they also had important fields in North Sumatra (1878), West Kalimantan (1885), North Sulawesi (1868), Timor (1883), southeast Maluku (1888), and southern Papua (1905). From 1859 until 1902, all mission fields in Indonesia were served by the Jesuits, who established successful missions, schools, and hospitals throughout the islands of Flores, Timor, and Alor. After 1902, most areas were gradually handed over to other orders and congregations, and the Jesuits retained only the capital city of Batavia and Central Java.

Despite their small number, Catholics in Indonesia have been major players in modern sectors and professions. Their schools and publications also enjoyed fame and prestige among Indonesians.

Percentage of Christians in "Southeast Asia"

Country	Population	Percentage of all Christians	Catholics	Protestants and others
Brunei Darussalam	374,000	10.00%	7.55%	2.45%
Cambodia	14,071,000	0.28%	0.20%	0.08%
East Timor (Leste)	876,000	93.00%	90.00%	3.00%
Indonesia	222,781,000	8.92%	3.05%	5.87%
Lao P.D.R.	5,924,000	2.00%	0.70%	1.30%
Malaysia	25,347,000	9.10%	3.30%	5.80%
Myanmar (Burma)	50,519,000	4.00%	1.05%	2.95%
Papua New Guinea*	5,887,000	76.00%	32.00%	44.00%
The Philippines	83,054,000	92.00%	80.40%	11.60%
Singapore	4,326,000	15.00%	4.00%	11.00%
Thailand (Siam)	64,233,000	0.50%	0.44%	0.06%
Vietnam	84,238,000	8.00%	7.00%	1.00%
Total**	561,630,000	20.67%	14.97%	5.70%

Notes:
* Despite the fact that Papua New Guinea is part of the whole island of Papua or Irian, it is not normally included in the standard geography of SEA; nor is it a member of ASEAN.

**SOURCES: Nation Master Online 2003-2005; The Reformist Church Online; Catholic Missionary Union of England and Wales Online; International Religious Freedom Report 2004; UN Population Division.

Table 1 THE GALE GROUP.

BRUNEI, MALAYSIA, AND SINGAPORE

About 20 percent of Brunei's population is ethnic Chinese, of which half is Christian and half is Buddhist. There is also a large workforce composed mainly of expatriates that includes Muslims, Christians, and Hindus.

Despite early encounters with Christianity, the gospel did not take root in Brunei until the second half of the nineteenth century. In 1857, for example, a mission of the Milan Foreign Missions was started at Barambangan, across from Brunei Town (now called Bandar Seri Begawan). Italian Father D. Antonio Riva was put in charge of this mission for a few years (1855–1859). By this time, some members of the Chinese and indigenous communities in the interior were attracted to Christianity.

The period of the British residency (1905–1959) in Brunei paved the way for the coming of British officials and their families, followed by Indians and Chinese who had accepted Christianity. When the first Catholic priest began regularly visiting Brunei from the beginning of the twentieth century, a few Catholic families were already living there. Brunei was regarded as an outstation of Labuan (Malaysia) for Mill Hill missionaries who had worked in Labuan since 1881. By 1937 resident Catholic priests were appointed for Kuala Belait and Brunei Town. The old church in Brunei Town was rebuilt and named Saint George's Church in 1957. The Catholic Church opened schools for boys and girls in Kuala Belait in 1929. In 1997 Pope John Paul II (1920–2005) issued a decree for the establishment of the Prefecture Apostolic of Brunei.

From the beginning, the Anglican mission in Brunei fell under the jurisdiction of the diocese of Kuching, a port city in present-day Malaysia. Although an institution was created in 1848 to raise funds to support the first mission on the island of Borneo, it was only in 1854 that the London-based Society for the Propagation of the Gospel in Foreign Parts became active in the region. The Borneo Mission Association was formed in 1909 to coordinate missionary activities in different parts of the island. The earliest Anglican parish in Brunei Town offered its services in a temporary shop building; only in 1934 was Saint Andrew's Church erected. This was followed in 1939 by the erection of Saint Philip's and Saint James's Church in Kuala Belait, mainly in response to the growing Christian population following the development of the oil industry in the area. Another church, Saint Margaret and All Hallows Church, was erected in Seria in 1954. Thus, in 2006 three Anglican parishes and several prestigious Christian schools prospered in Brunei Darussalam, which come under the jurisdiction of the Diocese of Kuching.

In British Malaya (now part of Malaysia), the Christianizing effort remained largely confined to the British possessions of Melaka, Penang, and Singapore, where evangelical work among the Chinese migrant communities became an important part of the missionary enterprise. The Muslim populations of the Malay Peninsula proved unresponsive to Christian evangelism.

In East Malaysia and Brunei, the indigenous adhered to traditional beliefs, the Chinese were both Buddhist and Christian historically, and the Malays were Muslims. In Singapore in the first decade of the twenty-first century, 15 percent of the population claimed to be Christian.

The formation of Christian churches in North Borneo is closely connected with the immigration of Chinese in the late 1860s. The British Chartered Company entered North Borneo in 1878 and offered new homes to Chinese settlers who founded the Roman Catholic and Anglican churches. The Basel Mission also began work there in 1882 that has continued into the twenty-first century.

Introduced by Portuguese colonists about 1511, the Roman Catholic Church was almost exclusively confined to Malacca until late in the eighteenth century. But the arrival of Francis Xavier in 1545 heralded a great era of expansion. He founded a school from which Roman Catholic missionaries eventually spread to Burma (Myanmar), Siam (Thailand), and the other parts of the archipelago.

The Vatican sent several Catholic missions to North Borneo as early as 1687. In 1881 the Vatican confided the mission of North Borneo and Labuan to the Society for Foreign Missions of Mill Hill, England. The society served two major stations in Labuan and Kuching, and supported the missionaries who regularly visited parishes throughout Sabah and Sarawak. Beginning with a tiny school at the port city of Sandakan in 1883, numerous Roman Catholic mission schools were established, and Catholic churches and vicariates also sprang up in East Malaysia.

The training of national clergy greatly enhanced the effectiveness of the missions. When Portuguese influence declined at the end of the sixteenth century, French Catholics took over. Concerted attempts were made in the mid-seventeenth century to launch missionary activities under the Society of Foreign Missions of Paris. From the late eighteenth century, French priests and nuns made a significant contribution. From the beginning of the nineteenth century, priests were trained locally. They established a seminary in 1806 at Penang, from which more than five hundred missionaries were sent to other Asian countries. The evangelism of Singapore was entrusted to the Society of Foreign Missions in 1830, and the society is still the predominant foreign group among Catholics in Sabah and Sarawak, where they began their missions in 1855. The expansion of the Roman Catholic Church has been rapid. Between 1885 and 1905, for example, the Chinese Catholic congregations trebled in numbers. Since the 1970s, leadership of the local Catholic Church has been entirely in Malaysian hands.

Protestant missions in the region initially followed the British flag. The London Missionary Society started its missions in Malaya and Singapore in 1814. The first Presbyterian church in Singapore was established in 1841. After the London Missionary Society officially left Malaya for China in 1847, more churches were founded and evangelism among the Chinese began. By 1925 there were nine Presbyterian congregations. After World War II (1939–1945), a further expansion of the Presbyterian Synod occurred. In 1962 the Chinese Presbyterian Synod formed three presbyteries: Singapore, South Malaysia, and North Malaysia. In 1971 the expatriate congregations decided to join the Chinese Synod and to form the Presbyterian Church of Singapore and Malaysia.

Following the Presbyterians, the Anglicans planted churches in Penang in 1819 and Singapore in 1834. The Anglican mission to the Chinese and other nationals was launched in 1856. Since 1970, Malaysia and Singapore have seen the formation of two independent Anglican dioceses. After launching missionary work in Sarawak and Labuan in 1854, the Society for the Propagation of the Gospel set up a center in Sandakan in 1882.

Other well-established Christian groups, such as the Brethren, Methodist, Lutheran, and Evangelical churches, also launched missions in Malaysia from the mid-nineteenth century. The Brethren focused on church planting in Penang (1859), Singapore (1866), and later in other cities of the Malay Peninsula. Many of the leaders in interdenominational movements in Malaysia and Singapore have come from among the Brethren.

The Methodists began their missions in the bustling port city of Singapore in 1885. From the beginning they focused on planting churches and schools among Asians. Churches were founded in Singapore (1885), Malaya (1891), and Sarawak (1900), and Methodist schools often followed or even predated church planting. The Australia-based Borneo Evangelical Church, founded in 1928, won the conversion of many indigenous groups in Sarawak. Following their successful mission in Sabah, in 1907, the Lutherans initiated church planting in Kuala Lumpur among the Tamils. After World War II, American and Swedish Lutherans began missionary work in Malaya. In 1962 the Evangelical Lutheran Church of Malaya and Singapore was formally constituted.

In addition, smaller but mobile and aggressive evangelical groups, such as the Overseas Missionary Fellowship, the Evangelical Free Church, the Southern Baptists of the United States, the Seventh-Day Adventists, the Mormons, and the Jehovah's Witnesses, have contributed to church growth in Malaysia and Singapore.

THE PHILIPPINES

The Philippines has been a predominantly Roman Catholic nation since the seventeenth century. Roman Catholic missionary work dates back to the mid-sixteenth century. The conquest of Manila in 1571 by the Spanish conquistador Miguel López de Legaspi (d. 1572) paved the way for Catholic evangelism in the Philippines. Despite the successful military pacification after 1571, Catholicism had yet to be propagated among the Filipino population. Once started, the work of evangelization went smoothly and rapidly.

The first Catholic bishop in the Philippines, the Spanish Dominican Domingo de Salazar (1512–1594), arrived in 1581, accompanied by a few Jesuits. More friars from the major orders, such as the Augustinians, Franciscans, Dominicans, and the Recollect Fathers, soon followed, and eventually dominated the archbishopric of Manila. The members of these orders penetrated farther and farther into the interior of the country, and established their missions. Religious books were written in the local dialects, and Catholic schools were opened. The early missionaries emphasized church planting in new settlements, along with the conversion of chiefs (datu), based on the principle of *cuius regio eius religio* (whose the region is, his religion). Since the principle of enforcing the religion of the ruler on the people had been endorsed by early Christian states, it was natural that Spanish missionaries adopted this approach in their work in the Philippines focusing, first of all, on winning the hearts of local chiefs.

From the beginning, the Spanish establishments in the Philippines were more like missions in character than colonies. They were founded and administered in the interest of religion rather than commerce or industry. Not surprisingly, the Catholic Church enjoyed a great deal of power on the local level. Even in the late nineteenth century, the friars of the Augustinian, Dominican, and Franciscan orders conducted many executive functions of government at the local level. The Catholic orders also had economic strength by virtue of their extensive landholdings. Moreover, the friars' monopoly on education guaranteed their dominant position in society and thus their control over cultural and intellectual life. When in 1863 the Spanish government introduced public primary education in the Philippines, the Catholic orders, including the Jesuits, remained indispensable.

There were several religious movements initiated by Filipinos during the nineteenth century. One of the most serious occurred in the 1840s. The movement was headed by a renegade cleric, Apolinario de la Cruz (1815–1841). Later, some native clergy participated in a revolt against Spanish authority in Cavite in 1872.

Three Filipino priests who were implicated in the uprising were executed. Moreover, although the Katipunan, a Filipino revolutionary society that emerged in 1896, originally did not explicitly endorse Catholic symbolism, it provided new life to the volatile antifriar movement when Gregorio Aglipay (1860–1940), a Catholic priest, was appointed chaplain-general of the rebel forces. In 1902 Aglipay accepted the leadership of the Philippine Independent Church (also known as the Aglipayan Church, which was founded and supported by Aglipay's followers) as its first supreme bishop. Under the slogan of religious independence, the church soon attracted new members, amounting to one-fifth of the total population.

The American Period and After. Following the establishment of American sovereignty in the Philippines in May 1898, the first non-Spanish archbishop of Manila, American Jeremiah Harty (1903–1916), a secular priest, who unlike a regular priest was not a member or friar of the locally dominant Roman Catholic orders, was appointed by the Vatican in 1903. In 1949 Gabriel M. Reyes (1892–1952), a Filipino, became the first Filipino archbishop of Manila. From the beginning, U.S. presidents and their representatives in the Philippines defined American colonial mission as tutelage, preparing the country for eventual independence. In 1902 the Catholic Church was formally disestablished as the state religion of the Philippines, and freedom of worship and the separation of church and state were instituted. After negotiations, the church agreed to sell the Spanish friars' estates and promised the gradual substitution of Filipino and other non-Spanish priests in the friars' posts.

Protestant missionaries first came to the Philippines following the U.S. takeover. The earliest groups included Presbyterians, Methodists, and Baptists. After World War II, many more groups entered the country, including denominational missions aiming at church planting and nondenominational agencies undertaking evangelism and training among the youth.

The first Presbyterian missionary arrived in Manila in 1899. From 1899 to 1902, eight Presbyterian church-planting missions worked in the Philippines, laying out a noncompetitive plan to evangelize the islands, commonly known as the comity agreements. Indeed, in 1901 these Protestant missionaries agreed to form the Evangelical Union and to fix geographical areas for each mission. Manila was kept open to all missionaries. However, two churches—the Seventh-Day Adventists and the Episcopalians—did not endorse the noncompetitive plan.

Movement toward an organic union of Protestant churches in the Philippines resulted in 1929 in the holding of the first general assembly of the United Evangelical

Church, the forerunner of the United Church of Christ in the Philippines, formed in 1948. The majority of the leaders who formed the new church were Filipinos. As of 2006, however, American Baptists and Methodists remained separate and distinct bodies.

The Protestant population of the Philippines continues to grow. The gains are chiefly from conversions among nominal Roman Catholics and Aglipayans. The principal Protestant churches, once predominantly rural, are becoming stronger in the towns and cities and evolving into urban middle-class denominations. Although the pioneer churches have continued to grow, a few non-Union-related groups, such as the Seventh-Day Adventists, Assemblies of God, and the Foursquare Gospel Church, have grown even faster.

MAINLAND SOUTHEAST ASIA

Mainland Southeast Asia provides an interesting pattern of Christian evangelism. In the countries that endorsed Theravada Buddhism, Christian missionaries, as can be seen in Table 1, were not very successful in evangelism, except among minorities and tribal groups, such as the Karen in Burma and the Hmong in Laos. In Vietnam, the situation is slightly different. In Cambodia and Siam, Portuguese Dominicans began to arrive as early as 1555. However, until 1584, local opposition prevented these missionaries from settling for long in the country. In Burma, Portuguese mercenaries under Diogo Soarez de Mello (d. after 1551) were instrumental in the wars of the Toungoo conquerors in the mid-sixteenth century. Overall, the Portuguese indirectly contributed to the introduction of Catholicism to various parts of mainland Southeast Asia.

The Spanish launched several missionary activities on the Southeast Asian mainland. In response to the invitation of King Satha (r. 1576–1594) of Cambodia, missionaries were sent from Manila in 1593. Rivalry among the elite in Phnom Penh, however, led to the elimination of Spanish influence in Cambodia by 1603 as Siam became increasingly powerful in the country.

In 1887 French Indochina was formed. Vietnam, which had been fertile ground for Confucianism, also saw the growth of Catholicism, whereas Cambodia and Laos, which had endorsed Theravada Buddhism, did not become an easy target for Christian evangelism.

Vietnam. Christianity was introduced to Indochina in the beginning of the sixteenth century by Portuguese and Spanish missionaries. However, the early missions seem to have made little impression on the population. In 1615 the Jesuits established a permanent mission in Annam in central Vietnam. Leading Jesuit missionaries advocated a policy of adaptation to traditional culture.

Among them, the French Jesuit missionary Alexandre de Rhodes (1591–1660) conceived a romanized Vietnamese alphabet *(quôc ngu)* that is still in use today. He also succeeded in baptizing many Vietnamese. After 1658, under the direction of missionaries from the French Society of Foreign Missions, Catholic churches were planted, parishes established, seminaries built, and many Catholic foundations instituted.

Jesuit missionaries spread their activities in practically all fields. They focused on influencing the cultural and political top echelons of Vietnamese society. The rapid growth of Catholics in the country, however, led both the Nguyen (circa 1510–1954) in the south and the Trinh rulers (1539–1787) in the north and the Trinh rulers in 1631 and 1663, respectively, to launch persecution of Catholics. By 1663 Catholicism had been formally banned in Vietnam. Only at the end of the eighteenth century were some French priests able to enter the country by acting as intermediaries in military affairs. Bishop Pierre Pigneau de Behaine (1741–1799) performed this service for Nguyen Anh (1762–1820), who in 1802 proclaimed himself the emperor with the title Gia Long. The presence of Christian communities came to be openly tolerated in Vietnam during this period. In fact, the Catholic Church at this time was more successful in Vietnam than in any other part of Asia except the Philippines. Spanish friars were active in Tonkin in northern Vietnam, and French priests worked in Annam and Cochin China in the south.

The privileges that the Catholic Church had enjoyed under Gia Long quickly gave way to excesses, which generated a negative response from the Vietnamese. Gia Long's successor, Minh Mang (1792–1841), was dominated by conservative Confucianists. In 1825 he inaugurated a policy aimed at harassing Christian missionaries and converts. The court at Hue was particularly alarmed in the 1820s by the arrival of aggressive French missionaries. In fact, persecution of Christians became more violent after 1833. King Minh Mang ordered that all foreign priests be held at the capital as virtual prisoners, and ten Catholic missionaries were killed between 1833 and 1840.

Vietnam's Catholic communities reacted by organizing revolts that were often directed by missionaries and supported by French national and commercial interests. After 1841, the Catholic missions were boycotted and the practice of Catholicism was again banned, although French missionaries continued to enter Tonkin secretly from Portuguese Macao in southern China. The French eventually retaliated against the ban. War vessels were sent to Vietnamese ports, and in June 1862 the French imposed a treaty on Vietnam. One of its clauses provided the Catholic Church with total religious freedom.

Not surprisingly, Vietnamese Catholicism came to be associated with French colonialism. By 1893, Vietnam, Laos, and Cambodia had become French colonies, and Roman Catholic missionaries were given privileges throughout the country. Indeed, prior to World War II, Catholics practically monopolized the entire civil and military administration.

When Catholics who resisted Vietnam's Communist guerrillas were defeated in the 1954 partition, many took refuge in the South, forming the largest Catholic concentrations around Saigon (now Ho Chi Minh City). In the north, major Catholic concentrations can be found in the provinces south of Hanoi. The unification of the two Vietnams in 1975 under Communist rule had a mixed effect on Christians. Despite many restrictions on religious missions, they were fundamentally allowed to evangelize, as long as they did not use religion against the state. In the mid-1990s Catholicism saw a modest revival and in 2004 the Vatican filled the vacant bishoprics, including the appointment of a cardinal for the country.

The first Protestant mission in the region was launched in the late 1820s by the British and Foreign Bible Society. Because of hostility from both the Vietnamese and the French, the society operated from abroad, particularly from Shanghai. In 1895 two missionaries from the American Christian and Missionary Alliance visited the north. In 1911 permission was granted by the French authorities to begin a Christian and Missionary Alliance mission in Da Nang in central Vietnam. The movement first spread north to Haiphong and Hanoi, and then by 1918 to Saigon and to other cities in the south. Missions among ethnic minorities, including the Montagnards in the south-central region, began in 1929.

The first Christian and Missionary Alliance missionaries focused on the training of national workers and the widespread use of literature to evangelize the French colony. The period 1922 to 1940 was a fruitful phase for the Christian and Missionary Alliance missions in Vietnam, particularly in the Mekong Delta region and in central Vietnam. In 1928 the Vietnamese congregations were organized into a church body, the Evangelical Church of Vietnam.

The turning point in Vietnam's missionary history took place with the Pacific segment of World War II, as a series of wars erupted in Vietnam for the next four decades almost without interruption. Evangelization efforts underwent adjustments that resulted in mixed outcomes. However, the division of the country in 1954 into North Vietnam and South Vietnam left fewer than two thousand Evangelical Church of Vietnam members in North Vietnam. In the south, the church soon recovered its strength. Between 1954 and 1965, the Evangelical Church of Vietnam made great gains, and by the early 1970s the church was one of the most successful foreign missions of the Christian and Missionary Alliance. The virtual monopoly of the organization came to an end when other missionary societies, such as the U.S.-based Seventh-Day Adventists and Assemblies of God, entered the south.

By the early twenty-first century, almost 70 percent of Vietnamese Protestants are ethnic minorities, especially those in the western and central highlands and rural villages. Hmong missionaries have contributed significantly to successful evangelism.

Cambodia. Roman Catholic missionary efforts began in the sixteenth century in Cambodia, but the Christian presence developed slowly. Portuguese missionaries arrived in the second half of the sixteenth century, but they had more success among the Vietnamese than among local Khmers. In 1658 Cambodia was included in the Apostolic Vicariate of Tonkin, administered by the Society of Foreign Missions. By 1842 there were four churches and approximately two hundred Roman Catholics in Cambodia.

In the mid-nineteenth century, numerous Vietnamese Catholics seeking refuge from persecution swelled the Cambodian Catholic population. In 1885 France declared Cambodia a protectorate. In 1953 Cambodia gained independence, and three years later the first Khmer priest was ordained. By 1962 the number of Catholics in Cambodia had increased to 62,000, but most of them were Vietnamese, Chinese, or European. In 1970 most Vietnamese Catholics were forced out of Cambodia by Khmer hostility, greatly reducing church membership.

From 1975 to 1979, the Cambodian government was seized by the Khmer Rouge, a repressive Communist regime that expelled all foreigners, including French missionaries, from the country. Many leaders of the Cambodian Catholic Church disappeared during this period. Following the signing of a peace treaty in 1991, the holding of elections in 1993, and the promulgation of a new constitution guaranteeing religious freedom, diplomatic relations were established with the Holy See (the office of the pope) in 1994, and in 1997 the Catholic Church was given official status by the new Cambodian government.

The American Christian and Missionary Alliance began a Protestant mission in the country in 1923. From the capital of Phnom Penh, evangelism and church planting were launched. By 1964 thirteen Protestant congregations were established in more than half of the provinces. The majority of the proselytes came from among the Khmer population. Missionaries also worked among the ethnic minorities in the northeastern part of the country, but they were forced to leave in 1965. Many returned in 1970 when Lon Nol (1913–1985) came to power.

During the regime (1975–1978) of Pol Pot (1925–1998), the leader of the Khmer Rouge, many Cambodians, including Christians, were either massacred or fled the country. During the subsequent pro-Vietnamese regime, Protestants, like other religionists, were again able to congregate. In 1996 an Evangelical Fellowship of Cambodia was founded. By 2006 some twenty-five Protestant denominations and congregations can be found in Cambodia, mainly in the capital city and in Battambang.

Laos. The capital city of Laos, Vientiane, possesses a special interest for Catholics as the scene of the first attempt to preach Christianity in the then-extensive Kingdom of Laos. Roman Catholic missionaries began visiting Laos in the seventeenth century, when the Portuguese Jesuit, Giovanni Maria Leria, proselytized in the country for five years until he was compelled to leave in December 1647. The Catholic missions did not resume their activities in Laos until the last quarter of the nineteenth century, concomitant with the French proclaiming a protectorate over the country. Although the Society of Foreign Missions began working in Laos in 1876 and established an apostolic vicariate on May 4, 1899, the country's Roman Catholic Church has been separated from that of Siam only since 1911. The mission won a significant number of proselytes in the late nineteenth century.

By 2006 most Lao members of the Roman Catholic Church were ethnic Vietnamese living in the most populous central and southern provinces of the country, where Rome has appointed three resident bishops.

The first Protestant mission in Laos was carried out by a Presbyterian missionary based in Chiang Mai, Thailand, who regularly visited northern Laos beginning in 1872. In 1902 the Brethren churches in Switzerland sent two missionaries to preach the gospel in southern Laos. The Brethren focused on church planting, establishment of a Bible school, and translation of the Bible into the Lao language.

The American Christian and Missionary Alliance sent missionaries into northern Laos in 1928. From then until 1975, when all missionaries had to leave the country, the Christian and Missionary Alliance worked in northern Laos and the Swiss Brethren worked in the south. Throughout this period, the two missions maintained cordial relations; thus, the church was eventually able to proclaim itself a single united body, the Lao Evangelical Church.

A change of government in 1975 had a dramatic impact on the church. Despite the exodus of about half of all Lao Protestants in 1975, by the late 1990s there were over 160 churches in the country. Since the early 1990s, concomitant with increased freedom, the Lao Evangelical Church has formally organized into an official church body. Several foreign Christian organizations and churches have increased their work in Laos. The vast majority of believers and churches are located in rural areas. In 2006 only three Protestant churches were located in the cities.

Although the present government recognizes two Protestant groups—the Lao Evangelical Church and the Seventh-Day Adventists—it does not permit public evangelism. In periodic state-sponsored political seminars, for example, the population has been taught that Roman Catholicism is a remnant of French colonialism and Protestantism is a remnant of American imperialism. Nevertheless, such evangelical churches as the Methodists and the Jehovah's Witnesses have found ways to preach the gospel in the country.

Thailand. Siam, officially renamed Thailand in 1939, has developed close ties with the Christian powers since the sixteenth century. Yet, like its Theravada Buddhist neighbors, it has not been fertile ground for Christianity.

The majority of Thai Roman Catholics are located in northeast Thailand and in Bangkok. Many are of Chinese, Vietnamese, and Cambodian origin. The earliest Christian incursions into Siam were by Catholic priests accompanying a Portuguese embassy of Alfonso de Albuquerque (d. 1515) in 1511; however, only in 1555 did the first resident Dominican missionaries arrive. They were followed in 1662 by missionaries from the Society of Foreign Missions under Bishop Pierre Lambert de la Motte (1624–1679), who set up his headquarters in Ayutthaya, where they found a sizeable Christian community.

The growth of the Society of Foreign Missions in Siam was clearly evident during the reign of King Narai (r. 1657–1688), who opened the country to foreigners and gave liberty to the missionaries to preach the gospel. Narai built closer ties with France and withdrew from the increasingly rampant Dutch power. On the other hand, the French influence in the country strengthened the role of the missionaries and the progress of evangelization. Between 1665 and 1669, the Society of Foreign Missions central seminary for Southeast Asia and the first hospital were erected in Ayutthaya. Despite the major debacle of 1688 and later restrictions, the Society of Foreign Missions continued working in Siam without interruption. More priests from Portuguese orders followed.

They worked until the fall of Ayutthaya in 1767, but the fruit of their evangelization was miniscule.

With the advent of the Chakri dynasty in 1782, particularly under the reign of kings Mongkut (1804–1868) and Chulalongkorn (1853–1910), the Catholic Church gradually enjoyed more peace, despite diplomatic complications between France and Siam in 1894. Significant results did not come until after World War II, however, when the community grew from approximately 3,000 Catholic adherents in 1802 to about 170,000 in 1972.

The Catholic Church in Thailand put great emphasis on building schools and convents, largely in Bangkok. Encouraged by the steady growth of the church, Pope Paul VI (1897–1978) divided the country into two church provinces in 1965 and appointed its first archbishop. By the early twenty-first century, the percentage of Thai clergy is increasing; half of the archbishops and bishops are Thai. In 2006 Thailand had two archbishops, eight bishops, thirty religious orders, and an apostolic delegate headquartered in Bangkok.

Protestants dominate in the north of the country. These are distributed among Thais and ethnic minorities. Protestantism was introduced to Siam through the works of diverse Protestant missionaries beginning in the 1810s. The first Protestant missionaries to live in Thailand, representing the Nederlandsch Zendelingsgenootschap and the London Missionary Society, arrived in 1828. In 1833 American Baptist missionaries arrived, and in 1837 they planted the first indigenous Protestant church in Southeast Asia, which survives today.

Early Protestant missionaries to Thailand saw the first fruits of their evangelism efforts mainly among the Chinese. The first American Presbyterian missionaries arrived in 1840. By 1910 the Presbyterian church was flourishing in the north. The English Disciples of Christ, who entered in 1903, joined their American counterparts in 1945 to evangelize within the Church of Christ in Thailand. The Seventh-Day Adventists arrived in 1918 and focused their activities on hospitals. The American Christian and Missionary Alliance followed in 1929, taking missionary responsibility for nineteen provinces in northeast Thailand.

Following World War II, new streams of Protestant missions grew steadily in Thailand, starting with the Worldwide Evangelization Crusade and the Finnish Free Foreign Mission. The largest of all these was the Overseas Missionary Fellowship, originally the China Inland Mission, which in 1949 sent hundreds of missionaries to all parts of the country. Their missions were followed both by major groups, such as the American Southern Baptists, the Church of Christ, the Scandinavian Pentecostal Mission, and the New Tribes Mission, and smaller ones, including the American Assemblies of God, the Pentecostal Assembly of Canada, and the Japan Christian Missions.

Two Protestant church bodies have been officially recognized by the Thai government. They are the Church of Christ in Thailand and the Evangelical Fellowship of Thailand. The Thailand Church Growth Committee, started in 1971, has served to bridge these two bodies with Baptist and Pentecostal organizations.

Myanmar. Although the majority of the population of Burma (renamed Myanmar in 1989) follows Theravada Buddhism, there are significant numbers of Christians, mostly Baptists but also some Catholics and Anglicans. The Kachin ethnic group in northern Burma and the Chin and Naga in the west are largely Christian, and Christianity is also widespread among the Karen and Karenni in the south and east. After World War II, the situation of Christian churches became more complicated when Christianity became a mark of identity for ethnic minorities that were opposed to the government in Yangon, the capital.

Christianity was introduced to Burma in the sixteenth century through the efforts of Roman Catholic missionaries and Portuguese traders and mercenaries. The actual work of evangelizing Burma did not begin until 1722 when two Barnabite fathers were sent there. In 1741 the Vatican mission was fully established after more Barnabites were sent to Burma. However, prolonged wars in Burma during the eighteenth century resulted in the termination of this mission. In 1842 Pope Gregory XVI (1765–1846) placed the Burmese mission under the Italian Oblates of Pinerolo, and appointed the first vicar apostolic, but the British invasion in 1852 led to the withdrawal of the mission almost immediately.

In response to the leadership vacuum in the Burmese vicariate, it was placed in 1855 under the control of the vicar apostolic of Siam for ten years. Burma was then divided into three independent vicariates: Northern, Southern, and Eastern Burma. In 1870 the vicariate of Eastern Burma was entrusted to the Milan Foreign Missions, and those in Northern and Southern Burma came under the control of the Society of Foreign Missions. The vicariate of Southern Burma was more successful in advancing Christianity than the other two, particularly among the Karenni. This is understandable in view of the intensity and number of rival Protestant missionaries in the north and east since the mid-nineteenth century and the near invincibility of Burmese Buddhism. The territorial division persists as of 2006, with three Catholic archdioceses headquartered in Mandalay, Taunggyi, and Yangon.

Protestant missionaries began their work in Yangon. The Baptist Missionary Society of England opened its first mission in 1807 and remained there until 1814. The London Missionary Society sent two missionaries to Yangon in 1808, but within a year the mission was abandoned. In 1813 an American Baptist began working in Burma and translated the Bible (1834). Other missions followed: Anglican (1852), Methodist (1879), Seventh-Day Adventist (1915), and Assemblies of God (1924). Efforts at evangelism made slow progress, however. While the Burmese Buddhist population showed little interest, the gospel was received by the highlanders, especially the Karen, Shan, Kachin, and Chin, beginning in the 1820s.

The Reformed churches owe their existence in the country both to missionary efforts and spontaneous movements. Reformed churches serve different parts of the Burmese hill population, especially the Chin and Kachin. American Baptist missionaries started work among the Chin in 1899. They remained in the Chin Hills until 1966, when the socialist government expelled all foreign missionaries from Burma. Apart from evangelism, the Baptists planted Bible schools and translated the Haka Bible.

A few American Pentecostal missionaries from the Assemblies of God were sent to Burma. Accompanying them were Pentecostal missionaries from Sweden and Finland, and the Go Ye Fellowship, which labored in Myanmar prior to World War II. In spite of the war and the absence of missionaries, especially after 1966, the Christian church showed progress under the leadership of indigenous workers.

Under the leadership of Assemblies of God missionaries from the United States, indigenous Pentecostal believers took up the challenge of evangelizing their own communities. This occurred in earnest after 1966, when authority and responsibility were handed over to the national church leaders. Local churches soon became centers for evangelism, outreach, and ministry among different people and groups in the capital city, as well as among the Kachin and Chin in the north. After 1966 many street preachers were trained by Burmese Christian leaders, and a Bible training school started by missionaries continued to operate.

SEE ALSO *London Missionary Society; Netherlands Missionary Society; Religion, Roman Catholic Church.*

BIBLIOGRAPHY

Andaya, Leonard, and Barbara Watson Andaya. *A History of Malaysia,* 2nd ed. Honolulu: University of Hawaii Press, 2001.

Aritonang, Jan Sihar. *Mission Schools in Batakland (Indonesia), 1861–1940.* Translated by Robert R. Boehlke. Leiden, Netherlands: Brill, 1994.

Aritonang, Jan Sihar. "The Encounter of the Batak People with Rheinische Missions." Ph.D. diss., Utrecht University, Netherlands, 2000.

Buchholt, Helmut. "The Impact of the Christian Mission on Processes of Social Differentiation in Indonesia." Working Paper No. 163. Southeast Asia Programme, University of Bielefeld. Bielefeld, Germany, 1992

Cady, John F. *Southeast Asia: Its Historical Development.* New York: McGraw-Hill, 1964.

Catholic Missionary Union of England and Wales. Available from http://www.cmu.org.uk/.

Cummins, J. S. *Jesuit and Friar in the Spanish Expansion to the East.* London: Variorum Reprints, 1986.

Durand, Frédéric. *Catholicisme et protestantisme dans l'île de Timor, 1556–2003: Construction d'une identite' chre'tienne et engagement politique contemporain.* Toulouse, France: Arkuiris; Bangkok: IRASEC, 2004.

Gall, Timothy L., ed. *Worldmark Encyclopedia of Cultures and Daily Life;* Vol. 3: *Asia & Oceania.* Detroit, MI: Gale, 1998.

Gani Wiyono. "Timor Revival: A Historical Study of the Great Twentieth-Century Revival in Indonesia." *Asian Journal of Pentecostal Studies* 4 (2) (2001): 269–293. Available from http://www.apts.edu/ajps/01-2/01-2_index.htm/.

Guillot, C. *L'Affaire Sadrac: Un essai de christianisation à Java au XIXe siècle.* Paris: Association Archipel, 1981.

Harper, George W. "Philippine Tongue of Fire? Latin American Pentecostalism and the Future of Filipino Christianity." *Journal of Asian Mission* 2 (2) (2000): 225–259.

Hunt, Robert, Lee Kam Hing, and John Roxborough, eds. *Christianity in Malaysia: A Denominational History.* Petaling Jaya, Malaysia: Pelanduk, 1992.

Keyes, Charles F. "Why the Thai Are Not Christians: Buddhist and Christian Conversion in Thailand." In *Conversion to Christianity: Historical and Anthropological Perspectives on a Great Transformation,* edited by Robert Hefner, 259–283. Berkeley: University of California Press, 1993.

Kipp, Rita Smith. *The Early Years of a Dutch Colonial Mission: The Karo Field.* Ann Arbor: University of Michigan Press, 1990.

Kipp, Rita Smith, and Susan Rogers, eds. *Indonesian Religions in Transition.* Tucson: University of Arizona Press, 1987.

Lee, Raymond L. M., and Susan E. Ackerman. *Sacred Tension: Modernity and Religious Transformation in Malaysia.* Columbia: University of South Carolina Press, 1997.

Lessard, Micheline. "Curious Relations: Jesuit Perception of the Vietnamese." In *Essays Into Vietnamese Pasts,* edited by K. W. Taylor and John Whitmore, 137–156. Ithaca, NY: Cornell University Press, 1995.

Maggay, Melba P. "Early Protestant Missionary Efforts in the Philippines: Some Intercultural Problems." *Journal of Asian Mission* 5 (1) (2003): 119–131. Available from http://www.apts.edu/jam/5-1/M-Maggay.pdf.

Mansurnoor, Iik Arifin. "Historical Burden and Promising Future Among Muslim and Christian Minorities in Western and Muslim Countries." In *Islam & the West: Dialogue of Civilizations in Search of a Peaceful Global Order*, edited by Dick van der Meij et al., 111–147. Jakarta, Indonesia: Konrad Adenauer Stiftung and Islamic State University, 2003.

NationMaster.com. Available from http://www.nationmaster.com/index.php.

Nguyen Huy Lai, Joseph. *La tradition religieuse, spirituelle, et sociale au Vietnam: Sa confrontation avec le christianisme*. Paris: Beauchesne, 1981.

Osborne, Milton. *Southeast Asia: An Introductory History*, 8th ed. Saint Leonards, NSW, Australia: Allen and Unwin, 2000.

Rabb, Clinton. "At the Crossroads for Mission in Vietnam." *New World Outlook: The Mission Magazine of the United Methodist Church* (May–June 2001). Available from *http://gbgm-umc.org/NWO/01mj/crossroads2.html*.

Reformist Church online. Available from http://www.reformiert-online.net/weltweit/.

Ricklefs, Merle C. *A History of Modern Indonesia Since c. 1200*, 3rd ed. Stanford, CA: Stanford University Press, 2001.

Rooney, John. *Khabar Gembira (The Good News): A History of the Catholic Church in East Malaysia and Brunei, 1880–1976*. London: Burns and Oates; Kota Kinabalu, Malaysia: Mill Hill Missionaries, 1981.

Saunders, Graham. *Bishops and Brookes: The Anglican Mission and the Brooke Raj in Sarawak, 1848–1941*. Singapore and New York: Oxford University Press, 1992.

Schrauwers, Albert. *Colonial "Reformation" in the Highlands of Central Sulawesi, Indonesia, 1892–1995*. Toronto: University of Toronto Press, 2000.

Smith, Ralph. *Viet-Nam and the West*. London: Heinemann, 1968.

Steinberg, David. *Burma*. Boulder, CO: Westview, 1982.

Subrahmanyam, Sanjay. *The Portuguese Empire in Asia, 1500–1700: A Political and Economic History*. London and New York: Longman, 1993.

Tarling, Nicholas, ed. *The Cambridge History of Southeast Asia*, 2 vols. Cambridge, U.K.: Cambridge University Press, 1992.

Tate, D. J. M. *The Making of Modern South-East Asia:* Vol. 2: *The Western Impact: Economic and Social Change*. Kuala Lumpur and New York: Oxford University Press, 1979.

Teixeira, Manuel. *The Portuguese Missions in Malacca and Singapore (1511–1958)*. 3 vols. Lisbon: Agência-Geral do Ultramar, 1961.

United Nations Population Division, Department of Economic and Social Affairs. World Population Prospects: 2004 Revision. Available from http://esa.un.org/unpp/.

U.S. Department of State. Bureau of Democracy, Human Rights, and Labor. International Religious Freedom Reports. Reports for 2001 to 2005 available from http://www.state.gov/g/drl/rls/irf/.

Wheatley, Paul. *The Golden Khersonese: Studies in the Historical Geography of the Malay Peninsula Before A.D. 1500*. Kuala Lumpur, University of Malaya Press, 1961; Westport, CT: Greenwood, 1973.

Iik Arifin Mansurnoor

RELIGION, WESTERN PRESENCE IN THE PACIFIC

The Christianization of the Pacific world can only loosely be described as a "Western" process. As in many parts of Africa, it was the large number of indigenous teachers and clergy who prompted conversion. The role of European or American missionaries was important, and Christianity arrived in conjunction with Western imperial expansion, but it was accepted (or not) for indigenous reasons.

The earliest attempts at Christianization are a case in point. Spain claimed the entire Pacific for its empire in the early modern period, but did little to explore or colonize it beyond the routes of the silver galleons between the Americas and the Philippines. One exception was a series of expeditions between 1567 and 1605 that produced brief and unsuccessful attempts to settle colonists in the Solomon Islands and elsewhere. These small, tentative settlements included Roman Catholic clergy but were abandoned quickly amid internal dissent, high mortality from disease, and indigenous hostility.

Only at the end of the eighteenth century were renewed attempts made to Christianize the Pacific, and this time it was the expanding empire of the British that took the lead. Some of the earliest British Protestant missions, which began in 1797 with the London Missionary Society, were as unsuccessful as the earlier Spanish ones had been. The sending societies persisted, however, and by the mid-nineteenth century, there were thriving British missions in many island groups, including New Zealand and a strong American presence in Hawaii.

British colonies had also been established in Australia (from 1788) and New Zealand (in 1840), although the connection between colonization and indigenous Christianization was not a straightforward one. Australia's Aboriginal peoples, nomadic and diverse, were relatively unenthusiastic about Christianity well after settlers had arrived in large numbers. Only later in the nineteenth century, when dispossession and disease began to bite more deeply, did the mission stations find it easier to persuade Aboriginal groups to stay with them. A partnership between governments, missions, and churches in Australia eventually led to the establishment of residential schools for Aboriginal children. The degree to which Christianization was a matter of choice under these conditions is debatable, and the legacy of the mission stations and schools is a deeply controversial one.

The story in New Zealand and other Pacific Island groups is very different. Here, indigenous Protestant teachers and their missionary patrons were extremely successful throughout most of Polynesia long before the islands were formally colonized by European powers or the United States. One explanation might be the hierarchical nature of Polynesian societies, including the Maori in New Zealand, whereby the conversion of chiefs led to the conversion of their people. Other explanations concern the nature of indigenous belief systems. Polynesia's polytheism, with its priesthoods and temples, could be compared with the polytheistic societies described in the Bible. For their own reasons, then, Polynesians were interested in the new faith and adopted it rapidly.

To counter these Protestant influences, French Roman Catholic missionaries arrived in the early nineteenth century with the fathers of the Society of the Sacred Hearts of Jesus and Mary (known as the "Picpus Fathers") in 1834. This society and others found that Roman Catholicism was welcomed by islanders, especially where indigenous power struggles created a fruitful climate for Christian sectarian rivalry. This situation mirrored the political rivalry by which Tahiti and the Society Islands became a French colony in 1843, followed by the western island of New Caledonia in 1853. Both Europeans and Islanders used religious commitments for their own purposes.

Sometimes a combination of acceptance and resistance was found in the shape of syncretic movements, such as the early "sailor cults" in Polynesia, where a rudimentary Christianity gained from European beachcombers was combined with indigenous religious practices. In other cases, indigenous prophets arose to create distinctive Christianities that were denounced by the mission stations. Western influences could also prompt the rejection of Christianity, as in the cargo cults of Vanuatu in the western Pacific. These cults drew inspiration from the sudden arrival of Western people and goods during World War II.

Where Christianization was most successful, the role of indigenous teachers and clergy was most critical. This did not mean an easy transition, however, from mission stations to indigenous-led churches. It was often difficult for indigenous teachers to obtain ordination, let alone independent leadership of their own congregations.

Indigenous ordination became more common by the early twentieth century, but the status of Pacific churches was still in question. Many remained under the supervision of missionary societies, or of Australian or New Zealand bishops, reflecting the degree to which Pacific peoples were often considered to be childlike Christians unready for full responsibility. By the early twentieth century, the Anglican mission in Papua New Guinea began recommending revised liturgy for islanders, acknowledging the importance of indigenous cultural perspectives, but treating them condescendingly as well.

Missionaries are still active in the Pacific, and Pacific Christianity is more diverse than ever, including Mormons, Seventh-Day Adventists, and Pentecostal groups alongside the long-established denominations. The process cuts both ways, however: the Pacific also sends missionaries to the Western world. Indigenous clergy concerned about liberalizing attitudes toward the ordination of women in the Anglican Church of Australia, for example, feel that their own conservatism better reflects true Christianity. Like their Asian and African counterparts, many Pacific Christian leaders feel that the Western world is losing its way. Historical distinctions between a "heathen" Pacific and a "Christian" Western world are being reversed.

SEE ALSO *Missions, China; Missions, in the Pacific; Religion, Roman Catholic Church; Religion, Western Perceptions of Traditional Religions; Religion, Western Perceptions of World Religions; Religion, Western Presence in East Asia.*

BIBLIOGRAPHY

Boutilier, James A., Daniel T. Hughes, and Sharon W. Tiffany, eds. *Mission, Church, and Sect in Oceania.* Ann Arbor: University of Michigan Press, 1978.

Crocombe, Marjorie Tuainekore. *Polynesian Missions in Melanesia: From Samoa, Cook Islands, and Tonga to Papua New Guinea and New Caledonia.* Suva, Fiji: Institute of Pacific Studies, University of the South Pacific, 1982.

Forman, Charles W. *The Island Churches of the South Pacific: Emergence in the Twentieth Century.* Maryknoll, NY: Orbis, 1982.

Garrett, John. *To Live Among the Stars: Christian Origins in Oceania.* Suva, Fiji: University of the South Pacific, 1982.

Garrett, John. *Footsteps in the Sea: Christianity in Oceania to World War II.* Suva, Fiji: University of the South Pacific, 1992.

Gunson, Niel. *Messengers of Grace: Evangelical Missionaries in the South Seas, 1797–1860.* Melbourne, Australia: Oxford University Press, 1978.

Hilliard, David. *God's Gentlemen: A History of the Melanesian Mission, 1849–1942.* St. Lucia, Australia: University of Queensland Press, 1978.

Langmore, Diane. *Missionary Lives: Papua, 1874–1914.* Honolulu: University of Hawaii Press, 1989.

Miller, Char, ed. *Missions and Missionaries in the Pacific.* New York: Edwin Mellen, 1985.

Munro, Doug, and Andrew Thornley, eds. *The Covenant Makers: Islander Missionaries in the Pacific.* Suva, Fiji: University of the South Pacific, 1996.

Wetherell, David. *Reluctant Mission: The Anglican Church in Papua New Guinea, 1891–1942.* St. Lucia, Australia: University of Queensland Press, 1977.

Wiltgen, Ralph M. *The Founding of the Roman Catholic Church in Oceania, 1825 to 1850.* Canberra: Australian National University Press, 1979.

Jane Samson

RHODES, CECIL
1853–1902

Cecil John Rhodes, a mining entrepreneur, colonial politician, and empire builder, was born in Bishop's Stortford (Hertfordshire, England) as the fifth son in a family of eleven children headed by Francis William Rhodes, the local vicar, and Louisa Taylor Peacock.

Cecil Rhodes was educated at the local grammar school, supervised by his father. A wished-for higher education in Oxford did not materialize. Instead, Rhodes went to South Africa in 1871 to join his eldest brother Herbert, a cotton planter in the British colony of Natal. On his arrival, Cecil left for the newly discovered diamond fields in Griqualand West. Rhodes set himself up as a cotton planter, but he was unsuccessful and became one of the region's many diamond prospectors within the year.

The brief Natal experience made Rhodes aware of his latent managerial skills, which he later exploited to the maximum, first as manager of his brother's diamond claims at Kimberley, and later as a businessman in his own right and as a politician. In the social conundrum of the diamond mines of the early 1870s, Rhodes formed a group of close friends, including John X. Merriman (1841–1926), a member of the Cape Legislative Assembly and future prime minister, and John Blades Currey (1829–1904), secretary of the British administration in Griqualand West. They introduced Rhodes to colonial politics.

By 1873 Rhodes had accumulated enough capital to go to Oxford University. The first phase of his Oxford career was short and incomplete, and it would take until 1881 and several more short periods of study before Rhodes acquired a degree. Although he was admitted at the Inner Temple in London (one of the traditional English "law schools") in March 1876, he never seriously pursued a career in the law. Though not much of an academic himself, Rhodes's relationship with academia extends to the present day with a legacy of scholarships and fellowships, the Rhodes House Library in Oxford, and funds set up to support several South African universities. In 1891 Rhodes received an honorary degree from his alma mater.

In the mid-1870s the diamond industry went through a crisis and rapid change. Adverse weather, the

Cecil Rhodes. *The nineteenth-century British diamond magnate, colonial politician, and empire builder, photographed with his pet collie.* © BETTMANN/CORBIS. REPRODUCED BY PERMISSION.

need for complex technologies to work hard rock in deep open pits, and the resulting squabbles between black and white small-claim holders led to unrest and the departure of many diggers from the business. On his return from Oxford, Rhodes positioned himself in the camp of the larger claim-holders and colonial authority. With his partner, Charles Dunnell Rudd (1844–1916), Rhodes strongly advocated rationalization and amalgamation of the mines, not only for the common good of the mining industry, but also with personal motives.

By the late 1880s, the De Beers Consolidated mining company, grown out of the De Beers mine set up by Rhodes and Rudd, had turned into a worldwide concern with a board in the Cape and in London and a virtual monopoly over diamond production and trade from South Africa. The amalgamation of the mines also meant extensive rationalization of business practices. De Beers introduced new systems of labor control, including the reorganization of black migrant labor into closed compounds, and rigorous and systematic strip searches of workers to prevent theft and smuggling of diamonds.

The enforcement of labor-control measures went hand in hand with British imperial expansion and the annexation of Griqualand West to the Cape Colony. It bought Rhodes a seat in the Cape parliament, and made his labor-control laws and institutions a model for twentieth-century South Africa.

Rhodes's entry into Cape politics in 1881 was forceful and set the tone for his imperial ambitions and handiwork in later years. He became the spokesman for the mining industry, pushing forward the Diamond Trade Act of 1882 in parliament, with the help of the *Cape Argus* newspaper, which he had bought for the purpose. Mining interests were soon allied to an expansionist imperial interest when Rhodes successfully argued for the disannexation of Basutoland (now Lesotho) from the Cape Colony and the expansion of British rule toward the north of Griqualand West in order to curb both Afrikaner and Tswana ambitions for control over land and water in the area.

After 1886, when gold was first prospected on the Witwatersrand, the northward expansion of British colonial control increased its pace. Rhodes was interested in gold, but decided to go for the exploration of this mineral north of the Limpopo River in the Ndebele kingdom, thus bypassing the Boer-controlled South African Republic (Transvaal) and at the same time leading the British effort in the scramble for this part of Africa, now contested by Britain, Germany, Portugal, and Belgium.

The formation of the British South Africa Company (BSAC), chartered by the British government in 1889, allowed Rhodes and his partners to exploit and extend administrative control over a vast, if ill-defined, area of southern and central Africa. Within a couple of years, the BSAC not only annexed most of the territory now known as Zimbabwe (formerly Southern Rhodesia), but the company also incorporated what are now Zambia and Malawi by way of treaties with local leaders. Underlying the BSAC's actions was a promise to populate the areas brought under its control with settlers, which would allow for an effective British occupation against contending European powers, and introduce the necessary capitalist development to the interior at minimum cost.

In the Cape, Rhodes's political star was rising. From the mid-1880s, Rhodes supported the policies of the powerful Afrikaner Bond, a political party founded in 1880, with regard to the control of African land ownership, franchise, and labor in the Cape. Through judicious agreements with the Afrikaner Bond and some of the liberal parliamentarians, Rhodes managed to become prime minister of the Cape Colony in 1890. When he lost the support of the liberals in 1893, a general election brought him back stronger and with enhanced support from the Afrikaner Bond.

Rhodes's second ministry, in which he also acted as minister for Native Affairs, saw the inclusion of all the remaining independent African polities into the Cape Colony. In Britain, his status as a colonial politician was confirmed with his appointment to the Privy Council, the traditional council of advisors to the British Crown, similar to a council of state, in 1895.

The construction of a railway line between the Cape and Transvaal in 1892 was popular with the Bond, but eventually led to a sharp conflict with the South African Republic led by Paul Kruger (1825–1904). In the next four years, the conflict built up and eventually led to a plan to incorporate the South African Republic. Rhodes and others, backed by British businessmen on the Witwatersrand and the British colonial secretary, made use of a trumped-up conflict about disenfranchised British immigrants (Uitlanders) in the South African Republic to stage an armed overthrow.

Leander Starr Jameson (1853–1917), a BSAC agent, invaded the Republic on his own accord, and against Rhodes's wish to postpone the invasion, in late 1895 with the British South Africa Police Force, only to find that there was no support from inside. The raid forced Rhodes to resign and lost him much of the Afrikaner sympathy he had so carefully built up. It also caused a final rift between Afrikaners and the British, both in the Cape and the Boer republics. The affair also lost Rhodes his position as managing director of the BSAC and threatened the charter of the company. It was only Liberal parliamentarian Joseph Chamberlain's (1836–1914) support of Rhodes before a House of Commons inquiry, in exchange for Rhodes's silence about the former's complicity, that prevented the revocation of the charter.

In the aftermath of the raid, the Ndebele of Southern Rhodesia rose against the white settlers in their area, and they were soon followed by the Shona people. Rhodes intervened personally and managed to diffuse the uprising by initiating successful secret negotiations with the Ndebele leadership, against the wishes of the white settlers. One result of the uprising was that the British government for the first time intervened directly in BSAC affairs by appointing a resident commissioner to the area. The era of colonialism and settler domination had started.

Despite the political setbacks of the 1890s, Rhodes returned to the political scene of the Cape Colony in the 1898 election, now as leader of the so-called Progressives in the Cape parliament, and against the Afrikaner Bond.

When the latter party won the general election, Rhodes's role in Cape politics was finally over.

In the last four years of his life, Rhodes stayed in England for a considerable time. He also took time to fight legal battles against accusations made over his role in the Jameson Raid, and against the Polish fortune-seeker Princess Catherine Radziwill (1858–1941), who first tried to attach herself to Rhodes and later—when unsuccessful in her attempts—blackmailed him. Suffering from deteriorating health, Rhodes died at his Cape cottage on March 26, 1902. At his own request, he was buried on the Matopo Plateau in Southern Rhodesia two weeks later.

SEE ALSO *Afrikaner; Cape Colony and Cape Town; Diamonds.*

BIBLIOGRAPHY

Marks, Shula and Stanley Trapido. "Rhodes, Cecil John (1853–1902)." *Oxford Dictionary of National Biography*, edited by H.C.G. Matthew and Brian Harrison. Oxford and New York: Oxford University Press, 2004.

Michell, Lewis. *The Life of the Rt. Hon. Cecil John Rhodes, 1853–1902*, 2 vols. London: Edward Arnold, 1910.

Rotberg, Robert, I. and Miles F. Shore. *The Founder: Cecil Rhodes and the Pursuit of Power*. New York: Oxford University Press, 1988.

Tamarkin, M. *Cecil Rhodes and the Cape Afrikaners: The Imperial Colossus and the Colonial Parish Pump*. London: Cass, 1996.

Vindex. *Cecil Rhodes, his Political Life and Speeches, 1881–1900*. London: Chapman and Hall, 1900.

Michel R. Doortmont

RIO DE JANEIRO

Rio de Janeiro means *River of January* in Portuguese. It was so named because the bay on which it is located, Guanabara Bay, was discovered on January 1, 1502, by European explorers who believed it to be the mouth of a river. The leader of the expedition was Gaspar de Lemos, a Portuguese captain following in the wake of Pedro Alvars Cabral (1468–1520) who was the first discoverer of the Brazilian coast in 1500. In 1530 the Portuguese court sponsored a further expedition, this time to colonize the region and establish a permanent settlement. There was much rivalry with French and Dutch colonists with whom there were frequent skirmishes. The first settlement in the bay area was called Antarctic France and was founded by Nicolas de

Rio de Janeiro. *Now Brazil's second largest city after São Paulo, Rio de Janeiro is pictured here in 1809 when it served as the capital of Brazil and the Portuguese Empire.* © HULTON-DEUTSCH COLLECTION/CORBIS. REPRODUCED BY PERMISSION.

Villegagnon (1510–1571) in 1555, but by the 1560s the Portuguese achieved preeminence despite the French alliance with the Tamoio. The city of Saint Sebastian of Rio de Janeiro was founded on March 1, 1565, by Estacio de Sá (1520–1567). It was named after the namesake of Sebastian (1554–1578), the king of Portugal. By 1585 Rio de Janeiro's population was 3,850, including some 750 Portuguese and approximately 100 Africans who had been brought to the Americas as slaves.

During the 1600s Rio de Janeiro developed into an important port, especially for the export of sugar derived from sugar cane production in the hinterland using enslaved indigenous people. Brazil wood (*Cesalpina echinata*), known as *pau-brasil,* a dense hardwood red in color, also became a major export. The city also benefited from the discovery of gold in the state of Minas Gerais (meaning General Mines) toward the close of the seventeenth century. This brought growth, wealth, and influence, and in 1764 Rio de Janeiro replaced Salvador as Brazil's capital. During the period 1808 to 1821 the Portuguese royal family, led by the prince regent (to become Dom João VI [1767–1826]) adopted it as their home as Napoléon Bonaparte (1769–1821) threatened their homeland. By the time they returned to Portugal, Brazil had declared independence in 1822, under the direction of Dom Pedro I (1798–1834), the son of Dom João VI, as its first emperor. He was a weak ruler abdicated in favor of his son, Dom Pedro II (1825–1891), who was then only five years old. A triple regency provided rule but only until Dom Pedro II came of age; he ruled for 50 years and established a state that would eventually deny the monarchy. The gold mines had been exhausted by this time but coffee production provided a new wealth to boost Rio de Janeiro's economy. The city continued to expand, first to the north and then to the south, and enjoyed a buoyant period until the late 1880s. The abolition of slavery and a series of poor harvests then resulted in economic hardship as labor and primary produce became increasingly expensive. Political problems ensued and in 1889 Brazil declared itself a republic after a military coup; the emperor was exiled and died in 1891. Rio de Janeiro remained the capital of the new republic until 1960 when it was moved to Brasília.

SEE ALSO *Brazilian Independence; Empire in the Americas, Portuguese; Minas Gerais, Conspiracy of.*

BIBLIOGRAPHY

Fausto, B. *A Concise History of Brazil.* Cambridge, U.K.: Cambridge University Press, 1999.

A. M. Mannion

ROYAL DUTCH-INDISCH ARMY

During the Java War (1825–1830), the Dutch government was forced to create a new type of military force to deal with that rebellion. This military force consisted of a professional army of Dutch officers, coupled with native Indonesian troops. These troops made up an army that operated against native populations, and a force that was not dependent on Dutch citizens to maintain its strength.

In 1830 Governor-General Johannes van den Bosch (1780–1844) officially organized these colonial forces into the Oost-Indisch Leger (East Indies Army). This army operated as the military arm of the colonial administration, with naval assistance provided by the Royal Netherlands Navy. From 1830 to 1870, the Oost-Indisch Leger was employed to control the numerous rebellions cropping up throughout the physical territory of the colony. Many wars, such as the Padri War (1821–1836), were ongoing conflicts that were downgraded to allow the Oost-Indisch Leger to concentrate on more pressing matters, like the Java War. In the case of Bali in 1846 and 1848, the Oost-Indisch Leger, or Leger, was employed to force the local raja to honor agreements, and to prevent other nations from influencing Indonesian trade.

In 1867 the "Accountability Law" separated the finances of the Netherlands and its colony in the East Indies. This ruling enabled the East Indies to create its own Department of War (Department van Oorlog), and the colony became responsible for its own financing of military operations.

Beginning in the late 1860s, the problem of Aceh, a province on the island of Sumatra, began to rise to prominence within the colony. Aceh had operated independently for several decades, but the opening of the Suez Canal renewed its importance to trade within the Dutch East Indies. The rising influence of other nations in the internal politics of Aceh compelled the Netherlands Indies to send forces to control the region and force its submission to Dutch authority.

The Aceh War lasted from 1873 to 1903, and the conflict forced the Oost-Indisch Leger to change its tactics in the field. Initially, efforts were made to control Aceh's territory through the use of a fortified line of outposts intended to contain the guerillas and marshal the limited resources of the colony. Soon, the Geconcentreerde Linie (Concentrated Line), which was a fortified line of sixteen forts protecting the town of Kutaraja, operated more as a prison for colonial troops that were constantly being harassed by Acehnese guerillas. The Leger employed a more modern force in the field that was made up of infantry battalions supported by artillery, cavalry, and engineers who were led by more professional officers like Colonel J. B. van Heutsz (1851–1924). These officers were also employed as civilian administrators *(officier-civiel gezaghebber)* as a way to control the outer reaches of the colony. These officers acted as civil administrators during times of peace, and as military officers during war.

To further control areas occupied by the government, a force known as the *Korps Marechaussee* (District Police) was created in 1893. This corps consisted of select native infantrymen commanded by Dutch officers. These companies were armed with carbines and *klewangs* (native short swords), and operated without coolie trains (supply trains consisting of forced native labor), which allowed them to rapidly move against a native threat. The operations of the Korps Marechaussee were mostly directed toward the native population in an effort to control the resistance. These light troops committed atrocities against local tribes in their attempts to control the Acehnese people and find suspected guerrillas.

By the twentieth century, the Leger began to change its focus from subjugation of rebellious island natives to the control of Indonesian society. The colony was nearly pacified, but the influence of Islamic and communist groups began to grow into a source of trouble for the colony. The Leger began to experiment with aircraft in 1914, and an airborne auxiliary was soon started for field service. To maintain force levels, laws were soon passed to make military service mandatory for Dutch citizens, and native conscription was being considered by the colony.

In the 1920s, two attempted revolts by the Indonesian Communist Party (Partai Komunis Indonesia) signaled efforts by both the colony's police and army to control dissent within the islands. Units were established to monitor political groups with the threat of exile or imprisonment in the Boven Digual Prison for political prisoners. In 1927 the Hague government set down the "Principles of Defense," whereby the colony was to protect Dutch authority within the islands against possible rebellion first, before assisting the Netherlands in its national obligations.

In 1933 the Oost-Indisch Leger was renamed *Koninklijk Nederlandsch Indsch Leger* (KNIL), or the Royal Netherlands Indies Army. During that time, the KNIL numbered around 35,000 men, of which 5,000 were deployed from the Netherlands. In addition, there was a militia *(landsturm)* that fielded a force of 8,000 men. The KNIL operated training facilities at Meester Cornelis and Magelang on the island of Java for all branches, as well as its small armor force. The air forces of the colony operated second-rate aircraft from counties such as the United States and Great Britain. The navy

remained under the control of the Royal Netherlands Navy, and consisted of three cruisers, seven destroyers, a number of smaller ships, and fifteen submarines.

With the German invasion and occupation of the Netherlands in 1940, the colony became one of the last areas of Dutch control. But the East Indies soon found itself facing an outside foe in Japan. The Netherlands declared war on Japan on December 8, 1941, but faced invasion in January 1942. The Japanese conquest of Indonesia lasted roughly three months. The KNIL found itself overwhelmed by the Japanese military forces, and the fighting renewed regional guerrilla activity in the field. The Dutch prisoners were sent to labor and prison camps, and native KNIL troops were given the opportunity to join the Japanese local forces, known as PETA (Pembela Tanah Air).

In 1945 Australian and Dutch forces landed in Tarakan to begin the liberation of the Dutch colony. The Japanese formally surrendered, and agreed to return the East Indies to the Dutch in August 1945. PETA units soon converted into an active revolutionary front against the Allied forces to win freedom for Indonesia. A month later, the government of the Netherlands East Indies was formally back in power, and KNIL prisoners were ordered back into service to regain control over the colony.

For a period of five years, the KNIL units fought to reestablish their colony against the Indonesian independence movement. Regular Royal Dutch Army units soon joined the KNIL in an attempt to win back their former colony. The KNIL units were mostly made up of troops of Dutch citizenry, and the total Dutch commitment ranged from 20,000 to 92,000 troops fighting in Indonesia. One of the worse units was the KorpsSpeciale Troepen, which was led by Captain Raymond Westerling (1919–1987). This force was similar to the Korps Marechaussee, and war crimes were committed to control the growth of the rebellion. In 1947 roughly 3,000 people were executed by elements of the KNIL over a period of two months. Due to pressure from the international community and a successful guerrilla movement, the Netherlands agreed to transfer control to the new Republic of Indonesia on November 2, 1949.

On July 20, 1950, the KNIL was officially disbanded by the government of the Netherlands. The effects of this force on Indonesian politics were still being felt after the collapse of the Dutch colonial administration. Much of the military training of the early leaders of the Indonesian independence movement was obtained when the men served as privates and noncommissioned officers of the KNIL. One example was Suharto (b. 1921), president of

Indonesia from 1967 to 1998, who rose from private to sergeant in the KNIL before World War II.

SEE ALSO *Aceh War; Empire, Dutch; Indonesian Independence, Struggle for.*

BIBLIOGRAPHY

Brown, Colin. *A Short History of Indonesia: The Unlikely Nation?* Crows Nest, NSW, Australia: Allen and Unwin, 2003.

Gimon, Charles A. "Sejarah Indonesia: An Online Timeline of Indonesian History." Available from www.gimonca.com.

Klerck, E. S. de. *History of the Netherlands East Indies,* Vol. 2. Rotterdam, Netherlands: Brusse, 1938.

Poeze, Harry A. "Political Intelligence in the Netherlands Indies." In *The Late Colonial State in Indonesia: Political and Economic Foundations of the Netherlands Indies, 1880–1942,* edited by Robert Cribb, 229-243. Leiden, Netherlands: KITLV, 1994.

Vandenbosch, Amry. *The Dutch East Indies: Its Documents, Problems, and Politics.* Berkeley and Los Angeles: University of California Press, 1942.

van den Doel, H. W. "Military Rule in the Netherlands Indies." In *The Late Colonial State in Indonesia: Political and Economic Foundations of the Netherlands Indies, 1880–1942,* edited by Robert Cribb, 1-75. Leiden, Netherlands: KITLV, 1994.

Willmott, H. P. *Empires in the Balance: Japanese and Allied Pacific Strategies to April 1942.* Annapolis, MD: Naval Institute Press, 1982.

William H. Brown

RUBBER, AFRICA

Rubber, also known as hydrocarbon polymer or latex, comes from plants and vines that once grew abundantly on the African continent. During the nineteenth century, French Guinea, Angola, the Gold Coast, French Congo, and the Congo Free State were among the five top rubber-producing states on the African continent. The Ivory Coast, German East Africa, and Nigeria also experienced rubber booms.

Nineteenth-century inventions, such as the pneumatic bicycle tire, and growing industrial uses of rubber products (tubing, hoses, springs, washers, and diaphragms) created a worldwide demand for rubber. During boom years, rubber was the most sought-after export commodity and the greatest income earner for many African states. The African rubber boom lasted from 1890 to 1913 with significant economic, social, and political consequences for many African states. Exploitation and hardship became standard for Africans in the colonies that produced rubber. However, the most devastating impact wrought by the demand for rubber occurred in the Congo Free State, the personal colony of King Leopold II of Belgium (1865–1909).

African rubber came from two sources, trees and vines. Rubber vines were far less durable than trees. Rubber-producing vines, *landolphia*, were fragile and easily killed. Areas in which rubber was harvested from vines were constantly threatened by the exhaustion of supplies. For example, in Angola, rubber extraction from vines began in the Quiboco forest in 1869; by 1875 no rubber was left in the forest. Similarly, rubber production from Dahomey (now Benin) reached a peak of 14.5 tons per year in 1900, and then declined to 5.9 tons in 1901 and 1.6 tons the year after that as the vines died. Likewise, in French Guinea, the majority of the rubber vines were used up between 1899 and 1905.

Unlike the vines, rubber trees, *Funtumia elastica*, were hearty and tolerated frequent tapping. If the trees were overtapped they went dormant, but they did not die. Generally, within five years an overused tree was once again producing rubber and could be tapped. Methods of tapping trees to harvest rubber varied greatly from state to state. Early in the rubber boom, in the Gold Coast for example, workers simply cut down the trees to extract as much rubber as possible. Later, they began to climb the trees and tap them with a series of shallow cuts to the tree trunk.

In the Ivory Coast, local people harvested rubber with great care so as to not damage the trees. Unfortunately, increased demand for rubber lead to poaching practices and rubber poachers, whose only goal was to extract as much rubber as quickly as possible, often invaded the Ivory Coast's forests and damaged the trees. The never-ending quest for rubber lead to boundary disputes between local peoples. Perpetual warfare broke out over access to rubber-harvesting territories as people crossed indigenous boundaries looking for rubber.

Rubber was acquired by colonial powers either through free-trade practices or by forced labor under the direction of a European-controlled concession company. In the areas in which rubber was bought and sold under free-trade agreements, world prices influenced the collection of rubber. High prices encouraged traders and harvesters to collect as much rubber as fast as possible. When worldwide rubber prices dropped, so did production; harvesters turned to other pursuits and traders moved on to more lucrative markets.

However, in areas in which rubber production was managed under a system of concession companies, rubber gatherers were not paid market rates for their rubber and the world price of rubber had little effect on demand. In areas controlled by concession companies, such as the Congo Free State, all rubber was gathered by using forced labor and coercion. When rubber prices dropped, in order to keep profits steady, concessionaires simply increased the quota demanded from rubber gatherers.

Rubber Gatherers in Cameroon. *Inspectors check the latex collected by native laborers in 1941 in Cameroon. Although the African rubber boom ended in about 1913, rubber production continued in Africa into the later decades of the twentieth century.* GEORGE RODGER/TIME LIFE PICTURES/GETTY IMAGES. REPRODUCED BY PERMISSION.

LEOPOLD'S RUBBER EXTRACTION IN THE CONGO

Using the premises of scientific exploration and the need to end the Arab slave trade in Africa, Leopold established the International Association of the Congo. He recruited Henry Morton Stanley (1841–1904), the famous Welsh-born explorer of Africa, to seek out and establish several trading and administrative stations along the Congo River and to establish monopoly control over the rich ivory trade in the Congo.

Stanley was instructed to secure treaties from local clan chiefs. Unbeknownst to the local chiefs, they signed documents that ceded their lands and the labor of their people to Leopold. Based on treaties that Stanley acquired with some 450 chiefs, Leopold was granted the Congo as a personal possession at the Congress of Berlin (1884–1885). Leopold's Congo encompassed a vast territory, covering nearly one million square miles and inhabited by twenty million people. It was larger than England, France, Germany, Spain, and Italy combined. The Congo region was primarily composed of thick, dense rain forest; however, savannahs and snow-covered volcanic mountains were also part of this terrain.

In the Belgian-controlled Congo Free State, Leopold carried out a massive plunder of the region's resources from 1885 to 1908. He designed policies to loot its rubber, brutalized the people, and ultimately slashed the population by 50 percent (some 10 million people). Almost all exploitable land was divided among concession companies.

The extraction of rubber was accomplished with the imposition of brutal practices against the local people. Forced labor, hostages, slave chains, starving porters, burned villages, paramilitary company "sentries," and the use of the chicotte were standard practices imposed on local peoples. (The *chicotte* was a whip made out of raw, sun-dried hippopotamus hide cut into long, sharp-edged corkscrew strips. It was most often applied to the bare buttocks of a man staked spread-eagle to the ground. These whippings left permanent scars. Twenty strokes of the chicotte sent a victim into unconsciousness, and one hundred or more strokes were often fatal. The chicotte was freely used in Leopold's Congo.)

In the Congo, concession companies were granted exclusive rights to exploit all the products of the forest for a period of thirty years. The people of the area were expected to collect ivory and wild rubber for the company in lieu of paying taxes to the state. Extra economic coercion in the form of beatings, kidnapping, mutilation, and rape of family members was necessary to force local people to gather rubber.

Rubber agents collected the names of all the men in the villages under their control; each man was given a quota of rubber to collect every two weeks. The rubber agents who worked for the concession companies signed two-year contracts. Their goal was to make a lot of money and return home as quickly as possible. In order to do this they assigned armed sentries, supported by the villages, to watch and ensure proper amounts of rubber were collected. The agents had a personal stake in the amount of rubber collected because they received a 2 percent commission on all rubber they shipped. More importantly, if an agent did not meet his quota he was docked the value of the missing rubber.

The majority of rubber in the Congo came from vines, which eventually died off. In order to increase the supply of rubber being produced, agents insisted that women and children gather rubber as well. In order to avoid exploitation and hardship, some rubber gatherers destroyed the vines on purpose. They believed that if the rubber was gone, the concession company would go away.

The search for rubber created a crisis in the Congo. The agents were irrationally harsh toward gatherers who could not produce enough rubber fast enough. Rubber gatherers abandoned their villages and went into hiding for fear of losing life, limb, or family members. Force Publique officers (Leopold's army) sent their soldiers into the forest to find and kill fleeing villagers and rebels hiding there. To prove they had succeeded, soldiers were ordered to cut off and bring back the right hand of every person they killed. Often, however, soldiers cut off the hands of living persons, even children, to satisfy the quota set by their officers.

This terror campaign succeeded in getting workers to collect rubber. A few villages attempted rebellion, attacking agents and killing sentries. However, resistance by villagers was met with extreme and immediate brutality. Whole villages would be massacred and burned to the ground. Some local people simply gave up and accepted massacre, preferring death to the ceaseless search for rubber that kept them searching in the forest for up to twenty-four days each month. The violence used against the people of the Congo was so extreme that in 1908 Leopold was forced to turn his colony over to the Belgian government.

The tactics used by the agents of the concession companies in Leopold's Congo were perhaps little different than methods used by other colonial powers. The striking thing about Leopold's Congo was the vast deception of his philanthropic mission there. Leopold convinced European powers and the United States to grant him the colony of the Congo. He promised to rid the area of the Arab slave trade and develop free trade on the Congo River. Leopold may have ended the Arab slave trade in the Congo, but he simply replaced it with his own form of slavery. He took possession of the land and its twenty million inhabitants and forced them to work for his personal enrichment and to the benefit of his business associates. He neither developed the region nor provided any benefit to the local people.

SEE ALSO *Belgium's African Colonies.*

BIBLIOGRAPHY

Gann, L. H., and Peter Duignan. *The Rulers of Belgian Africa, 1884–1914.* Princeton, NJ: Princeton University Press. 1979.

Harms, Robert. "The End of Red Rubber: A Reassessment." *Journal of African History* 16 (1) (1975): 73–78.

Hochschild, Adam. *King Leopold's Ghost: A Story of Greed, Terror, and Heroism in Colonial Africa.* Boston: Houghton Mifflin, 1998.

Morel, Edmund Dene. *Red Rubber: The Story of the Rubber Slave Trade Flourishing on the Congo in the Year of Grace 1906.* New York: Negro Universities Press, 1969.

Lorna Lueker Zukas

RUSSO-JAPANESE WAR

The Russo-Japanese War (1904–1905) was the struggle between the two dominant nations in northeastern Asia for supremacy in Korea and Manchuria (a region in northeastern China bordering Russia and Mongolia). Russia had begun its expansion into Siberia in the sixteenth century. Its first border conflicts with China were solved via the treaties of Nerchinsk (1689) and Kyakhta (1727). During the eighteenth century, Russia built an empire reaching as far as Alaska, and during the nineteenth century, Russia intensified its empire-building efforts in East Asia. In 1858 China ceded the Amur region to Russia, and in 1860 China further surrendered parts of the coast, where in the same year the Russians established a naval base with the programmatic name Vladivostok ("ruler of the east").

Japan Tramples Korea. *In this illustrated postcard, printed in Russia around 1905, Japanese soldiers heading toward Russia march over a prostrate Korean man.* © RYKOFF COLLECTION/CORBIS. REPRODUCED BY PERMISSION.

After the Japanese victory in the Sino-Japanese War (1894–1895), Russian and Japanese interests started to collide. When Japan demanded control of the strategically important harbor of Lüshun (Port Arthur) on China's Liaodong Peninsula, Russia combined forces with Germany and France and forced Japan to back down. Russia then took the harbor for itself in 1898. At the same time, Russia acquired the rights to build railways through Manchuria, providing a vital connection to Vladivostok and the new base at Port Arthur.

Under the pretext of aiding besieged legations in Beijing during the Boxer Uprising of 1900, Russia sent considerable reinforcements into Manchuria. In addition, Russia became interested in extending its influence into Korea, an area that Japan regarded as a potential future colony. Japan and Russia thus failed to reach an agreement on their mutual interests, causing Japan in 1903 to consider going to war. On February 4, 1904, Japan broke diplomatic relations with Russia.

Hostilities commenced without a declaration of war on the night of February 8, 1904, when Japan launched a torpedo boat attack on the Russian fleet at Port Arthur.

At the same time, the Japanese fleet under Admiral Heihachiro Togo (1847–1934) was on its way to blockade Russian harbors and secure landing operations for the Japanese army on the Korean Peninsula.

Several indecisive naval engagements ensued. At first, the Russian fleet mainly stayed near the coastal batteries at Port Arthur. A brief period of greater Russian activity under Admiral Stepan Osipovich Makarov (1849–1904) ended with the admiral's death when his flagship, *Petropavlovsk,* struck a mine on April 13, 1904. Meanwhile, the Japanese blockade gave their army cover for landing operations in Korea. Japanese forces occupied Korea in February and March 1904, and by the end of April, Japanese troops started to cross the Yalu River into Manchuria.

On May 1, 1904, Russia was defeated in the Battle of the Yalu. Japan combined the advance into Manchuria with further landings on the Manchurian coast, and the Russians were forced to fall back. Russia was thus cut off from Port Arthur, which came under siege from Japan. In August, the Russian fleet attempted to break through to Vladivostok, but was defeated by Togo's forces in the

Battle of the Yellow Sea (August 10). Russia's relief operations failed, and after the Battle of Liaoyang (August 26–September 3), Russian land forces were forced to fall back on Shenyang (Mukden).

After several attempts resulting in high numbers of Japanese casualties, Port Arthur fell to the Japanese on January 2, 1905. The Russians had originally counted on gaining the upper hand with the arrival of reinforcements via the Trans-Siberian Railway, but the connection was too slow and the Russian forces were continually driven back. After victory in the Battle of Mukden (February 19–March 10, 1905), Japanese forces gained the upper hand in Manchuria.

Russia had earlier dispatched its Baltic fleet under Admiral Zinovy Petrovich Rozhestvensky (1848–1909) to relieve Port Arthur. After a long journey around the Cape of Good Hope, the fleet was intercepted by Japan in the Tsushima Strait and was almost annihilated in the Battle of Tsushima (May 27–28, 1905).

Peace between Japan and Russia was negotiated by U.S. President Theodore Roosevelt (1858–1919), and on September 5, 1905, the Treaty of Portsmouth was concluded. Russia ceded Port Arthur and the Liaodong Peninsula to Japan and recognized Korea as a Japanese sphere of influence. Russia's disastrous defeat in the Russo-Japanese War led to the Russian revolution of 1905. After the war, Russia withdrew from the power struggle in East Asia and concentrated on inner reforms and the reconstruction of its military. This first major victory of an Asian power over a Western one came as a surprise. The Japanese success inspired resistance against Western imperialism in all of Asia, and especially in China. Without Russian competition, Japan rapidly expanded its sphere of influence, a development that eventually culminated in World War II in the Pacific.

SEE ALSO *Central Asia, European Presence in; Empire, Japanese.*

BIBLIOGRAPHY

Connaughton, Richard Michael. *The War of the Rising Sun and Tumbling Bear: A Military History of the Russo-Japanese War, 1904–5.* London: Routledge, 1988.

Nish, Ian. *The Origins of the Russo-Japanese War.* London: Longman, 1985.

Pleshakov, Constantine. *The Tsar's Last Armada: The Epic Voyage to the Battle of Tsushima.* New York: Basic Books, 2002.

Schimmelpenninck van der Oye, David. *Toward the Rising Sun: Russian Ideologies of Empire and the Path to War with Japan.* DeKalb: Northern Illinois University Press, 2001.

Warner, Denis, and Peggy Warner. *The Tide at Sunrise: A History of the Russo-Japanese War, 1904–1905*, 2nd ed. London: Cass, 2001.

Wells, David, and Sandra Wilson, eds. *The Russo-Japanese War in Cultural Perspective, 1904–05.* Basingstoke, U.K.: Macmillan, 1999.

Westwood, J. N. *Russia Against Japan, 1904–05: A New Look at the Russo-Japanese War.* Albany: State University of New York Press, 1986.

Cord Eberspaecher

S

SCIENCE AND TECHNOLOGY

The connections between science, technology, and Western colonialism are strong and complex. The connections were driven and shaped by the European scientific revolution of the seventeenth century, as well as the growing authority of science in the eighteenth century Enlightenment period. Together, these developments established a modern mentality of dominance and expansion, which differed significantly from the premodern period. The new methods of science drove and seemed to vindicate humankind's dominance over, and knowledge of, nature. This ambition frequently translated into exploration, expansion of territory, and consolidation of European authority over indigenous people.

There are four domains of activity where scientific and technological developments intersected most clearly with Western colonialism. First, ever-changing technologies of travel both facilitated and encouraged exploration and territorial expansion. These related both to ocean travel and land travel, in particular the railroad. Second, communication technologies evolved rapidly, especially in the nineteenth century, linking continents and people in novel ways. Innovations in transport and communication in the eighteenth and nineteenth centuries were spurred by industrializing Britain, and later France, Germany, and the United States. Crucial new technologies were created, themselves requiring extensive circuits of colonial trade in raw materials.

The third domain involves scientific advancements in the field of medicine and health care. Western colonialism created vast medical problems of illness, especially epidemics of infectious disease in indigenous communities. But conversely and paradoxically, one of the driving forces of Western colonialism came to be an apparently curing and caring one, whereby Western hygiene and public health were understood to be one of the great benefits brought to different parts of the world. Fourth, Western science and technology facilitated the development of new arms and weapons. While the contest of arms between colonizers and the colonized was not always as one-sided as might be expected, firearms technology permitted colonization of local people, often in the most brutal way. Differential arms technology also determined the outcome of territorial wars between colonial powers. Since 1450, the European idea of progress has applied to scientific knowledge, imperial territorial, military and administrative expansion, and the increasingly dominant adherence to a Western "civilizing" mission.

TRAVEL AND TRANSPORTATION

Technologies of transport and travel have enabled and shaped Western colonialism from the Renaissance period onward. The Iberian powers of the Mediterranean and the Atlantic honed sailing and navigating skills for military and fishing purposes over many generations. Square sails were increasingly used alongside lateen sails, an innovation from the Islamic world, which permitted ships to beat into the wind. Spanish and Portuguese sailors in particular developed skills, knowledge, and technology for increasingly wide Atlantic voyages, to the Cape Verde Islands, the Madeiras, and the Canary Islands; along the African coast; and to the Americas.

Technology to make great ocean voyages was within the grasp of not just the Europeans, however. Chinese

The Great Eastern. *This legendary ship, designed by the British engineer Isambard Kingdom Brunel and built in the 1850s, laid the first successful transatlantic telegraph cable, but was scrapped as financially unviable in 1889. This illustration appeared in 1859 in the* Illustrated London News. **ILLUSTRATED LONDON NEWS/HULTON ARCHIVE/GETTY IMAGES. REPRODUCED BY PERMISSION.**

navigation and shipping knowledge was comparable in the early period, and Polynesian cultures made long Pacific voyages, between the Hawaiian Islands and Aotearoa/New Zealand, for example. In the sixteenth- and seventeenth-century Atlantic, and in the eighteenth-century Pacific, European explorers, traders, missionaries, and military often adopted and adapted local means of transport, especially inland. Hudson Bay Company traders around the North American Great Lakes, for example, typically traveled by canoe. However, European navigating, sailing, mapping, and shipbuilding technology incrementally increased over many generations, facilitating the establishment of seasonal coastal trading posts, the permanent plantation settlements, and the commercial endeavors of the Atlantic: slavery and the sugar, tobacco, and fur trades.

Steam power and iron were the twin innovations of the British industrial revolution, and both revolutionized transportation, in turn shaping events in the colonial world. In the nineteenth century, there was a transition away from wooden to iron-hulled ships. With so many European forests denuded, and British shipbuilding

largely importing timber, iron offered many advantages for the shipbuilding industries. Wrought iron ships weighed far less, were more durable and the design of ships—their possible size and shape—was more flexible. From the late 1870s, a further transition from wrought iron to steel made ships lighter and more adaptable again.

The nineteenth-century transition from sail to steam affected both oceanic transport and river transport, and facilitated Western exploration of interior African, Asian, and American waterways. Especially in the African continent, steamships made travel possible deep inside a region previously largely closed to Europeans. Developing from the navigation of the Hudson River in New York in 1807, the steam-powered ship appeared in colonial contexts from the 1820s, especially in India, in British movement around China, and later in Africa.

As early as the 1830s, steamers were regularly carrying passengers and freight along the Ganges, and steamers came to be central to various military encounters, for example in the war between the British East India Company and the Kingdom of Burma from 1824. Steam navigation between Britain and India soon also became a reality. The British government invested in exploratory navigation by steamer across two overland routes: via Mesopotamia and via Egypt, the latter becoming the main route after the Suez Canal opened in 1869. Hybrid steam/sail transport across the Atlantic was possible from 1819, and from 1832 by steam alone. While the steamers did not entirely eclipse sail, especially for navies, they nonetheless reduced travel time considerably between west and east, north and south.

The development of railroads in the 1840s and 1850s consolidated internal expansion and investment in many areas, tying western and colonial economies ever more tightly. In Britain, for example, railroads interested the Lancashire cotton industry in particular, which sought rapid access to cotton-growing districts, as well as to Indian consumers of cotton garments. By the 1860s and 1870s, railway lines criss-crossed the Indian subcontinent. This involved building large bridges across frequently flooding rivers, themselves considerable engineering feats. In the same period, the transcontinental railroads spanned North America from east to west, bringing an infrastructure and a cultural and administrative permanence to territory and people, who had previously been in a more ambiguous and flexible frontier relationship with colonizers. Thus while railroads often brought easy transport, commercial reliability, and predictability to colonial sites, it was usually at the expense of local trade, communications, economies, and cultures.

COMMUNICATION

Part of the drive for quicker transportation was to speed up communication services between colonial peripheries and centers. By sail, letters between, for example, France and Indochina, between Britain and the Straits Settlements, took months, on both outward and return voyages. The steamer revolution steadily shortened this over the nineteenth century, and steam companies competitively coveted much-sought government contracts to deliver mail. For example, the Peninsular and Orient Steam Navigation Company (P&O) won the contract to deliver mail from Britain to Gibraltar and then to Alexandria in Egypt, connecting with the Indian Navy's mail service from Bombay to Suez, where mail was transported between seas on camels. The Suez Canal, opening in 1869, was largely a French initiative. It was impressive less in terms of engineering technology, than in terms of scale and significance. Built mainly by Egyptians, it was used largely by British ships. The territorial acquisition of Egypt in 1882 by the British was almost entirely about strategically securing the crucial Suez Canal route.

It was the technology of cable telegraphy—first land, and then submarine—that enabled even quicker communication. By 1865 a cable linked Britain with India, but ran across land, through much non-British territory. Land cables could always be sabotaged and cut, and it was not until a new line was laid in 1870—mainly submarine from Britain to Gibraltar, Malta, and Alexandria and then to Suez and India—that telegraph between Britain and India was rapid and reliable.

French colonies were also increasingly linked by telegraphy, with a line laid between France and Algeria in 1879. The increasing reliance on cables for communication was occasionally the rationale for gaining control of territory. At other points it was crucial for communication in times of war, for example the Anglo-Boer War. Telegraphy reduced global communication time from weeks and months, to hours and days, thus promoting and enabling ever-expanding trade and business around the colonial world of the late nineteenth century.

Cables and telegraphs were interrupted as a technology by the use of radio waves and wireless communication in the early twentieth century. In 1901 the first radio waves were transmitted across the Atlantic, from Cornwall to Newfoundland. Soon after, wireless stations appeared in the British, French, and German colonies, often with the ambition to create seamless "wireless chains" around the empires. After 1924 shortwave transmission gave another burst of energy to imperial telecommunications, bringing the most isolated places within instant reach. Much cable telegraphy business had switched to shortwave wireless communication by the late 1920s.

MEDICINE AND HEALTH

Questions of health and medicine were linked to the colonial enterprise from the outset. As soon as Europeans crossed the Atlantic, and explored and colonized the lands and people of Central America and the Caribbean, high mortality and illness rates became evident. Because of this experience of mortality, and because of longstanding climatic understanding of health and disease, in which elements of heat, moisture, air, and environment were seen to be causative, a new field of medicine and science emerged. Initially under the rubric of "the diseases of warm climates," the discipline of tropical medicine arose explicitly from the colonial experience. To some extent, this colonial medicine was concerned with the mortality of Africans on the slave ships and on American plantations, often less for humanitarian than commercial reasons. In the main, however, the concern was to reduce the massive mortality rates of European military, settlers, missionaries, and travellers.

The Maxim Gun. *This late nineteenth-century illustration depicts the first trial of the automatic Maxim machine gun by British Troops in Africa in 1887. The gun was designed by Hiram Maxim in the early 1880s.* © **BETTMANN/CORBIS. REPRODUCED BY PERMISSION.**

The colonial advance from the sixteenth century onward brought hitherto unknown microbes to the New World and brought others back to Europe, an interaction sometimes called the Columbian exchange. The demographic effects between colonizer and colonized populations were vastly different, however. For the Aztecs and Maya of Central America, for the Hawaiians, and for the Eora of eastern Australia, epidemics of infectious diseases meant illness, death, and often rapid depopulation. Smallpox and tuberculosis killed some people, diseases such as syphilis and gonorrhoea frequently rendered others infertile, seriously altering patterns of reproduction and population replacement. Moreover, the massive changes in land use that often accompanied European colonization seriously compromised indigenous people's health through hunger and starvation, thus unravelling the viability of traditional social and political organization.

Western colonialism, then, created health and medical problems for Europeans, for indigenous people, and for the growing diasporas of people in forced and free migration. But colonialism was also driven by a desire to ameliorate these problems, and increasingly so over the centuries. Thus, for example, if the Hudson Bay Company traders brought smallpox—both wittingly and unwittingly—they also sometimes brought the technology and the material of the smallpox vaccine. Often practical assistance with health and hygiene were the first moves made by colonial missionaries around the world. Western and Christian health care undoubtedly relieved some suffering, but it was also political: it was a means of buying goodwill and, not infrequently, dependence and obligation. By the nineteenth century, when European, North American, and Australasian governments were developing public health bureaucracies and infrastructures in their home countries, the extension of hygiene as rationale for colonial rule of indigenous people became increasingly common.

Pharmacological developments also had a mutual relationship to colonialism, both deriving from and facilitating European expansion. The anti-malarial drug quinine is one example. Local people in the Andes had long recognized the curative and preventive properties of the bark of the cinchona tree. Jesuits brought the bark to Europe in the seventeenth century, and thereafter securing sources of the bark was one reason for increasingly penetrating journeys into the region. Prompted by the need to reduce death rates from malaria in the military, French scientists successfully extracted quinine from the cinchona bark in 1820, undertook experimental research in Algeria, and began commercial production.

Thereafter, large quantities of quinine as anti-malarial prophylaxis were widely used, especially by British and French troops in tropical colonies. Its well-known efficacy clearly assisted British, U.S. and German explorations through Central Africa, and enabled a more permanent French presence in both North and West Africa. Mortality rates for European military as well as civilian populations in colonies began to fall dramatically, and the demand for the bark grew accordingly. This in turn spurred other colonial initiatives to cultivate the tree outside the Andes. The Netherlands East Indies government grew it successfully in Java, as did the British government in India. In the case of malaria, the cinchona tree, and quinine, colonialism created the conditions both of demand and supply.

ARMS

The history of colonialism is also the history of war. Armed combat took place between invading colonizers and indigenous people, from the Spanish invasion of central America, to the British expansion into the Australian continent, to Germans in the Congo. It also took place between competing colonial powers, often involving local people as well. The wars between the French and British in North America through the eighteenth century, for example, were consistently about securing territory on that continent. Especially from the middle of the nineteenth century, the technologies of firearms, and what historians sometimes call the arms gap, decided outcomes.

The arms gap sometimes enabled the massacre of local people by colonizers, with or without government consent. For example, the mass killing of the Kenyan Mau Mau rebels and civilians by the British after 1952 took the force it did partly because of technology available. But it was not always the case that those with firearms were at an unquestioned advantage in colonial wars. For example, when British colonists came to settle in Sydney from 1788, they were often anxious about the spearing skills of the local men, used both to kill and for ritual punishment. The muzzle-loading muskets, which British soldiers and settlers held in that instance, took

around one minute to load, and they had to be kept dry. They were simply not always a match for spearing technology. Nor was it consistently the case that colonized people were without firearms. People long involved in the slave trade in Africa, for example, were often armed with muskets and ammunition. The exchange of slaves for firearms was a basic one in that commercial circuit, although often the crudest and cheapest kind of firearm was bartered.

In another example, the Cree in present-day Canada exchanged furs for guns, dealing as middlemen between the Hudson Bay Company and other Native groups, who gradually incorporated traded firearms into their way of life. The world of colonialism was constantly involved in firearms dealing.

Partly because of this trade, and driven by the demands of Western warfare, firearms technology gained pace in the nineteenth century. The invention of the small metal cap for explosives meant that after 1814 the imperative to keep muskets dry was minimized. New oblong bullets were invented in France in 1848, and were tested in the colonies: the French used these bullets first in Algeria, and the British against the Xhosa in the Kaffir War of 1851–1852. Around the 1860s there was a crucial technological shift from muzzleloaders to breechloaders. It was the breechloading gun that created a major discrepancy in power between those with and those without. The American-developed "repeating rifle" and the Maxim, invented by Hiram S. Maxim in 1884, only increased this discrepancy in power. The Maxim was light and could shoot multiple bullets each second. The explorer of Africa, Henry Morton Stanley, had a Maxim gun on his 1886–1888 expedition, as did Lord Kitchener in his conquest of the Sudan in 1898. Both used the gun to achieve their respective colonizing goals.

Knowledge, technology, and power go together. The history of colonialism is a history of often vastly different knowledge systems encountering one other. It is a history of competing, transferring, and evolving technologies. And it is a history of power relations, not always expressed physically and technologically, but frequently so. Major changes in the European world from the Renaissance onward, including the scientific revolution, the development of mercantile capitalism, the industrial revolution, and the communications revolution—all occurred in the era of colonialism, not incidentally, but relatedly. The search for a newly valued scientific knowledge itself explicitly drove many European expeditions, especially in the eighteenth century. The development of technology often facilitated new places and means of travel, exploration, and colonization. Sometimes, science and technology were actively employed to rationalize extended colonial rule of people and territory, under a humanitarian and civilizing logic. Always, technologies established new Western infrastructures in foreign places, which created a momentum of exponential expansion for trade, commerce, government, and settlement.

SEE ALSO *China, Foreign Trade; Railroads, Imperialism; Sugar Cultivation and Trade; Tobacco Cultivation and Trade.*

BIBLIOGRAPHY

Ballantyne, Tony, ed. *Science, Empire, and the European Exploration of the Pacific.* Burlington, VT: Ashgate, 2004.

Chaplin, Joyce E. *Subject Matter: Technology, the Body, and Science on the Anglo-American Frontier, 1500–1676.* Cambridge, MA: Harvard University Press, 2001.

Crosby, Alfred W. *Ecological Imperialism: The Biological Expansion of Europe.* Cambridge, MA: Cambridge University Press, 2004.

Curtin, Philip. *Death by Migration: Europe's Encounter with the Tropical World in the Nineteenth Century.* Cambridge, U.K.: Cambridge University Press, 1989.

Headrick, Daniel R. *Tools of Empire: Technology and European Imperialism in the Nineteenth Century.* New York: Oxford University Press, 1981.

Headrick, Daniel R. *The Tentacles of Progress: Technology Transfer in the Age of Imperialism, 1850–1940.* New York: Oxford University Press, 1988.

Hobsbawm, E. J. *Industry and Empire: From 1750 to the Present Day.* Harmondsworth, U.K.: Penguin, 1987.

Lux, Maureen K. Medicine that Walks: Disease, Medicine, and Canadian Plains Native People, 1880–1940. Toronto, Canada: University of Toronto Press, 2001.

Alison Bashford

SCRAMBLE FOR AFRICA

Between 1875 and 1914, European countries invaded and subjugated almost all of the African continent. Historians have long debated the causes for this break with past European policies toward Africa. The rising European appetite for conquest, and the willingness of European governments to pay for imperialist ventures, has become known as the "New Imperialism" to distinguish it from older traditions of colonialism before 1850. Earlier policies focused more on seeking commercial influence rather than formal occupation.

CAUSES OF THE SCRAMBLE

No one cause can explain the Scramble. Rather, a conjunction of attitudes favorable to empire, technological advances, and political and social concerns led different governments to believe the occupation of Africa would be

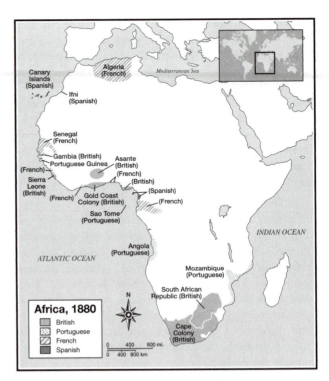

Europe's Colonies in Africa, 1880. Britain, France, Portugal, and Spain had established a number of colonies in Africa by 1880, four years before the Berlin Conference was convened to resolve territorial disputes between these and other colonial powers. **MAP BY XNR PRODUCTIONS. THE GALE GROUP.**

possible, necessary, and cheap. Technological developments created a short-lived, but radical, discrepancy between African and European countries. Quinine, steamboats, and new armaments like the machine gun gave Europeans a tremendous advantage over most African states. Many Europeans also considered technological prowess a sign of their moral superiority over Africans.

Economic needs also helped lead to occupation, although it was often done for getting quick profits rather than tangible benefits that resulted from colonization. J.A. Hobson (1858–1940) and Communist leader Vladimir Lenin (1870–1924) argued that imperialism stemmed from the need of capitalist societies to find new markets for their factories and raw materials so as to fuel production. However, this economic explanation fails to acknowledge that very few colonies turned a profit before World War I (1914–1918) and that most European investors preferred to put their money elsewhere. Only South Africa, where gold and diamonds were discovered before 1880, attracted many companies and extensive capital.

Other factors entered into the equation of African colonization. French politicians and military officers bitter at the loss of Alsace and Lorraine saw the domination of Africa as a chance for their country to remain a world power. Nationalists from many countries clamored for wars of conquest. Some politicians, like the Conservative Party minister Lord Salisbury and German premier Otto von Bismarck (1815–1898), personally disdained Africa, but felt the balance of power in Europe could only be kept through an equitable division of African spoils. Missionary writers like David Livingstone (1813–1873) presented Africa as ravaged by the slave trade and primitive superstition. The popularity of social Darwinist doctrines of European biological superiority led others to espouse empire, like South African magnate Cecil Rhodes (1853–1902). Finally, ambitious Europeans in Africa proved more willing to carve out empires using indigenous troops than their home country's regime ever planned.

HOW THE SCRAMBLE HAPPENED

Events in North and West Africa set the foundation for the occupation of Africa. The Egyptian government under Khedive Ismail (1830–1895) ran up enormous debts building the Suez Canal and other modernizing projects. Because of its debts, the British and French government took over much of Africa in 1879. European disagreements during the Balkan Crisis of 1875–1878 led to the British occupation of Cyprus. The French government received the tacit agreement of London to the occupation of Tunisia in 1881 as compensation. Once British forces put down a nationalist revolt in Egypt in 1882, French politicians demanded compensation. French officers also began expanding their authority in Senegal from 1879 onward.

By 1882 others entered the competition. Leopold II (1835–1909) of Belgium had long dreamed of creating an empire, and hired Anglo-American journalist Henry Morton Stanley (1841–1904) to help promote a supposedly scientific association, the African International Association, that had as its real goal the creation of a Central African state controlled by Leopold II himself. French officer Pierre Savorgnan de Brazza (1852–1905) and Stanley both persuaded African chiefs along the Congo River to sign dubious treaties on behalf of their rival sponsors. The Portuguese government, alarmed by British designs on Southern Africa as well as these moves into Central Africa on territory it had long claimed but never controlled, signed an agreement in 1884 with the British respecting Portuguese rights on the Congo River. To resolve these disputes, Bismarck organized the Berlin Conference of 1884–1885.

The Berlin Conference set up a procedure for how African territory could be taken over by European countries. France and Germany decided to permit Leopold II to form the Congo Free State as long as he allowed free

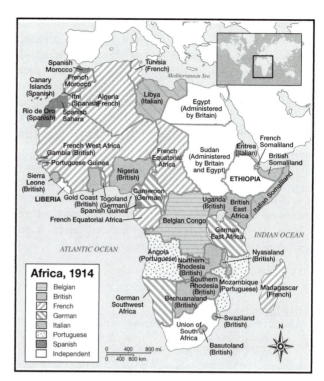

Colonized Africa, 1914. *The scramble for Africa began in the 1880s, when the European colonial powers raced to establish formal colonies in Africa. By the time World War I began in 1914, most of Africa was under European control.* **MAP BY XNR PRODUCTIONS. THE GALE GROUP.**

trade within its borders. Representatives from most European nations attended. The Niger and Congo Rivers were declared free for naval travel. Countries could claim territory with signed treaties and proof of "effective occupation." General "spheres of influence" were created, but the colonial borders were only fixed between 1885 and 1911.

After the Scramble, European countries did not immediately leap into invasion. French officers set their sights on the destruction of the Umarian Muslim kingdom in the late 1880s, but only succeeded in defeating it and other African leaders like Samory Touré (1830–1900) in the following decade. Attempts by European countries to rely on private companies, like Sir James Goldie's National African Company, to save expenses usually led to formal occupation once these firms proved unable to pay for and maintain colonial occupation. Competition between European countries for African land continued until World War I. French and English forces nearly squared off over the Sudan at the village of Fashoda in 1898, for example, but their disputes eventually were resolved through diplomacy.

African communities could sometimes fight guerilla wars for decades, but only once succeeded in completely defeating invaders. Ethiopia, led by Menelik II (1844–1913) and his well-prepared army, defeated Italian plans of conquest at the battle of Adowa in 1896, forcing Italy to recognize it as a sovereign nation. The white Boer republics defeated British forces in 1881, but a second war between the two resulted in English victory after a long conflict from 1899 to 1902. One of the reasons for European victory lay in the use of African auxiliaries. Another lay in political divisions between Africans. Vying factions in Buganda, the Tanzanian coast, and elsewhere tried to enlist European aid, often at the ultimate cost of their own independence. Some Africans profited from invasion, but many more suffered from taxes, forced labor, epidemics, and forced migrations in the initial years of European rule.

SEE ALSO *Berlin Conference; Stanley, Henry Morton.*

BIBLIOGRAPHY

Adas, Michael. *Machines as the Measure of Men: Science, Technology, and Ideologies of Western Dominance.* Ithaca, NY: Cornell University Press, 1989.

Baumgart, Winfried. *Imperialism: The Idea and Reality of British and French Colonial Expansion, 1880–1914.* New York: Oxford University Press, 1982.

Conklin, Alice and Ian Fletcher, eds. *European Imperialism, 1830–1930: Climax and Contradiction.* Boston: Houghton Mifflin, 1999.

Hargreaves, John. *West Africa Partitioned.* London: Macmillan, 1974–1985.

Headrick, Daniel. *The Tools of Empire: Technology and European Imperialism in the Nineteenth Century.* New York: Oxford University Press, 1981.

Mackenzie, John. *The Partition of Africa, 1880–1900 and European Imperialism in the Nineteenth Century.* London and New York: Meuthen, 1983.

Parsons, Timothy. *The British Imperial Century, 1815–1914: A World History Perspective.* Lanham, MD: Rowan and Littlefield, 1999.

Wesseling, H.L. *Divide and Rule: The Partition of Africa, 1880–1914.* Translated by Arnold Pomerans. Westport, CT: Praeger, 1996.

Jeremy Rich

SCRAMBLE FOR CONCESSIONS

China's defeats in the so-called Opium Wars brought on the unequal treaty system. Its main features, extraterritoriality and the 5 percent ad valorem tariff, clearly reflected imperialist imposition on China's integrity and the decline of the Qing dynasty. Still, led by Great Britain, and perhaps best symbolized by Sir Robert Hart and the China Maritime Customs Service, these efforts led to an informal empire, China's semi-colonial status, and rule, in a way, by missionaries and merchants, defended when necessary by military force.

Toward the end of the nineteenth century the situation changed greatly. In 1884–1885, France easily defeated China and took control of Indochina, a peripheral part of the traditional empire. Matters worsened when, in 1894–1895, Japan equally easily defeated Qing forces and demanded a series of territorial concessions including the island of Formosa, the nearby Pescadore Islands, Korea, and the Liaotung Peninsula in southern Manchuria.

The "triple intervention" in which France and Germany joined with Russia temporarily halted Japanese expansion onto the Asian mainland. Russia demanded a reward for keeping Japan from taking southern Manchuria, and used construction of the Trans-Siberian Railway to gain approval for a shortcut across Manchuria. This shortcut, the Chinese Eastern Railway, saved 1,036 square kilometers (400 square miles) on the 12,949-square-kilometer (5,000-square-mile) trip from Moscow to Vladivostok, and became a vehicle for Russian expansion into Manchuria. Similarly, Germany demanded a concession in eastern Shandong. France also used railway construction to move from Indochina into the Chinese provinces, Yunnan and Guangxi, along the border. Japan sought control over Fujian and Zhejiang provinces that faced Formosa across the Taiwan Straits. And Great Britain, not wanting to lose out as its informal empire gradually collapsed, sought control of Guangdong province adjacent to its leasehold in Hong Kong and Kowloon as well as territory along the lower Yangtze River.

Indeed, many Chinese feared that China would soon go the way of sub-Saharan Africa, and that the Middle Kingdom would disappear from world maps. This hatred of foreign imperialism and the Chinese who, in converting to Christianity, seemed to turn their back on tradition, led to the rise of a secret society, the Righteous and Harmonious Fists, the so-called Boxers that conservative elements of the Qing dynasty encouraged to throw off the foreign yoke. The resulting rebellion surged to Beijing in 1900 and besieged the foreign embassies and the Chinese Christian converts hiding in the legations; a relief expedition advanced to Beijing and rescued the besieged.

For the United States, the scramble for concessions was troubling. After the 1890s depression and America's new empire after war with Spain and the annexation of the Hawaiian Islands, American business wanted markets for surplus production, and the China market was tempting. The U.S. secretary of state, John Hay, with encouragement from the British government, issued two "Open Door" notes in which he called on the imperial powers not to cut China to pieces and not to incorporate those pieces into mercantile empires closed to American business. Most of the foreign powers ignored Hay, and the situation in China devolved as the Qing dynasty collapsed, and Yuan Shikai seized control and the world moved to World War I (1914–1918). Thereafter, in the 1920s and 1930s, Japan and China began to move down the road to war.

SEE ALSO *China, First Opium War to 1945; Open Door Policy.*

BIBLIOGRAPHY

Hunt, Michael H. *Frontier Defense and the Open Door: Manchuria in Chinese-American Relations, 1895–1911.* New Haven, CT: Yale University Press, 1973.

Joseph, Philip. *Foreign Diplomacy in China, 1894–1900: A Study in Political and Economic Relations with China.* New York: Octagon Books, 1971.

Tomimas, Shutaro. *The Open Door Policy and the Territorial Integrity of China.* Arlington, VA: University Publications of America, 1976.

Young, Leonard Kenneth. *British Policy in China, 1895–1902.* Oxford: Clarendon Press, 1970.

Charles M. Dobbs

SECULAR NATIONALISMS, MIDDLE EAST

Prior to World War I (1914–1918), secular nationalism in the Middle East was largely confined to military and administrative elites with Western educations. In the Islamic and multiethnic Ottoman Empire, such elites established Turkish and Arab cultural associations and secret nationalist societies after the constitutional revolutions of 1908 and 1909. Of the Middle Eastern provinces of the Ottoman Empire, only in Egypt did nationalism emerge as something approaching a popular movement before World War I. The country had become almost independent under a dynasty of governors established by the ethnic Albanian, Mehmet Ali (1770–1849).

By the end of the 1870s, bureaucrats, journalists, military officers, and landowners had begun to protest intensive political and economic intervention in Egyptian affairs by European powers. The protests were expressed in terms of Ottoman and Islamic identity as well as Egyptian territorial nationalism. A broadly based movement against European intervention and for constitutional government coalesced around Ahmad 'Urābī (1839–1911), a military officer and minister of war. In 1882 a British invasion force suppressed his movement and thus began the occupation of the country. Until after

World War I, the Egyptian independence movement remained primarily one of Western-oriented landowners, journalists, and lawyers, exemplified by Mustafa Kamil (1874–1908) and his National Party.

World War I brought the destruction of the Ottoman Empire. Soon after, ethnic Turks in Anatolia fought a two-year war of independence against Greek and Allied invaders. The leader of the independence movement, Mustafa Kemal Atatürk (1881–1938), along with other former Ottoman officers and officials, established the Turkish Republic in 1923 in the reconquered areas. The new state's ideology, known as Kemalism, emphasized secularism, Turkish nationalism, and republicanism as the basis of political identity. These ideas were inculcated with remarkable rapidity through the school system and the conscript army.

Egyptians resumed their struggle against British control after World War I with a popular revolt in 1919. The country gradually gained independence through a series of treaties signed with Great Britain in 1922, 1936, and 1954. The most influential party in this period was the secular, nationalist Wafd (Delegation) Party, led first by Sa'd Zaghlūl, (1857–1927), another landowning lawyer. The Wafd's influence peaked in the 1930s, while in the same period the Muslim Brotherhood emerged as a popular movement and a critic of the secularism of the Egyptian elite.

Egyptian nationalism was initially distinct from Arab nationalism, which became predominant in the Arab Levant and Fertile Crescent after World War I. During the war, in 1916, Sharif Husayn (1835–1931) of Mecca had launched a British-supported Arab revolt against the Ottoman Empire. Although some members of the prewar secret Arab nationalist societies joined his revolt, most of his followers were motivated by tribal loyalties and British subsidies, rather than by nationalist ideals. Following the war, the Arab Levant and Fertile Crescent were divided into four League of Nations mandates. These were Iraq, Syria (including Lebanon), Palestine, and Transjordan, each of which was promised eventual independence as a nation-state. Iraq, established as a monarchy under British supervision, gained independence in 1932. Iraqi Arab nationalism, with strong overtones of Pan-Arab nationalism, was inculcated through the newly established school system, youth organizations, and the conscript army. Army officers in particular resented continued British influence in Iraqi affairs. The mandate for Syria, under French tutelage, was constituted as two republics, Syria and Lebanon, both of which gained independence in 1946.

After an anti-French revolt lasting from 1925 to 1927, leading Syrian politicians formed the National Bloc as the principal association working for independence. The Bloc's

Hashemite King Hussein ibn 'Ali. *The king of Hejaz and the caliph al-Islam (front center), photographed on April 3, 1924, leaving the royal palace in Amman.* © BETTMANN/CORBIS. REPRODUCED BY PERMISSION.

supporters spread Syrian Arab and Pan-Arab nationalism through the school system, Boy Scout troops, and athletic clubs. Syrian and Pan-Arab nationalism expanded similarly in Lebanon, but they competed with a specifically Lebanese nationalism that was strong especially among Maronite Christians, who were traditionally close to the French. The most significant political party expressing Lebanese nationalism was the Phalange, established in 1936 by Pierre Gemayel (1905–1984).

Palestine, under British control, also saw the spread of Arab nationalism in much the same manner as Syria. However, the Zionist movement, benefiting by British protection, made the quest for Palestinian independence even more difficult. By 1935, five Arab nationalist political parties had been established in the country, though some had no popular followings. Palestinians launched an uprising against Great Britain and the Zionists in 1936, which the British put down by 1939.

The Arab world in the 1940s experienced the intensification of Pan-Arab nationalism. This was true even in Egypt, where the League of Arab States was headquartered after its creation in 1945. Widespread support in the Arab world for the struggle of the Palestinian Arabs

against Zionist colonization further magnified Pan-Arab sentiments, although allied Arab armies were defeated by the new state of Israel in the 1948 Palestine War.

Outside of the former Ottoman Empire, Iran also experienced secular nationalism after World War I. There, as in Turkey, the emergence of secular nationalism was a state-led development. In 1926, the army's commander in chief, Reza Khan (1878–1944), brought an end to the ruling Qajar dynasty and established himself as shah, taking the name of Pahlavi for his dynasty. Modeling his program on that of Atatürk, Reza Shah strove to inculcate in the Iranian people a secular Persian identity drawing on Iran's pre-Islamic traditions.

With considerably less success than Atatürk, Reza Shah advanced these ideas especially through a new secular school system and the military, and he created a secular legal system intended to replace Islamic courts. He abdicated and was replaced by his son, Mohammad Reza Pahlavi (1919–1980), in 1941, early in the British-Soviet occupation of the country. In the same year, the Iran Party was formed as a secular nationalist party opposed to the authoritarianism of the shah and to foreign interventionism. The Iran Party joined Islamist and leftist parties in the National Front, established in 1949 and led by the democratic reformer Muhammad Musaddiq (1881–1967). The National Front government of 1951–1953 was overthrown in a military coup supported by the United States and Great Britain, thus restoring effective authority to the shah.

SEE ALSO *Empire, Ottoman.*

BIBLIOGRAPHY

Abrahamian, Ervand. *Iran Between Two Revolutions.* Princeton, NJ: Princeton University Press, 1982.

Diekhoff, Alain. *Invention of a Nation: Zionist Thought and the Making of Modern Israel.* New York: Columbia University Press, 2003.

Khalidi, Rashid, Lisa Anderson, Muhammad Muslih, and Reeva S. Simon, eds. *The Origins of Arab Nationalism.* New York: Columbia University Press, 1991.

Khalidi, Rashid. *Palestinian Identity: The Construction of Modern National Consciousness.* New York: Columbia University Press, 1997.

Khoury, Philip S. *Syria and the French Mandate: The Politics of Arab Nationalism, 1920–1945.* Princeton, NJ: Princeton University Press, 1987.

Lewis, Bernard. *The Emergence of Modern Turkey,* 3rd ed. New York: Oxford University Press, 2002.

Massad, Joseph A. *Colonial Effects: The Making of National Identity in Jordan.* New York: Columbia University Press, 2001.

Salibi, Kamal. *A House of Many Mansions: The History of Lebanon Reconsidered.* Berkeley: University of California Press, 1988.

Simon, Reeva S. *Iraq Between the Two World Wars: The Militarist Origins of Tyranny*, updated edition. New York: Columbia University Press, 2004.

Weldon C. Matthews

SEGREGATION, RACIAL, AFRICA

The arrival of Europeans in southern Africa in 1487 set in motion a long period of upheaval that transformed the region and eventually led to white domination of the black population. Years of violent clashes between the Portuguese, Dutch, Germans, and numerous African peoples, Dutch settlers and the British, and the British and Africans left millions dead and black Africans subject to white laws and regulations. Foremost among these was segregation, expropriation of African property, the restricting of Africans' movement and activities within their own countries, and the forcing of blacks to relocate to special "reserves" apart from white society. Throughout the southern Africa region (South Africa, Swaziland, Lesotho, Botswana, Namibia, Mozambique, Angola, Zimbabwe, Malawi, and Zambia), whites claimed a monopoly over political power, the right to exploit local people economically, and eventually the right to determine where people lived and worked and the type of education they received.

From 1487 until the 1870s southern Africa was a hodgepodge of African kingdoms, white Afrikaner republics, and European colonies. However, by the late nineteenth century all of southern Africa's peoples fell within the domain of a European power. The segregation policies that transformed Africans from independent producers to squatters, wage laborers, and primarily rural-based female reproducers of laborers were first set out on the preindustrial frontier in the Afrikaner republics and in the British colony of Natal. In the Afrikaner republics, the principle was established that only those of white ancestry were eligible for citizenship rights, creating a white monopoly on political power; in Natal, policies of territorial segregation designated separate living areas for blacks and whites. Each group coexisted, with the British focused on commerce and trade and the Africans and the Afrikaners concerned with farming.

Developing economies and the need for cheap labor led to laws created by whites that legally separated races to the benefit of those of European descent and to the detriment of those of African descent. In 1809 the British introduced the Hottentot Code. This racially discriminatory legislation forced Khoikhoi and other free blacks to work for low wages. The law required that Africans carry passes stating where they lived and who their employers were. The law compelled

A Neighborhood in Soweto, South Africa. Soweto, a group of urban townships near Johannesburg, was built during South Africa's apartheid era. Many Soweto residents are poor and live in shacks in overcrowded neighborhoods like the one pictured here. © SERGE ATTAL/VISUM/THE IMAGE WORKS. REPRODUCED BY PERMISSION.

blacks to work for whites since whites issued the passes, and without a pass blacks could not move about freely.

In the late nineteenth century, when gold and diamonds were discovered in South Africa, and copper and other minerals, as well as rich agricultural lands, were encountered in other parts of southern Africa, white settlers established booming industries that relied heavily on low-paid black labor. These discoveries led to increased segregation and stratification between blacks and whites. To compel Africans to work in the migrant labor system, blacks throughout southern Africa were moved to reservations set aside as African homelands (sometimes called tribal trust lands, native purchase areas, or native reserves). Africans could not live outside the black areas without permission. The way they got permission was to work on a white-owned farm or in one of the many mines.

Mine owners organized a system to recruit and distribute black migrant labor from neighboring colonies. In South Africa, legislation was passed that required blacks to carry a pass stating their legal entitlement to work in an area, whether or not they had completed their contractual obligations, and whether they could leave the city. The passes limited the mobility of the workers and thus their ability to seek better-paying jobs. Segregation policies affected the rights of Africans to own land, to live or travel where they chose, and to enjoy job security or the freedom to switch jobs, leading finally to a limit on black power in southern Africa.

In the twentieth century, segregation restricted Africans to dangerous, unskilled, low-paid jobs in mining and industry or to laboring on white-owned farms, while supervisory jobs in all economic sectors were held by highly paid whites. Africans went to extensive lengths to avoid working in the white economy with its embedded discriminatory practices. Expropriation and hardship were not enough to force African men into mining work or work on commercial farms. In an effort to coerce the men to work, artificial monetary needs, mostly in the form of hut taxes, were introduced into the economy. Taxes—which had to be paid in cash—were imposed by white law. Unable to raise the necessary cash for taxes through subsistence farming, African men were forced to sell their labor-power in a white-designed system of male migratory work. The white political system completely colonized the life-world of black Africans. There was little room for autonomy on the part of Africans. By the 1940s many rural areas were nearly dependent on migrant remittances.

The men migrated to work, leaving their families in the rural native reserves; men were paid barely subsistence wages. Whites assumed that women and children in the African homelands produced their own income through subsistence farming, so they did not pay African males enough to support their families. This kept African wages very low and ensured poverty in the rural areas. The black homelands became domestic labor reservoirs and were used as a backup for the men when they were sick or could no longer work in the mines or on the farms.

Throughout southern Africa, whites maintained attitudes of superiority, paternalistic benevolence, and social distance toward Africans. Segregationist policies, legitimated by scientific claims from biologists, anthropologists, and other experts provided whites with higher social status and enabled them to maintain economic and political advantages. The system forced separation of African families, disenfranchised Africans from governance of their nations, and forced men to work in prison-like compounds. In South Africa, contemptuous superiority toward Africans created the most drastic form of white domination. South Africa's policy of segregation stripped nonwhite residents of virtually all their civil rights, including the right to move freely within the country. Blacks were forced into separate schools, driven out of white areas in towns and cities, and made into a permanent underclass with no chance of improving their lives. Apartheid sanctioned discrimination against nonwhites until it was abolished in the 1990s.

SEE ALSO *Apartheid.*

BIBLIOGRAPHY

Beinart, William, and Saul Dubow, eds. *Segregation and Apartheid in Twentieth-Century South Africa.* New York: Routledge, 1995.

Butler, Anthony. *Contemporary South Africa.* New York: Palgrave Macmillan, 2004.

Byrnes, Rita M., ed. *South Africa: A Country Study,* 3rd ed. Washington, DC: Library of Congress, Federal Research Division, 1997.

Denoon, Donald, and Balaam Nyeko. *Southern Africa Since 1800,* rev. ed. London: Longman, 1984.

Lapping, Brian. *Apartheid: A History,* rev. ed. New York: George Braziller, 1990.

Sparks, Allister. *The Mind of South Africa.* New York: Knopf, 1990.

Vieira, Sergio, William G. Martin, and Immanuel Wallerstein. *How Fast the Wind? Southern Africa, 1975–2000.* Trenton, NJ: Africa World Press, 1992.

Zeleza, Paul T., and Dickson Eyoh, eds. *Encyclopedia of Twentieth-Century African History.* New York: Routledge, 2003.

Lorna Lueker Zukas

SELF-DETERMINATION, EAST ASIA AND THE PACIFIC

While most of the former colonies of Asia achieved independence in the decade after 1945, only in the 1970s did the smaller, more remote and resource-poor colonies of Oceania gain sovereignty. Decolonization, however, did not satisfy all nationalist aspirations, and not all possessions have become independent states.

In Indonesia, for example, a secession movement in the Moluccas in 1949 proved unsuccessful; support for independence remains strong with both the local and diasporic populations. In the 1990s, pro-independence movements gained ground in Aceh (on the island of Sumatra) and in West Papua (on the island of New Guinea), although Indonesian authorities used military force to repress these contestatory movements. Only in East Timor did the campaign for independence succeed. The former Portuguese colony was annexed by Indonesia in 1975, but a long clandestine struggle finally secured a referendum favorable to independence. The Indonesian army and local anti-independence militias thereupon ravaged the territory, but intervention by United Nations troops allowed recognition of East Timor's sovereignty in 2002. The world's newest independent state faces formidable challenges of reconstruction, economic development, and the creation of a republican political culture.

Elsewhere in eastern Asia, the most prominent (and violent) movement for self-determination has occurred in the southern Philippines. In each of these cases, nationalist ideology has been based on ethnic, cultural, and regional differences between insurgent areas and the nation-state of which they sometimes unwillingly formed a part. Religious differences have pitted Christians in East Timor, the Moluccas, and West Papua against predominantly Muslim Indonesia, and stimulated Muslim sentiments in the largely Catholic Philippines. (Acehnese, who are Muslim, base their nationalism on the historical and cultural specificities of the region.)

Contemporary moves to self-determination in the Pacific islands have been most obvious in the French overseas territories, though there was a protracted, violent, and unsuccessful effort by Bougainville islanders to secede from Papua New Guinea. In New Caledonia, indigenous Melanesians undertook a campaign for independence that provoked strong "loyalist" reactions by descendants of settlers in the 1980s. Kidnapping, hostage taking, and assassination punctuated various attempts to solve the conflict, which ultimately resulted, in 1988, in the declaration of a moratorium on constitutional change for the next quarter century.

In French Polynesia, a similar but less intense and violent campaign brought together Polynesians in opposition to the French state and local elites. Both island groups remain integral parts of the French Republic with increased autonomy. Nationalist movements among Maoris in New Zealand and Polynesians in Hawaii have managed some political and cultural gains, but without major constitutional changes. West Papuans, who are Melanesian, see their efforts to win self-determination as part of a wider struggle by native populations of Oceania. Several island groups, particularly in Micronesia, have meanwhile opted for continuing formal ties with the United States, the former administering power. Throughout Oceania, rebel movements have based their ideologies on indigenous culture and heritage, Western-style nationalism and constitutionalism, and, in some cases, at least until the 1990s, vaguely Marxist analyses of economic exploitation. Christian ideals have been incorporated into the discourse of self-determination in a region where religion continues to play a strong role.

The boundaries of most Southeast Asian and island Pacific states are inherited from the colonial epoch, and populations seldom form homogeneous nations. The cohabitation of Europeans and indigenous peoples in New Zealand, New Caledonia, and Hawaii, of islanders and Indians in Fiji, of Malays and Chinese in Malaysia, and of a plethora of ethnic groups in such countries as Indonesia has inevitably created deep and abiding tensions. Political circumstances—most evident in the ideological and military clashes of the Korean War of the 1950s and Vietnam War of the 1960s and 1970s—are also linked with self-determination, state formation, and big-power intervention. The rise of a militantly political Islam and the resurgence of nationalism in such areas as West Papua, suggest renewed campaigns for self-determination, even while globalization continues to effect changes throughout the region.

SEE ALSO *Decolonization, East Asia and Pacific; French Polynesia; Moluccas.*

BIBLIOGRAPHY

Aldrich, Robert. *France and the South Pacific since 1940.* Honolulu: University of Hawaii, 1993.

Dunn, James. *East Timor: A Rough Passage to Independence,* 3rd ed. Double Bay, New South Wales: Longville Books, 2003.

King, Peter. *West Papua and Indonesia since Suharto: Independence, Autonomy or Chaos?* Kensington: University of New South Wales, 2004.

Robert Aldrich

SELF-STRENGTHENING MOVEMENTS, EAST ASIA AND THE PACIFIC

In the nineteenth century, the self-strengthening movement represented a common strategy among East Asian countries facing the challenge of Western imperialism. In China, Japan, and Korea, self-strengthening programs signaled a compromise between conservatives who longed for a return to Confucian tradition and radicals who embraced wholesale westernization.

The slogan "Eastern ethics and Western science" popularized by the Japanese samurai-scholar Sakuma Shōzan (1811–1864), and the distinction between base *(ti)* and utility *(yong)* articulated by the Chinese scholar-official Zhang Zhidong (1837–1909), indicate an implicit assumption among advocates of self-strengthening that culture and technology could be compartmentalized. The goals of self-strengthening—creating institutions and procedures for handling foreign affairs and acquiring Western technology to build up the military and industrial bases of the country—would not affect the fundamental nature or character of the national culture. Indeed, the ultimate purpose of self-strengthening, its sponsors insisted, was to protect the national essence by using Western techniques.

Among the East Asian countries, Japan emerged the strongest as a result of self-strengthening. Its long history of cultural borrowing and the tradition of Dutch learning provided precedents for learning from foreigners. Continuing with this practice, the Tokugawa shogunate created the Institute for the Investigation of Barbarian Books in 1857 and sponsored study-abroad expeditions. The immediate task was to strengthen Japan's military capabilities and land fortifications, which had grown weak after two centuries of relative peace. Embodying the spirit of the self-strengthening movement, the acquisition and application of Western knowledge and methods were accompanied by moral exhortations to strictly follow Confucian ethics. As Japan's self-strengthening program accelerated and the emperor system became the basis of the new national ideology, however, Japan's modernization program shed its Confucian veneer and opened the door to sweeping changes.

In contrast, the self-strengthening movement in China did not trigger dramatic transformations; the orthodox conservatives were too entrenched in the Qing bureaucracy and stymied any reforms they felt threatened the Confucian basis of Chinese civilization. Consequently, the Chinese self-strengthening movement was limited and gradual. Beginning with the Tongzhi Restoration in 1861, the Qing court initiated a program to modernize the military and create new institutions to deal directly with the foreign powers, the most notable of which was the Zongli Yamen (Office of General Management). In later years, the self-strengthening movement broadened to include modernization programs in transportation, communications, mining, and light industry.

Less cohesive and successful in Korea and elsewhere in the Pacific, self-strengthening movements nevertheless appealed to traditionalists who recognized the urgency of adopting Western techniques if they wished to preserve their civilization. Self-strengtheners did not promote assimilation, for they consciously sought to preserve the core of the original culture; East and West were never to merge. And although they relied on foreigners for advice and direction and were labeled traitors to their culture by those resistant to any interaction with the West, self-strengtheners were not collaborators; during the self-strengthening movement the countries in East Asia retained their territorial sovereignty.

SEE ALSO *Anticolonialism, East Asia and the Pacific; Self-Determination, East Asia and the Pacific.*

BIBLIOGRAPHY

Cumings, Bruce. *Korea's Place in the Sun: A Modern History.* New York: Norton, 1997.

Schirokauer, Conrad, and Donald N. Clark. *Modern East Asia: A Brief History.* Belmont, CA: Thomson/Wadsworth, 2004.

Tsunoda, Ryusaku, Wm. Theodore de Bary, and Donald Keene, eds. *Sources of Japanese Tradition,* vol. 2. New York: Columbia University Press, 1958.

Lisa Tran

SENGHOR, LÉOPOLD SÉDAR
1906–2001

Born on October 9, 1906, in Joal-la-Portugaise to a Serer father (Basile Diogoye Senghor) and a Fulani/Peul mother (Gnilane Bakhoum), Léopold Sédar Senghor was arguably Africa's best-known poet-statesman of the twentieth century. In 1922 he enrolled in a Dakar seminary (Collège Libermann) with the hope of becoming a Catholic priest, but his ambition ended abruptly when he was expelled for participating in a protest against racism. After graduating from high school in 1928, he received a scholarship to France where he studied French literature at the prestigious École Normale Supérieure. In 1932 he became a French citizen. He taught in French schools before serving in an all-African unit in the French army during World War II. Mobilized in 1940, he was captured by the Germans and spent eighteen months in a detention camp. In 1948 Senghor married Ginette Eboué, with whom he had two children; when that marriage ended in divorce in 1957, he married a French woman, Colette Hubert, from Verson, Normandy.

Senghor participated actively in the vibrant intellectual environment of "Black Paris" in the 1930s, when black students, artists, and writers from Africa, North America, and the Caribbean were reclaiming and reaffirming their heritage and defining their identities. In 1934 Senghor and two fellow students—Aimé Césaire and Léon Damas—founded the review *L'Etudiant noir* in which they first elaborated the concept of *negritude,* which evolved into an intellectual, cultural, and artistic movement—the Negritude Movement. In 1947 Senghor collaborated with Alioune Diop to found the journal *Présence africaine.* A gifted poet and prolific writer, Senghor produced numerous volumes of poetry and essays. Some of the themes explored in his writings include the identity crisis of the African intellectual, cultural *métissage* (cross-pollination), and the possibility of a universal culture based on a common humanity.

Senghor's political career began in 1945 when he was elected as a Senegalese representative in the French Assembly, where he served until 1958. In 1956 he was elected mayor of Thiès, Senegal. He became president of the legislative assembly of the Mali Federation in 1959 and the president of the newly formed Republic of Senegal in 1960. Senghor was drawn to pan-Africanism and a brand of African socialism that reserved a major role for the state, particularly in the economy. He worked vigorously for the creation of a pan-African organization—the Organization of African Unity—in 1963. He was, however, criticized for replacing the multiparty system in Senegal with an authoritarian one-party system that monopolized power and stifled debate and opposition.

Senghor registered many firsts in his long life and brilliant career. He was the first African to successfully complete the grammar *agrégation* (1935), which qualified him to teach in the French university system; the first African to be elected into the French Academy (1984); and the first president of Senegal (1960–1980). His extensive work in politics, arts, and culture earned him many international awards. After retiring from public life, he spent most of his time in Verson, where he died on December 20, 2001, at age ninety-five.

SEE ALSO *Negritude.*

BIBLIOGRAPHY

Bâ, Sylvia Washington. *The Concept of Negritude in the Poetry of Léopold Sédar Senghor.* Princeton, NJ: Princeton University Press, 1973.

Benoist, Joseph Roger de. *Léopold Sédar Senghor.* Paris: Beauchesne, 1998.

Girault, Jacques and Bernard Lecherbonnier. *Léopold Sédar Senghor: Africanité, universalité.* Paris: L'Harmattan, 2002.

Mezu, Sebastian Okechukwu. *The Poetry of Léopold Sédar Senghor.* London: Heinemann, 1973.

Nkashama, Pius Ngandu. *Négritude et poétique: une lecture de l'œuvre critique de Léopold Sédar Senghor.* Paris: L'Harmattan, 1992.

Senghor, Léopold Sédar. *Chants d'ombres.* Paris: Éditions du Seuil, 1945.

Senghor, Léopold Sédar. *Anthologie de la nouvelle poésie nègre et malgache de langue française.* Paris: Presses Universitaires de France, 1948.

Senghor, Léopold Sédar. *Hosties noires.* Paris: Éditions du Seuil, 1948.

Senghor, Léopold Sédar. *Chants pour Naëtt.* Paris: P. Seghers, 1949.

Senghor, Léopold Sédar. *Éthiopiques.* Paris: Éditions du Seuil, 1956.

Senghor, Léopold Sédar. *Nation et voie africaine du socialisme.* Paris: Présence Africaine, 1961.

Senghor, Léopold Sédar. *Nocturnes.* Paris: Éditions du Seuil, 1961.

Senghor, Léopold Sédar. *Liberté.* Paris: Éditions du Seuil, 1964.

Senghor, Léopold Sédar. *Les Fondements de l'africanité; ou, Négritude et arabité.* Paris: Présence Africaine, 1967.

Senghor, Léopold Sédar. *Négritude arabisme et Francité: Réflexions sur le problème de la culture.* Beyrouth, Lebanon: Éditions Dar Al-Kitab Allubnani, 1969.

Senghor, Léopold Sédar. *Ce que je crois : Négritude, Francité et civilisation de l'universel.* Paris: B. Grasset, 1988.

Senghor, Léopold Sédar. *Le dialogue des cultures.* Paris: Seuil, 1993.

Spleth, Janice, ed. *Critical Perspectives on Léopold Sédar Senghor.* Washington, DC: Three Continents, 1991.

Vaillant, Janet G. *Black, French, and African: A Life of Léopold Sédar Senghor.* Cambridge, MA: Harvard University Press, 1990.

Venev, Yvan Dimitrov. *La première bibliographie mondiale de Léopold Senghor, membre de l'Académie Française.* Paris: Y. Venev, 1999.

Obioma Nnaemeka

SEPOY

Derived from the Persian word *sipahi*, meaning "regular soldier," the term *sepoy* designates Indian infantrymen trained and equipped to European standards and employed in the armies of the East India Company and later the British Crown. A significant majority of the East India Company's armed forces from the middle decades of the eighteenth century, sepoys were absolutely crucial to the expansion, consolidation, and maintenance of the company's interests in India and Asia. As the British diplomat, soldier, and historian John Malcolm (1769–1833) wrote in 1826, "Our government of India is essentially military and our means of preserving and improving our possessions through the operation of our civil institutions depends on our wise and politic exercise of that military power upon which the whole fabric rests."

The sepoy was the foundation of this military power, and the mutiny that sparked the great Revolt of 1857 did not alter this reality. Though the proportion of sepoys to European troops was reduced thereafter, they remained majority participants in every campaign undertaken by the Indian Army through 1947.

From the early seventeenth century, the East India Company employed modest numbers of Indians as an economical solution to the need for guards and escorts, particularly in troubled times. However, these troops should not be confused with sepoys, since they were neither trained nor equipped in European fashion. The East India Company's first sepoy units were raised in

1748 by Major "Stringer" Lawrence (1697–1775). He simply emulated the French, who had shown the potential of Indian troops that were trained and equipped to European standards in the Anglo-French struggle over the Carnatic (1744–1748), a region in southeast India.

Sepoys proved to be cheaper than European recruits, as well as morally and physically superior. Thanks to the extensive military manpower market that existed in India, especially in the north, potential sepoys were also easy to find. From their perspective, service in the East India Company's armies was attractive because it provided relatively high and regular income, as well as certain legal and social privileges. These factors, combined with perceived threats from European rivals and local potentates, ensured that company armies became increasingly reliant on sepoys from the 1750s.

The British military leader and colonial administrator Robert Clive (1725–1774) was quick to appreciate their value: sepoys comprised two-thirds of the troops at his command during the heroic defense of Arcot (1751). It was he who raised the first battalion of sepoys, known as the "Lal Paltan" (red coats). Clive also took the innovative step of introducing three European officers to train and command each sepoy battalion. His expansion and reorganization of the sepoys paid considerable dividends at Plassey (1757) and Buxar (1764), where sepoy-dominated forces won the victories that made the East India Company a territorial power in Bengal. From this point forward there existed a profound disparity between the number of sepoys and the number of Europeans in the company's armies. By 1782 to 1783 the ratio was four to one. In 1805 it was six to one. As of 1856 it was nearly nine to one.

The prevalence of sepoys in the East India Company's armed forces made them the most significant military contributors to the expansion of company authority through the Indian Subcontinent. Sepoys participated in the campaigns against Mysore (concluded in 1799), as well as the long struggle against the Marathas (concluded in 1818). They were equally important in the conquest of the Sind (1843), the Punjab (1845–1849), and Awadh (1856). The systematic reduction of these regions enabled the growth of the East India Company's armies to 350,000 in 1856 by providing pools of newly unemployed, experienced soldiers from which to recruit.

Even as the process of expansion continued, sepoy units were deployed to consolidate the East India Company's authority in the face of "civil" disturbances, including communal disputes, agricultural and economic disaffection, succession crises in princely states, banditry, and religious or political movements bent on destroying or diminishing the company's influence. Nor was their

Sepoys in their Native Costume. *Sepoys were Indian infantrymen trained and equipped to European standards and employed in the armies of the East India Company and later the British Crown during the eighteenth and nineteenth centuries.* © CORBIS. REPRODUCED BY PERMISSION.

utility restricted to India. As early as the 1762 attack on Manila in the Philippines, sepoys were deployed overseas. From that point forward they were instrumental in the expansion of the East India Company's, as well as Britain's, power in the region. They provided the backbone of the forces used to secure Sumatra (1789), Ceylon (1795), Egypt (1800–1801), Java and Mauritius (1810–1811), Burma (1823–1824 and 1852), Aden (1839), Afghanistan (1839–1842), and the treaty ports in China (1839–1842).

In spite of all this, the British displayed a marked ambivalence toward the sepoys practically from the moment of their incorporation into the East India Company's armies. While most British officers praised the sepoys for their valor, discipline, regularity, and loyalty, certain company policies betrayed a degree of mistrust. When the first sepoy units were formed in 1748 they were excluded from the artillery, a proscription that was reaffirmed in 1770. Likewise, Clive's division of the

Bengal army into three separate brigades (1765), each with a sepoy and European element, has been interpreted as an attempt to divide and rule by ensuring that the sepoys would not form a single corporate identity. Moreover, payment and seniority policies placed sepoys on the lowest rung of the company's regular infantry forces, beneath Crown troops seconded to the company and the European troops in company service. Such inequities contributed to the series of sepoy mutinies that began in 1764 and culminated in 1857.

Pay became a particular point of acrimony from the 1820s, when the East India Company's position seemed secure enough to warrant a reduction in military expenditures. This meant stagnant salaries and the reduction of field pay, which lowered real wages and threatened the social standing of sepoys. Just as serious in terms of long-term sepoy disaffection was the issue of promotion. From the moment Clive introduced European officers into sepoy battalions in 1757, the status of Indian officers declined. The army reforms of 1796, which mandated twenty-two European officers for each sepoy battalion, effectively ended opportunities for promotions to positions of command.

The reforms of 1824 confirmed this situation. Continuing resentment over pay scales; changes in the conditions of service insensitive to sepoy religious and cultural concerns, such as those that sparked the Vellore mutiny of 1806; and the continued exclusion of sepoys from higher ranks provided fertile ground for more specific grievances to take root. While the East India Company's policies were intended to put the army that had won and maintained its empire on a more secure footing, they in fact progressively alienated the sepoys who were that army's mainspring, which ultimately sparked the mutiny of 1857.

SEE ALSO *Empire, British; Indian Army; Indian Revolt of 1857.*

BIBLIOGRAPHY

Alavi, Seema. *The Sepoys and the Company: Tradition and Transition in Northern India, 1770–1830.* Delhi: Oxford University Press, 1995.

Guy, Alan J., and Peter B. Boyden, eds. *Soldiers of the Raj: The Indian Army, 1600–1947.* London: National Army Museum, 1997.

Longer, V. *Red Coats to Olive Green: A History of the Indian Army, 1600–1974.* Bombay, India: Allied Publishers, 1974.

Malcolm, Sir John. *The Political History of India from 1784–1823.* London: J. Murray, 1826.

Menezes, S. L. *Fidelity and Honour: The Indian Army from the Seventeenth to the Twenty-First Century.* New Delhi, India: Penguin, 1993.

Singh, Madan Paul. *Indian Army Under the East India Company.* New Delhi, India: Sterling, 1976.

Chris Hagerman

SEX AND SEXUALITY

The various economic, social, and political underpinnings of European colonialism created a powerful psychosexual residue that asserted itself as a driving ambiguous impulse in the imperial project. Sex was the core of vulnerability at the center of colonialism. It undermined the presumed gender, race, and class or rank categories upon which colonizers constructed individuals' identity, rights, obligations, and behavior.

Colonizers and the colonized read sexuality from their own cultural scripts, and because they usually had very different ways of defining the meanings of sexuality, sex became a source of confusion, contention, manipulation, and transformation. Colonizers attempted to use sex with colonized people for pleasure, economic or political profit, and as a means of signifying their superior status; colonized people, caught in the economic, political, and often physical constraints imposed on them by colonizers, sometimes used their sexuality to gain favor or advantage with colonizers. In that process, both colonizers and the colonized labeled unfamiliar sexual characteristics and behaviors abnormal, used them as evidence of inferiority, and redefined themselves by claiming to be untainted by those characteristics or behaviors.

Through the coercive nature of colonial domination, colonizers sought to create a sexualized native bereft of will, desire, or gaze. This native was to be a tabula rasa for European sexual imaginings. But desire and the sexual gaze moved in two directions. Because the colonizer and colonized desired one another—even when laws or authorities prohibited such desire—the very characteristics and behaviors that were supposedly markers of inferiority became signifiers of exotic allure and therefore, perversely, emblems of superior sexual appeal and limited empowerment.

In Europe, during the entire colonial period, Europeans understood sexuality very differently from most of the people they colonized. Europeans' understandings were based on patriarchal hierarchies of gender, class, and race that placed men superior to women; aristocrats superior to common, indentured, and enslaved men; and white men superior to Moor, oriental, black, or savage men. In general, aristocratic white men encoded those differences of status in religious and civil laws that regulated rights, obligations, and behavior. Clothing and public behavior (also frequently regulated by law) exemplified status and signaled how men and women of different classes and races were to interact; it also indicated who was sexually available or exploitable. In practice if not in law, white aristocratic men had complete sexual liberty—even to the extent of sex with other men if they so chose—with very little repercussion.

Women and lesser-status men in Europe were vulnerable to the sexual demands of aristocratic men because they were politically and economically dependent on aristocratic men. Aristocratic white women were expected to remain virgins until they married, were usually only sexually available for marriage through explicit negotiations with their families, and were only sexually exploitable by members of the aristocracy. Common, indentured, and enslaved women could be exploited by both members of their own classes and the aristocracy, and were, in legal terms, available to anyone who wanted them or who they wanted. Lesser-status men could also be sexually exploited and, like their women, sometimes used that vulnerability to gain opportunity; they could sell sex or trade it for advantage. Courtesans, prostitutes, and an underground of establishments that catered to male same-sex eroticism and sex provided aristocratic men with a richly diverse sexual preserve.

Religious law dictated celibacy as the ideal state for Christians, and recognized only procreation as the valid justification for sexual relations within marriage. Men and women rarely conformed to those expectations. Although church officials refined confession to be a mechanism for revealing and discouraging unsanctioned sexual activity, confession became, too, a way for people to relieve themselves of the guilt and shame of perceived illicit sexuality. The common denominator of sexuality for all classes was that respectability and the full rights of adulthood could only be achieved through heterosexual marriage, but both men and women assumed some degree of secrecy and license was necessary in the various permutations of their sexual world.

Most of the people Europeans colonized held different attitudes toward sex because they were patrilineal or matrilineal, not patriarchal, and their identities, rights, obligations, and behaviors—including sexual interaction—were based on kinship and lineage rather than strict male control of political and economic power and individual behavior. While lineage, age, and gender defined identity and regulated behavior, sometimes hierarchically, in general both men and women had greater choice about what they did, how they dressed, and even what gender they were than Europeans did. In many matrilineal and patrilineal societies boys and girls could choose to take on the roles of men or women regardless of their biological sex, and in some societies they were granted sacred or third sex status if they did so. That initial freedom of choice was often reinforced by sexual

liberty prior to marriage, polygamy, and socially sanctioned participation in same-sex physical relationships even, with discretion, after marriage. Like people in patriarchal European societies, men and women in matrilinies and patrilinies could only achieve the full rights of adulthood through heterosexual marriage, but privacy rather than secrecy generally shaped their sexual world.

In the early colonial period (1450 to roughly 1800), when Europeans, Africans, Pacific Island peoples, Americans, South Asians, and Australians encountered one another in the lopsided relations of colonization, they read each other's personal appearance and behavior through their understandings of sexuality. Europeans' unequal layering of sexual rights and privileges permeated their interaction with the people they colonized. They exported their sexual practices, beliefs, and hierarchy to colonized societies. Europeans understood elaborate dress as a sign of high status that implied sexual exclusivity; they read nakedness as primitivity, sexual invitation, and promiscuity. The fact that African, Pacific Island, and American women had more sexual freedom than European women seemed to confirm European beliefs of native sexual promiscuity, and when high status men offered them women for sexual use those beliefs were reinforced, despite the fact that European men also trafficked in sexual favors.

European men were drawn to their own erotic projection of native sexuality because it reverberated with the stereotypes of Middle-Eastern harems and dancing girls, and the silent and accommodating boys and girls of the Far East, both known to European men through their own travels or, more prevalently, the tales that such men told about their adventures. They raved about the sexual appetites of colonized women and the pleasures to be found with them, and they also remarked on the beauty, virility, and manliness of colonized men. The explicit and implicit sexual praise they lavished on the bodies and behaviors of the people they colonized filtered back to Europe in contradictory ways. Colonized people were considered savage and primitive—and therefore uncivilized—but also they seemed to represent a pure and even noble connection with physical pleasure and freedom.

Colonized people read little more into clothing than the fact that Europeans rarely bathed and seemed dirty, but they welcomed Europeans as sexual equals, frequently forming emotional as well as physical bonds with them and sometimes marrying. In Africa, the Pacific, and the Americas, European men insinuated themselves into indigenous cultures by forming loving and often long-lasting relationships with colonized women and men. Those relationships eventually gave birth to an aristocracy of children of mixed racial descent who became minor bureaucrats, diplomats, interpreters, and merchants, often educated in

European schools. Such offspring frequently became part of a cosmopolitan elite that locked indigenous and European colonial cultures together.

In the 1740s in the British North American colony of Georgia, for example, Mary Musgrove (1700–1763), the daughter of a white man and a Creek woman, was a major landowner, trader, and negotiator on the Creek-Carolina border. Alexander McGillivray (1759–1793), the son of a Creek mother and a Scotch father, became a leader of the Creek Indians. He preferred to speak with his people through interpreters, claiming that he could not speak the Creek language, and he chose as his *tustenegee*, the highest Creek military office, a Frenchman, Leclerc Milfort, who was married to McGillivray's sister. During the U.S. Civil War (1861–1865) and its aftermath in Louisiana, the role of the French-descended, mixed-race community became a point of contention as efforts to limit the social, political, and economic mobility of newly freed people was disrupted, and these propertied, educated, and articulate elites represented the interests of the larger African-American community.

As colonial settlements stabilized and Europeans tried to establish more political and economic control of their colonies, European elites became alarmed at the number of European men who had adopted indigenous dress and behaviors, abandoning any pretense of being civilized and threatening the racial, cultural, economic, and political security of the colonies. Most colonial governments instituted strict anti-miscegenation laws to prohibit racial unity mixing and keep white men within colonial boundaries except for purposes of trade and military operations.

Though they rarely prosecuted elite white men for the rape or sexual abuse of colonized women, they fined and whipped white women and lesser-status white men for breaking those sexual laws, and sometimes castrated or killed colonized men. Rape or sexual coercion of colonized women became a way of demonstrating to colonized men that they were powerless. European elites intended such laws to reestablish the hierarchies of domination and power that were the essence of manhood and womanhood in Europe, but forbidden sex with exotic, primitive, and especially dark-skinned colonized people also became an exercise of rebellion against that domination.

By the nineteenth century the lure of sex with "Others" (those of different race, or economic and social status) was firmly embedded in European, Euro-American, and colonized psyches. European and Euro-American men—and women, though it was more dangerous—sought out sexual experiences with the colonized Others, which made rape and sexual coercion commonplace, and fed a growing sex industry among colonized populations. Colonized people saw sexual activity with colonizers as an opportunity for social, racial, and economic mobility. Colonized men and women recognized prostitution as a viable, often lucrative, and sometimes emancipatory career, and sought European men and women as sexual partners to improve their status and reassure themselves that they were equals to European men and women.

Sex with Others had not only the value of immediate experiential gratification, but also a patina of enhanced prowess for both men and women. They seldom recognized the ambivalent results of their desires, or the ways enacting them transformed both the worlds they came from and the worlds they were trying to inhabit. European and Euro-American men's taste for Other women masqueraded as rescue, conquering-hero, and freedom-from-restraint fantasies, but the women with whom they had sex often rejected any connection that was not purely financial, and used that income to buy themselves lives that were more European. Colonized people also flocked to imperial homelands to demonstrate their ability to be equals, in part by sexual liaison or marriage with white Europeans or Americans.

Sex subverted the imperial project. Colonizers attempted to transform colonies into replications of European and American political, economic, and social hierarchies, where whites dominated indigenous elites, and both white elites and indigenous elites dominated the urban and rural hinterlands of potential laborers and sex-workers. But Europeans adopted (often subconsciously) primitive styles, art, and fabrics as marks of their sophistication, and lost confidence in their repressive sexuality and sexual mores if not their sense of racial and cultural superiority. Europe's transformation is most memorably demonstrated with Sara Bartman (1790–1816). She was a twenty-year-old Khoikhoi captured by Englishmen in South Africa in 1810 and exhibited like an animal in European capitals as an example of African women's bodily makeup, her abnormally voluptuous buttocks receiving particular attention. She attracted and titillated crowds of European men and women whose horrified fascination was paralleled by the appearance of the bustle in the 1870s, which exaggerated women's posteriors as the height of feminine allure. White men in England and the United States began to worry publicly about their loss of manhood and praise primitive savagism as a mark of real manhood when recurring slave insurrections, the Indian Mutiny (1857), the post-U.S. Civil War emancipation of slaves, and the South African Boer War (1899–1902), among many other revolts, threatened notions of white male supremacy across the colonial world.

The irony of colonization is that it made primitive and exotic the hallmarks of a pure, undisturbed idea of humanity for Euro-American and North Atlantic cultures. Native American men became symbols of environmental unity, Asian men the embodiment of spiritual balance, and African men the personification of masculine virility; women of those colonies became the epitome of all that was proud, feminine, and sexually satisfying. Sex and sexuality in the colonial arena fundamentally remained yet another avenue of European control, determination, and domination of colonized people, but the appropriation and valorization of native bodies and cultures and the incremental subversion of imperial European ideas of racial, sexual, economic, political, and cultural superiority transformed sexual belief and practice in ways that remain etched on the lives of the former colonizers and formerly colonized to this day.

SEE ALSO *Imperialism, Gender and.*

BIBLIOGRAPHY

Aldrich, Robert. *Colonialism and Homosexuality.* London and New York: Routledge, 2003.

Aldrich, Robert and Garry Wotherspoon. *Who's Who in Gay and Lesbian History: From Antiquity to World War II.* London; New York: Routledge, 2001.

Axtell, James, ed. *The Indian Peoples of Eastern America: A Documentary History of the Sexes.* New York: Oxford University Press, 1981.

Bates, David. *Photography and Surrealism: Sexuality, Colonialism, and Social Dissent.* New York: I.B. Tauris, 2004.

Beckles, Hilary McD. *Natural Rebels: A Social History of Enslaved Black Women in Barbados.* New Brunswick, NJ: Rutgers, 1989.

Brown, Kathleen, *Good Wives, Nasty Wenches, and Anxious Patriarchs: Gender, Race, and Power in Colonial Virginia.* Chapel Hill: University of North Carolina Press, 1996.

Crompton, Louis. *Homosexuality and Civilization.* Cambridge, MA: Belknap Press of Harvard University Press, 2003.

D'Emilio, John, and Estelle B. Freedman. *Intimate Matters: A History of Sexuality in America.* New York: Harper and Row, 1988.

Davis, Angela. "Reflections on the Black Women's Role in the Community of Slaves." *The Black Scholar* 3(4): 2–16.

Dorsey, Joseph. *Slave Traffic in the Age of Abolition: Puerto Rico, West Africa, and the Non-Hispanic Caribbean, 1815–1859.* Gainesville: University Press of Florida, 2003.

Duberman, Martin, Martha Vicinus, and George Chancy Jr. *Hidden from History: Reclaiming the Gay and Lesbian Past.* New York: New American Library, 1989.

Fanon, Frantz. *Black Skin, White Masks.* Translated by Charles Lam Markman. New York: Grove Press, 1967.

Fischer, Kirsten. *Suspect Relations: Sex, Race, and Resistance in Colonial North Carolina.* Ithaca, NY: Cornell University Press, 2001.

Foucault, Michel. *The History of Sexuality: An Introduction.* New York: Random House, 1978.

Fradenburg, Louise, and Carla Freccero. *Pre-modern Sexualities.* New York: Routledge, 1996.

Gilman, Sander. *Difference and Pathology: Stereotypes of Sexuality, Race, and Madness.* Ithaca, NY: Cornell University Press, 1985.

Hayes, Jarrod. *Queer Nations: Marginal Sexualities in the Maghreb.* Chicago: University of Chicago Press, 2000.

Herman, Eleanor. *Sex with Kings: 500 Years of Adultery, Power, Rivalry, and Revenge.* New York: Morrow, 2004.

Higgins, Patrick, ed. *A Queer Reader.* London: Fourth Estate, 1993.

Jacobs, Harriet. *Incidents in the Life of a Slave Girl.* West Berlin, NJ: Townsend Press, 2004.

Kimmel, Michael. *Manhood in America: A Cultural History.* New York: Free Press, 1996.

Lancaster, Roger N., and Micaela di Leonardo, eds. *The Gender Sexuality Reader: Culture, History, Political Economy.* New York: Routledge, 1997.

Lavrin, Asunsion. *Sexuality and Marriage in Colonial Latin America.* Lincoln: University of Nebraska Press, 1989.

Lott, Eric. *Love & Theft: Blackface Minstrelsy and the American Working Class.* New York: Oxford University Press, 1993.

McClintock, Anne. *Imperial Leather: Race, Gender, and Sexuality in the Colonial Contest.* New York: Routledge, 1995.

McClintock, Anne, Aamir Mufti, and Ella Shohat. Social Text Collective, *Dangerous Liaisons: Gender, Nation, and Postcolonial Perspectives.* Minneapolis: University of Minnesota Press, 1997.

McLaurin, Melton A. *Celia, A Slave.* Athens: University of Georgia Press, 1991.

Nmanderson, Lenore and Margaret Jolly, eds. *Sites of Desire: Economies of Pleasure in Asia and the South Pacific.* Chicago: University of Chicago, 1997.

Pierson, Ruth Roach, and Nupur Chauduri, eds. *Nation, Empire, Colony: Historicizing Gender and Race.* Bloomington: Indiana University Press, 1998.

Prince, Mary. *The History of Mary Prince: A West Indian Slave.* London and New York: Penguin Books, 2001.

Rhodes, Colin. *Primitivism and Modern Art.* New York: Thames and Hudson, 1994.

Rubin, William, Kirk Varnedoe, and Philippe Peltier. *"Primitivism" in Twentieth Century Art: Affinity of the Tribal and the Modern.* New York: Museum of Modern Art; Boston: New York Graphic Society Books, 1984.

Said, Edward, *Orientalism.* New York: Pantheon Books, 1978.

Stoler, Ann Laura. *Race and the Education of Desire: Foucault's History of Sexuality and the Colonial Order of Things.* Durham, NC: Duke University Press, 1995.

Stoler, Ann Laura. *Carnal Knowledge and Imperial Power: Race and the Intimate in Colonial Rule.* Berkeley: University of California Press, 2002.

Williams, Walter. *Spirit and the Flesh: Sexual Diversity in American Indian Culture.* Boston: Beacon Press, 1986.

Karen Taylor

SHANDONG PROVINCE

Shandong Peninsula (156,008 square kilometers, or 60,235 square miles) borders the Yellow River, the Bohai Sea, and the Yellow Sea, making it northern China's most prosperous coastal trade center, with excellent natural ports at Weihaiwei and Qingdao. Historically, Shandong was home to the Shang dynasty (1766–1122 B.C.E.), the earliest Chinese state, and was the birthplace of Confucius (ca. 551–479 B.C.E.), China's most famous philosopher and teacher, as well as the fifth century B.C.E. Sun Wu (better known as Sunzi or "Master Sun"), the author of the classic military treatise *The Art of War*.

Although Japan invaded Shandong during the Sino-Japanese War (1894–1895), Shandong was not part of the Shimonseki Peace Treaty ending that war. However, in the 1895 "Triple Intervention," Germany, Russia, and France blocked Japan's claim for a concession in Manchuria's Liaodong Peninsula, to the north of Shandong. Soon afterward, in 1897, two German missionaries were killed in Shandong. Using this as a pretext, Germany forced China to cede Qingdao as an exclusive concession, establishing a port at Qingdao, constructing the Qingdao-Jinan railway, and opening coal mines to develop Shandong's industry.

With the beginning of World War I, Japan sought revenge against Germany for the Triple Intervention. It seized the Shandong concession in 1914, promising to return it to China after the war. In the 1919 Treaty of Versailles, the Allied Powers decided that Germany should first cede Shandong to Japan, which actually occupied Shandong, before Japan handed it over to China. While this decision assuaged the Japanese desire for vengeance against Germany, it outraged the Chinese, who considered it a "loss of face" that China—which also fought with the Allies in World War I—did not obtain the return of Shandong directly from Germany. The May Fourth movement was a student-led protest in Beijing demanding that China reject the Versailles Treaty.

Although the Chinese have long accused U.S. President Woodrow Wilson (1856–1924) of betraying China at the Paris Peace Conference, Wilson successfully negotiated a compromise with Japan guaranteeing Chinese sovereignty over the Shandong concession until Japan returned it in 1922. Rejecting this compromise, Chinese negotiators in Paris refused to sign the Treaty of Versailles, thus delaying the return of this concession to China. In 1921, while this question was still being negotiated, the Chinese Communist Party was founded, based in part on the Chinese desire to reclaim their lost colonial possessions.

Unfortunately, the resulting Nationalist-Communist United Front and then civil war during the late 1920s and early 1930s created the underlying conditions for the Soviet Union's increased influence in China, which spurred the Japanese reoccupation of Shandong during its 1937 invasion of China. Although the Nationalists temporarily reclaimed Shandong in 1945, the province changed hands for the final time in 1948, when it fell to the Communists, who proclaimed the creation of the People's Republic of China on October 1, 1949.

SEE ALSO *East Asia, American Presence in; East Asia, European Presence in; Empire, British, in Asia and Pacific; Empire, Japanese.*

BIBLIOGRAPHY

Buck, David D. *Urban Change in China: Politics and Development in Tsinan, Shantung, 1890–1949.* Madison: University of Wisconsin Press, 1978.

Elleman, Bruce A. *Wilson and China: A Revised History of the Shandong Question.* Armonk, NY: Sharpe, 2002.

Fifield, Russell H. *Woodrow Wilson and the Far East: The Diplomacy of the Shantung Question.* New York: Crowell, 1952. Reprint, Hamden, CT: Archon, 1965.

Myers, Ramon H. *The Chinese Peasant Economy: Agricultural Development in Hopei and Shantung, 1890–1949.* Cambridge, MA: Harvard University Press, 1970.

Schrecker, John E. *Imperialism and Chinese Nationalism: Germany in Shantung.* Cambridge, MA: Harvard University Press, 1971.

Bruce Elleman

SHANGHAI

Shanghai was not born in 1842 with the Nanjing Treaty that opened five Chinese port cities to foreign trade, nor in 1845 when the British were granted the right to establish a settlement (technically, "leased territory") in the outskirts of the walled city. For decades before these events, Shanghai had served as a major hub for trade between inland provinces and other port cities in China.

Located in the estuary of the Yangzi River, the main artery into inland China, Shanghai was connected to a vast hinterland through a dense network of rivers and canals that reached well into remote Sichuan Province 2,500 kilometers (about 1,550 miles) away. The Huangpu River that runs through the city provided a ready avenue both into the Yangzi River and Shanghai's surrounding area. In the foreign settlements, its bank—the Bund—became the place where westerners manifested their presence and power, with an impressive row of neocolonial-style multistoried buildings. With about 300,000 residents in the mid-nineteenth century,

Huangpu River in Shanghai, Circa 1920. *Shanghai was connected to a vast Chinese hinterland through a network of rivers and canals that reached well into remote Sichuan Province. The Huangpu River provided a ready avenue into both the Yangzi River and Shanghai's surrounding area.* **HULTON ARCHIVE/GETTY IMAGES. REPRODUCED BY PERMISSION.**

Shanghai was far from an empty land that awaited civilization from the outside.

There is no denying, however, that the inclusion of Shanghai into the extended trade routes that supplied Western countries with the materials and goods that their fast-growing economies consumed in increasing quantities changed the trajectory of the city. Initially, three groups of nationals obtained the right to open a settlement: British, American, and French. The first two merged their territory in 1863 to form the International Settlement, while the French, after some hesitation, eventually maintained their own autonomous concession. Both areas were repeatedly extended, up to 1914 when they reached their final limits. By that time, the two settlements had displaced the original walled city and its suburbs as the beating heart of Shanghai and its most populated section. Symbolically, but also to remove what was perceived as an obstacle to modernization, the local Chinese elites tore down the wall that confined the original city after China's 1911 revolution.

The population of Shanghai grew by leaps and bounds due to natural disasters, such as floods, but more often to wars and rebellions in the surrounding provinces. The Taiping Rebellion in the mid-1850s brought Shanghai's first wave of unwilling migrants. It marked the actual demographic takeoff of Shanghai. The internecine wars that raged between Chinese warlords in the 1920s, the 1931 Yangzi River flood, the Sino-Japanese War (1937–1945), and the civil war (1946–1949) all contributed to massive movements of population to Shanghai. Yet, population increase was also due to the growing attractiveness of the city. During the second half of the nineteenth century, Shanghai truly offered a "new frontier" that attracted all sorts of people from all over China, from poverty-driven peasants, to craftsmen and merchants. By the turn of the century, the emergence of a modern sector, both in industry and services (especially leisure), generated new waves of immigration. From half a million in 1852, the population of Shanghai jumped to 2 million in 1915, close to 4 million in 1937, and 5.5 million in 1948.

The change in population was not just quantitative. The establishment of the settlements brought migrants from a wide range of countries in the world, even if the larger communities came from Japan, the United Kingdom, the United States, and France. Yet, even with the Japanese that came to be Shanghai's largest foreign community by 1905, foreigners never represented a significant share of the population, ranging from a few thousand in the late nineteenth century to 150,000 at its peak in the 1940s. The Japanese alone formed a 100,000-strong community. Altogether, foreigners never represented more than 3.8 percent of Shanghai's total population. Nevertheless, by virtue of the privileges accorded in the treaties, foreigners enjoyed strong positions of power, at least formally, and benefited from conditions of life, even for the lower ranks of foreign residents, far better than in their home countries. The only foreigners who suffered from social debasement were the Russians who chose to flee the Bolshevik revolution and flocked in China's northeastern cities before moving to Shanghai. Deprived of diplomatic protection and extraterritorial rights, these Russian migrants struggled to make ends meet and by and large occupied menial jobs. In the late 1930s another group of Jewish refugees who had escaped Nazi persecution in Central Europe and Germany eventually settled in Shanghai. Because most of them had lost all resources, they also met a difficult fate until 1945.

The Land Regulations (1854) that defined the conditions for the establishment of settlements carried several provisions that foreigners took advantage of, especially in times of internal turmoil and the weakening of Chinese central power, to assert rights and powers far beyond those outlined in the original text. By virtue of the treaties, foreigners enjoyed extraterritorial rights that placed them beyond the reach of the Chinese legal and judicial system. In cases of misconduct or crime, foreigners were tried before their respective consular courts. But after the 1911 revolution, foreigners took full control of judicial administration, including the mixed courts where all Chinese residents were brought for civil and penal affairs.

By 1854, already, foreigners had taken over Shanghai's maritime customs, a major source of revenue for China. In the city proper, they set up their own municipal agencies: the Shanghai Municipal Council and the *conseil* (council) *municipal* in the International Settlement and French Concession respectively. When the Chinese organized their own local administrative bodies, first as elite-managed and district-based councils, then as a unified modern administration after 1927, the city ended up being administered by three different and unrelated municipal governments. This system was not dismantled until 1945.

The existence of foreign settlements in Shanghai created the conditions for the assertion of colonial power, though with limitations, but also an opportunity for complex games in politics, intellectual creativity, and social transformation. While formal power resided with Western institutions, the actual governance of the city relied very much on cooperation with local elites, especially the powerful Chinese merchant organizations that structured local society. Little could be achieved, in fact, without their support or against their will. Be it for tax matters, education, or in times of crisis and confrontation, foreigners had to deal with the Chinese representative organizations to implement a policy or to find a way out of a crisis.

Colonial power in Shanghai reached its limits with the existence of a well-organized polity within the broader context of a Chinese state that never lost its prerogatives and sovereignty, even with a weakened and at times powerless central administration. In other words, the system worked because both sides found it to its advantage to run a space that escaped the reach of a Chinese state perceived as predatory or simply unreliable.

Undoubtedly, Shanghai offered a place for great games. Chinese entrepreneurs benefited from an environment that was predictable in fiscal and legal matters. The protection afforded by the foreign settlements attracted a regular influx of capital that was available for investment in new economic ventures, especially industrial companies. The city developed sophisticated services that propelled it to the rank of first financial center in East Asia. Leisure and entertainment became not just a hallmark of Shanghai "glamour" but, in fact, an industry for its own sake on which thousands of people thrived.

From a plain commercial center in the mid-nineteenth century, Shanghai emerged as the major economic engine for the whole country, ranking first on all counts: industry, finance, and foreign trade. The wealth of the city, combined with the lack of strict controls on culture and education (except for political activism), also offered a breeding ground for the formation of a modern urban culture. Shanghai opened a whole new intellectual milieu that branched out in various directions with the creation of numerous modern schools and universities, the publication of a wide spectrum of journals and newspapers, the rise of a flourishing publication industry, the multiplication of associations of all sorts, and the broad circulation of new ideas among widening circles of the population. While still tainted with the suspicion of having been a Western Trojan horse in China, Shanghai played a major role in redefining the conditions of China's interaction with the outside world at the same time that it worked as a laboratory for the expression and construction of a modern Chinese society. After 1949 the city paid a dear price under the Communist regime, which literally milked Shanghai without making the necessary investments.

SEE ALSO *British American Tobacco Company; Chinese Revolutions; Compradors; Empire, Japanese; Extraterritoriality; Treaties, East Asia and the Pacific; Treaty Port System.*

BIBLIOGRAPHY

Bergère, Marie-Claire. *The Golden Age of the Chinese Bourgeoisie.* Cambridge, U.K.: Cambridge University Press, 1990.

Clifford, Nicholas R. *Spoilt Children of Empire: Westerners in Shanghai and the Chinese Revolution of the 1920s.* Berkeley: University of California Press, 1991.

Goodman, Bryna. *Native Place, City, and Nation: Regional Networks and Identities in Shanghai, 1853–1937.* Berkeley: University of California Press, 1995.

Henriot, Christian. *Prostitution in Shanghai. A Social History.* Cambridge, U.K. and New York: Cambridge University Press, 2001.

Lu, Hanchao. *Beyond the Neon Lights: Everyday Shanghai in the Early Twentieth Century,* Berkeley: University of California Press, 1999.

Wakeman, Frederic Jr., Yeh, Wen-hsin, eds. *Shanghai Sojourners.* Berkeley: University of California Press, 1993.

Christian Henriot

SHA'RAWI, HUDA
1879–1947

Huda Sha'rawi, an Egyptian nationalist, leading women's rights activist, philanthropist, and founder of the first Egyptian feminist organization, was also an inspiration to women throughout the Middle East and the colonized world.

Sha'rawi was born in Minya, Egypt, in 1879 to an elite Muslim family, and she was raised in Cairo. Her mother was a Turko-Circassian emigrant, and her father, who died when Sha'rawi was five years old, was a high-ranking government official. As was common for affluent Egyptian girls in the late nineteenth century, Sha'rawi studied French, her first language and the lingua franca of the elite, and music. Margot Badran, the translator of Sha'rawi's memoirs, notes that Sha'rawi was also allowed to participate in her younger brother's lessons on the Qur'an, Arabic, Turkish, and calligraphy.

Although many middle-class Egyptian girls attended primary schools by the turn of the century, most elite girls were still educated in their homes. Sha'rawi was an excellent student and memorized the Qur'an when she was nine years old, which was a remarkable achievement for a girl during this period. Sha'rawi was very close to her brother, and she was able to undertake more rigorous studies because of him, yet her memoirs indicate that her family's preferential treatment of her brother afflicted Sha'rawi throughout her childhood. Moreover, she was traumatized at the age of thirteen when her mother arranged Sha'rawi's marriage to an older man without her knowledge.

However, circumstances permitted Sha'rawi to suspend her marriage until she was twenty-one. During the interim, Sha'rawi became friends with Eugénie Le Brun, a Frenchwoman who had married an Egyptian. Along with the Egyptian elite's partiality for all things Western (save colonialism), Le Brun extended Sha'rawi's exposure to Western-oriented feminism. Badran suggests that Le Brun's influence contributed to Sha'rawi's unveiling in 1923 after returning from an international feminist conference. The removing of her face-veil symbolized Sha'rawi's unapologetic entry into the male-dominated public sphere and her determination to break traditional gender roles and restrictions.

Le Brun opened the first women's salon in Cairo in the 1890s, a public space in which women could meet to discuss current events and debate diverse issues from education to women's rights in Islam. After returning to her marriage in 1900, Sha'rawi had two children, founded a medical clinic for women and children, and arranged the first women's public lectures in Cairo. This period was one of significant changes for Egyptian women: middle and upper-class women were increasingly abandoning seclusion practices as they became more involved in charities and literary societies, women were entering the teaching profession, and a women's press was flourishing. However, gender separation was customary for the middle-upper classes until the events of 1919.

Sha'rawi played a leading role in the nationalist movement from 1919 until 1922, when Egyptians struggled to gain independence from Britain. After World War I (1914–1918), a delegation (*wafd*) appealed to the high commissioner, seeking to present their case for independence in London and at the Paris peace talks, but they were denied these opportunities. After publicizing their demands to the Egyptian people, the members of the *wafd* were arrested and spontaneous protests and strikes ensued. The *wafd* quickly morphed into a nationalist organization and would later become a political party; the Wafdist Women's Central Committee (WWCC) soon emerged to support it. Sha'rawi, the president-elect, led the WWCC in mobilizing women's demonstrations, sending petitions and protests to the colonial authority and Western governments, raising funds, and maintaining communications for their male counterparts. The WWCC was particularly critical to the male nationalists when *wafd* members were imprisoned or exiled. Sha'rawi also visited girls' schools and encouraged them to participate in the nationalist effort, and the WWCC helped mobilize women's groups nationwide to join the movement.

In 1922 Egypt won nominal independence from Britain, but the WWCC was frustrated because Britain retained a military presence and ultimate power over Egypt's foreign affairs. Egypt had gained control over internal matters, however; soon Egyptians promulgated a constitution and convened a representative parliament.

Sha'rawi continued to propagate her nationalist views, but she also promoted women's issues, often framing her arguments in nationalist or religious terms. In 1923 she founded the Egyptian Feminist Union (EFU) in order to advance a feminist agenda that addressed social and economic concerns, and to continue fighting for full independence. Only a month later, an electoral law that denied women suffrage rights was passed. Despite the tremendous support that Egyptian women had given male nationalists, women were now expected to withdraw to their homes as second-class citizens. The EFU was outraged by the affront and added equal political rights to their long agenda, which included socialist reforms, family law reforms, an end to legalized prostitution, more employment options for women, and equal educational opportunities for women. Along with other women's groups, the EFU also strove to increase social services, and established its own clinics, schools, scholarships, and literacy programs.

While Sha'rawi's feminism was rooted in her childhood, personality, and philanthropy, it certainly evolved in the nationalist context of the 1919 to 1923 resistance. This period was extremely valuable for Egyptian women because their contributions to the nationalist movement were indispensable; therefore, they were able to carve new public roles for themselves. Additionally, Sha'rawi's feminism was linked closely with her nationalism. Badran demonstrates that Sha'rawi and other feminists considered their struggle against patriarchy to be similar to that against colonialism.

When Sha'rawi died in 1947, Egyptian women had made progress in employment and education, but the only family law reform enacted was the raising of minimum marriage ages; women did not achieve political rights until the 1950s. Sha'rawi's legacy for the modern period is complicated by the "Islamic trend" since the 1970s; some Islamist women may remember Sha'rawi more for her comparatively secular, Western perspectives than for her feminist goals. However, many Egyptians continue to uphold Sha'rawi for her efforts to improve women's status, because she laid the groundwork for women's political activism and fought for many similar objectives, such as family law reform and greater employment opportunities. Furthermore, Sha'rawi's legacy extends beyond Egypt because of her support for women and movements in other colonized countries, her advocacy of the Palestinian cause, and her presidency of the Arab Feminist Union (1944–1947), which she founded a year before the formation in 1945 of the Arab League, an organization of Middle Eastern and African nations.

SEE ALSO *Egypt.*

BIBLIOGRAPHY

Ahmed, Leila. *Women and Gender in Islam: Historical Roots of a Modern Debate.* New Haven, CT: Yale University Press, 1992.

Badran, Margot. "Independent Women." In *Arab Women: Old Boundaries, New Frontiers*, edited by Judith Tucker, 129–148. Bloomington: Indiana University Press, 1993.

Badran, Margot. *Feminists, Islam, and Nation: Gender and the Making of Modern Egypt.* Princeton, NJ: Princeton University Press, 1995.

Baron, Beth. *The Women's Awakening in Egypt: Culture, Society, and the Press.* New Haven, CT: Yale University Press, 1994.

Sha'rawi, Huda. *Harem Years: The Memoirs of an Egyptian Feminist.* Translated by Margot Badran. London: Virago, 1986.

Elizabeth Brownson

SHIPPING, EAST ASIA AND PACIFIC

Western imperialism and colonialism took diverse forms in East Asia, from the formal colonies of the Dutch East Indies and French Vietnam to the multinational "informal empires" established by commercial treaties in China and Japan. Shipping was the lifeline of Western involvement in East Asia, as it both linked European metropoles and East Asian possessions and created new routes and relationships within East Asia itself.

During the sixteenth and seventeenth centuries, European powers entered the spice and luxury goods trades with Asia. In the 1500s, Portuguese merchant ships traveled along a network of trade settlements secured by the Portuguese navy, from Goa in western India, to Malacca (Melaka) in Malaysia, to Macao in southern China. The Portuguese were joined in the 1600s by Dutch ships journeying between the East Indian archipelago, Taiwan, and Japan. Later the "East Indiamen" of the British East India Company voyaged to India, the East Indies, and the China coast. By the early eighteenth century, British merchant sea power had outstripped its competitors, and would continue to dominate trade with Asia for the next two hundred years.

The withdrawal of the British East India Company's monopoly on trade with China (1834) introduced greater competition into Asian trades and drew greater numbers of merchant ships from Europe and the United States to Asia. Under these new conditions, the speed and efficiency of ships could have a much greater impact on trade profits. From the late 1840s, British and American clipper ships carried opium from India to the China coast, and delivered the freshest crops of China teas to London.

Although oceangoing steamships still burned too much coal to be viable for commercial shipping, a few lines such as the British Peninsular and Oriental Company and the French Messageries Maritimes received subsidies from their home governments to carry mail to colonies and settlements in Asia. Technological improvements in steamships and the completion of the Suez Canal in 1869 opened the routes to Asia to private steamship companies.

Steamship lines also traversed the Pacific to connect the ports of the western United States and Latin America to East Asia. After the American (1869) and Canadian (1885) transcontinental railways were completed, goods could be shipped via the Pacific and across the North American continent to Europe. British companies were the largest presence on these routes, challenged somewhat by German and Austrian companies in the late nineteenth century and by Japanese companies in the early twentieth century.

Shipping did not only intensify communication between Western countries and their interests in Asia, European ships also participated in intraregional and domestic carrying trades within Asia. Steamship companies established routes among the islands of the Indonesian Archipelago, carried agricultural goods and immigrants from China to settlements throughout Southeast Asia, and developed lines between China and Japan and later between East Asia and Australia. After the opening of multiple treaty ports in China, European shipping companies participated in China's domestic carrying trade by transporting goods among the open ports along the coast and Yangzi River. In some cases, these steamships displaced traditional carrying trades, but in others, steamships stimulated the demand for junk shipping between treaty ports and other places.

European domination of shipping in East Asia made it a significant field for contestation by emerging Asian nations. Japan's shipping industry saw the earliest and most dramatic success: while in the 1870s, 90 percent of Japan's foreign trade was carried in Western ships, a program of cooperation between government and industry developed Japan's merchant marine to the point that it participated not only on routes within Asia but also the Suez, Pacific, and Australian routes. By World War I (1914–1918), Japan was recognized as a world shipping power.

In China, officials of the Qing dynasty (1644–1911) established the China Merchants Steam Navigation Company in 1872 to compete with Western shipping companies in Chinese waters, and "take back" some of the profits of the domestic carrying trade for China. Although Western steamship companies (joined by Japanese in the late 1890s) continued to hold the largest share of China's coast and river traffic until the second Sino-Japanese War (1937–1945), the China Merchants Steam Navigation Company maintained a consistent presence on domestic routes, and was joined by several private Chinese companies in the 1920s. China, however, was not able to establish its own overseas lines until after World War II.

SEE ALSO *China Merchants' Steam Navigation Company.*

BIBLIOGRAPHY

Headrick, Daniel R. *The Tentacles of Progress: Technology Transfer in the Age of Imperialism, 1850–1940.* Oxford, U.K.: Oxford University Press, 1988.

Hyde, Francis E. *Far Eastern Trade, 1860–1914.* London: Adam & Charles Black, 1973.

Wray, William D. *Mitsubishi and the N.Y.K., 1870–1914: Business Strategy in the Japanese Shipping Industry.* Cambridge, MA: Harvard University Press, 1984.

Anne Reinhardt

SHIPPING, THE PACIFIC

The Pacific is the world's largest and deepest ocean, occupying one-third of the earth's surface. The countries along the western coast of North and South America have links in a North Pacific route with Japan and China, and in a South Pacific route with Australia, New Zealand, Indonesia, and southern Asia. Over half the world's merchant fleet capacity and more than one-third of the world's ships sail through straits between the Indian and Pacific oceans. The chief Pacific ports include those on the U.S. West Coast and the Chinese coast, as well as those in Tokyo-Yokohama, Japan; Manila, Philippines; and Sydney, Australia. The protection of these trade routes through Pacific waters has greatly affected the lives of Pacific Islanders.

There are about twenty thousand islands in the Pacific Ocean, and there has been continuous trade among Pacific Islanders since native settlement. Many of these original familial and ceremonial exchanges among Pacific Islanders are active today, connecting island-based populations with diaspora communities in the Americas and elsewhere who return cash remittances for the continuance of communal systems back home.

The potential of such early nineteenth-century industries as whaling and sandalwood were quickly exploited by Western countries and gave way to plantations and the establishment of coaling stations for shipping routes. It was the search for Pacific routes to Asia and Australia that prompted the United States to establish its hold on the great natural harbors at Pearl River in Hawaii and Pago Pago Bay in the Samoan Islands. Both were strategically mapped and explored in 1839 by a U.S. expedition led by the American naval officer Charles Wilkes (1798–1877).

Pandemics of Western diseases had greatly diminished the native populations of the Pacific islands by the mid to late nineteenth century. Missionaries from Europe and the Americas, who inevitably followed in the wake of these diseases while proselytizing Western monotheism as the best protection from them, exploited the much-weakened condition of the islanders by claiming their lands. Their actions eventually led to the takeover of many Pacific island nations by the United States and other Western nations.

U.S. naval strategists were inspired by the theory of sea power as a key to world power advanced by Alfred Thayer Mahan (1840–1914) in his 1890 book *The Influence of Sea Power Upon History, 1660–1783*. In this work, Mahan listed three key elements to sea power: "production, with the necessity of exchanging products, shipping, whereby the exchange is carried on, and colonies, which facilitate and enlarge the operations of shipping and tend to protect it by multiplying points of safety" (chap. 1). Following Mahan's advice, the U.S. Navy later based part of its Pacific Fleet in Hawaii. By the twenty-first century, most of the transpacific sea-lanes passed through the waters of the Hawaiian Islands, including a great deal of the drug traffic from Asia to the United States.

While international law guarantees foreign ships the right of passage through the waters of island nations, the United Nations Convention on the Law of the Sea, which went into effect in 1994, established "exclusive economic zones" within 200 nautical miles (370 kilometers, 230 miles) from each country's shoreline. Pacific island nations control undersea resources, primarily fishing and seabed mining, within these zones.

SEE ALSO *Exploration, the Pacific; Indigenous Responses, the Pacific.*

BIBLIOGRAPHY

Epeli Hau'ofa, ed. *A New Oceania: Rediscovering Our Sea of Islands*. Suva, Fiji: School of Social and Economic Development, University of the South Pacific, 1993.

Mahan, Alfred Thayer. *The Influence of Sea Power Upon History, 1660–1783*. Boston: Little, Brown, 1890. Available from Project Gutenberg at http://www.gutenberg.org/files/13529/13529.txt.

United Nations Convention on the Law of the Sea. UN Office of Legal Affairs, Division for Ocean Affairs and the Law of the Sea. Available from http://www.un.org/Depts/los/index.htm

Dan Taulapapa McMullin

SIAM AND THE WEST, KINGDOM OF

The Portuguese were the first Europeans to trade regularly with, and to settle in, the kingdom of Siam. They sent an envoy to the court of Ayutthaya around 1511, the year of their conquest of Melaka. The Portuguese wanted to ensure that there would continue to be Siamese shipping to their new possession, Siam being a major supplier of rice to that port. By 1516 a treaty had been signed, according the Portuguese the right to trade in Siam, in return for Portuguese sale of European firearms to the Ayutthayan court. Hundreds of Portuguese became mercenaries of the kings of Siam, who in the sixteenth century fought several wars against neighboring states. A Portuguese settlement, which became largely *mestizo*, sprang up in the city of Ayutthaya. Relations and trade with Spanish Philippines began in 1598, but were at best sporadic.

For the king and court of Siam, the seventeenth century was a time of intense commercial and diplomatic activity. The Dutch and English came to Siam in the first half of the century, and inevitably came into conflict and competition with the Portuguese and Spaniards. First to arrive were the Dutch, in the form of the United East India Company (Verenigde Oost-Indische Compagnie, or VOC), which sent envoys to Ayutthaya in 1604. The first Siamese embassy to Europe left Ayutthaya in 1607, traveling to the Dutch Republic, where the envoys were received by the *stadhouder* Prince Maurice. Dutch trade in Siam consisted largely in the export of the dye wood sapan and animal skins to Japan, and also the buying up of other produce and tin in exchange for Indian textiles, silver, and cash. The Dutch had a trading office and small settlement in Ayutthaya, which survived until late 1765, when the Burmese had begun to besiege Ayutthaya and there was no more trade to be done.

The English East India Company (EIC) arrived in Ayutthaya via Patani in 1612. The EIC established a factory at Ayutthaya, hoping to establish a lucrative Japan-Siam trade, but were disappointed. The EIC withdrew in 1623, and reestablished its Siam factory in 1675. But it was still not successful in its trade, closing down the office in 1684 amid much acrimony in its relations with the Siamese court. Anglo-Siamese relations were complicated by the roles of the "interlopers," many of whom had previously been employed by the EIC and were now undercutting or even obstructing the company's own trade. Some of these interlopers were in the employ of the king of Siam.

Among the many foreigners who joined Siamese royal service was the Greek Constantine Phaulkon, who had been an employee of the English EIC, but once he had entered the Siamese king's service, rose to a very high rank, becoming the de facto controller of the kingdom's foreign affairs and overseas trade in the 1680s. A supporter of the French cause in Siam, he was the favorite of Ayutthaya's most outward-looking king, Narai (r. 1656–1688).

The first French people to establish sustained contacts with Siam were the missionaries of the Société des Missions Etrangères, who first arrived in 1662. The missionaries of this society were to stay on until the fall of Ayutthaya in 1767, though they gained few native converts to Christianity. The French diplomatic initiatives in the 1670s and 1680s were based on a mistaken assumption that King Narai (along with the Siamese people) would convert to Roman Catholicism, and thus afford Louis XIV's government a secure political and commercial foothold in Asia. The French government sent garrisons to man fortresses at Bangkok and Mergui in 1687. In 1688 a palace revolution broke out against King Narai, ending with Phaulkon's execution and the withdrawal of the French officers, soldiers, and traders from Siam.

WESTERN INFLUENCE IN THE NINETEENTH CENTURY

After the fall of Ayutthaya in 1767 Europeans did not trade directly in Siam again until 1818. The Portuguese returned to Siam and set up a trading office on the banks of the Chao Phraya River in Bangkok. But the more significant arrivals during the first half of the nineteenth century were the British traders and diplomats and the American missionaries, the latter bringing in new medical knowledge, technology, and ideas.

The key geopolitical factor of this era was the establishment of the free port of Singapore by the British in 1819. The British, eager to increase trade with Bangkok, signed the Burney Treaty with Siam in 1826 but Siamese relations with the British and the Americans during the reign of King Rama III (r. 1824–1851) were notable for increasing Western impatience with Siam's refusal to give in to demands for free trade and extra-territorial rights.

The scholarly King Mongkut (Rama IV, r. 1851–1868) was deeply interested in the West, learning English from an American Protestant missionary and Latin from a French Roman Catholic missionary. It was during his reign that the Siamese court decided to begin a process of Westernization, to bring Siam up to the level of the modern Western world. The signing of the Bowring Treaty of 1855 with Great Britain was a key event in the history of Siam's relations with the West. It led to the end of the royal monopoly system in Siam (fixing import and export duty rates), and through the terms of the treaty extraterritorial rights protected the subjects of the British Empire. The treaty became the model on which all subsequent treaties with Western countries were based. Following the example of the British, the United States, France, Denmark, The Netherlands, and Portugal (among others) all concluded almost identical treaties with Siam. Siam became a major rice-exporting nation,

Mongkut, Circa 1859. *The scholarly Mongkut, who ruled Siam from 1851 to 1868 as King Rama IV, initiated a process of Westernization meant to raise Siam to the level of the modern Western world.* **HULTON ARCHIVE/GETTY IMAGES. REPRODUCED BY PERMISSION.**

and Western trade with the country increased. But serious problems also followed. First, the rights and activities of non-European subjects or protected persons of the imperial powers became an issue of contention between Siam and the Western countries, especially France. More importantly, the economic and territorial ambitions of Great Britain and France began to threaten the very independence of Siam.

Yet Siam, alone among the Southeast Asian countries, remained the only independent kingdom during the age of high imperialism. There were two major reasons for this. First, the Westernizing and modernizing reforms started by King Mongkut and carried forward with decisive vigor by his son Chulalongkorn (r. 1868–1910) transformed the country into a modern nation state, with institutions modeled on the West. Many Western experts and advisers were hired by the Siamese government to help reform of the country's legal, administrative, and military systems, and in the modernizing of transport and communications. Western nations and companies competed for contracts and an increased economic role in

Siam. As a result of the reforms, the monarchical government in Siam became more absolute than ever because Western technology and Western-inspired administrative reforms enabled the center to exert more effective control over most outlying provinces.

Second, a stalemate was reached between Britain and France in this region. From 1896 the two great powers agreed to use Siam or, more precisely, the Mekong River, as a "buffer" zone between their territories in Southeast Asia. The Siamese, however, still had to cede territories under its suzerainty to both France and Great Britain, notably the left bank of the Mekong (1893), the provinces of Siem Reap, Battambang, and Sisophon in Cambodia (1907), and the Malay states of Kelantan, Terengganu, Kedah, and Perlis (1909). The severest crisis occurred in 1893 when the French brought gunboats up the Chao Phraya River right into Bangkok, having forced the Siamese defenses at the river mouth. King Chulalongkorn was forced to accept a treaty giving France Siam's Lao territories on the east bank of the Mekong, and to pay an indemnity of 3 million francs for perceived offenses against the French in Laos.

The heartland of the kingdom, however, remained secure. In the reign of Chulalongkorn's son King Vajiravudh (1910–1925), Westernizing reforms continued to be implemented. The English-educated Vajiravudh also sent a Siamese expeditionary force to join the Allies in the later stages of World War I, thus earning Siam a place at the negotiations table at the Versailles Peace Conference. Although the Siamese delegation in Versailles lobbied unsuccessfully for an end to extraterritoriality and full autonomy in taxation, a negotiating strategy was soon put in place for a revision of all the nineteenth century treaties concluded with the Western powers. With the help of American advisers, Siam by 1926 was able to put an end to the Western powers' treaty privileges, thus regaining its full legal sovereignty.

SEE ALSO *Dutch United East India Company; English East India Company.*

BIBLIOGRAPHY

Bassett, D. K. "English Relations with Siam in the Seventeenth Century." *Journal of the Malayan Branch Royal Asiatic Society* 34, Part 2 (1961): 90–105.

Chandran, Jeshurun. *The Contest for Siam 1889–1902: A Study in Diplomatic Rivalry.* Kuala Lumpur: Penerbit Universiti Kebangsaan Malasia, 1977.

Cruysse, Dirk Van der. *Siam and the West 1500–1700.* Translated by Michael Smithies. Chiang Mai, Thailand: Silkworm, 2002.

Hutchinson, E. W. *Adventurers in Siam in the Seventeenth Century.* London: The Royal Asiatic Society, 1940.

na Pombejra, Dhiravat. "Ayutthaya at the End of the Seventeenth Century: Was There a Shift to Isolation?" In *Southeast Asia in the Early Modern Era: Trade, Power, and Belief,* edited by Anthony Reid. Ithaca, NY: Cornell University Press, 1993.

Smith, George Vinal. *The Dutch in Seventeenth-Century Thailand.* De Kalb: University of Northern Illinois, 1977.

Thongchai, Winichakul. *Siam Mapped: A History of the Geo-Body of a Nation.* Honolulu: University of Hawaii Press, 1994.

Tuck, Patrick. *The French Wolf and the Siamese Lamb. The French Threat to Siamese Independence 1858–1907.* Bangkok, Thailand: White Lotus, 1995.

Wyatt, David K. *Thailand: A Short History,* 2nd ed. New Haven, CT: Yale University Press, 2003.

Dhiravat na Pombejra

SIERRA LEONE

Sierra Leone is a strip of mountainous peninsula on the Atlantic coast of West Africa, 67 square kilometers (26 square miles) long and 31 square kilometers (12 square miles) wide, bounded by the Republics of Guinea and Liberia. The first European contact with Sierra Leonean coastline occurred in 1460 when Prince Henry the Navigator's sea captains voyaged beyond Cape Verde Islands in the quest for a sea route to the spice trade in the Far East. Christianizing the heathens camouflaged a crusading spirit and economic and political motives. Between 1418 and 1460 when the prince died, they had discovered Madeira, Canary Island, Cape Bojador, Cape Blanco, River Senegal, Cape Verde, and Sierra Leone.

In the seventeenth century, the Portuguese established about ten settlements, the major ones being Beziguiche (near the mouth of the Senegal River), Rio Fresco, Portudal, Joala, Cacheo, and Mitombo (in Sierra Leone). These depots sustained the shoe-string commercial empire from Iberia to Java and Sumatra. Portuguese power declined under the attack from other Europeans who took over the settlements, but various river tributaries and swaths of coastline contiguous to Sherbro, Turtle, and Banana Islands remained in the hands of mulatto offspring of Portuguese sailors and other adventurers, some of whom became "African" chiefs. These later contested the missionary work and colonization of Sierra Leone.

British settlement occurred in the bid to abolish slavery and slave trade by attacking the source of supply. The motives in the abolition campaigns by different groups changed over time. For instance, Lord Mansfield's legal declaration, in the case of the slave John Somerset in 1772, did not fully abolish slavery but catalyzed liberal opinions and philanthropists who promoted the abolitionist cause.

Freetown, Sierra Leone. *A neighborhood in the port city of Freetown, capital of Sierra Leone, photographed between 1900 and 1933.* © HULTON-DEUTSCH COLLECTION/CORBIS. REPRODUCED BY PERMISSION.

The Committee for the Black Poor's report that the numbers of slaves overburdened its capacity compelled the government's attention. Initially, Anglicans were prominent because the members of St. John's Church, Clapham, first concerned with the aftereffects of industrial revolution on the nation, came upon the inhuman slave trade. Other religious supporters, such as the Quakers, joined the affray. Some African ex-slaves, such as the Ghanaian Cugoano and the Nigerian Olaudah Equiano, published their experiences, urged military intervention in the coasts, and pointed to the economic inefficiency of the immoral trade that could be replaced with legitimate trade.

COLONIZING SIERRA LEONE

While sugar planters in the colonies were adamant, it was clear that their profit margin was in decline. Dubbed the Clapham Sect, the evangelicals advocated in Parliament, and organized the establishment of a colony in Sierra Leone as a means of countering the slave trade with a black community that engaged in honest labor and industry. A number of the leaders included Henry Smeatham, the amateur botanist and brain behind the project, the indefatigable Granville Sharp, who finally organized it, William Wilberforce, the parliamentarian

advocate, Henry Thornton, the banker who took over the consolidation of the Sierra Leone Company, and later Fowell Buxton, whose book, *African Slave Trade and Its Remedy* (1841) would summarize the basic contentions: deploy treaties with local chiefs to establish legitimate trade, use trading companies to govern, and spread Christianity to civilize and create an enabling environment.

The Sierra Leone experiment took three phases: On May 10, 1787, Captain T. Boulden Thompson arrived in Granville Town, situated in the "Province of Freedom" (as the settlement was called), with a few hundred black men and white women. By March the following year, one-third died because of harsh weather and infertile soil that had an underlying gravel stone. In 1791, as the Committee of the Privy Council heard the appeal against the slave trade, the Sierra Leone Company was incorporated, and Granville Town, a small community with only seventeen houses, relocated near Fourah Bay. Disaster struck when a local chief, Jimmy, sacked the town.

To salvage the colony, the British Buxton's book linked the experiment with the fate of African Americans who were promised freedom and land for fighting for the British during the American Revolution. The British lost but sent them to Canada, West Indies, and Britain. The experience in Nova Scotia was brutally racist, with little access to agricultural land. Thomas Peters, a Nigerian ex-slave, traveled to London to complain. He met Sharp, who enabled twelve hundred African Americans to sail for Freetown in May 1792. They arrived with their ready-made churches and pastors: Baptist, Methodist, Countess Huntingdon's Connection, and a robust republican ideology to build a black civilization based on religion. Their charismatic spirituality set the tone before the Church Missionary Society (CMS) was formed; their dint of hard work consolidated the colony through attacks by indigenous Temne chiefs at the turn of the 1800s.

THE NINETEENTH CENTURY

In September 1800, 550 ex-slaves, the "Maroons," arrived. These fought their slave owners in Trelawny Town, Jamaica, in 1738–1739 and set up free communities. But in 1795, hostilities broke out again with the slave holding state. Deported to Nova Scotia, they bombarded the government with petitions, memoranda, and sit-down strikes between 1796 and 1800. George Ross, an official of the Sierra Leone Company, was asked to organize their repatriation to Freetown. The Sierra Leone Company ruled the colony for seven years before the British government declared it a British "crown" colony in January 1808. But the French attack in 1894 hastened the conversion to a Protectorate status in 1896.

Before then, major transformations followed the Slave Trade Abolition Act of 1807 that provided for naval blockade against slave traders, and installed a Court of Admiralty that would seize slave ships and resettle the recaptives in Freetown. A process of evangelization intensified when the CMS started work in Sierra Leone with German missionaries in the 1840s. Soon, it became the dominant Christian body, enjoying the government's patronage while the Catholic and Quaker presence remained weak. The recaptives (67,000 in 1840) soon outnumbered the settlers, became educated, massively Christianized, enterprising, and imbued with the zeal that Africans must evangelize Africa. Representing the first mass movement to Christianity in modern Africa, they carried the gospel and commerce to their former homes along the coast. By the end of the nineteenth century, argued P. E. H. Hair, Sierra Leone "provided most of the African clerks, teachers . . . merchants, and professional men in Western Africa from Senegal to the Congo." Freetown became the "Athens of West Africa" (Hair 1967, p. 531).

SEE ALSO *Abolition of Colonial Slavery; Christianity and Colonial Expansion in the Americas; Slave Trade, Atlantic.*

BIBLIOGRAPHY

Fage, J. D. *An Atlas of African History.* London: Edward Arnold, 1978.

Fyfe, Christopher. *A History of Sierra Leone.* London: Oxford University Press, 1962.

Hair, P.E.H. "Africanism: The Freetown Contribution," *Journal of African Studies,* 5 (4) (December 1967): 521–539.

Hair, P.E.H. "Colonial Freetown and the Study of African Languages." *Africa* 57 (4) (1987): 560–565.

Hanciles, Jehu *Euthanasia of a mission: African church autonomy in a colonial context.* Westport, CT: Praeger, 2002.

Sanneh, Lamin. *Abolitionists Abroad: Americans and the Making of Modern West Africa.* Cambridge, MA: Harvard University Press, 1999.

Ogbu Kalu

SILK

Silk is a lightweight, soft, durable fiber produced from the cocoons of several related species of *Bombyx* or *Saturniidae* moths native to Asia, and the thread or cloth made from this fiber. *Bombyx mori,* a domesticated Chinese caterpillar that feeds on mulberry leaves *(morus),* is widely preferred for silk production, but lower-quality silk is also produced from other species that are generally grouped as wild silk or tussah, from the Hindi word *tussar.* The word *silk* originates from the Greek *serikos,* thus the manufacture of raw silk is called *sericulture.*

An estimated 300 pounds (136 kilograms) of mulberry leaves are necessary to feed the 1,700 to 2,000 caterpillars that produce 1 pound (.45 kilograms) of raw silk. Silk production is labor-intensive. Worms need to be kept clean, warm, and supplied with fresh leaves. Once the cocoon has formed, the worms are killed, usually by steaming. The cocoon is then submerged in boiling water to remove the gummy binding agent, after which it is carefully unraveled as a single thread. Sometimes these threads are spun into yarn (thrown).

Cocoons were first processed into silk in China, where silk remnants have been dated to as early as 3630 B.C.E. India, also home to a large variety of silk fauna, is the first region outside of China known to have cultivated silk, although it is not clear whether this technology spread from China or was developed independently; references to silk in India date from about 1400 B.C.E. Silk production later spread to other Asian nations, such as Korea (ca. 1100 B.C.E.), Persia (ca. 400 B.C.E.), and Japan (ca. 100 C.E.).

Silk textiles trickled to Europe along a land route, as evidenced by biblical references in the *Psalms* (ca. 950 B.C.E.) and in the works of the Greek poet Homer (ca. eighth century B.C.E.). That silk was rare is apparent

Selling Silk in China. *Cocoons were first processed into silk in China, where silk remnants have been dated to as early as 3630 B.C.E. This eighteenth-century woodcut depicts Chinese women buying and selling newly woven silk.* © **HISTORICAL PICTURE ARCHIVE/ CORBIS. REPRODUCED BY PERMISSION.**

in the sparsity of references before Alexander the Great (356–323 B.C.E.) invaded Persia in 334 B.C.E. Active use of the Silk Road, a land route from China to Europe used until the age of sail, dates from about the second century B.C.E. For centuries, Persia monopolized silk trade to the West by producing raw and woven silk, unraveling and reweaving Chinese fabrics, imitating Chinese designs in wool, and regulating any silk that passed across its borders.

In the West, silk was worn by important people in Greece, and later, the Republic of Rome, and Byzantium. War between the Persians and Romans cut off European silk supplies, so in 550 Byzantine Emperor Justinian I (482/3–565 C.E.) dispatched two Nestorian monks to China to find out how to produce silk. They returned about three years later with stolen mulberry seeds and silkworm eggs hidden in their staffs. Byzantine production was a royal monopoly until Justinian's death in 565 but then began to spread through the region.

European sericulture was limited, so Greek and Arab traders transported silk back to Europe in small boats from about the seventh century, and Moorish invasions of Spain introduced the silk industry there. The Crusades introduced many commoners to silk after knights brought back souvenirs from the Middle East.

Italy became the European capital of sericulture after 1130 when King Roger II of Sicily (1095–1154) brought weavers from the Middle East. Production on the mainland did not become significant until the mid-fifteenth century, fueling extravagant dress styles during the Italian Renaissance. Italian workers brought sericulture to southern France, but France never approached Italian production levels. Rather, by the eighteenth century the French focused on weaving, especially in Lyons. While Italian silk was regarded as of high quality, it could not be produced in sufficient quantities to replace foreign trade. Most imports were of raw silk because differing market demands made this more profitable than finished textiles.

Venice controlled European silk imports after successful conquests in the First Crusade of 1095 gave them virtual control of the Mediterranean. The Venetians carried Persian silk as the Mongols were disrupting Asian caravan trade, although demand temporarily dropped during the spread of the bubonic plague. Venetian domination lasted until 1453 when the Ottomans closed down shipping lanes and disrupted Persian silk production. Once Vasco da Gama (ca. 1469–1524) circumnavigated Africa in 1498, establishing a sea route east, Asian trade slipped to the Portuguese. Silk became an integral part of both East-West and intra-Asian commerce conducted by Europeans.

Throughout the early modern period, China, Persia, and Bengal were the most important suppliers of raw silk to Europe. Ming dynasty restrictions on trade caused Malacca (in present-day Malaysia) to become a major entrepôt for Chinese silk bound westward. Portuguese trade was fundamentally intra-Asian. Macao in southeast China was colonized by the Portuguese in 1557 to facilitate trade with Japan. Until the Spanish were banished in 1624 and the Portuguese in 1639, Japan trade consisted largely of Chinese silks purchased with New World silver, exchanged again for Japanese gold and silver. Similarly, the Spanish, who followed the Portuguese into Asia, traded New World silver for Chinese goods from a colony in Manila established in 1565. Profits were used to buy more silk and other luxuries to be brought to Europe or traded at Goa, Manila, Mexico, Peru, and Indonesia.

As a result, silk became widely available in the New World, leading to sumptuary legislation, such as a seventeenth-century Peruvian ban on blacks wearing silk. In 1718 and 1720 silk imports to the Spanish Americas were prohibited to halt the outflow of silver. Europeans brought Chinese silk to India, but there was no interest in China for Indian textiles. Rather, Indian textiles were sold in Europe, widely in Southeast Asia, and in the seventeenth century some Indian silks were used to trade for slaves in Africa.

The Dutch East India Company, the dominant trading force in seventeenth-century Asia, entered the Asian silk trade in 1604 after profiting from the captured Portuguese carrack *Santa Catharina*. Amsterdam became one of the most important silk markets in Europe. For much of the seventeenth century, Taiwan was an important source for Chinese silk bound for Japan, although Bengali raw silk was also sent. From 1623 Persia served as the main Dutch source for imports to Europe, but problems with the Persian shah led the Dutch to turn toward Bengal. Bengali silk came to replace Persian silk on the European market because it was of equal or better quality but could be produced more cheaply. Chinese silk remained the most desirable import.

Desire for silk spurred the English to expand into Bengal in the 1670s. Quality control was difficult and competition was stiff because Europeans were forced to deal through local brokers in Kasimabazar (the central market in Bengal). Both the Dutch and English East India companies brought European experts to Bengal to improve quality. From around 1700 to 1760 Bengali silk was an important East India Company commodity. The Bengal Revolution (1757) damaged the silk industry and caused the English to focus on obtaining silk from Canton (present-day Guangzhou) in China, even though they had expelled the Dutch completely from Bengal by 1825.

In China, sericulture generally benefited peasants by increasing the standard of living and creating cash that allowed imports of food. International demand for silk flooded the silver-based Chinese economy with New World and Japanese silver. New requirements of cash tax payments caused farmers to turn to cash crops like silk, which offered a high yield on land use and a quick return. More supply meant increased use among the Chinese populace. Once the Qing government lifted the export ban in 1683, foreign trade rose, but the larger market did not exploit the Asian producers because they fit into an already complex and sophisticated intra-Asian trade.

The Dutch brought less Chinese silk to Europe, using it for trade to Japan. The English East India Company usurped the Dutch position in China, trading through Canton after 1759. Exports increased so much that in the same year exports of raw silk were banned to keep weavers from becoming impoverished. The restrictions were partially lifted after two years but kept China from monopolizing the silk market.

Interest in Asian silk, especially woven silk, actually dropped in the eighteenth century as European production increased. Protective restrictions against imported silk were passed in the early eighteenth century in England and France. Silk became more affordable, and was used not just in clothing but also in bed hangings and covers and even wallpaper.

The Opium War (1839–1842) between China and England led to a colonial presence in China. The Treaty of Nanjing, which ended the war, facilitated silk exports, but they did not increase dramatically until foreign demand did. Rather than mechanization (although the first steam-powered filature, a silk reeling factory, dates from 1785), the spread of pebrine, a silkworm disease that ravaged European sericulture, created the need in

Europe for imported raw silk, which was paid for primarily with opium.

The sharp decrease of European supplies, the establishment of industrialized silk weaving in the United States, the opening of the Suez Canal in 1869, and the lower cost to westerners from the decline of the price of silver to gold in China created a huge demand for Chinese silk, overtaking tea in 1887. Production shifted from local producers to factories, and silk became available to the middle classes, usually in smaller pieces like shawls. Chinese sericulture came to comprise 30 to 40 percent of all Chinese exports until the 1911 revolution in China.

When Western imperialism opened East Asian trade, Japan was initially at a disadvantage to China, which supplied France. But Japan supplied the growing U.S. market, and quickly improved quality, mechanized faster, and lowered production costs. In addition, Japan's proximity to the United States offered lower freight and insurance prices. The Japanese silk industry also had government support, which Chinese producers had to do without. By 1912 Japan had overtaken China as the largest exporter of silk in the world.

The commercial manufacture of rayon, originally known as "artificial silk," along with the Great Depression and World War II, caused a sharp decline in silk production. Today China is the leading producer of silk.

SEE ALSO *Dutch United East India Company; Gama, Vasco da; Guangzhou.*

BIBLIOGRAPHY

Berg, Maxine, and Elizabeth Eger, eds. *Luxury in the Eighteenth Century: Debates, Desires, and Delectable Goods.* New York and Basingstoke, U.K.: Palgrave Macmillan, 2003.

Eng, Robert Y. *Economic Imperialism in China: Silk Production and Exports, 1861–1932.* Berkeley: University of California, Institute of East Asian Studies, 1986.

Feltwell, John. *The Story of Silk.* New York: St. Martin's Press, 1990.

Ma, Debin. "The Modern Silk Road: The Global Raw-Silk Market, 1850–1930." *Journal of Economic History* 56, no. 2 (1996): 330–355.

Prakash, Om. *The Dutch East India Company and the Economy of Bengal, 1630–1720.* Princeton, NJ: Princeton University Press, 1985.

Spring, Chris, and Julie Hudson. *Silk in Africa.* Seattle: University of Washington Press, 2002.

Vainker, Shelagh. *Chinese Silk: A Cultural History.* London and New Brunswick, NJ: The British Museum, Rutgers University Press, 2004.

Wills, John E. "European Consumption and Asian Production in the Seventeenth and Eighteenth Centuries." In *Consumption and the World of Goods,* edited by John Brewer and Roy Porter. London: Routledge, 1993: 133–147.

Martha Chaiklin

SINGAPORE

In 1827 George Windsor Earl, a British colonial official and ethnographer, having completed his tour of Java, Borneo, the Malay Peninsula, and Siam, had this to say of Singapore:

> Singapore is situated on an island at the extremity of the Malay peninsula which affords communication between the China Sea and the Bay of Bengal. In addition to the extensive commerce carried on by Europeans, native traders encouraged by freedom from duties enjoyed there, flock from all parts of the world, while the manufactures of Hindustan are there exchanged for rich productions of the archipelago. This port is visited by vessels of all nations and the flags of Britain, Holland, France and America may be seen intermingled with streamers of Chinese junks and fanciful colours of native prahus.
>
> (EARL 1837, P. 345)

Earl's observations were both penetrating and accurate. His description summed up the telescopic growth of Singapore in less than a decade after its establishment and suggested the immense potential the city had for its future expansion. From its very inception, Singapore was conceived of as a free port, a status that contributed to its rapid development.

The early history of Singapore remains obscure. Chinese sources refer to Temasek as an outpost of the Sumatran Sri Vijaya Empire; in the succeeding centuries, Singapore remained part of the sultanate of Johore.

The history of Singapore as a modern port city may be dated to the year 1819, when Sir Stamford Raffles (1781–1826), lieutenant governor of the English East India Company's settlement at Bencoolen (present-day Bengkulu, Indonesia), successfully persuaded company authorities to give him permission to find ports south of Malacca and thereby to further British trade in the Southeast Asian archipelago. In 1819 Raffles hoisted the British flag in the island, and established Singapore as a trading post and settlement after signing a treaty with the ruler of Johore. According to the treaty, British jurisdiction would extend over a limited part of the island. Five years later, final arrangements were made for the entire cession of the island and a treaty was concluded between the English East India Company with the sultan of Johore whereby "the island of Singapore together with the adjacent seas,

Singapore. *The British established Singapore as a trading post and settlement in 1819 after signing a treaty with the ruler of Johore. In the early twenty-first century, Singapore became one of the world's major centers of finance and industry.* **WENDY CHAN/IMAGE BANK/ GETTY IMAGES. REPRODUCED BY PERMISSION.**

straits and islets to the extent of 10 geographical miles from the coast of Singapore were given up in full sovereignty and property to the English East India Company."

For the first years of its founding, Singapore was one of the dependencies of Bencoolen. The city subsequently came under the control of the Bengal government and thereafter in 1826 was incorporated with Penang and Malacca to form the Straits Settlements under the control of British India. By 1832 Singapore had become the center of government for the three areas. On April 1, 1867, the Straits Settlements became a crown colony under the jurisdiction of the colonial office in London.

The founding of Singapore was largely intended to protect the China trade of the English East India Company and of its private servants, which consisted largely of the exchange of tea from Canton (present-day Guangzhou) with the opium of Bengal. The two principal routes for the trade between Europe, India, Southeast Asia, and China were the Straits of Malacca in the north and the Straits of Sunda in the south. The southern route

had been under Dutch control, but with the founding of Penang situated at the southern Straits of Malacca in 1781 and Singapore in 1819, both entrances to the straits came under British control, thereby assuring Britain full control over the China trade.

The Anglo-Dutch hostilities in the second quarter of the nineteenth century kept the situation fluid, but Singapore flourished, encouraging the English to press for its retention in the Anglo-Dutch Treaty of 1825. The treaty secured a division of the spheres of influence— with the British controlling the northern sector of the Straits of Malacca and the Dutch the southern segment. Even by this time, Singapore had become a much sought-after port by the English private traders who in 1813 had secured the opening of the India trade and had begun to participate extensively in the trade with China.

Singapore became a valuable transshipment base— Europeans picked up Chinese silks from Singapore and left English cloth to be shipped to China by Chinese traders. In 1833 the China trade was also thrown open with the result that Singapore's role as a transshipment center came to an end. But by this time, the status of Singapore as a free port had already established its potential for spectacular growth both within the region as well as within a larger global network.

The initial phase of Singapore's commercial development accommodated local and Asian enterprise, with the Chinese dominating the scene. The Bugis, for instance, were important carriers; from their headquarters in the Celebes (present-day Sulawesi, Indonesia), they made their way in sailing boats called *prahus*, collecting and distributing the produce of the eastern half of the archipelago to Singapore and taking away in exchange European and Indian textiles and other products. After 1837 the Chinese dominated the trade of Singapore. Around this date, Singapore was recorded to have imported British manufactures to the annual amount of several hundred thousand pounds and to have attracted a polyglot population of Chinese, Malays, Indians, Javanese, Bugis, Balinese, and Arabs.

With the advent of steam shipping, Singapore's advantages increased even further due to its location as a coaling depot. The expansion of steam-based commercial transport threatened to increase congestion and undermine trade, but this was averted with the development of the New Harbour (later known as Keppel Harbour), which began in earnest in the 1860s. Between 1860 and 1912, a number of companies competed against each other for contracts related to dock building and wharfing facilities. In 1912 the Singapore Harbour Board was reconstituted and the government began an extensive program of wharf accommodation and dock building.

The emergence of Singapore as the seventh largest port in the world in 1916 was a consequence of its strategic location as the hub of Southeast Asian steamship communication, lying as it did in the mainline shipping routes. Singapore's trade, as well as the trade of the Straits Settlements, was divided almost entirely between European and Chinese merchants. The Europeans handled the trade centered at New Harbour, while the Chinese monopolized the trade of Singapore River. These two sectors of trade were carried on in two different languages, English in the foreign markets and Chinese in the bazaar.

Singapore's trade flowed along two channels that may be called the east-west axis—that is, trade directed toward Europe involving the import of European manufactures and the export of Southeast Asian produce. In 1897 there were twenty European import-export firms engaged in the trade westward; the number had increased to sixty by 1908. These export-import firms took on the management of business enterprises, usually tin mines and rubber estates that were owned by companies located

in Europe, England, and elsewhere. European merchants worked through Chinese intermediaries on two to three months' credit. They bought from their Chinese connections the raw materials and foodstuffs for exportation to the West.

Chinese merchants were middlemen in a middleman's economy. They stood between the European merchants who imported Western manufactures and the producers of Southeast Asia, who bartered their produce for the manufactures. The Chinese merchants distributed manufactured goods by adopting three modes of exchange. One method was to barter cotton piece goods; a second method was for the merchant to dispose of goods to agents in Southeast Asia. Finally, the Chinese merchant could sell directly to native consumers, and this was occasionally done in the Malay Peninsula. Here, a greater degree of enterprise was required; besides textiles, the merchant took along necessities.

The ability of the Chinese to trade directly and effectively in Southeast Asia was due to the fact that they had established connections in all these islands and that they had agents stationed in Sumatra, Borneo, and the Indonesian mainland. The Chinese were also able to command corresponding facilities, which were enjoyed by European firms in the trade westward. Shipping in particular gave the Chinese a big advantage—Chinese steamers shipped European manufactures or intra-Asian commodities, such as fish and rice, and brought the produce to be sold to the Europeans. The development of Chinese shipping was encouraged by legislation passed in the colony in 1852, whereby old Chinese residents could become naturalized British subjects. By the 1860s Chinese-owned vessels flying British colors plied the ports between Singapore, Siam, Cochin in China, and the archipelago.

European and Chinese merchants complemented each others' activities. Europeans depended on the Chinese to dispose of their imports of manufactured goods and for a supply of exports of Southeast Asian produce. The Chinese depended on the Europeans for their credit facilities.

Euro-Asia trade constituted only one segment of Singapore's trade. A second component was the intra-Asian trade that involved huge exchanges with Southeast Asia, rice and fish being the most important commodities. Here, too, British political control was an important factor in the expansion of the colony's trade with the larger region. British control over Malaya had an appreciable effect on the trade of the Straits Settlements, whose merchants had substantial investment in tin and rubber, the natural resources of Malaya. Imports from and exports to Thailand were of equal value in 1870; imports increased thirteen times by 1915, exports increasing only by four and a half times. Thailand exported rice to Singapore and the Straits Settlements, while Malaysia exported rubber and tin.

Exports from Burma (Myanmar) were not appreciably significant; Burmese rice exports were diverted to the British and European market after the opening of the Suez Canal. The case of Borneo was different: Exports (rice, fish, cloth, opium, machinery, and railway materials) from Singapore made their way to Borneo, while the port received substantial imports of rattan, gambier, sago, gum, copra, coffee, and tobacco. Among the other items of Southeast Asian produce that entered Singapore's trade, mention must be made of such Indonesian imports as pepper, rattan, gambier, and small amounts of rubber.

Between 1870 and 1915, the trade of the Straits Settlements had become one of trade in Southeast Asian produce. By the end of the period, Malaysia had become Singapore's single most important trading partner, with tin and rubber figuring as the key imports. The phenomenal commercial expansion of the city was reflected in an impressive development of infrastructure related to expansion of dock facilities and civic amenities.

By the 1920s, Singapore became increasingly important in British perception as they began building a naval base in the city in 1923, partly in response to Japan's increasing naval power. A costly and unpopular project, construction of the base proceeded slowly until the early 1930s, when Japan began moving into Manchuria and northern China. A major component of the base was completed in March 1938, when the King George VI Graving Dock was opened; more than 300 meters (984 feet) in length, it was the largest dry dock in the world at the time. The base, completed in 1941 and defended by artillery, searchlights, and the newly built Tengah Airfield, caused Singapore to be hailed in the press as the "Gibralter of the East." The floating dock, 275 meters (902 feet) long, was the third largest in the world and could hold sixty thousand workers. The base also contained dry docks, giant cranes, machine shops, and underground storage for water, fuel, and ammunition.

The outbreak of World War II did not affect most Singaporeans until the first half of 1941. The main pressure on the Straits Settlements was the need to produce more rubber and tin for the Allied war effort. However, by 1942, following sustained bombing by Japan, Singapore came under Japanese control. During the period of Japanese occupation from 1942 to 1945, Singapore remained a witness to Japanese aggression and brutality. The occupation produced a huge wave of anti-Japanese agitation in Singapore, particularly among the Chinese population, which had borne the brunt of the occupation in retribution for support given by Singaporean Chinese to mainland China in its struggle against Japan.

The Japanese surrender in 1945 did not immediately guarantee Singapore's slow recovery to normalcy and prosperity. The end of the British Military Administration in March 1946 was followed by Singapore becoming a crown colony, while Penang and Malacca became part of the Malayan Union in 1946, and later the Federation of Malaya in 1948.

Postwar Singapore saw its merchants clamoring for a more active political role. Constitutional powers were initially vested in the governor, who had an advisory council of officials and nominated nonofficials. This evolved into the separate Executive and Legislative Councils in July 1947. The governor retained firm control over the colony, but there was provision for the election of six members to the Legislative Council by popular vote. These developments were followed by Singapore's first election on March 20, 1948.

The efforts of the Communist Party of Malaya take over Malaya and Singapore by force produced a state of emergency. The emergency that was declared in June 1948 lasted for twelve years. Towards the end of 1953, the British government appointed a commission under Sir George Rendel (1889–1979) to review Singapore's constitutional position and make recommendations for change. The Rendel proposals were accepted by the government and served as the basis of a new constitution that gave Singapore a greater measure of self-government.

The 1955 election was the first political contest in Singapore's history. David Marshall (1908–1995) became Singapore's first chief minister on April 6, 1955, with a coalition government made up of his own labor front, the United Malays National Organization and the Malayan Chinese Association.

Marshall resigned on June 6, 1956, after the breakdown of constitutional talks in London on attaining full internal self-government. Lim Yew Hock (1914–1984), Marshall's deputy and minister for labor became the chief minister. The March 1957 constitutional mission to London led by Lim Yew Hock was successful in negotiating the main terms of a new Singapore constitution. On May 28, 1958, the Constitutional Agreement was signed in London.

Self-government was attained in 1959. In May of that year Singapore's first general election was held to choose fifty-one representatives to the first fully elected Legislative Assembly. The People's Action Party (PAP) won forty-three seats, gleaning slightly more than 50 percent of the total vote. On June 3, the new constitution confirming Singapore as a self-governing state was brought into force by the proclamation of the governor, Sir William Goode, who became Singapore's first *yang di-pertuan negara* (head of state) from 1959–1961. The first government of the state of Singapore was sworn in on June 5, with Lee Kuan Yew (1923–) as Singapore's first prime minister.

The PAP had come to power in a united front with the Communists to fight British colonialism. The contradictions within the alliance soon surfaced and led to a split in 1961, with pro-Communists subsequently forming a new political party, the Barisan Sosialis. The other main players in this drama were the Malayans, who in 1961 agreed to Singapore's merger with Malaya as part of a larger federation. This federation was also to include the British territories in Borneo, with the British controlling the foreign affairs, defense, and internal security of Singapore.

On May 27, 1961, the Malayan prime minister, Tunku Abdul Rahman (1903–1990), proposed closer political and economic cooperation between the Federation of Malaya, Singapore, Sarawak, North Borneo, and Brunei in the form of a merger. The main terms of the merger, agreed on by Abdul Rahman and Lee Kuan Yew, were to have the central government responsible for defense, foreign affairs, and internal security, but local autonomy in matters pertaining to education and labor. A referendum on the terms of the merger held in Singapore on September 1, 1962, showed the people's overwhelming support for the PAP's plan to go ahead with the merger.

Malaysia was formed on September 16, 1963, and consisted of the Federation of Malaya, Singapore, Sarawak, and North Borneo (now Sabah). The merger proved to be short-lived. Singapore was separated from the rest of Malaysia on August 9, 1965, and became a sovereign, democratic, and independent nation.

Independent Singapore was admitted to the United Nations on September 21, 1965, and became a member of the Commonwealth of Nations on October 15, 1965. On December 22, 1965, it became a republic, with Yusof bin Ishak (1910–1970) as the republic's first president.

SEE ALSO *Batavia; Calcutta; Colonial Port Cities and Towns, South and Southeast Asia; Malaysia, British, 1874-1957; Raffles, Sir Thomas Stamford; Southeast Asia, Japanese Occupation of; Straits Settlements.*

BIBLIOGRAPHY

Chiang Hai Ding. *A History of Straits Settlements Foreign Trade, 1870–1915.* Singapore: National Museum, 1978.

Crawfurd, George. *History of the Indian Archipelago* (1820), 3 vols. Edinburgh: Constable, 1928.

Earl, George Windsor. *The Eastern Seas, or, Voyages and Adventures in the Indian Archipelago, in 1832–33–34.* London: W. H. Allen, 1837.

Greenberg, Michael. *British Trade and the Opening of China, 1800–1842.* Cambridge, U.K.: Cambridge University Press, 1951.

Hall, D. G. E. *A History of South-East Asia,* 4th ed. New York: Macmillan, 1981.

Harrison, Brian. *South-East Asia: A Short History,* 3rd ed. London: Macmillan; New York: St. Martin's Press, 1966.

Wilbur, Marguerite Knowlton Eyer. *The East India Company and the British Empire in the Far East.* New York: Richard R. Smith, 1945.

Lakshmi Subramanian

SLAVERY AND ABOLITION, MIDDLE EAST

The history of enslavement and abolition in the Middle East after 1450 is in fact mainly a chapter in the history of the Ottoman Empire. The Ottomans rose to the status of a major regional power in the course of the fourteenth century, becoming a universal empire during the second half of the fifteenth century, after the conquest of Constantinople in 1453. The Ottomans took over the heartlands of the Middle East, Egypt, and Syria in 1517, wresting these areas from the weakened Mamluk sultanate. Having later expanded their rule into North Africa, Arabia, and the Horn of Africa, and also northward and eastward to the Caucasus and Central Asia, the Ottomans came to control the entire network that acquired and distributed unfree labor within the Eastern Mediterranean basin and its hinterland for four centuries.

INTRODUCTION

During the fifteenth and sixteenth centuries, the main source of slaves in the Middle East was the series of wars that expanded the "abode of Islam" at the expense of the "abode of war," the territories ruled by non-Muslim sovereign powers. Prisoners of war were routinely reduced to slavery and employed in a variety of jobs, including agricultural, domestic, and other kinds of menial work. Although this practice continued into the nineteenth century, it became rare.

Consequently, because Ottoman expansion and large-scale conquests came to an end, importation from outside the Ottoman Empire and internal trade in already enslaved persons offered the main viable alternative. By the late eighteenth century, and until the demise of the Ottoman Empire following World War I, the slave trade was virtually the only source of unfree labor in the sultan's realm. From the second half of the nineteenth century, attempts to suppress the traffic, influenced to a large extent by British pressure, gradually reduced the number of slaves forcibly entering the Ottoman Empire.

The emergence in 1923 of the Republic of Turkey out of the ashes of the empire brought along a major social transformation under President Mustafa Kemal Atatürk (1881–1938). With the collapse of the sultanate, its major institutions and practices also disappeared, including slavery. But in some of the successor states, especially in Arabia and the Persian Gulf region, enslavement persisted for much longer, sustained by tribal monarchies that clung to their old ways, protected by a stubborn willfulness to preserve a lifestyle and a tradition that became an anathema to modernity. Using their oil wealth and other strategic assets, rulers and elites colluded to hold on to slavery and shield it from the outside world well into the second half of the twentieth century.

Enslavement of humans by other humans was a universal phenomenon, not peculiar to any culture, not deriving from any specific set of shared social values. Thus, there was nothing exceptional in the fact that it existed also in Islamic, Ottoman, Arab, Middle Eastern, or Mediterranean societies. Since biblical times, all monotheistic religions sanctioned slavery, though they did try to mitigate its harsh realities, and hardly any belief system was free from some form of bondage. Something in human nature made slavery possible everywhere, and it took major transformations in human thinking to get rid of it—and that too, barely a century and a half ago, an admittedly late stage in human history.

The Ottoman Empire, as one of the last great empires to survive into the modern period, inherited enslavement from its previous Islamic and non-Islamic predecessors, but developed its own version of it. The Ottoman brand was complex, with a variety of slave types, functions, countries of origin, cultural backgrounds, and modes of integration into society.

SOURCES OF SLAVES, NUMBERS, AND THE TRAFFIC

If during the earlier period of Ottoman history and up to the seventeenth century, the bulk of the enslaved population was recruited through conquest on the European and Black Sea frontiers, the majority of captured and enslaved persons in the following centuries came from Africa, with a small but significant minority originating in the Caucasus, mainly in Circassia and Georgia. Towards the end of the eighteenth and during the nineteenth centuries, Africans were being captured in the Sudan (the White and Blue Nile basins, Darfur, and Kordofan), Central Africa (mostly Waday, Bornu, and Bagirmi), and Ethiopia (mainly Galla, Sidamo, and Gurage provinces).

Africans were enslaved and forcibly transported along several historic trade routes crossing the Sahara Desert, then traversing the Mediterranean to reach Ottoman ports in the Balkans and the Middle East. Other major routes included the Nile Valley, the Red Sea, the Persian Gulf, and the network of pilgrimage roads leading to and from the holy cities in the Hejaz (a region along the Red Sea in present-day Saudi Arabia). From the Caucasus into the Ottoman Empire, enslaved people were being moved along the Black Sea and eastern Mediterranean routes and the overland roads of Anatolia (part of present-day Turkey). This human commodity was being transported via the same network as nonhuman merchandise, often by the same caravans and boats.

Scattered data and reasonable extrapolations regarding the volume of the slave trade from Africa to the Ottoman Empire yield an estimated number of approximately 16,000 to 18,000 men and women who were being coerced into the empire per annum during much of the nineteenth century. The large majority of these were African women. It is estimated that the total volume of involuntary migration from Africa into Ottoman territories was from the Swahili coasts to the Ottoman Middle East and India—313,000; across the Red Sea and the Gulf of Aden—492,000; into Ottoman Egypt—362,000; and into Ottoman North Africa (Algeria, Tunisia, and Libya)—350,000. Excluding the numbers going to India, a rough estimate of this mass population movement would amount to more than 1.3 million people. During the middle decades of the nineteenth century, the shrinking Atlantic traffic swelled the numbers of enslaved Africans coerced into both domestic African and Ottoman markets.

These figures should have resulted in a fairly noticeable African diaspora in Turkey and the successor states of the Middle East, North Africa, and even the Balkans. However, if one looks for persons of African descent in most of these regions, only scattered traces of them can be found. In Turkey, there are African agricultural communities in villages and towns in western Anatolia, with a larger concentration in areas around Izmir, as well as in the regions bordering the Mediterranean coastline. Even in the city of Izmir itself, where the largest African population in the Ottoman Empire lived at the end of the nineteenth century, an estimate of two thousand in the first half of the twentieth century is disputed as possibly too high.

Since Africans were considered as both Muslim and Ottoman (or later Turkish), they are statistically nonexistent in the official demographic records (e.g., yearbooks, directories, and statistically-compiled indexes). By comparison, in the post-Ottoman Levant (the countries bordering the eastern Mediterranean), as in Saudi Arabia, the Gulf states, and North Africa, one can find many more persons of African extraction among the various Bedouin tribes in desert areas and in settled villages bordering on them. In Egypt, Africans seem to have a larger presence than elsewhere in the Middle East.

The question is where have all the Africans gone to? One explanation is that many of the enslaved perished because they were not used to the colder weather, they suffered from contagious pulmonary diseases, and their life expectancy was quite low. An additional factor is that Islamic law and Ottoman social norm sanctioned concubinage and subsequent absorption into the host societies. An enslaved woman impregnated by her owner could not be sold, her offspring were considered free, and she herself would be freed upon the death of the owner. Thus, exogamy and the passing of several generations ensured not only the social absorption of free, mixed-race children, but also their visible disappearance from the observer's gaze.

In any event, by the end of the nineteenth century, the size of the enslaved population in the Ottoman Empire was around 5 percent, and slavers were a small, privileged minority, which scarcely reflected the experience of the majority. The overwhelming number of Ottoman families were monogamous, and did not own slaves nor employ free servants.

TYPES OF SLAVES AND TASKS THEY PERFORMED

Enslaved persons in the Ottoman Empire performed a variety of tasks, with the majority being employed as domestic servants in elite households, mostly in urban areas. Others engaged in menial jobs as mine workers, pearl divers, and manufacturers of various goods, but a certain number did work as agricultural laborers. Agricultural slavery was common in the Ottoman Empire until the sixteenth century, when captives in wars were sent to till the land in large, cash-crop farms. But this practice disappeared with the breakup of large estates into smallhold farms, and the loss of manpower supplies due to the end of military expansion by the end of the seventeenth century. Agricultural slavery resurfaced in the second half of the nineteenth century in two separate cases that were the exception rather than the rule.

During the late 1850s and early 1860s, the Russians drove out large numbers of Circassians from the Caucasus. Allowed to enter the Ottoman Empire, these refugees were settled in villages in strategic areas of Anatolia and the Balkans. Circassian landlords brought with them their serfs, who were classified by Ottoman law as slaves. Thus, several tens of thousands—some estimates go as high as 150,000, or 10 percent of the entire Circassian refugee population—worked as unfree agricultural laborers in the sultan's domains.

Another case was the employment of enslaved Africans on cotton farms in Egypt during the 1860s. This was the result of peaking demand for Egyptian cotton owing to shortages on world markets created by the American Civil War (1861–1865).

But the intriguing and analytically perplexing problem within Ottoman enslavement is that of military-administrative elite slavery. The men recruited to serve as the empire's generals, top ministers, provincial governors, and ranking bureaucrats were known as the sultan's household *kul*. They were levied as teenagers in Balkan villages according to certain criteria and entered into the Palace School, where they were trained to join the imperial elite. Legally, they were the sultan's slaves, but many of them attained powerful positions within the government, and enjoyed a lifestyle that one hardly would associate with the travails of the other types of slaves in the Ottoman Empire or elsewhere.

The corresponding female institution was elite harem servility. It was in the harem that the women and children of the sultan's household, and those of his elite members, lived. Contrary to Western perceptions of harem life, the women who ran those large and complex households were not mere sexual objects catering to the carnal pleasures of the sultan and his male elite members. Rather, the harem was a hub of political, social, cultural, and economic activity, where important decisions were being made by the sultan's mother and his wives, that were later negotiated with the leading men of the imperial court. Many, though not all, of the women in the harems were slaves bought in the Caucasus or the Balkans and educated in the palaces of the elite.

A small number of eunuchs served in the harems as intermediaries, facilitating contact between men and women in what was a gender-segregated environment. There were white and black eunuchs at the imperial palace, but during the seventeenth century, the corps of African eunuchs became dominant in court politics.

The question here is whether the *kul*-harem group of slaves should at all be subsumed under the category of Ottoman enslavement. Some leading Ottomanists have suggested alternative terms to describe the predicament of people in that group, feeling that they cannot properly be lumped together with domestic, menial, and agricultural slaves in Ottoman society. Thus, terms such as "the sultan's servants" or "servitors" were suggested, but since the privileges of these persons were of a temporary nature, they should be considered as essentially unfree. *Kul*-harem slaves were not allowed to bequeath their property nor their status to their offspring, and their wealth reverted to the treasury upon their death. The sultan not only controlled his enslaved servants' religious and cultural identity and their material assets, but also their right to life, which he could take if they were judged to have violated their bond of servitude. In fact, the status of elite slaves in the Ottoman Empire presents a true paradox at the heart of the Ottoman system—that is, that ordinary subjects enjoyed rights denied to those by whom they were governed, such as the right to immunity from the sultan's direct power over life and death.

Over the centuries of Ottoman imperial rule, certain aspects of *kul* servitude were gradually being mitigated in practice, especially during the major reforms of the nineteenth century, known as the *Tanzimat*. There was really no difference of kind between *kul*-harem slaves and other types of Ottoman slaves, although there certainly were differences of degree among them within the category of Ottoman slavery. It follows that the life-quality of enslaved people in the Ottoman Empire depended upon several criteria: (1) the task they performed (*kul*-harem, agricultural, domestic, or menial); (2) the status of the slaveholders whom they served (urban elite members, rural notables, smallhold cultivators, artisans, or merchants); (3) whether they were located in core or peripheral areas; (4) their type of habitat (whether urban, village, or nomad); and (5) their gender and ethnic background.

Thus, on the whole, enslaved domestic workers in urban elite households were better treated than enslaved people in other settings and predicaments. Slaves living farther from the core, on lower social strata, and in a less densely populated habitat, normally received better treatment, and the lives of enslaved Africans and enslaved women were usually harder.

WAS OTTOMAN ENSLAVEMENT MILDER? WERE THE ENSLAVED TOTALLY POWERLESS?

Slavery in Islamic societies has been deemed to have been of a milder nature than the stereotyped model of enslavement in the American antebellum South. Especially in the Ottoman case, the near-absence of agricultural slavery and the mitigating circumstances of domestic service were seen as offering the enslaved a better life than elsewhere. The path to freedom and relative protection bestowed upon concubines was also regarded as extenuating the lot of enslaved women in Ottoman and Islamic societies.

It is true that not a few slaves were better cared for than many of the sultan's free subjects and would not have traded their position for the uncertainties and vulnerabilities of the free poor and other marginalized persons in society. However, even in domestic slavery situations, especially when women were concerned, it would be inappropriate to describe the slaves' experience of enslavement as "mild." The intimacy of home, family, or household did not guarantee good treatment, nor was concubinage always bliss. A gendered view of female enslavement brings out a much harsher picture of realities.

There is ample evidence to show that, regardless of the alleged "mildness" of Ottoman slave experiences, bondage was a condition most enslaved people tried to extricate themselves from. Many went to a great deal of

trouble, took enormous risks, and fought against heavy odds to achieve freedom. In that, enslaved Ottoman subjects were not different from enslaved persons in any other society, and their efforts deserve to be recognized and appreciated.

Throughout Ottoman history, enslaved persons would abscond from abusive slavers, or commit acts classified as criminal by the state, in order to achieve freedom or register protest. But they also tried to work within the system to ameliorate their conditions. The latter occurred much more often during the second half of the nineteenth century, when the reforming Ottoman state was assuming the role of protector vis-à-vis the enslaved population of the empire, while at the same time attempting not to raise conservative opposition to its emancipatory moves.

By the latter part of the nineteenth century, absconding was becoming a legitimate way of getting out of enslavement in most societies under Ottoman rule. The Tanzimat state was increasingly siding with the enslaved and gradually abandoning its long-standing policy of supporting slaveholders' property rights. Its growing interference in the slaveholder-enslaved relationship benefited the weaker partner in that relationship, and many of the enslaved learned how to use the various means and opportunities made available to them by the state. The government also fully realized that once freed, ex-slaves were vulnerable and in need of protection—that is, of placement in a new job and of reattachment and patronage.

But absconding and assertion of freedom before the courts and government agencies were not the only types of action to which the enslaved resorted in their attempts to change their predicament. Some of these alternative actions were criminalized by the Ottoman state because the governing elite saw them as threatening to the existing order. Admittedly, the choices made by those enslaved Africans and Circassians who committed crimes were not always intended to achieve freedom, though not a few certainly were.

Another way of resisting enslavement in the Ottoman Empire was a cultural one. By retaining African and Circassian cultural components, enslaved persons served their spiritual and emotional needs and challenged the dominant culture of the slavers. Thus, for example, the trance and healing cult of Zar-Bori was carried by enslaved Africans into Ottoman territories and helped them cope with the tough realities of displacement and oppression.

CONCLUSION

To better understand enslavement in Ottoman and other societies, it needs to be viewed as a relationship between human beings, rather than as an institution with name-less and faceless structures. Enslaved persons were part and parcel of the network of social patronage that made up Ottoman society. Slaves were attached to a patron household regardless of the job they performed, and that attachment gave them social and economic protection and an identity as household members. Thus, after being brutally snatched out of their homes, successful attach-ment to the slaver's family was key to their absorption into the community at which they arrived. Resale to another slaveholder threatened that attachment, as did manumission, which despite its attraction to the enslaved, also raised fear of known and unknown vulner-abilities. This inevitably constrained the slaves' choice of action, such as when considering the consequences of insubordination, absconding, or mounting a challenge to criminalized and noncriminalized norms of conduct. Therefore, when they did resort to actions of this type, they had to be strongly motivated to achieve liberation.

It is therefore important to note the complexity of the phenomenon of slavery in general, and that of Ottoman enslavement in particular. As we strive to understand the social, economic, political, and cultural circumstances in which enslavement was widespread and universally acceptable in historic societies, we also should not hesitate to condemn it as reprehensible, regardless of where and by whom it was practiced. Understanding why enslavement was so natural in so many societies does not lead to condoning it. Ottomans and non-Ottomans alike had a choice in this matter regardless of sociocultural conventions: they could decide not to own slaves, and those who elected to use unfree labor could also choose not to mistreat their slaves, and—according to common Ottoman practice—manumit them after a reasonable period of service, commonly deemed in the empire as between seven and ten years. In addition, the enslaved had a measure of choice too, although theirs was much more constrained and involved greater risks and sacrifice.

SEE ALSO *Empire, Ottoman; North Africa; Slave Trade, Indian Ocean.*

BIBLIOGRAPHY

Austen, Ralph. "The 19th Century Islamic Slave Trade from East Africa (Swahili and Red Sea Coasts): A Tentative Census." In *The Economics of the Indian Ocean Slave Trade in the Nineteenth Century*, edited by William Gervase Clarence-Smith. *Slavery and Abolition* 9 (3) (1988): 21–44. Special issue.

Austen, Ralph. "The Mediterranean Islamic Slave Trade out of Africa: A Tentative Census." *Slavery and Abolition* 13 (1) (1992): 214–248.

Baer, Gabriel. "Slavery and its Abolition." In *Studies in the Social History of Modern Egypt*, 161–189. Chicago: University of Chicago Press, 1969.

Brunschvig, R. "'Abd." *Encyclopaedia of Islam*, 2nd ed. Vol. 1., 24ff. Leiden, Netherlands: Brill, 1960.

Durugönül, Esma. "The Invisibility of Turks of African Origin and the Construction of Turkish Cultural Identity: The Need for a New Historiography." *Journal of Black Studies* 33 (3) (2003): 281–294.

Erdem, Y. Hakan. *Slavery in the Ottoman Empire and its Demise, 1800–1909.* London: Macmillan, 1996.

Hunwick, John. "Black Africans in the Mediterranean World: Introduction to a Neglected Aspect of the African Diaspora." In *The Human Commodity: Perspectives on the Trans-Saharan Slave Trade*, edited by Elizabeth Savage, 5–38. London: Frank Cass, 1992.

Hunwick, John. "Islamic Law and Polemics Over Race and Slavery in North and West Africa (16th–19th Century)." In *Slavery in the Islamic Middle East*, edited by Shaun E. Marmon, 43–58. Princeton, NJ: Markus Wiener, 1999.

Hunwick, John. "The Religious Practices of Black Slaves in the Mediterranean Islamic World." In *Slavery on the Frontiers of Islam*, edited by Paul E Lovejoy, 149–172. Princeton, NJ: Markus Wiener, 2004.

Lewis, I. M., Ahmed Al-Safi, and Sayyid Hurreiz, eds. *Women's Medicine: The Zar-Bori Cult in African and Beyond.* Edinburgh: Edinburgh University Press, 1991.

Lovejoy, Paul E. "Commercial Sectors in the Economy of the Nineteenth-Century Central Sudan: The Trans-Saharan Trade and the Desert-Side Salt Trade." *African Economic History* 13 (1984): 87–95.

Lovejoy, Paul E., ed. *Transformations in Slavery: A History of Slavery in Africa*, 2nd ed. Cambridge, U.K., and New York: Cambridge University Press, 2000.

Lovejoy, Paul E. "Identifying Enslaved Africans in the African Diaspora." In *Identity in the Shadow of Slavery*, edited by Paul E. Lovejoy. London and New York: Continuum, 2000.

Lovejoy, Paul E., and David V. Trotman, eds. *Trans-Atlantic Dimensions of Ethnicity in the African Diaspora.* London and New York: Continuum, 2003.

Lovejoy, Paul E., ed. *Slavery on the Frontiers of Islam*, chap. 1. Princeton, NJ: Markus Wiener, 2004.

Miller, Joseph C., ed. *Slavery and Slaving in World History: A Bibliography.* 2 vols. Armonk, NY: Sharpe, 1999.

Toledano, Ehud R. "The Legislative Process in the Ottoman Empire in the Early *Tanzimat* Period: A Footnote." *International Journal of Turkish Studies* 11 (2) (1980): 99–108.

Toledano, Ehud R. "The Emergence of Ottoman-Local Elites (1700–1800): A Framework for Research." In *Middle Eastern Politics and Ideas: A History from Within*, edited by Ilan Pappé and Moshe Ma'oz, 145–162. London and New York: Tauris Academic, 1997.

Toledano, Ehud R. *Slavery and Abolition in the Ottoman Middle East.* Seattle: University of Washington Press, 1998.

Toledano, Ehud R. "The Concept of Slavery in Ottoman and Other Muslim Societies: Dichotomy or Continuum?" In *Slave Elites in the Middle East and Africa: A Comparative Study*, edited by Miura Toru and John Edward Philips, 159–176. London and New York: Kegan Paul, 2000.

Zilfi, Madeline C. "Servants, Slaves, and the Domestic Order in the Ottoman Middle East." *Hawwa* 2 (1) (2004): 1–33.

Ehud R. Toledano

SLAVE TRADE, ATLANTIC

Throughout history, there have been various forms of social oppression of the weak by the powerful and rich. These include, among many other forms, the exploitation of the labor of peasants by ruling elites (feudalism, serfdom), peonage, and slavery. Slavery is one of the oldest institutions in human history. For millennia, in different countries and continents, people have been enslaved. Unwritten rules of war in ancient times permitted the enslavement of prisoners of war, who were made to perform all kinds of tasks. Records from classical antiquity show that the Assyrians, Phoenicians, Hebrews, Egyptians, Greeks, Romans, Persians, and Chinese all utilized slave labor. In the Middle Ages, both Christians from Europe and Muslims from North Africa, the Middle East, and elsewhere enslaved each other during the struggle for supremacy between the Christian and Muslim worlds. Thus, in Europe, China, Japan, and Africa, slaves made important contributions to society.

The Atlantic slave trade, the trade that linked up Africa, the Americas, and Europe, differed from ancient slavery in one fundamental respect, though—it was predicated on race.

SLAVERY IN AFRICA

The nature of slavery in Africa has been the subject of much scholarly debate. Some scholars argue that slavery as practiced in Africa differed from slavery in the Americas in that slaves were not viewed as chattel and could be absorbed into the owner's family over time. This perspective is found in the work of Suzanne Meirs and Igor Kopytoff, who see slavery in Africa as existing along a continuum. In their view, the slave's position in traditional African society varied from total marginality to incorporation into the society or group. R. S. Rattray, who did field research in Asante in the 1920s, also belongs to this functionalist-assimilationist school of thought.

On the other hand, scholars like Claude Meillassoux, Paul Lovejoy, and Martin Klein belong to the economic paradigm school, which sees slavery in Africa as an economic institution predicated on the outsider status of the slave. They argue that as an outsider the slave had no rights and was only considered property. As a result, the slave could in no way become part of the owner's family, and could only live on the margins of society.

A Band of Captives Driven into Slavery. *This illustration of slaves captured in Zanzibar was published in* The Life and Explorations of David Livingston, LL.D. *(1875) by John S. Roberts.* © BETTMANN/CORBIS. REPRODUCED BY PERMISSION.

FROM AFRICAN SLAVERY TO THE ATLANTIC SLAVE TRADE

The gradual transformation of indigenous slavery into what became the largest intercontinental migration in history began with the trans-Saharan slave trade. The expansion of Islam into Africa led to the increased export of African slaves across the Sahara to the Mediterranean region and the Middle Eastern countries of the Persian Gulf. The wars of expansion into "infidel" territory that lasted several centuries enabled Muslim slave merchants to acquire Africans for enslavement. Some African slaves were used in the Mediterranean sugar islands, thus laying the basis for the plantation system that later developed in the Caribbean.

The number of Africans sent across the Sahara, while not as significant as the number of enslaved Africans sent across the Atlantic from the fifteenth to the nineteenth century, actually increased after the era of Portuguese exploration began. What eventually led to

The Middle Passage. *Sailors throw sick and dying slaves overboard during the Middle Passage, a term used to refer to the voyage of loaded slave ships across the Atlantic from Africa to the Americas.* © CORBIS. REPRODUCED BY PERMISSION.

the trans-Saharan trade petering out and the rapid growth of the Atlantic slave trade was the commercial revolution that occurred in Europe starting in the fifteenth century. This commercial revolution, which led to economic competition, was partly facilitated by a revolution in maritime technology in Europe between 1400 and 1600. Superior navigational and military technology gave Europe naval supremacy and enhanced the overseas activities and expansion of European states. Spain, Portugal, France, England, and Holland took advantage of these developments.

In the fifteenth century, Europeans began to search for new sources of wealth—gold, land for sugar production, and new routes to the Far East, with its spices and silk. The Portuguese led the way and soon "discovered" the Atlantic coast of Africa. They quickly monopolized the

production of sugar in the region by establishing sugar plantations worked by slave labor on the Atlantic islands of Madeira, Cape Verde, São Tomé, and Principé.

When the Reconquista diminished the number of captives available by largely ending warfare between the Christian and Islamic worlds, the Portuguese resorted to kidnapping, raids, and purchases from African traders in order to obtain slaves for the sugar plantations. Prince Henry the Navigator made their job easier by sanctioning the import of Africans—the first party of ten was sent to Portugal in 1441 (to be Christianized and for use in mission work). In addition, Pope Nicholas V (1447–1455) issued a papal bull granting Alphonso V of Portugal the right to enslave non-Christians captured in "just" wars in any regions that the Portuguese might discover.

Spain sought to challenge Portuguese supremacy and thus commissioned Christopher Columbus, whose voyages of exploration led to the 1492 contact with America and the subsequent exploitation of the hemisphere's aboriginal peoples.

SLAVERY IN THE NEW WORLD

Slaves were only imported to the New World in great numbers after other sources of labor proved inadequate. The new commercial enterprises first used forced aboriginal ("Indian") labor, but this approach met with little success for a number of reasons. First, the aboriginal lifestyle was not adapted to systematic agriculture. Second, Indians who escaped from the plantations could easily melt into the countryside. Third, Indians were very susceptible to European diseases and died in large numbers.

The persistent need for labor also led to the use of indentured servitude. Indentured servants, largely from Europe, were given free passage to the Americas and in return, worked for plantation owners for a fixed number of years (usually seven), after which they were freed from all obligations. However, indentured servitude proved inadequate as a source of labor because the labor it provided was temporary. Also, competition for labor in Europe made the cost of indentured servants high.

The Portuguese, the Spanish, and the English soon realized the advantages of using African slaves in the New World. Africans had had a longer period of contact with Europeans, and thus did not die of European diseases at the same alarming rate as the Indians, who were encountering diseases like syphilis for the first time. As transplants from Africa, it was harder for them to successfully escape. Because the Portuguese had used Africans as slaves in their Atlantic Islands, Europeans were also already familiar with the sources of African slave labor.

THE SOURCES OF AFRICAN SLAVES

Several studies have revealed that a large number of African slaves were acquired through warfare and that indeed warfare was the major cause of enslavement. As J. E. Inikori and others have shown, the high point of the Atlantic slave trade coincided with a period during which a large quantity of guns were being imported into Africa. Many wars were initiated for the purpose of acquiring slaves, but even wars whose origin had nothing to do with the Atlantic slave trade could produce large numbers of slaves. For example, the Yoruba civil wars, though inspired by political conflicts, became the largest single source of slaves during the last decades of the trade.

A different perspective has been offered by J. D. Fage, who argues that slaving wars and raids were not the outcome of the export slave trade, and would have occurred even without the trade. According to Fage, "the motive of warfare and raiding in Africa…was not to secure slaves for sale and export, but to secure adequate quantities of this resource and diminish the amounts available to rivals."

Besides warfare, other means of enslavement included raids and kidnapping. While recognized as illegal, slave-raiding parties roamed the countryside and snatched unsuspecting youth. One of the most famous enslaved Africans who was snatched in this way was Olaudah Equiano.

The judicial system was another vehicle through which people were enslaved. Some leaders exploited the judicial system by feeding people accused of heinous crimes like murder into the Atlantic slave trade.

EFFECTS OF THE TRANSATLANTIC SLAVE TRADE ON AFRICA

Scholars have long debated the impact of the transatlantic slave trade on Africa. Some, such as David Eltis, maintain that the impact of the trade on Africa was minimal; others claim the impact was profound. Different scholars focus on different aspects of the trade—including its economic impact, its political impact, its social impact, and a host of demographic issues.

THE ECONOMIC IMPACT

Among the most prominent of the scholars who argue that the slave trade led to the underdevelopment of the continent are Walter Rodney and J. E. Inikori. According to Rodney (1972), when the European slave trade removed millions of children and young adults, it robbed Africa of the most productive segment of its population. Furthermore, the slave trade and the wars it engendered created a climate of uncertainty and fear. As a result, economic development was rendered almost impossible in the areas affected by the trade. Many local industries that once existed no longer flourished. For example, many West African metallurgical and textile industries were partly ruined by the slave trade.

Rodney argues further that African industries were hurt by the type of imports that came with the slave trade. European imports into Africa did not stimulate the production process, but, rather, were items that were rapidly consumed or stored away. He adds that most of the imports were of the worst quality—cheap gunpowder, crude pots, and cheap gin. Inikori concurs, maintaining that the uncontrolled importation of cheap textiles and other manufactured goods from Europe and Asia retarded the development of manufacturing in Africa.

Henry A. Gemery and Jan S. Hogendorn (1979) conclude that the Atlantic slave trade caused not only enormous social dislocation, but also long-term economic decline in West Africa. They argue that when all

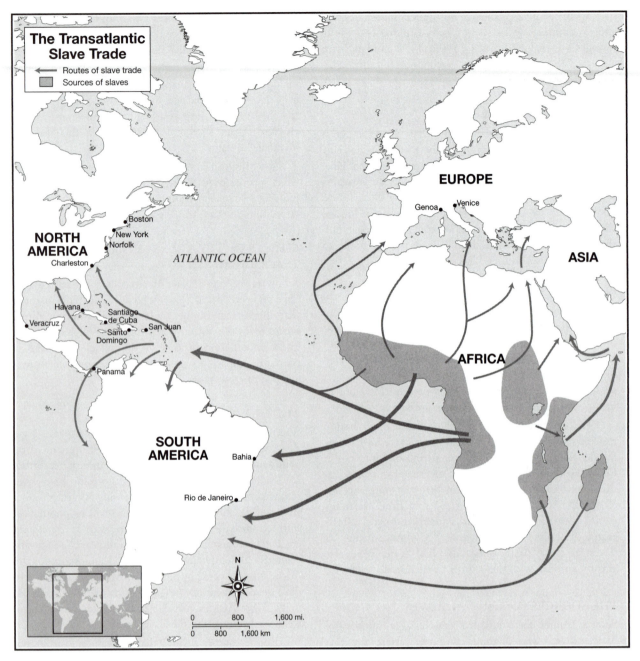

MAP BY XNR PRODUCTIONS. THE GALE GROUP.

costs are counted—social, political, and psychological—the welfare of West African society as a whole deteriorated markedly over the centuries of its involvement in the trade.

On the other hand, a number of scholars have argued that the economic impact of the Atlantic slave trade on Africa was minimal. Basil Davidson, for example, refutes the claim that indigenous industries collapsed. He points out that even after the trade was in place, Africans continued to weave textiles, smelt and forge metals, practice agriculture, and employ the manifold techniques of daily life.

In support of this view, A. G. Hopkins (1973) points out that as far as West Africa is concerned, no general evidence has been presented to support the claim that foreign imports led to the decline of local industries. To the contrary, he asserts that, "many indigenous manufactures, such as cloth and pottery, remained important, and it seems likely that the market was enlarged" (p. 121). He argues further that there is no evidence that the export of labor from Africa was one of the major causes of underdevelopment. Most of the slaves taken, he claims, were peasants lacking technical or entrepreneurial skills. He does agree, however, that in the late nineteenth century and early twentieth century, "when the economy began to expand very rapidly, there was undoubtedly a serious shortage of labor in West Africa, and it could be argued that at that point the pace of advance would have been faster if the slave trade had not retarded the population" (p. 122).

THE POLITICAL IMPACT

While some scholars maintain that the political impact of the slave trade on African society was minimal, most scholars now agree its impact was profound. One of the major political repercussions of the slave trade is related to the practice of exchanging firearms for slaves, which in turn led to an organization of force aimed at capturing more slaves to trade for more guns. According to some scholars, the slave trade and the importation of guns led to the expansion of militaristic states like Oyo and the subsequent devastation of the regions surrounding them. Due to this militarization, guns became important for national survival and prosperity, and because guns could only be bought with slaves, militaristic African states found themselves trapped in a "gun-slave-gun cycle." While some states acquired slaves in order to get more guns, other states sold slaves to get guns in order to protect themselves.

Inikori (1977) quantified the trade in firearms in some parts of West Africa and argued that there is a strong relationship between guns and the acquisition of slaves. Similarly, R. A. Kea and Richards point to the large volume of firearms imported into West Africa in the eighteenth century and the impact of these guns on interstate warfare, economic life, relations between Africans and Europeans, and the political organization of states along the Gold and Slave Coasts. Dahomey is often cited as a classic example of a militaristic state that expanded through the gun-slave-gun cycle. Dahomey maintained a slave-trade economy through a royal monopoly, exchanging slaves for guns. However, Werner Peukert (1978) points out, the bulk of the recent evidence seems to imply that there is nothing to suggest that Dahomey was completely subject to the influence of the Atlantic slave trade.

A number of scholars, including Paul Lovejoy, maintain that the export slave trade also indirectly increased the incidence of wars by exacerbating socioeconomic and political tensions within and between African states. Similarly, Inikori forcefully argues that "the export slave trade helped to create values, political and social structures, economic interests, social tensions, and intra-group

The Atlantic slave trade	
ARRIVALS IN AMERICA, 1451–1700	
Destination	**Imports**
Europe	50,000
Atlantic Islands	25,000
São Tomé	100,000
Spanish America	367,500
Brazil	610,000
English Colonies	263,700
French Colonies	155,800
Dutch Colonies	20,000

SOURCE: Adapted from Herbert S. Klein, *The Atlantic Slave Trade* (Cambridge: Cambridge University Press, 1999), Appendix, Table A.2, p. 210.

THE GALE GROUP.

or inter-territorial misunderstandings...which encouraged warfare" (1982, p. 20).

THE DEMOGRAPHIC IMPACT

Scholars have long debated the question of how many people were sent from Africa to the New World. Philip D. Curtin's pioneering work, *The Atlantic Slave Trade: A Census* (1969), estimates that the number of slaves sent to the Americas and other parts of the Atlantic basin from 1451 to 1870 was 9,566,100. Although his figures challenged old estimates, which ranged from 15 million to 50 million, Curtin nonetheless concluded that the impact on the continent was profound.

The debate over Curtin's figures has divided scholars into different camps: those who accept Curtin's estimates; those who essentially accept his conclusions, but argue that the estimates should be revised within a roughly 20 percent margin; and those who consider the estimates far too low to be meaningful. Paul E. Lovejoy (1982; 1983) and J. D. Fage (1978) are examples of scholars who have slightly modified Curtin's figures, but not his conclusions. Inikori, by contrast, believes that Curtin's estimate should be higher by about 40 percent. He argues (1982) that Curtin seriously underestimates the mortality rates of slaves between the time of their capture and their arrival in the New World; according to Inikori, at least 50 percent of slaves died before reaching the Americas.

There are also controversies about the demographic effects of slavery on African societies. Basil Davidson (*The African Trade*, 1961) and John Thornton (1977) argue that the demographic impact of the Atlantic slave trade on Africa was minimal. Thornton asserts that the population of the slave-exporting Sonyo province of the

Kongo kingdom did not decrease. Similarly, J. C. Miller (1982) concludes that depopulation in Angola was less a consequence of trade than of periodic droughts, famines, and epidemics—natural disasters that caused population movements, which in turn fed the slave trade and replenished the populations of slave-providing regions.

On the other side of the debate, scholars like Fage, Rodney, Lovejoy, Inikori, Reynolds (1985), and Manning (1981; 1988) are convinced that the demographic impact was profound. In *A History of Africa* (1978), Fage argues that substantial numbers of lives were lost in Africa as a result of the violent means used to secure slaves, and that as a result West Africa experienced an overall decline in population. Manning's simulation model (a statistical device used to measure demographic change under conditions of enslavement, slave trade, and slave exports) provides data that contradicts the findings of Thornton and Miller. For Western Africa, Manning's analysis shows that population growth declined in response to the slave trade, particularly between 1730 and 1850. This trend was accompanied by a change in the sex ratio, in which the number of men fell to under 90 for every 100 women. Manning's model suggests a cumulative decline of the West African population in the eighteenth and nineteenth centuries. The region's population in the early eighteenth century is estimated at twenty-two to twenty-five million with a growth rate of 0.3 percent throughout the era of the slave trade.

THE SOCIAL IMPACT

Patrick Manning (1981) shows that the ratio of males to females in the export trade affected marriage and birth rates in Africa. In support of this view, John Thornton (1983) points out that, among other things, imbalanced sex ratios altered the institution of marriage. While polygyny was already present in Africa at the time the trade began, the general surplus of women, he asserts, tended to encourage it and allowed it to become much more widespread. Claire Robertson and M. Klein, Inikori, and Lovejoy indicate that the ratio of women to men was generally 1:2. Be that as it may, gender imbalance had serious implications for population growth in many African states.

CONCLUSION

The Atlantic Slave Trade, the largest intercontinental migration in history, had serious implications for Africa as well as for those areas that received enslaved Africans. For one thing, it led to the emergence of African diasporic communities in the "New World." For another, it created serious economic, political, and social problems in Africa. The loss of about 10 million African people

The Atlantic slave trade

ARRIVALS IN AMERICA, 1701–1800

Destination	Imports
Spanish America	515,700
Brazil	1,498,000
British Colonies	1,256,600
French Colonies	1,431,200
Dutch Colonies	397,600
British North America/USA	547,500

SOURCE: Adapted from Herbert S. Klein, *The Atlantic Slave Trade* (Cambridge: Cambridge University Press, 1999), Appendix, Table A.2, p. 211.
Based on the estimates made by Philip Curtin and revised by David Eltis.

THE GALE GROUP.

severely hindered African development. The influx of firearms and the predatory activities of militaristic states and bands of individuals affected political development in many parts of the continent. The emergence of new lines of political allegiance and new political and economic elites altered centuries-old social formations. Finally, the gender imbalance that resulted from the slave trade affected African population growth. That the able-bodied segment of the population was the most desirable for slavers only worsened the demographic impact of the slave trade on Africa.

SEE ALSO *Abolition of Colonial Slavery; Commodity Trade, Africa.*

BIBLIOGRAPHY

Curtin, Phillip D. *The Atlantic Slave Trade: A Census.* Madison: University of Wisconsin Press, 1969.

Gemery, Henry A. and Hogendorn, Jan S (eds.), *The Uncommon Market: Essays in the Economic History of the Atlantic Slave Trade.* New York: Academic Press, 1979.

Inikori, J. E, ed. *Forced Migration: The Impact of the Export Slave Trade on African Societies.* London: Hutchinson, 1981.

Lovejoy, Paul E. "The Volume of the Atlantic Slave Trade: A Synthesis." *Journal of African History* 23, no. 4 (1982): 473–501.

Lovejoy, Paul E. *Transformations in Slavery: A History of Slavery in Africa.* New York and Cambridge, U.K.: Cambridge University Press, 1983.

Miers, Suzanne, and Igor Kopytoff, eds. *Slavery in Africa: Historical and Anthropological Perspectives.* Madison: University of Wisconsin Press, 1977.

Northrup, David, ed. *The Atlantic Slave Trade.* Lexington, MA: D. C. Heath, 2001.

Phillips, William D., Jr. *Slavery from Roman Times to the Early Transatlantic Trade.* Minneapolis: University of Minnesota Press, 1985.

Rodney, Walter. *How Europe Underdeveloped Africa.* Dar es Salaam, Tanzania: Tanzania Publishing House, 1976.

Edmund Abaka

SLAVE TRADE, INDIAN OCEAN

Whereas the Atlantic slave trade has been mapped out in detail in numerous studies, its Indian Ocean counterpart has remained largely uncharted territory. Two notable exceptions exist to the "history of silence" surrounding the Indian Ocean slave trade: the east coast of Africa (though mostly centered on the period after 1770) and the Dutch Cape Colony (1652–1796/1805). The "Afrocentric" focus of Indian Ocean historiography is a derivative of the Atlantic slave trade in general, and reflects the "take off" of plantation slavery on the Swahili coast and the Mascarene Islands (Mauritius and Réunion) in the late eighteenth century along with its obvious connections with the modern biracial system of Apartheid in South Africa (1948–1994) in particular.

Slavery was a defining component, slaves constituting 20 to 40 percent or more of the populations of European colonial settlements throughout the Indian Ocean. Slavery in this region was grafted onto a preexisting open system of slavery in the commercialized, cosmopolitan cities of Southeast Asia and elsewhere in the Indian Ocean region. In the open system, the boundary between slavery and other forms of bondage was porous and indistinct, and upward mobility was possible. In contrast, in the closed systems of South and East Asia, it was almost inconceivable for slaves to be accepted into the kinship systems of their owners as long as they remained slaves because of the stigma of slavery; instead they were maintained as separate ethnic groups.

The European Indian Ocean slave systems drew captive labor from three interlocking and overlapping circuits: (1) the westernmost, African circuit of East Africa, Madagascar, and the Mascarene Islands; (2) the middle, South Asian circuit of the Indian Subcontinent; and (3) the easternmost, Southeast Asian circuit of Malaysia, Indonesia, New Guinea (Irian Jaya), and the southern Philippines. The Indian Subcontinent remained the most important source of forced labor until the 1660s. The eastward expansion of the Mughal Empire (1526–1857), however, cut off supplies from Arakan and Bengal, though Coromandel remained the center of an intermittent slave trade that occurred in various short-lived booms accompanying natural and human-induced disasters.

After 1660 more slaves came from Southeast Asia, especially following the collapse of the powerful sultanate of Makassar in southwest Sulawesi (in present-day Indonesia) in 1667 to 1669. The slave-trade network in the archipelago revolved around the dual axis of Makassar and Bali. East Africa, Madagascar, and the Mascarenes provided a regular supply of slaves to the Portuguese, English, and French, and in the eighteenth century the Dutch. These European powers profited from African and Afro-Portuguese slaving expeditions on the mainland, as well as from frequent warfare among the major confederations and kingdoms of Madagascar, a situation compounded by the rise of militant Islamic sultanates, such as Maselagache, on the northwest coast of the island.

Europeans supplemented the slavery-related prescriptions of preexisting indigenous traditions and normative texts (Hindu law books, Islamic authoritative sources, and Southeast Asian legal codes) with an intellectual, theoretical mentality steeped in Christian humanism combined with a healthy dose of pragmatism. In Europe, pro-slavery apologists used the authority of the Old and New Testaments—most notably, the so-called Ham-ideology, based on Noah's cursing of Ham's son, Canaan, for pointing his two other brothers, Shem and Japheth, to the nudity of their drunken father (Genesis 9:25–27). David Goldenberg (2003) believes that the biblical name Ham bears no relationship at all to the notion of blackness, and is now of unknown etymology. Instead, the growing insistence on the chimerical curse coincided with increasing numbers of black Africans taken as slaves, first in the Islamic East in the seventh century and then in the Christian West in the fifteenth century. Biblical sources were supplemented by the writings of Greco-Roman authors, to condone slavery "within natural limits."

In Asia, slavery found virtually universal acceptance on a practical level among self-righteous religious, military, and civil officials. A variety of ad hoc arguments included Christian humanitarian compassion (saving the body and soul of the slave); the need to establish and populate settlement colonies; the right of war and conquest; the uncivilized nature of the "servile" indigenous peoples; natural law based on the inviolability of contractual agreements (*pacta sunt servanda*) and financial-budgetary considerations.

The Europeans acquired the majority of their slaves indirectly through purchase from indigenous suppliers. Throughout the Indian Ocean region, war captives came largely from animist, stateless upstream societies of slash-and-burn farmers or hunter-gatherers and from micro-states too weak to defend themselves against the stronger and wealthier downstream Muslim societies of the region's cities and rice-growing lowlands.

Inheritance and judicial punishment were the most common avenues to forced labor in closed systems where

Numbers of Dutch East India Company slaves and total Dutch slaves along with estimates of the size of the accompanying annual slave trades, ca. 1688.

	Year	Company slaves	Year	Total Dutch slaves	Size of annual Company slave trade	Size of annual total Dutch slave trade
Ambon	1687–1688	74	1688	10,569	6–7	800–900
Banda	1687–1688	166	1688	3,716	10	150–200
Batavia	1687–1688	1,430	1689	26,071	70–140	1,300–2,600
Cape	1688	382	1688	931	20–40	45–60
Ceylon	1687–1688	1,502	1688	c. 4,000	75–150	200–400
Makassar	1687–1688	112	1687–1688	c. 1,500	6–11	75–150
Malabar	1687–1688	32	1687	c. 1,000	2–4	50–100
Malakka	1687–1688	161	1682	1,853	8–16	90–180
Moluccas	1687–1688	0	1686	c. 400	0	20–40
Others	1687–1688	268	1688	16,308	15–30	1,000–1,800
Total	1687–1688	4,127	1688	c. 66,348	c. 200–400	3,730–6,430

SOURCE: Adapted from Vink, Markus, " 'The World's Oldest Trade': Dutch Slavery and Slave Trade in the Indian Ocean in the Seventeenth Century." *Journal of World History* 14(2) (2003): Table 4, 166–167.

THE GALE GROUP.

a money economy was little developed. Sale and indebtedness were more important routes to slavery in cities and other areas open to the money economy. Numerous "just wars" with indigenous societies also provided Europeans with a major source of captive labor, though the distinction between legal acquisition and illegal kidnapping and robbery was often nebulous. In addition, "rebellious" peoples, once subdued, were frequently forced at gunpoint to sign treaties with slaving clauses whereby they promised to deliver a fixed number of slaves and other commodities as fines or tribute. Enslavement of indigenous subjects via debt bondage also arose, despite recurrent prohibitions. People suffering judicial punishment as political exiles and convicts represented a small but distinct category of captive labor.

Slaves were general laborers who worked in a wide variety of occupations in the European slave societies across the Indian Ocean basin. Specialization, however, occurred in accordance with the size of the household and the particular position the settlement occupied within the overall trade network. The majority of slaves acted as domestic servants. They also performed heavy coolie labor, and worked in agriculture, mining, fishing, manufacturing, trade, and the service sector.

The division of slave labor roughly followed ethnic, gender, and age lines based on colonial classification schemes and preexisting indigenous beliefs and practices that characterized local slave systems. Indian and Southeast Asian slaves in general were deemed to be cleaner, more intelligent, and less suited to hard physical labor than African slaves. Slave women did not regularly perform fieldwork, but were mostly involved in domestic labor. Slave children could be employed in seasonal

work, or they could serve as companions to their master's children or guard younger white children and babies.

The number of slaves and the annual volume of the slave trade were subject to great volatility and varied significantly from year to year. Famine, wars, epidemics, and natural disasters could wreak havoc among local slave populations, which already had a tendency to melt away due to high mortality rates, low levels of reproduction or creolization, manumission, and widespread desertion. Whereas the slave population of the Iberian crown enterprises (Spain and Portugal) and northern European chartered companies and their officials was relatively stable, that of European and Asian subjects in areas under European jurisdiction displayed a distinct upward trend between the sixteenth and late eighteenth centuries.

According to a 1688 "tentative census" (Table 1), there were about 4,000 Dutch East India Company slaves and perhaps 66,000 total slaves in the various Dutch settlements scattered across the Indian Ocean basin. To replenish or increase these numbers, 200 to 400 Dutch East India Company slaves and 3,730 to 6,430 total Dutch slaves had to be imported each year. Assuming average mortality rates en route of around 20 percent on slaving voyages, 240 to 480 company slaves and 4,476 to 7,716 total Dutch slaves were exported annually from their respective area of capture.

To put these numbers in a comparative framework: the annual volume of the total Dutch Indian Ocean slave trade was 15 to 30 percent of the Atlantic slave trade (29,124 slaves per year), and 1.5 to 2.5 times the size of the Dutch West India Company slave trade (2,888 slaves per year) during the last quarter of the seventeenth century. Further research will be necessary to fill in the details and shed more light on the "world's oldest trade" in the Indian Ocean basin, but the protracted history of silence has finally ended.

SEE ALSO *Indian Ocean Trade; Slavery and Abolition, Middle East.*

BIBLIOGRAPHY

Arasaratnam, Sinnappah. "Slave Trade in the Indian Ocean in the Seventeenth Century." In *Mariners, Merchants, and Oceans: Studies in Maritime History*, edited by Kenneth S. Mathew, 195–208. New Delhi, India: Manohar, 1995.

Armstrong, James C. "Madagascar and the Slave Trade in the Seventeenth Century." *Omaly sy Anio* 17/18/19/20 (1983–84): 211–233.

Barendse, René. "Slaving on the Malagasy Coast, 1640–1700." In *Cultures of Madagascar: Ebb and Flow of Influences*, edited by Sandra Evers and Marc Spindler, 137–155. Leiden, Netherlands: International Institute for Asian Studies, 1995.

Campbell, Gwyn, ed. *The Structure of Slavery in Indian Ocean Africa and Asia*. London, U.K., and Portland, OR: Frank Cass, 2004.

Goldenberg, David M., *The Curse of Ham: Race and Slavery in Early Judaism, Christianity, and Islam*. Princeton, NJ: Princeton University Press, 2003.

Patnaik, Utsa, and Manjari Dingwaney, eds. *Chains of Servitude: Bondage and Slavery in India*. Madras and Hyderabad, India: Sangam, 1985.

Reid, Anthony, ed. *Slavery, Bondage and Dependency in Southeast Asia*. New York: St. Martin's Press, 1983.

Scarr, Deryck. *Slaving and Slavery in the Indian Ocean*. New York: St. Martin's Press, 1998.

Shell, Robert Carl-Heinz. *Children of Bondage: A Social History of the Slave Society at the Cape of Good Hope, 1652–1838*. Hanover, NH: Wesleyan University Press, 1994.

Vink, Markus. "'The World's Oldest Trade': Dutch Slavery and Slave Trade in the Indian Ocean in the Seventeenth Century." *Journal of World History* 14 (2) (2003): 131–177.

Watson, James L., ed. *Asian and African Systems of Slavery*. Berkeley: University of California Press, 1980.

Worden, Nigel, with Ruth Versfeld, Dorothy Dyer, and Claudia Bickford-Smith. *The Chains that Bind Us: A History of Slavery at the Cape*. Kenwyn, South Africa: Juta, 1996.

Markus Vink

SNOUCK HURGRONJE, CHRISTIAAN
1857–1936

Christiaan Snouck Hurgronje, born in Oosterhout in the Netherlands on February 8, 1857, was one of the most important Dutch scholars of Arabic studies and Islam. On account of his position as government adviser in the Netherlands Indies during a crucial stage of colonial development, his publications about Islam, and his role as professor of Arabic language and culture in Leiden, he was and remains a scholar of international standing.

Snouck Hurgronje went to the Dutch equivalent of a grammar school in the provincial town of Breda, where he studied classical languages. In 1874 he went to the prestigious University of Leiden to study theology, in which subject he acquired his first degree. He then continued his studies in Semitic languages, more specifically Arabic, under the tutorship of the well-known professor M. J. de Goeje. In 1880 Snouck finished his Ph.D. thesis with the successful defense of his dissertation, *Het Mekkaansche feest* (The Mecca Festival). After his graduation Snouck spent a year in Strasbourg, where he studied with professor Th. Nöldeke, before returning to Leiden to take up a position as lecturer at the College for East Indian Officials (Opleiding voor Oost-Indische Ambtenaren) and at the Higher Military School. These institutions trained civil and military personnel, respectively, for service in the Netherlands Indies. In 1887 Snouck returned to the university as a lecturer in Islamic organizations.

Snouck Hurgronje was quite unique in his approach to the study of Islam, which up until then had received little systematic scholarly analysis. First and foremost, his interest was in the language of Islam. His dissertation was a first effort at a new critical historical examination of Islam, and promised much in the way of new and original departures and a possible paradigm shift. After his dissertation, in which the emphasis is on religious culture, Snouck started to study Islamic law, or rather, as Snouck himself preferred to call it, the "Islamic duties." This subject has been at the heart of Islamic scholarship for many centuries, but was much neglected by European scholars in Snouck's time. Through a range of publications in article form, Snouck paved the way for new and original research focusing on the basis and content of Islamic law. These writings also made him one of the founders of the modern study of Islam.

Snouck, trained in the ethnographic tradition of Leiden, was not content to remain in the Netherlands, however: he wished to visit Mecca as a participant-observer and to discuss his ideas at first hand with fellow Muslim scholars. For this it was necessary for Snouck to convert to Islam, and thus his study of Islamic law and duties had a functional as well as scholarly purpose. After setting off for the Middle East, Snouck stayed in Djeddah, the port of Mecca for almost six months, before traveling on to Mecca, where he concluded the welcoming ceremony of encircling the Ka'aba seven times. However, here Snouck's scientific and personal adventure came to an abrupt halt. In a French newspaper article,

Snouck was accused of trying to steal the possessions of the murdered French scholar C. Huber, which were left behind in Mecca. The French consul had a hand in this intrigue and stopped short what Snouck later called "the great event in my life" and "the beginning of a medieval dream." Just before the beginning of the Hajj, the annual pilgrimage at the heart of the Islamic belief system, Snouck was deported from Mecca. The unfairness of the incident could still make Snouck angry many years later. It did not, however, diminish his scholarly energies in any way, because soon after he concluded his second large publication, *Mekka*. This two-volume book, based on his experiences during his travels in the Middle East, reports the results of his fieldwork research in Mecca, and is one of the first Western scholarly descriptions and analyses of the town. The first volume describes the town and its rulers, while the second looks at day-to-day life in the town as Snouck found it in 1885. In addition, Snouck included an atlas with images to complete the set. The fact that the book was published in German made Snouck's research and ideas accessible to an international public for the first time, and made him internationally famous. In later years, Snouck would publish several other overview studies that were received well.

After the publication of *Mekka*, Snouck began a period of strong academic and political involvement with the Netherlands Indies. While in Mecca, he had encountered numerous Muslim pilgrims from the Netherlands Indies. At the time, this Dutch colonial possession was providing more pilgrims than any other region. These encounters imbued in Snouck the conviction that the Netherlands, then confronting frequent revolts in the Islamic state of Aceh in northern Sumatra, should study Islam thoroughly if it wished to rule its colony without problems. Snouck convinced the Dutch Ministry of the Colonies to let him make a study trip to the Netherlands Indies, though they would not permit him to start work in Aceh. During 1889 and 1890 Snouck first traveled through West and Central Java as a government advisor, tasked with making suggestions for the supervision of Islamic education and the functional improvement of Islamic councils. He produced numerous volumes of travel notes, which remain unpublished and have hardly been touched since they were deposited in his archives in Leiden. The Java trip did, however, yield several well-received articles on Javanese customs and traditions.

Finally, in 1891, Snouck had the opportunity to travel to Aceh, now as a government advisor on Asian languages and Islamic law. The visit lasted just over six months, but Snouck was not allowed to travel outside the Dutch military safety zone, which restricted the scope of his fieldwork studies considerably. Nevertheless, within three months he produced his report, the first two chapters of which were to form the basis for the two-volume government-sponsored publication *De Atjehers* (1893–1895; published in English in 1906 as *The Achenese*). The other chapters of the original report outlined Snouck's iconoclastic ideas about Dutch policies on Aceh. Snouck proposed a departure from the wait-and-see policy that had dominated Dutch actions for over a decade, and advised the government to break the resistance with force in the district of Aceh and Dependencies and thus achieve pacification of the whole area. The government was not enthusiastic about Snouck's proposal, however, and it would take several incidents in the area and a change of governor-general before his policy advice was implemented, starting in 1896.

The policy of pacification by force turned out to be very effective, in no small part due to the military skills of Colonel J. B. van Heutsz, who was in charge of the operations. Van Heutsz and Snouck cooperated closely in the field for several years. The chemistry between them was good, and in terms of devising policies and executing them in the greater Aceh area the two men were complementary. Snouck pushed strongly for the appointment of Van Heutsz as civil and military governor of Aceh, as he felt Van Heutsz was the best man to complete the task of full pacification. Snouck himself was appointed as advisor for Indigenous and Arabic Affairs in 1898, and in this position he was Van Heutsz's second-in command from 1898 to 1903, though he was only in Aceh until 1901. At the end of this period the relationship between the two men turned sour. Snouck did not agree with the way in which Van Heutsz pushed through the final submission of Aceh. In 1903, the same year a final treaty heralded an end to hostilities between the Dutch government and the sultan-pretender, Snouck asked to be relieved from his post. His request was honored, but it meant the end of his involvement with matters of colonial policy for five years. Only in 1908, when the new Dutch governor of Aceh, G. C. E. van Daalen—Van Heutsz's successor since the latter had been appointed governor-general of the Netherlands Indies in 1904—was sacked because of gross misbehavior during a number of military campaigns, did Minister A. W. F. Idenburg propose that Snouck be given a government commission to undertake an inquiry in Aceh. Snouck refused this offer, however, because, he claimed, his acceptance would cause Van Heutsz's resignation. Snouck, although not in agreement with Van Heutsz policy-wise, did not find Van Heutsz's resignation a viable option at that time.

In the following years, Snouck focused on the problem of pacification in other parts of the archipelago, and limited his political advice to those areas. It was only in Djambi that Snouck did research on the ground and kept a somewhat strong interest in developments over time. This put him in the position to advise the Dutch government concerning the Djambi Rebellion of 1916.

Mecca, Saudi Arabia, 1880s. *Christiaan Snouck Hurgronje, the Dutch government advisor and scholar of Islam, photographed this scene during the 1880s in Saudi Arabia, where he had traveled to study the practices of Muslim pilgrims.* © CORBIS. REPRODUCED BY PERMISSION.

In the meantime, Snouck published prolifically, both under his own name and under several pen names. He wrote about topical issues in the press, but also kept up his academic work. Snouck prepared an orthography in Latin characters for the Aceh language, and wrote two important articles about the language. He began studying the Gajos language and culture in 1900, and in 1903 published *Gajosland en zijn bewoners* (Gajosland and Its Inhabitants). Though only based on materials collected outside of Gajos, the book became a standard work, and the linguistic material in it found its way into the dictionary prepared by another scholar, G. A. J. Hazeu, some years later.

Snouck's social skills were well developed, and during his life he developed friendly relationships with numerous people in the Netherlands Indies and the Arab world. For this reason, he was often better informed about developments in the Islamic world than were many

of his contemporaries. The numerous opinions and recommendations Snouck offered during his long career—he would remain an official adviser to the colonial minister until 1933—comprised over two thousand pages in print and were published twenty years after his death.

Snouck left the Netherlands Indies for good in 1906, in order to escape his contentious relationship with Governor-General Van Heutsz. Having refused the offer of a chair in the Malay language in Leiden in 1891, and several other offers of a professorship in later years, Snouck was ready to return to academia. In 1907 he accepted the chair of Arabic language and culture in Leiden, succeeding his teacher De Goeje. His inaugural lecture, presented on January 23, 1907, was entitled *Arabia and the East Indies*, and dealt with the subject of study Snouck had first embraced in his Ph.D. dissertation, though now set in a mature context of a quarter of a century of personal involvement, field research, and extensive study.

Professor C. van Vollenhoven, occupying the chair in East Indian law, transferred his lecture series on Islam to Snouck. Snouck used these as a platform for his ideas on Islamic politics based on neutrality toward religion as such, and a strict intolerance toward politics based on (extremist) religion. In many respects, Snouck showed himself to be a child—if not a proponent—of the Ethical Policy in both its theoretical form and its development over time. Beginning in the 1890s as a proponent of the unification of the colonial state through the subduing and incorporating of rebellious regions, Snouck shifted in the 1910s and 1920s toward support for emancipation and the development of an indigenous administration. This was most evident in the pleasure he took in educating the sons of traditional political leaders. Snouck and his colleague Van Vollenhoven became staunch defenders of the thorough reform of the administrative structure of the Netherlands Indies through Western education and the association of elites on both sides of the political divide. In reaction to this, a conservative group set up and financed alternative courses at the University of Utrecht aimed at preparing aspiring civil servants for service in the East Indies. At the same time, Snouck kept on promoting the interests of the population of the Netherlands Indies in his lectures and publications.

After 1903 Snouck published no large works. The list of his smaller and often topical publications is impressive, however. He wrote about the demise of the Ottoman caliphate and the rise of the Turkish state, about the Arab revolt against the Turks, about the rise of the Saudi kingship in Arabia, and about Islam and race relations. In this period several articles were also published in English or French, which enhanced his international status further. He was asked repeatedly to give advice on international matters, and in 1925 he was offered the chair in Arabic language and culture of the National Egyptian University in Cairo. In 1927 Snouck resigned his chair in Leiden, though he remained closely connected to the university until his death, not least because of his appointment to a special chair in modern Arabic and the language of Aceh.

Snouck's family ties were interrelated with his work as an academic. The son of a Dutch Reformed minister, he married Ida Maria Oort, who came from a family that boasted several Leiden-based scholars of early Christianity, the Old Testament, the history of the Middle East, and law. His main teacher, De Goeje, was also part of this family group. At the same time, during his years in the Netherlands Indies, Snouck married two women according to Islamic rites, and had five children with them. For political reasons he never publicly acknowledged either of these wives or his children with them, although he did look after them. Snouck died in Leiden on June 26, 1936.

SEE ALSO *Aceh War; Ethical Policy, Netherlands Indies.*

BIBLIOGRAPHY

Benda, H. J. *The Crescent and the Rising Sun.* The Hague: W. van Hoeve, 1958.

Benda, H. J. "Christiaan Snouck Hurgronje and the foundations of Dutch Islam policy in Indonesia," *The Journal of Modern History* 30 (1958): 338–347.

Drewes, G. W. J. *Snouck Hurgronje en de Islamwetenschap.* Public lecture on the event of the 100th birthday of Dr. C. Snouck Hurgonje, 10 Februrary. Leiden, Netherlands: Universitaire Pers, 1957.

Drewes, G. W. J. "Snouck Hurgronje, Christiaan (1857–1936)." In: *Biografisch Woordenboek van Nederland.* Available from http://www.inghist.nl/Onderzoek/Projecten/BWN/lemmata/bwn2/snouckc.

Gobée, E. and C. Adriaanse, eds. *Ambtelijke adviezen van C. Snouck Hurgronje 1889–1936.* 3 vols. Gravenhage, Netherlands: Nijhoff, 1957–1965.

Pedersen, J. *The Scientific Work of Snouck Hurgronje.* Public lecture for the members of the Oosters Genootschap in the Netherlands, on the event of the 100th birthday of Snouck Hurgonje, 8 Febr. 1857. Leiden, Netherlands: Brill, 1957.

van Niel, R. "Christiaan Snouck Hurgronje." *Journal of Asian Studies* 16 (1956–57): 591–594.

Wertheim, W. F. "Counter-insurgency research at the turn of the Century–Snouck Hurgronje and the Acheh war." *Sociologische Gids* 19 (1972): 320–328.

Michel R. Doortmont

SOCIAL DARWINISM

The term *Darwinism* refers most centrally to the theory of natural selection, according to which only the fittest species in organic nature survive, whereas the unfit become extinct. The extension of these ideas to social thought is known as *Social Darwinism*.

The application of models of evolution to human societies long preceded the publication of Charles Darwin's *Origin of Species* in 1859, however. Already in the eighteenth century, historians influenced by the Scottish Enlightenment—including William Robertson and Adam Smith—had constructed a universal vision of history in which all societies advanced through four stages (from hunter-gathering to commercial society) as they progressed from "rudeness to refinement." This theory of development by stages influenced European notions of progress and of civilization among non-Europeans: peoples engaged in trade were held to be superior to those who relied exclusively on agriculture while the latter, in turn, were considered more advanced than subsistence hunter-gatherers.

In the early nineteenth century, the notion that world history and human society proceeded in evolutionary stages was purveyed in the works of Auguste Comte, G. W. F. Hegel, and Karl Marx, each of whom searched for general laws that underpinned social change. Unlike later theorists, these earlier political writers had a universal outlook that did not exclude non-European peoples from following the road already taken by European nations. By the time of Herbert Spencer (1820–1903), however, this optimism had given way to a bleaker, Malthusian conception of competition between human beings for the scarce resources required for subsistence. In the late nineteenth century, this notion became linked directly to imperialism. It provided a framework for understanding the rise and decline of nations and enlivened competition among European nations.

Spencer—who coined the term *survival of the fittest* several years before Darwin set forth his theory—developed an all-encompassing conception of human society and relations based on evolutionary principles. His conviction that a general law for all processes of the earth could be formulated led him to apply the biologic scheme of evolution to society. The principles of social change must be the same, he supposed, as those of the universe at large. Although Spencer clung to outdated scientific ideas, such as Jean-Baptiste Lamarck's debunked thesis concerning the inheritance of acquired characteristics, it would be inaccurate to argue that he corrupted Darwin's pristine scientific ideas. Many of Darwin's ideas emerged from the social context in which he lived. As Marx noted, "it is remarkable how Darwin recognizes in beasts and plants his English society with its divisions of labor, competition, [and] opening up of new markets" (Dickens 2000, p. 29).

Spencer's ideas about selection also were born from his political beliefs: He repudiated government interference with the "natural," unimpeded growth of society. He maintained that society was evolving toward increasing freedom for individuals and so held that government intervention should be kept to a minimum. This belief led him to oppose all state aid to the poor, a group he maintained were unfit and should be eliminated. Spencer viewed state intervention to ameliorate their condition as the "artificial preservation of those least able to take care of themselves." As Spencer wrote, "the whole effort of Nature is to get rid of such, to clear the world of them, and make room for better" (Hofstadter 1955, p. 41). Although he personally was against colonization and the European rivalry this activity engendered, Spencer's ideas were catalysts for a generation of influential writers on

Herbert Spencer. The English philosopher Herbert Spencer—who coined the phrase survival of the fittest—developed an all-encompassing conception of human society and relations based on evolutionary principles. EDWARD GOOCH/HULTON ARCHIVE/ GETTY IMAGES. REPRODUCED BY PERMISSION.

international relations and empire. Social Darwinism played a key role both in imperial rivalry among European states and in the justification of empire over non-European peoples. Social Darwinistic arguments about the struggle to be the "fittest" were utilized to justify rising military expenditure, to press for increased national efficiency, and to promote certain types of government. For example, Walter Bagehot harnessed biology to defend liberal democracy in the 1870s. Emphasizing cultural rather than individual selection, he sought to prove that the institutions and practice of liberal democracy were the guarantor of evolutionary progress. "In every particular state in the world," Bagehot wrote in *Physics and Politics* (1872), "those nations which are the strongest tend to prevail over the others; and in certain marked peculiarities the strongest tend to be the best" (Baumgart 1982, p. 84). In 1886 the Russian sociologist Jacques Novikov defined the foreign policy of a state as "the art of pursuing the struggle for existence among social organisms." War, in this view, was a determinant of the "fittest" nation: Karl Pearson claimed that should war cease, "mankind will no longer progress," for "there will be nothing to check the fertility of inferior stock, [and] the relentless law of heredity will not be controlled and guided by natural selection" (Baumgart 1982, p. 87).

Darwinism was put at the service of imperialism, as a new instrument in the hands of theorists of race and civilizational struggle. Competition with other European states urged the securing of colonies to prevent raw material, land, and potential markets from being seized by rapacious rivals. In Theodore Roosevelt's "The Strenuous Life" (1899), the future American president warned against the possibility of elimination in an international struggle for existence. America, he said, could not shrink from "hard contests" for empire or else the "bolder and stronger peoples will pass us by, and will win for themselves the domination of the world" (Hofstadter 1955, p. 180). Successful imperial ventures thus were perceived to indicate the vitality, and hence "fitness," of a nation.

Social Darwinism also proved to be a justification for the subjugation of non-European peoples, who were deemed less "fit" than Europeans. Nature, theorists argued, intended the rule of superior European nations over inferior colonial races. Racial arguments permeated the language of adherents of Social Darwinism as well. The French political leader Jules Ferry (1832–1893) explicitly argued that "the superior races have rights over the inferior races" (Baumgart 1982, p. 89). After World War I, the mandate and trusteeship system set up by the victors over much of the colonized world utilized arguments that derived from Social Darwinism. In 1922 Baron F. D. Lugard argued that the British Empire had a "dual mandate" in tropical dependencies "unsuited for white settlement," calling for the "advancement of the subject races" and "the development of [the territories'] material resources for the benefit of mankind." He insisted that indigenous populations were benefiting from "the influx of manufactured goods and the substitution of law and order for the methods of barbarism" (Lugard 1922, pp. 616–618). Social Darwinism thus lent a pseudoscientific veneer to colonial subjugation and bolstered the alleged civilizing mission of Europeans to non-Europeans.

The most extreme form of Social Darwinism was eugenics. Proponents of eugenics claimed that particular racial or social groups were naturally superior, and sought the enactment of laws that would control human heredity by forbidding marriage between people of different races and restricting the reproductive activities of people they considered unworthy, such as criminals and the mentally ill. In the late 1920s and 1930s, Nazis drew on such extreme precepts of Social Darwinism in their attempt to create an idealized Aryan race, an effort that culminated in the Holocaust and the brutal deaths of millions of

Jews, Roma (gypsies), and members of other groups considered inferior by the Nazis.

SEE ALSO *Imperialism, Liberal Theories of; Imperialism, Marxist Theories of.*

BIBLIOGRAPHY

Ballantyne, Tony. "Empire, Knowledge, and Culture: From Proto-Globalization to Modern Globalization." In *Globalization in World History*, edited by A. G. Hopkins. London: Pimlico, 2002.

Bannister, Robert C. "Social Darwinism." In *Microsoft Encarta Online Encyclopedia 2004*. Available from http://encarta.msn.com.

Baumgart, Winfried. *Imperialism: The Idea and Reality of British and French Colonial Expansion, 1880–1914*. Oxford, U.K.: Oxford University Press, 1982.

Dickens, Peter. *Social Darwinism: Linking Evolutionary Thought to Social Theory*. Buckingham, U.K.: Open University Press, 2000.

Hofstadter, Richard. *Social Darwinism in American Thought*. Boston: Beacon, 1955.

Jones, Greta. *Social Darwinism and English Thought: The Interaction between Biological and Social Theory*. Sussex, U.K.: Harvester, 1980.

Lugard, F. D. *The Dual Mandate in British Tropical Africa*. London and Edinburgh: Blackwood, 1922.

Semmel, Bernard. *Imperialism and Social Reform: English Social-Imperial Thought, 1895–1914*. London: Allen and Unwin, 1960.

Spencer, Herbert. *Social Statics*. London: J. Chapman, 1851.

Spencer, Herbert. *Study of Sociology*. London: King, 1873.

Sweet, William. "Herbert Spencer (1820–1903)." In *The Internet Encyclopedia of Philosophy*, edited by James Fieser. Available from http://www.iep.utm.edu/s/spencer.htm.

Wiltshire, David. *The Social and Political Thought of Herbert Spencer*. New York: Oxford University Press, 1978.

G. B. Paquette

SOUTHEAST ASIA, JAPANESE OCCUPATION OF

The Japanese occupation of Southeast Asia developed out of what was arguably the first international conflict that was truly "global," in that it mounted a challenge to the Eurocentric world system and to increasing American intervention in the region. Japan's leaders in the occupation championed the fight for Japanese hegemony in East Asia, which they saw as a legitimate right, and led what they conceived as a pan-Asian struggle to throw off the yoke of Western imperialism.

Prior to World War II (1939–1945), Japan controlled Korea (formally annexed in 1910), Taiwan (colonized in 1895), Karafuto (or Sakhalin Island), the Guangdong Leased Territory, and the Pacific Islands (most of Micronesia), and sought to integrate their economies with its own as suppliers of raw materials and foodstuffs in exchange for Japanese investment and technology.

In September 1931, units of the Japanese army stationed in Manchuria in northeastern China took steps to protect the security of the Russian-built railroad that Japan had acquired a quarter-century earlier. Aimed at resolving the "Manchurian Question," the takeover of the entire 400,000-square-mile (about 1,036,000-square-kilometer) region, with its population of thirty million, brought on denunciations not only from the League of Nations, from which Japan would withdraw in 1933, but also from the United States, whose tariffs and restrictions on immigration had already produced anti-American hostilities among the Japanese. The subsequent freezing of Japanese financial assets by the United States and its embargo on all oil exports to Japan led to the latter's decision to wage war against its Western adversaries.

The powerful Japanese army subscribed to the colonialist theory that the key to Japan's future prosperity and strength as a world power lay in control of Chinese raw materials and the vast market that that country had to offer. The Great Depression of the 1930s meant a loss of sales to foreign clients and the imposition of tariffs on Japanese imports. Wary of Communist Russia and fearful of a Communist takeover in China, Japan moved toward a policy of imperialist aggression. In 1937 Prime Minister Konoye Fumimaro (1891–1945) declared a "New Order in East Asia"; in political reality, its mission was to erect a buffer or Asian hinterland to ensure the security of an expanded Japanese Empire. Indeed, the slogan of "Asia for the Asians" pointed to an Asia liberated from Western domination but unified under Japanese rule.

In September 1940 Japan signed the Tripartite Pact, becoming therewith the ally of Germany and Italy. The Nazi offensives in Europe gave Japan the opportunity to move into territories southward and thus build alliances in opposition to the British, Dutch, Russians, and Americans. On invading northern Indochina, Japanese troops tried to close the Burma Road by which the Americans and the British brought supplies to the Chinese Nationalists. This action on the part of the Japanese brought them into opposition with the Allied powers. Japan subsequently proclaimed the expansion of its new order into French Indochina and the Dutch East Indies.

Japan had joined Vichy France in enforcing a protectorate over the entire French colony. Japanese troops invaded French-controlled Cochin China (southern Vietnam), entering Saigon (later called Ho Chi Minh City) in July of 1941. With the conclusion of the Hanoi convention in Spring of 1940, Japan had obtained permission from France to occupy northern Indochina. Japan in these movements was seeking to acquire control over the tin, rubber, and oil of Indonesia. Once the Nazis had taken over the Netherlands in May of 1940, Japan sent its delegates to Batavia (Jakarta), but it was not until after Japan's incursions in 1942 and its subsequent occupation that the Dutch conceded rights to oil and other resources in the Indonesian archipelago. With the internment of some 100,000 Dutch and Eurasians, many Javanese rejoiced, welcoming the invasion as a step in the process of "liberation from the colonial yoke."

Japan invaded British-controlled Malaya in December 1941 from the east coast at the same time that Singapore was bombarded. In this confrontation, the British fleet was sunk in the South China Sea. North Borneo would be occupied, then, in February, Singapore and Bali. Japan finally conquered Malaya in January 1942 and soon thereafter the Dutch East Indies, the great prize in this contest, in March 1942. British rule in Asia had ended. Wanting control over raw materials in Malaya, the Japanese chose to impose direct rule. By January 4, 1942, the Japanese took control of Manila, and the Japanese Imperial High Command announced the "liberation" of the formerly American-controlled Philippines.

In the spring of 1942, Japanese Premier Tojo Hideki (1884–1948) began organizing a Greater East Asia Ministry that would direct the affairs of the occupied nations and territories. The Greater East Asian Coprosperity Sphere was inaugurated in November 1942 with a promise to create a pan-Asian union. A year later, leaders of Japan, China, Manchukuo (Japanese Manchuria), Malaya, Thailand, Burma (Myanmar), Singapore, and the Philippines met at the Greater East Asia Conference in Tokyo, where they declared their solidarity and united opposition to Western imperialism. The Coprosperity Sphere was heralded as a pact of "mutual cooperation" between the signatory nations that aimed to "ensure stability of their region and construct an order of common prosperity and well-being based upon justice."

In reality, the Japanese occupation entailed harsh measures of control over national governments, economies, and cultures, with the settlement in the colonized countries of thousands of Japanese officials and laborers, all mainly for the benefit of Japan itself. Typically, Japanese officials held the bulk of authority in colonial administrations, whereas locals were consigned to subordinate functions. Indeed, Japan had promised independence to the Dutch East Indies but placed more than 23,000 Japanese officials in its colonial bureaucracy. Throughout the occupied territories, Japanese soldiers acted under no obligation to obey officers or even sentries of the "host" countries' military forces.

In the countries it occupied, Japanese authorities imposed educational reforms that would replace Western teachings with principles consistent with the "new order." Textbooks and periodicals were censored or banned, and *Nippongo* (the Japanese language) became a required part of the curriculum. Yet the brutality of Japanese rule and the establishment of a pro-Japanese hierarchy produced disillusionment throughout Southeast Asia. Japan suppressed shows of anti-Japanese nationalism in the occupied countries and exacted forced labor from their peoples. In mobilizing the masses for their cause, the Japanese high commands broadcast pro-Japanese propaganda on the radio and controlled the media. Throughout the occupied territories, moreover, Japanese troops inflicted violence on the local populations, which included the forcing of females into sexual slavery as "comfort women." Such outrages bred dissatisfaction but also catalyzed nationalist movements. Indonesia's Sukarno (1901–1970) would declare independence for his country on August 17, 1945, eight days after the atomic bomb fell over Nagasaki.

The temporary victory of Japan in Asia signified an end to the myth of Western invincibility and gave the European colonial regimes in Southeast Asia a shock from which they never recovered. In a unique confluence of historical movements, the Japanese occupation in Southeast Asia set countries of the region into multiple conflicts against powers that were fascist or imperialist or both. Japan's own imperialist drive extended its control over the broadest expanse of territory that Japan would ever know. Yet the defeat of Japan at the end of the Pacific War meant both the end of the Japanese Empire in Southeast Asia and the sunset of Western colonialism in the region.

SEE ALSO *Empire, Japanese; Occupations, East Asia; Occupations, the Pacific.*

BIBLIOGRAPHY

Brown, Roger H. "Japanese Expansion." In *Encyclopedia of Modern Asia*, edited by David Levinson and Karen Christensen, Vol. 3, 258–260. New York: Scribner's Sons, 2002.

Busch, Noel F. "A Flawed Democracy Falters." In *Japan*, edited by Clay Farris Naff, 106–111. San Diego: Greenhaven, 2004.

Gluck, Carol. "World War II in Asia." In *Encyclopedia of Asian History*, edited by Ainslee T. Embree, Vol. 4, 230–235. New York: Scribner's Sons, 1988.

Iriye, Akira. *The Origins of the Second World War in Asia and the Pacific*. London: Longman, 1987.

Keay, John. *Empire's End: A History of the Far East from High Colonialism to Hong Kong*. New York: Scribner, 1997.

Meyer, Milton W. "The Pacific War." In *Japan*, edited by Clay Farris Naff, 120–132. San Diego: Greenhaven, 2004.

Naff, Clay Farris, ed. *Japan*. San Diego: Greenhaven, 2004.

Worden, Robert L. "The Militarists Take Power." In *Japan*, edited by Clay Farris Naff, 112–119. San Diego: Greenhaven, 2004.

Eugenio Matibag

SPANISH AMERICAN INDEPENDENCE

The humiliating defeats suffered by Spanish forces during the Seven Years War (1756–1763) included the capture by British forces of Havana, one of the economic and strategic jewels in the imperial crown. In response, the administration of Charles III (1716–1788), who ruled from 1759 to 1788, sought to increase the rate of the reform of colonial government in order to secure its grasp on its overseas possessions in the second half of the eighteenth century. José Gálvez (1729–1787) came to epitomize these Bourbon reforms; he was appointed minister of the Indies in 1776. New administrative territories were created (such as the viceroyalty of the Río de la Plata and the captaincy-general of Venezuela) in order to increase efficiency and hence revenues. The new position of intendant was established in order to centralize power and increase accountability to Spain. In addition, measures were introduced to facilitate colonial trade, and to increase mining output and taxation yields. The Bourbon reforms were aimed at maintaining and reinforcing colonial America's economic dependence on Spain; they were essentially a program of modernization within the established order.

IMPERIAL REFORMS, COLONIAL TENSION

The reforms were generally successful in bringing about growth in colonial commerce and income from taxation. They also brought to a head simmering tensions about taxation and identity in the colonial world, particularly in the Andean regions that saw themselves as benefiting less from imperial rule than coastal urban centers. This contributed to some major rebellions against colonial rule. Tax increases fostered resentment and, often, a desire to return to the colonial consensus when imperial officials and their local alliances had enjoyed considerable autonomy to interpret official laws in accordance with local circumstances. Two major rebellions seriously threatened the colonial project in the Andes. The 1780 and 1781 rebellions in Andean Peru and Upper Peru (now Bolivia), headed by the indigenous leader Tomás Katari in the latter and José Gabriel Condorcanqui (1742–1781), a Creole noble of indigenous heritage who renamed himself Túpac Amaru II, in the former, were particularly violent and memorable expressions of the resentment and bitterness that lurked beneath the predominantly peaceful Spanish rule in the region.

In 1781 the Comuneros of New Granada physically protested against the increased tax burden and demanded the king to remedy the bad policies being enacted upon them by his representatives in America. These rebellions (eventually contained by the imperial authorities and, particularly in the case of Túpac Amaru, harshly repressed) were staged in defense of identity and interests, although they later became seen as stages on the road to the development of national self-awareness. The late eighteenth century saw a series of political uprisings against Spain evoking freedom and independence and causing anxiety about the consequences should such sentiments spread among indigenous peoples, slaves, and freed people of color. The shadow of the Haitian Revolution was never far away, particularly in the Spanish circum-Caribbean where slavery was most prevalent.

CRISIS IN 1808

As historian F. X. Guerra argued, the absolutist vision of imperial rule collapsed among Creoles after Napoléon Bonaparte (1769–1821) imposed his brother Joseph (1768–1844) as king of Spain in 1808. Old forms of representation such as *cabildos* (town councils) and *municipios* (municipalities) continued to be important, but loyalty to the king as the supreme representative of the *pueblo* (people) was destroyed. During 1808 to 1810 cities and towns across Spanish America declared their own autonomy and sovereignty while they awaited the return of the legitimate king, *el deseado* Ferdinand VII (1784–1833). Creoles filled the political vacuum in order to safeguard their own lives and property, and to preserve their positions at the top of the colonial social and racial hierarchies. The juntas formed on the basis of these fears and these colonial institutions, and the limited autonomies they represented became pathways toward independence during the subsequent extended period of confusion regarding the Spanish metropolitan political situation. But once the ties to Spain had been broken, they would never be fully repaired. In the words of historian John Lynch (1994), Spanish America could not remain a colony without a metropolis, or a monarchy without a monarch. In addition, the often violent and unsympathetic policy pursued by Spanish officials in their attempts to reconquer the rebellious colonies contributed to the disintegration of the colonial world.

INTER-IMPERIAL CONFLICT AND COLONIAL RELATIONS

In the decades preceding 1808, the Americas were a zone of conflict between Britain, France, and Spain for imperial control and influence, just as they had been in preceding centuries. Around 1796 Spain lost economic control of its American colonies, which increasingly convinced Creoles that they had been abandoned to their fate by a weakened, incapable, and indifferent imperial power. The Bourbon reform innovation of *comercio libre* did not mean the free trade of Adam Smith (1723–1790), but rather a protectionist policy of freedom for Spaniards to trade within the confines of an empire that was supposed to shelter them from economic rivals such as Britain. Nevertheless, the destruction of the Spanish fleet at Trafalgar in 1805 represented only the confirmation of a process that had developed over several decades in which British merchants became the principal agents for the import and export of goods to and from Spanish America. Repeated warfare between Spain and Britain disrupted official trade between the metropole and colonies and shifted large sections of trade into the hands of smugglers and those who dealt with them.

In addition, the wars surrounding Haitian independence entailed massive loss of life, and their geopolitical consequences were also considerable. Britain asserted itself further by taking Trinidad from Spain and Tobago and St. Lucia from France: All three were important staging posts toward influence on the Spanish American mainland. The constantly shifting geopolitical situation in the Western hemisphere between 1756 and 1808 meant that moves toward Hispanic American independence fully embraced contemporary Atlantic currents of ideology and commerce. In the subsequent attempts to establish republics independent of Spanish rule, Creoles repeatedly angled for the support and assistance of major foreign powers. They attempted to play off one against the other by offering commercial concessions and promises of future support. Diplomatic missions were repeatedly sent to London, Paris, Washington, and the Vatican. Receptions were almost always guarded and cautious with the powers, anxious not to offend Spanish sensibilities by explicitly supporting independence movements that in private they often welcomed or encouraged. British diplomatic recognition was predicated on the abolition of the slave trade by the new republics, something that each government promised to do with varying degrees of reluctance, depending on the importance of that trade to their economy. (Cuba, not coincidentally, was the most reliant on slave labor, and remained both a colony of Spain and a trader in slaves.)

MOVEMENTS FOR CONTINENTAL LIBERATION

From the beginning, farsighted Creoles saw that the fate of independence in their own locality would depend upon the success or otherwise of revolutions elsewhere in Hispanic America. There were two continental

***Simón Bolívar,* El Libertador.** *The South American revolutionary, statesman, and soldier Simón Bolívar, known as The Liberator, in an engraving rendered circa 1820.* HULTON ARCHIVE/GETTY IMAGES. REPRODUCED BY PERMISSION.

movements for liberation coming out of Buenos Aires and Caracas. In 1806 a British force operating somewhere between its official orders and own initiative in the South Atlantic attacked Buenos Aires, an event that was reported in newspapers across Hispanic America. Initially successful, the British were repelled within weeks by a Creole militia under Santiago Liniers (1753–1810) responding to the complete incapacity and inaction of the colonial defense forces. The British returned a year later and were again denied, and the seeds of independence were planted in Buenos Aires.

In 1810 the viceroy was deposed but the ambitions of the new Buenos Aires political and commercial elite to rule over its hinterland as the viceroy had done were to be frustrated. Upper Peru, Paraguay, Santiago de Chile, and the regions of present-day Argentina all refused to be ruled from Buenos Aires, triggering a decade of warfare for control of the new independence, and the establishment

of several new republics outside of Buenos Aires' sphere of influence. Nevertheless, in 1814 the revolutionary government in Buenos Aires chose José Francisco de San Martín (1778–1850) as its military leader, and he went on to form the Army of the Andes and defeat Royalists in battles in Chile, most famously at Maipo in 1818. San Martín planned to assure the independence of Buenos Aires by expelling the viceroy of Peru from Lima—this he did in 1821.

The other movement toward independence, led by Simon Bolívar (1783–1830), came out of Venezuela, one of the first areas to declare independence from Spain. Patriotic declarations of independence and worthy and wordy constitutions were little defense, however, when a Spanish expedition under Pablo Morillo (1778–1837) finally arrived in Venezuela to begin a reconquest in 1814. The expedition encountered a population that had been ravaged by civil war and that had by no means irrevocably cast off its adherence to the Crown. Many people were easily persuaded to show allegiance to the reconquerors. Exploiting considerable differences between the patriotic factions, between rival towns, and between groups of diverse ethnic loyalties, by the end of 1815 virtually all of Venezuela, New Granada, and Ecuador was back under imperial rule, along with all of the viceroyalty of Peru that remained faithful to the Crown.

Forced into exile by the reconquest, Bolívar took up residence in Jamaica and then Haiti, where he wrote long letters justifying the struggle for independence and prepared new expeditions of liberation. In 1816 he sailed for Venezuela and began a long but eventually successful military campaign, building on the successes of other regional *caudillos* who had remained in Venezuela resisting the *reconquista.* Bolívar was successful in attracting over 7,000 European (mainly Irish) mercenaries to his cause between 1817 and 1820. In 1819 at the Congress of Angostura, in a small town on the side of the River Orinoco, Bolívar and his allies formally declared the Independence of the Republic of Colombia, encompassing the territories of Venezuela, New Granada, and Ecuador, where over the next three years Bolívar's armies would formally take control from the disintegrating and increasingly demoralized Royalist armies.

In Mexico, wherein uniquely Spanish American substantive ideas about national identity had developed during the colonial period, events took a different course. The symbol of the Mexican Virgin of Guadelupe was adopted by rebels in their struggle against Spain: the priest Miguel Hidalgo (1753–1811) took the Virgin of Guadelupe as his emblem when he declared an uprising with his *Grito de Dolores* on September 16, 1810. The situation in Mexico was made worse by drought and high food prices, which brought the hunger and despair of the rural poor more fully into the equation. Popular insurgency was essentially local, social, and agrarian rather than national or utopian, however, despite the Creole patriotism and belief in a Mexican identity, which united many intellectuals.

The uprising was eventually quelled by force and both Hidalgo, and his successor as leader José María Morelos (1765–1815), were executed. Spanish rule continued in Mexico, albeit weakened, until 1821. It finally fell when Agustin de Iturbide (1783–1824), a former Royalist soldier turned revolutionary leader, articulated plans for independent nationhood in his Plan de Iguala. In this appealing compromise, Mexico was to be an independent constitutional monarchy, closely linked to the Catholic church. Iturbide was independent Mexico's first emperor but he was powerless to overcome the economic, regional, and political problems that continued to beset the region and he was executed upon his return from an early exile in 1824. In the rest of Central America independence was a more fractured process, in which local power centers fought successfully to establish autonomy from Spain, from Mexico, and from Guatemala.

THE ANDEAN CLIMAX

The two separate trajectories of military movements for independence in Hispanic South America, symbolized by their respective leaders Bolívar and San Martín, met in the coastal port of Guayaquil in 1822. The latter went into exile, whereas Bolívar orchestrated the Andean climax of the independence movements, leading his forces to victory over Royalists at Junín in 1824 and then retiring to Lima while his young general Antonio José de Sucre (1795–1830) finished the job at Ayacucho on December 10, 1824. Royalist resistance was finally defeated in the highlands during 1825, and in coastal strongholds such as Callao and Chiloe in 1826. (The Caribbean island colonies of Cuba, Puerto Rico, and Santo Domingo remained loyal to the Crown for several decades more.)

In the same year of 1826 Bolívar unveiled his constitution for the new republic of Bolivia, to be administered in the old colonial jurisdiction of Upper Peru, named after its great liberator. Bolívar's democratic ideals had been tempered by years of experience of popular protest, race conflict, and elite factionalism, and his constitution aimed to provide stability and authority for lands whose futures he feared would become ungovernable. The failure of Bolívar's constitution prefigured half a century in which elites sought to build nations, safeguard property and avoid bloodshed while remaining true to at least the rhetoric of liberty that had catalyzed their struggles for independence.

WAS THERE A CRISIS OF SPANISH COLONIALISM?

Lynch (1994) has argued that political independence had a demographic inevitability. The increasing numbers of Creoles and their consequent desire for influence became a constant and pressing thorn in the side of imperial policy. The ideological effects of intellectual innovations reverberating across the Atlantic world in the first quarter of the nineteenth century were also important in maintaining the conflict. Many of the Creoles involved in the juntas and the subsequent military and political struggles for independence formed part of the same liberal Atlantic world of the Enlightenment that fostered the 1812 Constitution of Cádiz in Spain. Bolívar, San Martín, Iturbide, and many others had traveled to London, read widely, and interpreted new ideas of freedom and equality in terms of what they saw as the unique circumstances of Hispanic America.

Nevertheless, the tipping-point toward inevitability had certainly not been reached by 1808. It was metropolitan crisis that combined with new colonial articulations of the revolutionary Atlantic in the wake of the American, French, and Haitian examples to create a unique Hispanic American (and not, at least initially, anticolonial) revolution and then independence. Despite fears of informal imperialism, and the shackles of debt and unfavorable trading relationships that beset the new republics in their early years, the events between 1808 and 1825 set into motion both short and long-term changes in social arrangements and relationships that would have been impossible under Spanish rule.

SEE ALSO *Empire in the Americas, Spanish; Haitian Revolution; Túpac Amaru, Rebellion of.*

BIBLIOGRAPHY

Fisher, J., A. McFarlane, and A. Kuethe, eds. *Reform and Insurrection in Bourbon New Granada, and Peru.* Baton Rouge: Louisiana State University Press, 1990.

Guerra, F. X. *Modernidad e independencias,* Madrid: Mapfre, 1992.

Kinsbruner, J. *Independence in Spanish America: Civil Wars, Revolutions, and Underdevelopment.* Albuquerque: University of New Mexico Press, 1994.

Lynch, J. *Latin American Revolutions, 1808–1826: Old and New World Origins.* Norman: University of Oklahoma Press, 1994.

Rodriguez, J. E. *The Independence of Spanish America.* Cambridge, U.K. and New York: Cambridge University Press, 1998.

Matthew Brown

SPICE ISLANDS
SEE *Moluccas*

SRI LANKA
SEE *Ceylon*

STANLEY, HENRY MORTON
1841–1904

Born as John Rowlands in Denbigh, Wales, on January 28, 1841, Henry Morton Stanley spent most of his unfortunate youth in a workhouse, from which he was released in 1856. He embarked on a ship to the United States as a cabin boy in 1858, but jumped ship upon his arrival in New Orleans. There he met a wealthy cotton broker, Henry Hope Stanley, who offered him protection and gradually began treating him as a son. Out of gratitude to his adoptive father, John Rowlands took the name "Stanley" from 1859 onwards. After a quarrel with his benefactor, he resumed his errant lifestyle.

He was, among other things, a sailor, a soldier in the Confederate (1861–1862) and the Union army (1864–1865), and a journalist. In this capacity, he traveled widely in the Far West, in Ethiopia, and in many countries around the Mediterranean. In 1869 the *New York Herald* asked him to organize an expedition in order to search for Dr. David Livingstone (1813–1873), the British missionary and explorer, who was reported lost in Central Africa. This expedition met with success and took place between 1871 and 1872. Stanley found Livingstone in Ujiji. After this, he convinced the *New York Herald* and the *Daily Telegraph* to finance another expedition in this region.

Starting from Bagamoyo, on the East African coast, on November, 17, 1874, he crossed the continent in approximately 1,000 days, arriving in Boma, at the mouth of the Congo River, on August, 9, 1877. On his return to Europe, Stanley tried to persuade the British authorities to develop a more active political interest in the Congo area. These demarches being unsuccessful, he then accepted the offer of Leopold II (1835–1909), king of the Belgians, to become the managing agent of the *Comité d'Etudes du Haut-Congo* and, later, of the *Association Internationale du Congo* (AIC). Both organizations were created by Leopold II to realize his commercial and political ambitions in the Congo region.

From 1879 to 1884, Stanley remained intensely active. During this period, he explored the Congo basin, built a military force, concluded treaties with African

Henry Morton Stanley. *The Welsh-born explorer and journalist Henry Morton Stanley led expeditions across Central Africa during the 1870s and 1880s. In this illustration he consults a map with the assistance of African guides and other members of his expedition.* © BETTMANN/CORBIS. REPRODUCED BY PERMISSION.

chiefs recognizing the AIC's sovereignty, and founded many colonial stations, some of which were to become major cities such as Kinshasa and Kisangani. Upon his return to Europe in June 1884, he became a technical adviser of the American delegation at the Berlin Conference (1884–1885), while still on Leopold's payroll. Consequently, he contributed to the international recognition of the AIC as the legitimate authority of the vast area, which was, from then on, called the Congo Free State.

Stanley led a last important expedition in Africa from March 1887 to December 1889. With Eduard Schnitzer (1840–1892), also called Emin Pasa, white province governor in Southern Sudan, being threatened by the Mahdists, a campaign was launched in Europe to rescue him. Stanley was chosen as the leader of this expedition, which succeeded in finding Emin Pasa and bringing him back to the east coast of Africa. Leopold II, still eager to expand his African dominion toward the Nile, then asked Stanley to lead a huge military campaign to take Khartoum from the Mahdists, but Stanley declined the offer. Stanley's career as an explorer was now over, but in the early 1890s he made one last contribution to the shaping of colonial Africa, when he led a campaign aimed at bringing and maintaining Uganda under British rule.

During the last years of his life, Stanley retired to the English countryside. In 1890, he married a wealthy lady, Dorothy Tennant, and adopted a son in 1896. Stanley served as a Member of Parliament (1895–1900) and was knighted in 1899. He died in his domain of Furze Hill, Surrey, on May 10, 1904.

Stanley was a controversial figure, even in his own time. He met with hostility in influential British circles, but, at the same time, was hailed as a heroic personality—most notably by the Belgians. The many books Stanley wrote, as well as his numerous conferences held in Europe and the United States largely contributed to his extraordinary fame. Stanley's writings must nevertheless be read with great caution, since their author more than once takes liberty with the facts. This tendency to hide or to embellish things is but one aspect of Stanley's complex psychology. On the one hand, he was tortured by his troubled sexuality; on the other, he acted in an authoritarian, ruthless, and often violent way during his African journeys, both toward the African population and the members of his expedition. With that being said, Stanley undoubtedly left a historic imprint on the political fate of contemporary Africa.

SEE ALSO *Belgium's African Colonies; Berlin Conference.*

BIBLIOGRAPHY

Liniger-Gaumaz, Max, and Gerben Helling. *Henry Morton Stanley. Bibliographie.* Genève: Editions du Temps, 1972.

McLynn, Frank. *Stanley, the Making of an African Explorer.* Chelsea, MI: Scarborough House Publishers; Chicago: Independent Publishers Group, 1990.

McLynn, Frank. *Stanley. The Sorcerer's Apprentice.* Oxford, U.K.: Oxford University Press, 1992.

Newman, James L. *Imperial Footprints: Henry Morton Stanley's African Journeys.* Washington, DC: Brassey's, 2004.

"Stanley Private Papers." The Africa Museum of Tervuren, Belgium. Available from http://www.africamuseum.be/research/dept4/history/publications/StanleyArchives.

Guy Vanthemsche

STRAITS SETTLEMENTS

The Straits Settlements, a British colonial administrative unit comprised of three city ports flourishing along the Strait of Malacca, was established in 1826 and administered from Penang, overseeing Malacca and Singapore.

Penang, the first Straits settlement, was ceded to the English East India Company on August 11, 1786, by Sultan Abdullah Mukarram (r. September 23, 1778–September 1, 1797), the ruler of Kedah, who was eager to seek British protection from Siamese and Burmese threats.

As a trading center and port of call, Penang (in present-day Malaysia) left much to be desired. Despite the reluctance of the British government, Singapore, located at the southern tip of the Strait of Malacca, was sought, therefore, as an additional settlement by Stamford Raffles (1781–1826), a farsighted and industrious British colonial administrator. Notwithstanding Dutch attempts to forestall it, Singapore was successfully acquired from Sultan Hussein Muazzam Shah (r. February 6, 1819–September 2, 1835), the lawful but displaced ruler of Johor, on February 6, 1819. Malacca (Malaysia), the other settlement, was obtained from the Dutch through the Anglo-Dutch Treaty of March 17, 1824, in exchange for the British colony Bencoolen (present-day Bengkulu, Indonesia) that was situated on the west coast of Sumatra. Among the three settlements, Singapore stood out as the most prosperous.

The British presence in the Far East came on the heels of the Portuguese and the Dutch. The efforts to seek a wider market for woolen cloth and other manufactured goods produced by the blooming industries in Europe brought the British government, through the English East India Company, first to India and later to the Malay Archipelago, which was popularly known as the East Indian islands. As a major sea route connecting the Indian and Pacific oceans, the Strait of Malacca was indispensable because of the increasing trade between Europe and China in the eighteenth century. By then, tea had become a social beverage in Europe, and the growing demand for Chinese tea made a free passage to China a central concern of European merchants and governments.

For the British, the Strait of Malacca remained the most important sea route for Indian opium and Strait produce, such as pepper and tin, to be shipped to China in exchange for its tea. Fearing a possible monopoly of the burgeoning trade by the Dutch, the British government eventually searched for a staging post for both commercial and military vessels from British India to the Far East. Penang, located at the northern entrance of the Strait of Malacca, was chosen, owing to its strategic position.

As a new British settlement, Penang saw a rapid expansion of trade and immigrants; in 1805, it was made the fourth presidency of British India. The high expectations for Penang, however, remained unfulfilled. Not suitable as a dockyard due to the unavailability of quality timber nearby, Penang, in 1812, was abandoned as a naval base. The waning importance of Penang, however, lay chiefly in its unsuccessful bid to become a great trading center among the East Indian islands. Situated on the western edge of the Malay Archipelago, Penang failed to summon adequate trade to be financially independent and remained a constant drain to the coffers of British India.

When Singapore was established as a new British settlement in 1819, Penang's strategic value diminished even further. As a free port located closer to the center of the Malay Archipelago, Singapore became the darling of the day, endearing itself to local and international sea merchants. Singapore's success was made more distinct as it was the only settlement in the Straits Settlements able to foot its own expenditure. In 1832 it replaced Penang as the administrative center of the Straits Settlements. Under Penang's watch, the Straits Settlements had forfeited its presidency status and been reduced to a residency in June 30, 1830, because of financial strain.

As commercial interests in Singapore gained strength, its mercantile community began to demand more attention and voice over Singapore's affairs. However, the English East India Company, which administered the Straits Settlements, lost interest in Singapore after losing its monopoly on the China trade in 1833, and it took little note of the grievances of Singapore's merchants. The residents of Singapore were rarely consulted on such matters as the dumping of Indian convicts on the island to the proposed port tax that threatened the very foundation of Singapore's success as a free port.

The mercantile community eventually brought their concerns to the British Parliament, and after long decades of public meetings and petitioning, Singapore was finally made a crown colony on April 1, 1867, and received direct rule from the Colonial Office in London. With the advent of steamships in the mid-1860s and the opening of the Suez Canal in 1869, Singapore's position as the port of call between Europe and China was further strengthened; it became at once "the Gibraltar and the Constantinople of the East."

SEE ALSO *Malaysia, British, 1874-1957; Raffles, Sir Thomas Stamford; Singapore.*

BIBLIOGRAPHY

Andaya, Barbara Watson, and Leonard Y. Andaya. *A History of Malaysia*, 2nd ed. Honolulu: University of Hawaii Press, 2001.

Mills, Lennox Algernon. *British Malaya, 1824–67*. Kuala Lumpur and New York: Oxford University Press, 1966.

Swettenham, Frank Athelstane. *British Malaya: An Account of the Origin and Progress of British Influence in Malaya,* rev. ed. London: Allen and Unwin, 1948.

Turnbull, C. M. *The Straits Settlements, 1826–67: Indian Presidency to Crown Colony.* London: Athlone, 1972.

Choon-Lee Chai

SUB-SAHARAN AFRICA, EUROPEAN PRESENCE IN

The first European contact with sub-Saharan Africa was a byproduct of the Portuguese desire to bypass the Muslim world and to tap the gold trade from Africa and the spice trade from the Indies. By 1444, the Portuguese had passed the Senegal River and entered into contact with black African peoples. They reached the Gold Coast in 1471 and the Congo River in 1483. In 1488 Bartolomeo Dias (ca. 1450–1500) rounded the Cape of Good Hope. Ten years later, Vasco da Gama (ca. 1469–1524) reached India. In the process, the Portuguese also discovered a series of islands in the Atlantic Ocean: Madeira in 1418, the Cape Verde Islands in 1460, and São Tomé in 1470.

European settlement in Africa was limited. In 1482 the Portuguese began construction of a fort, El Mina, on the Gold Coast, which became the major center of their gold trade. Many Portuguese settled on the Atlantic islands, which became either commercial entrepôts or centers of plantation agriculture, usually using African slaves. There was also an important Portuguese presence in the Congo kingdom and on the East African coast, where they tried to control the Indian Ocean trade that was profitable for Arab traders.

The Portuguese diaspora was largely made up of men, who often married local women. They thus developed Luso-African populations, Catholic in belief, but linked by language and culture to both Portugal and various African cultures. Cape Verdians developed trading communities along the West Africa coast. In the Zambezi Valley, the Portuguese gave land grants called *prazos* to men, who married locally and exploited their ties with Portugal and with local African rulers to form small states.

Portugal was a small country, which by the late sixteenth century was being challenged by the Dutch, British, and French, who wanted to participate in the slave and gold trades. In East Africa, Arab traders and a Swahili resistance won control of all areas north of Mozambique. Few of the other Europeans settled in Africa. This was partly a result of African resistance. African states generally restricted the European presence to coastal ports of trade. It was also due to the high mortality rate Europeans experienced along most of the African coast. Europeans had little resistance to diseases like malaria and yellow fever that decimated their numbers. Slave traders generally traded from their ships or from temporary installations in various ports of trade. African merchants often prolonged negotiations over slave cargoes, knowing that disease would press Europeans to settle quickly in order to get back to the sea. The mortality rate of sailors on slaving expeditions was higher than that for the slaves themselves.

EARLY SETTLEMENT

There were some European installations. The French had bases at Saint-Louis and Gorée in what is now Senegal. All trading nations maintained castles on the Gold Coast, where the climate was somewhat more favorable than elsewhere. There were small European installations on the Slave Coast, particularly at Whydah in what is now Benin. The Portuguese founded Luanda (in Angola) in 1576 and maintained settlements on the Mozambique coast, most notably on Mozambique Island.

The number of Europeans in these settlements was very small. As late as the early nineteenth century, there were little more than two hundred French-born males in the two Senegalese settlements. The majority of the population of most of these settlements was slaves, some of them trusted figures who led trading expeditions and played key roles in military and economic life.

Most of the "Europeans" were either of mixed descent or were Africans who learned European languages and participated in Atlantic culture. The slave trade was lucrative enough to attract Europeans willing to risk the possibility of an early death. A small number survived their first bouts with malaria and lived many years. Many others left their trading establishments in the hands of their African wives, many of whom proved to be shrewd traders. Those who lived long enough also left behind offspring, some of whom were educated in Europe and many of whom expanded family trading operations.

This persisted into the nineteenth century. When the British abolished the slave trade, they pressured other European nations to do the same and eventually to sign treaties allowing each other the right to search and seize ships in the slave trade. Over about sixty years, the British freed more than 180,000 people, who were taken to Freetown in Sierra Leone, where the only international prize court was available. The function of this court was to decide whether the ships seized were slavers and thus subject to seizure under international law. Entrusted to European missions, these people, known as Creoles or Krio, eagerly absorbed education and usually became Christians. They provided West Africa's first modern professionals: doctors, lawyers, judges, civil servants, ministers, teachers, and journalists. They also helped staff the nascent colonial administrations, the missions, and British commercial operations.

The most important area of European settlement was South Africa, where the climate was more temperate than areas further north. South Africa was also strategic because of its commanding position on the only trade route to India and Indonesia. The voyage to the Indies was a long one, generally about five months. Ships usually stopped at several places to pick up supplies and fuel.

The Dutch East India Company founded Cape Town as a refreshment station. The climate was favorable, but the hinterland was inhabited by hunters and herders, who lacked a surplus and were not eager for trade. The company thus settled a small number of colonists to provide food for passing ships. After the arrival of French Huguenot settlers in the 1680s, the Dutch East India Company stopped further immigration because it did not want the cost of a real colony. Still, the disease environment was favorable, native people were a limited threat, and good land was available. In 1717 there were only two thousand free people in the colony, but the population grew rapidly.

In spite of company efforts, the frontier pushed rapidly inland. The residents of Cape Town itself focused on servicing ships going to and from Asia. In the area around the city, grain and wine production provided supplies for the boats. The frontier saw the emergence of a more extensive economy based on ways of using cattle learned from the local Khoi. Better armed than native people, the frontiersmen tended to be poor in goods, but wealthy in land, cattle, and dependants.

Some of the local Khoi and San were decimated by European diseases like smallpox. Others retreated into the far interior. A large group moved into service on the European farms. Some were children of San hunters taken prisoner when their parents were killed and raised as virtual slaves on farms of the Dutch frontiersmen. The Cape Town slaves, the frontier servants, and the offspring of mixed marriages eventually merged into a group labeled *Coloured*. Others passed into the European population, which grew rapidly, largely as a result of natural increase.

NINETEENTH CENTURY

In the nineteenth century, the European presence in Africa changed dramatically and well before European medical science came to terms with Africa's tropical diseases. The first change was the attack on slavery. Britain abolished the slave trade in 1807 and slavery itself in 1833. The French abolished slavery in 1848 but were not as resolute as the British in their efforts to try to exterminate the Atlantic slave trade. Though the slave trade persisted into midcentury and actually grew in East, Central and Northeast Africa, the closing of American markets and improved methods of steam navigation destroyed the Atlantic trade by the 1860s. Fueled by abolitionist groups in Britain, the United States, and Europe, the fight against slavery increased European involvement in Africa.

It did so largely through the second change, the development of Christian missions in Africa. Catholic missionaries under Portuguese auspices played an earlier role, particularly in the Congo, where they created a

Christian community. In the eighteenth century, the Catholic Church lacked both funds and personnel to continue these efforts, but Protestants, led by newer churches like the British Methodists and Quakers or German Pietists, became involved in mission efforts.

South Africa became an important field for mission activity. Freetown in Sierra Leone became a particularly important center as missions responded to the needs of the recently freed recaptives, as those freed by the British Navy were called. The Catholic Church reemerged as a major factor in mission activity from the 1840s. In 1856 the Scottish explorer David Livingstone (1813–1873) gave an important speech at Westminster Abbey in London calling for young missionaries to carry the faith to Africa and to struggle against the slave trade. As a result, by the time the scramble for Africa took place in the 1880s, Christian missions were found in all parts of Africa.

Many of the first converts were runaway slaves, who took refuge at mission stations and, like the Creoles of West Africa, eagerly sought education. Missions depended on the ability to raise money, and thus lectures by returning missionaries and publications by and about them helped spread information on Africa in Europe.

The third change was an increase in exploration. The primary drive for the first explorations was scientific curiosity about unknown parts of the world. From 1768 to 1773, James Bruce (1730–1794), a Scottish landowner, explored Ethiopia. In 1788 the African Association was founded in Great Britain to encourage exploration. Many of the early explorers paid with their lives. In 1796 the Scottish explorer Mungo Park (1771–1806) became the first European to see the Niger River, but he died in 1806 on a second exploration seeking to find out where the river went. Scottish explorer Hugh Clapperton (1788–1827) died in the same effort, but in 1830 the British explorer Richard Lander (1804–1834) found the Niger's outlet.

Many explorers were also missionaries, the most famous being Livingstone, who covered much of Central and southern Africa between 1851 and his death in 1873. German scholar Heinrich Barth (1821–1865) spent four years in central Sudan. French military officers included Louis-Gustave Binger (1856–1936), who explored western Sudan, and Pierre Savorgnan de Brazza (1852–1905), who explored the area north of the Congo River. Many, like Park and de Brazza, traveled alone or with one or two companions. Others, like the brutal British explorer Henry Morton Stanley (1841–1904), traveled in large, well-armed, and well-funded caravans, which could shoot their way out of difficult situations.

Underwriting all of this was the Industrial Revolution, which dramatically increased European wealth and power. This wealth created an industrial bourgeoisie

---

Estimated populations of Sub-Saharan Africa, 1500

West Africa	14,000,000
East Africa	12,800,000
Central Africa	8,000,000
Southern Africa	3,500,000
Total	38,300,000

SOURCE: Adapted from table 6.1 'African Population, 1–2001 A.D.,' in Angus Maddison, *The World Economy: Historical Statistics* (Paris: Development Centre of the Organization for Economic Co-operation and Development 2003), p. 190.

THE GALE GROUP.

---

convinced of the value of free labor and hostile to slavery. It provided the funding for the missionaries and explorers. European wealth also changed the pattern of European economic involvement with Africa. It reduced the price of products European commerce sold in Africa. The cost of cotton cloth, for example, was reduced to about 5 percent of what it had been. Cheaper commodities provided an incentive for Africans to produce cash crops.

The Industrial Revolution also created new needs and intensified old ones. From the 1790s, European demand for vegetable oils increased dramatically. Palm oil and peanut oil were used to lubricate machines and to produce soap and, later, margarine. European hopes that Africa would provide a new source of cotton produced limited results, but Zanzibar (in present-day Tanzania) became the world's largest producer of cloves. Cocoa, coffee, gum, wool, and copra were all important, and after 1870 Africa became a major source of rubber, which was used to make tires for bicycles and later automobiles.

New products created new structures. The French expanded their presence in Senegal in the 1850s. The British established a protectorate over Lagos (a port in present-day Nigeria) in 1851 and then occupied the city in 1861. European commercial houses increased their activity in various places along the coasts of Africa. All major powers established consulates in Zanzibar. The British also created a consulate for the bights of Benin and Biafra. Credit machinery, some based on the trust system of the slave trade, was expanded and facilitated the commercial penetration of the interior. In West Africa, European merchants and banks provided credit, while in East Africa, it was Indian financiers.

This slow expansion took place in spite of the continued high mortality. In an 1841 expedition up the Niger, forty-eight Europeans lost their lives to malaria. Thirteen years later, the Scottish explorer William Balfour Baikie (1825–1864) sent another expedition up the Niger with instructions that all Europeans were to use quinine to prevent disease. Not a single person died. The use of quinine made it possible for Europeans to operate in the interior of Africa, though the discovery of the parasites that caused malaria and yellow fever did not take place until the early twentieth century. The European military presence was still mostly African soldiers. The armies that conquered Africa in the latter part of the century were largely armies of African soldiers, often of slave origin, under the command of European officers.

Technological progress was also important. The steamboat dramatically reduced the cost of shipping, making it possible for bulkier items to be shipped profitably. By the middle of the century, mail steamers were calling at major ports in Africa, making it possible for both European and African traders to buy space and ship relatively small lots of goods. Improvements in weaponry—breach-loader rifles, repeaters, field artillery, and toward the end of the century, the machine gun—made killing much more efficient. Many of these weapons could be obtained by African military leaders, but the cost was high and the long-term effect was to facilitate the European ability to dominate any field of combat. European business interests also began talking of railroads opening up the interior, though as late as 1870 there was only one small line in Africa, in Cape Town.

PARTITION OF AFRICA

In 1880 the area actually under European sovereignty was minuscule, but the seeds of change were already there. Britain and France had spheres of influence they were anxious to protect. The French were talking about building rail lines to connect coastal Senegal to the Niger River. New competitors were emerging. Many in Germany, which was challenging British industrial ascendancy, were convinced that Germany needed empire to protect its interests. The chancellor, Otto von Bismarck (1815–1898), was skeptical, but procolonial interests were sending explorers like Carl Peters (1856–1918) to Africa and publishing procolonial books. Leopold II (1835–1909), the king of the Belgians, was financing exploration and the development of stations in the Congo Basin.

In South Africa, Afrikaner dissidents had trekked into the interior in the 1830s and 1840s to create republics free of the control of Great Britain. The stakes in a struggle for control of the South African interior were increased when the discovery of diamonds in 1867 and gold in 1884 made South Africa a potentially rich and powerful country.

The French were the first to move. In 1879 Captain Joseph-Simon Gallieni (1849–1916) was sent to Sudan to chart a route for the railroad. A year later, Major Gustave Borgnis-Desbordes (1839–1900) began the conquest. By 1883, the French were in Bamako (in present-day Mali) and on the Niger River. During the same period, the British were involved in a series of wars in South Africa, but their effort to occupy the Transvaal led to an Afrikaner revolt and British withdrawal. Then, in 1884 and 1885, Bismarck took treaties that various German explorers had signed with African chiefs and claimed four colonies: German East Africa (later Tanganyika), South-West Africa (now Namibia), Togo, and Cameroon. In doing so, they opened up the race for control of Africa.

The Congress of Berlin, convened in late 1884, recognized Leopold II as ruler of the Congo Basin, provided guarantees for free trade, and set up ground rules for partition. The major precondition to a claim was effective occupation, though that often meant a treaty with an African leader and the establishment of a post with a flag. During the succeeding years, there were a series of races for control of places of limited interest and often with limited wealth. This was preemptive colonization, seizing areas of unknown value to keep rivals out. In general, European leaders resolved all border conflicts in Europe, sometimes to the dissatisfaction of colonial proconsuls, who often had exaggerated views of the value of these territories.

The colonial states created by the scramble were unusual in that men from one culture ruled people of a totally different culture and in a totally different part of the world. It was unusual too in that the colonizers did not seek to become part of the world of the colonized, nor did they make it possible for the colonized to enter large parts of their world. All of West Africa, Uganda, and parts of equatorial Africa were colonies of exploitation with relatively few European settlers.

The European parliaments that had authorized the conquest of Africa were reluctant to appropriate funds for its administration. With most of Africa's wealth produced by hoe-wielding peasants, there was little surplus to be taxed. Thus, colonial administration was very thin and often staffed by administrators who relocated regularly and thus had only a superficial knowledge of the people they governed. They depended heavily on a larger group of African chiefs, clerks, interpreters, guards, and messengers. Colonial administrators did not come to stay. The economic benefits of the peasant-based colonies were controlled by export-import houses.

There were a series of areas that attracted settlers. The Rhodesian territories were a product of the South African frontier. Colonized under a charter to the British South Africa Company, they were settled by British and Afrikaner settlers from South Africa. Southern Rhodesia had the largest settler population. The white invaders never numbered more than 4 percent of the total population, but they eventually received about half the land, including most of the best land and the land closest to the rail line. The early years were difficult for many settlers, who often had little capital, but with time they became a wealthy and privileged community. In Northern Rhodesia, there were fewer settlers, but many of them received large land grants near the rail line in order to provide food for the copper mines. Whites ran the government and benefited from segregation and discrimination.

The second large settler area was the East African Protectorate, later Kenya, which was colonized partially to keep the Germans out. The British built a railroad to make it possible to tap the fertile lands of Uganda, but once built, they were worried that it could not pay for itself. The railroad traversed a highland area, which was quite comfortable for European settlers. Much of this highland area was set aside for white settlement. At its peak, there were only about seventy thousand settlers. Kenya attracted a wealthier and more privileged body of settlers than Rhodesia. Many of them were originally attracted to the area to hunt. While most white settlers became wealthy, they were able to do so largely because they were subsidized. Africans in Kenya and Rhodesia paid the highest taxes in Africa, which forced many of them to take work at low wages. White settlers also benefited from better roads and from government agricultural policy.

There were also small nuclei of white settlement in other areas: French planters in Guinea and the Ivory Coast, Belgians in the eastern Congo, Germans around Mount Kilimanjaro in German East Africa, and Portuguese in coffee-growing areas of Angola. There were also European colonists in many of the cities, especially Dakar, Senegal; Nairobi, Kenya; Lourenço Marques (now Maputo, Mozambique); Léopoldville (now Kinshasa, Democratic Republic of the Congo); and Luanda. As colonization became more comfortable, many of these urban settlers, often merchants or restaurant owners, sometimes skilled mechanics or teachers, came to stay. Missionaries also came to stay and with medical progress, often lived out long lives in Africa. With the exception of the missionaries, most of the settlers had little interest in Africa except as a place to live a comfortable life.

Other areas that attracted white settlement were colonies heavily dependent on mineral wealth. There were small mining enterprises in many colonies—for example, gold in the Gold Coast and tin in Nigeria. The major mineral complexes, however, were gold in South Africa and Rhodesia, diamonds in South Africa, and copper in the Congo and Northern Rhodesia. These large mining complexes involved both substantial investment and a large labor force. High taxes and coercive recruitment policies were used to drain labor flow into the mines.

Most colonies were autocracies. A corps of white administrators ruled through African chiefs and were responsible only to a governor and to superiors in the mother country. The only Africans who had the vote were the inhabitants of the Four Communes of Senegal (Saint-Louis, Dakar, Rufisque, and Gorée) and propertied Africans in the Cape Colony. In some colonies, there was a legislative council that included a small number of settlers or wealthy Africans. In general, Africans played no role in their own government.

NATIONALISM AND DECOLONIZATION

To govern Africa at minimal cost, European states had to educate Africans. They generally tried to educate relatively few, though for the missionaries, education was a prerequisite to religious knowledge. Education, however, opened the door to nationalistic and anticolonial activity. So too did foreign travel, which was one reason the Belgians prevented the Congolese from coming to Belgium for many years.

The earliest nationalist response came from Creoles who in the late nineteenth century were disturbed that discrimination deprived them of positions they once occupied. Religion was an important area of protonationalist activity, some people seeking only to separate themselves from the missions, others to develop African churches with independent theologies. Some educated groups also formed early: the African National Congress in South Africa in 1912, the Kikuyu Association in Kenya in 1919, and the National Congress of British West Africa in 1920.

During the 1930s, economic hardship led to strike activity and the formation of a number of radical youth movements. An important role was played by "been-tos," Africans such as future Nigerian president Nnamdi Azikiwe (1904–1996) who had studied abroad and returned to Africa to oppose colonial rule and seek radical economic change.

World War II was the beginning of the end of colonial rule. Africans were influenced by the democratic propaganda of the Allies. Many also served abroad in both European and Asian theaters of war and came back determined to struggle. But the war affected European colonialism in other ways. The war crushed right-wing forces in Europe. An important role in new regimes was played by Communists, who were hostile to colonialism, and by Socialists, who were committed to a more democratic form of colonialism. The new French constitution provided African nations with representation in the French Parliament. Britain willingly granted independence to India and Pakistan, setting an example for Africa.

MUNGO PARK

Scottish explorer Mungo Park was born on September 10, 1771, in Foulshiels, Scotland, the seventh of thirteen children of a tenant farmer. After studying anatomy and surgery at the University of Edinburgh without earning a degree, Park joined his sister and her husband, James Dickson, in London. An amateur botanist, Dickson was acquainted with Joseph Banks, the founder of the African Association, and managed to find his brother-in-law work as a doctor on a ship bound for the island of Sumatra. During his trip, Park gathered many native plants as well, which he showed to Banks upon his return. Impressed, Banks suggested that the young Scotsman attempt an expedition to reach the Niger River, a journey tried three times by the African Association without success. The British government was also interested in expanding their settlements in West Africa and desired new information about waterways in the region.

Park set out for Africa in May of 1795, and one month later reached the British outpost of Pisania on the Gambia River. There he remained until December, preparing his journey into the heartland and studying Mandingo, the local language. Setting out with four porters, a guide, and a servant, Park began a northeast trek, passing through friendly and unfriendly towns and villages. Abandoned by most of his entourage, Park was taken prisoner by the king of Benown and held for several months until he escaped in June 1796. Alone, he continued on his journey and eventually reached Segou,

situated on the banks of the Niger River, making him probably the first European to have seen the African river.

Park returned to London on December 25, 1797, wrote a popular book about his exploits, and established a medical practice in Scotland. However, the quiet life of medicine in a small town failed to stimulate Park, and when the British government contacted him about further exploring the Niger and contesting French presence in the region, Parks accepted the offer and returned to the Gambia River on April 6, 1805. Leaving Pisania on May 4, Park reached the Niger a second time on August 19, but with only seven of the forty or so Europeans that had begun that leg of the trip, the others having died of malaria and dysentery. Rather than returning, Park decided to follow the path of the Niger to the sea, searching for new trade routes, and took a new guide, Ahmadi Fatouma.

Before he left the town of Sansanding on the Niger, Park wrote one final letter home, which his old guide, Isaaco, took to the coast. After five years passed without another letter, the British government hired Isaaco to learn the fate of Park. Eventually, Isaaco found Fatouma, who said the expedition had sailed past the city of Goa, nearly 1,500 miles from their starting point at Bamako. Here, in March or April of 1806, Park met his end after a local king, dissatisfied with the gifts the Scotsman offered, commanded his men to attack Park, who drowned in the Niger.

Europe was also weak and threatened by the high cost of repression. Britain won a difficult war in Malaya; the French lost in Indochina, as did the Dutch in Indonesia. In Kenya, a small, poorly armed Mau Mau force tied up parts of the British army for four years. And some Europeans began to ask whether European countries benefited in any way from colonial rule.

All of this might have been meaningless if Africans were not insistent. Protest in Ghana led to a form of self-government in 1951. In French Africa, the left-wing Rassemblement Democratique Africain (African Democratic Assembly) grew in strength in elections, and in 1958 French president Charles de Gaulle (1890–1970) offered the African colonies self-government or independence. Only Guinea rejected de Gaulle's form of self-

government, but in doing so it put pressure on all the others. By 1960, all of France's African colonies were independent.

In the Belgian Congo, riots in 1959 led to a total collapse of Belgian authority. One by one, various colonies negotiated their independence. Only South Africa, Rhodesia, and the Portuguese colonies resisted what British prime minister Harold Macmillan (1894–1986) called "the winds of change," but in 1974 the collapse of the dictatorship in Portugal of Marcello Caetano (1906–1980) led to the independence of Angola, Mozambique, and Guinea-Bissau. A harsh guerilla war wore down Rhodesia to the point where it lacked the resources and the will to continue fighting.

South Africa conceded independence to Namibia in 1989. A year later, South Africa released Nelson Mandela

(b. 1918) from prison and lifted bans on the major opposition parties, the African National Congress (ANC) and the Pan-African Congress. After a period of negotiation, a democratic election was held in 1994, which brought Mandela and the ANC to power.

Europeans, however, are still in Africa, particularly in those countries that have achieved some measure of peace and social order. The colonial officials have been replaced by diplomats, aid officials, representatives of nongovernmental organizations, businesspeople, and tourists. South Africa has become a multiracial democracy. The churches are still there, but the leadership is African.

SEE ALSO *Decolonization, Sub-Saharan Africa; Nationalism, Africa; Scramble for Africa.*

BIBLIOGRAPHY

Clarence-Smith, William Gervase. *The Third Portuguese Empire, 1825–1975: A Study in Economic Imperialism.* Manchester, U.K.: Manchester University Press, 1985.

Cohen, William B. *Rulers of Empire: The French Colonial Service in Africa.* Stanford, CA: Hoover Institution Press, 1971.

Crowder, Michael. *West Africa Under Colonial Rule.* Evanston, IL: Northwestern University Press, 1968.

Elphick, Richard, and Hermann Giliomee, eds. *The Shaping of South African Society, 1652–1840.* Middletown, CT: Wesleyan University Press, 1989; Cape Town, South Africa: Maskew, Miller, Longman, 1989.

Hallett, Robin. *The Penetration of Africa: European Enterprise and Exploration Principally in Northern and Western Africa Up to 1830.* London: Routledge, 1965.

Hargreaves, John D. *Decolonization in Africa,* 2nd ed. London: Longman, 1996.

Kennedy, Dane. *Islands of White: Settler Society and Culture in Kenya and Southern Rhodesia, 1890–1939.* Durham, NC: Duke University Press, 1987.

Kirk-Greene, Anthony. *Britain's Imperial Administrators, 1858–1966.* New York: St. Martin's Press, 2000.

Lovejoy, Paul. *Transformations in Slavery: A History of Slavery in Africa,* 2nd ed. Cambridge, U.K.: Cambridge University Press, 2000.

Moodie, T. Dunbar. *The Rise of Afrikanerdom: Power, Apartheid, and Afrikaner Civic Religion.* Berkeley: University of California Press, 1975.

Oliver, Roland. *The Missionary Factor in East Africa.* London: Longmans, 1952.

Martin Klein

SUDAN, EGYPTIAN AND BRITISH RIVALRY IN

The independent Republic of Sudan emerged in 1956 after two phases of colonial rule—the Turco-Egyptian

(1820–1881) and Anglo-Egyptian (1898–1956) periods respectively—and as a result of encounters with two competing powers, namely Egypt and Britain.

NINETEENTH-CENTURY COLONIALISM

Under orders from Muhammad 'Ali, who carved out an autonomous dynasty in Egypt under nominal allegiance to the Ottoman Empire, Turco-Egyptian armies invaded in 1820 the region that is present-day northern Sudan and consolidated control from Khartoum. Eager to secure new sources of military manpower, the Turco-Egyptian regime tapped into an escalating local slave trade by seizing male slaves for the armies of Egypt and by allowing private traders to sell females and children in northern Sudanese, Egyptian, and Arabian markets. The regime also forced the development of a Sudanese cash-crop economy and extracted taxes from the free population. At its peak by 1880, the Turco-Egyptian regime had a sphere of administrative and economic influence that extended to the Red Sea in the east, to Darfur in the west, and into parts of what is now southern Sudan.

British influence began to creep into the Sudan in the third quarter of the nineteenth century, when Britain was already flexing its political and economic muscles in Egypt. In the 1870s, the Egyptian ruler Khedive Ismail (a grandson of Muhammad 'Ali) appointed several British and other English-speaking military officers to the Sudan and entrusted some of them with suppressing the slave trade. This last measure was part of an effort to satisfy Britain's antislavery foreign policy in Africa. In the 1870s, Khedive Ismail also attempted to assert Egypt's presence in northeast Africa by deploying armies in the regions that are present-day Eritrea and Ethiopia. However, these plans for Egyptian imperial expansion crumbled after Egypt went bankrupt in 1876 and yielded to British and French financial regulation.

Six years later, in 1882, Britain occupied Egypt and placed the country under its own imperial subjection. In the decades that followed, Egyptian nationalists struggled to remove British control over Egypt even while continuing to press Egyptian claims to Sudan—a situation that prompted one historian to call Egypt in the late nineteenth and early twentieth centuries a country of "colonized colonizers."

By the time Britain occupied Egypt in 1882, the Turco-Egyptian regime in Sudan was already fighting for its survival. One year earlier, a Sudanese Muslim scholar named Muhammad Ahmad had declared himself to be the *mahdi*, a millenarian figure who according to popular Sunni Muslim thought would restore order at a time of chaos and repression prefiguring Judgment Day. Muhammad Ahmad, the Mahdi, rallied support among

Riots in Sudan, 1924. *Anti-British protestors run along the banks of the Atbara River in Sudan on September 1, 1924. Troops and ships were rushed to the scene to quell the disorders.* © BETTMANN/CORBIS. REPRODUCED BY PERMISSION.

many Sudanese Muslims by condemning what he described as the un-Islamic practices of the Turco-Egyptian regime, notably their excessive taxation, their appointment of Christian military officers, and their efforts to end the slave trade (which Sudanese Muslims then regarded as a practice sanctioned by Islamic law). The Mahdi's movement, in short, was a kind of anti-colonial jihad (Muslim holy war) that succeeded in defeating Turco-Egyptian forces in a string of battles after 1881.

At the decisive battle for the city of Khartoum in 1885, Mahdist soldiers killed the British general, Charles Gordon, who had gone to evacuate the city. A decade later, when the European powers were pursuing their Scramble for Africa, memories of Gordon's death in Khartoum helped to rally popular British support for the colonial invasion of the Sudan, set out to destroy the Sudanese Mahdist state (1881–1898) that had supplanted the Turco-Egyptian regime.

THE ANGLO-EGYPTIAN CONDOMINIUM

In 1898 Britain justified and bolstered its claims to Sudanese territory and thwarted competing French interests in the region by declaring that its invasion had been a "Reconquest": a shared British-Egyptian effort to reassert political claims that the Mahdists had usurped. Britain went still further in 1899 by framing the new colonial regime as an Anglo-Egyptian "Condominium" in which Britain and Egypt would be co-domini, or joint rulers. To reinforce the Sudan's special status, Britain refused to call the country a colony (akin to say, Nigeria or Hong Kong) and placed the Sudan under British Foreign Office rather than Colonial Office supervision. In reality, Britain dominated the Sudanese government. In the first half of the Anglo-Egyptian period Egyptians nevertheless made their mark on the colonial regime both in the army, where they served as officers, and in the bureaucracy, where they functioned as accountants, clerks, and educators.

Beginning in 1919, a year of nationalist revolt in Egypt, Britain became increasingly concerned about Egypt's capacity to inspire anticolonial, that is, anti-British, sentiment within the Sudan. These concerns reached a climax in 1924 following a spate of urban anticolonial activities in the Sudan followed by the assassination in Cairo of the Sudan's British governor-general. Responding to this crisis, Britain expelled the Egyptian army from the Sudan and fired or retired Egyptian bureaucrats in the Sudan. By 1930 the British had replaced almost all Egyptian employees with young, educated northern Sudanese men who were members of a nascent nationalist class.

In the second quarter of the twentieth century Egypt continued to insist on its rights to the Sudan even while struggling to reverse its own subjection to British imperialism—a subjection that remained palpable notwithstanding Egypt's official "independence" in 1922. Ongoing frustrations over Egypt's status in the Sudan sharpened nationalism in Egypt. Meanwhile, within the Sudan itself, nationalism was coming into focus among the educated northern Sudanese who closely followed and admired Egyptian popular culture as manifest in newspapers and poetry and increasingly, too, in movies and songs.

Despite these cultural ties, political sentiments toward Egypt varied among budding Sudanese nationalists. Whereas some insisted that Sudanese identity was distinct and autonomous from its Egyptian counterpart, others stressed the political and cultural affinities between Sudanese and Egyptians (even while rejecting Egyptian paternalism). These two camps of early Sudanese nationalism—represented by the slogans Sudan for the Sudanese and Unity of the Nile Valley respectively—came to dominate the local political scene in the late Anglo-Egyptian period.

DECOLONIZATION

Many of the political dramas of the immediate post–World War II years in the Sudan revolved around the questions of when and how Britain would devolve political authority on Sudanese nationalists (who were pressing for a greater role in local government) and what Egypt's future status in the country would be. The situation became clearer after the signing of the Anglo-Egyptian Agreement of 1953, which set out plans for parliamentary elections in the Sudan and acknowledged the right of the "graduates" (that is, members of the educated class who enjoyed exclusive suffrage at this time) to decide whether to unify with or separate from Egypt. Sudanese parliamentarians ultimately chose separate autonomy. Thus the Sudan gained independence on January 1, 1956, barely six months after the start of a civil war that went on to blight the country during most of the late-twentieth-century postcolonial period.

Meanwhile, in 1956 (four years after the Free Officers Revolution of 1952), Egypt entered the final phase of its own decolonization as British troops finally withdrew from the Suez Canal zone. A few months later, the Nasser government nationalized the Suez Canal, an event that precipitated the Suez Crisis. Historians suggest that the Suez Crisis confirmed the demise of British and French colonialism in the Middle East and ushered in the cold war era of U.S.-Soviet regional dominance.

SEE ALSO *Egypt; Empire, British; Empire, Ottoman; Suez Canal and Suez Crisis.*

BIBLIOGRAPHY

Collins, Robert O. *The Nile.* New Haven, CT: Yale University Press, 2002.

Daly, M. W. *Empire on the Nile: The Anglo-Egyptian Sudan, 1898–1934.* Cambridge, U.K.: Cambridge University Press, 1986.

Daly, M. W. *Imperial Sudan: The Anglo-Egyptian Condominium, 1934–1956.* Cambridge, U.K.: Cambridge University Press, 1991.

Holt, P. M., and M. W. Daly. *A History of the Sudan: From the Coming of Islam to the Present Day.* London: Longman, 2000.

Johnson, Douglas H., ed. *Sudan.* 2 vols. British Documents on the End of Empire series. London: Stationery Office, 1998.

Powell, Eve M. Troutt. *A Different Shade of Colonialism: Egypt, Great Britain, and Mastery of the Sudan.* Berkeley: University of California Press, 2003.

Sharkey, Heather J. *Living with Colonialism: Nationalism and Culture in the Anglo-Egyptian Sudan.* Berkeley: University of California Press, 2003.

Warburg, Gabriel R. *Historical Discord in the Nile Valley.* Evanston, IL: Northwestern University Press, 1992.

Heather Sharkey

SUEZ CANAL AND SUEZ CRISIS

The idea of constructing a canal connecting the Mediterranean and the Red Sea had been discussed by French engineers during Napoleon Bonaparte's (1769–1821) occupation of Egypt in 1798–1801, but miscalculations concerning water levels at the time saw the project dropped. Proved feasible soon after, it was not until 1854 that Sa'id Pasha (1822–1863), the Egyptian ruler, granted a concession to the Suez Canal Company (SCC) headed by Ferdinand-Marie de Lesseps (1805–1894), to construct and operate the canal for ninety-nine years. Excavation began in 1859 with labor being

Ceremonies Marking the Opening of the Suez Canal. *Ceremonies were held in Egypt to celebrate the opening of the Suez Canal in November 1869.* © BETTMANN/CORBIS. REPRODUCED BY PERMISSION.

imported from Italy, Greece, and Syria to assist an estimated 1.5 million Egyptian workers.

For a time, British and Turkish opposition saw work suspended, but French support and Sa'id's purchase of 44 percent of company shares (later assumed by the Egyptian government) kept the project going. Stretching from Port Said to Suez, a distance of 170 kilometers (106 miles), the canal was officially inaugurated in grand style on November 17, 1869, by Khedive Ismail (1830–1895), who had invited a large number of European dignitaries, including the French Empress Eugénie (1826–1920), and commissioned Giuseppe Fortunino Francesco Verdi (1813–1901) to compose Aïda for the occasion.

In 1875, in severe financial straits, the Egyptian government sold its company shares to the British government, an important factor in the British decision to occupy Egypt in 1882. The Convention of Constantinople of 1888, signed by the major European powers, declared the canal neutral and granted its use to all during peace and wartime with Britain acting as guarantor. A vital waterway for British imperial communications, particularly the route to India and access to Middle Eastern oil, the canal also facilitated the colonization of East Africa by other European powers, particularly the Italian conquest of Ethiopia. Under the terms of the 1936 Anglo-Egyptian treaty Britain retained control

of the canal zone, which proved a crucial advantage during World War II (1939–1945) and a significant military base in the early Cold War years.

In the postwar period the continuing British occupation of the canal attracted mounting Egyptian criticism. When the Free Officers took power in Egypt in July 1952, negotiations were reopened with the British who, in an accord reached in 1954, agreed to withdraw all of its troops from the country by June 1956. In July, when the Americans reneged on their offer to finance the Aswan High Dam, Gamal Abd al Nasir (1918–1970) responded by dramatically announcing the nationalization of the canal before a large crowd in Alexandria on July 26, asserting that the revenue from canal dues would help finance the dam. The right of the Egyptian government to nationalize the SCC, an Egyptian company, was a well-recognized principle in international law, but the British, French, and other Western governments called for the internationalization of the canal, an idea stoutly resisted by Nasir.

While the Egyptians, to the surprise of many, continued to operate the canal competently, the British Prime Minister Anthony Eden (1897–1977) entered into a secret agreement with the French and Israeli governments to attack Egypt. Under its terms, when Israeli forces invaded the Sinai on October 29, 1956 and met with Egyptian resistance, France and Britain would issue a joint ultimatum the next day calling for a halt to hostilities. When, as expected, Egypt rejected this, British and French planes bombed Egyptian airfields on October 31 and landed Anglo-French troops on November 5 to secure the canal, now rendered inoperative by ships sunk by the Egyptian government. A United Nations Security Council resolution condemning the Israeli aggression had been vetoed by the British and French, but with the threat of Soviet military intervention and American displeasure towards the British action, expressed by its withdrawal of support for the British pound, a cease-fire was accepted by all sides at midnight on November 6. A United Nations Emergency Force (UNEF) was constituted and supervised the withdrawal of British and French forces in December and of the Israelis in March the next year.

Despite being defeated in the field—Egypt suffered by far the greatest losses in the war—Suez was a substantial diplomatic victory for Nasir that greatly enhanced his international standing as an anti-imperialist leader. By contrast, Eden was discredited and resigned from office the following year. Suez witnessed an important break between two traditional allies, the United States and Britain, and more significantly, came to symbolize the decline of British imperial power. It also gave notice of Israeli military capabilities. Now run by the Egyptian Canal Authority, the canal was reopened in April 1957, and compensation paid to shareholders. United Nations forces remained in place until the lead-up to the six-day war of June 1967 when the canal was closed again.

SEE ALSO *Egypt; Empire, British; Empire, French; Nasir, Gamal Abd al.*

BIBLIOGRAPHY

Heikal, Mohamed. *Cutting the Lion's Tail: Suez through Egyptian Eyes.* New York: Arbor House, 1987.

Kyle, Keith. *Suez: Britain's End of Empire in the Middle East.* London: I.B. Tauris, 2003.

Louis, W. R. and Roger Owen, eds. *Suez 1956: The Crisis and its Consequences.* Oxford: Clarendon Press; New York: Oxford University Press, 1989.

Anthony Gorman

SUGAR AND LABOR: TRACKING EMPIRES

Sugar, the refined granules of crystallized juice extracted from the sugarcane plant, was transformed during the era of European colonialism from a medicine, spice, and rare luxury in parts of Asia, the Pacific, and Europe to a ubiquitous staple ingredient of postcolonial diets. The story of this transformation is entwined with the story of European colonialism and the related forces of change that swept the globe since 1450.

In contrast to the ever-increasing demand that takes sugar for granted, and the ease with which it has been consumed, the sugarcane plant is in fact notoriously delicate, disease prone, and resource hungry during cultivation. Moreover, it only yields sugar through a labor-intensive process of extraction and refinement that is unforgiving of any time lag between harvesting and processing. Unprecedented levels of exploitation of labor, land, and environment have therefore characterized the economic viability of its mass production. Sugar demanded endless acres of tropical and subtropical land for cultivation, as well as armies of cheap enslaved, indentured, or enforced labor to grow, harvest, and process it. As such, sugarcane worked its way into the heart of the economies and trades that would fund and drive European expansion.

While sugar was used as a spice and sweetener in Asia and the Pacific before the colonial era, in Europe it remained a medicinal and luxury item. This status would change after 1492 when Christopher Columbus (1451–1506) took sugarcane to the New World, and throughout the sixteenth century, sugar was produced in Brazil for export to Lisbon and the European market.

Brazilian sugar was grown with the use of African slaves and plantation-based cultivation and production, which was a system founded in relations of exploitation that would continue to characterize sugar production well into the twentieth century. Until the middle of the seventeenth century, while Portugal and Spain supplied Europe with sugar, the majority of sugar production worldwide occurred in Asia in Bengal, Java, southern China, and Taiwan. Here it was produced for local consumers and exported to Europe through trading links established by such companies as the Dutch East Indies Company. From early in the seventeenth century, however, the prominence of Asian sugar as an export commodity would be overtaken by sugar grown in the Caribbean.

The arrival of the British and French in the Caribbean in the early seventeenth century marked the beginning of the never-ending expansion of sugar production and the deepening of its identification with slavery. For the first half of the seventeenth century, plantation cultivation relied for labor on varied combinations of African and indigenous slaves and European indentured laborers. From the middle of the seventeenth century, however, sugar was exclusively produced by enslaved Africans on plantations that monopolized land use and transformed entire islands like Barbados and Jamaica into virtual "sugar factories" (Ashcroft 1999, p. 44).

Cutting Sugarcane in the West Indies. *With supervisors looking on, laborers cut sugarcane on a nineteenth-century plantation in the West Indies. The production of sugar was laborious, and plantations required large numbers of enslaved and indentured workers.* © CORBIS. REPRODUCED BY PERMISSION.

By the end of the seventeenth century, sugar had become an inextricable link in an economic triangle that entwined the fates, desires, and wealth of people in three continents. While sugar and molasses were traded from West Indian possessions to ever-expanding European and New England markets, the finished goods exported from Europe and New England, such as rum, clothes, or tools, were traded in Africa for slaves, who in turn produced the raw sugar products that would be exported for trade in Europe and European colonies. Sugar was therefore integral to the three-way trade between colonial possessions (the West Indies), colonies of exploitation (the African continent), and imperial centers (Britain). This was an interrelationship that turned sugar from being a by-product of colonial expansion to an enabling and driving force.

As Sidney Mintz explored in his classic *Sweetness and Power* (1985), the eighteenth century saw a growth in the demand for sugar in Europe and North America that was driven by the increased production in the Caribbean, which was fueled by the roaring slave trade. To create demand, British sugar producers, as represented by such organizations as the West India lobby, actively promoted the consumption of other colonial products, such as bitter coffee and tea that was imported from Asia by the British East India Company and rendered palatable and desirable with the addition of sugar.

Aided by falling prices, by the middle of the eighteenth century, sugar was no longer a luxury item. It had become a basic dietary ingredient indicated by the twentyfold increase in consumption that took place in England and Wales between 1663 and 1775. So successful was its promotion that by the end of the century, sugar was not only being widely consumed, it was also well on its way, along with other such colonial products as tea, tobacco, cocoa, and coffee, to being thoroughly appropriated as icons of European cultures. As James Walvin (1999, p. 24) put it in relation to Britain, where consumption had increased by 2,500 percent in the hundred and fifty years preceding 1800, what could be more British than a sweet cup of tea?

By the middle of the nineteenth century, sugar was a necessity in many European and North American households. British consumption alone increased in sixty years from 572,000 tons in 1830 to a staggering six million tons by 1890. Still, sugar production continued to rise, outstripping and, as a consequence, driving demand.

In the United States, sugar became so cheap and available that North American sugar refineries deliberately lowered production. The reason for this massive increase in productive capability was multifaceted. First, from 1850, beet sugar, which was grown in temperate climates in Europe and the United States, had expanded to supplant cane sugar by 1880. Second, slavery was abolished in the European colonies from 1838 onward, so that by 1884 all the major sources of sugar in the Caribbean were being produced by varied forms of contracted and paid, and therefore relatively expensive, labor. Finally, the rapid expansion of European colonies from the eighteenth century led to an opening up of new land for cane cultivation, along with seemingly inexhaustible pools of cheap labor. By the end of the nineteenth century, sugar production was diversified and was flourishing throughout Europe, Southeast Asia, southern Africa, the Pacific, and northeastern Australia. Hence, while the plantation-based Caribbean was the sole producer of export-oriented sugar at the opening of the nineteenth century, it had been displaced by the century's close. By 1900 Germany was the biggest producer and exporter of sugar from beets, followed by Cuba and Java as the second and third largest producers of sugar from cane.

The combination of the economic crises caused by this increased competition and the added expense of labor forced sugar producers to modernize and industrialize during the nineteenth century. From mid-century, steam-powered technology aiding both harvesting and refining was introduced to most sugar-producing centers. Although this helped to lower the cost of production, the demand for cheap, unskilled, and coercible labor remained strong in the post-emancipation period. With few exceptions, many sugar producers turned to indentured or contracted, and usually imported labor supplied by colonial empires.

The French West Indies, for example, used labor from French India. British planters transferred labor from the Pacific to Australia, from India to the Pacific, and from southern Africa and the Caribbean. Dutch planters in Sumatra used labor imported from Java. While not using indentured or contracted labor, the sugar exported from Asian industries in Taiwan, the Philippines, or Java was produced utilizing existing social relations to extract labor and sugar from peasants. In Java, for example, the existing sugar industry was co-opted, centralized, and enforced by the Netherlands Indies state after 1830 when, under the so-called Cultivation System, Javanese peasants were obligated to grow commercial and export crops. The essential low cost of labor and land that characterized colonial sugar production was therefore retained.

Although the production of sugar for ever-expanding and disparate European and American markets diversified in the nineteenth century beyond the antiquated Caribbean-style plantations, essential features remained unchanged into the twentieth century. The global sugar industry continued to dedicate vast tracts of productive and fertile tropical land to a single crop, at the same time that the economic viability of such cultivation remained reliant on supplies of cheap, expendable, and usually nonwhite labor. For this reason it remained an essentially colonial crop, dependent for its production on the land and labor made available through European expansion and appropriation of territory.

Sugar, or the industry and market that grew up around it, has been described by Sidney Mintz (1985, p. 71) as one of the most powerful demographic forces in world history. Sugar, perhaps more than any other tropical product, funded and necessitated the transformation of millions of acres of forest, ecosystems, and indigenous lands into enormous agricultural factories. This resulted in the displacement of indigenous agricultures, technologies, and economies, and the uprooting and dispossession of entire populations.

While European nations leaked their populations all over the globe in search of sugar-fed riches, African, south Asian, and Pacific countries hemorrhaged their populations to produce these riches. More than eight million enslaved Africans were displaced to produce Caribbean sugar. So too, 1.25 million Indian laborers were moved around the British Empire for sugar, and hundreds of thousands of Pacific Islanders were moved around the Pacific and to Queensland for sugar industries in Kanaky/New Caledonia, Fiji, Hawaii, and Queensland. Indeed, the demographic diversity of the postcolonial world can be traced to the diasporic force of sugar.

In five hundred years of colonialism, sugar has become a staple item in every Western kitchen, and an almost mandatory ingredient of processed foods. As a cheap, rapidly consumed, and high-energy food that so perfectly suits the demands of time-disciplined industrial societies, its production and demand continue to grow. But more than a food, as a demographic, social, and economic force, sugar both reflects and encapsulates the era of European colonialism. It was, and arguably remains, a thoroughly colonial product steeped in the social relations, political phenomena, and economic drives and imperatives that shaped the colonial era.

SEE ALSO *African Slavery in the Americas; Caribbean; Sugar Cultivation and Trade.*

BIBLIOGRAPHY

Ahluwalia, Pal, Bill Ashcroft, and Roger Knight. "Introduction." In *White and Deadly: Sugar and Colonialism*, edited by Pal Ahluwalia, Bill Ashcroft, and Roger Knight, 1–20. Commack, NY: Nova Science, 1999.

Albert, Bill, and Adrian Graves. "Introduction." In *Crisis and Change in the International Sugar Economy, 1860–1914*, edited by Bill Albert and Adrian Graves. Norwich, U.K.: ISC, 1984: 1–7.

Ashcroft, Bill. "A Fatal Sweetness: Sugar and Post-Colonial Cultures." In *White and Deadly: Sugar and Colonialism*, edited by Pal Ahluwalia, Bill Ashcroft, and Roger Knight, 33–50. Commack, NY: Nova Science, 1999.

Burrows, Geoff, and Clive Morton. *The Canecutters*. Carlton, Victoria, Australia: Melbourne University Press, 1986.

Knight, G. Roger. *Narratives of Colonialism: Sugar, Java, and the Dutch*. Huntington, NY: Nova Science, 2000.

Lal, Brij V., Doug Munro, and Edward D. Beechert, eds. *Plantation Workers: Resistance and Accommodation*. Honolulu: University of Hawaii Press, 1993.

Marks, Shula, and Peter Richardson, eds. *International Labour Migration: Historical Perspectives*. Hounslow, Middlesex, U.K.: Institute of Commonwealth Studies, 1984.

Mintz, Sidney W. *Sweetness and Power: The Place of Sugar in Modern History*. New York: Viking, 1985.

Robbins, Richard. *Global Problems and the Culture of Capitalism*, 3rd ed. Boston: Pearson Allyn and Bacon, 2005.

Saunders, Kay, ed. *Indentured Labour in the British Empire, 1834–1920*. London: Croom Helm, 1984.

Schwartz, Stuart B., ed. *Tropical Babylons: Sugar and the Making of the Atlantic World: 1450–1680*. Chapel Hill: University of North Carolina Press, 2004.

Shineberg, Dorothy. *The People Trade: Pacific Island Laborers and New Caledonia, 1865–1930*. Honolulu: University of Hawaii Press, 1999.

Stoler, Anne Laura. *Capitalism and Confrontation in Sumatra's Plantation Belt, 1870–1979*, 2nd ed. Ann Arbor: University of Michigan Press, 1995.

Walvin, James. "Sugar and the Shaping of Western Culture." In *White and Deadly: Sugar and Colonialism*, edited by Pal Ahluwalia, Bill Ashcroft, and Roger Knight, 21–31. Commack, NY: Nova Science, 1999.

Wertheim, Wim F. "Conditions on Sugar Estates in Colonial Java: Comparisons with Deli." *Journal of Southeast Asian Studies* 24 (2) (1993): 268–285.

Woloson, Wendy A. *Refined Tastes: Sugar, Confectionery, and Consumers in Nineteenth-Century America*. Baltimore, MD: Johns Hopkins University Press, 2002.

Tracey Banivanua Mar

SUGAR CULTIVATION AND TRADE

Sugar, a sweet crystallizable material that consists essentially of sucrose, is transparent or white when pure, brownish when less refined. It is obtained primarily from sugarcane, and, since the early nineteenth century, from sugar beet as well. Other, minor sources are sorghum, maples, and palms. Nutritionally, sugar is important as a source of dietary carbohydrate but little else, although it is also employed as a sweetener, and to cure and preserve other foods. Sugarcane, the main source, is a stout, coarse, tall perennial grass (*Saccharum officinarum*) with juice or sap high in sugar content. In a tropical climate the cane may be planted at almost any season as the plant does not require a rest period, but temperatures slightly below freezing kill the leafy tops, substantially reducing the sugar yield.

Prior to 1500 sugar had entered Europe from the east as a flavoring spice. Venetian and Sicilian supplier-producers sold small quantities at exorbitant prices to wealthy elites, but by the early 1600s the Italian industry had been ruined by cheap slave-produced sugar from the New World.

Canary Island sugarcane arrived in the Americas in 1493 on Christopher Columbus's second voyage, which introduced many European foodstuffs with the goal of establishing a permanent colony on Hispaniola. Sugarcane easily prospered in the New World environment and its cultivation spread across tropical America as it was colonized during the following centuries.

The fundamental requirements for the growth of sugarcane and the development of a plantation system were numerous, but were met in many regions of tropical America. These included:

1. extensive, fertile lands near navigable coasts and rivers, with a deep water port nearby to facilitate the movement of large, bulky cargos;

2. abundant timber reserves for construction and firewood—the latter used for the extensive boiling, and eventually the steam power, necessary for the refining process;

3. the importation of tools and implements, especially cast iron gears, levers, axes, and the omnipresent machete;

4. readily available foodstuffs for the large labor population, often grown on the plantation itself;

5. a continuing supply of cheap labor—slaves—including both women and men, who were employed in planting, cultivation, and harvesting.

Sugar production in the Atlantic, 1500–1860

Producer	Tonnage	Year
Madeira	1,500	1500
São Tomé	5,000	1550s
Hispaniola	1,000	1570
Brazil	20,000	1620s
Dutch Brazil	4,000	1639
Barbados	10,000	1660s
Jamaica	48,000	1775
Saint Domingue	78,000	1791
Cuba	447,000	1860

THE GALE GROUP.

The Spanish initially employed Indian slaves as a labor force, but sparse populations and devastating epidemics soon made it clear that native labor was insufficient. African slaves began to be imported in 1512, first to compliment and then to replace the Indians. Before long the terms *sugar* and *slave* had become indelibly linked, an association that lasted up until the end of the nineteenth century.

The Spanish did not fully develop the sugar industry, however, as the great mineral riches of the mainland distracted them. The Portuguese colony of Brazil was the site of the first major success with sugar cultivation. Immediately upon the founding of Pernambuco in 1526, and São Vicente and Espiritu Santo in 1530 to 1532, Madeira Island sugarcane was introduced. The Atlantic island techniques of cultivation, however, would be extensively modified. A new agricultural system appeared: the plantation. Substantially large landholdings—coupled with Brazil's proximity to Africa, which made for lower importation costs and higher survival rates for slaves—assured the expansion of large-scale sugar production.

The monoculture society that developed was multifaceted, as numerous goods and service industries were necessary. Food, as mentioned, was crucial and many times produced on the estates themselves, creating hybrid plantation-farms with their attendant needs. Sizable initial capital investments were needed, and credit was obtained both locally and from overseas sources—though dependence upon the mother country for financing tended to decrease over time. On the increase continually, though, was the consumption of goods and services for the planter class, and in some areas absentee ownership appeared.

The success of Brazil encouraged other European countries to become involved in sugar production. The Dutch West Indies Company occupied Recife and Olinda (Pernambuco) in the Portuguese sugar region of Brazil in 1630, but was expelled in 1654. Subsequently, the Dutch focused on establishing their own settlements, which they did on the islands of Curaçao (1634), St. Eustatius (1636), and St. Martin (1631–1648)—the latter shared with the French. The English settled St. Christopher (1624), Barbados (1627), Nevis (1628), Montserrat (1632), Antigua (1632), and Jamaica (1655). The French concentrated on St. Christopher (Kitts, 1624)—where they joined forces with the English to thwart the Spanish and Carib Indians—Guadeloupe (1635), and Martinique (1635).

Irrespective of which European power was involved, the planting, cultivation, harvesting, and processing of sugar followed the same pattern. For planting, mature cane stalks are cut into sections and laid horizontally in rows about six feet apart. Like other grasses, the stem produces nodes—four to ten inches apart along the above-ground section. The mature stems reach twelve feet or more in height. The stem between the nodes is made up of a hard, thin tissue or rind and a soft, fibrous core. In this center is the juice, with its high concentration of sugar. More than one crop may be harvested from a planting, but once cut the cane must be milled as soon as possible, as delay results in loss of sugar content. Once the harvest starts, milling becomes a twenty-four-hour job.

Sugar mills are located in the center of the cultivation area to facilitate prompt transportation. After being washed, the cane is sent through roller mills—large grooved rollers—that crush and macerate it, producing the liquid runoff containing the extracted sugar juice. This slightly acid juice is neutralized with lime and then boiled. The nearly clear juice at the top of the tanks is drawn off and sent to evaporators, where a progressive process leaves a sludge. This sludge is centrifuged to separate the brown sugar crystals from the liquid molasses. To produce transparent or white sugar, the brown sugar crystals are passed through an additional round of melting, filtering, and boiling, after which drying is necessary. The molasses from the sludge, or "poor man's sugar," is used as an additive for foods and livestock feed, and to manufacture alcohol and alcoholic beverages—the famous *eau de vie de molasses, aguardiente de caña,* and rum bullion.

The early Caribbean production was characterized by its low quality crystallized sugar and high volume of molasses. The by-product came to rival the refined sugar in volume and value as a large quantity of the sticky syrup was transformed into rum at both local and New England distilleries. And although Brazil continued to produce an enormous crop, by the late seventeenth century the West Indies had become the world's largest source of sugar. In both places, slave labor and easy

An Abandoned Sugar Mill in Saint Croix. *The arrival of the British and French in the Caribbean in the early seventeenth century marked the beginning of the never-ending expansion of sugar production. The remains of this old sugar mill stand on the grounds of the Buccaneer Resort on Saint Croix in the Virgin Islands.* © **BUDDY MAYS/CORBIS. REPRODUCED BY PERMISSION.**

transportation permitted lower prices than was possible for sugar imported from the East or grown in Europe, and as a result the American trade dwarfed all other rivals combined. By the early eighteenth century the term *Sugar Islands* had become quite literal: the economies of entire islands such as Barbados, Guadalupe, and Martinique centered on sugar production. In 1750 the French colony of Saint Domingue (Haiti) was the largest sugar producer in the world.

Larger-volume production and lower prices allowed sugar consumption to extend to almost all social groups in Europe; sugar became enormously popular and experienced a series of booms. The principal reason for the increased demand was the great change in the eating habits of Europeans. They consumed candy, cocoa, coffee, jams, and tea in greater quantities than even before, creating a larger demand that stimulated greater

production. It is estimated that the "sugar islands" produced up to 90 percent of the sugar consumed in Western Europe. By the end of the eighteenth century, monoculture sugar production monopolized the economies of numerous islands; in the case of Barbados and the British Leeward Islands, for example, sugar accounted for, respectively, 93 and 97 percent of overall exports.

Cuba, the largest of the Antilles and one of the oldest colonies in the region, withstood the onset of sugar monoculture until the end of the eighteenth century. Until that time, it possessed a multifaceted economy based on diversified agriculture (cattle leather, foodstuffs, sugar, and tobacco), heavy industry (the largest shipyard in the Spanish empire, plus a canon foundry and other metal works), and substantial service industries and bureaucracy. A nascent planter class, stimulated by Bourbon reforms in commerce and communication, appeared just as the age of revolutions began, however. Bourbon commercial and communications reforms that legalized the importation of large numbers of slaves and the access to heretofore closed markets stimulated the nascent planter class to expand production. The Saint Domingue slave revolt of 1791 drove up sugar prices worldwide and signaled the entry of Cuba as the major sugar/slave colony for the next century.

Despite Cuba's dominance, American pioneers on various colonial frontiers attempted to be self-sufficient as far as sugar production was concerned. This led to some curious sugar experiments, and to some of the worst or strangest sugars ever manufactured. One of the most unique efforts was the extraction of sugar and molasses from watermelons attempted in the southeastern United States—the volume of watermelons and firewood necessary for the production of one pound of sugar was staggering. Obviously, this experiment was a commercial failure.

In the nineteenth century, the price of sugar declined as production volumes increased. Multiple sources made for fewer market fluctuations, and the "white gold" became just another commodity. While sugar lost much of its uniqueness, all of the sugar colonies displayed enduring hallmarks. The plantations had stripped the environment of timber and had sown flowing seas of sugarcane, destroying the preexisting ecological system. The indigenous population had long since disappeared, replaced by imported, ethnically mixed Africans who produced a new amalgamated culture. And a new economic order had appeared. No longer were the colonies dependent upon the mother country; now their fortunes were shaped by the rise and fall of world prices, and by their ability to survive in the face of stiff international competition.

SEE ALSO *Plantations, the Americas.*

BIBLIOGRAPHY

Bethell, Leslie, ed. *Colonial Brazil*. Cambridge, U.K.: Cambridge University Press, 1987.

Deerr, Noël. *The History of Sugar*. 2 vols. London: Chapman and Hall, 1949–1950.

Dunn, Richard S. *Sugar and Slaves: The Rise of the Planter Class in the English West Indies, 1624–1713*. Chapel Hill: University of North Carolina Press, 1972.

Moreno Fraginals, Manuel. *El ingenio: Complejo económico social cubano del azúcar*. 3 vols. Havana: Editorial de Ciencias Sociales, 1978.

Sauer, Carl Ortwin. *The Early Spanish Main*. Berkeley: University of California Press, 1966.

Sheridan, Richard. *Sugar and Slavery: An Economic History of the British West Indies, 1623–1775*. Bridgetown, Barbados: University of the West Indies Press, 1974.

G. Douglas Inglis

T

TAIPING REBELLION

The Taiping Rebellion (1850–1864) was the largest peasant rebellion in Chinese history and one of the bloodiest civil wars in the annals of human experience. The conflict ravaged the most cultivated parts of the Qing dynasty, encompassing eighteen of its most populous provinces, claiming the lives of at least 25 million. It also fundamentally changed China's political, social, economic, and military structures.

The Taiping Rebellion took place in the aftermath of Western powers' forced entrance into China's coastal areas after the Sino-British Treaty of Nanjing (Nanking) of 1842. The Western influence was particularly strong in the Pearl River Delta area where Western merchants, Christian missionaries, and adventurers congregated. This presence naturally brought about increased economic instability as a result of foreign competition, political tension as a result of nascent nationalism, and cultural and intellectual revolution as a result of the introduction of Christian tenets to a fundamentally Confucian society. The rebellion's leader, Hong Xiuquan, keenly felt these new forces that had been growing to challenge the Chinese state, society, and mindset. As a failed degree-seeking Confucian scholar, Hong accepted prototypical Christianity from roaming missionaries based in Hong Kong. Convinced he was the younger brother of Jesus Christ, Hong in January 1851 announced the establishment of a Christianity-based state called Taiping Tianguo (Heavenly Kingdom of Grand Peace), which immediately attracted frenzy attacks organized by the ruling Qing dynasty.

Starting in the southern province of Guangxi, the Taiping rebels set out to obliterate what they believed were "demons" that would include the Manchu rulers, all Confucian icons, landed interests, and eventually the imperial court itself. Superb command structure with unparalleled leadership cohesion, plus rejuvenated energy and dedication from the rank and file of the Taiping Army—who were inspired by Hong's prototypical Christian socialism and Utopian egalitarianism—gave the Taiping rebels great victories in the first years of their relentless campaign. They swept most of China's southern provinces and in 1853 captured the metropolis Nanjing near the Yangtze Delta. Hong settled there and made Nanjing his capital.

Yet the efforts to storm into Beijing to destroy the Qing court, lasting from 1853 to 1855, failed miserably, despite the temporary victory of a westward military expedition to secure Taiping's left flank. A devastating blow befell the Taiping cause in 1856 when Hong went on a fanatic killing spree of his top lieutenants, forcing his remaining generals of the highest caliber to flee.

Seizing these opportunities, the Qing court took dramatic measures to strike back. An age-old ban on granting ethnic Chinese the power to command military units was lifted, opening the door to the rise of a gentry army system pioneered by the renowned court scholar Zeng Guofan. Zeng and his Hunan army represented the landed interests whose land and privileges had been the main targets of the Taiping rebels wherever they went. Contrary to the Taiping's puritanical and egalitarian principles of organizing and training, Zeng's Hunan army stressed the Confucian ideals of hierarchy, loyalty, and family. Following the example of Zeng's Hunan army, several of Zeng's protégés set up gentry armies in their own provinces, the most renowned of which was

Li Hongzhang's Huai army in the eastern province of Anhui.

Westerners played an important role during the Taiping Rebellion. In the early years of the war, many westerners were hired by the Taiping rebels as mercenaries. The Qing court and Zeng Guofan, however, had even a larger number of mercenaries at their disposal. The best known is the Ever-Victorious Army, initiated by the American adventurer Frederick Ward, and after Ward's death in the battle, by the Royal Army officer Charles "Chinese" Gordon. When Hong decided to attack Shanghai and other treaty ports where foreign commercial interests concentrated, and when Hong showed strong signs of millenarian fanaticism, Western governments uniformly lent strong support to the government's counterinsurgent efforts against the Taiping rebels. In the summer of 1864, soon after Hong's sudden death, Zeng's Hunan army captured Nanjing, marking the end of the momentous Taiping Rebellion.

The Taiping Rebellion severely shattered the confidence of the ruling dynasty. Emerging from the rubbles of the devastation was a generation of Chinese scholar-generals who had learned the efficacy of modern weaponry imported from the West. Combined with a Confucian revival, these scholar-generals undertook concerted measures, collectively known as the Self-Strengthening movement, to upgrade China's military hardware. As a result, the scholar-generals became the harbingers of China's modern warlords.

SEE ALSO *Boxer Uprising; China, First Opium War to 1945; Chinese Revolutions; Mercenaries, East Asia and the Pacific.*

BIBLIOGRAPHY

Jen, Yu-wen. *The Taiping Revolutionary Movement.* New Haven, CT: Yale University Press, 1973.

Michael, Franz H. *The Taiping Revolution: History and Documents.* Seattle: University of Washington Press, 1966.

Spence, Jonathan D. *God's Chinese Son: The Taiping Heavenly Kingdom of Hong Xiuquan.* New York: W.W. Norton, 1996.

Maochun Yu

TEA

Tea became the subject of enormous consumer demand in the seventeenth century, and this demand sparked the creation of a European tea empire. An infusion drink, tea is made when tea leaves are soaked in boiling water. The heat kills off water-borne diseases, while the resulting drink contains a mild amount of caffeine. As a tasty, healthy source of quick energy, tea is best known as the national drink of the British, but it has wide appeal throughout the world.

Tea comes from the *Camellia sinensis* plant. This plant developed in the Himalaya Mountains in an indefinite area to the southeast of the Tibetan plateau. It was discovered by the Chinese, who were the first to consume tea as a beverage. The Chinese cultural influence throughout East Asia spread the popularity of tea. Buddhist monks brought the cultivation of *Camellia sinensis* to Japan around the twelfth century. Consumption of tea was limited to upper-class Japanese, who regarded the beverage only as a medicinal drink.

When tea leaves were packed into bricks, it became easy to trade tea. Turkish traders moved the Chinese tea bricks westward to the Mongolian border by the end of the fifth century. They exchanged the bricks for various goods. It is not clear why the spread of tea slowed, but the cost of the product may have reduced its popularity. Tea was a luxury item, and the leaves did not reach Europe for several hundred more years.

Tea was first mentioned in European sources in 1559, but it did not arrive in Europe until Dutch traders imported it from Japan in the early seventeenth century. Tea arrived in Amsterdam in 1610 before appearing in France in the 1630s and in England in 1657. The first tea served to the British public, a Dutch import, was offered at Garraway's Coffee House in London in 1657. Thomas Garraway touted the medicinal effects and virtues of the drink in the first British advertisement for tea. This new beverage captured the imagination of the English to the extent that the British East India Company commenced importing tea directly from China in its heavily armed ships in 1689.

The supply of tea brought into England by the East India Company led to a reduction in the price of the drink. It became easily affordable for most Britons. By the mid-1750s, tea houses and tea gardens were appearing throughout London. The East Indian Company made hefty profits with its tea monopoly. Sir Joseph Banks (1743–1820), a famed English explorer-botanist and the president of the Royal Society, suggested to the East India Company in 1788 that tea would grow on the southern slopes of the Himalayas. His advice was ignored until 1833 when the company's monopoly of the tea trade ended.

The Chinese knew that tea was an enormously valuable commodity. To protect their dominance of the tea industry, they prohibited tea seeds and tea makers from leaving the country. The Chinese government placed a price on the head of any merchant thought to be engaged in botanical sabotage and tried to capture the ships of suspected smugglers. The East India Company, desperate

Tea Laborers in Indonesia. *Indonesian women sort tea leaves in the sorting room of a tea factory in Java.* © BETTMANN/CORBIS. REPRODUCED BY PERMISSION.

to make profits, sent one of its officers to China in 1834 to capture these industrial secrets. The trip was enormously risky, but G. J. Gordon returned to London with tea seeds and a few tea makers willing to emigrate.

Meanwhile, the Dutch had managed to acquire tea-making knowledge as well. The first five hundred tea plants to reach Java were procured from Japan by the Dutch government. The Dutch established tea estates in Java in 1828. The following year, J. I. L. L. Jacobson produced the first Javanese black tea for export by the Dutch East India Company.

In test plantings undertaken by the British, the best growing success occurred in the Brahmaputra Valley in Assam in northern India. As a result, the area was selected for major development, and the British commenced chopping down the heavy Indian forest. The Assam plantings would grow to become the largest area of tea in the world. Although Chinese tea makers were crucial

in the establishment of the Assam tea industry in India, the British described them as both troublesome and insubordinate. Once others had acquired their skills and knowledge, the Chinese workers were replaced by local labor.

The Chinese method of tea manufacture was used in the East Indies until the coming of machinery. However, the planting, growing, and plucking of tea leaves is impossible to mechanize to any extent. To begin, the heavy forest growth in the jungle must be cleared. Tea plants are then set, with hoeing and weeding occurring periodically. Plucking tea leaves is the most labor intensive stage because only the top shoots can be picked. Women typically do the plucking. It has been estimated that a worker using both hands can pluck as many as thirty thousand shoots in a ten-hour day or fifty shoots per minute. Plucking takes place about every ten days, and 3,200 shoots are needed to make a pound (.45 kilograms) of tea. The tea is then carried to collection points.

The actual method of processing the tea has been industrialized. To produce dried tea leaves, moisture is first partially removed. The leaf is cut and rolled until it partially disintegrates, then it is exposed to air to ferment. Then the tea is dried or fired to completely remove moisture, after which it is sieved into size fractions, with fiber sorted out.

The tea workers, segregated from outside forces on tea estates, are typically illiterate. While the employers have always had powerful associations to protect their interests, workers have been unable to organize. As in centuries past, they suffer from low wages, poor housing, no pensions, and open drains that contribute to the spread of diseases. The death rate among tea workers is high.

The popularity of tea has expanded its range. It is produced in Sri Lanka (formerly Ceylon), Malaysia, Bangladesh, Vietnam, Argentina, Bolivia, Brazil, Ecuador, and Peru, as well as in East and Central Africa.

SEE ALSO *Dutch United East India Company; English East India Company; Shipping, East Asia and Pacific.*

BIBLIOGRAPHY

Forrest, Denys. *Tea for the British: The Social and Economic History of a Famous Trade.* London: Chatto and Windus, 1973.

Macfarlane, Alan, and Iris Macfarlane. *The Empire of Tea: The Remarkable History of the Plant That Took Over the World.* Woodstock, NY: Overlook, 2004.

Willson, K. C. *Coffee, Cocoa, and Tea.* New York: CAB International, 1999.

Willson, K. C., and M. N. Clifford, eds. *Tea: Cultivation to Consumption.* London: Chapman and Hall, 1992.

Caryn E. Neumann

THIRTEEN COLONIES, BRITISH NORTH AMERICA

The thirteen colonies of British North America that eventually formed the United States of America can be loosely grouped into four regions: New England, the Middle Colonies, the Chesapeake, and the Lower South. Each of these regions started differently, and they followed divergent paths of development over the course of more than a century of British settlement; yet they shared enough in common to join together against British rule in 1776.

New England was characterized from its earliest days by the religious motivation of most settlers. The Pilgrims who settled at Plymouth in 1620 were followed by a large group of Puritans in 1630. While religiously distinct from each other, the Pilgrims and Puritans had each left England because of religious persecution from conservative Anglicans, and each hoped to find a safe haven where they could worship without restrictions. The strictly moral societies founded in New England were intended to shine as beacons to the rest of the world, showing how life should be lived. The everyday lives of settlers revolved around religious worship and moral behavior, and while normal economic activities were understood to be necessary they were not intended to be the main focus of settlers' lives.

A majority of the settlers who arrived in New England before 1642 came in family groups, and many came as community groups as well. The communities they reformed in America were immediately demographically self-sustaining, and were often modeled on villages and towns left behind in England. Consequently, New England settlements often closely resembled English ones in ways that settlements elsewhere in the thirteen colonies did not. Migration during the English Civil War almost dried up completely, and when migration restarted after 1660, the increase in more commercially minded settlers began to alter the fundamental structure of New England society.

The Middle Colonies of New York, New Jersey, and Pennsylvania were all "Restoration Colonies," so-called because they came under English control after the Restoration of Charles II (1630–1685). New York was conquered from the Dutch in 1664, and although many Dutch settlers remained, large numbers of English and Scottish migrants arrived to alter the ethnic makeup of the colony. Pennsylvania probably bore more resemblance to the New England colonies than the rest of the Middle Colonies because it was founded by Quaker William Penn (1644–1718) as a religious haven. However, in contrast to most New England colonies, Penn adopted a policy of religious toleration, and his colony quickly attracted migrants from all over western Europe, particularly from Germany. The climate of Pennsylvania made it ideal farming country, and corn became its main staple product.

The Chesapeake was the earliest region colonized by the English. From the initial settlement at Jamestown the English spread very slowly around the tidewater of Chesapeake Bay, partly because of hostile local Native-American tribes, but also because the young men who constituted most of the settlers in Virginia before 1618 were not interested in forming stable communities. Instead, from 1612 onward they grew tobacco, which they knew would bring riches, but which also brought instability. The tobacco plant exhausted the soil and

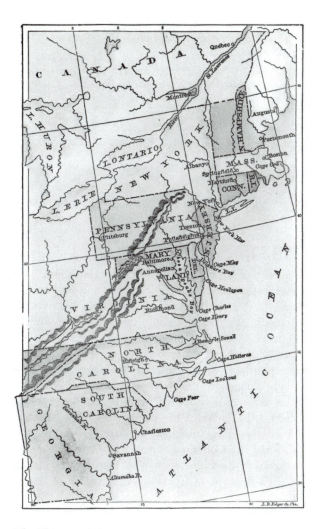

The Thirteen Colonies. *Great Britain's thirteen colonies in North America later formed the first thirteen states in the new United States.* © BETTMANN/CORBIS. REPRODUCED BY PERMISSION.

many were Catholic. The proprietor of Maryland, Lord Baltimore (Cecil Calvert, 1605?–1675), was a leading English Catholic and saw Maryland, like the Puritans saw New England and Penn saw Pennsylvania, as a religious refuge for those who shared his faith. Consequently, many of those in positions of authority and influence in Maryland were Catholic, something that caused friction among residents who were not Catholic. As a result, Lord Baltimore approved the passage of the Toleration Act of 1649, guaranteeing religious freedoms to the population.

The popularity of tobacco cultivation in the Chesapeake necessitated a regular supply of labor. Initially this demand was met by indentured servants who served for a period of seven years in return for passage to the New World and a promise of free land once the indenture was complete. Although the system of indentured labor was not perfect it served the colony well enough and was generally preferred to the alternative—slave labor—until the 1680s. This was mainly an economic decision; slaves were more expensive than indentured servants. And because significant numbers of servants did not live to see their freedom, the additional investment required for slave labor was simply not worth it. However, as death rates fell in Virginia and the ready supply of white indentured servants to the Chesapeake began to decline, slave labor became a more attractive alternative.

While there had been Africans in Virginia since before 1620, their status as slaves was not fixed and at least some Africans obtained their freedom and began farming. However, by 1660 discriminatory laws began to appear on the Virginia statute book, and after 1680, when the number of enslaved Africans began to rise quickly, they entered a full-fledged slave society that increasingly defined the Chesapeake colonies.

The Lower South colonies consisted of the Carolinas, first settled in 1670, and Georgia, not settled until 1733. Since the climate of the Carolinas was known to be conducive to plantation-style agriculture and many of the proprietors were also directors of the Royal African Company, slaves followed hard on the heels of the first white settlers. Finding large numbers of white settlers proved difficult, and the earliest migrants to Carolina were English and Scottish dissenters and a large group of Barbadian Anglicans who brought their slaves with them. The tidal waters around Charles-Town were ideally suited to rice cultivation, the techniques of which were most likely taught to planters by Africans, and large plantations growing the staple quickly became the norm. The numbers of workers required for rice cultivation were large, and as early as 1708 the coastal regions of Carolina had a black majority population.

therefore virgin land was constantly needed to continue production. The quest for more land to bring under cultivation brought the English into further conflict with local tribes, and it was partly responsible for provoking the devastating Indian attacks of 1622 and 1644.

Although the English appetite for tobacco remained undiminished, oversupply of the crop meant that prices after 1620 were not high enough to sustain the get-rich-quick mentality that had pervaded between 1615 and 1620. As the Virginia Company began to transport more women to the colony after 1618, the society became more demographically stable, though still heavily reliant on inward migration to maintain its population levels.

In 1632 Maryland was created out of northern Virginia, and although the colonists shared with those farther south a desire to make money from tobacco,

The trustees of Georgia initially intended their colony to be both a buffer between South Carolina and Spanish Florida and a haven for persecuted European Protestants, and believing that slavery would not be conducive to either of these aims, they prohibited it in 1735. However, the colony languished economically, failing to keep settlers who could see the wealth on offer in neighboring South Carolina, and eventually the trustees were forced to back down and permit slavery from 1750. Georgia quickly became a plantation colony like South Carolina.

The significant differences that existed between these four regions lessened during the eighteenth century but never entirely disappeared. The society of New England became more heterogeneous and less moralistic due to increased migration of non-Puritans. Chesapeake society gradually stabilized as death rates fell, and by 1700 the population was demographically self-sustaining. Significant events began to have an impact throughout the colonies, creating a shared American colonial history. The Glorious Revolution of 1688 affected New England, New York, Maryland, and South Carolina as colonials successfully struggled against what they believed were the pro-French absolutist tendencies of James II (1633–1701) and his followers in America. In the eighteenth century the pan colonial religious revivals collectively known as the Great Awakening made household names of evangelists such as George Whitefield (1714–1770). Continued migration brought hundreds of thousands of new settlers to the colonies, not only from England but increasingly from Ireland, Scotland, France, and Germany. The dispersal of these settlers in America, together with half a million enslaved Africans, made the colonial population a truly diverse one.

While it is difficult to speak of a common colonial culture, given the diverse experiences of Boston merchants, Pennsylvanian farmers, and Georgian planters, most shared a belief in traditional English freedoms, such as the rule of law and constitutional government. When these freedoms were thought to be threatened by actions of the British Parliament in the 1760s and 1770s, most colonists were quick to find common cause as Americans against British tyranny, though significant loyalist sentiment lingered in New York, South Carolina, and Georgia.

SEE ALSO *Caribbean; Empire, British; New Spain, The Viceroyalty of; Peru Under Spanish Rule.*

BIBLIOGRAPHY

Fischer, David Hackett. *Albion's Seed: Four British Folkways in America.* New York: Oxford University Press, 1989.

Geiter, Mary, and W. A. Speck. *Colonial America: From Jamestown to Yorktown.* Basingstoke, U.K.: Palgrave Macmillan, 2002.

Greene, Jack P. *Pursuits of Happiness: The Social Development of Early Modern British Colonies and the Formation of American Culture.* Chapel Hill: University of North Carolina Press, 1988.

Simmons, R. C. *The American Colonies from Settlement to Independence.* New York: McKay, 1976; reprint, Norton, 1981.

Tim Lockley

TIBET

Remote and largely inaccessible until recent times, Tibet never experienced Western colonial rule. Its strategic location, however, incited competition between the Mongols, Manchus, Chinese, Russians, and British for influence or control. China's Qing empire (1644–1912), established when the Manchus conquered China in the seventeenth century, exercised loose suzerainty over Tibet, while allowing it to be essentially self-governing. Tibet achieved de facto independence when the dynasty fell in 1912, although the Republic of China that succeeded the Qing continued to claim Tibet. In 1950, following the Communist victory in China, Tibet was occupied by the Chinese army and incorporated into the People's Republic of China. In 1959 it lost its vestigial autonomy.

By the mid-seventeenth century, the Dalai Lama, head of the reformed Geluk (Yellow Sect) branch of Tibetan Buddhism, exercised both temporal and spiritual authority over a theocratic Tibetan government. Each successive Dalai Lama, identified by oracles in infancy, was considered a living buddha, the incarnation of the bodhisattva Avalokiteśvara.

In the meantime, the Manchus conquered China and established the Qing dynasty. In 1656 the Fifth Dalai Lama (1617–1682) visited Beijing and met the Qing emperor Shunzhi (r. 1644–1661). The priest-patron relationship between the two, between a religious teacher and a lay patron, did not imply Tibet's subordination to the Qing. Nevertheless, the death of the Fifth Dalai Lama ultimately led to conflict over control of Tibet between the Manchus and their rivals, the Jungar Mongols, who had established hegemony over Tibet.

In 1720 a Qing army, accompanied by a Manchu-sponsored reincarnation of the Dalai Lama, expelled the Jungars and occupied Tibet. The Manchus established a protectorate, leaving Tibet essentially autonomous under the Dalai Lama while controlling Tibet's relations with its neighbors. A Qing garrison was stationed in Lhasa,

Tibet's capital. Two Qing imperial commissioners *(ambans)* were assigned to Lhasa to protect Qing interests and supervise the oracles identifying new incarnations of the Dalai Lama and other incarnated lamas. Parts of eastern Tibet were placed under direct Qing administration. Manchu hegemony over Tibet eventually weakened, however, as the Qing dynasty went into decline. By the beginning of the twentieth century, Tibet was, for practical purposes, independent.

Few westerners traveled to Tibet before the twentieth century. In 1707 Capuchin friars established a Catholic mission in Lhasa, and the Jesuit Ippolito Desideri (1684–1733) lived there from 1716 to 1721. The Catholic mission was abandoned in 1745. Soon the Tibetan authorities closed Tibet to westerners. Nonetheless, by the end of the nineteenth century, two Western empires, British India and Russian Central Asia, abutted Tibet. Despite British suspicions of Russian designs on Tibet, however, Russia had little influence in Lhasa. Britain, on the other hand, was eager to develop trade with Tibet, but the Tibetan government rebuffed British diplomatic contacts. In 1904 a British military expedition commanded by Francis Younghusband (1863–1942) fought its way to Lhasa, forcing the flight of the Thirteenth Dalai Lama (1876–1933) to Mongolia. The British established a consular office in Lhasa, the only Western country to do so. In 1947, upon independence, India inherited the British mission there.

The fall of the Qing dynasty in 1912 severed Tibet's subordination to China. The new Republic of China was unable to enforce its claim to Tibet as part of its territory. China did, however, continue to control ethnic Tibetan areas in Qinghai Province (Amdo) and Western Sichuan (Kham). In the decades that followed, Tibet isolated itself and did not seek international recognition or diplomatic representation until the 1940s. It also sometimes compromised its claims to independence in its dealings with the Nationalist government in China. The international community generally acquiesced in China's claims to Tibet.

The People's Republic of China, established in 1949, inherited its predecessor's territorial claims. China invaded Tibet in 1950. Tibetan resistance collapsed quickly, and the government of the Fourteenth Dalai Lama (b. 1935) signed an agreement recognizing Chinese sovereignty over Tibet. The agreement, however, stipulated that Tibet would be self-governing under the Dalai Lama. Nevertheless, the Chinese government undermined the old order by cultivating the Panchen Lama, the second-ranking leader of Tibetan Buddhism, and recruiting Tibetan collaborators. The Chinese organized serfs in Tibet, carried out antireligious propaganda, and recruited and trained Tibetan cadres. Nonetheless,

the Chinese government worked officially through the Dalai Lama's government. In most of Tibet, life continued on with little interference by the Chinese authorities through the 1950s.

Resentment over Chinese occupation sparked an uprising and the Dalai Lama's flight to India in 1959. Chinese forces crushed the rebellion and used it as a pretext for ending Tibetan autonomy, imposing martial law, and instituting severe political and religious persecution. In 1964 the Panchen Lama was arrested and imprisoned for fourteen years. After 1966, China's Cultural Revolution (1966–1976) reached Tibet, with devastating effects. Monasteries were closed, monks and nuns were forced to return to lay life, and "struggle sessions" were carried out against Buddhist clergy and landlords. Red Guards—militant young Maoist activists—both Chinese and Tibetans, destroyed much of Tibet's cultural heritage.

Cultural and religious liberalization began in the 1980s, but Tibet remains securely under Chinese control. In recent decades a significant number of Chinese immigrants have moved to Tibet, and Chinese now constitute the majority of Lhasa's population.

SEE ALSO *China, After 1945.*

BIBLIOGRAPHY

Fleming, Peter. *Bayonets to Lhasa: The First Full Account of the British Invasion of Tibet in 1904.* New York: Harper, 1961.

Goldstein, Melvyn C. *A History of Modern Tibet, 1913–1951: The Demise of the Lamaist State.* Berkeley: University of California Press, 1989.

Goldstein, Melvyn C. *The Snow Lion and the Dragon: China, Tibet, and the Dalai Lama.* Berkeley: University of California Press, 1997.

Goldstein, Melvyn C., Dawei Sherap, and William R Siebenschuh. *A Tibetan Revolutionary: The Political Life and Times of Bapa Phüntso Wangye.* Berkeley: University of California Press, 2004.

Grunfeld, A. Tom. *The Making of Modern Tibet,* rev ed. Armonk, NY: Sharpe, 1996.

Shakya, Tsering. *The Dragon in the Land of Snows: A History of Modern Tibet Since 1947.* New York: Columbia University Press, 1999.

Robert Entenmann

TOBACCO CULTIVATION AND TRADE

Tobacco (any of the species of plants belonging to the genus *Nicotiana*, especially *Nicotiana tabacum*) is native to the Americas. The tobacco plant had been domesticated by Native American peoples thousands of years before the arrival of Europeans.

Native Americans smoked tobacco for a variety of social and religious reasons, and its use was widespread throughout the Americas. The first recorded European sight of tobacco smoking came from the first voyage of Christopher Columbus (1451–1506) in 1492, when Columbus's men recorded the Indians' use of "certain herbs which they inhale," evidently for pleasure. Tobacco was not only used by the native peoples of the Caribbean islands, but it was also consumed in many other regions of the Americas. Archaeologists in Mexico City have unearthed decorative pipes in Indian burial mounds. Some tribes participated in the ceremonial smoking of tobacco in rituals such as baptism. In Peru, tobacco served as medicine and was taken in the form of snuff. In the 1530s, members of Jacques Cartier's (1491–1557) expedition to Canada saw Iroquois Indians smoking pipes in their homes close to what is now Montreal. Toward the end of the sixteenth century, the English visitors to Roanoke smoked tobacco with the natives before relations between the two groups turned sour.

It was not long before the European settlers began cultivating tobacco themselves. The Spanish pioneered its commercial production. They cultivated it for export to Europe on the island of Hispaniola in the 1530s, and commercial cultivation subsequently spread to other regions in and on the fringes of the Caribbean, especially Trinidad and Venezuela. From the mid-sixteenth century, the taste for tobacco began to spread in Europe, encouraging further growth in its cultivation and sale.

In 1559 the French ambassador to Portugal, Jean Nicot (1530–1600), after whom the plant was named, took to Lisbon some tobacco seeds that a sailor returning from Florida had given him. From this beginning, the desire for tobacco grew throughout the Mediterranean among people of all levels of society. In response, the Portuguese started growing tobacco in Brazil from early in the seventeenth century and subsequently made it Brazil's most important export crop after sugar. Portuguese traders took tobacco to their Asian trading ports and to West Africa, where it became a key item in the trade for slaves on the Guinea coast. Tobacco thus became part of the infamous triangular trade that saw millions of Africans taken to the Americas to work on plantations growing tobacco, sugar, and later cotton.

The first detailed description of tobacco in English was in Thomas Hacket's 1568 version of Andre Thevet's narrative of his travels in Brazil, although more influential was the book by Nicolas Monardes, a physician from Seville who in 1571 suggested to the English that tobacco smoking was a panacea. This opinion did not go unchallenged, however. The most famous author to write of the

evils of smoking tobacco was King James I (1566–1625) in 1604. He referred to himself as the doctor of the body politic, and in his *A Counterblaste to Tobacco* he condemned smoking as a "custome lothesome to the eye, hateful to the nose, harmful to the brain, dangerous to the lungs, and in the black and stinking fume thereof, nearest resembling the horrible stygian smoke of the pit that is bottomless" (James I 1604, p. 5).

England had, however, entered the tobacco trade thanks to Sir Francis Drake (ca. 1543–1596), who introduced pipe smoking into Britain, and Sir Walter Raleigh (ca. 1554–1618), the most significant supporter of tobacco smoking in the Elizabethan court. Indeed, Raleigh is said to have smoked throughout his imprisonment in the Tower of London and to have smoked a final pipe just before his execution.

The English trade relied at first on tobacco grown in the Spanish colonies, but the British soon sought to develop their own production of the commodity. Tobacco was indeed to play a key role in promoting English settlement in the Americas. When English settlers in Virginia were searching for a way to finance their colony, they turned to tobacco for a solution. In 1612 John Rolfe (1585–1622), influenced by native cultivation and curing techniques, began experimenting with a tobacco crop to rival that of the Spanish, who marketed their South American–grown tobacco to the whole of Europe.

In the 1620s tobacco cultivation also underpinned English settlement and trade in the Caribbean, where, after failing to establish tobacco-growing colonies in Guiana, English adventurers set up colonies based on tobacco cultivation in Barbados and other islands of the Lesser Antilles. The advantage of tobacco cultivation was that a small amount of seed could produce a large number of plants; the disadvantage was that the soil was soon exhausted. For this reason, tobacco cultivation soon proved less suitable for the English Caribbean islands than for Virginia, where land was in seemingly boundless supply and where tobacco quickly became the mainstay of the Chesapeake economy.

Initially, yeoman farmers grew tobacco on small plantations, but because of soil exhaustion, large-scale planters quickly dominated the trade, and large plantations soon spread along the banks of the James River. By 1620 the crop was well established, and growers were receiving high prices for the commodity on the European market. By 1624 Virginia's crop was secure enough for Edward Bennett, a merchant of Virginia, to propose to the British House of Commons that the importing of Spanish tobacco into England should be banned. Tobacco growing in England itself was also forbidden by James I, who, despite his personal dislike of tobacco,

Colonial Tobacco Laborers. *Slaves and other laborers process leaves and operate machinery at a North American tobacco plantation in this illustration engraved in 1754 for* Universal Magazine. **HULTON ARCHIVE/GETTY IMAGES. REPRODUCED BY PERMISSION.**

wanted to protect the new Virginia trade in which he now had a strong personal interest following the collapse of the Virginia Company and the region's emergence as a royal colony.

Much of the tobacco grown in Virginia arrived in Europe via Amsterdam, which became extremely wealthy on the profits from the curing and processing trades. Many of the leading merchants were Jews exiled from Spain and Portugal during the *reconquista* of the late fifteenth century. The English also realized how lucrative the trade could be, importing far more tobacco than they consumed.

Elizabeth I (1533–1603) saw the tax potential of tobacco imports, too, and placed a duty of two pence per pound on tobacco, infuriating small-scale importers on Britain's south coast. But this was nothing compared to the duty raised by James I in October 1604 when he pushed up the duty to six shillings and eight pence per pound of tobacco. Although James disliked smoking, he was sufficiently pragmatic to turn it to his financial

advantage: his was the first government to tax tobacco heavily.

Although tobacco was much less lucrative for Spain than the trade in precious metals, the profitability of the tobacco trade encouraged government taxation and regulation. The Spanish Crown established an *estanco* (royal monopoly) on the sale and distribution of tobacco within Spain as early as 1636; Portugal followed in 1659. In the eighteenth century, Virginia and Maryland were still the largest growers of tobacco in the New World, but several other colonies produced it on a smaller scale. French settlers grew it in Louisiana and Canada, but it was never their main source of income.

In the Spanish and Portuguese colonies of Central and South America, tobacco was invariably produced for local consumption, but for some colonies it was an important export crop. Venezuelan tobacco was particularly highly prized and was such an attraction to foreigners that the Spanish government was willing to suppress tobacco growing there in order to stop illicit trade with the Dutch, whose contraband in Venezuelan tobacco threatened Spanish dominance of European tobacco markets. During the eighteenth century, Cuba became the most notable of the Spanish tobacco-exporting colonies, although from 1764 the imposition of a government monopoly restricted sales of Cuban tobacco and drove many traders toward cheaper Virginian tobacco.

During the eighteenth century, the Spanish Crown gradually extended *estanco* regulations throughout its colonies, and in the second half of the century turned tobacco sales into a major source of state revenues. At their peak, these revenues were second in value only to taxes on gold and silver, which remained the major exports of the Spanish colonies.

State controls on tobacco cultivation and sales did not pass without protest: indeed, it triggered resistance ranging from tax evasion through illegal sales to violent riots and rebellions. The most important of these was the 1781 *comunero* rebellion in the viceroyalty of New Granada, where resistance by small farmers to restrictions on tobacco cultivation played a part in an uprising that forced the Spanish government temporarily to suspend its program of fiscal and administrative reforms. On the international market, Cuban tobacco remained an important commodity because of the perception of the world's smokers that it made the best cigars. By the early 1820s, hand-rolled "Havanas" had become famous among English smokers and were to remain so, though in the later nineteenth century Cuba was to export more unprocessed tobacco leaf than finished cigars.

After independence, tobacco continued to figure strongly in American exports, not only from the traditional export regions of the American South, Brazil, and Cuba, but also from some of the new Spanish American republics, where free trade encouraged export, and governments continued to find the tobacco trade a convenient source of revenue, sometimes even reviving the *estancos*. Colombia briefly became a major tobacco exporter around the mid-nineteenth century, mainly to Germany, while most Spanish American countries produced tobacco for their own consumption or for neighboring markets.

In the late nineteenth and twentieth centuries, another phase in the history of the tobacco trade opened when foreign companies from Europe and the United States extended their search for sources of tobacco production and their influence on consumer markets. By the early years of the twenty-first century, tobacco was produced for local markets and consumed widely in Asia and Africa, while its use had become less fashionable in Europe and America.

SEE ALSO *British American Tobacco Company; Native Americans and Europeans; Plantations, the Americas; Virginia Company.*

BIBLIOGRAPHY

Breen, T. H. *Tobacco Culture: The Mentality of the Great Tidewater Planters on the Eve of the Revolution.* Princeton, NJ: Princeton University Press, 1985.

Deans-Smith, Susan. *Bureaucrats, Planters, and Workers: The Making of the Tobacco Monopoly in Bourbon Mexico.* Austin: University of Texas Press, 1992.

Gateley, Iain. *Tobacco: A Cultural History of How an Exotic Plant Seduced Civilization.* New York: Grove Press, 2001.

James I [King of England]. *A Counterblaste to Tobacco.* London: [Unknown binding], 1604.

McFarlane, Anthony. *Colombia before Independence: Economy, Society, and Politics under Bourbon Rule.* New York: Cambridge University Press, 1993.

Catherine Armstrong

TOBACCO PROTEST, IRAN

The Tobacco protest of 1891–1892 was the first mass nationwide popular movement in Iran and was directed both against a tobacco concession given to a British subject in 1890 and, implicitly, against the shah, Nasir al-Dīn, who granted it, and several other concessions, especially to the British and Russians. Great Britain and Russia in the nineteenth century were the main foreign powers with political and economic interests in Iran, which neither of them could conquer due to the opposition of the other. Russia had been gaining ground after the mid-nineteenth century, especially with the creation in 1879 of the Russian-officered Cossack Brigade, the only modern military force in Iran. From 1888 to 1890 the aggressive British minister to Iran, Sir Henry Drummond Wolff, tried to further British power via a series of concessions. These included one for the new Imperial Bank of Persia, giving it exclusive rights to issue banknotes, opening up the Karun River to navigation, and a concession in March 1990 to a friend of Wolff's, Major G. F. Talbot, for the purchase, sale, and export of all tobacco products. Because tobacco was a major domestic and export crop, the latter concession aroused both merchants whose economic interests would be harmed and the *ulama* (religious scholars), who objected (partly at the urging of merchants) to foreigners controlling such an important item. At this time Sayyid Jamal al-Dīn al-Afghānī was in Iran, and his followers distributed leaflets against the shah's concession-granting, which led to Afghānī's expulsion to Iraq in January 1891.

Mass protests against the concession in several major cities began in the spring of 1891, when tobacco company representatives began to arrive and post six-month deadlines for the sale of all local tobacco to them. Demonstrations began first in Shiraz, from which a leader of the *ulama* was exiled as a result, and then spread to Tabriz, where demonstrations were so widespread and threatening that the shah suspended the concession there. The Russians aided some of the protests. From his Iraqi exile, Afghānī wrote to Mirza Hasan Shirazi, the top religious leader in the Shi'i shrine cities of Iraq, asking him to lead a protest. Several Iranian Ulama also asked Shirazi to act, and Shirazi telegraphed the shah to condemn foreign interference and the killing of people in the recent protests, and called for an end to concessions to foreigners.

In the fall the movement spread to Isfahan and Mashhad. In December the protest reached its culmination in the nationwide boycott of the use and sale of tobacco, ordered by a fatwa attributed to Shirazi that, at least in public, was universally observed, even by non-Muslims. The universality of observance amazed observers, and it was reliably reported that even the shah's wives and servants refused to smoke. The shah was forced to cancel the internal concession, but further disorders ensued, and in January in Tehran troops fired on a growing crowd of male and female demonstrators and killed seven or more people. This event brought the definitive end of the whole concession, which the shah was forced to cancel. The local head of the tobacco company agreed to cancellation and to a cessation of operations, although Iran was forced to pay exaggerated compensation for company expenses.

Although the shah was now able to sow division in the *ulama* via threats and favors, the oppositional role of the groups allied in the anti-concession movement—merchants, *ulama*, and reformers—was to reappear in greater force in the constitutional revolution of 1905 to 1911 and afterward. More immediately, Iran was saddled with a large debt as a result of the concession's cancellation, and Drummond Wolff's project lay in ruins as Russian influence increased. This example of a successful mass movement against internal and foreign exploitation helped spark later oppositional movements in Iran. Iran indeed has had, beginning with the Tobacco Movement, more nationwide and multi-city rebellions and revolutions than any other Muslim country, which may in part be due to the *ulama*-merchant alliance and to the fact that merchants in Iran, unlike in many other countries, were overwhelmingly locally born Muslims who had close family and business ties to the *ulama*. Several reformers who, before the Tobacco Movement, had attacked the *ulama* and institutional Islam as reactionary now came to see them as potential allies against governmental and foreign oppression and exploitation.

SEE ALSO *Afghānī, Jamal ad-Dīn al-*.

BIBLIOGRAPHY

Keddie, Nikki R. *Religion and Rebellion in Iran: The Tobacco Protest of 1891–1892*. London: Frank Cass, 1966.

Lambton, Ann K. S. "The Tobacco Regie: Prelude to Revolution." *Studia Islamica* 22 (1965): 119–157 and 23 (1965): 71–90.

Nikki Keddie

TRAVELOGUES

Eyewitness accounts by those "on the spot" at the cutting edge of Western expansion figure frequently in the primary sources used by students of colonialism. No doubt the best known are those book-length narratives that were aimed at a public eager to read about bold exploits in exotic places. But alongside them were logs, diaries, letters, field notes, official reports, news stories, and scientific monographs, addressed to more specialized audiences. Indeed many of them were not intended for publication.

Some still only exist as rare manuscripts in national archives and private collections. Others have been lost altogether. The nearest we have to the journal of Columbus's first voyage, for example, is a later summary by Bartolemé de Las Casas. The main—and sometimes only—source for early accounts (often in abridged and reworked versions) are the multivolume collections of voyage literature that appeared during the sixteenth to eighteenth centuries, such as those assembled by Giovanni Ramusio, Richard Hakluyt, and Theodore de Bry, to name some early examples.

In addition, one finds valuable testimony—if only in passing—in works that would not normally be considered travel narratives. First-hand reports appear in the memoirs or biographies of public figures, whose colonial experiences may have been short-lived. Indeed, they may be implicit in works that do not take a narrative form at all. The bilingual *Allada Catechism* (1670), prepared for missionaries in West Africa, can tell us a good deal about prevailing attitudes and local conditions, as can maps, charts, and atlases. Scholars of travel writing have also paid attention to the novels of writers such as Herman Melville, Pierre Loti, or Joseph Conrad, which owe so much to their authors' experiences on the imperial frontier. In addition, they have considered imaginative works that draw heavily on contemporary travel literature, even if, as with William Shakespeare's *The Tempest* or Daniel Defoe's *Robinson Crusoe*, their authors never left Europe.

The titles of anthologies and academic studies of travel writings indicate the prevailing tendency to classify such material in one of three ways: based on the nationality or gender of the author, the area of the world being traveled and written about, or the historical period in which the work was written. Sometimes one finds combinations of all three: "English Women and the Middle East, 1718–1918" or "Twentieth-Century African American Writing about Africa," to pick two subtitles almost at random.

But it may be more useful here to offer a schematic grouping in terms of what might be called the positioning of the author; in other words, his or her role in the colonial project. While one cannot deduce from such positions the ideological stance of the text or its factual reliability, their very diversity should begin to indicate that colonial travel writing is not at all written in a single voice or from the same point of view.

First, there are those senior figures who were appointed as leaders of expeditions, or rulers of territory, and are better known perhaps for what they did than for what they wrote. Their writings—shaped as they often are by the desire to impress the monarch or government that appointed them—were used to promote and justify the colonial enterprise, or at least easily lend themselves to such readings. Examples would include Hernán Cortés's letters detailing the conquest of Mexico, Walter Ralegh's account of his search for El Dorado, and the famous narratives of circumnavigation by Louis Antoine de Bougainville and James Cook. Both Edward Eyre and Marie-Joseph-François Garnier, administrators in Australia and Indochina respectively, wrote extensively of their explorations in regions unknown to Europeans at the time.

Second, there are those who played a more intermediary role—as traders, interpreters, missionaries, diplomats, sometimes at the cutting edge of expansion, sometimes following in its wake. Here we might place the letters of Dutch merchant Willem Bosman from the coast of West Africa in 1705, the record of Isabella Bird's missionary work in the Far East, or Edward Lane's seminal study of Egypt and of Arabic language and literature. These diverse roles often overlap, as they do quite explicitly in the life and work of Roger Williams, whose *Key into the Language of America* (1643) is about conversion and trade as much as translation. Their writings are more likely to demonstrate an engagement with native beliefs and practices, an engagement most vividly symbolized by famous cases of cultural cross-dressing: for instance, the pilgrimage to Mecca carried out by British diplomat Richard Burton or the French religious scholar Alexandra

David-Néel's epic journey to Lhasa, both undertaken in disguise.

A third group comprises those whose journeys to—and experiences on—the colonial frontier were in the capacity of rank-and-file employees, such as laborers, servants, sailors, and soldiers. They include Richard Henry Dana, whose experiences as a common seaman trading for hides on the Californian coast in the 1830s are recorded in *Two Years before the Mast*, and Hans Staden, who was captured by Tupinamba in the 1550s while serving as a gunner at a Portuguese fort off the coast of Brazil. George Orwell's *Burmese Days* (1934), based on his experiences as a colonial policeman, is a more recent example, but it is quite rare that such perspectives find their way into print. More marginalized still are the voices of fugitives, slaves, prisoners, and pirates, whose stories usually come down to us in the words of others.

Finally, there are those who traveled as more independent observers. Not directly involved in the colonial enterprise, their writings exhibit perhaps a greater variety of perspectives than the others. News coverage, for example, ranges from the investigative and critical journalism of Albert Londres in French Guiana or Michael Herr in Vietnam to the sensationalist reporting associated with the Spanish American and Boer Wars. More extended stays by those on professedly scientific missions are less obviously partisan. Alexander von Humboldt's delineations of the physical geography of the Americas or Margaret Mead's anthropological study of the sexual mores of Samoa are classics in their fields—but so too once was the racial classification proposed by the anatomist Josiah Nott and Egyptologist George Gliddon in *Types of Mankind* (1854), which drew on the latter's research while U.S. vice-consul in Cairo.

ASSESSING COLONIAL TRAVEL WRITING

It was only in the wake of decolonization in the post–World War II period that this vast body of writing began to receive sustained critical attention. One approach made extensive use of travel literature to trace a history of the attitudes of Europeans toward people of color, as they evolved from the confusions and misunderstandings of first contact through the development of more standardized prejudice, to modern racism. Another, by contrast, saw early accounts as marking an advance on medieval ignorance and paving the way for the systematic description and interpretation of other cultures by modern anthropologists.

When anthropologists began to take a more critical view of their own discipline and interrogate its colonialist assumptions (signaled by two influential collections of essays, edited by Talal Asad and Dell Hymes), this contrast began to lose its force. During the 1970s, the analysis of travel accounts moved away from the assessment of their accuracy or the scrutiny of their motives toward an attempt to understand the deeper rhetorical structures of the writings themselves and the institutional frameworks that lend them authority.

This new approach was pioneered, above all, by Edward Said, a literary critic drawing on Michel Foucault's concept of "discourse." His *Orientalism* (1978) takes to task a wide range of writings on the Middle East, from the Napoleonic *Description de l'Egypte* to the *Cambridge History of Islam*. His target is the very notion of an essentially unchanging "Orient," which they unquestioningly presuppose, whatever their ostensible sympathies. It was not so much what the "West" said about the "East" that is at issue here, but the assumed distinction between an "us" and a "them" that makes such statements meaningful in the first place.

Orientalism proved hugely influential on the growing number of studies of travel writing and colonialism that followed, and not only those concerned specifically with the Middle East. A case in point is Mary Louise Pratt's elaboration of the notion of "anti-conquest" in *Imperial Eyes* (1992), which finds apparently innocent descriptions of landscape serving the imperialist project as much as those accounts that celebrate the acquisition of territory, precisely because they disavow the relations of power that make them possible. Another is David Spurr's *Rhetoric of Empire* (1993), which investigates twelve basic tropes used to represent non-Western peoples, including *affirmation* and *idealization* as well as *debasement* and *negation*.

In a related and parallel development, similar concerns were evident in close readings of modern anthropological texts. Johannes Fabian, James Clifford, and others examined the conventions of the "classic" monograph, such as its use of the "ethnographic present," which suppresses the dialogue and negotiation of the fieldwork experience in order to generalize about a way of life that seems always to have been so.

Much of this scholarship has involved tracing recurrent themes and preoccupations across a wide range of writings. It has produced its own terminology— "monarch-of-all-I-survey" scenes (Mary Louise Pratt) or "allegories of salvage" (James Clifford)—and scrutinized familiar categories: *wonder* (Stephen Greenblatt), *curiosity* (Nigel Leask). William Pietz's rich, politicized etymology of the term *fetish* offers another approach. Many specific studies (of authors or geographical regions) have shed light on the relationship between colonial travel writing and broader issues, such as indigeneity (Peter Hulme), forms of exchange (David Murray), exoticism (Charles Forsdick), and the female gaze (Indira Ghose).

The field has been characterized by lively debate. Cannibalism has been a contested topic since William Arens raised doubts about the claims made in many travel accounts regarding the practice and argued that there is no evidence that it ever existed anywhere as a socially accepted custom. The interpretation of narratives is also at the heart of a famous disagreement between Marshall Sahlins and Gananath Obeyesekere over the reception of Captain Cook when he landed in Hawai'i in 1778, a debate that touches on many key issues of cross-cultural judgment.

Sara Mills and others have fine-tuned the terms in which the issue of gender has been discussed in a colonial context. The general question of whether women write differently from men—and why—is of course complicated when the relationship between women and the people they write about is taken into account. This work has been accompanied by the extensive republication and anthologization of the accounts of women travelers, among them Lady Mary Wortley Montagu, who accompanied her husband to Constantinople when he was appointed ambassador in 1716, and Mary Kingsley, the Victorian explorer and author of *Travels in West Africa* (1897).

A good number of studies of European and North American travel writings show how such works tended to legitimate the colonial project by presenting the colonized as peoples without history. While some of this scholarship has been legitimately criticized for its tendency to treat what it sometimes refers to as "colonial discourse" as monolithic and inescapable, with travel writing as its inevitable servant, much of it is more sophisticated than this. Many scholars, for instance, now acknowledge that even the most unsympathetic and propagandistic work can nevertheless tell us much not only about the practices and psychology of conquest and settlement but also about the places and peoples described, and can be used to theoretically reconstruct precolonial cultures for which there is precious little other evidence.

This is at least partly because the kind of colonial encounters described in travel writings—the day-to-day exchanges of words, ideas, and things between the colonizer and colonized—exhibit, despite the radically uneven power relations at play, a fair amount of negotiation and improvisation. For Mary Louise Pratt this is why the colonial frontier is perhaps better described as a *contact zone*, a term that has since been widely used by those who have read "classic" texts against the grain, paying attention to the hesitations, uncertainties, and contradictions in the writing that allow the complexities of this interaction to become visible—sometimes in conjunction with the (re)discovery of private notes, diaries,

THREE WRITERS OF TRAVELOGUES

From the accounts of expedition leaders, explorers, and traders to adventurers, pilgrims, and everyday people, travelogues allow us to view colonial history from varying perspectives. Among the many writers associated with travelogues, three of the most significant are Giovanni Battista Ramusio, Edward John Eyre, and Mary Kingsley.

The Italian geographer and Renaissance scholar Giovanni Battista Ramusio (1485–1557) did not write travelogues based on his own experiences; rather, he compiled the travelogues of others. By obtaining as many as possible and translating them into Italian, along with maps, images, and his own commentary, Ramusio played an instrumental role in making the accounts of European explorers available to others. The fruit of his labor was a three-volume work titled *Delle navigationi et viaggi*.

The English explorer Edward John Eyre (1815–1901) was one of the first persons to begin the exploration of central Australia, and was the first to make an overland trip across Australia. His original goal was to find a way to drive livestock overland—but he ended up proving that there was no practical way of doing this. Eyre and his companions suffered through an extreme scarcity of water and food, and were slowed down by wind-blown sand. In addition, the Aborigines with whom Eyre traveled murdered a member of his party. These hardships are detailed in *Journals of Expeditions of Discovery into Central Australia and Overland from Adelaide to King George's Sound in the Years 1840–1*. In this book, Eyre describes natives who thrived in what Europeans would deem impossible conditions.

The Englishwoman Mary Kingsley (1862–1900) published various accounts of her pioneering trips to West Africa, including the book *Travels in West Africa* (1897) and a large number of articles on African subjects. As a trader, Kingsley gained access to the Fan tribe, who were known to be cannibals. Only one European, a Frenchman, had visited them previously, and he had disappeared without a trace. Through their travels together, Kingsley and the Fan developed a sense of mutual respect.

In one village, Kingsley recounts in *Travels in West Africa*, she stayed in a chief's house, where she had difficulty sleeping because of a strong and disgusting odor. She soon discovered the odor was coming from a bag hanging from the roof beams. She shook the bag's contents "out in my hat, for fear of losing anything of value. They were a human hand, three big toes, four eyes, two ears, and other portions of the human frame. The hand was fresh, the others only so so, and shrivelled. Replacing them I tied the bag up, and hung it up again. I subsequently learnt that although the Fans will eat their fellow friendly tribesfolk, yet they like to keep a little something belonging to them as a memento" (Kingsley, London: Macmillian and Co, 1897).

and letters never meant for publication, in which these complexities are often in greater evidence.

But more obviously "postcolonial" perspectives on travel writing are apparent in two other broad currents of scholarship. One approach focuses on a certain crisis of authority in the writings of Western travelers and tourists of the post–World War II period. In the last half-century or so, authors—having previously enjoyed an apparently exclusive relationship with the people they described—have begun to acknowledge (if only obliquely) that their accounts might be open to question. They sense the possibility of criticism not only by other Western travelers (who have been visiting "remote" locales in growing numbers) but also, more significantly, by the people they write about, people who must increasingly be counted among their readers. No longer feeling confident to repeat the imperious generalizations of the past, contemporary travelers often undercut them with self-parody (such as Eric Newby's shambling exploration of the Hindu Kush) or overwhelm them with pessimistic despair (Graham Greene's cynical portrayals of Liberia and Haiti, for instance).

Some travel writers have responded to this crisis more directly and reflexively by experimenting with the form of the travel narrative or anthropological monograph itself, producing "polyphonic" texts that mix genres and intentionally make it difficult for older, patronizing certainties to take hold. They may critically engage with earlier writers or work closely with interpreters and informants to produce what are in effect jointly authored texts, and they frequently reflect on their own practice and institutional location. Many of these techniques are evident in the various publications of Richard and Sally Price on Surinam that have appeared since the 1970s. But if such bold experiments have become increasingly common, it also has become clear that they were anticipated by modernist writers of the 1920s and 1930s such as Zora Neale Hurston and Michel Leiris, whose unconventional ethnographies have recently been reappraised.

Another postcolonial approach to travel writing has focused on travel writings by authors from colonized and formerly colonized countries, especially those that recount journeys to Europe and North America. These range from the slave narrative of Olaudah Equiano, to Domingo Faustino Sarmiento's *Viajes por Europa, Africa, y América* (1849–1851), which records an attempt to seek overseas models for the young republic of Argentina to follow. Twentieth-century examples include the Ivorian Bernard Dadié's impressions of Paris and New York and the Egyptian Nawal al-Saadawi's *My Travels Around the World* (1991).

In *Home and Harem* (1996), Inderpal Gewal discusses the travels to Britain and the United States of Indian men and women toward the end of the nineteenth century. Accounts like these tend to be found, not in recognizable "travel books," but in diaries, letters, and autobiographies. But the memoirs of public figures who traveled to the West—whether to publicize a cause, secure an education, earn a living, or escape arrest—form a wealth of material. The experiences of lesser-known travelers are more likely to be recorded by oral history projects or evoked in the many fictional narratives of immigration, such as the multigenerational epics *The Gunny Sack* (1989), by M. G. Vassanji, and *La Vie Scélérate* (1987), by Maryse Condé.

However, the type of "writing back" that has, arguably, attracted most attention is the contemporary, self-consciously postcolonial travel narrative written by a successful author based in the West. Examples include the works of V. S. Naipaul and Caryl Phillips, whose writings—both fictional and nonfictional—offer, in effect, multiple ways of engaging with the Indian diaspora and "Black Atlantic," respectively. Perhaps more controversial—and certainly more unusual and striking—is *A Small Place* (1988), Jamaica Kincaid's scathing polemic addressed to tourists who visit her native Antigua.

The search for travel writing that challenges the Eurocentric legacy of the genre has been undertaken with some caution. Colonial discourse may not be monolithic and all-embracing, but it is nonetheless not easy to identify a straightforward alternative. Even when travel writing undermines colonial discourse through inversions, revisions, or uncertainties, colonial assumptions may remain. As Patrick Holland and Graham Huggan suggest

in *Tourists with Typewriters* (1998), the comic self-deprecation that marks a certain type of popular travel book diverts attention from serious questions of power and privilege, while the "counter-travel" of cosmopolitan writers of color run the risk of perpetuating the long-standing Western investment in the "exotic." Every attempt to subvert the tradition may always come close to being co-opted by it.

SEE ALSO *Columbus, Christopher; Cortés, Hernán; Hakluyt, Richard.*

BIBLIOGRAPHY

Arens, William. *The Man-Eating Myth: Anthropology and Anthropophagy.* New York: Oxford University Press, 1979.

Asad, Talal, ed. *Anthropology and the Colonial Encounter.* London: Ithaca, 1973.

Boehmer, Elleke, ed. *Empire Writing: An Anthology of Colonial Literature, 1870–1918.* Oxford: Oxford University Press, 1998.

Clark, Steve, ed. *Travel Writing and Empire: Postcolonial Theory in Transit.* London and New York: Zed, 1999.

Clifford, James. "On Ethnographic Allegory." In *Writing Culture: The Poetics and Politics of Ethnography*, edited by James Clifford and George E. Marcus, 98–121. Berkeley, Los Angeles, and London: University of California Press, 1986.

Clifford, James. "On Ethnographic Authority." In his *The Predicament of Culture: Twentieth-Century Ethnography, Literature, and Art*, 21–54. Cambridge and London: Harvard University Press, 1988.

Fabian, Johannes. *Time and the Other: How Anthropology Makes Its Object.* New York: Columbia University Press, 1983.

Forsdick, Charles. *Victor Segalen and the Aesthetics of Diversity: Journeys between Cultures.* Oxford and New York: Oxford University Press, 2000.

Fulford, Tim, and Peter Kitson, eds. *Travels, Explorations, and Empires: Writings from the Era of Imperial Expansion, 1770–1835.* 8 vols. London: Pickering and Chatto, 2001.

Greenblatt, Stephen J. *Marvelous Possessions: The Wonder of the New World.* Oxford: Clarendon, 1991.

Grewal, Inderpal. *Home and Harem: Nation, Gender, Empire, and the Cultures of Travel.* Durham, NC: Duke University Press, 1996.

Holland, Patrick, and Graham Huggan. "After Empire." In their *Tourists with Typewriters: Critical Reflections on Contemporary Travel Writing*, 27–65. Ann Arbor: University of Michigan Press, 1998.

Hulme, Peter. *Colonial Encounters: Europe and the Native Caribbean, 1492–1797.* London: Methuen, 1986.

Hulme, Peter. *Remnants of Conquest: The Island Caribs and Their Visitors, 1877–1998.* Oxford and New York: Oxford University Press, 2000.

Hulme, Peter, and Tim Youngs, eds. *The Cambridge Companion to Travel Writing.* Cambridge, U.K.: Cambridge University Press, 2002.

Hymes, Dell, ed. *Reinventing Anthropology.* New York: Pantheon, 1972.

Pettinger, Alasdair, ed. *Always Elsewhere: Travels of the Black Atlantic.* London: Cassell, 1998.

Quinn, David B., ed. *New American World: A Documentary History of North America to 1612.* 5 vols. New York: Arno, 1979.

Pratt, Mary Louise. *Imperial Eyes: Travel Writing and Transculturation.* London and New York: Routledge, 1992.

Murray, David. *Indian Giving: Economies of Power in Indian-White Exchanges.* Amherst: University of Massachusetts Press, 2000.

Sahlins, Marshall. *How "Natives" Think: About Captain Cook, for Example.* Chicago: University of Chicago Press, 1995.

Said, Edward. *Orientalism.* London: Routledge and Kegan Paul, 1978.

Speake, Jennifer, ed. *The Literature of Travel and Exploration: An Encyclopedia.* 3 vols. London: Fitzroy Dearborn, 2002.

Spurr, David. *The Rhetoric of Empire: Colonial Discourse in Journalism, Travel Writing, and Imperial Administration.* Durham, NC, and London: Duke University Press, 1993.

Alasdair Pettinger

TREATIES, EAST ASIA AND THE PACIFIC

In international law, a *treaty* is defined as a written instrument whereby two or more states signify their intention to establish a new legal relationship, involving mutually binding contractual obligations. Any such agreement that is not based on the mutual recognition by the contracting parties of their respective equality and sovereignty, and that does not contain the element of reciprocity insofar as rights and obligations are concerned, must appear to be legally somewhat incongruous. However, it has long been held that a substantial part of what constitutes international law rests upon the usage and practice of sovereign states. International treaties ought to be studied from the point of history and international law. The so-called Unequal Treaties concluded between the Western powers and China in the nineteenth century are a case in point.

The concept of the Unequal Treaties originated with contemporary Western writers on international law. While the treaties furnished a legal basis for the Western presence in China's Qing empire (1644–1911), the term *Unequal Treaties* came to symbolize the special type of Western imperialism in Asia. The beginnings of the Unequal Treaties can be found in the peace treaty of Nanjing (1842), which brought to a conclusion the first Anglo-Chinese War (1839–1842), usually somewhat misleadingly referred to as the first Opium War.

What began as a punitive expedition led to a profound alteration of China's external relations. Under the Treaty of Nanjing, China was forced to open five ports to British commerce, and British merchants had the right to settle and trade there. Crucially, British subjects residing in these so-called treaty ports enjoyed extraterritoriality, that is, they were not subject to Chinese jurisdiction. Exploiting the country's weakness, other colonial powers, led by France and the United States, forced China to conclude similar agreements.

All the treaties concluded in this period contained a most-favored-nation clause, and all the privileges conferred in them were automatically extended to the other treaty powers. In this sense, it is possible to talk of the "treaty system." In its essence, the system was completed by 1860 with the conclusion of the Treaty of Tianjin at the end of the so-called Second Opium War (1856–1860). Under the provisions of the treaty, China was forced to accept the establishment of permanent diplomatic relations with the outside world. Further provisions included the opening of eleven more treaty ports, now even in the interior of the country, and more especially in the prosperous Yangzi Basin (the number of treaty ports would eventually rise to forty-eight by the eve of World War I in 1914); the freedom of travel for all foreigners; and, controversially, the freedom of movement and religious practice for Christian missionaries.

The Treaty of Tianjin marked the end of the dramatic phase of the opening of China. Yet, the treaty systems continued to evolve, so much so that by the beginning of the twentieth century it had grown to such an extent and to such a complexity that it was impenetrable to all but highly specialized legal experts. In fact, Chinese lawyers now began to challenge the Western powers with their own legal weapons. The Unequal Treaties remained in force until their negotiated abrogation in November 1943.

Although the treaty system was avowedly "unequal" in that the treaties constituted an enforced, unilateral infringement of Chinese sovereignty, in practice the system was more ambiguous. The extraterritoriality clauses meant that the citizens of the treaty powers were exempted from Chinese jurisdiction, and could only be tried in a foreign, and in practice this usually meant consular, court. However, judicial exemption did not constitute a claim to separate territorial rights.

The treaty ports were not colonies; in most of them Chinese authority was not infringed. A partial exception was the small number of "concessions"—clearly delimited residential districts leased to foreign governments, such as those in Shanghai and Tianjin. The treaty system

Singing of the Treaty of Tianjin, 1858. Under the provisions of this treaty, China was forced to accept the establishment of permanent diplomatic relations with the outside world. © BETTMANN/CORBIS. REPRODUCED BY PERMISSION.

cloaked the Western (and later Japanese) presence in the Qing empire in excessive legalism. It furnished the juridical basis of informal imperialism, while the treaty ports were the "bridgeheads" of the foreign presence in China.

The historical significance of the treaties is beyond doubt. Between 1842 and 1943 China was a country of at least partially impaired sovereignty, underscoring its position as an object of Great Power politics. The almost automatic extension of commercial privileges to all treaty powers was a de facto institutionalization of the "open door," that is, the notion of equal opportunities in the economic penetration of China.

To some degree, the treaties also represented a mid-nineteenth-century confluence of Western and Chinese interests; both sides were anxious to establish standardized commercial practices and to minimize the disruptive influence of smuggling and piracy. In the longer term, however, the treaties provided the main focus for an emerging Chinese nationalism and an ideal vehicle for anti-imperialist and anti-Western propaganda.

SEE ALSO *China, After 1945; China, First Opium War to 1945; China, to the First Opium War; Empire, Japanese; Extraterritoriality; Korea, from World War II; Korea, to World War II; Missions, China; Open Door Policy; Opium Wars; Perry, Matthew; Treaty Port System.*

BIBLIOGRAPHY

Keeton, G. W. *The Development of Extraterritoriality in China.* 2 vols. London: Longmans, 1928.

Pope Alexander VI with Clerics and Noblemen. *In 1493 Pope Alexander VI, depicted in this mid-eighteenth-century engraving, established the line of demarcation that defined the spheres of Spanish and Portuguese influence in the world; the line was later renegotiated with the Treaty of Tordesillas, signed in 1494.* **HULTON ARCHIVE/GETTY IMAGES. REPRODUCED BY PERMISSION.**

MacMurray, John van Antwerp,, ed. *Treaties and Agreements with and Concerning China, 1894–1919.* 2 vols. New York: Oxford University Press, 1921.

Morse, Hosea Ballou. *The International Relations of the Chinese Empire.* 3 vols. London: Longmans, 1910–1918.

Osterhammel, Jürgen. *China und die Weltgesellschaft: Vom 18,, Jahrhundert bis in unsere Zeit.* Munich: Beck, 1986.

Trouche, Marcel. *Le Quartier diplomatiquediplomatique de Pékin: Etude historique et juridique.* Paris: Subervie, 1935.

Tung, William L. *China and the Foreign Powers: The Impact of and Reaction to the Unequal Treaties.* Dobbs Ferry, NY: Oceana, 1970.

Willoughby, Wester. *Foreign Rights and Interests in China,* rev. ed. 2 vols. Baltimore, MD: Johns Hopkins University Press, 1927.

T. G. Otte

TREATY OF TORDESILLAS

Between 1418 and 1492, Portugal was the dominant maritime power in the Atlantic Ocean, sending numerous naval and military expeditions to explore the African coast, enforce colonial claims, and find a sea route around Africa to the rich markets of the Indies.

Bolstered by Christopher Columbus's (1451–1506) accounts of his voyage in 1492, Spain claimed sovereignty over the lands Columbus touched, which Columbus believed included the East Indies, the object of Portuguese mercantile ambitions. It was clear that conflict would soon arise over the rival claims of Spain and Portugal to lands previously unclaimed by Europeans. To prevent serious conflict between their expansionist nations, the wary monarchs of Spain and Portugal divided the non-Christian world outside Europe in the Treaty of Tordesillas (1494).

The papal bull (edict) *Inter Caetera* ("among other works," often incorrectly spelled as "coetera") laid the framework for the Treaty of Tordesillas. Spain and Portugal were major Catholic powers and the possibility of a clash between them was of great concern to leaders of the Catholic Church. In response, the Spanish-born Pope Alexander VI (1431–1503) issued *Inter Caetera* on May 4, 1493; the bull established a line of demarcation running north-south through the Atlantic Ocean, 100 leagues (about 345 statute miles or 556 kilometers) west of the Cape Verde Islands. With the exception that lands already claimed by a Christian sovereign would remain under that ruler's control, the pope granted Spain possession of undiscovered territories west of the line and awarded Portugal possession of undiscovered territories east of the line. Spanish interests heavily influenced the bull, which threatened to exclude Portugal from Asia: After Columbus's return the Spanish believed East Asia lay a little west of the pope's line.

Protesting the specifics of the papal edict while endorsing its assumption of Spanish and Portuguese global dominance, King John II (1455–1495) of Portugal negotiated with King Ferdinand (1452–1516) and Queen Isabella (1451–1504) of Spain to move the line west. John argued that the pope's line extended around the world, limiting Spanish influence in Asia. In the course of a year the line was renegotiated and the agreement was formally ratified by both nations in the Castilian town of Tordesillas (Spain) on June 7, 1494. The treaty shifted the papal line to a meridian 370 leagues (about 1,277 statute miles or 2,056 kilometers) west of the Cape Verde Islands.

Pope Julius II (1443–1513) gave the treaty formal papal sanction in a bull of 1506. In all of these diplomatic developments, other European nations were expressly denied access to new overseas territories with the result that England, France, and the Netherlands utlimately rejected the pope's legal authority to divide undiscovered regions and the legitimacy of Spanish and Portuguese territorial claims based on it.

In any case, at the time that the treaty was negotiated, only a very small area of the world had actually been explored by Europeans, and the exact position of the boundary line was unclear due to the difficulty of establishing longitude accurately. Spain ultimately claimed most of the Americas and the easternmost parts of Asia, while Portugal claimed Brazil and most of the lands around the Indian Ocean. The Treaty of Saragossa (1529) formally extended the demarcation line around the entire globe.

SEE ALSO *Columbus, Christopher; Empire in the Americas, Portuguese; Empire in the Americas, Spanish; Religion, Roman Catholic Church; Religion, Western Perceptions of Traditional Religions.*

BIBLIOGRAPHY

Bell, Christopher R. V. *Portugal and the Quest for the Indies.* New York: Barnes and Noble, 1974.

McAlister, Lyle N. *Spain and Portugal in the New World, 1492–1700.* Minneapolis: University of Minnesota Press, 1984.

"Tordesillas, Treaty of." *Gale Encyclopedia of U.S. Economic History.* Edited by Thomas Carson and Mary Bonk, Vol. 2, 1009–1010. Detroit: Gale, 1999.

Alexander M. Zukas

TREATY PORT SYSTEM

While European commercial interest in Asia stretches back to the sixteenth century with the establishment of the Portuguese colony of Macau in southwestern China, the direct precursor to the *treaty port system* developed between Great Britain and China in the eighteenth century. Concomitant with Britain's industrial development was its new interest in the untapped markets of Asia. China, however, rebuffed repeated requests to expand commercial relations beyond the open port of Canton (present-day Guangzhou), which since 1759 had been the only place where foreign trade was permitted by the Chinese government.

By the nineteenth century, Britain and the other imperialist powers had begun to chafe under the restrictions of this so-called Canton system. Over and above issues of profit and loss was the adamant desire among the countries of the West for diplomatic representation and equality. China, in turn, remained set on its own notions of cultural superiority and expressed little willingness to reform its policies.

The growing influence of illegal opium smuggling, generally but not exclusively, practiced by the British, further exacerbated these matters. Chinese Commissioner Lin Zexu's (ca. 1785–1850) celebrated destruction of foreign opium stores in 1839 was used as a pretext by the British Parliament to authorize the deployment of men and ships into battle. The immediate aftermath of the one-sided Opium War (1839–1842) was the Treaty of Nanking (1842), a document that dictated the West's relationship with China for the remainder of the century. The treaty (and those subsequently forced upon China by the other Western powers) contained several stipulations, the most significant of which were the following: five port cities, including Shanghai and Canton, were opened to residence and trade; tariff rates were fixed by the European powers; the Cohong (a Chinese merchant guild given monopoly rights over foreign trade by the Chinese government) was abolished; the right of extraterritoriality was granted to foreigners in criminal cases; and Hong Kong was ceded to Britain. The period of "unequal treaties" had begun.

THE TREATY PORT SYSTEM IN CHINA

What resulted was a new and unique system. At Canton, to take one example, the Western powers obtained from the Chinese grants of land known as *concessions,* upon which foreign merchants could live and construct commercial buildings. The concession territories were not sold, but rather leased to the foreign powers, who individually split them up into lots and rented them out to the members of their own countries. Each country provided its own municipal government, which was presided over by the consul of that country; as a result, within one port there were often multiple areas of sovereignty, multiple municipal governments with individual authority.

In Shanghai, the situation was somewhat different. In that case, the Chinese and the British agreed to a system in which the British bought land from the Chinese and in turn paid rent to the government. The land still belonged nominally to the Chinese emperor, but it was leased "in perpetuity." This agreement was generally referred to as a *settlement*.

Despite these differences, there were several features that characterized the Chinese treaty ports. Most had their own newspapers, churches, chambers of commerce, and other features of Victorian life. The bund (an embankment or quay upon which foreign businesses and residences were often located), the "club," and the racecourse were all important parts of treaty port culture. For many Chinese, these cities were an exciting introduction to Western literature, philosophy, and institutions.

By the 1850s, many problems in this system were apparent (exacerbated by growing anti-Western sentiment in China). Although Great Britain had won a series of military conflicts, the fact remained that they had imposed an alien presence on an unwilling people, and a system of trade that was repellent to traditional Confucian morality and Chinese conceptions of world order. A second round of conflicts—the Arrow War or second Opium War (1856–1860)—between the Western powers and China resulted in the extraction of further concessions from the Chinese government, including the right for diplomatic representatives to reside in Beijing and for foreigners to travel in the Chinese interior.

THE TREATY PORT SYSTEM IN JAPAN

Although spared from the international military conflicts that marked China's entry into the world of global capitalism, in 1853 to 1854 and in 1858 Japan was coerced into signing its own series of unequal treaties. These treaties allowed foreigners to set up embassies and port facilities in five cities; the most crucial of these was Yokohama, a port close to Tokyo, which became the hub of interaction between the Japanese government and people and the foreign community. Other ports opened to foreign residence and trade included Hakodate, Nagasaki, Kobe, and eventually even Edo (now Tokyo) itself.

The treaties contained provisions similar to those forced upon the Chinese government: the right of extraterritoriality for foreign citizens, as well as the right of the foreign powers to set tariff rates. Following the dissolution of the Tokugawa shogunate in 1868 it became a major goal of Japan's new Meiji government to revise the unequal treaties. The Western powers, eager to expand commercial and trading rights into the interior, proved receptive to overtures to end the system, and in 1899 the treaty ports were abolished.

THE END OF THE TREATY PORT SYSTEM

In contrast to Japan, China's treaty ports persisted well into the twentieth century. Through "most-favored-nation" provisions in Sino-foreign bilateral treaties, each new signatory gained the benefits of extraterritoriality and the treaty port system. Indeed, Japan's forays into China, which eventually led to the Pacific war during World War II, came by virtue of Japanese privileges in that country.

In the 1920s and 1930s, urban culture in cities such as Shanghai flourished, a topic of continued interest in the arenas of academe and popular culture alike. For China, as well other counties such as Thailand, Korea, and Vietnam, the process of treaty revision generally extended until the end of World War II. Extraterritoriality effectively ended during the war, when beleaguered China joined the Allies. The Chinese Communists came to power largely on the strong antiforeign sentiments that had grown up around treaty port culture.

At the beginning of the twenty-first century, places that were once treaty ports—Shanghai, Yokohama, and Hong Kong—are among the world's largest and most vibrant cities. While seen by some as humiliating reminders of the colonial past, many of the former treaty ports play indispensable roles in the global economy of the twenty-first century.

Recent years have witnessed new perspectives on the legacy of Asia's treaty ports. Scholars such as Robert Bickers and Gail Hershatter have broadened our understanding of the historical conditions in the treaty ports from a social and cultural perspective, and done much to revise outdated impressions of the ports as simply outposts on the fringes of empire.

SEE ALSO *China, First Opium War to 1945; China, Foreign Trade; Extraterritoriality; Guangzhou; Hong Kong, from World War II; Hong Kong, to World War II; Japan, Colonized; Japan, Opening of; Nagasaki; Shanghai.*

BIBLIOGRAPHY

Bickers, Robert, and Christian Henriot, eds. *New Frontiers: Imperialism's New Communities in East Asia, 1842–1953.* Manchester, U.K.: Manchester University Press, 2000.

Fairbank, John King, and Merle Goldman. *China: A New History*, enl. ed. Cambridge, MA: Belknap, 1998.

Hershatter, Gail. *Dangerous Pleasures: Prostitution and Modernity in Twentieth-Century Shanghai.* Berkeley: University of California Press, 1997.

Jansen, Marius B. *The Making of Modern Japan.* Cambridge, MA: Belknap, 2000.

Todd S. Munson

TRIBUTE

Queen Isabella of Spain (1451–1504) considered the natives of the Americas, from the start of Spanish colonization, as free vassals with certain rights and duties. In exchange for the crown's promise of fair rule, protection, and access to resources, native vassals were expected to serve Spain. This service took the form of tribute, first levied as labor and goods, and then gradually commuted to specie (money in the form of coins).

Crown representatives—first Christopher Columbus (1451–1506) and subsequently governors, viceroys, and other royal officials—assigned the right to exact tribute from the natives to Spaniards whom the crown rewarded for their service with grants of *encomienda*. Called *encomenderos*, these beneficiaries promised to protect and Christianize the natives in return for taking their labor and goods. During the first generation or two, the *encomenderos*, unfettered by peninsular controls, forced the natives to work on personal or public construction projects and in their homes, fields, and mines.

The precipitous fall of the native population from the combined effects of disease, overwork, abuse, and flight led to increasing government control. Early efforts took the form of laws, often observed in the breach. Later, tribute lists *(tasas)* specified the type and duration of labor service and the types and quantities of items to be delivered on given dates. The problem with these tribute lists was that the population decreased faster than *tasas* could be revised downward, often leaving the natives overcharged and in arrears. This untenable situation brought eventual reforms. The crown abolished personal service as a form of tribute. Officials restricted tribute items to a limited number of goods produced locally. Quotas were set on an individual basis, not by community. Finally, goods were commuted to silver.

In the second half of the sixteenth century the *encomienda* came under increasing attack, the crown became a stronger presence in America with the appointment of royal officials, and the native population continued its disastrous decline. Eventually, the crown mandated that scattered native families be moved into new native villages, patterned after the Spanish villas. This concentration of the native population facilitated more effective evangelization and increased Spanish control over native labor, as continued commutation of high tribute quotas into silver forced the natives into the money economy.

SEE ALSO *Columbus, Christopher; Empire in the Americas, Spanish; Encomienda.*

BIBLIOGRAPHY

Bouysse Cassagne, Thérèse. "Tributo y etnias en Charcas en la epoca del virrey Toledo." *Historia y cultura* (La Paz, Bolivia) 2 (1976): 97–113.

Cook, Noble David. *Demographic Collapse: Indian Peru, 1520–1620.* New York: Cambridge University Press, 1981.

Hampe Martínez, Teodoro. "Notas sobre población y tributo indígena en Cajamarca." *Boletin del Instituto Riva-Agüero* 14 (1986–1987): 65–81.

Mansilla, Ronald Escobedo. *El tributo indígena en el Perú: Siglos XVI y XVII.* Pamplona, Spain: Ediciones Universidad de Navarra, 1979.

Ramírez, Susan Elizabeth. *The World Upside Down: Cross-Cultural Contact and Conflict in Sixteenth-Century Peru.* Stanford, CA: Stanford University Press, 1996. See especially chapter 4.

Sempat Assadourian, Carlos. "De la renta de la encomienda en la decada de 1550." *Revista de Indias* 48 (182–183) (1988): 109–146.

Tord Nicolini, Javier. "El corregidor de indios del Perú: Comercio y tributos." *Historia y cultura* (Lima) 8 (1974): 173– 214.

Susan E. Ramírez

TRUSTEESHIP

At the conclusion of World War I, and under the leadership of South African statesman Jan Christiaan Smuts (1870–1950), the League of Nations established the *mandate system*, which gave broad authority to the victorious Allies over the former colonial empires of Imperial Germany and the Ottoman Turks. The mandated territories were divided into three classes and were assigned to individual powers to govern until they were deemed capable of self-rule.

The territories of the Arab world were declared Level A mandates because they were perceived to be at an advanced stage of development that would require only a short period of British (Iraq and Palestine) and French (Lebanon and Syria) oversight before they could choose their own leaders and become autonomous states. Comprising former German colonies in Central Africa and the Pacific, Level B and C mandates were believed to be less advanced areas not yet ready for political independence. They were to be governed for an undetermined period of time as integral parts of the respective empires of Britain (Tanganyika, Togoland, and Cameroons); France (Togoland, Cameroons); Belgium

(Ruanda-Urundi); South Africa (South-West Africa); New Zealand (Samoa); Australia (New Guinea, Nauru); and Japan (Pacific Islands north of the equator).

As these powers raised and expended revenues, appointed officials, and enforced laws, the mandates were in many ways little different from colonial regimes. However, as stipulated in Article 22 of the Covenant of the League of Nations, an eleven-member Permanent Mandates Commission (PMC) had the authority to pressure the colonial powers to promote the material and moral well-being of native peoples, and to protect their inalienable rights. The colonial powers had to present an annual report for acceptance and suggestions by the PMC detailing their efforts in this regard. Thus, mandate was to replace might as the guiding principle in colonial affairs, a notion that also served as the foundation of the United Nations trusteeship system that was established once the League of Nations ceased to exist in 1946.

Under Chapters XII and XIII of the United Nations Charter, many of the former mandates, as well as those territories taken from enemy states at the end of World War II, were administered through the United Nations Trusteeship Council (UNTC). Its primary goal was to help native peoples work toward independence, while respecting their right to permanent sovereignty over their natural resources. Therefore, while the states of Australia (Nauru, New Guinea); Belgium (Ruanda-Urundi); New Zealand (Western Samoa); Britain (Tanganyika, Cameroons, and Togoland); France (Cameroons, Togoland); Italy (Somalia); and the United States (Trust Territory of the Pacific Islands) possessed full legislative, administrative, and judicial authority, they had to administer the territories they held in trust for the benefit of the inhabitants and not for their own aggrandizement.

To ensure that trust territory guidelines were followed, the UNTC—comprised of the five permanent members of the Security Council: China, France, the United Kingdom, the Russian Federation, and the United States—met once a year to consider petitions from inhabitants of the territories, to examine detailed reports on measures to increase self-governance and educational opportunities, and to adopt recommendations by majority vote (not subject to veto), such as taking special missions to trust territories. As with the PMC, the UNTC observed and placed a limit on colonial governance and formally guaranteed an end to colonialism.

There was opposition to the trusteeship system however, as the one territory not turned over to the United Nations was South-West Africa, which South Africa insisted remain under the League of Nations mandate. In particular, South Africa objected to trust guidelines that stipulated that lands prepared for independence be subject to majority rule; a stance that was a tacit indictment of their own apartheid regime (South Africa and the United Nations would contest the status of South-West Africa until 1990, when it was finally granted its independence and became Namibia).

In 1949 the United Nations General Assembly, by virtue of the League of Nations mandate over Palestine, declared Jerusalem a trust territory. However, because the two occupying states, Israel and Jordan, opposed this move, implementation of this recommendation was postponed indefinitely.

Of the earlier trusteeships, Italian Somaliland joined British Somaliland, becoming Somalia in 1960; British Togoland joined Ghana in 1956 and French Togoland became Togo in 1960; the French Cameroons became Cameroon in 1960, joined by the British Cameroons in 1961; Tanganyika gained independence in 1961; Western Samoa became Samoa in 1961; Ruanda-Urundi became the states of Rwanda and Burundi in 1962; Nauru gained independence in 1968; New Guinea joined with Papua to become Papua New Guinea in 1975; and the Trust Territory of the Pacific Islands gained independence under a compact of free association with the United States in 1986. The last trust territory, Palau, gained independence in 1994, and the UNTC ceased operation that same year.

SEE ALSO *Pacific, American Presence in; Pacific, European Presence in.*

BIBLIOGRAPHY

Murray, James. *The United Nations Trusteeship System.* Urbana: University of Illinois Press, 1957.

Toussaint, C. E. *The Trusteeship System of the United Nations.* New York: Praeger, 1956. Reprint, Westport, CT: Greenwood, 1976.

Wright, Quincy. *Mandates Under the League of Nations.* Chicago: University of Chicago Press, 1930. Reprint, Westport, CT: Greenwood, 1968.

Stephen A. Toth

TÚPAC AMARU, REBELLION OF

In 1780, José Gabriel Condorcanqui (ca. 1742–1781), who claimed descent from Túpac Amaru (d. 1572), the last Inca to resist Spanish authority in the sixteenth century, took the name Túpac Amaru and led a rebellion against Spanish colonial rule, even though it was initiated in the name of the Spanish monarch and was not necessarily meant to sever all ties with Spain. This insurgency was the most serious challenge to colonial domination between the sixteenth-century wars of encounter and conquest and the early nineteenth-century wars of independence.

The rebellion was centered in the rural provinces of Canas y Canchis (Tinta) and Quispicanchis in Peru. In this region near the former Inca capital of Cuzco, the authority of traditional *kurakas* (ethnic leaders) remained strong, despite more than two centuries of Spanish rule. Túpac Amaru and much of his family, several of whom were also to play important leadership roles in the rebellion, lived in Canas y Canchis. Under the leadership of Túpac Amaru, who declared himself the *Inca* (ruler), the rebellion spread like wildfire over the southern Andean highlands from Cuzco to Lake Titicaca and beyond.

Other uprisings, such as that of Túpac Katari (Julián Apasa, d. 1781) near La Paz and the Katari brothers (d. 1781) closer to Potosí and Sucre, challenged colonial rule in what is now Bolivia—then the viceroyalty of Río de la Plata—at the same time. The Bolivian rebellions have been historically associated with the Túpac Amaru rebellion, even though the Katari insurgency began before the Cuzco movement.

Although often responding to similar demands and exploitation, the Katari and Túpac Katari rebellions had significant internal differences from the Cuzco-based movement. To secure his legitimacy, Túpac Amaru harkened back to the Inca and called for concerned and accountable hereditary ethnic leaders *(kurakas)* who governed their communities with a just hand. The movements led by Túpac Katari and the Katari brothers not only challenged colonial rule but also the rule of many *kurakas*, arguing that many of these ethnic leaders had sold out to the Spanish, or to their own self interests, and no longer represented the values and needs of their communities.

ECONOMIC TENSION

These upheavals erupted during a period of growing economic tension in the Andes, especially for indigenous society. Like other colonial powers in the eighteenth century, Spain was trying to streamline its colonial rule, make its rule more secure, and force the colonies to yield a higher return to the mother country.

In the Andes, one of the measures designed to enforce these policies was an effort to increase the efficiency of tribute collection. Spanish officials tried to eliminate the practice of hiding tributaries, while noncommunity members who had previously been effectively exempt from tribute were now more consistently forced to pay some tribute. Items of indigenous production, such as *ají* (chili peppers) and textiles produced in relatively small operations *(chorillos),* which had not been subject to taxation, were now included on the list of taxable items.

To enforce this new regime of taxation, customs houses were built in cities such as Arequipa, La Paz, and Cochabamba. In addition, the sales tax *(alcabala)* was increased twice in the 1770s. This caused great discontent among those involved in trade and led to rioting against the new taxes not only by indigenous peoples but also by criollos (people of Spanish descent born in the New World) and others who saw these taxes as a threat to their well-being. The disruption of commercial and trade networks caused by such reforms was further exacerbated by the annexation of much of what is now Bolivia from the viceroyalty of Peru into the newly created viceroyalty of Río de la Plata (Argentina) in 1776.

In the mid-eighteenth century the crown had also legalized, and set quotas for, the *reparto*, a system for the forced sale of goods primarily to indigenous people, but in reality to some nonindigenous people as well; this became an increasing cause of friction. The local Spanish authorities *(corregidores),* often in concert with urban merchants, pressed the indigenous population ever harder after the *reparto* was legalized. The quotas were commonly ignored as *corregidores* abused the *reparto*, sometimes "selling" double or even triple the amount of goods to which they were entitled by colonial law. This abuse was one of the factors that began to undermine the legitimacy of colonial rule as indigenous people began to balk at excessive economic coercion.

At first these protests took the form of an increasing number of village revolts directed at local officials, such as the Spanish district officers *(corregidores),* who were regarded as the chief cause of exploitation. In the period between 1750 and 1780, these tumults increased greatly in frequency, and a number of tax collectors and *corregidores* were even killed. This, however, did not lead to any direct changes in policy.

Another of the other great grievances of indigenous peoples in the southern Andes was the system of forced labor *(mita)* for the silver mines of Potosí. Created in the 1570s, the *mita* was imposed on indigenous peoples in certain provinces, caused severe hardship to those affected by it, and thus played a part in arousing indigenous anger against the authorities.

DIMINISHING RESOURCE BASE

At the same time that colonial exactions pressed indigenous people ever harder, these same villagers began to experience serious concerns related to their diminishing resource base. The introduction of Old World diseases devastated the Andean world, as it did almost all of the Americas. The last great epidemic had swept the Andes from 1719 to 1720. After this long and terrible decline, however, indigenous people began a period of rapid population growth; they finally had developed sufficient immunities against Old World diseases to not be devastated by each new outbreak. Somewhat altered, but still intact as distinct indigenous peoples, they had managed to survive not only biologically but also culturally. This rapid growth threatened to leave them short of land, however, for the Spanish had sold off or appropriated lands considered to be in excess of community needs.

Thus, at the very same time that the colonial regime was pressuring indigenous peoples with new and enhanced economic demands, the per capita resource base for the communities was threatened. This not only put their ability to meet colonial exactions in doubt, but it also threatened their communal cultural survival. By 1780 a conjuncture of international colonial policies with local and regional changes created a situation in which the legitimacy of colonial rule was increasingly questioned, and large scale rebellion became possible.

INCA CULTURAL REVIVAL

It was in these circumstances that Túpac Amaru, a *kuraka* of noble heritage, sought recognition in colonial courts as the rightful heir to the Inca throne. The implications of his actions were enhanced by a growing respect for, and revival of, things Inca during this period. The "Incas" were allowed back into public festivals, such as parades, thus securing a public presence for a vision of indigenous history. This celebration of the past was also reflected in the practice among indigenous individuals and families of royal heritage of having their portraits painted as Incas. The literate indigenous elite also began to read the *Royal Commentaries* (1609) of Garcilaso de la Vega (1539–1616), the son of an Inca princess and a conquistador, who had glorified the period of Inca rule and the relatively equitable system of social control that had kept most people from suffering and misery.

At the same time, myths or legends surrounding *Inkarrí*, in which the *Inca* (and symbolically the empire) was regenerating from the buried head of the *Inca*, also grew and gained further strength. When this regeneration was complete, it was said, the *Inca* would come back to life, assume his proper role as leader, and reestablish the empire, just social order, and benevolent rule that had prevailed before the Spanish invasion.

Thus, during a period of growing exploitation, increasing population pressure, and abusive treatment, a consciousness of the Inca past that revered Inca justice and society was also emerging, so that, when the second Túpac Amaru claimed the Inca throne, many indigenous people were receptive to his leadership. When he executed the *corregidor* of Canas y Canchis, Antonio de Arriaga, on November 10, 1780, in the name of the Spanish king, while claiming his Inca heritage, thousands of indigenous people rallied to a cause that offered to end bad Spanish rule and to restore the *Inca*.

The rebellions of Túpac Amaru, Túpac Katari, and the Katari brothers shook the very foundations of colonial society. By most estimates, some one hundred thousand people were killed in the course of these uprisings. Túpac Amaru and his family were captured, tortured, executed, and dismembered in the central plaza of Cuzco, and their body parts were displayed throughout the region as a warning to others. Túpac Katari and the Kataris were also captured and executed. Together, however, they had provided the leadership to challenge colonial rule and give voice to the suffering and exploitation of Andean peoples under colonial rule.

With their cultural survival at stake, these rebels had risked, and often lost, their lives to put an end to continued exploitation and to replace it with a system of just rule that was culturally relevant to their existence. In the wake of the rebellion, the Spanish rulers granted some of the changes desired by the rebels, but Andean villagers also lost a degree of autonomy and the racial divide between indigenous peoples and others was enhanced. This divide left indigenous peoples marginalized in the early years following independence, but it may also have bought them the time to regroup and survive as indigenous communities in the centuries that followed.

SEE ALSO *Empire in the Americas, Spanish; Peru Under Spanish Rule; Potosí.*

BIBLIOGRAPHY

Fisher, Lillian Estelle. *The Last Inca Revolt, 1780-1783.* Norman: University of Oklahoma Press, 1966.

Flores Galindo, Alberto. *Buscando un Inca.* Lima, Peru: Instituto de Apoyo Agrario, 1987.

Lewin, Boleslao. *La rebellion de Túpac Amaru y los origenes de la emancipacion Americana.* Buenos Aires, Argentina: Hachette, 1957.

O'Phelan Godoy, Scarlett. *Rebellions and Revolts in Eighteenth Century Peru and Upper Peru.* Koln, Germany: Bohlau Verlag, 1985.

Serulnikov, Sergio. *Subverting Colonial Authority: Challenges to Spanish Rule in Eighteenth-Century Southern Andes.* Durham, NC: Duke University Press, 2003.

Stavig, Ward. *The World of Túpac Amaru: Conflict, Community, and Identity in Colonial Peru.* Lincoln: University of Nebraska Press, 1999.

Stern, Steve, ed. *Resistance, Rebellion, and Consciousness in the Andean Peasant World, Eighteenth to Twentieth Centuries.* Madison: University of Wisconsin Press, 1987.

Szeminski, Jan. *La utopia tupamarista.* Lima: Pontificia Universidad Catolica de Peru— Fondo Cultural, 1983.

Thompson, Sinclair. *We Alone Will Rule: Native Andean Politics in the Age of Insurgency.* Madison: University of Wisconsin Press, 2002.

Ward Stavig

U

UNITED STATES COLONIAL RULE IN THE PHILIPPINES

The United States exercised formal colonial rule over the Philippines, its largest overseas colony, between 1899 and 1946. American economic and strategic interests in Asia and the Pacific were increasing in the late 1890s in the wake of an industrial depression and in the face of global, interimperial competition. Spanish colonialism was simultaneously being weakened by revolts in Cuba and the Philippines, its largest remaining colonies.

The Philippine Revolution of 1896 to 1897 destabilized Spanish colonialism but failed to remove Spanish colonial rule. The leaders of the revolution were exiled to Hong Kong. When the United States invaded Cuba and Puerto Rico in 1898 to shore up its hegemony in the Caribbean, the U.S. Pacific Squadron was sent to the Philippines to advance U.S. power in the region, and it easily defeated the Spanish navy. Filipino revolutionaries hoped the United States would recognize and assist it. Although American commanders and diplomats helped return revolutionary leader Emilio Aguinaldo (1869–1964) to the Philippine Islands, they sought to use him and they avoided recognition of the independent Philippine Republic that Aguinaldo declared in June 1898.

In August 1898 U.S. forces occupied Manila and denied the Republic's troops entry into the city. That fall, Spain and the United States negotiated the Philippines' status at Paris without Filipino consultation. The U.S. Senate and the American public debated the Treaty of Paris, which granted the United States "sovereignty" over the Philippine Islands for $20 million. The discussion emphasized the economic costs and benefits of imperialism to the United States and the political and racial repercussions of colonial conquest.

When U.S. troops fired on Philippine troops in February 1899, the Philippine-American War erupted. The U.S. Senate narrowly passed the Treaty of Paris, and the U.S. military enforced its provisions over the next three years through a bloody, racialized war of aggression. Following ten months of failed conventional combat, Philippine troops adopted guerrilla tactics, which American forces ultimately defeated only through the devastation of civilian property, the "reconcentration" of rural populations, and the torture and killing of prisoners, combined with a policy of "attraction" aimed at Filipino elites. While Filipino revolutionaries sought freedom and independent nationhood, a U.S.-based "anti-imperialist" movement challenged the invasion as immoral in both ends and means.

Carried out in the name of promoting "self-government" over an indefinite but calibrated timetable, U.S. colonial rule in the Philippines was characterized politically by authoritarian bureaucracy and one-party state-building with the collaboration of Filipino elites at its core. The colonial state was inaugurated with a Sedition Act that banned expressions in support of Philippine independence, a Banditry Act that criminalized ongoing resistance, and a Reconcentration Act that authorized the mass relocation of rural populations.

In the interests of "pacification," American civilian proconsuls in the Philippine Commission, initially led by William Howard Taft (1857–1930), sponsored the Federalista Party under influential Manila-based elites. The party developed into a functioning patronage network and political monopoly in support of

1095

American Soldiers in the Philippines, 1899. *American soldiers fire their rifles from behind a makeshift barricade at the West Beach Outpost in San Roque during the Philippine insurrection that followed the 1898 Spanish-American War.* © CORBIS.
REPRODUCED BY PERMISSION.

"Americanization" and, initially, U.S. statehood for the Philippines. When the suppression of independence politics ended in 1905, it gave rise to new political voices and organizations that consolidated by 1907 into the Nationalista Party, whose members were younger than those of the Federalista Party and rooted in the provinces. When the Federalista Party alienated its American patrons and its statehood platform failed to win mass support, U.S. proconsuls abandoned it for the Nationalista Party, which over the remainder of the colonial period developed into a vast, second party-state, under the leadership of Manuel Quezon (1878–1944) and Sergio Osmeña (1878–1961).

Following provincial and municipal elections, "national" elections were held in 1907 for a Philippine Assembly to serve under the commission as the lower house of a legislature. The 3 percent of the country's population that was given the right to vote swept the Nationalistas to power. The Nationalistas clashed with U.S. proconsuls over jurisdiction and policy priorities, although both sides also manipulated and advertised

these conflicts to secure their respective constituencies, masking what were in fact functioning colonial collaborations. Democratic Party dominance in the United States between 1912 and 1920 facilitated the consolidation of the Nationalista party-state in the Philippines.

When Woodrow Wilson (1856–1924), a Democrat, was elected president in 1912, he appointed as governor-general Francis Burton Harrison (1873–1957), who, working closely with the Nationalistas, accelerated the "Filipinization" of the bureaucracy and allowed the Philippine Assembly to assume additional executive power. When Democrats passed the Jones Act in 1916, which replaced the commission with a Philippine senate and committed the United States to "eventual independence" for the Philippines, Quezon claimed credit for these victories and, despite his own ambivalence about Philippine independence, translated them into greater power. During the 1920s, Quezon dominated the Nationalista Party, using clashes with Republican governor-general Leonard Wood (1860–1927) to secure his *independista* credentials.

Under pressure from protectionists, nativists, and military officials fearful of Japanese imperialism, the U.S. Congress passed the Tydings-McDuffie Act in 1934. The act inaugurated a ten-year "Philippine Commonwealth" government transitional to "independence." While serving as president of the commonwealth in the years prior to the 1941 Japanese invasion of the Philippine Islands, Quezon consolidated dictatorial power. Colonial political structures, constructed where the ambitions and fears of the Filipino elite connected with the American imperial need for collaborators, had successfully preserved the power of provincial, landed elites, while institutionalizing this power in a country-wide "nationalist" politics.

In economic terms, American colonial rule in the Philippines promoted an intensely dependent, export economy based on cash-crop agriculture and extractive industries like mining. American capital had initially regarded the Philippines as merely a "stepping stone" to the fabled China market, and American trade with the Philippine Islands was initially inhibited by reciprocity treaties that preserved Spanish trade rights. When these rights ended, U.S. capital divided politically over the question of free trade. American manufacturers supported free trade, hoping to secure in the Philippines both inexpensive raw materials and markets for finished goods, whereas sugar and tobacco producers opposed free trade because they feared Philippine competition. The Payne-Aldrich Tariff of 1909 established "free trade," with the exception of rice, and set yearly quota limits for Philippine exports to the United States.

American trade with the Philippine Islands, which had grown since the war, boomed after 1909, and during the decades that followed, the United States became by far the Philippines' dominant trading partner. American goods comprised only 7 percent of Philippine imports in 1899, but had grown to 66 percent by 1934. These goods included farm machinery, cigarettes, meat and dairy products, and cotton cloth. The Philippines sold 26 percent of its total exports to the United States in 1899, and 84 percent in 1934. Most of these exports were hemp, sugar, tobacco, and coconut products.

Free trade promoted U.S. investment, and American companies came to dominate Philippine factories, mills, and refineries. When a post–World War I economic boom brought increased production and exports, Filipino nationalists feared economic and political dependence on the United States, as well as the overspecialization of the Philippine economy around primary products, overreliance on U.S. markets, and the political enlistment of American businesses in the indefinite colonial retention of the Philippine Islands.

Meanwhile, rural workers subject to the harsh terms of export-oriented development challenged the power of hacienda owners in popular mass movements. While some interested American companies did lobby against Philippine independence, during the Great Depression powerful U.S. agricultural producers—especially of sugar and oils—supported U.S. separation from the Philippines as a protectionist measure to exclude competing Philippine goods. The commonwealth period and formal Philippine independence would be characterized by rising tariffs and the exclusion of Philippine goods from the U.S. markets upon which Philippine producers had come to depend.

Philippine-American colonialism also transformed both the Philippines and the United States in cultural terms. In the Philippines, the colonial state introduced a secular, free public school system that emphasized the English language (believed by U. S. officials to be the inherent medium of "free" institutions), along with industrial and manual training to facilitate capitalist economic development. While the Filipino elite retained and developed Spanish as a language of literature, politics, and prestige into the 1920s—often contrasted with "vulgar" Americanism—Filipinos increasingly learned and transformed English and used it to their own purposes. Filipinos also reworked forms and elements from American popular culture, especially in film, fashion, and literature. In addition, this period saw the development of popular and literary culture in other Philippine languages. With the advent of the commonwealth, Tagalog was declared the unifying "national" language.

The struggle for Philippine independence fundamentally shaped emerging Filipino modes of self-identification, as Filipinos sought to prove their "capacity" for "self-government." Where the U.S. colonial state administered "non-Christian" regions inhabited by animists and Muslims through separate, American-dominated political and military controls (insulating them from emerging "national" politics), Filipino nationalists sought to integrate these regions and peoples into the "nation" by arguing for their rights to administer them undemocratically on the basis of the "civilizational" superiority of Christian Filipinos.

American culture would also be transformed culturally by Philippine-American colonialism. Beginning in the 1920s, mass Filipino labor migration to Hawaii and the American West would alter both region's culture and demography, bridging the Philippine and U.S. cultural and social worlds. At the same time, official justifications of conquest and colonial administration helped accommodate Americans more generally to the notion that overseas empire was compatible with a "republic." American colonial rule in the Philippines was held up domestically and internationally as symbolic of the United States' own exceptional democracy and foreign policy. American policy toward the Philippines following World War II—characterized by Cold War anticommunism—suggested continuities with the colonial period.

SEE ALSO *Empire, United States; Pacific, American Presence in.*

BIBLIOGRAPHY

Cullinane, Michael. *Ilustrado Politics: Filipino Elite Responses to American Rule.* Quezon City: Ateneo de Manila University Press, 2005.

Go, Julian, and Anne Foster, eds. *The American Colonial State in the Philippines: Global Perspectives.* Durham: Duke University Press, 2003.

Guerrero, Milagros C. *Under Stars and Stripes.* Vol. 6, *Kasaysayan: The Story of the Filipino People.* Asia Publishing Co., 1998.

Kramer, Paul A. *The Blood of Government: Race, Empire, the United States and the Philippines.* Chapel Hill: University of North Carolina Press, 2006.

Miller, Stuart Creighton. *"Benevolent Assimilation": The American Conquest of the Philippines, 1899-1903.* New Haven, CT: Yale University Press, 1982.

Paredes, Ruby, ed. *Philippine Colonial Democracy.* Quezon City: Ateneo de Manila University Press, 1989.

Paul A. Kramer

UNITED STATES INTERVENTIONS IN POSTINDEPENDENCE LATIN AMERICA

Great Britain formally acknowledged the independence of the United States in the Treaty of Paris on September 3, 1783. Surrounded by the New World empires of Britain, France, and Spain, the United States was concerned about its weakness and isolation. The second successful independence movement in the Western Hemisphere occurred in the French Caribbean colony of Saint Domingue on the island of Hispaniola. The French colonists appealed for help and received, in addition to volunteer soldiers, U.S. federal and state government aid in the form of loans, provisions, and weaponry. Despite U.S. assistance, the French were unable to suppress the slave revolt that devastated Saint Domingue and led to the creation of the sovereign nation of Haiti in 1804. Due to its origins in slave rebellion, Haiti was subsequently denied U.S. diplomatic recognition until 1862. Yet U.S. leaders who believed the

extension of republicanism would ensure their government's stability and survival sought to attract the hemisphere's European colonial subjects to republican ideas.

THE ROAD TO SPANISH-AMERICAN INDEPENDENCE

One of the earliest advocates of Spanish-American independence, the Venezuelan Francisco de Miranda, was inspired by the American Revolution (1775–1781). Miranda believed that the rebellion that created the United States was a prelude to independence in the entire Western Hemisphere. With the assistance of private U.S. citizens, Miranda outfitted a ship in 1806 and launched the first expedition against royalists in South America. Miranda's attempt proved unsuccessful, but when the Spanish-American wars of independence began in earnest in 1810, there was sympathy in the United States for the colonial rebels.

The rebels were fighting the Spanish Catholic monarchy, which, despite having aided rebellious North Americans in their independence struggle from Britain, remained an object of U.S. hatred and contempt. U.S. leaders relished the prospect of the loss of European influence and hoped for increased trade in the hemisphere. In July 1815 U.S. president James Madison announced that rebel ships would be treated on the same basis as other foreign ships in U.S. ports, thereby granting belligerent rights to the Spanish-American rebels. The following year, Venezuelan patriots bought gunpowder from the administration on credit, but this was the only time the U.S. government proffered a loan or grant to the insurgents.

As the wars of independence progressed, the noncommittal attitudes and policies of the U.S. government frustrated Spanish-American independence leaders like Simón Bolívar, who complained of U.S. indifference toward what he believed to be the just conflict for Spanish-American independence. Bolívar later came to view U.S. power as a threat to Spanish-American sovereignty. As speaker of the U.S. House of Representatives, Henry Clay argued that the liberation of Latin America from European colonial rule was an ongoing aspect of the American Revolution and urged an active policy of support for the wars of independence. But most U.S. leaders wanted the United States to remain uninvolved. In a test vote in the House of Representatives in 1818 on the possible recognition of the United Provinces of the Rio de la Plata, the Clay faction lost by a vote of 115 to 45.

Many U.S. leaders doubted that the principles of the American Revolution were applicable to Latin Americans, who were deemed ill-prepared for republicanism. Secretary of State John Quincy Adams did not believe in a community of interests between North and

South America. Like many of his contemporaries, Adams inherited negative attitudes toward Catholic Spaniards from his Protestant English forbears. Adams and former U.S. president Thomas Jefferson doubted Latin Americans had the right religion, laws, manners, customs, and habits for good independent republican governance. The Spanish Americans were also of dubious whiteness and considered racial inferiors by their North American neighbors. Those who were white were considered to come from degraded Spanish stock mixed with Indian and African blood.

Many U.S. observers were uneasy over the presence of men of African descent in the Spanish-American liberation armies. Another issue for concern was the rebel privateers in Caribbean and South American waters who sought loot under the pretext of independence, thereby hurting U.S. shipping. But when Spanish-American rebels sought privateers to attack Spanish shipping, U.S. ship owners and sailors, enticed by economic gain, contributed to the cause of Spanish-American independence. Volunteers from the United States served in the rebel government navies. U.S. merchants were also eager to profit. When they were able to pay, the Spanish-American rebels received military and other supplies that were of great importance to their struggle.

Official U.S. opinion changed in response to the successes of the Spanish-American wars of independence after 1820. As president of the United States, Adams now optimistically asserted that Latin American independence spelled the end of the European mercantilist system of commercial restrictions on U.S. trade. The United States recognized the independence of Spanish-American nations in 1822, three years before any European government. In December 1823, U.S. president James Monroe boldly asserted that the Western Hemisphere was henceforth closed to both Europe's political system and future European colonization. The Monroe Doctrine declared any European threat to the new nations of Latin America would be viewed as a threat to the United States. After the liberation of the Spanish-American mainland, colonists who remained loyal to Spain retreated to the islands of the Spanish Caribbean.

MANIFEST DESTINY AND THE MEXICAN-AMERICAN WAR

In the first half of the nineteenth century, the United States progressively expanded its frontiers west and southward. Believing that the United States was divinely ordained to extend across the continent and overseas, advocates of manifest destiny argued that northern Europeans were superior peoples fated to spread their social, political, economic, and religious culture. While many of the prejudices of manifest destiny can be found

among early British North American settlers, the term was coined in 1845 by the Irish-American intellectual John L. O'Sullivan, who used his *United States Magazine and Democratic Review* to help win the vote for James K. Polk, the U.S. Democratic presidential candidate in 1844. Polk won on a platform of U.S. acquisition of Texas.

Since independence in 1821, Mexican authorities had increasingly attracted thousands of U.S. colonists into the once sparsely populated region of Texas, where Stephen F. Austin founded the first legal settlement of U.S. immigrants, who by and large refused to adapt to Mexican society. By the 1830s, U.S. immigrants living in Texas far outnumbered Mexicans.

The Republic of Texas declared its independence from Mexico in 1836 after rebellious Texans under Sam Houston defeated Antonio López de Santa Ana's Mexican troops. Texas's expansive territorial claims and Mexico's reluctance to acknowledge Texas's annexation to the United States in December 1845 resulted in the outbreak of the Mexican-American War in April 1846. Manifest destiny became a catchphrase in the war, which was terminated by the Treaty of Guadalupe Hidalgo in February 1848. Mexico gave up all claims to Texas and ceded its land between Texas and the Pacific Ocean. Mexico lost nearly one-half of its territory, including all or parts of the present-day U.S. states of Arizona, California, Colorado, Nevada, New Mexico, Wyoming, and Utah. Army officer Zachary Taylor became a national hero and won the U.S. presidency in the war's aftermath. The military disaster in Mexico deeply impressed Latin Americans, who feared for their national existence in the face of additional U.S. expansion.

FILIBUSTERS

The persistent political disorder in Spanish America in the postindependence period greatly affected the region's foreign affairs. In the 1850s, private U.S. citizens known as filibusters intervened militarily in Latin American affairs. Always encouraged by instability and sometimes invited by rival national political factions, U.S. citizens joined filibuster expeditions by the thousands in search of private wealth. Yet filibustering is mostly associated with the U.S. South seeking to extend slavery in the face of the North's efforts to halt its expansion in the contiguous United States. William Walker, who succeeded in ruling Nicaragua for a short time in the mid-1850s, is the most famous filibuster. Although unsuccessful, the filibustering expeditions further contributed to anti-U.S. sentiment throughout Latin America. Many Latin Americans identified filibustering as a manifestation of U.S. imperialism and attempted territorial expansion inspired by ideas of manifest destiny.

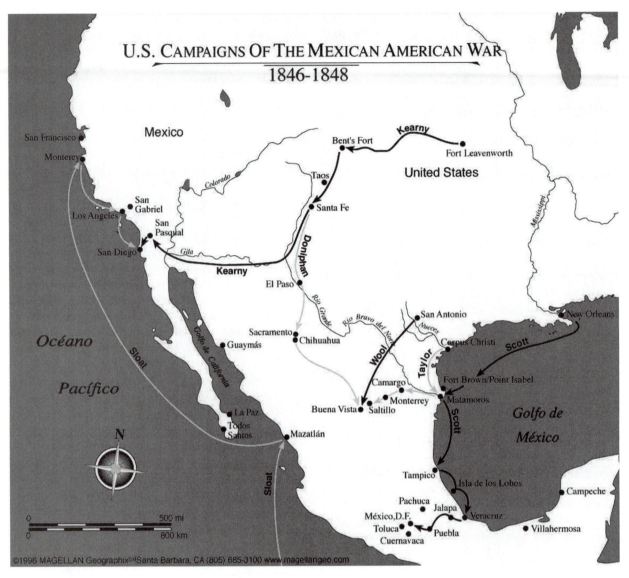

U.S. Campaigns of the Mexican-American War. *Texas's territorial claims and Mexico's reluctance to acknowledge the U.S. annexation of Texas resulted in the outbreak of the Mexican-American War. By the war's end, Mexico had lost nearly half of its territory, including all or parts of present-day Arizona, California, Colorado, Nevada, New Mexico, Wyoming, and Utah.* © MAPS.COM/CORBIS. REPRODUCED BY PERMISSION.

Several failed filibustering attempts against Cuba began in U.S. ports, and played a significant role in triggering the Spanish-American War. Jefferson was the first U.S. president to consider annexing Cuba, but most U.S. officials opposed the liberation of Cuba from Spanish rule because they feared Cuba's slaves might take advantage of the conflict and seize power, making the island a second Haiti. They also worried that European powers could occupy a weak, independent Cuba and that democratic, self-governing Cubans would resist future U.S. annexation. U.S. leaders who advocated joining the late nineteenth-century European scramble for overseas imperial possessions were given their opportunity in

1895 when José Martí and Cuban rebels renewed their efforts to win Cuban independence from Spain.

As U.S. leaders argued over intervention and fretted about the protection of U.S.-owned property on the island, U.S. president William McKinley sent the battleship *Maine* to Havana's harbor. On February 15, 1898, the *Maine* exploded, killing 260 U.S. sailors. A subsequent investigation incorrectly determined that the accidental blast was caused by an underwater mine. The tragedy broke the will of U.S. leaders who had resisted the pressure of those calling for war, including Cuban lobbyists and emotionally charged U.S. citizens captivated by reports in the newspapers of William Randolph Hearst and Joseph

Pulitzer. The victorious exploits of the Rough Riders fighting in Cuba helped their leader Theodore Roosevelt to win the U.S. vice-presidential nomination in 1900. Roosevelt subsequently became president in 1901 after an anarchist assassinated President McKinley.

CUBA AND PUERTO RICO IN THE AFTERMATH OF THE SPANISH-AMERICAN WAR

Cubans and Puerto Ricans did not participate in the Treaty of Paris of December 1898 that ended both the Spanish-American War and the reign of the Spanish Empire in the Western Hemisphere by calling for Spain's withdrawal from Puerto Rico and Cuba. Puerto Rico became a U.S. possession. Cuba became independent in May 1902, but a special U.S.–Cuban relationship was established. The Roosevelt administration granted Cuban independence while maintaining control over Cubans, whom it considered unfit for self-government, through an amendment to the U.S. Army appropriations bill for fiscal year 1902 known as the Platt Amendment. Named for Connecticut Senator Orville Platt, the amendment severely curtailed the new nation of Cuba's autonomy. U.S. troops left the island only after the Cubans incorporated the amendment's provisions into the Cuban constitution, where it remained until withdrawn with U.S. approval in 1934. The amendment granted the U.S. the right to militarily intervene in Cuban national affairs.

The United States demanded land for a naval base in Guantánamo Bay following U.S. naval officer and historian Alfred Thayer Mahan's recommendation that overseas coaling and naval stations needed to be acquired to assert U.S. power around the world. The amendment provided that the Cuban government would not assume any extraordinary public debt, reflecting the U.S. fear of European intervention in the Caribbean to collect on defaulted debts. U.S. interventions to take over public finances and protect U.S. private capital in Central America and the Caribbean became a major theme in U.S.–Latin American relations at the beginning of the twentieth century.

SEE ALSO *Monroe Doctrine.*

BIBLIOGRAPHY

Francaviglia, Richard V., and Douglas W. Richmond, eds. *Dueling Eagles: Reinterpreting the U.S.-Mexican War: 1846–1848.* Fort Worth: Texas Christian University Press, 2000.

Gleijeses, Piero. "The Limits of Sympathy: The United States and the Independence of Spanish America." *Journal of Latin American Studies* 24 (3) (October 1992): 481–505.

Haynes, Sam W., and Christopher Morris, eds. *Manifest Destiny and Empire: American Antebellum Expansionism.* College Station: Texas A&M University Press, 1997.

Johnson, John J. *A Hemisphere Apart: The Foundations of United States Policy toward Latin America.* Baltimore, MD: Johns Hopkins University Press, 1990.

LaFeber, Walter. The *New Empire: An Interpretation of American Expansion, 1860–1898,* 35th anniversary ed. Ithaca, NY: Cornell University Press, 1998.

Smith, Angel, and Emma Dávila-Cox, eds. *The Crisis of 1898: Colonial Redistribution and Nationalist Mobilization.* New York: St. Martin's Press, 1998.

David M. Carletta

UNITED STATES POLICY TOWARDS THE MIDDLE EAST

The Middle East lies across the shortest route by sea connecting Europe with South and Southeast Asia and exports a major share of the oil and natural gas that fuels the world's industrial economies. The Persian Gulf has two-thirds of the world's proven oil reserves. Saudi Arabia alone has more than a fourth of world reserves and Iraq is believed to have the second largest reserves.

Soon after World War II (1939–1945) and as the Cold War was beginning, the Gulf began to produce a significant share of the world's oil: 17 percent in 1950, 25 percent in 1960, and 27 percent in 1990. The United States had just become a net oil importer and economic recovery in Europe and Japan depended upon Middle East oil. As Britain withdrew from the Middle East, the Americans stepped in to secure a steady supply of oil at low and stable prices and to limit Soviet influence; oil security remained a basic policy goal even after the dissolution of the Soviet Union. In response to successive crises and challenges, the United States involved itself more directly in the Persian Gulf and Central Asia instead of retreating. Although the invasions of Afghanistan and Iraq were no more predictable than the September 11, 2001, terrorist attacks that led to them, they were consistent with a trend of more direct U.S. involvement in the Gulf since the early 1970s.

The American–Israeli alliance developed at the height of the Cold War in the 1960s. The alliance offered strategic advantages but also entailed political disadvantages in the Arab world. Since the 1970s U.S. policy has sought to close the gap between its alliance with Israel and its relations with the Arabs by mediating an Arab-Israeli peace. In the 1990s, as the United States intervened more directly in the Persian Gulf, it took a more active role in promoting Israeli–Palestinian negotiations.

BEGINNINGS

American involvement in the Middle East was quite limited before World War II. American Protestant missionaries contributed to the development of education, founding what are now the American University of Beirut, the American University in Cairo, and Bogazici University in Istanbul. American policymakers regarded the Middle East as a British sphere and usually supported British policy there. President Woodrow Wilson (1856–1924) and the congress endorsed the Balfour Declaration (1917), in which Britain declared itself in favor of establishing a Jewish national home in Palestine, and Wilson acquiesced in postwar British and French colonial rule in the Fertile Crescent.

The British were the first to develop Persian Gulf oil in Iran. After World War I (1914–1918) the United States demanded an open door policy for its oil companies, and so in the early 1920s the Iraq Petroleum Company (IPC) was formed with British, American, and French participation. Standard Oil of California (Socal, now Chevron), which was not a participant in the IPC, struck oil in Bahrain in 1933 and in Saudi Arabia in 1938. The Arabian-American Oil Company (ARAMCO) was formed in 1944 as a consortium of several U.S. oil companies to exploit Saudi oil.

FROM BRITISH TO AMERICAN HEGEMONY

The United States became the major power in the Middle East in little more than a decade after World War II, to a large extent stepping in as Britain withdrew. The two powers had similar interests, especially the containment of communism and protection of the oilfields, but they did not see eye to eye on everything nor always act in concert. In 1947 Britain informed the United States that it could no longer bear the cost of supporting Greece and Turkey. Greece was facing a communist insurgency and Turkey was under Soviet pressure over territory and its sovereignty in the Bosphorus and Dardanelles. The Americans responded in the Truman Doctrine by pledging aid to both countries and support for their independence and territorial integrity.

In 1953 the United States joined Britain in boycotting Iranian oil after it was nationalized by Prime Minister Muhammad Musaddiq (1882–1964). In August the Central Intelligence Agency (CIA) assisted a coup that overthrew Musaddiq's elected government and secured the throne of Shah Muhammad Reza Pahlavi (1919–1980). The Eisenhower administration was alarmed by the participation of the communist Tudeh Party in the parliament, even though Musaddiq was an anticommunist nationalist. The coup marked the ascendance of American influence in Iran. The British Anglo-Iranian Oil Company (now British Petroleum, or BP) had controlled Iran's oil since the beginning of the century. Now a new consortium was organized with American companies holding a 40 percent share. The United States also began to provide military and economic assistance to Iran. Over the next three decades the shah would remain a close ally of the United States while creating a royal dictatorship.

The United States supported and later emulated Britain's postcolonial strategy of maintaining hegemony in the Middle East through defense treaties and regional security pacts such as the Baghdad Pact alliance of 1955. Later known as the Central Treaty Organization (CENTO), it included Turkey, Iraq, Iran, and Pakistan along with Britain, and was aimed at containing the Soviet Union on its southern flank.

Britain withdrew from the Persian Gulf in 1971 as its remaining Middle Eastern colonies—Bahrain, Qatar, and the United Arab Emirates—became independent. With Britain's exit the Nixon administration turned to Iran and Saudi Arabia as allies that could maintain regional stability. Both received weapons and military training under this twin pillar policy, and as major oil producers they paid in cash. President Richard M. Nixon's (1913–1994) strategy of relying on regional allies to protect U.S. interests in vital areas pragmatically acknowledged the unpopularity of the Vietnam War (1955–1975) and the certainty of public opposition if large numbers of U.S. troops were deployed abroad elsewhere.

In the Gulf the United States sought to block threats from perceived Soviet allies. The United States encouraged the rise of the Baath Party in Iraq because of their ruthless anticommunism. Yet the Baathist regime of Ahmad Hassan al-Bakr (1914–1982) and Saddam Hussein (b. 1937) that seized power in 1968 later signed a treaty of friendship and cooperation with the Soviet Union. At the bottom of the Arabian Peninsula, the People's Democratic Republic of Yemen, independent since 1967, was openly Marxist. With U.S. blessing, Iran aided a Kurdish insurrection in northern Iraq (1972–1975) that distracted and weakened the Baathist regime and sent troops to Oman's Dhofar province, on the border with Yemen, to put down a Marxist insurgency.

There was far less agreement between Britain and America when it came to postwar Palestine/Israel and Egypt. British policy in Palestine restricted Jewish immigration and aimed at creating a state with the existing population in which there was an Arab majority. The Truman administration favored a version of the Zionist or Jewish nationalist program that called for large-scale Jewish immigration and the creation of a state for the Jews, who at the time were a large minority in Palestine. The United States lobbied for the November 1947

Anti-American Demonstration in Tehran, June 1, 1951. *A large poster depicting Uncle Sam being thrown out of Iran is carried in a demonstration organized by the Tudeh Party (an Iranian communist party) in Tehran. The script on the poster criticizes American "junk sellers" who import preservatives and dolls into Iran.* © BETTMANN/CORBIS. REPRODUCED BY PERMISSION.

United Nations (UN) General Assembly resolution partitioning Palestine into Jewish and Arab states and quickly recognized the new State of Israel proclaimed in May 1948. A more dramatic breach between the United States and Britain occurred during the Suez War, launched in October 1956 by Britain, France, and Israel against Egypt, in response to the nationalization of the Suez Canal. The Eisenhower administration distrusted Egypt's President Gamal 'Abd al Nasir (1918–1970), who opposed the Baghdad Pact, espoused neutrality, and received Soviet-bloc weapons. Yet, believing that the assault on Egypt was a disaster for Western interests, they joined the Soviets in demanding a cease-fire and the withdrawal of the invaders.

The Suez debacle marked the eclipse of Britain by the United States as the leading power in the Middle East. Two other consequences were soon apparent. The Soviets gained a firmer foothold in Egypt—their first in the region—not only supplying arms but agreeing in 1958 to assist in building the Aswan High Dam. Second, the war turned Nasir into a pan-Arab hero. Already before the war Egypt's Voice of the Arabs radio,

broadcast with a high-power transmitter throughout the region, was attacking the Baghdad Pact and the Arab allies of Britain and the United States—Jordan, Iraq, Saudi Arabia, and Kuwait. The wave of Arab nationalist and Nasirite sentiment that now broke over the region was seen in Washington and London as favoring the spread of Soviet influence. In January 1957, before Israeli troops withdrew from the Sinai, the Eisenhower Doctrine asserted that the Soviets were manipulating regional instability and offered assistance including the use of troops to countries facing communist aggression, direct and indirect.

In the first half of 1958 it appeared that the Arab nationalist goal of political unity might be achieved, and with it a setback to Western interests. In February Syria and Egypt signed a pact of union, forming the United Arab Republic (UAR) under Nasir's leadership. Then in July the Iraqi monarchy was overthrown by officers using revolutionary, nationalist rhetoric similar to that of the Egyptians. The United States and Britain responded by sending troops to Lebanon and Jordan. Lebanon was in the throes of a local political struggle now known as its first civil war (1958). The arrival of U.S. Marines in Beirut brought an end to the conflict while British troops propped up the remaining Hashemite Kingdom. The specter of Arab unity turned out to be just that, however. Within months the Iraqi and Egyptian regimes were trading invective, and three years later the UAR dissolved.

THE U.S.–ISRAELI ALLIANCE

Although American public opinion consistently favored Israel, a close political–military alliance was cemented only in the aftermath of the June 1967 Six Day War. France was Israel's main source of military equipment before 1967 and provided the know-how and probably the fuel for Israel's nuclear program, begun in 1958. The French–Israeli relationship was based on mutual antipathy toward Arab nationalism and especially Nasir, during the Algerian War of Independence (1954–1962).

The United States proposed more than one Arab-Israeli peace scheme before 1956, but Cold War geopolitics drew the United States closer to Israel as self-styled progressive regimes emerged in Egypt (1954), Iraq (1958), and Syria (1966) that espoused Arab unity and socialism, opposed U.S. hegemony, and received Soviet weapons and aid. Like prerevolutionary Iran, Israel was a counterweight to these states. A strategic relationship including the supply of heavy weapons began to develop between the United States and Israel after 1956, and a threshold to more sophisticated weapons was crossed when President John F. Kennedy (1917–1963) authorized the supply of Hawk anti-aircraft missiles in 1963. While the emerging alliance with Israel balanced Egypt and other Soviet clients, both Presidents Dwight D. Eisenhower (1890–1969) and Kennedy hoped that Israel would abandon its nuclear weapons program if it received sufficient conventional arms.

In the June 1967 war Israel conquered Egypt's Sinai peninsula, the Palestinian West Bank (including East Jerusalem) and Gaza, and Syria's Golan Heights. Israel's decisive victory over the Arabs was celebrated in the United States as the triumph of an ally against Soviet proxies. The United States now became Israel's main patron, and aid—especially military aid—grew exponentially. In part this was driven by a postwar arms race. The Soviets supplied Egypt and Syria with new and more advanced weapons after 1967 and, again, after the Yom Kippur/Ramadan War of October and November 1973. U.S. policy was to ensure that Israel kept an advantage in conventional weapons. The doctrine that Israel is a strategic asset became fixed in U.S. policy circles during the Nixon administration.

The 1973 war showed the dangers of letting the Arab-Israel conflict fester. Israel threatened to use nuclear weapons if not resupplied promptly, resulting in a U.S. airlift of weapons. Saudi Arabia and Kuwait responded by declaring a boycott of oil sales to the United States and the Netherlands and reducing output. Separately the Organization of Petroleum Exporting Countries (OPEC) quadrupled the price of oil. Near the end of the war a Soviet–American confrontation was narrowly averted. A more positive inducement to pursue peace was Egyptian President Anwar al-Sadat's (1918–1981) courtship of the Americans and the opportunity of replacing the Soviets as Egypt's patron. Secretary of State Henry Kissinger's (b. 1923) shuttle diplomacy produced disengagement agreements in the Sinai and Golan Heights in 1974 and 1975.

In November 1967 the United States had cosponsored UN Security Council Resolution 242, which called upon Israel to withdraw from (unspecified) territories occupied in the recent war in exchange for peace with its Arab neighbors. This land-for-peace formula remains the basis of proposals to settle the Israeli-Arab/Palestinian conflict. In the 1970s and 1980s the United States supported Israel's desire for treaties of peace and normalization with the Arab states, refusing to deal with the Palestine Liberation Organization (PLO), led by Yasir Arafat's (1929–2004) Fatah organization. The Americans envisioned the return of most of the West Bank to Jordan, but the Jordan option was undermined by PLO diplomatic gains and Israeli colonization in the occupied territories. In December 1988 the United States opened a formal dialogue with the PLO after it declared its goal of a state in the West Bank and Gaza and accepted Israel.

In the 1980s the strategic relationship between the United States and Israel deepened, whereas differences persisted over the path to regional peace. Israel annexed greater East Jerusalem in 1981 and stepped up settlement activity in the occupied territories over ineffectual opposition by Presidents Jimmy Carter (b. 1924) and Ronald Reagan (1911–2004). Israel entangled the United States in its bid for mastery in Lebanon between 1982 and 1984, resulting in the death of 241 U.S. marines in Beirut and a rare instance of U.S. retreat.

In the 1990s Presidents George H. W. Bush (b. 1924) and Bill Clinton (b. 1946) took an active role in promoting Israeli–Palestinian negotiations. The 1991 Madrid conference and subsequent working groups made little headway politically but established a framework for discussing economic ties between Israel and the Arab states. After Israel and the PLO agreed to the 1993 Oslo Declaration of Principles, Clinton strove to move the Oslo process forward over the next several years. Though it failed, the Oslo process showed how the land-for-peace and two-state concepts might be applied in a viable settlement.

Egyptian Billboard in Support of Peace Negotiations with Israel, March 1979. *This billboard in Cairo carries the images of American president Jimmy Carter and Egyptian president Anwar el-Sadat along with an expression of support for Carter's efforts to achieve peace between Egypt and Israel.* © CORBIS. REPRODUCED BY PERMISSION.

Between the 1970s and 2000s the Arab–Israeli conflict was transformed from a conflict between states in a Cold War context into an asymmetrical struggle between Israel and the Palestinians for possession of the occupied territories. Egypt normalized relations with Israel in 1979, followed by Jordan in 1994. After Madrid several other Arab states established sub-ambassadorial contacts with Israel. A 1982 Arab League peace plan envisioned creating a Palestinian state in the territories occupied by Israel in 1967 and called on the U.N. to ensure "guarantees for peace for all the states of the region," including Israel. In March 2002 the Arab League explicitly offered full normalization of relations with Israel in exchange for Israel's withdrawal from the occupied territories.

In the same period U.S. policy evolved dramatically from tacit acceptance of Israel's territorial gains soon after the 1967 war to President George W. Bush's June 2002 statement envisioning a Palestinian state alongside Israel. American opinion remained divided over whether the continuing conflict is part of the larger "war on terrorism" or itself something that feeds anti-Americanism and terrorism. Pro-Israel pressure groups gained a place in policy discussions that they lacked earlier, complicating policymaking in unusual ways. Israel's 2005 withdrawal of military forces and settlements from the Gaza Strip

was seen by many as a step toward an eventual political settlement. However, Israel's policy of annexing several large settlement blocks in East Jerusalem and the West Bank seemed an obstacle to the creation of a viable Palestinian state.

THE UNITED STATES IN THE PERSIAN GULF FROM 1979 TO 2003

Four events in 1979 shaped U.S. policy as it is today. In April Egypt became the first Arab state to normalize relations with Israel, regaining the Sinai. This enabled the United States to develop a strategic alliance with Egypt, which became the second greatest recipient of American aid after Israel.

Two months earlier the Ayatollah Ruhollah Khomeini (1902–1989) returned to Iran at the culmination of a popular revolution that overthrew the shah. The United States lost its strongest ally in the Persian Gulf and the twin pillars policy was in ruins. The November takeover of the U.S. embassy and the imprisonment of American personnel for 444 days, known as the hostage crisis, poisoned what was left of American–Iranian relations. In July Saddam Hussein assumed the presidency of Iraq in a bloody purge. A year later he invaded Iran's oil-rich Khuzistan province, claiming it for the Arab nation.

In December the Soviet Union sent troops into Afghanistan to save a beleaguered communist regime, raising old fears of a Russian advance toward the Gulf.

The United States responded to the Iranian revolution and the Soviet invasion of Afghanistan by becoming more directly committed in the Gulf. The Carter Doctrine of January 1980 declared, "Any attempt by any outside force to gain control of the Persian Gulf region will be regarded as an assault on the vital interests of the United States of America, and such an assault will be repelled by any means necessary, including military force." To put teeth in this policy the United States created a Rapid Deployment Force that later evolved into the Central Command (Centcom) of the U.S. military. The new strategy, carried forward by the Reagan administration, still relied on local allies—Saudi Arabia and the smaller Gulf Arab states—while planning for the direct use of American forces. State of the art military and air bases were constructed in Saudi Arabia, and the Saudis purchased Airborne Warning and Command Systems (AWACS) planes and advanced fighter aircraft. Supplies and equipment were prepositioned in Saudi Arabia, other Gulf states, and Egypt. The navy acquired a forward base in the Indian Ocean by leasing the island of Diego Garcia from Britain. These preparations enabled the United States to respond rapidly and effectively when Iraq invaded Kuwait in 1990.

At the same time it prepared for the defense of the Gulf, the United States intervened against the Soviets in Afghanistan. Even before the Soviet invasion, the United States and its allies, Pakistan and Saudi Arabia, had supported anticommunist *mujahideen* (holy warrior) fighters in Afghanistan. During the Reagan administration money, expertise, and materiel flowed into Afghanistan through Pakistan. Allies such as Saudi Arabia encouraged volunteers to join the mujahideen, and thousands of Muslims did so. After the Soviets withdrew in 1989, some of these Arab-Afghan veterans joined radical Islamist movements back home, in places such as Algeria, Egypt, and Saudi Arabia. The most famous of the Arab-Afghan veterans is Osama Bin Laden (b. 1957).

During the Iran-Iraq war (1980–1988) the Reagan administration assisted Iraq, judging Iran's revolutionary regime to pose the greater danger. Aid to Iraq was stepped up in 1982 after a successful Iranian counteroffensive. In 1986 and 1987 the Soviets and the United States reflagged Kuwaiti tankers to protect them from Iranian attack, and the U.S. Navy engaged in the tanker war with Iran in 1988, leading to Iran's acceptance of a ceasefire that year.

The United States supported Iraq without illusions, except in underestimating Saddam's capacity for miscalculation. Condemnation of his invasion and annexation of Kuwait in August 1990 was nearly universal. President George H. W. Bush assembled a broad coalition of forces that ejected the Iraqis from Kuwait in February 1991. The coalition had a UN mandate to liberate Kuwait, not to carry the war to Iraq itself or to overthrow Saddam. Nevertheless, Bush compared Saddam to Adolf Hitler (1889–1945) and made his removal a goal. A postwar UN Security Council resolution imposed economic sanctions on Iraq to force it to divest itself of unconventional weapons (weapons of mass destruction, or WMD). However, the Bush and Clinton administrations, backed by Britain, sought to use the sanctions for regime change. Several covert operations were launched in the 1990s, and the no-fly zones in the south and north of Iraq were used aggressively. Some analysts argued that American policy gave Saddam no incentive to cooperate in disarming, and controversy grew over the effect of the sanctions on Iraqi civilians, which included high child mortality.

Bin Laden and other radical Islamists have articulated the goal of establishing a new caliphate. However, his war against the United States and its allies, including his native Saudi Arabia, appears to have been triggered by the stationing of American forces on Saudi soil during and after the Kuwait war, which he found intolerable. President George W. Bush declared a "war on terror" in response to the September 11, 2001 (9/11) attacks by Bin Laden's al-Qaeda organization on New York and Washington, DC. Between October and December 2001 the United States and its allies including Afghan militias defeated the Taliban regime in Afghanistan, which harbored Bin Laden, but he eluded capture. The United States invaded Iraq in March 2003 with far less international support, alleging that Saddam still possessed WMD and was reviving WMD programs, and that he posed a threat. Less directly Iraq was alleged to be involved in the 9/11 attacks. Neither allegation proved to be true. American and allied forces made little headway against a post-invasion insurgency, while an Iraqi transitional assembly was unable to achieve consensus on a new constitution scheduled to be voted upon in an October 2005 plebiscite.

In addition to invading and occupying two countries in the Middle East and Central Asia, Bush introduced two novel foreign policy ideas. In January 2002 he announced a policy of preventive war to keep adversaries from developing the capacity to pose a threat. The Iraq war was justified mainly on that basis. The other idea, invoked before and since the war, was the promotion of democracy and free markets, which he associated with peace and development.

President Bush in Aqaba, June 4, 2003. *American president George W. Bush strolls with (left to right) Palestinian Authority president Mahmoud Abbas, Israeli prime minister Ariel Sharon, and King Abdullah II of Jordan following a meeting in the Jordanian Red Sea port of Aqaba. The four leaders had met to discuss peace efforts in the region.* © REUTERS/CORBIS. REPRODUCED BY PERMISSION.

A NEW GREAT GAME?

Nineteenth-century Anglo–Russian rivalry in Central Asia was once known as the Great Game. Since the dissolution of the Soviet Union in 1991, a version of the Great Game appears to have revived, with the United States in Britain's role. During the twenty-first century more U.S. troops are deployed by Centcom in Central and Southwest Asia than in Europe and East Asia combined, and the United States has basing and military aid agreements with numerous countries in the two regions. There is likely to be a long-term American presence in Central and Southwest Asia (including the Persian Gulf) regardless of the short-term outcome of the Iraq war, due to the perception that American hegemony is the surest way to protect the industrial world's—and America's—supply of oil. Efforts to mediate an Israeli-Palestinian settlement will continue out of a recognition that failure to do so would undermine this and other U.S. policy goals in the rest of the region.

SEE ALSO *Oil; Suez Canal and Suez Crisis.*

BIBLIOGRAPHY

Brands, H.W. *Into the Labyrinth: the United States and the Middle East, 1945–1993.* New York: McGraw-Hill, 1994.

Cleveland, William L. *A History of the Modern Middle East*, 3rd ed. Boulder, CO: Westview, 2004.

Dawisha, Adeed. *Arab Nationalism in the Twentieth Century: From Triumph to Despair.* Princeton, NJ: Princeton University Press, 2003.

Hourani, Albert, Philip Khoury, and Mary Wilson, eds. *The Modern Middle East: A Reader*, 2nd ed. New York and London: I.B. Tauris, 2004.

Lesch, David W. *The Middle East and the United States: A Historical and Political Reassessment*, 3rd ed. Boulder, CO: Westview, 2003.

Little, Douglas. *American Orientalism: The United States and the Middle East since 1945.* Chapel Hill: University of North Carolina Press, 2002.

Ovendale, Ritchie. *Britain, the United States, and the Transfer of Power in the Middle East, 1945–1962.* London and New York: Leicester University Press, 1996.

Quandt, William B. *Peace Process: American Diplomacy and the Arab-Israeli Conflict since 1967.* Washington, DC: Brookings

Institution Press; Berkeley: University of California Press, 2001.

Reich, Bernard. *A Brief History of Israel*. New York: Facts on File, 2005.

Smith, Charles. *Palestine and the Arab-Israeli Conflict*, 5th ed. Boston: Bedford/St. Martins, 2004.

Yergin, Daniel. *The Prize: The Epic Quest for Oil, Money, and Power*. New York: Simon and Schuster, 1991.

Kenneth M. Cuno

'URABI REBELLION

The 'Urabi Rebellion (1881–1882) occurred when an Egyptian army colonel, Ahmad 'Urabi, led a movement to subject Egypt's hereditary Ottoman governor, Khedive Tawfiq, to constitutional rule and lessen the country's reliance on European advisors. The rebellion provoked the British occupation of Egypt in 1882, which, although it officially ended in 1922, continued in the Suez Canal Zone until 1956.

Prior to the rebellion, Egypt had become deeply indebted to European creditors as a result of expensive development projects, such as the digging of the Suez Canal. Egypt declared bankruptcy in 1876 and accepted British and French control of its revenues (called the Dual Control) to ensure repayment of the debt. When in 1879 Khedive Isma'il threatened to repudiate the debt, he was deposed and replaced by his more pliable son, Tawfiq. In part because Tawfiq accepted the Dual Control and a financial system that assigned 60 percent of revenues to debt payment, people from many different social classes opposed his rule. Matters worsened in 1880, when Tawfiq passed a law excusing native Egyptians from serving more than four years in the Egyptian army. This decision was intended to ease the burden of military service on peasants but also prevented native Egyptians from rising to any rank higher than colonel. All other officers were descended from the Turco-Circassian elite that had ruled the country during the Mamluk Empire (1249–1517) or were European. Tawfiq attempted to ease matters by appointing an Egyptian colonel, Ahmad 'Urabi, to be his war minister.

'Urabi used his position to demand limits on the khedive's power. On September 9, 1881, 'Urabi, a group of native officers, and urban supporters marched up to Tawfiq's palace. The French and British Controllers came out with Tawfiq to meet the demonstrators. 'Urabi stood in front of the palace and said to Tawfiq: "We are not slaves, and shall never from this day forth be inherited" (Blunt 1967, p. 114). Egypt would be governed by Egyptians, he proclaimed, which inspired the movement to take "Egypt for the Egyptians!" as its rallying cry. The army threatened to withdraw support from Tawfiq unless he allowed the people some form of representative government and a constitution. Unwillingly, he agreed to give legislative powers to the Chamber of Deputies, an advisory council established by Khedive Isma'il. Wilfrid S. Blunt, a British observer, commented, "The three months which followed this notable event were the happiest time, politically, that Egypt has ever known" (Blunt 1967, p. 116). The Egyptians participated in their own government for the first time since the Persians conquered Egypt in 343 B.C.E.; they had a constitution and an elected legislature.

The European Controllers and the Ottoman sultan sided with the khedive against 'Urabi. The British were uneasy, worried that the Chamber of Deputies might repudiate the debt, abrogate the Dual Control, and encourage violence against Europeans and Egyptian Christians. In fact, 'Urabi's government met with religious scholars who signed a *fatwa* (legal opinion) stating that all Egyptians were brothers regardless of religion, but the British, fearing conflict, moved in ships to patrol the harbor of Alexandria.

The presence of British ships contributed to rising tensions in Alexandria, which had a large European population. On June 11, 1882, the tensions climaxed. A fight in a Christian neighborhood turned into a riot that spread rapidly throughout the city. Homes were looted; parts of the city went up in flames. Europeans began to flee to the British ships. Tawfiq saw this as an opportunity to reestablish his control and ordered the British ships to bombard the city with cannons. He then declared 'Urabi a rebel, accused him of inciting the riots in Alexandria, and told his Chamber of Deputies that the rebels were attacking and that they should resist to the last man. Then Tawfiq escaped the chaos and took refuge on a British ship. Subsequently 393 Egyptian leaders, including officials, officers, religious scholars, merchants, artisans, and village headmen, signed a decree on July 29 deposing Tawfiq and declaring him a traitor.

The British launched a full-scale invasion to return Tawfiq to power. The great battle of the British invasion, Tel al-Kabir, was disastrous for the Egyptians. 'Urabi and his followers were arrested, subjected to a trial for rebellion against their rightful ruler (Tawfiq), and exiled. Tawfiq invited the British in to restore his authority.

The 'Urabi constitutionalist movement ended in British occupation. The period from 1882 to 1914 is known as the Veiled Protectorate. Officially, Tawfiq still ruled Egypt as an Ottoman province, and the government was still administered by Ottoman officials. However, British commissioners governed, notably Lord Cromer (1883–1907), and each ministry was attached to a British "adviser" who heavily influenced its policies.

SEE ALSO *Egypt; Empire, British; Empire, Ottoman.*

BIBLIOGRAPHY

Blunt, Wilfrid S. *Secret History of the English Occupation of Egypt.* New York: Howard Fertig, 1967 [1922].

Cole, Juan R. I. *Colonialism and Revolution in the Middle East: Social and Cultural Origins of Egypt's 'Urabi Movement.* Princeton, NJ: Princeton University Press, 1993.

Scholch, Alexander. *Egypt for the Egyptians! The Socio-Political Crisis in Egypt, 1878–1882.* London: Ithaca Press, 1981.

Indira Falk Gesink

V

VALENTIJN, FRANÇOIS
1666–1727

François Valentijn was born on April 17, 1666, in the city of Dordrecht, the Netherlands, as the eldest of seven children of Abraham Valentijn and Maria Rijsbergen. He studied theology at the universities of Utrecht and Leiden. During his life he spent nearly fifteen years as a minister in the Dutch East-Indies (1685–1694 and 1706–1713), mostly in the Moluccan Archipelago. In 1692 he entered into matrimony with Cornelia Snaats (1660–1717) who bore him two daughters. Valentijn died on August 6, 1727, in the city of The Hague. Valentijn is often noted for his role in discussions about early translations of the Bible into Malay. However, his established reputation rests on his multivolume work on Asia titled *Oud en Nieuw Oost-Indië* (Old and New East-Indies).

REVEREND VALENTIJN IN THE MOLUCCAS

At the age of nineteen, Valentijn was called to the ministry on Ambon Island, the chief trade and administrative hub of the Moluccan Archipelago. In the city of Ambon, he preached in the Malay language and trained local Ambonese assistant ministers, while also having to inspect some fifty Christian parishes in the region.

In the 1600s the catechism and liturgy were offered in so-called High-Malay, which most local Christians did not understand. Valentijn fervently opposed the use of High-Malay and instead propagated Ambon-Malay because, in his opinion, all Christian communities in the Indies understood this local dialect.

During his stay in Ambon, a number of Valentijn's colleagues blamed him for paying too much attention to his wife and making a living from usury. On top of these accusations, he was found guilty of manipulating official church records. The relationship with his colleagues grew tense because Valentijn disliked his task of inspecting the Christian parishes on other islands. In 1694 he returned to the Netherlands where he spent much time on his Bible translation.

In 1705 Valentijn returned to Ambon. During this period, Reverend Valentijn got into a conflict with the governor of Ambon about too much interference of the secular administration in church affairs without the consent of the church administration. This conflict worsened after Valentijn rejected his call by the central colonial administration to the island of Ternate. In 1713 his repeated request for repatriation was finally met.

THE MALAY BIBLE TRANSLATION

In 1693 during a meeting with the Church Council of Batavia, Valentijn announced that he had completed the translation of the Bible into Ambon-Malay. The Church Council refused to publish Valentijn's translation because two years earlier they assigned the task of translating the Bible into High-Malay to the Batavia-based Reverend Melchior Leydecker.

After Valentijn returned to the Netherlands in 1695, he rallied support for his translation. A heated discussion unfolded, in which Valentijn and, amongst others, the Dutch Reformed synods of both the provinces of North- and South-Holland, opposed the critique of Leydecker and the Church Council of Batavia. The Council's criticism largely concerned Valentijn's use of a poor dialect of Malay. The synods in the Netherlands were not in the position to participate in the debate as most relevant linguists resided in the Indies, but Valentijn's personal network most likely contributed to the support for Valentijn's translation.

In 1706 a special commission of ministers in the Indies inspected a revised edition of Valentijn's translation but still noticed a number of shortcomings. Although Valentijn told the commission that he would redo the translation, the final revised edition was never presented to the Church Council. The Council eventually decided to publish Leydecker's High-Malay translation, which was used in the Moluccas from 1733 onward into the twentieth century.

OUD EN NIEUW OOST-INDIË

From 1719 onward, Valentijn, as a private citizen, devoted himself chiefly to his magnum opus, *Oud en Nieuw Oost-Indië* (*ONOI*), comprising his own notes, observations, sections of writings from his personal library, and materials trusted to him by former colonial officials. In 1724, the first two volumes were published in the cities of Dordrecht and Amsterdam, followed by the following three volumes in 1726. This work comprises geographical and ethnological descriptions of the Moluccas and the trading contacts of the Dutch East India Company (VOC) throughout Asia.

Scholars consider this substantial work the first Dutch encyclopedic reference for Asia. *ONOI* contains factual data, descriptions of persons and towns, anecdotes, ethnological engravings, maps, sketches of coastlines, and city plans, as well as excerpts of official documents of the church council and colonial administration.

Valentijn wrote in an uncorrupted form of Dutch, which many contemporary writers were not able to compete with. The structure of Valentijn's colossal work is rather chaotic: the descriptions of more than thirty regions are erratically spread over a total number of forty-nine books in five volumes, each consisting of two parts, and held together in eight bindings.

Since the publication of *ONOI*, numerous scholars have accused Valentijn of plagiarism. It is true that he included abstracts of other works, such as the celebrated account on the Ambon islands by Rumphius, without referencing them properly. However, general acknowledgment of sources can be found in several places, for example, in his preface to the third volume.

THE INFLUENCE OF VALENTIJN'S WORK

For almost two centuries, Valentijn's work was the single credible reference for Asia. *ONOI* was therefore used as the main manual for Dutch civil servants and colonial administrators who were sent to work in the East Indies.

Valentijn's work is still a major source for historical studies on the Dutch East Indies. For example, the reference book on Dutch-Asiatic shipping in the seventeenth and eighteenth centuries (*The Hague*, 1979–1987) was compiled on the basis of materials derived from Valentijn's work. The importance of *ONOI* for the historical reconstruction of other regions is clearly demonstrated by the publication of English translations of Valentijn's parts concerning the Cape of Good Hope (1971–1973) and the first twelve chapters of his description of Ceylon (1978).

Valentijn's work also proved to be of great importance for the natural history of the Moluccas. Valentijn included in *ONOI* descriptions by Rumphius on, for example, Ambonese animals, while Rumphius's original unpublished manuscript was later lost. In 1754 Valentijn's part on sea flora and fauna was separately published in Amsterdam, and some twenty years later translated into German. It was only in 2004 that the complete *ONOI* was reprinted and made available to a larger public.

SEE ALSO *Dutch United East India Company; Moluccas; Religion, Western Perceptions of Traditional Religions; Religion, Western Perceptions of World Religions; Travelogues.*

BIBLIOGRAPHY

Boetzelaer van Asperen en Dubbeldam, dr. C.W.Th. baron. "De geschiedenis van de Maleische bijbelvertaling in Nederlandsch-Indië" [The history of the Malay bible translation in the Netherlands-Indies]. *Journal of the Humanities and Social Sciences of Southeast Asia and Oceania* (Bijdragen tot de Taal-, Land- en Volkenkunde), 100 (1941): 27–48.

Habiboe, R. R. F. *Tot verheffing van mijne natie. Het leven en werk van François Valentijn* [For the elevation of my nation. The life and work of François Valentijn] *(1666–1727)*. Franeker: Uitgeverij Van Wijnen, 2004.

Keyzer, dr. S. *François Valentijn's Oud en Nieuw Oost-Indiën*. (1856–58). 1st ed. Amsterdam: Wed. J. C. van Kesteren & Zoon, 1862.

Valentijn, François. *Deure der waarhyd* [Door of Truth]. Dordregt: Cornelis Willegaarts, 1698.

Valentijn, François. *Oud en Nieuw Oost-Indiën* [Old and New East-Indies] (1724–1726). 1st ed. Franeker: Uitgeverij Van Wijnen, 2002–2004.

Valentijn, François. *Verhandeling der Zee-Horenkens en Zee-gewassen in en omtrent Amboina, dienende tot een vervolg van de Amboinsche Rariteitenkamer beschreven door Georgius Everhardus Rumphius* [Discourse concerning sea-whelks and sea-plants in and around Amboina, as a sequel to The Ambonese Curiosity Cabinet described by Georgius Everhardus Rumphius]. Amsterdam: J. van Keulen, 1754.

Nationalist Leader Jimmy Stevens, June 1980. *Nagriamel leader Jimmy Stevens, who declared the independence of Espiritu Santo Island in June 1980, stands before local supporters prepared to resist Vanuatu's Prime Minister, Walter Lini.* © **ALAIN DEJEAN/SYGMA/ CORBIS. REPRODUCED BY PERMISSION.**

Valentijn, François. "Description of the Cape of Good Hope with Matters Concerning It, Amsterdam 1726." *Van Riebeeck Society Publications*, 2nd series, no. 2, 4. Cape Town: Van Riebeeck Society, 1971–1973. Edited and annotated by Prof. P. Serton, Maj. R. Raven-Hart, and Dr. W. J. de Kock. Final editor Dr. E. H. Raidt. Introduction by Prof. P. Serton. English translation by Maj. R. Raven-Hart.

Valentijn, François. "François Valentijns description of Ceylon." *Works Issued by the Hakluyt Society,* 2nd series, no. 149. Translated from the Dutch and edited by Sinnappah Arasaratnam. London: Hakluyt Society, 1978.

R. F. F. Habiboe

VANUATU

Vanuatu, which assumed this name at independence in 1980, had been known during the previous seventy-four years of colonial administration as the New Hebrides. An archipelago lying within a region of the South Pacific known as Melanesia, only about one-quarter of Vanuatu's eighty-three islands are inhabited. Although the nation's total population is only about 200,000, linguists credit Vanuatu with the greatest number of languages per capita. (A type of pidgin English, called Bislama, serves as lingua franca and the nation's national language.)

Vanuatu's major resources are coconuts, processed and exported as coco and copra (dried coconut meat from which coconut oil is extracted), as well as timber and livestock. The largest importers of these products are Belgium, Chile, and Germany. Vanuatu's tropical island locus makes it a destination for approximately fifty thousand tourists a year, mostly from Australia. Tourism is consequently a major revenue earner, as is Vanuatu's status as an offshore financial center.

Vanuatu is unique in the annals of colonial history. As a *condominium* under joint sovereignty by two nations, administration of the territory and inhabitants of the New Hebrides was shared by France and Britain. The land was not divided into French and British zones, nor were indigenous islanders (unlike European and Australian settlers) subjects of either the British Crown or the French Republic. Rather, three distinct sets of government operated simultaneously (and often competitively): the British Residency, the French Residency, and the Joint (or Condominial) Administration. Competition was more prevalent than coordination and cooperation.

For example, health, education, and policing systems were established separately by the British and French. The two even released separate sets of weights and measures, stamps, and currency. Certain services were conducted jointly as part of the condominium (e.g., transportation, communications, agriculture, and livestock). Most distinctive was the Joint Court, responsible for dispensing justice for the stateless New Hebrideans. (Nonindigenes were subject, according to their own choice, to either French or British law.)

Greater than the rivalry between the national residencies in Vanuatu was that between missionary churches (Catholic and various Protestant). By competing for the souls of the otherwise animistic Melanesians, the churches indirectly fostered linguistic and political cleavages among the population. Mission schools became the prime venue for formation of the two major competing camps among native New Hebrideans: Anglophone (English-speaking) Protestants and Francophone (French-speaking) Catholics.

Most proindependence leaders emerged from the ranks of Protestant-trained (and often ordained) mission graduates. Most notable was the Anglican priest Walter Lini (1942–1999), who became Vanuatu's first prime minister. Some anticolonial movements were also anti-Western or antimissionary. These included the John Frum cargo cult and the pro-"custom" Nagriamel headed by Jimmy Stevens (1926–1994). The latter spent a decade in prison for his role in an aborted secessionist campaign in the lead-up to independence.

A major challenge to Vanuatu's nationalism and development is overcoming the divisions inherited by the condominial rule, particularly that between Anglophones and Francophones. Prominent Francophone politicians include Maxime Carlot Korman (b. 1941), Jean-Marie Léyé (b. 1932), and Serge Vohor (b. 1955). Anglophone leaders who have tried to succeed the late Walter Lini are John Bani (b. 1941), Donald Kalpokas (b. 1943), and Barak Sope (b. 1951). Political parties have nevertheless created Anglophone–Francophone alliances. France's role as a regional power is periodically contested in Vanuatu's foreign policy, while Australia represents the most significant Anglophone counterweight.

SEE ALSO *Empire, British; Empire, French; Melanesia; Missions, in the Pacific.*

BIBLIOGRAPHY

Beasant, John. *The Santo Rebellion, An Imperial Reckoning.* Honolulu: University of Hawaii Press, 1984.

Bresnihan, Brian J., and Keith Woodward, eds. *Tufala Gavman, Reminiscences from the Anglo-French Condominium of the New Hebrides.* Suva, Fiji: University of the South Pacific, 2002.

Miles, William F. S. *Bridging Mental Boundaries in a Postcolonial Microcosm: Identity and Development in Vanuatu.* Honolulu: University of Hawaii Press, 1998.

William F. S. Miles

VESPUCCI, AMERIGO
1451–1512

The continent of America was named after the explorer Amerigo Vespucci, who was born on March 9, 1451, in Florence, Italy. He was the third of four sons of Nastagio and Elisabetta Vespucci, whose family was influential in the city-state that was governed by the Medici family, for whom Amerigo Vespucci later worked. He was well educated and developed interests in astronomy, geometry, physics, mathematics, and maps. These interests also fostered a desire for travel. From 1478 to 1480 Vespucci was attached to the Florentine embassy in Paris, France. In 1492 he left Florence for Seville to look after Medici interests in Spain. This was the same year in which the New World was "discovered" by Christopher Columbus, whose explorations were much admired by Vespucci. At the age of forty-one, Vespucci became director of a mercantile company that supplied ships for long journeys, including the many voyages of discovery that were taking place at this time.

How many voyages Vespucci undertook is disputed; it could have been as many as six. In any case, the earliest voyages were under the Spanish flag, and those of 1501 and 1503 were under the Portuguese flag. Vespucci began his first voyage to the New World on May 10, 1497, and returned in 1498. His company comprised three ships, provided by King Ferdinand of Castille, and explored the north coast of South America with a landing in either Brazil or Guiana. During this first voyage he also sailed into the Caribbean and then west toward Costa Rica; after following the Mexican Gulf coast and going past Florida, the company sailed north and eventually reached the Gulf of St Lawrence. On his second voyage, which departed Cadiz on May 16, 1499, Vespucci served as navigator, and was accompanied by Alonso de Ojeda and Juan de la Cosa. The expedition touched the Cape Verde Islands off the coast of Africa, explored the northeast coast of South America, including the mouth of the Amazon River, and visited the Caribbean islands of Hispaniola and Cuba, as well as the Bahamas. During this voyage Vespucci also used his mathematical and cartographical skills to calculate the circumference of the earth to within fifty miles.

Soon after the return to Spain in 1500, another voyage was planned and on May 14, 1501, Vespucci departed from Lisbon. This expedition explored the southeastern coast of South America, including the Rio de la Plata, and the southern coast to within 400 miles of Tierra del Fuego, the last southerly land before Antarctica. His fourth voyage was made with Gonzalo Coelho and departed Lisbon on June 19, 1503. These latter voyages led Vespucci to realize that the New World was not Asia/India, the goal of Columbus and other contemporary explorers. His revelation led European mapmakers to redraw maps of the world, among them the German cartographer Martin Waldseemuller, whose proposal to call the newly discovered continent "America" immortalized Vespucci. In 1505 and in 1507 Vespucci undertook two further voyages with Juan de la Cosa in search of gold, pearls, and wood.

Vespucci's contribution to European knowledge of the New World also took the form of letters to contacts in Europe and written descriptions of indigenous peoples of South America and their cultural and agricultural practices. His expeditions facilitated commerce between the New and Old Worlds and the annexation of colonies. Vespucci became a naturalized citizen of Spain in 1505, the same year in which he married Maria Cerezo. In 1508 he was declared Pilot Major of Spain, a distinguished position that he occupied until his death from malaria in Seville on February 22, 1512.

SEE ALSO *Columbus, Christopher; European Explorations in South America.*

BIBLIOGRAPHY

Pohl, Frederick J. *Amerigo Vespucci, Pilot Major.* New York: Octagon, 1966.

Ray, Kurt. *Amerigo Vespucci: Italian Explorer.* New York: Rosen, 2003.

A. M. Mannion

VIRGINIA COMPANY

The Virginia Company was formed in 1606 to restart English colonial ambitions in North America after the failure of the Roanoke colony in the 1580s. Its aims were broadly similar to those that had motivated the first settlement attempts at Roanoke a generation earlier. Among those aims were the discovery of a short route to Asia (the Northwest Passage); to ease English dependence on imported goods from Europe by growing and shipping produce from America; to provide raw materials such as timber or precious metals that were valued in England; to provide an outlet for a surplus population in England; to reestablish the English claim to North America in the face of French and Dutch interest in settlement; and to prove that the Americas were not a Spanish or Catholic monopoly.

The Virginia Company was a joint-stock company, with investors sharing the risks and the potential profits of colonization, and was closely modeled on the East India Company that had been founded just six years earlier. Although many of those investing in the Virginia Company were merchants with a strong commercial drive for profits, leading politicians and nobles eager to promote English imperial ambitions were also shareholders. The initial charter granted to the Virginia Company in 1606 actually distinguished between two groups of investors, one based in London and the other in Plymouth. Each was given a distinct geographic area to settle in: The London Company was allocated the land between 34 and 41 degrees North, whereas the Plymouth Company was allocated land between 38 and 45 degrees North. Although the Plymouth Company made a short-lived attempt to colonize in what later became New England in 1607–1908, the main colonization effort made by the Virginia Company was that of the London Company in Chesapeake Bay.

The Virginia Company of London was led by men such as Sir George Somers (1554–1610), who had experience fighting the Spanish in the Caribbean; Richard Hakluyt (1552–1616), whose *Principal Navigations, Voyages, and Discoveries of the English Nation* had raised the profile of colonization among the English elite; Sir Thomas Smith (1558–1625), also involved in the East India Company; and Captain Edward Maria Wingfield (1560–1613), a soldier with experience fighting the Spanish in the Netherlands. These men had powerful connections with merchants and politicians in London, which ensured that money and supplies were far more forthcoming than had been the case with the Roanoke Colony.

As a joint-stock company, the Virginia Company received no royal finance, but that did not mean the monarchy was completely sidelined from the project. Joint control of the Virginia Company was entrusted to two councils of thirteen individuals, one based in London and appointed by King James I (1566–1625), the other residing in Virginia and appointed by the company. The latter also was permitted to elect the colony's governor.

It was under these conditions that the company successfully recruited 144 men to journey to Virginia in the spring of 1607, but the earliest years of the colony

Landing at Jamestown. *In 1607 the Virginia Company sent three ships to the Atlantic Coast of North America. Those onboard established the Jamestown settlement in present-day Virginia.* © BETTMANN/CORBIS. REPRODUCED BY PERMISSION.

were plagued by poor leadership in Virginia and high mortality rates among settlers. The second charter issued in 1609 altered the political structures of the Virginia Company significantly. James surrendered his role in the company's affairs, in part to allow him to disavow the Virginia Company if they overantagonized Spain, and the Governor became an appointee of the company in London. The changes led to a successful share issue among London's merchants and trade guilds, and the company rapidly equipped a new fleet led by Sir Thomas Gates (1585–1621), with another to follow led by Lord Delaware (1577–1618) in 1610.

The terrible conditions of the "Starving Time" during the winter of 1609–1610 nearly led to the colony being abandoned, and serious doubts were raised in London about the long-term viability and profitability of the colony despite the publication of a number of promotional tracts designed to encourage migration. Lord Delaware had to return to England because of his failing health, which led to a financial low point for the

Virginia Company in 1613. The third and final charter of the Virginia Company, issued in 1612, permitted the establishment of a lottery that eventually became the company's main source of income, since few new investors were forthcoming given the dismal prospects of Virginia.

Experiments with tobacco provided the first hints that the colony might have a profitable future, and by 1614 the first shipments of tobacco from Virginia arrived in London. The crop would be the saving of the colony, since the fabulous profits to be made attracted new migrants. While recognizing the benefits of a cash crop to the viability of the colony, the Virginia Company also tried to prevent overproduction and to promote economic diversity. Unfortunately, oversupply eventually led to a collapse in the price of tobacco in the early 1620s and economic instability throughout the colony.

In 1616 the company paid a dividend to its shareholders of 50 acres of land in Virginia per share. A year later the company extended its use of free land in an attempt to restart colonization by instituting the head-right of 50 acres to go to whomever bore the costs of passage to the New World. This policy encouraged the growth of the system of indentured labor, with the wealthy paying for the passage of workers in return for seven years of free labor. Moreover, in response to the negative publicity that was generated by those returning from Virginia, the company permitted the election of a House of Burgesses in 1619, giving settlers a direct voice in their government.

With these changes and a new man in charge of the Virginia Company, Sir Edwin Sandys (1561–1629), 3,500 people left England for Virginia between 1619 and 1622. However, internal divisions among company officials, and an inadequate response to the 1622 massacre of colonists by local Native Americans, showed how weak the Virginia Company actually was. In 1623 the Privy Council ordered an inquiry into the company's affairs and on May 24, 1624, the charter was recalled and the Virginia Company was officially disbanded.

SEE ALSO *Colonization and Companies; Company of New France; Conquests and Colonization; Massachusetts Bay Company; Tobacco Cultivation and Trade.*

BIBLIOGRAPHY

Craven, Wesley Frank. *The Virginia Company of London, 1606–1624.* Charlottesville: University Press of Virginia, 1957.

Morgan, Edmund. *American Slavery, American Freedom: The Ordeal of Colonial Virginia.* New York: Norton, 1975.

Tim Lockley

VOC (VERENIGDE OOST-INDISCHE COMPAGNIE)

SEE *Dutch United East India Company*

W

WAITANGI, DECLARATION OF INDEPENDENCE

In August 1839 the British Colonial Secretary, Lord Normanby, issued instructions for a treaty to be concluded between the British Crown and the Maori chiefs of New Zealand. The instructions were prompted by a growing British population in New Zealand (around 2,000 by the end of 1839) that was effectively beyond the scope of British law. The resulting Treaty of Waitangi was first signed on February 6, 1840, and by September of that year around 542 chiefs had put their names to the agreement.

In the Treaty's English text, Maori ceded sovereignty to the Crown, but whether this was sovereignty over Europeans in the colony, or over Maori as well, is subject to debate. The English text also guaranteed Maori full possession of their lands and fisheries, and gave them the same rights as British subjects.

However, there were discrepancies in the Maori version of the Treaty, which was translated by the Anglican missionary Henry Williams. Whether Williams deliberately mistranslated the Treaty is in dispute, but in the Maori version, the chiefs ceded some form of government to the Crown, while retaining their chieftainship—an arrangement that, ironically, was tantamount to a form of sovereignty.

Not all chiefs signed the Treaty, and it is unlikely that every signatory fully comprehended its provisions. Despite this, on May 1840, William Hobson, the colony's Governor and one of the authors of the Treaty, proclaimed British sovereignty over the entire country—satisfied that sufficient Maori endorsement of the Treaty had been received.

SEE ALSO *Pacific, European Presence in; New Zealand.*

BIBLIOGRAPHY

Moon, Paul. *Te Ara Ki Te Tiriti: The Path to the Treaty of Waitangi.* Auckland, New Zealand: David Ling, 2002.

Orange, Claudia. *The Treaty of Waitangi.* Wellington, New Zealand: Bridget Williams, 1987.

Paul Moon

WARS AND EMPIRES

As the fifteenth century was drawing to a close, the nations of western Europe began a process of expansion that would lead, over the next several centuries, to the development of colonial empires in the Americas, Asia, and Africa. The urge to explore, conquer, and settle beyond the boundaries of Europe was manifested in the medieval Crusades to the Middle East, but the major stimulus to overseas expansion came from the discovery in southern and eastern Asia of exotic and valuable goods, especially spices, that became prized objects of trade. The desire of monarchs and merchants in western Europe to gain direct access to these commodities, avoiding Italian and Arab middlemen, encouraged competition to open new sea routes and establish overseas colonies, justified by a commitment to spread the doctrines of Christianity.

The Portuguese and Spanish were leaders in exploration eastward and westward from Europe, and in the

English Fire Ships Attack the Spanish Armada. *Colonization halted briefly during the years of conflict between Spain and England and the appearance in 1588 of the Spanish Armada. In this engraving, England's "fire ships" are shown infiltrating the Armada near Calais, France.* HULTON ARCHIVE/GETTY IMAGES. REPRODUCED BY PERMISSION.

sixteenth century they created great maritime empires in Asia and the Americas. Other powers followed where they had led, and during the seventeenth and eighteenth centuries England, France, and the Netherlands established colonial dominions in the Americas.

The first real colonization began with Spain. Christopher Columbus (1451–1506) sailed west from Spain in 1492, believing the world was not as wide as it actually is at the equator. He thus "discovered" the Caribbean Islands rather than Japan and East Asia. Soon thereafter, other explorers sought a seaborne passage through or around the Americas and began to map the extensive coastlines of the New World.

Columbus's return to Spain in 1493 put Portugal and Spain on a potential collision course as King João II (1455–1495) of Portugal worried about the value of Portugal's expeditions around Africa, and Ferdinand (1452–1516) and Isabella (1451–1504) of Spain wanted to exploit Columbus's discovery. After appealing to the pope, and tensing for a fight, the Iberian neighbors recognized the need to compromise, and they signed the Treaty of Tordesillas in 1494. It established a line of demarcation, some 370 leagues west of the Cape Verde Islands. West of that line, Spain could establish colonies, and this included all of the New World except Brazil. East of the line of demarcation, Portugal could dominate in Africa and in Asia. The exact line was never clearly established, and the other western European nations did not feel bound by this pact. However, the Treaty of Tordesillas did reduce the chances of conflict between Spain and Portugal, and it created a boundary that was largely respected, with Spain concentrating on the New World and Portugal focusing on Africa and Asia.

European colonization was usually achieved by making war on native peoples. Between about 1500 and 1540, Spain gained a great empire in the Americas by engaging in several wars of conquest, of which the most famous were those conducted in Mexico and Peru. The Spanish wars of conquest invariably succeeded in overcoming much larger Indian forces, thanks to the superiority of European weaponry and other factors, including

Spanish efforts to make alliances with Indian kingdoms, nations, or groups in campaigns against their dominant Indian enemy. This was also true for the Portuguese in Brazil, and the French, English, and Dutch in North America. Spaniards and Portuguese were fighting Indians (with Indian and African assistance) throughout the colonial era. According to John Hemming, "All the Indian wars exploited fatal rivalries between tribes. No Portuguese ever took the field without masses of native auxiliaries to attack their traditional enemies" (1978, p. 178).

In general, the sixteenth-century wars of conquest between Europeans and Native Americans tended to be quite short and of relatively slight mortality (much greater mortality came from epidemic diseases). The fighting between the European colonial powers in the New World also occurred on a very small scale during the sixteenth century, being largely limited to raiding along Spanish trade routes and at poorly guarded ports. European contest for empire in the Americas became more serious in the seventeenth century, as the English and French settled areas neglected by Spain, and the Dutch briefly seized Portuguese territories in Brazil; nonetheless, these occupations were invariably peaceful, because Spain did not have the resources to resist

In 1519 Hernán Cortés (ca. 1484–1547), after participating in the conquest of Cuba, sailed to the coast of Mexico with six hundred soldiers, one hundred sailors, and some horses. He landed near present-day Veracruz, Mexico, and strengthened by Indian allies, he conquered the Aztecs in their capital of Tenochtitlán (now Mexico City). A decade after Cortés's conquest brought the lands and peoples of Mexico under Spanish rule, Francisco Pizarro (ca. 1475–1541) learned of the riches of the Inca empire. In 1533 he seized the Inca capital at Cuzco. Two years later he founded Lima, and thereby initiated the Spanish conquest and colonization of Peru. From these centers, the Spaniards fanned out into neighboring territories, often using violence to overcome native kings and take control of their lands and peoples, while at the same time unintentionally spreading a variety of Old World diseases that decimated the Native American populations of the New World and undermined their ability to resist.

The French moved into North America following the waterways and animals whose fur had value for coats and hats. Private companies had moved up the Saint Lawrence River by the end of the sixteenth century seeking valuable furs. In 1603 Samuel de Champlain (ca. 1570–1635) explored the area and founded Quebec. In the 1670s Louis Jolliet (1645–1700) moved along the lakes and rivers, found the headwaters of the Mississippi River, and floated down to the Ohio River, claiming the entire basin for New France. The French sent few settlers, and fur trappers and soldiers frequently coupled with Native American women.

Finally, the English arrived, seeking to recreate parts of the societies they had left. The first English colony, established in 1587 on Roanoke Island off the coast of present-day North Carolina, disappeared mysteriously. In 1607 the English established a second colony at Jamestown in Virginia. In 1620 English Puritans seeking freedom to follow their religion settled at Plymouth Rock in Massachusetts. William Penn (1644–1718), a Quaker, spurred settlement of Pennsylvania in the 1680s, and during the mid-1600s Lord Baltimore (Cecil Calvert, ca. 1605–1675) established Maryland as a refuge for Catholics.

Settlers soon moved from Virginia into North Carolina, then to South Carolina, and thereafter across the Cumberland Gap into present-day Kentucky and the great lands across the Appalachian Mountains. There were small pockets of Dutch and Swedish settlement, but the English soon overran them. While Penn, a devout Quaker, signed treaties with Native Americans and tried to befriend them, relations between European settlers and Native Americans were generally difficult, marked by fighting, allegations of massacres, and profound cultural differences.

As Europe engaged in several hundred years of warfare, those conflicts evidenced themselves in the New World. During the late seventeenth and eighteenth centuries, European wars tended to spill over into the Americas, especially into the Caribbean, but increasingly into North America as well. Colonization halted briefly during the years of conflict between Spain and England and the appearance in 1588 of the Spanish Armada, a fleet of warships sent to invade England. Four major conflicts ensued in Europe; these were complemented by wars between the French and British colonists in North America.

The first three wars—King William's War (1689–1697), Queen Anne's War (1702–1713), and King George's War (1744–1748)—resulted in few changes in the colonies. The British gained Acadia (in eastern Canada) from the French during Queen Anne's War, and renamed it Nova Scotia. Generally, however, despite depredations along the thinly settled frontier between the British colonies in New England and French and Indian areas in French Canada, there was little change.

The fourth war, known as the French and Indian War (1754–1763) in America and the Seven Years' War (1756 to 1763) in Europe, resulted in a total British victory after the capture from the French of Fort Duquesne in Pennsylvania and Louisbourg in Nova Scotia in 1758, Quebec in 1759, and Montreal in

General Washington Captures Fort Duquesne. *The French and Indian War resulted in a total British victory after the capture from the French of several key forts, including Fort Duquesne in Pennsylvania in 1758. George Washington's men are shown in this nineteenth-century engraving raising the British flag at Fort Duquesne after seizing the fort from the French.* **HULTON ARCHIVE/ GETTY IMAGES. REPRODUCED BY PERMISSION.**

1760. France also subsequently ceded New France to Great Britain in the Treaty of Paris of 1763. Louisiana had been transferred to Spanish control a year earlier. When Europeans came to fight one another for empire in North America in the seventeenth and especially the eighteenth century, what are known as the "French and Indian" wars actually amounted to "European and Indian" wars that involved African and black soldiers, militia, and various rebels as well.

Britain amassed large debts during the French and Indian War, and expected its North American colony to pay its share for the removal of the French and Indian threat. The change in British policy met with strong colonial opposition, shaping a movement of protest and resistance that ultimately led to the American Revolution. From 1763 through 1775, it became increasingly clear that a mature English society and polity had developed in North America, and the bonds of empire were broken. Fighting between British soldiers and American colonists began in April 1775 at Lexington and Concord in Massachusetts, and thereafter a series of campaigns

indicated the depth of the challenge facing the British. After the surrender in 1777 of British General John Burgoyne (1723–1792) at Saratoga in New York, France openly supported the American rebels, and Great Britain found itself involved in a broader conflict. In 1783 Britain conceded independence to the thirteen colonies.

More important than the fate of Britain's North American colonies were the valuable island holdings in the Caribbean. There, slave labor helped satisfy profitable markets in sugar and other commodities that were rare in Europe. When enslaving Native Americans proved inadequate to labor demands, as it did for the Spanish in America, European nations engaged in a lively slave trade with West Africa, forcing the migration of millions of sub-Saharan Africans to the New World. In the sixteenth and seventeenth centuries, British privateers (ship captains chartered by the English Crown) preyed on Spanish treasure ships laden with gold and silver returning to Spain, although weather was as much a threat as piracy. Later, as sugar plantations spread, European navies led attacks on different islands to secure better port anchorages, to gain improved farm lands, and to defend other holdings.

The Napoleonic Wars of the late 1700s and early 1800s further weakened colonial power in the Americas. A slave rebellion begun in 1791 in Haiti eventually succeeded, and Haiti gained independence from France. Although the French received help from Spanish and British forces, none of whom were eager to see slave revolts hurt lucrative holdings in the Caribbean, the slave army, commanded mostly by Toussaint L'Ouverture (1743–1803), achieved its final victory at Vertiéres, and Napoléon Bonaparte (1769–1821) conceded Haitian independence in 1803. Without Haiti as a gateway, Napoléon forced the retransfer of Louisiana from Spain and then sold the vast territory between the Mississippi River and the Continental Divide, including the port of New Orleans, to the United States for $15 million.

As the Napoleonic Wars ended, and as the Congress of Vienna (1814–1815) sought to impose stability and restore the old order, the New World continued to evolve. Napoléon had sold French Louisiana and thus he created a potential juggernaut, which soon would push for West Coast ports and access to the Pacific Ocean. The Spanish Empire was straining at the seams, as Simón Bolívar (1783–1830) and José de San Martín (1778–1850) led independence movements that would liberate Central and South America. The nineteenth century would bring even greater changes to the New World. The "Indian wars" continued in the Americas until the late nineteenth century, not only in the United States, but in Mexico, Central America, Brazil, Argentina, and Chile.

SEE ALSO *Buccaneers; Treaty of Tordesillas.*

BIBLIOGRAPHY

Black, Jeremy. *Europe and the World, 1650–1830.* New York: Routledge, 2002.

Bray, Warwick, ed. *The Meeting of Two Worlds: Europe and the Americas, 1492–1650.* Oxford: Oxford University Press, 1993.

Curtin, Philip D. *The World and the West: The European Challenge and the Overseas Response in the Age of Empire.* New York: Cambridge University Press, 2000.

Daniels, Christine, and Michael V. Kennedy. *Negotiated Empires: Centers and Peripheries in the Americas, 1500–1820.* New York: Routledge, 2002.

Dunn, Richard S. *Sugar and Slaves: The Rise of the Planter Class in the English West Indies, 1624–1713.* Chapel Hill: University of North Carolina Press, 1972.

Hart, Jonathan Locke. *Comparing Empires: European Colonialism from Portuguese Expansion to the Spanish-American War.* New York: Palgrave MacMillan, 2003.

Hemming, John. *Red Gold: The Conquest of the Brazilian Indians.* Cambridge, MA: Harvard University Press, 1978. Rev. ed., London: Papermac, 1995.

Means, Philip Ainsworth. *The Spanish Main: Focus of Envy, 1492–1700.* New York: Scribner's, 1935.

Muldoon, James. *The Americas in the Spanish World Order: The Justification for Conquest in the Seventeenth Century.* Philadelphia: University of Pennsylvania Press, 1994.

Parry, J. H. *The Establishment of the European Hegemony, 1415–1715: Trade and Exploration in the Age of the Renaissance,* 3rd rev. ed. New York: Harper & Row, 1966.

Ringrose, David R. *Expansion and Global Interaction, 1200–1700.* New York: Longman, 2001.

Scammell, Geoffrey Vaughn. *The First Imperial Age: European Overseas Expansion, c. 1400–1715.* London: Unwin Hyman, 1989.

Schlesinger, Roger. *In the Wake of Columbus: The Impact of the New World on Europe, 1492–1650.* Wheeling, IL: Harlan Davidson, 1996.

Wesselring, H. L., ed. *Imperialism and Colonialism: Essays on the History of European Expansion.* Westport, CT: Greenwood Press, 1997.

Charles M. Dobbs

WARRANT CHIEFS, AFRICA

The British administrative system of indirect rule incorporated the indigenous elite in the administration of some African colonies. Although the powers of African collaborators have been exaggerated, British rule would have faced severe difficulties of finance and personnel if Africans were not employed to administer local regions. British officials were paid higher salaries and were available in very limited numbers.

In areas with centralized political institutions, such as the Buganda Kingdom in present-day Uganda and the Islamic emirates of northern Nigeria, the British employed a policy of indirect rule in which existing indigenous chiefs helped to govern Britain's African possessions. The indirect rule system was elevated to the level of an administrative ideology by Frederick Lugard (1858–1945), first colonial governor of Nigeria, and the system was applied vigorously to Nigeria and other colonial territories in Africa.

The warrant chief system emanated as a matter of necessity from the lack of preexisting chieftaincy traditions in some parts of Africa. There were parts of British colonial territories, such as the Igbo region of eastern Nigeria, which had no tradition of chieftaincy intuitions. The British appointed willing participants or collaborators and gave them "warrants" to act as local representatives of the British administration among their people. The French, Belgians, and Portuguese, practicing

British Colonial Administrators Meet with Nigerian Representatives. *During the colonial period in Africa, the British appointed African collaborators and gave them "warrants" to act as local representatives of the British among their people. This meeting between British administrators and African representatives took place in Lagos, Nigeria, in the early twentieth century.* © HULTON-DEUTSCH COLLECTION/CORBIS. REPRODUCED BY PERMISSION.

so-called direct administration, also appointed provincial chiefs to assistant in local administration. The appointment of warrant and provincial chiefs was an invention of traditions that have continued in different forms today.

The British failed to realize, however, that some parts of Africa were unfamiliar with the idea of "chiefs" or "kings." Among the Igbo, for example, decisions were made by protracted debate and general consensus. The new powers given to the warrant chiefs and enhanced by the native court system led to an exercise of power and authority unprecedented in precolonial times. Warrant chiefs also used their power to accumulate wealth at the expense of their subjects. Through this process, colonial officials tended to create or recreate a patriarchal society because only men were appointed as warrant chiefs.

The appointment of warrant chiefs created significant problems and engendered large-scale resentment among African people. The warrant chiefs were hated because they were corrupt and arrogant. One of the most important acts of resistance to the warrant chief system

occurred among the Igbo of eastern Nigeria during the famous 1929 women's revolt in which thousands of peasant women protested against the introduction of taxes, the warrant chief system, and the low prices of agricultural produce emanating from the global depression of the late 1920s. The indirect rule and warrant chief systems were particularly foreign to existing political structures.

The women's protests, which started in Oloko Bende Division in eastern Nigeria, quickly spread throughout the Owerri and Calabar provinces, culminating in massive revolts called *Ogu Umunwanyi* or the "Women's War" among the Igbo. By December 1929, when troops restored order in the region, the women had destroyed ten native courts and damaged a number of others, and about fifty-five women were killed by the colonial troops. In addition, the houses of warrant chiefs and native court personnel were attacked, European factories at Imo River, Aba, Mbawsi, and Amata were looted, and prisons were attacked and prisoners released.

The women called for the revocation of the warrant chief system, the removal of warrant chiefs whom they accused of high-handedness, bribery, and corruption, and their replacement with indigenous clan heads appointed by the people rather than by the British.

Throughout late December 1929 and early January 1930, the commission of inquiry set up to investigate the remote and immediate causes of the women's movement sat in over thirty locations throughout the eastern region to collect evidence and recommend punishment for the actors or their communities. Nevertheless, the 1929 Women's War brought about fundamental reforms in British colonial administration. The British finally abolished the warrant chief system and reassessed the nature of colonial rule among the natives of Nigeria. Several colonial administrators condemned the prevailing administrative system and agreed to the demand for urgent reforms based on the indigenous system. Court tribunals that incorporated the indigenous system of government that had prevailed before colonial rule were introduced to replace the old warrant chief system.

SEE ALSO *Britain's African Colonies; Igbo Women's War; Indirect Rule, Africa.*

BIBLIOGRAPHY

Afigbo, A. E. *The Warrant Chiefs: Indirect Rule in South-Eastern Nigeria, 1891–1929.* London: Longman, 1972.

Isichei, Elizabeth. *A History of the Igbo People.* London: Macmillan, 1976.

Chima J. Korieh

WESTERN THOUGHT, MIDDLE EAST

The interest taken by the Islamic world in Western thought prior to the colonial period was selective and spasmodic. The expansion of Islam in the centuries following the death of the Prophet Muhammad in 632 C.E. quickly brought Muslims into contact with populations rooted in other cultural traditions, such as those of ancient Greece and Persia, and during the Abbasid period (749–1258 C.E.), an institution known as the House of Wisdom (Bayt al-Hikma) was established in Baghdad to facilitate the translation of Greek and other texts.

A large number of important works were translated into Arabic during this period, often through the intermediate language of Syriac, including works by Aristotle (384–322 B.C.E.), Plato (ca. 427–347 B.C.E.), and Ptolemy (second century C.E.), but the selection of works was primarily practical and utilitarian. Greek learning was translated when it was felt that it could supply a

need or serve the interests of those in positions of authority, either religious or political. Many works of philosophy, mathematics, medicine, and other sciences were accordingly translated into Arabic, but little or no attention was paid to works of Greek literature, from which the Muslims felt they had nothing to learn.

At the other end of the Islamic world, Islamic Spain provided a forum for the cross-fertilization of cultures (Muslim, Jewish, and Christian) from the eighth century C.E. to the fall of Granada in 1492—a phenomenon that has been much studied, though its precise ramifications remain in some cases obscure. Despite its obvious importance for the history of contacts between Islam and the West, however, Islamic Spain was more significant as a channel for the transmission of Greek and Islamic ideas to Christian Europe than for any transmission in the opposite direction. Contact between the two cultures of a different kind was provided by the Crusades, a series of Western military expeditions to the Holy Land between 1095 and 1270, but these are of little or no significance in the present context.

THE OTTOMANS

From the fifteenth to the early twentieth century, much of the Middle East and North Africa remained under the control of the Ottoman Empire, centered on Constantinople (Istanbul, Turkey). Early Ottoman rulers seemed eager to learn from European ideas, both contemporary and classical. Sultan Mehmed II (1432–1481), for example, who had conquered Constantinople in 1453, had the works of Ptolemy and Plutarch (ca. 46–120 C.E.) translated into Turkish, and gathered Italian and Greek scholars around him at his court.

These initiatives, however, lost their impetus as the Ottoman Empire generally lost its vitality, so that, despite contacts on various levels, intellectual exchanges between Europe and the Ottoman Middle East were not of major significance during the succeeding period. It was not until the latter part of the eighteenth century that Sultan Selim III (r. 1789–1807) made serious attempts to reform the empire, by then threatened with economic and administrative chaos, on the basis of European ideas, opening embassies in major European capitals in order to promote links, and opening the way for the formation of a new educated class of reform-minded intellectuals later in the nineteenth century.

Meanwhile, within the Ottoman Empire, particular ethnic and religious groups had, for different reasons, been maintaining regular intellectual contacts of their own with their counterparts in the West. The Christian Maronite community, centered on Lebanon, had had a college in Rome since 1584, and members of that community were later to play a prominent role in the *nahda*

Napoléon in Egypt. *Napoléon Bonaparte's expedition to Egypt in 1798 gave large numbers of a Middle Eastern population direct exposure to Western ideas in practice. The French emperor is shown in this illustration gazing at the Great Sphinx near Giza.* © BETTMANN/CORBIS. REPRODUCED BY PERMISSION.

(the Arab literary and cultural revival) of the nineteenth century.

NAPOLÉON IN EGYPT, 1798–1801

Although a case can be made for other dates as the starting point for the history of the modern Middle East, there can be little doubt that the expedition of Napoléon Bonaparte (1769–1821) to Egypt in 1798 played a major role in laying the foundations for the relationships—intellectual and otherwise—that subsequently developed between the West and the central Islamic world. Itself largely a product of Anglo–French colonial rivalry, Napoléon's expedition for the first time gave large numbers of a Middle Eastern population direct exposure to Western ideas in practice: these included not only intellectual and cultural institutions, such as the printing press, newspapers, and Western-style theater, but also representative institutions, such as administrative councils, embodying the ideals of democracy and of the French Revolution (1789–1799). Meanwhile, teams of scholars and savants roamed Egypt constructing a detailed survey of the country, subsequently published in several volumes as the *Description de l'Egypte* (1810–1829).

The reaction of educated Egyptians to these developments was, not surprisingly, an ambiguous one. The most prominent Egyptian intellectual to have witnessed the invasion, 'Abd al-Rahman al-Jabarti (1753–1825), expressed contempt for the French as materialists and the enemies of Islam; in other passages of his account, however, he speaks with enthusiasm not only of their scientific and cultural achievements, but also of their sense of justice and fair play, which he regarded as superior to that of the Ottomans. This ambiguous attitude toward the ideas of the West—a combination of suspicion and admiration—forms the starting point for many of the subsequent discussions during the nineteenth century, when Muslim reformers and the champions of secularism alike strove to reformulate the guiding principles of Middle Eastern society in the light of the perceived new challenges of the West.

EARLY VIEWS OF EUROPE

These nineteenth-century debates were fueled by an interchange of ideas in which travel, both east to west and west to east, played a large part. In Egypt, the reign of Muhammad 'Ali (1769–1849), who established himself as a virtually independent ruler in the wake of the departure of the French, and who modeled himself to some extent on Selim III, saw foreign instructors imported into Egypt to provide the military and administrative expertise required to run the country. At the same time, Egyptian students were dispatched to study in the West, mainly France. On their return, these students were often required to translate the textbooks from which they had studied—a process that laid the foundations for the nineteenth-century translation movement that played a significant part in the transmission of Western ideas to the Islamic world during this period.

Among the most interesting of these early travelers to the West was Rifa'a Rafi'al-Tahtawi (1801–1871), a religious imam who served as leader of the first Egyptian educational mission to France from 1826 to 1831. On returning to Egypt, he embarked on a distinguished career in public service that included the directorship of the School of Translation. His *Takhlis al-ibriz ila talkhis? Bariz* (The refinement of gold for the summary of Paris) (1869), which offers a lively account of his encounter with Western society, set a pattern for many subsequent works, both autobiographical and fictional, inspired by visits to Europe. Al-Tahtawi's account of his stay in French society, which included meetings with some of the leading Orientalists of the day, is often surprisingly sympathetic, and his writing reveals the influence of wide reading in the works of eighteenth-century French thought, including Voltaire (1694–1778), Jean-Jacques Rousseau (1712–1778), and Montesquieu (1689–1755).

Although al-Tahtawi's views on the nature of the state and the relationship between ruler and ruled—topics treated at some length in *Manahij al-albab al-misriyya fi mabahij al-adab al-'as?riyya* ("The ways of Egyptian minds in the delights of modern manners") (1869)—remained essentially rooted in the Islamic tradition, his writings introduce a number of themes that were shortly to be commonplaces among Arab and Muslim thinkers. These included the idea that within the Islamic community *(umma)* there could be national communities demanding the loyalty of the subject, and the suggestion that the Islamic world should not shy away from adopting modern European science in order to adapt to the modern world. Implicit in much discussion of this sort was a central problematic: how to reconcile the belief in a divinely revealed religion and the all-embracing set of religious law (the Islamic *shari'a*) that accompanied it, with the idea that laws should be made by governments in the interests of their subjects? Or, to pose the problem more generally, how could the practice of Islam be reconciled with the needs of the modern world? And if Islam had claim to be the definitive divine revelation, how was it that the Islamic world had fallen behind Europe in so many material respects?

It was not only in Egypt that these questions were acquiring an importance in the middle years of the nineteenth century. In Tunis, the capital of Tunisia, the reformist Khayr al-Din al-Tunisi (1822/3–1889) produced a monumental work, *Aqwam al-masalik fī ma'rifat al-mamalik* (1867), in which he reviewed the history and political and economic structures of a number of European countries, as well as those of the Ottoman Empire itself. In the most interesting part of the work, the *Muqaddima* (meaning "Introduction," a title borrowed from his illustrious fellow-countryman Ibn Khaldun [1332–1406]), the author argued in favor of trying to emulate the progress of the West, which in his view sprang from a combination of representative government and the fruits of the Industrial Revolution.

In the meantime, similar sets of questions were being addressed in a somewhat different form further east by members of Christian communities centered on Lebanon and Syria, whose perspective, unencumbered by the weight of Islamic tradition, was in some respects more flexible. Among the most prominent of these were the ruggedly individualist Faris (later Ahmad Faris) al-Shidyaq (1804–1887) and Butrus al-Bustani (1819–1893), a member of the extensive Bustani family who collectively were to play a leading role in the nineteenth-century *nahda* (revival) in its Syro-Lebanese form.

One of the most fascinating characters of the nineteenth-century Middle East, al-Shidyaq's loyalties embraced at least two sects of Christianity before his conversion to Islam around 1865. His *al-Saq 'ala al-Saq* (Leg Over Leg) (1855), which has been likened to the sixteenth-century narrative *Gargantua and Pantagruel* by the French satirist François Rabelais (ca. 1483–1553), has some claim to be considered the first attempt at modern fiction in Arabic. For his part, many of al-Bustani's ideas echoed those of Ottoman reformists such as the Young Turks—though for obvious reasons, Lebanese Christian intellectuals generally laid more emphasis on notions of religious tolerance and equality than their Muslim counterparts elsewhere.

RELIGIOUS REFORM AND SECULAR THOUGHT

The religious strand implicit or explicit in many of these debates found perhaps its most eloquent expression in the lives and works of the two most prominent religious reformers active in nineteenth-century Egypt, Jamal al-Din al-Afghani (1839–1897) and his disciple Muhammad 'Abduh (1849–1905), whose lives were closely intertwined. The origins of al-Afghani are slightly obscure, but as his name suggests he certainly hailed from the eastern part of the Islamic world, from either Iran or Afghanistan. His roving life included spells not only in the West but also in India, and both his life and his work (though he in fact wrote rather little) have a strongly anti-imperialist tone to them. In 1883 al-Afghani published a vigorous article taking issue with the argument of French historian Ernest Renan (1823–1892) on the incompatibility of Islam and science, and it was largely through al-Afghani that the modern European concept of civilization, as expounded by French historian and statesman François Guizot (1787–1874) and others, reached the Islamic world.

Al-Afghani's disciple, the Egyptian Muhammad 'Abduh, was not only a less flamboyant figure than his master but also a more systematic thinker. His association with al-Afghani started when the latter was lecturing at the traditionalist Azhar University in Cairo in around 1869. The two men's collaboration found its most obvious expression in their cooperation on the short-lived weekly periodical *al-'Urwa al-Wuthqa* (the Firmest Bond), published in Paris from March to October 1884, which struck a note that simultaneously embraced both anti-imperialism and Islamic reformism.

Muhammad 'Abduh's career was intertwined with the politics of the time, including the resistance to British interference expressed in the 'Urabi Rebellion of 1882. He was for a time imprisoned, but in later life he became a much respected figure both in his native Egypt and beyond. His thought, which found its expression in a commentary on the Qur'an, as well as in an important theological treatise, *Risalat al-tawhid* (Treatise on the Unity of God, 1897), laid emphasis on the reinterpretation of the Islamic *shari'a* in the light of modern conditions, with considerable stress on the idea of the public interest, clearly derived from contemporary European thinking.

Although never universally accepted, Muhammad 'Abduh's influence was undoubtedly greater than that of any other Islamic thinker of his period, and his ideas found echoes in groups of intellectual Muslims in many parts of the Islamic world, from North Africa to Iraq and even beyond. Some thinkers, such as the Syrian Rashid Rida (1865–1935), may be regarded primarily as Islamic modernists, whose work lay in extending and carrying forward the ideas of al-Afghani and 'Abduh without radically changing their direction.

At the same time, however, a number of other, more radical intellectual currents were beginning to gain ground in the region. As in the previous generation, Middle Eastern Christians—whose acquaintance with modern Western ideas had in many cases been fostered through missionary schools—were prominent in this process. Two Arab thinkers in particular may be mentioned in this context: Shibli Shumayyil (1853–1917) and Farah Antun (1874–1922), both of whom made major contributions to Arab secularist thought of the period.

The Syrian-born Greek Catholic Shibli Shumayyil, who trained and practiced as a doctor, played a prominent role during the 1880s and later in popularizing modern European scientific theories, including those of Charles Darwin (1809–1882), but he also wrote extensively on society more generally, many of his ideas being derived from European thinkers such as Herbert Spencer (1820–1903) and Georg Büchner (1813–1837), and he was mainly responsible for spreading the concepts of socialism widely in the Arab world.

This strand of thinking, which openly espoused Darwinian and Freudian ideas, was carried forward by, among others, the Egyptian Copt Salama Musa (1887–1958), who had studied in England, where he made the acquaintance of the playwright and critic Bernard Shaw (1856–1950) and the novelist H. G. Wells (1866–1946) and adopted the philosophy of the Fabian Society, a socialist organization founded in 1884. Marxist ideas were by this time circulating widely among groups of Middle Eastern intellectuals. Although the popularity of Marxism in its more extreme forms has been limited in the Middle East by its often aggressively atheistic associations, this more moderate form of socialism as espoused by Shumayyil and Salama Musa was later to underlie the social and economic structures of a large part of the Arab world following independence in the latter half of the twentieth century.

Unsurprisingly, Shumayyil's ideas, which he advanced with considerable vigor, provoked controversy and opposition among the more conservative elements of the intelligentsia. Equally controversial was the Lebanese-born Farah Antun, whose omnivorous interests may be gauged from the range of his translations, which included not only Rousseau's novel *Émile* (1762), but also German philosopher Friedrich Nietzsche's (1844–1900) *Also sprach Zarathustra* (Thus Spake Zarathustra, 1883–1885), Renan's *Vie de Jésus* (Life of Jesus, 1863), and works by Maxim Gorky (1868–1936), Anatole France (1844–1924), Chateaubriand (1768–1848), and others. An admirer of Renan, Shumayyil's views on the medieval Arab philosopher Ibn Rushd (Averroës, 1126–1198) provoked a vigorous confrontation with Muhammad 'Abduh in which the relative merits of Islam and Christianity played a prominent part.

In the meantime, other followers and disciples of Muhammad 'Abduh were developing his ideas in a variety of different directions. Qasim Amin (1863–1908), like Salama Musa, had studied in both England and France, where his experiences and exposure to the liberal intellectual tradition of Europe prompted him to propose changes in the status of women in Egyptian society.

Although his proposals were in fact rather modest, they predictably provoked controversy among his more conservative colleagues. Another of Muhammad 'Abduh's followers, Ahmad Lutfi al-Sayyid (1872–1963), played a prominent role in the development of a modern educational system in Egypt, as well as making contributions to political life and to journalism.

The extent to which the culture of contemporary Arabic thought and writing was by now being influenced by Western ideas can perhaps be most clearly seen, however, in the career and output of the great Egyptian litterateur Taha Husayn (1889–1973), who had learned Greek and Latin in France, attending courses at the Sorbonne in Paris in classical civilization, history, philosophy, and psychology. Much influenced by his Orientalist teachers, who included Eno Littmann, Carlo Alfonso Nallino, and David Santillana, he set out to apply the principles of Western literary criticism to pre-Islamic poetry, provoking an outcry among his conservative colleagues with his claim (no longer accepted) that much pre-Islamic poetry had been forged. Taha Husayn subsequently went on to argue, contrary to much contemporary nationalist debate, that Egypt had always belonged to a wider Mediterranean civilization—in effect, arguing that the future of Egypt lay with Europe rather than the Arab or Islamic world.

NATIONALISM

Religion excepted, the most important debate, or rather, series of debates, preoccupying the Middle East during the last years of the nineteenth and first half of the twentieth century revolved around different varieties of nationalism. Space does not permit a detailed discussion of this complex phenomenon, but the general political and intellectual context may be summed up briefly in a number of interrelated factors: the progressive weakening of the Ottoman Empire in the nineteenth century, prompting both dissent and a number of attempts at internal reform in response to threats from Europe; the growth of European influence on, and control over, many parts of the region, as exemplified by Napoléon's expedition of 1798 and by the British occupation of Egypt from 1881; and the growing sense of self-identity of the various ethnic groups who formed a large proportion of the population of the Ottoman Empire. The last of these factors can be paralleled in several parts of Europe during the same period.

A notable feature of the various national movements active around this time was the extent to which they cross-fertilized each other intellectually. Unlike in India, for example, nationalism in the Arab Middle East was almost always formulated in terms derived from European experience, and its emergence and

development was closely bound up with events in the Ottoman Empire itself, including the progress of the reformist Young Turks (Turkish: Jöntürkler) movement.

Influenced by positivist thinkers such as Auguste Comte (1798–1857) and Georg Büchner, the Young Turks—a loose coalition of various reform groups—had their origins in the Istanbul student communities of the late 1880s. An initial conspiracy to unseat the authoritarian Sultan Abdülhamid II (1842–1918) was uncovered before it could be put into effect and several of the group's leaders fled to Paris. Following the formation of the Committee of Union and Progress (CUP) in Turkey, they succeeded in establishing a constitutional government in 1908, consolidating their power in 1913. Despite some success in internal reform, however, including education and the status of women, the Young Turks proved inept in the handling of foreign affairs, and it was only after the collapse of the Ottoman Empire at the beginning of the 1920s that Mustafa Kemal (Atatürk, 1881–1938) was able to begin to articulate a fully modern Turkish nationalism based on European models.

Arab nationalist thinkers such as Sati' al-Husri (1880–1968) drew on the ideas of Ziya Gökalp (ca. 1875–1924), the Young Turks' theoretician, together with those of such European thinkers as Johann Fichte (1762–1814) and Johann Herder (1744–1803), to produce a sort of Romantic cultural nationalism that later found expression in different countries in various forms, many of them modeled on the regime of Gamal Abdel Nasser (1918–1970) that came to power in Egypt in 1952.

A somewhat different slant to the Arab nationalist movement was provided by the Syrian Michel 'Aflaq (1910–1989), whose four years of study in France had enabled him to develop a wide-ranging acquaintance with European history and philosophy—studies that underlay the foundation in 1947 of the Ba'th (Renaissance) Party, which subsequently assumed power in Syria and Iraq. In Turkey itself, the final collapse of the Ottoman Empire in the wake of World War I (1914–1918) was followed by the establishment of an officially secular state modeled on European principles, and by the introduction of language reform measures including the substitution of Latin script for the Arabic alphabet. But these measures were nowhere followed in the Arab world.

By contrast with the Arab regions of the Middle East, European influences on Iran, initially at least, came mainly through Russia rather than the countries of western Europe. Russian influence in the area increased dramatically following the Russian invasion of 1826, and the country soon found itself in an unenviable position, sandwiched between the competing economic, political, and diplomatic rivalries of Russia to the north and

British imperial interests in the Indian Subcontinent to the east. The economic and social chaos brought about by World War I was followed by the ousting of the Qajar regime, to be replaced in 1925 by the Pahlavis, who embarked on a program of rapid westernization, accompanied in later years by an increasingly unrestrained apparatus of repression.

The frustration of many Iranians, not least the religious hierarchy, at what appeared to be an increasing loss of national identity was expressed most vividly, if a little belatedly, by the writer Jalal Al-e Ahmad (1923–1969) in his polemical work *Gharbzadegi* (an untranslatable term, broadly equivalent to "westoxication" or "westomania"), first published in 1962. Banned by the Pahlavis, the work circulated underground until the Islamic Revolution of 1979, when it quickly acquired almost cult status—its radically anti-Western tone echoing some aspects of the ideas of Ayatollah Ruhollah Khomeini (1900–1989). It remains among the most controversial and thought-provoking essays to emerge from modern Iran, and arguably, indeed, from the whole of the Islamic Middle East.

POSTSCRIPT

An interesting twist to debates in the Arab world on relations with the West in the period following World War II (1939–1945) was provided by the existentialist philosophy of Jean-Paul Sartre (1905–1980), whose idea of commitment, in both literary and political senses, appeared to mirror the mood of the Arab Middle East following the Arab defeat in the Palestine War of 1948 and the Egyptian Free Officers' Revolt of 1952. Commitment *(iltizam)* quickly became the dominant literary and cultural mood of the period, echoing the Romanticism—again, largely derived from Western models—of the interwar years.

The next sea change in the prevailing mood among Arab intellectuals coincided with the Arab defeat in the Six-Day War of 1967, which initiated a period of widespread bitterness and frustration among Arab writers and other intellectuals in the region. More recently, globalization, the rise of Islamic fundamentalism, and the failure to find a lasting solution to the Arab–Israeli conflict have again radically shifted both the tone and the focus of the Middle Eastern response to the West. Despite that, it is arguable that the underlying problematic continues to be the one that dogged Muslim intellectuals in the nineteenth century—how to adapt to modern civilization while remaining true to the revelation of Islam.

SEE ALSO *Education, Middle East; Empire, Ottoman; Ideology, Political, Middle East.*

BIBLIOGRAPHY

al-Jabarti, 'Abd al-Rahman. *Al-Jabarti's Chronicle of the First Seven Months of the French Occupation of Egypt: Muharram-Rajab 1213, 15 June–December 1798: Tarikh muddat al-Faransis bi-Misr.* Edited and translated by S. Moreh. Leiden, Netherlands: Brill, 1975.

Al-e Ahmad, Jalal. *Plagued by the West (Gharbzadegi).* Translated by Paul Sprachman. Delmar, NY: Caravan, 1982.

Gökalp, Ziya. *Turkish Nationalism and Western Civilization: Selected Essays.* Translated and edited by Niyazi Berkes. London: Allen and Unwin, 1959.

Hourani, Albert. *Arabic Thought in the Liberal Age, 1798–1939.* Cambridge, U.K., and New York: Cambridge University Press, 1983.

Kedourie, Elie. *Afghani and 'Abduh: An Essay on Religious Unbelief and Political Activism in Modern Islam.* London: Cass, 1966.

Le Gassick, Trevor J. *Major Themes in Modern Arabic Thought: An Anthology.* Ann Arbor: University of Michigan Press, 1979.

Lewis, Bernard. *The Emergence of Modern Turkey,* 3rd ed. London: Oxford University Press, 2002.

Reid, Donald M. *The Odyssey of Farah Antun: A Syrian Christian's Quest for Secularism.* Minneapolis, MN: Bibliotheca Islamica, 1975.

Starkey, Paul. "Modern Egyptian Culture in the Arab World." In *The Cambridge History of Egypt;* Vol. 2: *Modern Egypt from 1517 to the End of the Twentieth Century,* edited by M. W. Daly, 394-426. Cambridge, U.K.: Cambridge University Press, 1998.

Tahtawi, Rifa'a Rafi'. *An Imam in Paris: al-Tahtawi's visit to France (1826–1831).* Translated by Daniel L. Newman. London: Saqi, 2002.

Tibi, Bassam. *Arab Nationalism: A Critical Enquiry,* 2nd ed. Edited and translated by Marion Farouk-Sluglett and Peter Sluglett. New York: St. Martin's Press, 1990.

Paul Starkey

WILSONIANISM

If a single moment can be marked as sounding the death knell of Western colonialism, then surely it was in 1917, as the United States declared war on Germany, when Woodrow Wilson (1856–1924, president from 1913 to 1921) announced that:

> The nations should with one accord adopt the doctrine of President Monroe as the doctrine of the world: that no nation should seek to extend its polity over any other nation or people but that every people should be left free to determine its own polity, its own way of development, unhindered, unthreatened, unafraid, the little along with the great and powerful.

(ADDRESS TO THE U.S. SENATE, JANUARY 22, 1917)

Woodrow Wilson. *President Wilson (standing center) waves to a crowd in Saint Louis, Missouri, on September 6, 1919, during a speaking tour to promote the League of Nations.* © BETTMANN/CORBIS. REPRODUCED BY PERMISSION.

Hence, as the United States had said in 1823 with the Monroe Doctrine that it would interpose itself between the newly freed countries of Latin America, now Washington was proposing guidelines for Europe, the Middle East, and perhaps beyond. Here was the call for "national self-determination" (Wilson's pet phrase) for peoples subjected to colonial rule, Western or otherwise, uttered with clear determination by the greatest power of the twentieth century. To be sure, the chaos of the interwar years made Wilson's announcement appear illusory, and three decades stretched between those momentous words and the independence of India and Pakistan. Still, Wilson attempted to implement the promise of democratic national self-determination immediately, at Versailles, as the victors in World War I deliberated what to do with the peoples released from imperial control with the disintegration of the German, Ottoman, Russian, and Austro-Hungarian empires.

The League of Nations, the precursor organization to the United Nations, was born of his hope, as was the independence of a number of countries of Eastern Europe and the mandate system that prepared certain peoples of the Middle East and Africa for eventual self-government. If only Czechoslovakia emerged much as the American leader had hoped from these grand designs, a framework had nevertheless been established that would guide later American presidents as they worked to refashion international order in the aftermath of World War II and the Cold War. Washington would work, in a word, to create a politically plural world, one free of imperial domination and constituted instead by democratic states linked by multilateral institutions for the sake of preserving the common peace.

The genius of Wilson's design for world order was that it put American traditions and interests together in a package attractive for many of the peoples of the world. The basis of international order, Wilson held, should be democratically constituted states created by self-determining peoples. These states should interact with one another in terms of an open, nondiscriminatory international economic system. Disputes among them should be settled by a system of multilateral institutions based on

WOODROW WILSON'S MESSAGE TO CONGRESS

In 1917, Woodrow Wilson urged the United States Congress to declare war on Germany. What follows is part of this speech.

"We are glad, now that we see the facts with no veil of false pretence about them, to fight thus for the ultimate peace of the world and for the liberation of its peoples, the German peoples included: for the rights of nations great and small and the privilege of men everywhere to choose their way of life and of obedience. The world must be made sage for democracy. Its peace must be planted upon the tested foundations of political liberty. We have no selfish ends to serve. We desire no conquest, no dominion. We seek no indemnities for ourselves, no material compensation for the sacrifices we shall freely make. We are but one of the champions of the rights of mankind. We shall be satisfied when those rights have been made as secure as the faith and the freedom of nations can make them."

---

the premise of collective security (rather than on the standard appeal to balance of power). In short, here was a framework for domestic and international order based on American interests and principles that corresponded to the hopes of nationalists in many other lands as well. Its consequence would be "a world safe for democracy," an international order composed of mutually respecting states interacting with peaceful reciprocity, the best guarantee the United States could have that its national security as a democracy would be preserved. As a result, the term *Wilsonianism* was born, the only *ism* attached to the name of an American president so far as world affairs is concerned. In due course, Wilsonianism was to become synonymous with *liberalism* in world affairs, and as such it has been an active ingredient in American foreign policy ever since.

At the time and since, there were many who disparaged Wilsonianism. Some doubted that democratic government held much appeal for many of the peoples of the world. Others were skeptical that even if democracy were to flower in much of the world it would create [what later liberals came to call] a "pacific union," a "zone of democratic peace" (Russett and Oneal 2001, Chapter 1)—notions that harkened back to the writings of the German philosopher Immanuel Kant (1724–1804) in the late eighteenth century that democratic regimes were different from those based on authoritarian rule in that they would be more pacific toward one another. And yet others resisted these liberal appeals as solvents of the authoritarian and imperial systems they vowed to maintain.

The interwar years seemed to prove the skeptics right. The rise of communism and fascism, compounded by the Great Depression, made any hopes of a perfectible future seem utopian indeed. Nevertheless, the framework proposed by Wilson returned to inspire President Franklin Delano Roosevelt (1882–1945) as he called for the creation of the Bretton Woods Accords (1944), which presided over the greatest liberalization of trade and investment in world history; as he oversaw the opening of the United Nations (1945–1946), which sought a new basis for conflict resolution among states; and as he promoted the Atlantic Charter (in 1941) and the Declaration on Liberated Europe (in 1945), which foresaw national self-determination for peoples liberated from Axis domination in World War II, as well as implicitly (and in due course) eventual self-government for those under European colonial rule.

Wilsonianism rested on four essential legs: (1) a call for democratic governments worldwide; (2) an appeal for an open and integrated international economic system; (3) a proliferation of multilateral organizations; and (4) the active involvement of the United States in maintaining this framework for order understood to be working for its own national security. However, of the four legs it is surely the emphasis on national self-determination, understood as democratic state building, that is justifiably understood as its most basic ingredient, even if its reassurance to an American public that primary security interests were guaranteed made it palatable at home.

It was on the basis of this political thinking that during World War II Roosevelt called for the independence of the peoples under British and French colonial rule and that he called upon Soviet leader Joseph Stalin (1879–1953) to restore the independence of those people liberated from Nazi rule by the Red Army. Roosevelt died in April 1945, but his successor Harry Truman (1884–1972) carried forth with this policy, pushing for European decolonization, opposing Soviet expansionism, and presiding over the democratization of occupied Germany and Japan.

Reagan Helps Dismantle the Remnants of the Berlin Wall, September 12, 1990. *The presidency of Ronald Reagan marked a high point in the resurgence of Wilsonianism. With the fall of Germany's Berlin Wall in November 1989, Wilsonianism stood supreme as the premier blueprint for domestic and international order.* © **MICHAEL PROBST/REUTERS/CORBIS. REPRODUCED BY PERMISSION.**

As the Cold War grew in intensity, Wilsonianism became something of a "second track" in the conduct of American foreign policy. The "first track" was called *containment* and aimed to prevent the spread of international communism. Yet at the same time a commitment to multilateralism, economic openness, and democratic government typified relations among Washington's closest allies and its hopes for a wider network of contacts. When President John F. Kennedy (1917–1963) launched the Alliance for Progress with Latin America, or President Jimmy Carter (b. 1924) initiated his campaign for human rights, they were clearly within the Wilsonian tradition.

The presidency of Ronald Reagan (1911–2004) marked a highpoint in the resurgence of Wilsonianism not seen since the 1940s. Although Reagan eschewed the multilateralism typical of liberalism, he forcibly advanced the cause of democratic government worldwide, most

notably within not only the Soviet empire but for the Soviet Union itself. Soviet leader Mikhail Gorbachev's (b. 1931) eventual embrace of this liberal creed was meant to reform, not to destroy, the leadership of the Communist Party and the legitimacy of the Soviet empire, but in short order these monolithic entities disintegrated, as did the Soviet Union itself. With the fall of the Berlin Wall in November 1989, Wilsonianism stood supreme as the premier blueprint for domestic and international order.

The administrations of presidents George H. W. Bush (b. 1924) and Bill Clinton (b. 1946) continued in this liberal democratic internationalist tradition. The newly independent countries of central and east Europe were encouraged to democratize, and one way of aiding the process was to involve them in the multilateral organizations that had been born of World War II (including especially the North Atlantic Treaty Organization and the

European Union). At the same time, democratic transitions in South Africa and South Korea could be saluted, marking as they did the spread of liberal values and institutions in still other parts of the world.

The presidency of George W. Bush (b. 1946) was at first distinguished by a distinct hostility toward democracy promotion abroad. The president, his first-term national security advisor Condoleezza Rice (b. 1954), and secretary of state Colin Powell (b. 1937), all declared their skepticism that "state and nation building" should enjoy a high priority for American foreign policy. However, following the terrorist attacks of September 11, 2001, a "born-again" version of Wilsonianism appeared, one that claimed that American security could only be preserved if the Arab Middle East (or a good portion of it) were democratized. The war on Iraq, launched in March 2003, was in this sense a democratic crusade designed to reform a foreign people in ways in keeping with American security interests.

In the minds of many, the question raised by the war on Iraq was whether Wilson's old pledge to "make the world safe for democracy" had perhaps taken a perverse turn so that now democracy was itself not safe for world order. The demands placed by the Bush administration on the governmental institutions of others seemed so high, and the means put at the disposal of achieving these ends appeared so brutal, that a doctrine that once had looked forward to undergirding world peace now seemed to have transformed itself into one destined to promote perpetual war. To be sure, Wilsonianism had always had American security as its primary concern, and many in Latin America especially had always felt that the call for democratic governments there served as a pretext for Washington to intervene in their affairs. This regional perspective now began to be more widely shared. How ironic that the "neo-Wilsonianism" of the years after 9/11 had put aggressive self-interest so high on the American agenda that what had once been an anti-imperial framework for world order now threatened instead to become an imperial framework in its own right.

SEE ALSO *Self-Determination, East Asia and the Pacific.*

BIBLIOGRAPHY

Cox, Michael, et al. *American Democracy Promotion: Impulses, Strategies and Impacts.* New York: Oxford University Press, 2000.

Ikenberry, G. John. *After Victory: Institutions, Strategic Restraint, and the Rebuilding of Order after Major Wars.* Princeton, NJ: Princeton University Press, 2001.

Macmillan, Margaret Olwen. *Paris 1919: Six Months That Changed the World.* New York: Random House, 2002.

Russett, Bruce M., and John R. Oneal. *Triangulating Peace: Democracy, Interdependence, and International Organizations.* New York: Norton, 2001.

Smith, Tony. *America's Mission: The United States and the Worldwide Struggle for Democracy in the Twentieth Century.* Princeton, NJ: Princeton University Press, 1994.

Tony Smith

WORLD WAR I, AFRICA

World War I, which began as a European civil war, soon engulfed thirty-two nations, twenty-eight of which constituted the Allied and Associated Powers, ranged against the Central Powers made up of Germany, Austria-Hungry, Bulgaria, and the Ottoman Empire. The war was not contained within the Balkan theater where competing nationalisms and old ethnic rivalries had been simmering. It quickly expanded to include a wider area of Europe and beyond and eventually spilled into Africa as well. In Africa, where the British and the French had extensive colonial interests to protect, the conflict engrossed a number of European nations battling it out among themselves in different regions of Africa with armies that consisted mostly of soldiers from the colonies, including India.

In the African phase of the war, the British and the French (using African troops under European command) quickly overran German Togo, which was surrounded by British and French colonies. The German Cameroon took a little longer to subdue, although it too did not have many white settlers or a significant number of German troops, which would have prolonged the military campaign.

Further south, the Allied forces, South African troops in particular, occupied German South-West Africa (Namibia) by 1915 without much struggle. The military campaign (given South African racist opposition) was carried out by white troops with a substantial number of Africans being used mainly as support labor. In German East Africa (Tanganyika) the conflict between the British (who relied heavily on white South Africans, Indians, and Africans, though South African racist objections against Africans serving as combatants surfaced once again) and the German forces (consisting mostly of African soldiers) became quite bloody. Some troops from India on their way to serving in Egypt were instead sent to East Africa to attack the enemy from the coast. This attempt proved to be a disaster and was quickly replaced by an invasion from the hinterland, that is, Nairobi. The campaign was a difficult one given the incidence of disease that affected horses, and African porters became the substitute for moving supplies for

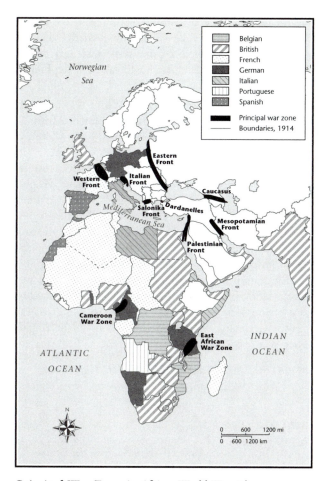

Principal War Zones in Africa. *World War I began as a European civil war, but quickly expanded beyond Europe and eventually spilled into Africa, where the European colonial powers had extensive interests to protect. The conflict engrossed a number of European nations battling it out among themselves in different regions of Africa.* **MAP BY XNR PRODUCTIONS. THE GALE GROUP.**

the troops. Needless to mention, African labor was not voluntary but coerced as the British needed extensive labor to maintain the military supply lines.

The German army was led by Colonel Paul von Lettow-Vorbeck (1870–1964), who conducted a very effective guerrilla campaign by avoiding direct confrontations and keeping constantly on the move. He succeeded in widening the battle zone into a spectacular theater of operations that extended into Portuguese-controlled Mozambique, British Nyasaland (Malawi), and northeastern Rhodesia (Zambia). Von Lettow-Vorbeck managed to tie down more than 100,000 British-led Allied troops over this vast territory (rich with mining resources) in a dogged resistance that did not end until Germany suffered defeat in Europe. Scorched-earth tactics were utilized by both sides, with disastrous results on the local populations' food supply.

What were the consequences of the war for Africa? What were African perceptions of the war? Clearly Africans had nothing to look forward to (as they were not fighting for some principle or, as in the case of the French, to preserve what they had lost four decades earlier in the Franco-Prussian war), being drawn into conflicts and wars that were not of their making. As a matter of fact, Africans were themselves recent victims of European aggression that had resulted in, with the exception of Liberia and Ethiopia, the whole continent being carved up into colonies dominated by European powers (with a number of primary resistance movements cropping up here and there to deal with this situation). Quite understandably, therefore, they resented the sacrifices they were being asked to make on behalf of someone else or some other nation's wars.

The war campaigns created such untold hardship that around 100,000 people died of disease, malnutrition, and overwork. Famine and such diseases as influenza, malaria, and dysentery took their toll, killing large numbers of people in East, West, and Central Africa from 1918 to 1919. On both sides of the conflict, the African fighting men were killing one another for European causes. For instance, Kenya alone lost tens of thousands of people who died, mainly from disease, from the forcible recruitment of Africans into the fighting forces. Moreover, about 150,000 Africans in French colonies fought in Europe, where as many as 30,000 died in the savage battle of attrition against the Germans. The French had recruited several hundred thousand combat troops in North Africa and West Africa, a good many of whom fought in the trenches while others provided much needed labor or were employed in support roles.

The war disrupted Africa's international trade with the outside while raising commodity prices far above the rise in incomes. The increase in taxes to help finance the war efforts only added further burdens to Africa's subsistence producers, who had no other sources of income to fall back on. There were also heavy demands being placed on newly established health and medical programs, whose benefits were being mitigated by the disease factor, which had been made worse by the war.

Moreover, the developmental policies that were implemented in the period between the two wars resulted in migrations, voluntary or coerced, by people who were seeking employment from agriculturally marginal regions to mining or cash-crop-producing areas. In other areas of Africa, such as French West Africa, the return of a large number of ex-soldiers with no jobs waiting for them affected the employment situation. So did the disappearance of jobs that had been associated with ports and other facilities that had been heavily used during the duration of the war. There was a lot of hardship for people in urban centers who were trying to cope as best they could away from their homes in the villages.

There were other repercussions as well: a number of African uprisings occurred both before and during World War I. Among the most serious were the Maji Maji uprising in German East Africa in 1905 and Elliot Kamwana's (1870–1956) Watchtower movement in Nyasaland in 1908. These religious revitalization movements were motivated by a strong sense of resentment against European domination, overtaxation, and forced labor. The movements, with their religious or messianic overtones, received a receptive ear among Africans (especially those in areas where Africans had lost their lands to white-settler communities, as in Rhodesia).

There were stirrings of revolt, as in the Shire Highlands (an area of white plantation settlement in northern Malawi) in 1915 when Africans protested against colonial injustices and the shedding of African blood in World War I. Though the leader of the uprising, John Chilembwe (d. 1915), was eventually captured and executed, his inspiration won him folklore status among people who had been increasingly subjected to colonial oppression. Similarly, strikes and protests took place in colonies such as Dahomey (now Benin) and Kenya. Among the most prominent of these protest organizations was the Young Kikuyu Association headed by Harry Thuku (1895–1970), who was later detained and exiled to a remote area of Kenya. This laid the foundations for the later struggles for independence in Kenya.

The above examples indicate that the war did not end colonial subjugation, despite the European propaganda about fighting for democracy; on the contrary, it ushered in a new era of colonial consolidation, especially in the absence of any external competition for the control of Africa. This was the era when the tiny educated African elite did not demand collective rights but rather sought to work within the system by seeking concessions with respect to participation in the political and decision-making process. The mood, of course, would change after the end of World War II, when Africans became more assertive in terms of their demands for total liberation, not piecemeal change for only certain sectors of the population. The colonial authorities dismissed such demands as premature, arguing that Africans were not ready to assume such practices as an open press and free speech, which were associated with the liberal traditions of countries like Britain.

The war had also weakened the European powers, which had been forced to borrow heavily from the United States to finance the war. This made the European powers look for ways in which the colonies could pay for themselves, while hopefully generating wealth for the imperial country. As a result, the theory of the dual mandate, developed by Frederick Lugard (1858–1945), attempted to put a respectable face to this British policy, as did its French equivalent in the French colonies.

Finally, it should be noted that World War I did not lead to the redrawing of the map of colonial Africa, as had occurred in Europe and the Middle East, where old empires had collapsed. Nothing of the sort happened in Africa. The war simply meant that Germany lost its former territories to the French (for instance, Togo), the British (Tanganyika), and the South Africans (Namibia, which was mandated by the League of Nations to be administered by South Africa). In the case of South Africa, the war had divided the white population into two camps: those who saw South Africa as a British dominion (and therefore took the country to war on the side of the British), and those (Afrikaner nationalists) who were vehemently opposed to going to war against Germany, which had aided them in the Anglo-Boer War (1880–1881).

SEE ALSO *Dual Mandate, Africa; Maji Maji Revolt, Africa; Sub-Saharan Africa, European Presence in.*

BIBLIOGRAPHY

Katzenellenbogen, S. E. "Southern Africa and the War of 1914–18." In *War and Society: Historical Essays in Honour and Memory of J. R. Western, 1928–1971,* edited by M. R. D. Foot, 107–122. London: Elek, 1973.

Rathbone, Richard. "World War I and Africa: Introduction." *Journal of African History* 19 (1) (1978): 1–9.

Shillington, Kevin. *History of Africa.* New York: St. Martin's Press, 1989; rev. ed., 1995.

Abdin Chande

WORLD WAR I, MIDDLE EAST

Despite the romance of associations with the Holy Land and iconic figures such as T. E. Lawrence (Lawrence of Arabia, 1888–1935) and Mustafa Kemal Atatürk (1881–1938), the Middle East was strategically insignificant with respect to the outcome of World War I (1914–1918). Viewed from a regional perspective, however, World War I was both a profound human tragedy and an exceedingly important formative episode. It brought the end of the Ottoman Empire and established successor states that are the foundation of the modern Middle East. The war also drew virtually the whole of the Middle East into the imperial embrace of Great Britain and France.

War came to the Middle East through Ottoman ambition as much as the imperialism of the great

European powers. Prompted by imperial ambition, awareness of Russian designs on their territory, and the inability of France and Great Britain to provide effective guarantees for their security, a prowar, pro-German cabal within the Ottoman cabinet led by Enver Paşa (1881–1922) signed a secret alliance with imperial Germany on August 2, 1914. With aid and expertise from Germany, Enver and his supporters saw an opportunity to inflict a decisive defeat on Russia and recover the territory and prestige lost during the preceding half century.

From the German perspective, the Ottoman alliance was intended to distract the Entente powers (Britain, France, and Russia) from the European theater and promote rebellion among their Muslim subjects. It was also hoped that the Ottoman Empire might provide a base from which to threaten Britain's communications with India via the Suez Canal. Though well aware of these dangers, the French and British were unable to maintain their traditional support of the Ottoman Empire against Russia because they needed Russian support against Germany in Europe. In the event, the Ottoman Turks made good their alliance with Germany and brought the Middle East into the war on October 29, 1914, when their fleet, led by German Admiral Wilhelm Souchon (1864–1946), attacked Sevastopol, a Black Sea port on the Crimean Peninsula in Ukraine. Though the sultan-caliph quickly proclaimed a jihad (a Muslim holy war) against the Entente powers, it had no significant impact on the course of the war in the Middle East or among the Muslim subjects of Britain, France, and Russia.

The British seized the initiative in the Middle East in late 1914. They declared a protectorate over Egypt and deployed Indian troops to secure Basra and Kurna, which provided a buffer for the strategically vital Abadan oil refinery at the head of the Persian Gulf. Before the end of 1914, however, Ottoman forces retook the initiative on two fronts. In the Caucasus, Enver Paşa led an ambitious but ultimately disastrous winter offensive against the Russians. His initial gains were offset by the decimation of his best troops in the fighting at Sarikamish and a retreat to Erzurum in northeastern Turkey. A Russian counteroffensive in early 1915 put the Ottoman forces in Anatolia and the Caucasus on the defensive until 1917. As Enver Paşa's offensive collapsed in January 1915, Jemal Paşa (1872–1922) led a daring but futile attack across the Sinai Desert against the Suez Canal.

Frustrated by the stalemate on the Western Front, the British soon turned to the Middle East in hopes of finding a way to break the deadlock from their rapidly growing base in Egypt. The initial result was the Dardanelles campaign, which ran from February through December 1915. A disaster for the French, British, and ANZAC (Australian and New Zealand Army Corps)

forces involved, it was a triumph for the Turks under General Otto Liman von Sanders (1855–1929) and the beginning of Mustafa Kemal's rise to notoriety.

The failure of the Dardanelles campaign preserved the Ottoman Empire. Yet in the long term its greatest significance lay in the arrangements it spawned among the Entente powers. As early as March 1915, when victory yet seemed a possibility, representatives of the Entente powers—Sergei Sasanov (1861–1927), Raymond Poincaré (1860–1934), and Edward Grey (1862–1933)—discussed the partition of the Ottoman Empire, though negotiations persisted through the conclusion of the Sykes-Picot Agreement of May 1916. This secret arrangement confirmed earlier Russian claims to Constantinople (now Istanbul, Turkey) and the Straits of Bosporus and Dardanelles, and assigned areas of direct and indirect control to the French in Syria and Lebanon and the British in Mesopotamia and the port cities of Acre and Haifa in Palestine. It also provided for international administration of Palestine and a limited degree of independent Arab control over parts of Syria, Arabia, and Transjordan.

Despite the concessions secured by the French, they were unable to commit substantial land forces to the Middle East after the Dardanelles debacle. This left Britain and Russia to carry on the war with the Ottoman Empire. While the Russians remained locked in a largely static struggle with Ottoman forces in the Caucasus and Anatolia, the British focused their efforts on two fronts: Mesopotamia and Syria-Palestine.

Having resisted Ottoman counterattacks against the buffer zone acquired in late 1914, the British commander in Mesopotamia, General John Nixon (1857–1921), advanced northward in June 1915. After initial successes that drew Amra and Kut under their control and threatened Baghdad, British forces suffered a major defeat at Ctesiphon (September 22–26). Nixon retreated to Kut, where his troops were surrounded and cut off in early December. Ottoman forces under Field Marshal Colmar von der Goltz (1843–1916) thwarted efforts to relieve Kut and on April 29, 1916, the remnants of the British force surrendered.

The Egyptian Expeditionary Force (EEF) under General Archibald Murray (1860–1945) had meanwhile gone on the offensive, beginning a slow push toward Palestine through the Sinai Desert, relying heavily on Egyptian transport and auxiliary labor corps. As of June 10, 1916, they were aided by a revolt against Ottoman authority led by Sharif Hussein (1853–1931) of Mecca. Though labeled an "Arab Revolt," this movement was in fact restricted to the tribes of the Hejaz and aimed primarily at preserving Hussein's power in the face of Ottoman attempts to reassert their authority over the province. This made Hussein and his followers natural allies of the British, who hoped to exploit existing anti-Ottoman sentiments among the Arab subjects of the Ottoman Empire.

By the spring of 1916, Hussein and the British high commissioner of Egypt, Sir Henry McMahon (1862–1949), reached an agreement. In exchange for Arab assistance in the war against the Ottoman Empire, the British pledged their support for the foundation of independent Arab states in certain areas liberated from Ottoman control. Though certain vital particulars of this agreement were left deliberately vague, with the consent of both parties, its spirit is difficult to reconcile with that of the Sykes-Picot Agreement. This contradiction presented significant difficulties in later stages of the war and during the postwar settlement.

In the meantime, the "Arab Revolt" distracted Ottoman attention and resources at the very moment when Murray was moving against Palestine. Arab tribesmen under Hussein's son Faisal (1883–1933) and his advisor T. E. Lawrence took the Red Sea port of Aqaba (July 5), after which they were reorganized as the Northern Arab Army and deployed alongside the EEF for the advance into Palestine. After a key victory at Romani (August 4–5, 1916), Murray was twice rebuffed in attempts to reduce the Ottoman stronghold of Gaza (February and April 1917). His replacement, General Edmund Allenby (1861–1936), spent the next several months building a significant numerical and logistical superiority over Ottoman forces, and in November (5–7) he triumphed at the Third Battle of Gaza. British and Allied forces entered Jerusalem on December 9, 1917.

Events followed much the same pattern in Mesopotamia. After the disaster at Kut, Nixon's replacement, General Frederick Maude (1864–1917), drew on the Indian Army to build a massive numerical superiority over the Ottoman forces. His offensive began in December 1916 and lasted through March 1917, during which time British forces retook Kut and occupied Baghdad. Ottoman plans for a counteroffensive were thwarted by the British advance into Palestine and the initiative remained with the British.

Some relief for the overburdened Ottoman forces came in late 1917 via the Russian Revolution. Despite continuing pressure from the British on the Mesopotamian and Syria-Palestine fronts, the Turks were able to mount an offensive against the Russians in the Caucasus and Anatolia, recovering the territory lost in early 1915. It also offered an opportunity to drive a wedge between Hussein and the British, when the Bolsheviks made public the secret treaties of the czarist government, including the Sykes-Picot Agreement. The British succeeded in allaying Hussein's concerns about their commitment to French control over Syria by downplaying Sykes-Picot and reiterating their promises of independent Arab successor states to the Ottoman Empire. Hussein had staked so much on the British connection that he had little choice but to accept their reassurances and carry on in hopes of realizing his own ambitions.

The Anglo-Arab connection survived the nearly contemporary shock of the Balfour Declaration (November 2, 1917) for similar reasons. Designed to play on American sympathies and on Zionist sensibilities within the international Jewish community, the declaration promised British support for a Jewish homeland in Palestine. It therefore had the potential to alienate the Arab inhabitants of the region. Again a combination of British reassurances and Hussein's pragmatism succeeded in allaying the concerns of Britain's Arab allies, if only for a time.

From late 1917 through the fall of 1918 the fronts in Mesopotamia and Syria-Palestine remained static. Events in Europe, specifically the massive German offensive launched in the spring of 1918, precluded the British from any forward move in the Middle East. Only when the situation in Europe had stabilized was Allenby able to begin his final offensive against northern Palestine and Syria. The Battle of Megiddo (September 19–21) broke the Ottoman forces in Palestine and opened Syria to the EEF. Damascus fell on October 1 and Faisal immediately established a nominally independent Arab administration there as per his understanding of British promises. By the final week of October, elements of the EEF had broken the last Ottoman resistance and reached Aleppo.

The collapse of Ottoman forces in Syria was paralleled by a similar collapse in Mesopotamia. Seeing an opportunity to bring all the rich oil fields in the region under their control, the British launched one final offensive in October 1918, which culminated in the capture of Mosul. Military defeat on both southern fronts, in addition to the imminent collapse of their German ally, forced the Turks to sign the Mudros Armistice on October 30, 1918, effectively ending World War I in the Middle East.

For the Ottoman Empire, the war was a catastrophe. Politically it meant the end of the Ottoman Empire. The territorial losses delineated in the Treaty of Sèvres (August 1920) reduced the Ottoman state to an Anatolian rump. The humiliation of these losses, Entente occupation, and the human and economic costs of the war sparked the crisis that spurred Mustafa Kemal to abolish the sultanate in November 1922.

In economic and human terms, the war was equally disastrous. Public debt quadrupled under the pressures of total war. The army suffered some 1.45 million casualties, while famine and economic contraction spread

General Allenby Enters Jerusalem. *General Edmund Allenby, commander of British forces in Palestine, rides through the Jaffa Gate in January 1918 as part of his formal entry into the newly captured city of Jerusalem.* © **HULTON-DEUTSCH COLLECTION/ CORBIS. REPRODUCED BY PERMISSION.**

suffering among the civilian population. In Syria alone some estimates put civilian deaths from disease and privation brought on by corruption, hoarding, locust infestation, and blockade as high as half a million.

The harsh measures taken by the Ottoman government to ensure internal stability only added to the suffering. In 1915 the specter of nationalist rebellion among the Ottoman Empire's Armenian subjects led to the episode of mass eviction, starvation, and murder known as the "Armenian genocide." Similarly unfounded fears that Syrian Arabs might use the war to launch a nationalist uprising inspired Jemal Paşa to inaugurate an era of violent repression that earned him the epithet "Blood Shedder."

For their part, the British had attained all of their Middle Eastern desiderata. At a cost of 145,000 casualties and substantial diversions from the Western Front, they had wrested Palestine, Syria, and Mesopotamia from the Ottoman Empire. The short route to India was secure, as was their access to the vast oil reserves of Mesopotamia.

They were also in a position to ensure that these interests were enshrined in the postwar settlement.

The problem was negotiating a settlement that would also fulfill British promises to Hussein and his followers, implement the Balfour Declaration, and placate the French, who desired a rigid implementation of the Sykes-Picot Agreement. It proved impossible to do so. The British were unable to reconcile the Sykes-Picot Agreement with the promises to Hussein and his cohorts regarding Arab independence. And the overwhelming need to maintain a strong tie to the French for European purposes ensured that British prime minister David Lloyd George (1863–1945) chose French imperial over Arab national aspirations.

Anglo-French supremacy in the Middle East was formalized in the San Remo Conference of April 1920, and later confirmed by the League of Nations. Britain received "mandates" over Mesopotamia and Palestine, including Transjordan. France received "mandates" over Syria and Lebanon. Though envisioned as a temporary arrangement meant to provide for a gradual transition to independence under Western tutelage, mandate status amounted to colonial status and marks the formal incorporation of the Middle East into the orbit of the European empires.

Satisfactory to imperial powers, whose primary interests were recognition of their supremacy and access to oil, to Zionists, and even to members of the puppet regimes that quickly appeared in the region, such arrangements engendered profound resentment among the majority of Arab nationalists, who felt betrayed by their erstwhile allies. The destabilizing effects of frustrated Arab nationalism, European political and economic domination, and active support of Zionism must stand beside the end of Ottoman domination and the appearance of the successor states comprising the modern Middle East as the key legacies of World War I in the Middle East.

SEE ALSO *British Colonialism, Middle East; Empire, Russian and the Middle East; French Colonialism, Middle East; Germany and the Middle East.*

BIBLIOGRAPHY

Bruce, A. P. C. *The Last Crusade: The Palestinian Campaign in the First World War.* London: John Murray, 2002.

Cleveland, William L. *A History of the Modern Middle East,* 3rd ed. Boulder, CO: Westview, 2004.

Davis, Paul K. *Ends and Means: The British Mesopotamian Campaign and Commission.* Rutherford, NJ: Fairleigh Dickinson University Press, 1994.

Fromkin, David. *A Peace to End All Peace, The Fall of the Ottoman Empire and the Creation of the Modern Middle East.* New York: Henry Holt, 1989.

Kedourie, Elie. *England and the Middle East: The Destruction of the Ottoman Empire 1914–1921,* 2nd ed. Hassocks, U.K.: Harvester Press, 1978.

Macfie, A. L. *The End of the Ottoman Empire, 1908–1923.* London and New York: Longman, 1998.

Mansfield, Peter. *The Ottoman Empire and its Successors.* New York: St. Martin's Press, 1973.

Monroe, Elizabeth. *Britain's Moment in the Middle East, 1914–1971,* 2nd ed. Baltimore: Johns Hopkins University Press, 1981.

Strachan, Hew. *The First World War.* New York: Oxford University Press, 2001.

Tauber, Eliezer. *The Arab Movements in World War I.* London and Portland, OR: Cass, 1993.

Chris Hagerman

WORLD WAR II, AFRICA

World War II was ignited by competing territorial ambitions or claims on land in Europe, where tensions that would precipitate the war had been simmering since 1918, when a vindictive peace had been forced on Germany. Africa became embroiled in this conflict, which saw Germany make a bid to regain territories as well as colonies that it had lost during World War I. Earlier, Mussolini, seeking to revive the glory of Rome, had invaded Ethiopia in 1935 to avenge the defeat that Italy had suffered at the hands of Ethiopia in 1896. This unprovoked invasion aroused much anger and indignation on the part of Africans, who saw it as yet another instance of European colonial violence—in this case directed against one of only two remaining independent African countries.

Africa was called upon by the colonial powers (as it had been during World War I) to supply manpower for combat purposes both on and outside the continent. The numbers were quite staggering: half a million men were recruited by the French and the British to serve in the war. It was only in South Africa (given the racial politics of its white-led minority governments) that African soldiers were not allowed to bear arms.

Africa was drawn into the war in Tunisia and Egypt, where Italian and German armies (led by Erwin Rommel) were pitted against Allied forces (a significant number of whom were Africans); by 1943 allied victories had reversed earlier gains by Germany. In 1941 Allied forces and African troops liberated Ethiopia, which had been under fascist Italian occupation for at least six years. In addition, large numbers of Africans recruited by European powers saw action in Europe and in Burma against the Japanese, who had overrun most of Southeast Asia.

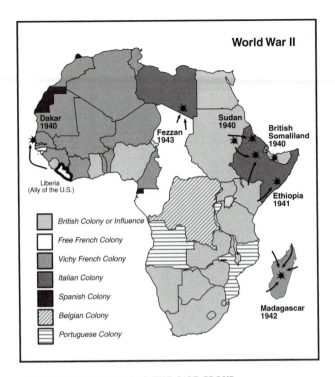

MAP BY XNR PRODUCTIONS. THE GALE GROUP.

Africans also contributed to the war effort in other ways, including the production of food staples to feed the fighting men. Moreover, funds raised in Africa in support of the war effort were crucial to the production of munitions for the colonial powers.

Colonial recruiting strategies were quite sophisticated and often alarmist—antifascist propaganda focused on what life would be like under fascist/racist German rule for people of color—and anger over the Italian invasion may also have induced some to enlist. Nonetheless, more coercive pressure was also exerted on local chiefs to induce them to round up recruits and forced labor was used in key sectors of the economy to mobilize resources for the war effort. As a result, there were, as in the previous war, some Africans who were opposed to Africa's involvement in a war that called for sacrifice and a life of hardship (conscripted labor, increased taxation, declining cash crop prices, reduced imports, etc.) ostensibly to "make the world safe for democracy." This was, for instance, the case in the Congo, where Africans were forced to work in difficult and inhuman conditions in the mines. Such forced labor was considered necessary because during the war years Africa became a major supplier of raw materials such as rubber, sisal, and minerals (such as tin in Nigeria), especially after a number of Asian countries fell to imperialist Japan.

What did Africa have to show for its war effort in the service of the colonial masters? To begin with, prior to World War II Europeans had not seriously entertained the idea of granting African countries their independence. In fact, the period after World War I was characterized by European expansion or consolidation of colonial administration. While there were some movements here and there seeking a greater role for Africans in the administration of colonies, none of these efforts resulted in significant progress toward independence. World War II led to African aspirations being placed in check while the war was being waged. It soon became apparent, however—particularly as hundreds of thousands of Africans were drafted to fight in Burma and in Europe—that some future reward would have to be offered in recognition of the African war effort. In 1941 British Prime Minister Winston Churchill and American President Franklin D. Roosevelt signed the Atlantic Charter, which promised Africans the right to choose the form of government they wanted to live under after the war. Many Africans thus had high hopes for a new future with better jobs and better opportunities.

Not surprisingly, the end of the war ushered in a new era in which Africans expected to earn their freedom; after all, hadn't they fought so well in the name of freedom and democracy to liberate Europe? Yet, European colonial rule was anything but democratic; it was autocratic, authoritarian, and even racist—especially in those colonies with a substantial European population. Despite this European intransigence, African movements for self-rule—and indeed freedom movements around the world—received a major boost in 1947 when India gained independence. Mahatma Gandhi in particular provided an ideological example for the independence fighter Kwame Nkrumah of the Gold Coast, later renamed Ghana.

World War II had also shattered any notions of European superiority, as African soldiers in Europe had witnessed the purveyors of a so-called higher civilization slaughtering each other. Africans began to revise their thinking about their place in the world and formed organizations or movements to express their nationalist sentiments. African intellectuals, who articulated African grievances against the colonial order, were at the head of these postwar movements, which sought to organize rural and urban populations into mass political parties. Nationalist parties emerged all over Africa and spearheaded the struggle for independence, whether through civil disobedience, as in the Gold Coast, or guerrilla warfare, as in Algeria. Clearly, African nationalism had been transformed (through a process that began as early as the 1930s) from a reformist movement to a revolutionary one.

Africans had flocked into the cities both before and during the war as colonial economies shifted to the production of war matériel. This demographic shift both expanded the population of Africa's urban centers and made the formation of mass parties more possible. At the same time a new elite, either locally or foreign educated, had emerged (as a product of the colonial order), which now had a mass audience (including proletarianized African workers) for its nationalist ideas. This elite realized that slavery and racism had created common bonds between Africans and people of African descent living in the areas of the African diaspora. More specifically, the Garveyist idea of racial pride filtered back to Africa through major African nationalists such as Nkrumah. Nkrumah saw Africans wherever they were as being united by their colonial experience or oppression at the hands of Europeans. These sentiments were expressed at the first Pan-African Congress, which was held in London in 1945 and brought together like-minded people from both the continent and the areas of the African diaspora. Among those present were future leaders of future independent African nations, including Nkrumah, Jomo Kenyatta, and Hastings Banda.

French African colonies had served France well during its hour of need (when France fell to Germany in 1940), first of all by providing a base or capital for Charles de Gaulle's Free France movement in Brazzaville, French Congo. Moreover, a significant number of French divisions that fought in France were made up of African soldiers. France fulfilled some of the promises it had made during the war: it abolished both the unpopular *indigenat* legal system and forced labor, and granted citizenship to all inhabitants of its colonies. Nevertheless, by not spelling out clearly what the rights of citizens were, the French managed to deny citizenship to indigenous African populations on the paternalistic pretext that they were not ready for it. Moreover, the colonies sent only a small number of delegates to the Chamber of Deputies in France, well below the proportion of their population relative to that of France. Worse, the French did not plan to grant independence to their African colonies. They only did so after the costly Algerian revolution forced them to work out an arrangement that provided independence to their colonies while maintaining French influence through formal economic and other ties.

In France after the war, French soldiers were welcomed as heroes, but African soldiers were pushed into the background. In fact, France repatriated African soldiers to Africa, thus giving the impression that they wanted to weed them out of the army to keep it white. Some Africans believed that De Gaulle did not want French colonies to see Africans as liberators of France, as this would have serious implications for France's

African Troops in the French Colonial Army. *African soldiers, in training for duty in World War II as part of the French colonial army, stand in formation in 1941 in the Central African Republic, then a colony of France.* **GEORGE RODGER/TIME LIFE PICTURES/ GETTY IMAGES. REPRODUCED BY PERMISSION.**

relations with its colonies. France did make an exception for Africans in France who were French citizens, as these soldiers were allowed to stay. Nevertheless, repatriation exposed the assimilation policy as a sham, because Africans were treated differently despite their efforts in the service of the French motherland.

The repatriated Africans were kept in temporary camps, as it was believed that once out of the army they would not be tied down by discipline. Disturbances did, in fact, break out in some of the camps where the ex-servicemen complained against white racism and low wages. In one such camp in Dakar, for instance, disgruntled protesters held a French commander-in-chief hostage. By the time order was restored, thirty-five people had been killed and over a hundred injured. Some of these ex-soldiers, despite being war heroes, were tried and some were marched through the city to humiliate them.

Riots and general strikes in the post–World War II period were not limited to Francophone areas of Africa only. Ex-soldiers and a new industrial class of workers, as well as other social groups, were involved in disturbances

that brought educated elite leaders of the nationalist struggle, such as Nkrumah, into the political limelight. Nkrumah's Convention People's Party (CPP) organized protests and strikes that effectively paralyzed the colonial administration and forced it to negotiate with nationalist leaders over some of their demands. The catalyst for these actions was first provided by a mass demonstration in 1948, in which several ex-soldiers who had served in Burma were killed after security forces began firing into the crowd. With this disturbance, the Gold Coast in particular entered into a new era of full-fledged nationalism in which European colonial rule was no longer acceptable. Africans, especially the ex-servicemen, felt that the British had not been quick enough to honor the pledges made in the Atlantic Charter. They believed that only protests and demonstrations or, if necessary, resorting to violence (as was the case in Kenya, though loss of prime farming land to white settlers was the crux of the problem there) would convince Europeans that the old colonial order had died with World War II. More significantly, the superpower rivalry of the Cold War era, which saw the Soviets willing to finance nationalist struggles in Africa, revealed the inability of weaker colonial powers such as Portugal to hold on to their colonies indefinitely.

The war had other consequences for Africa as well: large numbers of African soldiers were either killed (one quarter of those who served in France) or injured. Others suffered from physical disabilities and, more seriously, psychological trauma as a result of racist mistreatment in Nazi prison camps. Furthermore, unlike their white counterparts in postwar Europe, the widows and families of servicemen were not sufficiently cared for or supported.

During the war itself, not only African soldiers but also the general African population suffered many difficulties, such as recurring shortages both of imported foodstuffs (rice and flour in particular) and local staples. The supply of staple foods had been partly affected already in some areas by the prewar colonial policy of diverting labor away from the raising of subsistence crops to the production of cash-crops such as sisal and commodities such as copper. As living conditions got worse in the countryside (partly exacerbated by the practice of forced labor, both for public projects and also for military service), a significant number of rural people migrated to the cities to avoid production geared toward satisfying external needs.

Kenya was amongst the countries most seriously affected by migration to its urban centers, especially Nairobi. The pressure for increased agricultural production that caused this migration was brought about, ironically, by African troops and their Italian prisoners, whose presence promoted a demand for both beef and maize. Moreover, the increased demand for sisal (a plantation crop), which was no longer available from Southeast Asia following the Japanese occupation of that region, benefited mainly European settler farmers. The migration of land-deprived Africans from rural areas to cities not only weakened African family bonds, it also led to the development of shantytowns in Nairobi and the creation of health, employment, and crime-related problems.

The war witnessed a number of infrastructural projects (using forced labor, which until then had been limited mainly to rural areas), such as the construction of airstrips in West and East Africa to aid in the transportation of fighting men and goods to North Africa and the Middle East. Africans were called on not only to build these projects, but also to provide housing for European and American settlers and personnel who came to Africa during the war years. More significantly, it was during this period that the United States' role in Africa increased as its need for vital mineral resources from the central Southern Africa region grew.

The war stimulated the South African economy with respect to the production of industrial goods and munitions. South Africa, which had derived its industrial base from the gold and diamonds discovered in the second half of the nineteenth century, now become a major manufacturing power as well. Indeed, the size of the industrial labor force and the level of industrial output grew by leaps and bounds. The South African economy therefore underwent its second major transformation in less than a century.

SEE ALSO *Decolonization, Sub-Saharan Africa; Nationalism, Africa.*

BIBLIOGRAPHY

Akurang-Parry, Kwabena. "Africa and World War II." In *Africa, Vol. 4: The End of Colonial Rule: Nationalism and Decolonization*, edited by Toyin Falola. Durham, NC: Carolina Academic Press, 2000.

Killingray, David, and Richard Rathbone, eds. *Africa and the Second World War*. London: Macmillan, 1986.

Abdin Chande

X

XAVIER, FRANCIS
1506–1552

Francis Xavier, the first great missionary of the Society of Jesus (the Jesuits), was born in Navarre, Spain, on April 7, 1506, and died on the island of Sancian, off the Chinese mainland, on December 3, 1552.

Xavier left his native Spain in 1525 to take up studies at the University of Paris. It was here that he met Ignatius Loyola (1491–1556) and other founding members of the future Society of Jesus. Xavier was at first resistant to Loyola's attempts to bring about a spiritual conversion in his life. By 1533, however, the two men had developed a close friendship and they were among the group of seven students who, on August 15, 1534, assembled at a chapel in Montmartre and took private vows of poverty and chastity.

After finishing their studies in Paris, the friends aimed to travel to Jerusalem to help in the work of converting the infidels. If this proved impossible (as it did), they pledged to visit Rome and allow the pope to use them in whatever way he thought "most useful to the glory of God and the good of souls." Official papal recognition of the new Society of Jesus arrived in September 1540 with the bull *Regimini militantis ecclesiae*.

At this stage, there was little, if any, talk of some of the activities (combating the burgeoning Protestant Reformation; setting up educational establishments) that would come to characterize the Society's history. However, it was not long before another familiar sphere of Jesuit endeavor began to open up. Over the next four centuries, Jesuit missionaries would travel extensively across Asia, Africa, and the Americas: in the vanguard of such efforts was Francis Xavier, who, in response to a request from the Portuguese king, departed for India on April 7, 1541.

Xavier would spend the next decade evangelizing across southern and eastern Asia. He spent several months in Goa, on the western coast of India, ministering to the sick in the city's hospitals and striving to win converts among the city's children. In October 1542 he traveled south to Cape Comorin, where, armed with prayers translated into Tamil, he worked among the local pearl-fishing community. A trip to Malacca (1545) and the Spice Islands (1546–1547) followed, after which Xavier turned his attentions to the two greatest evangelical prizes Asia had too offer: Japan and China.

Xavier arrived at Kagoshima, Japan, on August 15, 1549. He was immediately impressed by what he perceived as the enormous Japanese potential to understand and embrace the Christian gospel. "We shall never find among heathens another race equal to the Japanese," he wrote, "they are people of excellent minds—good in general and not malicious." Drawing broad, usually reductive, conclusions about the relative worth of various Asian populations would be a hallmark of Christian evangelism throughout the early modern era. Although Xavier met with some resistance from local Buddhist leaders, his two and a half years in cities such as Hirado, Kyoto, and Yamaguchi proved worthwhile. By the time of his departure in 1551 he had won over several thousand converts.

Xavier was back in Goa by January 1552. He set sail for China in May but was destined never to enter the

Saint Francis Xavier. *Canonized in 1622, Xavier's memory would inspire missionary priests from Ethiopia to New France to Arizona.* HULTON ARCHIVE/GETTY IMAGES. REPRODUCED BY PERMISSION.

That said, Xavier was more than capable of criticizing what he perceived as the lax morality of European settlers. Also, while he shared the prejudices and assumptions of his contemporaries, he did make efforts to genuinely understand the cultures in which he found himself. This, along with a willingness to adapt evangelical strategies according to local circumstances, would emerge as a defining characteristic of Jesuit missionary activity across the globe. Such an ethos certainly carried serious risks.

The accommodationist approach of Jesuit missionaries such as Xavier, Matteo Ricci (1552–1610) in China, and Roberto de Nobili (1577–1656) in India drew enormous criticism from commentators who feared that too much adaptation of the gospel message would result in syncretic, impure versions of the Christian faith. Nor was the work of reacting to local circumstances ever straightforward. In Japan, Xavier had turned to words in the local vernacular to translate concepts such as god, soul, and sacrament. It turned out that he had been badly advised, and the meanings carried by the chosen Japanese words were very different from what Xavier had intended. He was forced to employ Japanese "versions" of Latin words—*Deusu, anima, eucaristia*—which, to a Japanese audience, were essentially devoid of any inherent meaning.

Perhaps Xavier's greatest significance lay in his role as an icon and model of all subsequent Jesuit missionary activity. Canonized in 1622, his memory would inspire priests from Ethiopia to New France to Arizona. Relics of the saint would be a much sought-after spiritual commodity during the seventeenth century. The lower part of his right arm would be shipped off to Rome, the remainder would be divided in three and shared between the Jesuit communities in Macao, Cochin, and Malacca. By the eighteenth century, "Xavier-Water," in which medals or relics of the saint had been immersed, had become a popular central-European cure for fevers and bad eyesight. Even today, his body, housed in the Church of the Bom Jesus in Goa, remains a cherished sight of pilgrimage and adoration.

SEE ALSO *China to the First Opium War; Mission, Civilizing; Missions, China; Religion, Western Presence in East Asia.*

BIBLIOGRAPHY

Alden, Dauril. *The Making of an Enterprise: The Society of Jesus in Portugal, its Empire, and Beyond, 1540–1750.* Stanford, CA: Stanford University Press, 1996.

Brodrick, James. *Saint Francis Xavier, 1506–1552.* New York: Wicklow, 1952.

empire's territories. He was taken ill on Sancian Island in late November and died on the morning of December 3, within sight of the Chinese mainland.

Throughout Xavier's Asian career the links between evangelism and the colonial enterprise were plain to see. Xavier was a papal legate, but he was also under commission from the Portuguese king, arriving in Goa on board the *Santiago* in the company of Governor Martim Afonso de Sousa (ca. 1500–1564). There were clear advantages to be wrung from the association with empire. The awe and fear that the European colonists inspired could always be exploited, and satisfaction could be derived from the compulsive European habit of destroying the idols and temples of indigenous faiths. Perhaps most significantly, it could be made abundantly clear to local leaders that allowing missionaries to work in their territories (perhaps even converting to Christianity themselves) might bring military, political, and economic advantages.

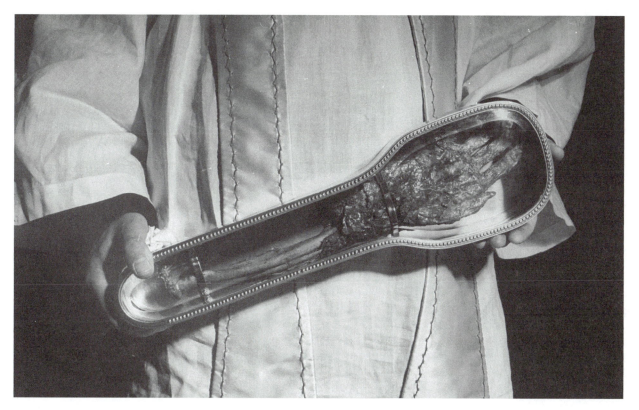

Xavier's Arm. *Xavier died en route to China in 1552, and relics of the saint became sought-after spiritual commodities during the seventeenth century. The lower part of his right arm was sent to Rome, where it remains in a reliquary in the Church of Gesù.* **AL FENN/ TIME LIFE PICTURES/GETTY IMAGES. REPRODUCED BY PERMISSION.**

Coleridge, Henry, ed. *The Life and Letters of St. Francis Xavier*, 4th ed., 2 vols. London: Burns and Oates, 1912.

Elison, George. *Deus Destroyed: The Image of Christianity in Early Modern Japan.* Cambridge, MA: Harvard University Press, 1973.

Neill, Stephen. *A History of Christianity in India: The Beginnings to AD 1707.* New York: Cambridge University Press, 1984.

Ross, Andrew. *A Vision Betrayed: The Jesuits in Japan and China, 1542–1742.* Maryknoll, NY: Orbis, 1994.

Schurhammer, Georg. *Francis Xavier: His Life, His Times*, 4 vols. Translated by M. Joseph Costelloe. Rome: Jesuit Historical Institute, 1973–1982.

Jonathan A. Wright

Z

ZONGLI YAMEN (TSUNGLI YAMEN)

The Zongli Yamen (Office of General Management) was established by the Qing state to deal with the foreign presence in China. Although the Qing state preferred the traditional tribute system that had long regulated China's relations with foreign countries, China's weakness in the face of Western military might, combined with the demands of the Western powers for diplomatic relations on an equal basis, made it impossible for China to maintain its traditional model of foreign relations with its assumption of Chinese supremacy and Western barbarity. A new institution was called for to formally manage relations with the Western countries.

In 1861 the conservative Qing court reluctantly agreed to the creation of the Zongli Yamen, which it emphasized was to be a temporary measure to manage relations with the Western countries until they could be removed from China. The Qing court refused to grant the Zongli Yamen complete institutional autonomy, making it instead accountable to the Grand Council and appointing five high-ranking officials to serve as a powerful advisory board. Among the five, the most important was Prince Gong (1833–1898), the uncle of the Tongzhi emperor.

Under the leadership of the reform-minded Prince Gong (Kung) and his capable right-hand man, Wenxiang (1818–1876), the Zongli Yamen played a vital role in the Tongzhi Restoration, the chief aim of which was to strengthen China's hand in the game against Western imperialism. To this end, in 1862 the Zongli Yamen authorized American missionary W. A. P. Martin's translation of Henry Wheaton's *Elements of International Law,* published in 1836. Widely accepted in diplomatic circles in the West, Wheaton's work was required reading for those in the foreign service; ignorance of its contents placed Chinese ambassadors at a serious disadvantage.

Besides publishing a translation of Wheaton's text, the Zongli Yamen also launched a movement to create foreign language schools. Beginning with the opening of a small school in Beijing in 1862, the Zongli Yamen in short order set up similar language institutes in Shanghai, Canton (Guangzhou), and Fuzhou. Despite staunch opposition from the conservative members of the Qing court, Prince Gong and Wenxiang converted the Beijing school to a college; expanded the curriculum beyond foreign languages to include subjects in math, the sciences, and law; and invited foreign teachers to lead instruction. By sponsoring translations of Western texts and financing language schools, the Zongli Yamen sought to provide Chinese diplomats with the training and knowledge they needed to deal with the West.

Less successful was the Zongli Yamen's project to build a navy. In 1862 the Zongli Yamen purchased from Britain a fleet of ships. Problems arose when the fleet arrived a year later, and Captain Sherard Osborn (1822–1875) of the Royal Navy, having been promised in writing full command of the fleet, refused to hand over control to his Chinese counterpart. Seeing no other alternative, the Zongli Yamen abandoned its plans for a modern navy. Overall, however, the greater cooperation between China and the West in the late 1860s attests to the relative success of the Zongli Yamen in negotiating relations with the West until its replacement by the

Ministry of Foreign Affairs as mandated by the Boxer Protocol of 1901.

SEE ALSO *Boxer Uprising; China, First Opium War to 1945; Chinese Revolutions; Qing Dynasty; Self-Strengthening Movements, East Asia and the Pacific; Taiping Rebellion.*

BIBLIOGRAPHY

Schoppa, R. Keith. *Revolution and Its Past: Identities and Change in Modern Chinese History,* 2nd ed. Upper Saddle River, NJ: Pearson, 2005.

Spence, Jonathan D. *The Search for Modern China,* 2nd ed. New York: Norton, 1999.

Lisa Tran

ZULU WARS, AFRICA

The Anglo-Zulu War of 1879 was fought between Britain and the Zulu nation in South Africa. The war remains one of the most dramatic in both British and southern African history during the colonial period. It marked the end of the independence of the Zulu nation and the entrenchment of British colonialism in South Africa.

The Zulu kingdom emerged early in the nineteenth century along the eastern seaboard of southern Africa under its legendary ruler Shaka Zulu (1787–1828). The background to the war must be located in contestations over land between the Zulu, the Boers, and the British. British adventurers were attracted to Zululand in search of trade and by the 1840s the British colony of Natal had sprung up on the southern borders of Zululand. The expansion of the Boer into the southern African interior from 1835, the attempt by the Zulu to defend their own independence, and the aggressive policy of the British to control South Africa by imposing their authority over the Boer and the Zulu led to a chain of events that resulted in the war of 1879, in which the British suffered humiliating defeat before they eventually subdued the Zulu.

The prelude to the war was the dispute that emerged between the Zulu king, Cetshwayo (ca. 1836–1884), and his brother Umtonga. In 1861 Umtonga fled to the Utrecht district. Cetshwayo offered the Boer farmers a strip of land along the border if they would surrender his brother. But he later rescinded his endorsement of the deal after his brother fled to Natal. The contestation over this ceded land and the boundary issue that developed attracted the British into what could be regarded as a local dispute. Indeed, by the 1870s the British began to adopt a policy that would bring the various British colonies, Boer republics, and independent African groups under common British control. The British high commissioner in South Africa, Sir Henry Bartle Frere (1815–1884), believed that an independent and self-reliant Zulu kingdom was a threat to this policy. Frere was convinced that economic development and peace in South Africa could only be achieved by curtailing the power of Cetshwayo and the Zulu nation.

To achieve this goal, the British pursued a policy of unwarranted aggression. In 1878, Cetshwayo was presented with an ultimatum as part of the British plan to bring about the confederation of states in South Africa, including Zululand. One of the demands made of Cetshwayo was that he disband his armies within one month and accept a British resident commissioner as co-ruler. This ultimatum was rejected. On January 20, 1879, British troops under the command of Lt. Gen. Lord Chelmsford (1827–1905) invaded Zululand in a three-pronged attack. The initial outcome was a humiliating defeat of British forces by the Zulu army at Isandlwana Mountain. Over 1,300 British troops and their African allies were killed. In the aftermath of one of the worst disasters of the colonial era, the Zulu reserves mounted a raid on the British border post at Rorke's Drift, but the Zulu were driven off after ten hours of ferocious fighting. The British collapse at Isandlwana left the flanking columns at Nyezane River and Hlobane Mountain vulnerable. But the success at Isandlwana exhausted the Zulu army and Cetshwayo was unable to mount a counteroffensive into Natal. The British rushed reinforcements to South Africa from various parts of the British Empire.

The war entered a new phase in March when Lord Chelmsford assembled a column to march to the relief of the other embattled commands. On April 2, Lord Chelmsford broke through the Zulu cordon around Eshowe at kwaGingindlovu, and relieved Pearson's column. The defeat of the Zulu king's forces in two battles demoralized the Zulu. British troops continued to advance toward the Zulu capital, Ulundi, which they reached at the end of June. Chelmsford defeated the Zulu army in the last great battle of the war on July 4, 1879. The Zulu capital of Ulundi was burned and Cetshwayo became a fugitive. But it took several weeks for the British to suppress lingering resistance outside the capital. Cetshwayo was captured on August 28, and exiled to Cape Town. The end of the war had many implications for the Zulu and for the British. The British divided the Zulu kingdom among pro-British chiefs—a deliberately divisive move that resulted in a decade of destructive civil war among various Zulu chiefdoms.

SEE ALSO *Britain's African Colonies.*

African Warriors in Natal, January 1, 1879. *A contingent of African soldiers fighting for the British stand in formation behind British officers in the colony of Natal during the 1879 Zulu War.* HULTON ARCHIVE/GETTY IMAGES. REPRODUCED BY PERMISSION.

BIBLIOGRAPHY

Greaves, Adrian. *Crossing the Buffalo: The Zulu War of 1879.* London: Orion, 2005.

Knight, Ian. *The Sun Turned Black: Isandlwana and Rorke's Drift, 1879.* Rivonia, South Africa: Waterman, 1996.

Morris, Donald R. *The Washing of the Spears: A History of the Rise of the Zulu Nation under Shaka and Its Fall in the Zulu War of 1879.* New York: Simon and Schuster, 1965.

Chima J. Korieh

Glossary

abolition: the ending of the practice of slavery.

aboriginal: an original inhabitant or native of a region or country. In the eighteenth century this term came to be associated with a native of a country colonized by European countries.

absolutist: characterizing a form of government in which the ruler or rulers have complete and unrestricted power to govern. Absolute power is vested in the authorities.

acculturation: the process by which one's culture is influenced by prolonged contact with a different culture. In the process of colonization, a composite culture emerges.

aldeias: a Portuguese term referring to mission villages of native Americans supervised by Portuguese clergy, generally, Jesuits; similar to Spanish *reducciónes* and French *reserves*.

anarchy: the lack of any formal system of government; political and social disorder created by the absence of government or law.

Ancien Régime: the dominant political and social order in France before the French Revolution. The Ancien Regime was characterized by absolute monarchy and the divine right of kings.

Annexation: the act by which one governmental entity asserts its sovereignty over another previously outside its boundaries.

Apartheid: Afrikaans word meaning "separation" or literally "apartness," Apartheid was the system of laws and policy implemented and enforced by the "White" minority governments in South Africa from 1948 until it was repealed in the early 1990s. As the idea of Apartheid developed in South Africa, it grew into a tool for racial, cultural, and national survival.

apologist: derived from the Greek word *apologia*, meaning defense of a position against an attack, an apologist is someone who participates in apologetics, the systematic defense of a position.

archipelago: a group or cluster of islands, sometimes including the body of water surrounding the islands.

asiento: a Spanish term referring to the trading contract and official license awarded to kingdoms and charter companies to supply African slaves to Spanish America.

assimilation: the integration of one entity into another entity. Assimilation as a colonial policy sought the integration of colonized peoples into the colonizer's cultural, social, and political institutions. The philosophy that drove this practice emphasized the Enlightenment ideas of such thinkers as the French philosopher Jean-Jacques Rousseau (1712–1778), who wrote in his *The Social Contract and Discourses* that men "who may be unequal in strength and intelligence, become every one equal by convention and equal right."

autarchy: a national policy aimed at economic independence and self-sufficiency. Under this system foreign economic aid and imports are relied on as little as possible.

Ayatollah: a religious leader of Shiite Muslims, often carrying political as well as religious importance.

Baathism: belief system of the Arab Socialist Baath Party founded in 1945. Baathism is a mostly secular ideology combining Arab socialism, nationalism, and Pan-Arabism.

balance of trade: the difference between the value of a nation's merchandise exports and imports.

Balfour Declaration: The Balfour Declaration of November 1917 was a letter from the British Foreign Secretary, Arthur Balfour, to Lord Rothschild, a prominent British member of the Zionist movement. On behalf of the British government, Balfour declared that "His Majesty's Government view with favour the establishment in Palestine of a National Home for the Jewish people."

Balkans, Balkan: the Balkans are the major mountain range running through the center of Bulgaria into eastern Serbia. The history of the Balkan region is one dominated by wars, rebellions, invasions and clashes between empires, from the Roman Empire to the Yugoslav wars of the twentieth century. The term Balkan has a broader meaning associated with its fragmented and often violent history.

Berber: an ethnic group indigenous to northwest Africa, speaking the Berber languages and principally concentrated in present-day Morocco and Algeria.

betel: evergreen climbing plant indigenous to parts of Asia and cultivated as a commercial crop in Madagascar, Bourbon and the West Indies; its leaves contain a stimulant and digestive aid.

Boer: The Dutch word for farmer, Boer refers to Dutch colonists settling in the Cape region of South Africa since the seventeenth century.

bossal/bozal: a slave brought directly to the New World from Africa and therefore speaks no European language, has no knowledge of Christianity, and is outside of civilization.

British Raj: historical period during which most of the Indian subcontinent (present-day India, Afghanistan, Pakistan, Bangladesh, and Myanmar) was under the colonial authority of the British Empire.

bull, papal: Bulls are papal letters or edicts during the Middle Ages, the name of which derives from the Latin *bulla* or leaden seal, which most often sealed the documents. Papal bulls were bulls of donation. These letters gathered more weight as the Middle Ages progressed. Donations were gifts or endowment of lands.

bullion: uncoined silver or gold in the form of ingots or bars. In the early modern period, bullion, silver in particular, was the most essential commodity of European-Asian trade.

bureaucracy: the hierarchical administrative structure of a large organization.

cabal: a small group of persons united to promote a common scheme, often operating in secrecy.

cacao: *Theobroma cacao*, known as "the food of the gods," and its main byproduct, chocolate, come from the seeds or nibs of a pod, the fruit of a tree native to tropical America. The cacao tree usually requires shade trees, often the so-called *madre de cacao* (mother of cacao), also an American native.

caliph: term or title for an Islamic leader; Anglicized/Latinized version of the Arabic word meaning "successor" or "representative," and sometimes referred to as a successor to the prophet of God, or representative of God.

canon law: body of laws governing the faith and practice of a Christian church, also called ecclesiastical law.

capitalism: an economic system based on private ownership of property in general, capital in particular. Production decisions are made and income is distributed as a result of a system of markets.

captaincy: a grant of dominion in the overseas territorial empire of Portugal to a private individual, a *donatorio,* who is given the authority to govern, assign land, and profit from the territory.

Carib: the name or language of a group of American Indian peoples of the Lesser Antilles, northern South America, and the eastern coast of Central America. The Caribbean Sea was named after the Caribs.

cartel: an alliance of producers of a similar or identical product formed to control pricing and competition.

casbah: the older section of a North African city, sometimes a walled citadel, castle, or palace.

casta: a term for all persons of mixed blood including freed blacks in Spanish America.

chartered company: a firm founded under a government grant (charter) giving it specified rights and privileges to trade to and in a certain region. Chartered companies were often given monopolies in their trade area, and were frequently established to compete with foreign businesses.

Cold War: the term used to describe the state of hostility, political tension, and military rivalry characterizing the struggle for supremacy between the Western powers and the Communist bloc from the end of World War II until the collapse of Communism in 1989.

Columbian Exchange: the widespread exchange of agricultural products, livestock, slave labor, communicable diseases, and related ideologies between the Eastern and Western Hemispheres (the Old World and the New World) that occurred in the decades following Christopher Columbus's first voyage to the New World in 1492.

commonwealth: originally a small group of self-governing white dominions within the British Empire. The evolution of the Commonwealth paralleled the deconstruction of the British Empire through the twentieth century, and the changing meaning and purpose of the Commonwealth reflected British efforts to maintain some influence as formal empire declined. The Commonwealth is now a voluntary association of over fifty nations, independent of British control, but linked by the culture of a common colonial heritage.

Communist: characterizing a political and economic system in which all property is owned by the community and the distribution of income is to each according to his or her need. This put the State in charge of organizing every aspect of the economy. The Communist movement, or Communism, is based on the ideas of Karl Marx (1818–1883) and Friedrich Engels (1820–1895).

conquistador: Spanish for conqueror, a term referring to sixteenth-century conquerors (military leaders) of Mexico, Peru, and Central America. Within just a few years of landing on the coasts of Mexico (1519) and Peru (1532), Spanish conquistadores under the leadership of Hernán Cortés (ca. 1484–1547) and Francisco Pizarro (ca. 1475–1541) respectively, had taken possession on behalf of the Spanish Crown of the large, rich, and densely populated empires of the Aztecs and the Incas.

coup d'état: the sudden, often violent overthrow of an existing government by a small group of subversives.

crown colony: a British overseas territory under the direct authority of the British Crown. As such, a Crown Colony does not possess its own representative government and is not represented in the British Parliament. The colony is administered by a governor appointed by the Crown and responsible to the colonial office (or its forerunners) and, from 1966 onward, to the Foreign and Commonwealth Office in London.

decolonization: a term referring to the European imperial retreat from sub-Saharan Africa in the aftermath of World War II and one of the most sudden and momentous transformations in the history of the modern world. Although the granting of self-government was not entirely novel prior to the end of the war in 1945, given the independence of Liberia in 1848, South Africa in 1910, and Ethiopia in 1943, the postwar imperial transformation was nevertheless unprecedented. Between 1945 and 1965, almost all European African colonies—except the former Portuguese territories, Zimbabwe and Namibia—regained their independence.

demography: branch of sociology that studies the characteristics of human populations.

coureurs de bois: a French term for backwoodsmen who traveled into the interior of New France to trade with Native Americans.

criollo: a Spanish term for a Spaniard born in America; the English equivalent is *creole;* the Spanish also used this term to refer to African American slaves who were American born and acculturated into Spanish American society. The equivalent Portuguese word is *crioulo.*

dependency (as form of colonial governance): emphasizing informal imperialism, dependency theory focuses on the subjugation by core nations of peripheral and semi-peripheral economies through new forms of domination, such as financial coercion (dollar diplomacy) and, at times, military action. Since the 1940s international organizations, such as the International Monetary Fund, have been created by core powers to continue this dependency. Any economic development was primarily in the service of the core nations.

despotism: rule by a despot or tyrant; a form of government in which the ruler is an absolute dictator (not restricted by a constitution, laws or opposition).

diaspora: the out-migration of peoples from traditional homelands, often in times of crisis. Among the best-known modern example are African slaves, persons of Jewish descent (who have been forced to move at many times throughout history), and persons of Irish descent (who settled in places like the United States and Australia after the great famine of 1847–1851).

direct rule: a system of government wherein the central or national government is in direct control of the regional governmental entities.

divide-and-rule system: Roman system of colonization whereby the Romans willingly and freely incorporated newly conquered people into their own society, freely giving citizenship to outsiders in order to Romanize them and make them willing participants (instead of unwilling subjects or enemies) in the Roman imperial system. egalitarianrelating to the doctrine that all people are equal and should be treated on equal terms, such as legally, economically, politically, and socially.

emancipation: setting free from slavery or oppression; for example, in the Emancipation Proclamation, U.S. president Abraham Lincoln set free all slaves in the Confederate States in 1863.

encomienda: a Spanish term for a royal grant of the tribute or labor of a population of native Americans to a private individual, an *Encomendero,* usually as a reward for service to the crown in a military campaign.

endemic: relating to a limited geographic region; native or restricted to a limited geographic region.

engagé: a French term referring to an indentured servant who contracted to work a certain number of years for payment of passage to New France or another French colony.

entrepôt: a center of trade, often a port, to which goods are shipped for storage and distribution to buyers in other areas. In the nineteenth century Liverpool was an important entrepôt for Britain's west coast.

ethnocentric: perceiving one's own culture as the center of everything and other cultures as its periphery; relating to the inherent superiority of one's cultural or ethnic group.

exogamy: the custom of marrying outside one's social group.

extraterritoriality: the practice of exempting certain foreign nationals from the jurisdiction of their country of residence. The most common application of extraterritoriality is the custom of exempting foreign heads of state and diplomats from local jurisdiction. Another form of extraterritoriality is the limited immunity from local jurisdiction that U.S. servicemen on overseas duty enjoy under the Status of Force Agreements. In the nineteenth and early twentieth centuries, extraterritoriality was often used synonymously with consular jurisdiction, which was the practice of consuls exercising jurisdiction over their nationals in certain non-Western countries.

fascism: a political movement characterized by rabid nationalism, authoritarianism, and opposition to Communism. It insisted on state control of the economy.

Fertile Crescent: the historic, fertile region of the Middle East including all or parts of Israel, the West Bank, Jordan, Lebanon, Syria, and Iraq; spans the northern part of the Syrian desert, bordered on the west by the Mediterranean Sea and on the east by the Tigris and Euphrates rivers.

feudalism: the form of political and social organization characteristic of Western Europe in the Middle Ages whereby a king rewarded chosen nobles with land in return for their loyalty and military service, and the nobility's subsequent use of the peasantry to farm the land in return for labor and a portion of the produce.

free trade: a system of trade that gradually replaced mercantilism in the nineteenth century. In theory it allows for the international exchange of commodities without imposition of tariffs or duties.

galleon: large oceangoing vessel used by Spanish and Portuguese from the fifteenth to eighteenth centuries for commerce and warfare. Their size and weight distribution gave them a military disadvantage.

globalization: worldwide exchange of technology, economics, politics, and culture facilitated by modern technological advances.

Glorious Revolution: events of 1688–1689 in English history resulting in the deposition of James II and the ascension of William III also referred to as the Bloodless Revolution because there was little armed resistance, the Glorious Revolution established the power of parliament over the monarch.

guerrilla: Spanish for "little war," a small unofficial military group and its members.

hacienda: a Spanish word referring to a diversified agricultural estate in Spanish America.

hegemony: a degree of informal control exerted by a country with the economic, political, and military power to set and enforce the prevailing rules of the international system. Unlike an empire, the hegemon does not have to exert formal control over other states or powers in the global arena; instead, it exercises a degree of informal control known as hegemony. The power and influence of the United States on world affairs in the twentieth century is often cited as an example of hegemony.

Hispaniola: an island in the Greater Antilles of the Caribbean, home to the largest of the first Spanish settlements in North America. Today Hispaniola is shared by the Dominican Republic and Haiti.

home rule: self-government by a local jurisdiction in their own matters; originated in the nineteenth century as a political term used by Irish nationalists in their fight for self-government for Ireland.

Huguenot: French Protestants and the Protestant movement in the sixteenth century. French Huguenots expanded into the Atlantic and attempted to create colonies in Florida and Brazil without success. Although Protestants formed a majority of the population in the sixteenth century, French Catholics with support from the King of Spain gained power and in the Edict of Nantes in the late sixteenth century, freedom of worship was proclaimed. Huguenot revolts in La Rochelle and other centers in the early seventeenth century were repressed.

imam: title of a Muslim leader; successor to Muhammad as the leader of Shiite Islam.

imperialism: assumption of control by one society or nation over others, often by force; creating an empire. Because of the use of power, imperialism is often considered an objectionable foreign policy.

ingenio: a Spanish term for a sugar plantation and mill.

isolationist: referring to a country's policy of isolation by refraining from participating in alliances or international relations.

jihad: Islam for holy war of some type, a war ordained by God.

ladino: a Christianized African slave who spoke Spanish or had some knowledge of Spanish of culture.

League of Nations: international organization established after World War I under the provisions of the Treaty of Versailles to promote cooperation and peace among nations; forerunner of the United Nations.

Leninism: modification of Marxism by Lenin; political and economic theories stressing imperialism as the highest form of capitalism

letter of marque and reprisal: a government's official warrant or commission authorizing a designated agent to search, seize, or destroy specified assets or personnel belonging to foreign or hostile parties. Often used to authorize private ships to raid and capture an enemy's merchant vessels.

Levant: from the French *lever*, (to rise), the countries bordering the eastern shore of the Mediterranean Sea, Cyprus, Egypt, Israel, Lebanon, Syria, and Turkey. This term first came into use with the French mandate of Syria and Lebanon from 1920 until the mid-1940s, which were called the Levant States.

lingua franca: a common language used between speakers of different native languages.

Madrasa: a term derived from the Arabic word for Islamic institution of higher learning.

malaria: disease caused by a blood parasite transmitted through the bite of an infected Anopheles mosquito, most often in tropical and subtropical regions. Characterized by recurring chills and fever.

mameluco: a Portuguese term referring to the offspring of Portuguese and Indian parents.

mandate: defined in Article 22 of the Covenant of the League of Nations (1919) as a new form of political supervision created after World War; the mandate system gave broad authority to the victorious Allies over the former colonial empires of Imperial Germany and the Ottoman Turks. The mandated territories were divided into three classes and were assigned to individual powers to govern until they were deemed capable of self-rule.

manumission: the act of liberating a slave from bondage.

Marshall Plan: the program by which the United States helped European countries rebuild after the devastation of World War II by giving them significant economic aid. Named after its proponent, U.S. secretary of state General George C. Marshall, the Marshall Plan was a comprehensive program of targeted investments, run by American economic advisers, aimed at rebuilding the European economies on the basis of free market policies.

maroon: from the Spanish word *cimarróm* (wild) for runaway slave, a Maroon is both a runaway slave and a community of runaway slaves.

martial law: temporary rule and control by domestic military authorities when war or civil crisis prevents civil authorities from enforcing the law.

Marxism: the political and economic theories of Karl Marx (1818–1883) and Friedrich Engels (1820–1895) in which economic determinism (the theory that political and social institutions are economically determined) figures prominently and class struggle is central to social change.

mercantilism: a term encompassing the diverse trade practices followed by European states from the sixteenth until the late eighteenth century; a collection of policies designed to keep the state prosperous through economic regulation. Mercantilism assumed that wealth is an absolutely indispensable means to achieve geopolitical power; that such power is valuable as a means to acquire or retain wealth; that wealth and power constitute the dual ends of national policy; and that these two ends are compatible and, indeed, complementary.

Mercator projection: created by Gerardus Mercator in 1569, a method of showing the three-dimensional world on a two-dimensional map that satisfied many of the requirements of explorers and other mariners.

mercenary: soldiers hired into foreign service. For example, the most renowned mercenaries in colonial Asia were those hired by both sides of the momentous military campaigns during China's Taiping Rebellion (1850–1864).

Mesoamerica: the pre-Columbian region of Central America and southern North America in which diverse civilizations flourished, including the Mayan and the Olmec.

mestizo: Hispanic for a person of mixed or combined racial ancestry, especially referring to a person in Latin America with both Native American and European ancestry.

metropole: a developed urban center, often associated with the provision of financial/industrial goods and services to associated rural areas (hinterlands) from which they receive raw materials.

Middle Passage: term for the journey of slaves in slave ships from Africa across the Atlantic to the Caribbean or the Americas; a horrific experience marked by inhuman conditions of transport, insufficient food, and disease.

miscegenation: intermarriage between people of different races.

Moors: Muslim North Africans; nomadic people of the northern shores of Africa, largely Arab and Berber.

most favored nation: status accorded by one nation to another in international trade whereby the nation receiving most favored nation status will be awarded all trade advantages that other trading nations receive.

mulatto: a derivation of the word mulo, which refers to the hybrid offspring of a horse and a mule. It became a term used to designate a person of mixed blood, usually someone with a Caucasian father and an African or African-American mother.

multilateral: involving multiple nations or groups.

nationalism: assertion of a nation's right to independence and self-government. Nations were normally those groups with a shared culture, religion, language and history. A frequent nationalist goal has been the creation of a "nation-state," or country, in which to realize cultural aspirations.

negritude: an African diasporic, self-affirming idea that evolved into an artistic and cultural movement and later became a lightening rod for controversy and ideological disputes. The (re)valorization of the black world, the affirmation of the humanity of black people, and the glorification of the richness of black culture had antecedents in the works of earlier thinkers and scholars such as Edward Wilmot Blyden (1832–1912), Martin Delany (1812–1885), and W. E. B. Du Bois (1868–1963), and writers of the Harlem Renaissance such as Claude McKay (1890–1948) and Langston Hughes (1902–1967), who reclaimed "blackness" with pride, reinvested it with positive meanings, and rejected the negativity heaped on it by racism, slavery, colonialism, and imperialism.

new imperialism: a sophisticated manifestation of free trade imperialism resulting from the rising European appetite for conquest and the willingness of European governments to pay for imperialist ventures; distinguished from older traditions of colonialism before 1850, which focused more on seeking commercial influence than formal occupation.

Occidentalism: scholarly study of the characteristics of Western civilizations; Occidentalism has become associated with Eastern views of Western culture, peoples, and languages.

Oceania: geographic region usually considered to include the central and southern Pacific, but excluding the North Pacific and Australia. Oceania consists of three principal areas: Polynesia, Micronesia, and Melanesia.

oligarchy: system of government in which power is held by a small group. When referring to governments, the classical definition of oligarchy, as given for example by Aristotle, is of government by a few, usually the rich, for their own advantage.

open door policy: a policy proposed by U.S. secretary of state John Hay in September 1899 in which all nations would have equal trading and development rights throughout all of China, as an effort by the U.S. government to preserve China's territorial and administrative integrity at a time when it seemed the major imperial powers intended to carve China into a series of concessions, perhaps presaging the end of a unified China.

Pacific Rim: the term used to describe the nations bordering the Pacific Ocean, but not always the island countries. situated in it. In the post–World War II era, the Pacific Rim became an increasingly important and interconnected economic region. The socioeconomic concept of a "Pacific Rim" exploits the region's sea-lanes and sea resources, including fishing rights.

pass law: a reference to the Pass Laws Act of 1952, which required all black South Africans over the age of 16 to carry a pass book, the terms and conditions of which effactually controlled the movement of black people within South Africa.

Penal colonies: colonies created for detaining prisoners for penal labor. Penal colonies were located at a substantial distance from the homeland to discourage prisoners from returning to their native country once their terms expired.

patroonship: an Anglicized Dutch term referring to a grant of land and political authority (a fief) awarded to an individual, a patroon, who had the obligation to settle fifty colonists within four years. In New Netherland, Rensselaerswijck was a patroonship founded by Kiliaen van Rensselaer that measured nearly one million acres in what are today the counties of Albany and Rensselaer, New York.

Persia: conventional European designation of the country now known as Iran. This name was in general use in the West until 1935, although the Iranians themselves had long called their country Iran. The name of Persia is often employed for that part of the country's history concerned with the ancient Persian Empire until the Arab conquest in the seventh century c.e.

pidgin: a non-native language of simplified grammar and vocabulary, used between people speaking different languages.

pre-Columbian: relating to North, Central, or South America before the arrival of Christopher Columbus in 1492; generally referring to the cultures indigenous to the New World, in the era before significant European influence.

privateer: private ship of war. Issued a "Letter of Marque" authorizing it to attack enemy vessels. Privateers earned profits by capturing ships, then selling the vessel and its cargo. Remained important until after the War of 1812.

protectionism: the economic policy of restricting import trade to protect domestic producers from competition.

Quilombos: remote Brazilian settlements of runaway slaves (Maroons) and free-born African slaves. These settlements were active in helping slaves escape and fighting groups commissioned to recapture escaped slaves. One well-known quilombo was Palmares, or Quilombo dos Palmares, a large, independent, and self-sustaining settlement founded about 1600 in northeastern Brazil.

raj: Indian word for prince or royalty; empire.

reconquista: Spanish and Portuguese word meaning "reconquest," often referring to the reestablishment of Christian rule in the Iberian Peninsula between 718 and 1492, the seven-century-long process of reconquest of much of Iberia (the peninsula now occupied by Spain and Portugal) from Muslims who first invaded the region in 711.

repatriate: referring to someone who has been returned to his or her country of birth, or an artifact which has been returned to its country of origin (or the act of returning someone or something to its country of birth or origin).

revisionism: a socialist movement arguing for the revision of revolutionary Marxist theory, toward nonviolent achievement of social progress through reform.

Royal African Company: founded in 1672, one of many joint-stock companies of the English Atlantic from the mid-sixteenth through the seventeenth century. A good number of these companies lasted only decades, but they laid the foundations for the English slave trade, Atlantic commerce, and "foreign plantations" in the Americas.

royal charter: a written grant by royalty creating an entity such as a university or organization.

Safavid Empire: an empire reaching from southern Iraq to the borders of Herat in modern Afghanistan, from Baku in present-day Azerbaijan to Kandahar in Afghanistan, and from the Caspian Sea to Bahrain. The Safavid Empire's boundaries have come to define where Iran is (or ought to be) in the contemporary Iranian national imagination.

satellite state: an independent country dominated by a larger power; initially coined during the Cold War era in reference to Central and Eastern European countries of the Warsaw Pact being "satellites" of the Soviet Union.

scorched-earth (adj, as in scorched-earth tactics): referring to a policy whereby armed forces destroy anything of use in an area to prevent its use by enemy forces.

scurvy: illness or deficiency disorder resulting from the lack of vitamin C, or ascorbic acid, characterized by gums becoming spongy, anemia, and skin hemorrhaging. Scurvy became especially common among sailors when ready sources of vitamin C, such as fresh fruits and vegetables, could not be stocked aboard ship.

secession: withdrawal from an established union, such as when the eleven southern states withdrew from the Union at the onset of the U.S. Civil War.

Self-Determination: the power of a nation to decide how it will be governed. Self-Determination was integral to "Wilsonianism," named for U.S. president Woodrow Wilson.

sepoy: Derived from the Persian word *sipahi*, meaning "regular soldier," the term sepoy designates Indian infantrymen trained and equipped to European standards and employed in the armies of the East India Company and later the British Crown. A significant majority of the East India Company's armed forces from the middle decades of the eighteenth century, sepoys were absolutely crucial to the expansion, consolidation, and maintenance of the company's interests in India and Asia.

sericulture: the manufacture of raw silk, originating from the Greek word *serikos*.

shogunate, shogun: A shogunate was the Japanese military administrative system between the twelfth and nineteenth centuries; the shogun was an emporer's military deputy and the practical ruler of Japan.

Silk Road: a land route from China to Europe actively used in the trading of silk textiles until the age of sail, dating from about the second century b.c.e.

Slave Coast: European trading term for the coast bordering the Bight of Benin on the Gulf of Guinea, West Africa; served as the principal source of West African slaves from the sixteenth to the mid-nineteenth century.

socialism: theories calling for a more fair and egalitarian society usually to be attainted through government action. By 1900 socialism was the major force representing working-class interests. From Socialist ideals have sprung reforms like social security benefits, national health care, and worker representation through trade unions.

sovereignty: referring to a nation or state's supreme power within its borders.

trust territory: United Nations Trust Territories were the successors of the League of Nations mandates and came into being when the League of Nations ceased to exist in 1946. All of the trust territories were administered through the UN Trusteeship Council.

vassal state: a state that is dependent on or subordinate to another, often involving military support or protection.

Voortrekkers: Afrikaans word for pioneers; Voortrekkers were Boers (Afrikaner farmers) who emigrated from Cape Colony in the 1830s and 1840s to what is now South Africa.

welfare state: a political system in which a government assumes the primary responsibility for assuring the basic health, education, and financial well-being of all its citizens through programs and direct assistance.

Zionist: pertaining to the political movement begun in the late nineteenth century for reconstituting a Jewish national state in Palestine.

Primary Sources

HISTORICAL TEXT

ANGLO-RUSSIAN ENTENTE OF 1907

INTRODUCTION *The Anglo-Russian Entente of 1907 was an agreement between Russia and Britain that fixed the boundaries of Persia, Afghanistan, and Tibet. Persia was divided into spheres of Russian interest in the North and British interest in the southeast, keeping the Russians away from the Persian Gulf and the Indian border. As the Ottoman Empire began to decline in power in the 1700s, the rivalry between Russia and Great Britain became a major factor in geopolitics as both countries took measures to gain influence in southeastern Europe, in the Middle East, and in Central Asia. After nearly two centuries of tension, the Anglo-Russian Entente formalized British and Russian spheres of interest over economic development in the region.*

AGREEMENT CONCERNING PERSIA

The Governments of Great Britain and Russia having mutually engaged to respect the integrity and independence of Persia, and sincerely desiring the preservation of order throughout that country and its peaceful development, as well as the permanent establishment of equal advantages for the trade and industry of all other nations;

Considering that each of them has, for geographical and economic reasons, a special interest in the maintenance of peace and order in certain provinces of Persia adjoining, or in the neighborhood of, the Russian frontier on the one hand, and the frontiers of Afghanistan and Baluchistan on the other hand; and being desirous of avoiding all cause of conflict between their respective interests in the above-mentioned provinces of Persia;

Have agreed on the following terms:

I. Great Britain engages not to seek for herself, and not to support in favour of British subjects, or in favour of the subjects of third Powers, any Concessions of a political or commercial nature\emdash such as Concessions for railways, banks, telegraphs, roads, transport, insurance, etc. – beyond a line starting from Kasr-i-Shirin, passing through Isfahan, Yezd, Kakhk, and ending at a point on the Persian frontier at the intersection of the Russian and Afghan frontiers, and not to oppose, directly or indirectly, demands for similar Concessions in this region which are supported by the Russian Government. It is understood that the above-mentioned places are included in the region in which Great Britain engages not to seek the Concessions referred to.

II. Russia, on her part, engages not to seek for herself and not to support, in favour of Russian subjects, or in favour of the subjects of third Powers, any Concessions of a political or commercial nature – such as Concessions for railways , banks, telegraphs, roads, transport, insurance, etc. – beyond a line going from the Afghan frontier by way of Gazik, Birjand, Kerman, and ending at Bunder Abbas, and not to oppose, directly or indirectly, demands for similar Concessions in this region which are supported by the British Government. It is understood that the above-mentioned places are included in the region in which Russia engages not to seek the Concessions referred to.

III. Russia, on her part, engages not to oppose, without previous arrangement with Great Britain, the grant of any Concessions whatever to British subjects in the regions of Persia situated between the lines mentioned in Articles I and II. Great Britain undertakes a similar engagement as regards the grant of Concessions to Russian subjects in the same regions of Persia.

All Concessions existing at present in the regions indicated in Articles I and II and maintained.

IV. It is understood that the revenues of all the Persian customs, with the exception of those of Farsistan and of the Persian Gulf, revenues guaranteeing the amortization and the interest of the loans concluded by the Government of the Shah with the "Banque d'escompte et des Prits de Perse" up to the date of the signature of the present Agreement, shall be devoted to the same purpose as in the past. It is equally understood that the revenues of the Persian customs of Farsistan and of the Persian Gulf, as well as those of the fisheries on the Persian shore of the Caspian Sea and those of the Posts and telegraphs, shall be devoted, as in the past, to the service of the loans concluded by the Government of the Shah with the Imperial Bank of Persia up to the date of the signature of the present Agreement.

V. In the event of irregularities occurring in the amortization or payment of interest of the Persian loans concluded with the "Banque d'escompte et des Prits de Perse" and with the Imperial Bank of Persia up to the date of the signature of the present Agreement, and in the event of the necessity arising for Russia to establish control over the sources of revenue guaranteeing the regular service of the loans concluded with the first-named bank, and situated in the region mentioned in Article II of the present Agreement, or for Great Britain to establish control over the sources of revenue guaranteeing the regular service of the loans concluded with the second-named bank, and situated in the region mentioned in Article I of the present Agreement, the British and Russian Governments undertake to enter beforehand into a friendly exchange of ideas with a view to determine, in agreement with each other, the measures of control in question and to avoid all interference which would not be in conformity with the principles governing the present Agreement.

ATLANTIC CHARTER

INTRODUCTION *The Atlantic Charter, a declaration of principles issued by U.S. president Franklin D. Roosevelt and British prime minister Winston Churchill in 1941, echoed Woodrow Wilson's Fourteen Points and called for the rights of self-determination, self-government, and free speech for all peoples. The charter stipulated that at the end of World War II, all Allied nations could determine their own political destinies. Many African and Asian nationalists capitalized on the promise of the Atlantic Charter to argue for political independence from colonial control.*

AUGUST 14, 1941

The President of the United States of America and the Prime Minister, Mr. Churchill, representing His Majesty's Government in the United Kingdom, being met together, deem it right to make known certain common principles in the national policies of their respective countries on which they base their hopes for a better future for the world.

First, their countries seek no aggrandizement, territorial or other;

Second, they desire to see no territorial changes that do not accord with the freely expressed wishes of the peoples concerned;

Third, they respect the right of all peoples to choose the form of government under which they will live; and they wish to see sovereign rights and self government restored to those who have been forcibly deprived of them;

Fourth, they will endeavor, with due respect for their existing obligations, to further the enjoyment by all States, great or small, victor or vanquished, of access, on equal terms, to the trade and to the raw materials of the world which are needed for their economic prosperity;

Fifth, they desire to bring about the fullest collaboration between all nations in the economic field with the object of securing, for all, improved labor standards, economic advancement and social security;

Sixth, after the final destruction of the Nazi tyranny, they hope to see established a peace which will afford to all nations the means of dwelling in safety within their own boundaries, and which will afford assurance that all the men in all lands may live out their lives in freedom from fear and want;

Seventh, such a peace should enable all men to traverse the high seas and oceans without hindrance;

Eighth, they believe that all of the nations of the world, for realistic as well as spiritual reasons must come to the abandonment of the use of force. Since no future peace can be maintained if land, sea or air armaments continue to be employed by nations which threaten, or may threaten, aggression outside of their frontiers, they believe, pending the establishment of a wider and permanent system of general security, that the disarmament of such nations is essential. They will likewise aid and encourage all other practicable measure which will lighten for peace-loving peoples the crushing burden of armaments.

Franklin D. Roosevelt

Winston S. Churchill

THE BALFOUR DECLARATION

INTRODUCTION *The Balfour Declaration of November 2, 1917, was a letter from the British foreign secretary, Arthur Balfour, to Lord Rothschild, a prominent British supporter of the Zionist movement. On behalf of the British government, Balfour expressed support for the establishment of a Jewish homeland in Palestine. Although the Balfour Declaration reflected a degree of British official sympathy with Zionist aspirations, it also served British strategic and colonial interests: first, by building wartime support among Jews in Europe and North America, and second, by bolstering Britain's postwar claims to the territory northeast of the Suez Canal.*

Foreign Office
November 2nd, 1917
Dear Lord Rothschild,

I have much pleasure in conveying to you, on behalf of His Majesty's Government, the following declaration of sympathy with Jewish Zionist aspirations which has been submitted to, and approved by, the Cabinet.

"His Majesty's Government view with favour the establishment in Palestine of a national home for the Jewish people, and will use their best endeavours to facilitate the achievement of this object, it being clearly understood that nothing shall be done which may prejudice the civil and religious rights of existing non-Jewish communities in Palestine, or the rights and political status enjoyed by Jews in any other country."

I should be grateful if you would bring this declaration to the knowledge of the Zionist Federation.

Yours sincerely,
Arthur James Balfour

CHARTER OF PRIVILEGES AND EXEMPTIONS, THE DUTCH WEST INDIA COMPANY

SOURCE The Federal and State Constitutions Colonial Charters, and Other Organic Laws of the States, Territories, and Colonies Now or Heretofore Forming the United States of America, *Compiled and Edited Under the Act of Congress of June 30,* 1906 by Francis Newton Thorpe Washington, DC : Government Printing Office, 1909.

INTRODUCTION *The States-General (parliament) of the Netherlands granted this charter to the Dutch West India Company in 1621. According to the charter, the company held a monopoly in shipping and trade in a territory that included Africa south of the Tropic of Cancer, all of America, and the Atlantic and Pacific islands between the two meridians drawn across the Cape of Good Hope and the eastern extremities of New Guinea. Within this territory the States-General authorized the company to set up colonies, sign treaties with local rulers, erect fortresses, and wage war against enemies. Although its main objective was to establish and defend a commercial network in the Atlantic, in practice the West India Company spent more money on privateering and war against Spain and Portugal.*

JUNE 3, 1621

The States-General of the United Netherlands, to all who shall see these Presents, or hear them read, Greeting.

Be it known, that we knowing the prosperity of these countries, and the welfare of their inhabitants depends principally on navigation and trade, which in all former times by the said Countries were carried on happily, and with a great blessing to all countries and kingdoms; and desiring that the aforesaid inhabitants should not only be preserved in their former navigation, traffic, and trade, but also that their trade may be encreased as much as possible in special conformity to the treaties, alliances, leagues and covenants for traffic and navigation formerly made with other princes, republics and people, which we give them to understand must be in. all parts punctually kept and adhered to: And we find by experience, that without the common help, assistance, and interposition of a General Company, the people designed from hence for those parts cannot be profitably protected and mantained in their great risque from pirates, extortion and otherwise, which will happen in so very long a voyage. We have, therefore, and for several other important reasons and considerations as thereunto moving, with mature deliberation of counsel, and for highly necessary causes, found it good, that the navigation, trade, and commerce, in the parts of the West-Indies, and Africa, and other places hereafter described, should not henceforth be carried on any otherwise than by the common united strength of the merchants and inhabitants of these countries; and for that end there shall be erected one General Company, which we out of special regard to their common well-being, and to keep and preserve the inhabitants of those places in good trade and welfare, will maintain and strengthen with our Help, Favour and assistance as far as the present state and condition of this

Country will admit: and moreover furnish them with a proper Charter, and with the following Priveleges and Exemptions, to wit, That for the Term of four and twenty Years, none of the Natives or Inhabitants of these countries shall be permitted to sail to or from the said lands, or to traffic on the coast and countries of *Africa* from the *Tropic of Cancer to the Cape of Good Hope,* nor in the countries of *America,* or the West-Indies, beginning at the fourth end of *Terra Nova,* by the streights of *Magellan, La Maire,* or any other streights and passages situated thereabouts to the straights of *Anian,* as well on the north sea as the south sea, nor on any islands situated on the one side or the other, or between both; nor in the western or southern countries reaching, lying, and between both the meridians, from the Cape of Good Hope, in the East, to the east end of New Guinea, in the West, inclusive, but in the Name of this United Company of these United Netherlands. And whoever shall presume without the consent of this Company, to sail or to traffic in any of the Places within the aforesaid Limits granted to this Company, he shall forfeit the ships and the goods which shall be found for sale upon the aforesaid coasts and lands; the which being actually seized by the aforesaid Company, shall be by them kept for their own Benefit and Behoof. And in case such ships or goods shall be sold either in other countries or havens they may touch at, the owners and partners must be fined for the value of those ships and goods: Except only, that they who before the date of this charter, shall have sailed or been sent out of these or any other countries, to any of the aforesaid coasts, shall be able to continue their trade for the sale of their goods, and cosine back again, or otherwise, until the expiration of this charter, if they have had any before, and not longer: Provided, that after the first of July sixteen hundred and twenty one, the day and time of this charters commencing, no person shall be able to send any ships or goods to the places comprehended in this charter, although that before the date hereof, this Company was not finally incorporated: But shall provide therein as is becoming, against those who knowingly by fraud endeavour to frustrate our intention herein for the public good: Provided that the salt trade at *Ponte del Re* may be continued according to the conditions and instructions by us already given, or that may be given respecting it, any thing in this charter to the contrary notwithstanding.

II. That, moreover, the aforesaid Company may, in our name and authority, within the limits herein before prescribed, make contracts, engagements and alliances with the limits herein before prescribed, make contracts, engagements and alliances with the princes and natives of the countries comprehended therein, and also build any forts and fortifications there, to appoint and discharge Governors, people for war, and officers of justice, and other public officers, for the preservation of the places, keeping good order, police and justice, and in like manner for the promoting of trade; and again, others in their place to put, as they from the situation of their affairs shall see fit: Moreover, they must advance the peopling of those fruitful and unsettled parts, and do all that the service of those countries, and the profit and increase of trade shall require: and the Company shall successively communicate and transmit to us such contracts and alliances as they shall have made with the aforesaid princes and nations; and likewise the situation of the fortresses, fortifications, and settlements by them taken.

III. Saving, that they having chosen a governor in chief, and prepared instructions for him, they shall be approved, and a commission given by us, And that further, such governor in chief, as well as other deputy governors, commanders, and officers, shall be held to take an oath of allegiance to us and also to the Company.

IV. And if the aforesaid Company in and of the aforesaid places shall be cheated under the appearance of friendship, or badly treated, or shall suffer loss in trusting their money or Goods, without having restitution, or receiving payment for them, they may use the best methods in their power, according to the situation of their affairs, to obtain satisfaction.

V. And if it should be necessary for the establishment, security and defence of this trade, to take any troops with them, we will, according to the constitution of this country, and the situation of affairs furnish the said Company with such troops, provided they be paid and supported by the Company.

VI. Which troops, besides the oath already taken to us and to his excellency, shall swear to obey the commands of the said Company, and to endeavour to promote their interest to the utmost of their ability.

VII. That the provosts of the Company on shore may apprehend any of the military, that have inlisted in the service of the aforesaid company, and may confine them on board the ships in whatever city, place, or jurisdiction they may be found; provided, the provosts first inform the officers and magistrats of the cities and places where this happens.

VIII. That we will not take any ships, ordnance, or ammunition belonging to the company, for the use of this country, without the consent of the said company.

IX. We have moreover incorporated this company, and favoured them with privileges, and we give them a charter besides this, that they may pass freely with all their ships and goods without paying any toll to the United Provinces; and that they themselves may use their liberty in the same manner as the free inhabitants of the cities of this country enjoy their freedom, notwithstanding any person who is not free may be a member of this company.

X. That all the goods of this company during the eight next ensuing years, be carried out of this country to the parts of the West Indies and Africa, and other places comprehended within the aforesaid limits, and those which they shall bring into this country, shall be from outward and home convoys; provided, that if at the expiration of the aforesaid eight years, the state and situation of these Countries will not admit of this Freedom's continuing for a longer time, the said goods, and the merchandises coming from the places mentioned in this Charter, and exported again out of these countries, and the outward convoys and licenses, during the whole time of this Charter, shall not be rated higher by us than they have formerly been rated, unless we should be again engaged in a war, in which case, all the aforesaid goods and merchandises will not be rated higher by us than they were in the last list in time of war.

XI. And that this company may be strengthened by a good government, to the greatest profit and satisfaction of all concerned, we have ordained, that the said government shall be vested in five chambers of managers; one at Amsterdam,-this shall have the management of four-ninths parts; one chamber in Zealand, for two-ninth parts; one chamber at the Maeze, for one-ninth part; one chamber in North Holland, for one-ninth-part; and the fifth chamber in Friesland, with the city and country, for one-ninth part; upon the condition entered in the record of our resolutions, and the Act past respecting it. And the Provinces in which there are no chambers shall be accommodated with so many managers, divided among the respective chambers, as their hundred thousand guilders in this company shall entitle them to.

XII. That the chamber of Amsterdam shall consist of twenty managers; the chamber of Zealand of twelve; the chambers of Maeze and of the North Part, each of fourteen, and the chamber of Friesland, with the city and country, also of fourteen managers; if it shall hereafter appear, that this work cannot be carried on without a greater number of persons; in that case, more may be added, with the knowledge of nineteen, and our approbation, but not otherwise.

XIII. And the States of the respective United Provmces are authorized, to lay before their High Mightinesses' ordinary deputies, or before the magistrates of the cities of these Provinces, any order for registering the members, together with the election of managers, if they find they can do it according to the constitution of their Provinces. Moreover, that no person m the chamber of Amsterdam shall be chosen a manager who has not of his own in the fields of the company, the sum of five thousand guilders; and the Chamber of Zealand four

thousand Builders, and the chamber of Maeze, of the North Part, and of Friesland, with the city and country. the like sum of four thousand guilders.

XIV. That the first managers shall serve for the term of six years, and then one-third part of the number of managers shall be changed by lot; and two years after a like third part, and the two next following years, the last third part; and so on successively the oldest in the service shall be dismissed; and in the place of those who go off, or of any that shall die, or for any other reason be dismissed, three others shall be nominated by the managers, both remaining and going oaf, together with the principal adventures in person, and at their cost, from which the aforesaid Provinces, the deputies, or the magistrates, shall make a new election of a manager, and successively supply the vacant places; and it shall be held before the principal adventurers, who have as great a concern as the respective managers.

XV. That the accounts of the furniture and outfit of the vessels, with their dependencies, shall be made up three months after the departure of the vessels, and one month after, copies shall be sent to to us, and to the respective chambers: and the state of the returns, and their sales, shall the chambers (as often as we see good, or they are required thereto by the chambers) send to us and to one another.

XVI. That evry six years they shall make a general account of all outfits and returns, together with all the gains and losses of the company; to wit, one of their business, and one of the war, each separate; which accounts shall be made public by an advertisement, to the end that every one who is interested may, upon hearing of it, attend; and if by the expiration of the seventh year, the accounts are not made out in manner aforesaid, the managers shall forfeit their commissions, which shall be appropriated to the use of the poor, and they themselves be held to render their account as before, till such time and under such penalty as shall be fixed by us respecting offenders. And notwithstanding there shall be a dividend made of the profits of the business, so long as we find that term per Cent shall have been gained.

XVII. No one shall, during the continuance of this charter, withdraw his capital, or sum advanced? from this company; nor shall any new members be admitted. If at the expiration of four and twenty years it shall be found good to continue this company, or to erect a a new one, a final account and estimate shall be made by the nineteen, with our knowledge, of all that belongs to the company, and also of all their expences, and any one, after the aforesaid settlement and estimate, may withdraw his money, or continue it in the new company, in whole or in part, in the same proportion as in this; And the new company shall in such case take the remainder, and pay the members which do not think fit to continue in the company their share, at such times as the nineteen, with our knowledge and approbation, shall think proper.

XVIII. That so often as it shall be necessary to have a general meeting of the aforesaid chambers, it shall be by nineteen persons, of whom eight shall come from the chamber of Amsterdam; from Zealand, four; from the Maeze, two; from North Holland, two; from Friesland, and the city and country, two, provided, that the nine-teen persons, or so many more as we shall at any time think fit, shall be deputed by US for the purpose of helping to direct the aforesaid meeting of the company.

XIX. By which general meeting of the aforesaid chambers, all the business of this Company which shall come before them shall be managed and finally settled, provided, that in case of resolving upon a war, our approbation shall be asked.

XX. The aforesaid general meeting being sum-moned, it shall meet to resolve when they shall fit out, and how many vessels they will send to each place, the company in general observing that no particular chamber shall undertake any thing in opposition to the foregoing resolution, but shall be held to carry the same effectually into execution. And if any chamber shall be found not following the common resolution, or contravening it, we have authorized, and by these presents do authorize, the said meeting, immediately to cause reparation to be made of every defect or contravention, wherein we, being desired, will assist them.

XXI. The said general meeting shall be held the first six years in the city of Amsterdam, and two years there-after in Zealand. and so on from time to time in the aforesaid two places.

XXII. The managers to whom the affairs of the company shall be committed, who shall go from home to attend the aforesaid meeting or otherwise, shall have for their expences and wages, four guilders a day, besides boat and carriage hire; Provided, that those who go from one city to another, to the chambers as managers and governors, shall receive no wages or travelling charges, at the cost of the company.

XXIII. And if it should happen that in the aforesaid general meeting, any weighty matter should come before them wherein they cannot agree, or in case the vote are equally divided, the same shall be left to our decision; and whatever shall be determined upon shall be carried into execution.

XXIV. And all the inhabitants of these countries, and also of other countries, shall be notified by public advertisements within one month after the date hereof, that they may be admitted into this Company, during five months from the first of July this year, sixteen hundred and twenty one, and that they must pay the

money they put into the Stock in three payments; to wit, one third part at the expiration of the aforesaid five months, and the other two-thirds parts within three next succeeding years. In case the aforesaid general meeting shall find it necessary to prolong the time the members shall be notified by an advertisement.

XXV. The ships returning from a voyage shall come to the place they sailed from; and if by stress of weather. the vessels which sailed out from one part shall arrive in another; as those from Amsterdam, or North Holland, in Zealand, or in the Maeze; or from Zealand, in Holland; or those from Friesland, with the city and country, in another part; each chamber shall nevertheless have the direction and management of the vessels and goods it sent out, and shall send and transport the goods to the places from whence the vessels sailed, either in the same or other vessels: Provided, that the managers of that chamber shall be held in person to find the place svhere the vessels and goods are arrived, and not appoint factors to do this business; but in case they shall not be in a situation for travelling, they shall commit this business to the chamber of the place where the vessels arrived.

XXVI. If any chamber has got any goods or returns from the places included within the Limits of this char-ter, with which another is not provided, it shall be held to send such goods to the chamber which is unprovided, on its request, according to the situation of the case, and if they have sold them, to send to another chamber for more. And in like manner, if the managers of the respec-tive chambers have need of any persons for fitting out the vessels, or otherwise, from the cities where there are chambers or managers, they shall require and employ the managers, of this company, without making use of a factor.

XXVII. And if any of the Provinces think fit to appoint an agent to collect the money from the inhab-itants, and to make a fund in any chamber, and for paying dividends, the chamber shall be obliged to give such agent access, that he may obtain information of the state of the disbursements and receipts, and of the debts; provided, that the money brought in by such agent amount to fifty thousand builders or upwards.

XXVIII. The managers shall have for commissions one per cent. On the outfits and returns, besides the Prince's; and an half per cent. On gold and silver: which commission shall be divided; to the Chamber of Amsterdam, four-ninth parts; the Chamber of Zealand, two-ninth parts; the Maeze, one-ninth part; North Holland, one-ninth part, and Friesland, with the city and country, a like ninth part.

XXIX. Provided that they shall not receive commis-sions on the ordnance and the ships more than once. They shall, moreover, have no commissions on the ships, ordnance, and other things with which we shall strengthn the Company; nor on the money which they shall collect for the Company, nor on the profits they receive from the goods, nor shall they charge the Company with any expenses of traveling or provisions for those to whom they shall commits the providing a cargo, and purchasing goods necessary for it.

XXX. The book-keepers and cashiers shall have a salary paid them by the managers out of their commissions.

XXXI. The manager shall not deliver or sell to the Company, in whole or in part, any of their own ships, merchandise or goods; nor buy or cause to be bought, of the said Company, directly or indirectly, any goods or merchandize nor have any portion or part therein on forfeiture of one year's commissions for the use of the poor, and the loss of Office.

XXXII. The managers shall give notice by advertisement, as often as they have a fresh importation of goods and merchandize, to the end that every one may have seasonable knowledge of it, before they proceed to a final sale.

XXXIII. And if it happens that in either Chamber, an of the managers shall get into such a situation, that he cannot make good what was entrusted to him during his administration, and in consequence thereof any loss shall happen, such Chamber shall be liable for the damage, and shall also be specially bound for their administration, which shall also be the case with all the members, who, on account of goods purchased, or otherwise, shall become debtors to the Company, and so shall be reckoned all cases relating to their stock and what may be due to the Company.

XXXIV. The managers of the respective chambers shall be responsible for their respective cashiers and book-keepers.

XXXV. That all the goods of this Company which shall be sold by weight shall be sold by one weight, to wit, that of Amsterdam; and that all such goods shall be put on board ship, or in store without paving any excise, import or weigh-money; provided that they being sold; shall not be delivered in any other way than by weight; and provided that the impost and weigh-money shall be paid as often as they are alienated, in the same manner as other goods subject to weigh-money.

XXXVI. That the persons or goods of the managers shall not be arrested, attached or encumbered, in order to obtain from them an account of the administration of the Company, nor for the payment of the wages of those who are in the service of the Company, but those who shall pretend to take the same upon them, shall be bound to refer the matter to their ordinary judges.

XXXVII. So when any ship shall return from a voyage, the generals or commanders of the fleets, shall be obliged to come and report to us the success of the voyage of such ship or ships, within ten days after their arrival, and shall deliver and leave with us a report in writing, if the case requires it.

XXXVIII. And if it happens (which we by no means expect) that any person will, in any manner, hurt or hinder the navigation, business, trade, or traffic of this Company, contrary to the common right, and the contents of the aforesaid treaties, leagues, and covenants, they shall defend it against them, and regulate it by the instructions we have given concerning it.

XXXIX. We have moreover promised and do promise, that we will defend this Company against every person in free navigation and traffic, and assist them with a million of Builders, to be paid in five years, whereof the first two hundred thousand guilders shall be paid them when the first payment shall be made by the members; Provided that we, with half the aforesaid million of Builders, shall receive and bear profit and risque in the same manner as the other members of this Company shall.

XL. And if by a violent and continued interruption of the aforesaid navigation and traffic, the business within the limits of their Company shall be brought to an open war, we will, if the situation of this country will in any wise admit of it, give them for their assistance sixteen ships of war, the least one hundred and fifty lasts burthen; with four good well sailing yachts, the least, forty lasts burthen, which shall be properly mounted and provided in all respects, both with brass and other cannon, and a proper quantity of ammunition, together with double suits of running and standing rigging, sails, cables, anchors, and other things thereto belonging, such as are proper to be provided and used in all great expeditions; upon condition, that they shall be manned, victualled, and supported at the expense of the Company, and that the Company shall be obliged to add thereto sixteen like ships of war, and four yachts, mounted and provided as above, to be used in like manner for the defence of trade and all exploits of war: Provided that all the ships of war and merchant-men (that shall be with those provided and manned as aforesaid) shall be under an admiral appointed by us according to the previous advise of the aforesaid General Company, and shall obey our commands, together with the resolutions of the Company, if it shall be necessary, in the same manner as in time of war; so notwithstanding that the merchantmen shall not unnecessarily hazard their lading.

XLI. And if it should happen that this country should be remarkably eased of its burthens, and that this

Company should be laid under the grievous burthen of a war, we have further promised, and do promise, to encrease the aforesaid subsidy in such a manner as the situation of these countries will admit, and the affairs of the Company shall require.

XLII. We have moreover ordained, that in case of a war, all the prizes which shall be taken from enemies and pirates within the aforesaid limits, by the Company or their assistants; also the goods which shall be seized by virtue of our proclamation, after deducting all expenses and the damage which the Company shall suffer in taking each prize, together with the just part of his excellency the admiral, agreeable to our resolution of the first of April sixteen hundred and two; and the tenth part for the officers, sailors and soldiers, who have taken the prize, shall await the disposal of the managers of the aforesaid Company; Provided that the account of them shall be kept separate and apart from the account of trade and commerce; and that the nett proceeds of the said prizes shall be employed in fitting our ships, paying the troops, fortifications, garrisons, and like matters of war and defence by sea and land; but there shall be no distribution unless the said nett proceeds shall amount to so much that a notable share may be distributed without weakening the said defence, and after paying the expenses of the war, which shall be done separate and apart from the distributions on account of Trade: And the distribution shall be made one-tenth part for the use of the United Netherlands, and the remainder for the members of this Company, in exact proportion to the capital they have advanced.

XLIII. Provided nevertheless, that all the prizes and goods, taken by virtue of our proclamation, shall be brought in, and the right laid before the judicature of the counsellors of the admirality for the part to which they are brought, that they may take cognizance of them, and determine the legality or illegality of the said prizes: the process of the administration of the goods brought in by the Company remaining nevertheless pending, and that under a proper inventory; and saving a revision of what may be done by the sentence of the admirality, agreeable to the instruction given the admiralty in that behalf. Provided that the vendue-masters and other officers of the Admiralty shall not have or pretend to any right to the prizes taken by this Company, and shall not be employed respecting them.

XLIV. The managers of this Company shall solemnly promise and swear, that they will act well and faithfully in their administration, and make good and just accounts of their trade: That they in all things will consult the greatest profit of the Company, and as much as possible prevent their meeting with losses: That they will not give the principal members any greater advantage in the payments or distribution of money than the least: That they, in getting in and receiving outstanding debts, will not favour one more than another: that they for their own account will take, and, during the continuance of their administration, will continue to take such sum of money as by their charter is allotted to them; and moreover, that they will, as far as concerns them, to the utmost of their power, observe and keep, and cause to be observed and kept, all and every the particulars and articles herein contained.

XLV. All which privileges, freedoms and exemptions, together with the assistance herein before mentioned, in all their particulars and articles, we have, with full knowledge of the business, given, granted, promised and agreed to the- aforesaid Company; giving, granting, agreeing and promising moreover that they shall enjoy them peaceably and freely; ordaining that the same shall be observed and kept by all the magistrates, officers and subjects of the United Nethelands, without doing anything contrary thereto directly or indirectly, either within or out of these Netherlands, on penalty of being punished both in life and goods as obstacles to the common welfare of this country, and transgressors of our ordinance: promising moreover that we will maintain and establish the Company in the things contained in this charter, in all treaties of peace, alliances and agreements with the neighboring princes, kingdoms and countries, without doing anything, or suffering any thing to be done which will weaken their establishment. Charging and expressly commanding all governors, justices, officers, magistrates and inhabitants of the aforesaid United Netherlands, that they permit the aforesaid Company and managers peaceably and freely to enjoy the full effect of this charter, agreement, and privilege, without any contradiction or impeachment to the-contrary. And that none may pretend ignorance hereof, we command that the contents of this charter shall be notified by publication, or an advertisement, where, and in such manner, as is proper; for we have found it necessary for the service of this country.

Given under our Great Seal, and the Signature and Seal of our Recorder, at the Hague, on the third day of the month of June, in the year sixteen hundred and twenty one.

Was countersigned
J. MAGNUS, Secr.
Underneath was written,
The ordinance of the High and Mighty Lords the States General.
It was subscribed,
C. AERSSEN.
And has a Seal pendant, of red Wax, and a string of white silk.

CHRISTOPHER COLUMBUS

SOURCE The First Ocean Decade of Peter Martyr of Anghiera and Milan, *1511. From Geoffrey Eatough, Editor and Translator, Selections from Peter Martyr in* Repetorium Columbianum, *Volume V (Turnhout, Belgium: Brepols, 1998), pp. 43-44.*

INTRODUCTION *This account of Christopher Columbus's first voyage to the New World in 1492 appeared in* The First Ocean Decade of Peter Martyr of Anghiera and Milan *(1511) by Peter Martyr, an Italian-born historian at the Spanish court. Martyr's goal, like other Spanish historians of the period, was to emphasize the glory of Spain. As such, Martyr cast Columbus's voyage as a great adventure that would lead to "an unimaginable abundance of pearls, spices, and gold." As Martyr foresaw, Columbus's discoveries of new lands, mineral wealth, and new people and animals launched a new era of European exploration, expansion, and colonialism.*

The ancients, to show their gratitude, used to respect as gods men whose vision and toil revealed lands which had been unknown to their ancestors. We, however, who hold that beneath his three persons there is only one God to be worshipped, can nonetheless feel wonder at men such as these, even if we have not worshipped them. Let us revere the sovereigns under whose leadership and auspices it was granted these men to fulfill their plans; let us praise to heaven sovereigns and discoverers; and let us use all our powers to make their glory seen as is right and proper. Here then what is reported about the islands recently discovered in the western seas and about the authors of this event. Since in your letter you seem most eager to know, I intend to start my account from the beginning of the event to avoid doing harm to anyone.

A certain Christopher Columbus, a man from Genoa, made a proposal to Ferdinand and Isabela, our Catholic majesties, and persuaded them that he would find to the west of us the islands neighboring on India, if they would equip him with ships and items required for the voyage. By these means the Christian religion could increase and an unimaginable abundance of pearls, spices and gold be easily had. He persisted and it was arranged that he should have three ships paid out of the royal treasury: one a cargo ship, with a crow's nest; the other two light merchant ships, without crow's nests, which the Spaniards call caravels. When he had taken possession of them Columbus began his proposed voyage around the first of September in the 1492nd year of our salvation with about two hundred twenty Spaniards.

Out in the deep ocean are islands which in many people's opinion are the Fortunate Islands, named the Canaries by the Spaniards, discovered Sometime ago, 1200 miles from Cádiz by their reckoning, for they say that the distance is three hundred leagues, while the experts in navigation say that on their calculations each league contains four miles. Antiquity called them the Fortunate Isles on account of the mildness of their climate: for the inhabitants are not oppressed by intolerable winters or fierce summers, because they are situated in the south beyond Europe's climate. Some, however, would like those which the Portuguese call the Cape Verde to be the Fortunate Islands. The Canaries have, right up to the Present day, been inhabited by men who are naked and who exist without any religion. Columbus made for there in order to take on water and refurbish the ships, before committing himself to hard toils ahead.

From these islands Columbus sailed for thirty-three continuous days, Always following the westerning sun, though for a little while towards the left of it, happy with just the sea and sky. His Spanish companions began first to mutter in secret, then to harass him with open abuse and to think about murdering him; indeed in the end they deliberated on hurling him into the sea: they had been deceived by a fellow from Genoa; the were being dragged headlong into an abyss from where they would never be able to return. After what was not the thirtieth day, roused to fury, they shouted out to be taken back and urged the man to go no further; but he tried to soothe their anger and restrain their excesses, coaxing them, giving large grounds for hope, protracting the issue from one day to the next. He also stated that their majesties would change them with treason, if they made a hostile move against him, of if they refused to obey. In the end to their delight they gained sight of the land for which they had longed.

On this first voyage he revealed just six islands, and two of these were of Unprecedented magnitude. He called one of these Hispaniola, the other Juana, but he was not sure that Juana was an island. As they were shaved the shores of some of them, they heard, in the month of November, the song of the nightingale in the dense groves. They also found huge rivers of fresh water and natural harbors with room for large fleets. Licking the coast of Juana, north west on a straight line, they ran out not much less than eight hundred miles, for they say it was one hundred and eighty leagues. Thinking it was mainland, because there was no apparent end nor sign of any end on the island, for as far as their eyes commanded a view, they decided to retreat. The sea surge also forced them to turn back, for the shore of Juana with its twists and turns eventually bends and curves so far to the north that the ships were assailed by severe gales from the north, for the storms of winter were beginning.

DE ORIGINE, POPULI (ON THE ORIGINS OF THE NATIVES OF VIRGINIA) 1612

SOURCE *William Strachey,* The Historie of Travell into Virgina Britania, *Edited by Louis B. Wright and Virginia Freund. (London: The Hakluyt Society, 1953), pp. 53-55.*

INTRODUCTION *The early English settlers in North America brought with them the perception of native peoples as suffering from savagery and barbarism. The Protestant colonists associated Native American forms of ritual with those practiced by Roman Catholics, and thus referred to both traditions as idolatrous. Although the English believed that Indians were susceptible to Christian education and conversion, the English process of converting native peoples required that their religious and social habits be reduced to the level of false religion. In this passage from* The Historie of Travell into Virginia Britania *(1612), William Strachey, a resident of the Jamestown settlement, speculates on what he considers the biblical origins of the natives of Virginia and their descent into "prophane worshippe."*

It were not perhappes too curious a thing to demand, how these people might come first, and from whom, and whence, to inhabited these so far remote westerly parts of the world, having no entercourse with Africa, Asia nor Europe, and considering the whole world, so many years, (by all knowledge received, was supposed to be only contained and circumscribed in the discovered and traveled Bounds of those three: according to that old Conclusion in the Scholes Quicquid prceter Africam, et Europeam est, Asia est. Whatsoeuer Land doth neither appertayne vnto Africk, nor to Europe, is part of Asia: as also to question how yt should be, that they (if descended from the people of the first creation) should maynteyne so generall and grosse a defection from the true knowledg of God, with one kynd, as yt were of rude and savadge life, Customes, manners, and Religion, yt being to be graunted, that with vs (infallably) they had one, and the same discent and begynning from the vniversall Deluge, in the scattering of Noah his children and Nephewes, with their famelies (as little Colonies) some to one, some to other borders of the Earth to dwell? as in Egypt (so

wryting Berosus) Esenius, and his howshold, tooke vp their Inhabitacion: In Libia, and Cyrene, Tritames: and in all the rest of Africa, Iapetus Priscus; Attalaas in East-Asia; Ganges, with some of Comerus Gallus children, in Arabia-Fwlix, within the confines of Sabaea, called the Frankincense bearer; Canaan in Damascus, vnto the vtmost bowndes of Palestyne; ect.

But, yet is observed that Cham, and his famely, were the only far Travellors, and Straglers into divers and unknowne countries, searching, exploring and sitting downe in the same: as also yet is said of his famely, that what country so ever the Children of Chain happened to possesse, there beganne both the Ignorance of true godliness, and a kynd of bondage and slavery to be taxed one vpon another, and that no inhabited Countryes cast forth greater multytutes, to raunge and stray into divers remote Regions, then that part of Arabia in which Cham himselfe (constrayned to fly with wife and Children by reason of the mocking that he had done to his father) tooke into possession; so great a misery (saith Boem of Auba) brought to mankynd, the vnsatisfyed wandring of that one man: for first from him, the Ignoraunce of the true worship of god took beginning, the Inventions of Hethenisme, and adoration of falce godes, and the Deuill, for he himself, not applying him to leame from his father, the knowledge and prescrybed worship of the etemall god, the god of his fathers, yet by a fearfull and superstitious instinct of nature, carryed to ascribe vnto some supernaturall power, a kynd of honour and power, taught his successors new and devised manner of Gods, sacryfices, and Ceremonies; and which he might the easierympresse into the Children, by reason they were carryed with him so young away from the Elders, not instructed, nor seasoned first, in their true Customes, and religion:

In so much as then we may conclude, that from Cham, and his tooke byrth and begynning the first vniversall Confusion and diversity, which ensued afterwardes throughout the whole world, especially in divine and sacred matters, while yt is said agayne of the Children of Sem, and Iaphet, how they being taught by their elders, and content with their owne lymitts and confynes, not travelling beyond them into new Countryes as the other, retayned still (vntill the comming of the Messias,) the only knowledge of the eternall, and the never chaungeable triuth.

By all which yet is very probable likewise, that both in the travells and Idolatry of the famely of Cham, this portion of the world (west-ward from Africa, vpon the Atlantique Sea) became both peopled, and instructed in the forme of prophane worshippe, and of an vnknowne Diety: nor is yt to be wondred at, where the abused triuth of Religion is suffred to perish, yf men in their owne

Inventions, and lives, become so grosse and barbarous as by reading the processe of this history will hardly be perceaved, what difference may be betweene them and bruit beasts, sometymes worshipping bruit beasts, nay things more vyle, and abhorring the inbredd motions of Nature itself, with such headlong and bloudy Ceremonies, of Will, and Act.

But how the vagabond Rance of Cham might discend into this new world, without furniture (as may be questioned) of shipping, and meanes to tempt the Seas, togither how this great Continent (divided from the other three) should become stoared with beasts, and some Fowle, of one, and the same kynd with the other partes, especially with Lions, Beares, Deare, Wolues, and such like, as from the first Creation tooke begynning in their kynd, and after the generall floud were not anew created, nor haue their being or generation (as some other) ex putredine, et sole, by corruption and Heate. Let me referre the reader to the search of Acosta in his booke of his morall and naturall History of the West-Indies, who hath so officiously laboured herein, as he should but bring Owles to Athens, who should study for more strayned, or new Aucthority Concerning the same.

Thus much then may be in brief be sayd, and allowed, Concerning their originall, or first begynning in generall, and which may well reach even downe vnto the particuler Inbabitants of this particuler Region, by vs discovered, who cannot be any other, then parcell of the same, and first mankynd.

DISCOURSE OF WESTERN PLANTING

SOURCE *Richard Hakluyt, 1584.*

INTRODUCTION *This table of contents for Richard Hakluyt's* Discourse of Western Planting *(1584) outlines a text that established English legal claims to North America and discussed in depth the commercial and strategic advantages of settling the region. Hakluyt (1552-1616) was a geographer, historian, editor, and leading promoter of English colonial expansion in North America. He presented his* Discourse of Western Planting *to Queen Elizabeth I in manuscript, but it was not actually printed until almost three hundred years later. Although Elizabeth was in agreement with the sentiments of the* Discourse, *England was engaged in a rivalry with Spain and unable to finance the colonial project that Hakluyt proposed, though Hakluyt's* Discourse *probably had an influence on the formation of the unsuccessful colony*

established in 1585 on Roanoke Island, off the coast of present-day North Carolina.

A particuler discourse concerninge the greate necessitie and manifolde comodyties that are like to growe to this Realme of Englande by the Westerne discoveries lately attempted, Written In the yere 1584 by Richarde Hackluyt of Oxforde at the requeste and direction of the righte worshipfull Mr. Walter Raghly [Raieigh] nowe Knight, before the comynge home of his Twoo Barkes: and is devlded into xxi chapiters, the Titles whereof followe in the nexte leafe.

1. That this westerne discoverie will be greately for the inlargement of the gospell of Christe whereunto the Princes of the refourmed relligion are chefely bounde amongste whome her Majestie is principall.

2. That all other englishe Trades are growen beggerly or daungerous, especially in all the kinge of Spaine his Domynions, where our men are dryven to flinge their Bibles and prayer Bokes into the sea, and to forsweare and renownce their relligion and conscience and consequently theyr obedience to her Majestie.

3. That this westerne voyadge will yelde unto us all the commodities of Europe, Affrica, and Asia, as far as wee were wonte to travell, and supply the wantes of all our decayed trades.

4. That this enterprise will be for the manifolde imployment of nombers of idle men, and for bredinge of many sufficient, and for utterance of the greate quantitie of the commodities of our Realme.

5. That this voyage will be a great bridle to the Indies of the kinge of Spaine and a means that wee may arreste at our pleasure for the space of teime weekes or three monethes every yere, one or twoo hundred saile of his subjectes shippes at the fysshinge in Newfounde Iande.

6. That the rischesse that the Indian Threasure wrought in time of Charles the late Emperor father to the Spanishe kinge, is to be had in consideracion of the Q. moste excellent Majestie, leaste the contynuall commynge of the like threasure from thence to his sonne, worke the unrecoverable annoye of this Realme, whereof already wee have had very dangerous experience.

7. What speciall meanes may bring kinge Phillippe from his high Throne, and make him equal to the Princes his neighbours, wherewithall is shewed his weakenes in the west Indies.

8. That the limites of the kinge of Spaines domynions in the west Indies be nothinge so large as is generally

imagined and surmised, neither those partes which he holdeth be of any such forces as is falsely geven oute by the popishe Clergye and others his suitors, to terrffie the Princes of the Relligion and to abuse and blinde them.

9. The Names of the riche Townes lienge alonge the sea coaste on the northe side from the equinoctiall of the mayne lande of America under the kinge of Spaine.

10. A Brefe declaracion of the chefe Ilands in the Bay of Mexico beinge under the kinge of Spaine, with their havens and fortes, and what commodities they yeide.

11. That the Spaniardes have executed most outragious and more then Turkishe cruelties in all the west Indies, whereby they are every where there, become moste odious unto them, whoe woulde joyne with us or any other moste willingly to shake of their moste intollerable yoke, and have begonne to doo it already in dyvers places where they were Lordes heretofore.

12. That the passage in this voyadge is easie and shorte, that it cutteth not nere the trade of any other mightie Princes, nor nere their Contries, that it is to be perfourmed at all tymes of the yere, and nedeth but one kinde of winde, that Ireland beinge full of goodd havens on the southe and west sides, is the nerest parte of Europe to it, which by this trade shall be in more securitie, and the sooner drawen to more Civilitie.

13. That hereby the Revenewes and customes of her Majestie bothe outwardes and inwardes shall mightely be inlarged by the toll, excises, and other dueties which without oppression may be raised.

14. That this action will be greately for the increase, mayneteynaunce and safetie of our Navye, and especially of great shippinge which is the strengthe of our Realme, and for the supportation of all those occupacions that depende upon the same.

15. That spedie plantinge in divers fitt places is moste necessarie upon these luckye westerne discoveries for feare of the daunger of being prevented by other nations which have the like intentions, with the order thereof and other reasons therewithall alleaged.

16. Meanes to kepe this enterprise from overthrowe and the enterprisers from shame and dishonor.

17. That by these Colonies the Northwest passage to Cathaio and China may easely quickly and perfectly be searched oute aswell by river and overlande, as by sea, for proofe whereof here are quoted and alleaged divers rare Testymonies oute of the three volumes of voyadges gathered by Ramusius and other grave authors.

18. That the Queene of Englande title to all the west Indies, or at the leaste to as moche as is from Florida to the Circle articke, is more lawfull and righte then the Spaniardes or any other Christian Princes.

19. An aunswer to the Bull of the Donacion of all the west Indies graunted to the kinges of Spaine by Pope Alexander the VI whoe was himselfe a Spaniarde borne.

20. A brefe collection of certaine reasons to induce her Majestie and the state to take in hande the westerne voyadge and the plantinge there.

21. A note of some things to be prepared for the voyadge which is sett downe rather to drawe the takers of the voyadge in hande to the presente consideracion then for any other reason for that divers thinges require preparation longe before the voyadge, without which the voyadge is maymed.

THE EARL OF CROMER: WHY BRITAIN ACQUIRED EGYPT IN 1882

SOURCE *The Earl of Cromer, Modern Egypt, 2 Vols., (New York: Macmillan, 1908), Vol. I.xvii-xviii.*

INTRODUCTION *Evelyn Baring, the Earl of Cromer, served as consul-general of Egypt from 1883 to 1907. In this passage from Comer's Modern Egypt (1908), he explains the British rationale for taking control of Egypt in 1882. A nationalist uprising had broken out in Egypt in 1881 against a backdrop of widespread economic distress and growing anti-European sentiment. Known as the Urabi Revolt, this uprising prompted deep concern among Britons, who feared that instability in Egypt could threaten the Suez Canal—the British imperial lifeline to India—as well as local British investments. Britain took action in 1882 by bombarding the coast of Alexandria and occupying Egypt. British authorities maintained that the occupation would be a short-term affair, but in fact Britain kept a hold over Egypt for the next seventy years and only withdrew its last troops from the Suez Canal in 1956.*

Egypt may now almost be said to form part of Europe. It is on the high road to the Far East. It can never cease to be an object of interest to all the powers of Europe, and especially to England. A numerous and intelligent body of Europeans and of non-Egyptian orientals have made Egypt their home. European capital to a large extent has been sunk in the country. The rights and privileges of

Europeans are jealously guarded, and, moreover, give rise to complicated questions, which it requires no small amount of ingenuity and technical knowledge to solve. Exotic institutions have sprung up and have taken root in the country. The capitulations impair those rights of internal sovereignty which are enjoyed by the rulers or legislatures of most states. The population is heterogeneous and cosmopolitan to a degree almost unknown elsewhere. Although the prevailing faith is that of Islam, in no country in the world is a greater variety of religious creeds to be found amongst important sections of the community.

In addition too these peculiarities, which are of a normal character, it has to be borne in mind that in 1882 the [Egyptian] army was in a state of mutiny; the treasury was bankrupt; every branch of the administration had been dislocated; the ancient and arbitrary method, under which the country had for centuries been governed, had received a severe blow, whilst, at the same time, no more orderly and law-abiding form of government had been inaugurated to take its place. Is it probable that a government composed of the rude elements described above, and led by men of such poor ability as Arabi and his coadjutators, would have been able to control a complicated machine of this nature? Were the sheikhs of the El-Azhar mosque likely to succeed where Tewfik Pasha and his ministers, who were men of comparative education and enlightenment, acting under the guidance and inspiration of a first-class European power, only met with a modified success after years of patient labor? There can be but one answer to these questions. Nor is it in the nature of things that any similar movement should, under the present conditions of Egyptian society, meet with any better success. The full and immediate execution of a policy of "Egypt for the Egyptians," as it was conceived by the Arabists in 1882, was, and still is, impossible.

History, indeed, records some very radical changes in the forms of government to which a state has been subjected without its interests being absolutely and permanently shipwrecked. But it may be doubted whether any instance can be quoted of a sudden transfer of power in any civilized or semi-civilized community to a class so ignorant as the pure Egyptians, such as they were in the year 1882. These latter have, for centuries past, been a subject race. Persians, Greeks, Romans, Arabs from Arabia and Baghdad, Circassians, and finally, Ottoman Turks, have successively ruled over Egypt, but we have to go back to the doubtful and obscure precedents of Pharaonic times to find an epoch when, possibly, Egypt was ruled by Egyptians. Neither, for the present, do they appear to possess the qualities which would render it desirable, either in their own interests, or in those of the civilized world in general, to raise them at a bound

to the category of autonomous rulers with full rights of internal sovereignty.

If, however, a foreign occupation was inevitable or nearly inevitable, it remains to be considered whether a British occupation was preferable to any other. From the purely Egyptian point of view, the answer to this question cannot be doubtful. The intervention of any European power was preferable to that of Turkey. The intervention of one European power was preferable to international intervention. The special aptitude shown by Englishmen in the government of Oriental races pointed to England as the most effective and beneficent instrument for the gradual introduction of European civilization into Egypt. An Anglo-French, or an Anglo-Italian occupation, from both of which we narrowly and also accidentally escaped, would have been detrimental to Egyptian interests and would ultimately have caused friction, if not serious dissension, between England on the one side and France or Italy on the other. The only thing to be said in favor of Turkish intervention is that it would have relieved England from the responsibility of intervening.

By the process of exhausting all other expedients, we arrive at the conclusion that armed British intervention was, under the special circumstances of the case, the only possible solution of the difficulties which existed in 1882. Probably also it was the best solution. The arguments against British intervention, indeed, were sufficiently obvious. It was easy to foresee that, with a British garrison in Egypt, it would be difficult that the relations of England either with France or Turkey should be cordial. With France, especially, there would be a danger that our relations might become seriously strained. Moreover, we lost the advantages of our insular position. The occupation of Egypt necessarily dragged England to a certain extent within the arena of Continental politics. In the event of war, the presence of a British garrison in Egypt would possibly be a source of weakness rather than of strength. Our position in Egypt placed us in a disadvantageous diplomatic position, for any power, with whom we had a difference of opinion about some non-Egyptian question, was at one time able to retaliate by opposing our Egyptian policy. The complicated rights and privileges possessed by the various powers of Europe in Egypt facilitated action of this nature.

There can be no doubt of the force of these arguments. The answer to them is that it was impossible for Great Britain to allow the troops of any other power to occupy Egypt. When it became apparent that some foreign occupation was necessary, that the Sultan would not act save under conditions which were impossible of acceptance, and that neither French nor Italian cooperation could be secured, the British government acted with promptitude and vigor. A great nation cannot throw off the responsibilities which its past history and its position in the world have imposed upon it. English history affords other examples of the government and people of England drifting by accident into doing what was not only right, but was also most in accordance with British interests.

FOURTEEN POINTS

INTRODUCTION *United States President Woodrow Wilson's Fourteen Points were delivered during an address to the U.S. Congress on January 8, 1918. Wilson intended the Fourteen Points to serve as a plan to end World War I and establish a lasting peace. In his fourteenth point, Wilson suggested the creation of an association of nations to facilitate the sovereignty and independence of all nations based upon self-determination, a proposal that led to the formation of the League of Nations at the Paris Peace Conference in 1919. The Fourteen Points encouraged a number of nationalist leaders, including Vietnam's Ho Chi Minh, to attend the Paris Peace Conference and present petitions for autonomy and independence.*

It will be our wish and purpose that the processes of peace, when they are begun, shall be absolutely open and that they shall involve and permit henceforth no secret understandings of any kind. The day of conquest and aggrandizement is gone by; so is also the day of secret covenants entered into in the interest of particular governments and likely at some unlooked-for moment to upset the peace of the world. It is this happy fact, now clear to the view of every public man whose thoughts do not still linger in an age that is dead and gone, which makes it possible for every nation whose purposes are consistent with justice and the peace of the world to avow nor or at any other time the objects it has in view.

We entered this war because violations of right had occurred which touched us to the quick and made the life of our own people impossible unless they were corrected and the world secure once for all against their recurrence. What we demand in this war, therefore, is nothing peculiar to ourselves. It is that the world be made fit and safe to live in; and particularly that it be made safe for every peace-loving nation which, like our own, wishes to live its own life, determine its own institutions, be assured of justice and fair dealing by the other peoples of the world as against force and selfish aggression. All the peoples of the world are in effect partners in this interest, and for our own part we see very clearly that unless justice be done to others it will not be done to us. The programme of the world's peace, therefore, is our programme; and that programme, the only possible programme, as we see it, is this:

I. Open covenants of peace, openly arrived at, after which there shall be no private international understandings of any kind but diplomacy shall proceed always frankly and in the public view.

II. Absolute freedom of navigation upon the seas, outside territorial waters, alike in peace and in war, except as the seas may be closed in whole or in part by international action for the enforcement of international covenants.

III. The removal, so far as possible, of all economic barriers and the establishment of an equality of trade conditions among all the nations consenting to the peace and associating themselves for its maintenance.

IV. Adequate guarantees given and taken that national armaments will be reduced to the lowest point consistent with domestic safety.

V. A free, open-minded, and absolutely impartial adjustment of all colonial claims, based upon a strict observance of the principle that in determining all such questions of sovereignty the interests of the populations concerned must have equal weight with the equitable claims of the government whose title is to be determined.

VI. The evacuation of all Russian territory and such a settlement of all questions affecting Russia as will secure the best and freest cooperation of the other nations of the world in obtaining for her an unhampered and unembarrassed opportunity for the independent determination of her own political development and national policy and assure her of a sincere welcome into the society of free nations under institutions of her own choosing; and, more than a welcome, assistance also of every kind that she may need and may herself desire. The treatment accorded Russia by her sister nations in the months to come will be the acid test of their good will, of their comprehension of her needs as distinguished from their own interests, and of their intelligent and unselfish sympathy.

VII. Belgium, the whole world will agree, must be evacuated and restored, without any attempt to limit the sovereignty which she enjoys in common with all other free nations. No other single act will serve as this will serve to restore confidence among the nations in the laws which they have themselves set and determined for the government of their relations with one another. Without this healing act the whole structure and validity of international law is forever impaired.

VIII. All French territory should be freed and the invaded portions restored, and the wrong done to France by Prussia in 1871 in the matter of Alsace-Lorraine, which has unsettled the peace of the world for nearly fifty years, should be righted, in order that peace may once more be made secure in the interest of all.

IX. A readjustment of the frontiers of Italy should be effected along clearly recognizable lines of nationality.

X. The peoples of Austria-Hungary, whose place among the nations we wish to see safeguarded and assured, should be accorded the freest opportunity to autonomous development.

XI. Rumania, Serbia, and Montenegro should be evacuated; occupied territories restored; Serbia accorded free and secure access to the sea; and the relations of the several Balkan states to one another determined by friendly counsel along historically established lines of allegiance and nationality; and international guarantees of the political and economic independence and territorial integrity of the several Balkan states should be entered into.

XII. The turkish portion of the present Ottoman Empire should be assured a secure sovereignty, but the other nationalities which are now under Turkish rule should be assured an undoubted security of life and an absolutely unmolested opportunity of autonomous development, and the Dardanelles should be permanently opened as a free passage to the ships and commerce of all nations under international guarantees.

XIII. An independent Polish state should be erected which should include the territories inhabited by indisputably Polish populations, which should be assured a free and secure access to the sea, and whose political and economic independence and territorial integrity should be guaranteed by international covenant.

XIV. A general association of nations must be formed under specific covenants for the purpose of affording mutual guarantees of political independence and territorial integrity to great and small states alike.

In regard to these essential rectifications of wrong and assertions of right we feel ourselves to be intimate partners of all the governments and peoples associated together against the Imperialists. We cannot be separated in interest or divided in purpose. We stand together until the end.

For such arrangements and covenants we are willing to fight and to continue to fight until they are achieved; but only because we wish the right to prevail and desire a just and stable peace such as can be secured only by removing the chief provocations to war, which this programme does remove. We have no jealousy of German greatness, and there is nothing in this programme that impairs it. We grudge her no achievement or distinction of learning or of pacific enterprise such as have made her record very bright and very enviable. We do not wish to injure her or to block in any way her legitimate influence or power. We do not wish to fight her either with arms or with hostile arrangements of trade if she is willing to associate herself with us and the other peace-loving nations of the world in covenants of justice and law and fair dealing. We wish her only to accept a place of equality among the peoples of the world,—the new world in which we now live,—instead of a place of mastery.

HOMESTEAD ACT

INTRODUCTION *After the American Revolution, both the federal government and the states jockeyed to acquire as much Native American land as possible, leading the United States Congress to pass a series of ordinances in the 1780s to bring order to the process of land development. One such ordinance established the land grid that is visible on any flight over the American Midwest—what had been Indian country was divided into perfect squares. The final result of this process was the Homestead Act, passed by Congress on May 20, 1862, which made 160-acres plots of unappropriated public land available for free, to women and men alike. Thousands of settlers from the eastern United States and Europe seized on the opportunity to become landowners. The Indian inhabitants of these lands had little choice but to retreat, and retreat again.*

May 20, 1862

AN ACT to secure homesteads to actual settlers on the public domain.

Be it enacted, That any person who is the head of a family, or who has arrived at the age of twenty-one years, and is a citizen of the United States, or who shall have filed his declaration of intention to become such, as required by the naturalization laws of the United States, and who has never borne arms against the United States Government or given aid and comfort to its enemies, shall, from and after the first of January, eighteen hundred and sixty-three, be entitled to enter one quarter-section or a less quantity of unappropriated public lands, upon which said person may have filed a pre-emption claim, or which may, at the time the application is made, be subject to pre-emption at one dollar and twenty-five cents, or less, per acre; or eighty acres or less of such unappropriated lands, at two dollars and fifty cents per acre, to be located in a body, in conformity to the legal subdivisions of the public lands, and after the same shall have been surveyed: Provided, That any person owning or residing on land may, under the provisions of this act, enter other land lying contiguous to his or her said land, which shall not, with the land so already owned and occupied, exceed in the aggregate one hundred and sixty acres.

Section 2. And be it further enacted, That the person applying for the benefit of this act shall, upon application to the register of the land office in which he or she is about to make such entry, make affidavit before the said register or receiver that he or she is the head of a family, or is twenty-one years or more of age, or shall have performed service in the army or navy of the United States, and that he has never borne arms against the Government of the United States or given aid and comfort to its enemies, and that such application is made for his or her exclusive use and benefit, and that said entry is made for the purpose of actual settlement and cultivation, and not either directly or indirectly for the use or benefit of any other person or persons whomsoever; and upon filing the said affidavit with the register or receiver, and on payment of ten dollars, he or she shall thereupon be permitted to enter the quantity of land specified: Provided, however, That no certificate shall be given or patent issued therefor until the expiration of five years from the date of such entry; and if, at the expiration of such time, or at any time within two years thereafter, the person making such entry; or, if he be dead, his widow; or in case of her death, his heirs or devisee; or in the case of a widow making such entry, her heirs or devisee, in the case of her death; shall prove by two credible witnesses that he, she, or they have resided upon or cultivated the same for the term of five years immediately succeeding the time of filing the affidavit aforesaid, and shall make affidavit that no part of said land has been alienated, and he has borne true allegiance to the Government of the United States; then, in such case, he, she, or they, if at that time a citizen of the United States, shall be entitled to a patent, as in other cases provided for by law: And, provided, further, That in case of the death of both father and mother, leaving an infant child, or children, under twenty-one years of age, the right and fee shall enure to the benefit of said infant child or children; and the executor, administrator, or guardian may, at any time within two years after the death of the surviving parent, and in accordance with the laws of the State in which such children for the time being have their domicil, sell said land for the benefit of said infants, but for no other purpose; and the purchaser shall acquire the absolute title by the purchase, and be entitled to a patent from the United States, on payment of the office fees and sum of money herein specified.

Section 3. And be it further enacted, That the register of the land office shall note all such applications on the tract books and plats of his office, and keep a register of all such entries, and make return thereof to the General Land Office, together with the proof upon which they have been founded.

Section 4. And be it further enacted, That no lands acquired under the provisions of this act shall in any event become liable to the satisfaction of any debt or debts contracted prior to the issuing of the patent therefor.

Section 5. And be it further enacted, That if, at any time after the filing of the affidavit, as required in the second section of this act, and before the expiration of the five years aforesaid, it shall be proven, after due notice to the settler, to the satisfaction of the register of the land office, that the person having filed such affidavit shall have actually changed his or her residence, or abandoned the said land for more than six months at any time, then and in that event the land so entered shall revert to the government.

Section 6. And be it further enacted, That no individual shall be permitted to acquire title to more than one quarter section under the provisions of this act; and that the Commissioner of the General Land Office is hereby required to prepare and issue such rules and regulations, consistent with this act, as shall be necessary and proper to carry its provisions into effect; and that the registers and receivers of the several land offices shall be entitled to receive the same compensation for any lands entered under the provisions of this act that they are now entitled to receive when the same quantity of land is entered with money, one half to be paid by the person making the application at the time of so doing, and the other half on the issue of the certificate by the person to whom it may be issued; but this shall not be construed to enlarge the maximum of compensation now prescribed by law for any register or receiver: Provided, That nothing contained in this act shall be so construed as to impair or interfere in any manner whatever with existing preemption rights: And provided, further, That all persons who may have filed their applications for a preemption right prior to the passage of this act, shall be entitled to all privileges of this act: Provided, further, That no person who has served or may hereafter serve, for period of not less than fourteen days in the army or navy of the United States, either regular or volunteer, under the laws thereof, during the existence of an actual war, domestic or foreign, shall be deprived of the benefits of this act of account of not having attained the age of twenty-one years.

Section 7. And be it further enacted, That the fifth section of the act entitled An act in addition to an act more effectually to provide for the punishment of certain crimes against the United States, and for other purposes, approved the third of March, in the year eighteen hundred and fifty-seven, shall extend to all oaths, affirmations, and affidavits, required or authorized by this act.

Section 8. And be it further enacted, That nothing in this act shall be so construed as to prevent any person who has availed him or herself of the benefits of the first section of this act, from paying the minimum price, or the price to which the same may have graduated, for the quantity of land so entered at any time before the expiration of the five years, and obtaining a patent therefor from the government, as in other cases provided by law, on making proof of settlement and cultivation as provided by existing laws granting preemption rights.

Approved, May 20, 1862.

IMPERIALISM: A STUDY, 1902

SOURCE *John A. Hobson.* Imperialism. *(London: Allen and Unwin, 1948), p. 35.*

INTRODUCTION *In this excerpt from* Imperialism: A Study *(1902), the British economist and political philosopher J. A. Hobson offers a criticism of the economic benefits of colonialism. Hobson, a follower of Marx, argued in* Imperialism *that the financial sector was the only area of the economy that actually benefited from colonies. In other areas, the military and administrative costs of empire outweighed any financial gains. Hence, Hobson contended that imperialism only benefited a small group of elites and did not provide long-range economic gains for the lower and working classes.*

Amid the welter of vague political abstractions to lay one's finger accurately upon any "ism" so as to pin it down and mark it out by definition seems impossible. Where meanings shift so quickly and so subtly, not only following changes of thought, but often manipulated artificially by political practitioners so as to obscure, expand, or distort, it is idle to demand the same rigour as is expected in the exact sciences. A certain broad consistency in its relations to other kindred terms is the nearest approach to definition which such a term as Imperialism admits. Nationalism, internationalism, colonialism, its three closest congeners, are equally elusive, equally shifty, and the changeful overlapping of all four demands the closest vigilance of students of modern politics.

During the nineteenth century the struggle towards nationalism, or establishment of political union on a basis of nationality, was a dominant factor alike in dynastic movements and as an inner motive in the life of masses of population. That struggle, in external politics,

sometimes took a disruptive form, as in the case of Greece, Servia, Roumania, and Bulgaria breaking from Ottoman rule, and the detachment of North Italy from her unnatural alliance with the Austrian Empire. In other cases it was a unifying or a centralising force, enlarging the area of nationality, as in the case of Italy and the PanSlavist movement in Russia. Sometimes nationality was taken as a basis of federation of States, as in United Germany and in North America.

It is true that the forces making for political union sometimes went further, making for federal union of diverse nationalities, as in the cases of AustriaHungary, Norway and Sweden, and the Swiss Federation. But the general tendency was towards welding into large strong national unities the loosely related States and provinces with shifting attachments and alliances which covered large areas of Europe since the breakup of the Empire. This was the most definite achievement of the nineteenth century. The force of nationality, operating in this work, is quite as visible in the failures to achieve political freedom as in the successes; and the struggles of Irish, Poles, Finns, Hungarians, and Czechs to resist the forcible subjection to or alliance with stronger neighbours brought out in its full vigour the powerful sentiment of nationality.

The middle of the century was especially distinguished by a series of definitely nationalist revivals, some of which found important interpretation in dynastic changes, while others were crushed or collapsed. Holland, Poland, Belgium, Norway, the Balkans, formed a vast arena for these struggles of national forces.

The close of the third quarter of the century saw Europe fairly settled into large national States or federations of States, though in the nature of the case there can be no finality, and Italy continued to look to Trieste, as Germany still looks to Austria, for the fulfilment of her manifest destiny.

This passion and the dynastic forms it helped to mould and animate are largely attributable to the fierce prolonged resistance which peoples, both great and small, were called on to maintain against the imperial designs of Napoleon. The national spirit of England was roused by the tenseness of the struggle to a selfconsciousness it had never experienced since "the spacious days of great Elizabeth." Jena made Prussia into a great nation; the Moscow campaign brought Russia into the field of European nationalities as a factor in politics, opening her for the first time to the full tide of Western ideas and influences.

Turning from this territorial and dynastic nationalism to the spirit of racial, linguistic, and economic solidarity which has been the underlying motive, we find a still more remarkable movement. Local particularism on the one hand, vague cosmopolitanism upon the other, yielded to a ferment of nationalist sentiment, manifesting itself among the weaker peoples not merely in a sturdy and heroic resistance against political absorption or territorial nationalism, but in a passionate revival of decaying customs, language, literature and art; while it bred in more dominant peoples strange ambitions of national "destiny" and an attendant spirit of Chauvinism.

No mere array of facts and figures adduced to illustrate the economic nature of the new Imperialism will suffice to dispel the popular delusion that the use of national force to secure new markets by annexing fresh tracts of territory is a sound and a necessary policy for an advanced industrial country like Great Britain....

But these arguments are not conclusive. It is open to Imperialists to argue thus: "We must have markets for our growing manufactures, we must have new outlets for the investment of our surplus capital and for the energies of the adventurous surplus of our population: such expansion is a necessity of life to a nation with our great and growing powers of production. An ever larger share of our population is devoted to the manufactures and commerce of towns, and is thus dependent for life and work upon food and raw materials from foreign lands. In order to buy and pay for these things we must sell our goods abroad." During the first threequarters of the nineteenth century we could do so without difficulty by a natural expansion of commerce with continental nations and our colonies, all of which were far behind us in the main arts of manufacture and the carrying trades. So long as England held a virtual monopoly of the world markets for certain important classes of manufactured goods, Imperialism was unnecessary.

After 1870 this manufacturing and trading supremacy was greatly impaired: other nations, especially Germany, the United States, and Belgium, advanced with great rapidity, and while they have not crushed or even stayed the increase of our external trade, their competition made it more and more difficult to dispose of the full surplus of our manufactures at a profit. The encroachments made by these nations upon our old markets, even in our own possessions, made it most urgent that we should take energetic means to secure new markets. These new markets had to lie in hitherto undeveloped countries, chiefly in the tropics, where vast populations lived capable of growing economic needs which our manufacturers and merchants could supply. Our rivals were seizing and annexing territories for similar purposes, and when they had annexed them closed them to our trade The diplomacy and the arms of Great Britain had to be used in order to compel the owners of the new markets to deal with us: and experience showed that the safest means of securing and developing such markets is by establishing 'protectorates' or by annexation....

It was this sudden demand for foreign markets for manufactures and for investments which was avowedly responsible for the adoption of Imperialism as a political policy.... They needed Imperialism because they desired to use the public resources of their country to find profitable employment for their capital which otherwise would be superfluous....

Every improvement of methods of production, every concentration of ownership and control, seems to accentuate the tendency. As one nation after another enters the machine economy and adopts advanced industrial methods, it becomes more difficult for its manufacturers, merchants, and financiers to dispose profitably of their economic resources, and they are tempted more and more to use their Governments in order to secure for their particular use some distant undeveloped country by annexation and protection.

The process, we may be told, is inevitable, and so it seems upon a superficial inspection. Everywhere appear excessive powers of production, excessive capital in search of investment. It is admitted by all business men that the growth of the powers of production in their country exceeds the growth in consumption, that more goods can be produced than can be sold at a profit, and that more capital exists than can find remunerative investment.

It is this economic condition of affairs that forms the taproot of Imperialism. If the consuming public in this country raised its standard of consumption to keep pace with every rise of productive powers, there could be no excess of goods or capital clamorous to use Imperialism in order to find markets: foreign trade would indeed exist....

Everywhere the issue of quantitative versus qualitative growth comes up. This is the entire issue of empire. A people limited in number and energy and in the land they occupy have the choice of improving to the utmost the political and economic management of their own land, confining themselves to such accessions of territory as are justified by the most economical disposition of a growing population; or they may proceed, like the slovenly farmer, to spread their power and energy over the whole earth, tempted by the speculative value or the quick profits of some new market, or else by mere greed of territorial acquisition, and ignoring the political and economic wastes and risks involved by this imperial career. It must be clearly understood that this is essentially a choice of alternatives; a full simultaneous application of intensive and extensive cultivation is impossible. A nation may either, following the example of Denmark or Switzerland, put brains into agriculture, develop a finely varied system of public education, general and technical, apply the ripest science to its special manufacturing industries, and so support in progressive comfort and character a considerable population upon a strictly limited area; or it may, like Great r Britain, neglect its agriculture, allowing its lands to go out of cultivation and its population to grow up in towns, fall behind other nations in its methods of education and in the capacity of adapting to its uses the latest scientific knowledge, in order that it may squander its pecuniary and military resources in forcing bad markets and finding speculative fields of investment in distant corners of the earth, adding millions of square miles and of unassimilable population to the area of the Empire.

The driving forces of class interest which stimulate and support this false economy we have explained. No remedy will serve which permits the future operation of these forces. It is idle to attack Imperialism or Militarism as political expedients or policies unless the axe is laid at the economic root of the tree, and the classes for whose interest Imperialism works are shorn of the surplus revenues which seek this outlet.

IMPERIALISM: A GERMAN VIEWPOINT

SOURCE *Fabri, Friedrich.* Does Germany Need Colonies, *1879.*

INTRODUCTION *This excerpt from Friedrich Fabri's 1879 pamphlet* Bedarf Deutschland der Colonien? *(Does Germany Need Colonies?) presents an argument for the development of German imperialism, which Fabri believed would invigorate the German economy and renew the national spirit. Fabri was the director of a German missionary society, and his propagandistic writings in favor of colonization were part of a procolonial movement that arose in Germany after unification in 1871. Advocates of colonization exerted pressure on the government to acquire colonies abroad, especially in Africa, by arguing that Germany needed territories to maintain its economic preeminence among European nations.*

Should not the German nation, so seaworthy, so industrially and commercially minded, ... successfully hew a new path on the road of imperialism? We are convinced beyond doubt that the colonial question has become a matter of life-or death for the develo pment of Germany. Colonies will have a salutary effect on our economic situation as well as on our entire national progress.

Here is a solution for many of the problems that face us. In this new Reich [i.e., the new Imperial Germany] of ours there is so much bitterness, so much unfruitful, sour, and poisoned political wrangling, that the opening of a new, promising road of national effort will act as a kind of liberating influence. Our national spirit will be renewed, a gratifying thing, a great asset. A people that has been led to a high level of power can maintain its historical position only as long as it understands and proves itself to be the bearer of a culture mission. At the same time, this is the only way to stability and to the growth of national welfare, the necessary foundation for a lasting expansion of power.At one time Germany contributed only intellectual and literary activity to the tasks of our century. That era is now over. As a people we have become politically minded and powerful. But if political power becomes the primal goal of a nation, it will lead to harshness, even to barbarism. We must be ready to serve for the ideal, moral, and economic culture-tasks of our time . . . .

No one can deny that in this direction England has by far surpassed all other countries. . . . . .I has been customary in our age of military power to evaluate the strength of a state in terms of its combat-ready troops. But anyone who looks at the g lobe and notes the steadily increasing colonial possessions of Great Britain [will perceive] how she extracts strength from them, the skill with which she governs them, how the Anglo-Saxon strain occupies a dominant position in the overseas territories . . . .

The fact is that England tenaciously holds on to its world-wide possessions with scarcely one-fourth the manpower of our continental military state. That is not only a great economic advantage but also a striking proof of the solid power and cultural fib er of England. Great Britain, of course, isolates herself far from the mass warfare of the continent, or only goes into action with dependable allies; hence, the insular state has suffered and will suffer no real damage. In any case, it would be wise for us Germans to learn about colonial skills from our Anglo-Saxon cousins and to begin a friendly competition with them. W hen the German Reich centuries ago stood at the pinnacle of the states of Europe, it was the Number One trade and sea power. If the New Germany wants to protect its newly won position of power for a long time, it must heed its Kultur-mission and, above all, delay no longer in the task of renewing the call for colonies.

KINGDOM OF CONGO

SOURCE A Reporte of the Kingdome of Congo, a Region of Africa, and of the Countries that border rounde about the same. *Drawn out of the writings and discourses of Odordo Lopes, a Portingal, by Philippo Pigafetta. Translated out of Italian by Abraham Hartwell. London, Printed by John Wolfe, 1597, pp. 118-121.*

INTRODUCTION *Slave traders and Catholic missionaries from Portugal who landed on the west coast of Africa during the fifteenth and sixteenth centuries brought with them very little knowledge of the region's traditional religions, but they quickly recognized the difficulty in converting Africans to Christianity without first gaining the support of African monarchs. As missionaries serving at the pleasure of African kings, Portuguese priests had to tread softly when it came to the conversion of Africans, and African leaders largely controlled the process. In this passage from* A Report of the Kingdom of Congo *(1588), the Portuguese historian Duarte Lopes describes the delicate, diplomatic conversion of a Congolese prince and king.*

Of the Original beginning of Christendom in the Kingdom of Congo, And how the Portuguese obtained this traffic.

The K. of Portugal Don Gionanni, the second, being desirous to discover the East Indies, sent forth divers ships by the coast of Africa to search out this Navigation, who having found the Islands of Cape Verde, and the Isle of Saint Thomas, and running all along the coast, did light upon the River Zaire, whereof we have made mention before, and there they had good traffic, and tried the people to be very courteous and kind. Afterwards he sent forth (for the same purpose) certain other vessels, to entertain this traffic with Congo, who finding the trade there to be so free and profitable, and the people so friendly, left certain Portuguese behind them, to learn the language, and to traffic with them: among whom one was a Mass-priest. These Portuguese conversing familiarly with the Lord of Sogno, who was Uncle to the King, and a man well up there in years, dwelling at that time In the Port of Praza (which is in the mouth of Zaire) were very well Entertained and esteemed by the Prince, and reverenced as though they Had been earthly Gods, and descended down from heaven into those Countries. But the Portuguese told them that they were men as themselves Were, and professors of Christianity. And when they perceived in how great estimation the people held them, the foresaid Priest & others began to reason with the Prince touching the Christian religion, and to show unto them the errors of the Pagan supersition, and by little and little to teach them the faith which we possess, insomuch as that which the Portuguese spoke unto them, greatly pleased the Prince, and so he became converted.

With this confidence and good spirit, the prince of Sogno went to the Court, to inform the King of the true doctrine of the Christian Portuguese, and to encourage him that he would embrace the Christian Religion which was so manifest, and also so wholesome for his soul's health. Hereupon the king commanded to call the Priest to Court, to the end he might himself treat with him personally, and understand the truth of that which the Lord of Sogno had declared unto him. Whereof when he was fully informed, he converted and promised that he would become a Christian.

And now the Portuguese ships departed from Congo, and returned to Portugal: and by them did the King of Congo write to the King of Portugal, Don Gionanni, the second, with earnest resquest, that he would send him some Priests, with all other orders and ceremonies to make him a Christian. The Priest also that remained behind, had written at large touching this business, and gave the King full information of all that had happened, agreeable to his good pleasure. And so the King took order for sundry religious persons, to be send unto him accordingly, with all ornaments for the Church and other service, as Crosses and Images: so that he was thoroughly furnished with all things that were necessary and needful for such an action.

At the last the ships of Portugal arrived with the expected provisions (which was in the year of our salvation 1491) and landed in the port which in in the mouth of the River Zaire. The Prince of Sogno with all show of familiar joy, accompanied with all his gentlemen ran down to meet them, and entertained the Portuguese in most courteous manner, and so conducted them to their lodgings. The next day following according to the direction of the Priest that remained behind, the Prince caused a kind of Church to be built, with the bodies and branches of certain trees, which he in his own person, with the help of his servants, most devoutly had felled in the wood. And when it was covered, they erected therein three Altars, in the worship and reverence of the most holy Trinity, and there was baptized himself and his young son, himself by the name of our Savior, Emanuel, and his child by the name of Anthonie, because that Saint is the Protector of the City of Lisbon.

MONGO: MULATTO CHIEF OF THE RIVER, 1854

SOURCE *From Capt. Theodore Canot,* Adventurers of an African Slaver: An Account of the Life of Captain Theodore Canot, Trader in Gold, Ivory and Slaves on the Coast of Guinea. *Written out and edited from the* Captain's Journals, Memoranda and Conversations *by Brantz Mayer [1857] (Mineola, New York: Dover Publications, 2002), pp. 76-78, 94.*

INTRODUCTION *Theodore Canot was a French-Italian slave trader whose vivid memoirs,* Adventures of an African Slaver *(1857), record the Atlantic slave trade as it was practiced during the early to mid-nineteenth century. One of his African associates in the slave trade was known as Mongo, or "Chief of the River." Mongo was, in fact, a man named Jack Ormond, the son of an English slave trader and an African woman. He had been educated in England, but returned to Africa to claim his father's property and pursue his father's business. Canot describes Mongo as "a type of his peculiar class in Africa," and Mongo's political machinations as he positions himself as a powerful slave trader illustrate the serious implications that the slave trade had on politics and society within Africa.*

It is time I should make the reader acquainted with the individual who was the presiding genius of the scene, and, in some degree, a type of his peculiar class in Africa.

Mr. Ormond was the son of an opulent slave-trader from Liverpool, and owed his birth to the daughter of a native chief on the Rio Pongo. His father seems to have been rather proud of his mulatto stripling and dispatched him to England to be educated. But Master John had make little progress in belleslettes, when news of the trader's death was brought to the British agent, who refused the youth further supplies of money. The poor boy soon became an outcast in a land which had not yet become fashionably addicted to philanthropy; and, after drifting about awhile in England, he shipped on board a merchantman. The press-gang soon got possession of the likely mulatto for the service of his Britannic Majesty. Sometimes he played the part of dandy waiter in the cabin; sometimes he swung a hammock with the hands in the forecastle. Thus, five years slipped by, during which the wanderer visited most of the West Indian and Mediterranean stations.

At length the prolonged cruise was terminated, and Ormond paid off. He immediately determined to employ his hoarded cash in a voyage to Africa, where he might claim his father's property. The project was executed; his mother was still found alive; and, fortunately for the manly youth, she recognized him at once as her first born.

The reader will recollect that these things occurred on the west coast of Africa in the early part of the present century, and that the tenure of property, and the interests of foreign traders, were controlled entirely by such customary laws as prevailed on the spot. Accordingly, a 'grand palaver' was appointed, and all Mr. Ormond's brothers, sisters, uncles, and cousins, - many of whom were in possession of his father's slaves or their descendants, - were summoned to attend. The 'talk' took place at the appointed time. The African mother stood forth staunchly to assert the identity and rights of her first-born, and, in the end, all of the Liverpool trader's property, in houses, lands, and negroes, that could be ascertained, was handed over, according to coast-law, to the returned heir.

When the mulatto youth was thus suddenly elevated into comfort, if not opulence, in his own country, he resolved to augment his wealth by pursuing his father's business. But the whole country was then desolated by a civil war, occasioned, as most of them are, by family disputes, which is was necessary to terminate before trade could be comfortably established.

To this task Ormond steadfastly devoted his first year. His efforts were seconded by the opportune death of one of the warring chiefs. A tame opponent, - a brother of Ormond's mother, - was quickly brought to terms by a trifling present; so that the sailor boy soon concentrated the family influence, and declared himself 'Mongo,' or Chief of the River.

Bangalang had long been a noted factory among the English traders. When war was over, Ormond selected this post as his permanent residence, while he sent runners to Sierra Leone and Goree with notice that he would shortly be prepared with ample cargoes. Trade, which had been so long interrupted by hostilies, poured from the interior. Vessels from Goree and Sierra Leone were seen in the offing, responding to his invitation. His stores were packed with British, French, and American fabrics; while hides, wax, palm-oil, ivory, gold, and slaves were the native products for which Spaniards and Portuguese hurried to proffer their doubloons and bills.

It will be readily conjectured that a very few years sufficed to make Jack Ormond not only a wealthy merchant, but a popular Mongo among the great interior tributes of Foulahs and Mandingoes. The petty chiefs, whose territory bordered the sea, flattered him with the title of king; and, knowing his Mormon taste, stocked his harem with their choicest children as the most valuable tokens of friendship and fidelity....

I was a close watcher of Mongo John whenever he engaged in the purchase of slaves. As each negro was brought before him, Ormond examined the subject, without regard to sex, from head to foot. A careful manipulation of the chief muscles, joints, arm-pits and groins was made, to assure soundness. The mouth, too, was inspected, and if a tooth was missing, it was noted as a defect liable to deduction. Eyes, voice, lungs, forgers and toes were not forgotten; so that when the negro passed from the Mongo's hands without censure, he might have been readily adopted as a good 'life' by an insurance company.

Upon one occasion, to my great astonishment, I saw a stout and apparently powerful man discarded by Ormond as utterly worthless. His full muscles and sleek skin, to my unpractised eye, denoted the height of robust health. Still, I was told that he had been medicated for the market with bloating drugs, and sweated with powder and lemon juice to impart a gloss to his skin. Ormond remarked that these jockey-tricks are as common in Africa as among horse-traders in Christian lands; and desiring me to feel the negro's pulse, I immediately detected disease or excessive excitement. In a few days I found the poor wretch abandoned by his owner, a paralyzed wreck in the hut of a villager at Bangalang.

MONROE DOCTRINE

INTRODUCTION *The Monroe Doctrine was enunciated by U.S. President James Monroe in his annual message to the United States Congress on December 2, 1823. It amounted to a statement that the United States would treat any attempt to extend European influence in the New World as a threat to its security. This was, in effect, an assertion that the Western Hemisphere was closed to European colonization in the face of U.S. ascendancy in the region. The Monroe Doctrine was one of the strongest early American expressions of anticolonialism, but it also demonstrated the dichotomous nature of U.S. policy since the United States would oppose some colonial ventures but accept others, including British efforts in Canada.*

December 2, 1823

... At the proposal of the Russian Imperial Government, made through the minister of the Emperor residing here, a full power and instructions have been transmitted to the minister of the United States at St. Petersburg to arrange by amicable negotiation the respective rights and interests of the two nations on the northwest coast of this continent. A similar proposal has been made by His Imperial Majesty to the Government of Great Britain, which has likewise been acceded to. The Government of the United States has been desirous by this friendly proceeding of manifesting the great value which they have invariably attached to the friendship of the Emperor and their solicitude to cultivate the best understanding with his Government. In the discussions to which this interest has given rise and in the arrangements by which they may terminate the occasion has been judged proper for asserting, as a principle in which the rights and interests of the United States are involved, that the American continents, by the free and independ-

ent condition which they have assumed and maintain, are henceforth not to be considered as subjects for future colonization by any European powers...

It was stated at the commencement of the last session that a great effort was then making in Spain and Portugal to improve the condition of the people of those countries, and that it appeared to be conducted with extraordinary moderation. It need scarcely be remarked that the results have been so far very different from what was then anticipated. Of events in that quarter of the globe, with which we have so much intercourse and from which we derive our origin, we have always been anxious and interested spectators. The citizens of the United States cherish sentiments the most friendly in favor of the liberty and happiness of their fellow-men on that side of the Atlantic. In the wars of the European powers in matters relating to themselves we have never taken any part, nor does it comport with our policy to do so. It is only when our rights are invaded or seriously menaced that we resent injuries or make preparation for our defense. With the movements in this hemisphere we are of necessity more immediately connected, and by causes which must be obvious to all enlightened and impartial observers. The political system of the allied powers is essentially different in this respect from that of America. This difference proceeds from that which exists in their respective Governments; and to the defense of our own, which has been achieved by the loss of so much blood and treasure, and matured by the wisdom of their most enlightened citizens, and under which we have enjoyed unexampled felicity, this whole nation is devoted. We owe it, therefore, to candor and to the amicable relations existing between the United States and those powers to declare that we should consider any attempt on their part to extend their system to any portion of this hemisphere as dangerous to our peace and safety. With the existing colonies or dependencies of any European power we have not interfered and shall not interfere. But with the Governments who have declared their independence and maintain it, and whose independence we have, on great consideration and on just principles, acknowledged, we could not view any interposition for the purpose of oppressing them, or controlling in any other manner their destiny, by any European power in any other light than as the manifestation of an unfriendly disposition toward the United States. In the war between those new Governments and Spain we declared our neutrality at the time of their recognition, and to this we have adhered, and shall continue to adhere, provided no change shall occur which, in the judgement of the competent authorities of this Government, shall make a corresponding change on the part of the United States indispensable to their security.

The late events in Spain and Portugal shew that Europe is still unsettled. Of this important fact no stronger proof can be adduced than that the allied powers should have thought it proper, on any principle satisfactory to themselves, to have interposed by force in the internal concerns of Spain. To what extent such interposition may be carried, on the same principle, is a question in which all independent powers whose governments differ from theirs are interested, even those most remote, and surely none of them more so than the United States. Our policy in regard to Europe, which was adopted at an early stage of the wars which have so long agitated that quarter of the globe, nevertheless remains the same, which is, not to interfere in the internal concerns of any of its powers; to consider the government de facto as the legitimate government for us; to cultivate friendly relations with it, and to preserve those relations by a frank, firm, and manly policy, meeting in all instances the just claims of every power, submitting to injuries from none. But in regard to those continents circumstances are eminently and conspicuously different.

It is impossible that the allied powers should extend their political system to any portion of either continent without endangering our peace and happiness; nor can anyone believe that our southern brethren, if left to themselves, would adopt it of their own accord. It is equally impossible, therefore, that we should behold such interposition in any form with indifference. If we look to the comparative strength and resources of Spain and those new Governments, and their distance from each other, it must be obvious that she can never subdue them. It is still the true policy of the United States to leave the parties to themselves, in hope that other powers will pursue the same course....

MUNDUS NOVUS

SOURCE *Amerigo Vespucci,* Mundus Novus: Letter to Lorenzo Pietro de Medici, *translation G.T. Northrup (Princeton: Princeton University Press, 1916), pp. 1, 4.*

INTRODUCTION *In this excerpt from Amerigo Vespucci's Mundus Novus (1502), the Italian explorer describes the native peoples he encountered as he explored South America. Vespucci realized during a voyage to Brazil in 1501 that the landmass was part of a hitherto-unknown continent, which he called Mundus Novus, Latin for "New World." His revelation led European mapmakers to redraw maps of the world, among them the German cartographer Martin Waldseemüller, whose proposal to call the newly discovered continent*

America immortalized Vespucci. Vespucci's contribution to European knowledge of the New World also took the form of letters to contacts in Europe, and written descriptions of the indigenous peoples of South America and their cultural and agricultural practices.

Amerigo Vespucci Views the Natives of South America, 1502

We found in those parts such a multitude of people as nobody could enumerate (as we read in the. Apocalypse), a race I say gentle and amenable.

All of both sexes go about naked, covering no part of their bodies; and just as they spring from their mothers' wombs so they go until death. They have indeed large square-built bodies, well formed and proportioned, and in color verging upon reddish. This I think has come to them, because, going about naked, they are colored by the sun. They have, too, hair plentiful and black.

In their gait and when playing their games they are agile and dignified. They are comely, too, of countenance which they nevertheless themselves destroy; for they bore their cheeks, lips, noses and ears. Nor think those holes small or that they have only one. For some I have seen having in a single face seven borings any one of which was capable of holding a plum. They stop up these holes of theirs with blue stones, bits of marble, very beautiful crystals of alabaster, very white bones, and other things artificially prepared according to their customs. But if you could see a thing so unwonted and monstrous, that is to say a man having in his cheeks and lips along seven stones some of which are a span and a half in length, you would not be without wonder. For I frequently observed and discovered that seven such stones weighed sixteen ounces, aside from the fact that in their ears, s, each perforated with three holes, they have other stones dangling on rings; and this usage applies to the men alone. For women do not bore their faces, but their ears only.

They have another custom, very shameful and beyond all human belief. For their women, being very lustful, cause the private parts of their husbands to swell to such a huge size that they appear deformed and disgusting; and this is accomplished by a certain device of theirs, the biting of certain poisonous animals. And in consequence of this many lose their organs which break through lack of attention, and they remain eunuchs.

They have no cloth either of wool, linen or cotton, since they need it not; neither do they have goods of their own, but all things are held in common. They live together without king, without government, and each is his own master. They marry as many wives as they please; and sons cohabits with mother, brother with sister, male cousin with female, and any man with the first woman he meets. They dissolve their marriages as often as they please, and observe no sort of law with respect to them. Beyond the fact that they have no church, no religion and are not idolaters, what more can I say? They live according to nature, and may be called Epicureans rather than Stoics.

NORTHWEST ORDINANCE; JULY 13, 1787

INTRODUCTION *The Northwest Ordinance was passed by the United States Congress on July 12, 1787, to establish a system of governance for "the Territory of the United States northwest of the River Ohio." With this ordinance, Congress worked out a new system of colonies to be called territories. The territories were granted the right to advance to full statehood and membership in the union. Section 14 of the Northwest Ordinance enumerates the rights of the inhabitants of the territories. Congress hoped that this ordinance would preempt the development of inequality between the residents of the thirteen colonies and the settlers of the country's western territories.*

AN ORDINANCE FOR THE GOVERNMENT OF THE TERRITORY OF THE UNITED STATES NORTHWEST OF THE RIVER OHIO.

Section 1. *Be it ordained by the United States in Congress assembled,* That the said territory, for the purposes of temporary government, be one district, subject, however, to be divided into two districts, as future circumstances may, in the opinion of Congress, make it expedient.

Sec 2. *Be it ordained by the authority aforesaid,* That the estates, both of resident and nonresident proprietors in the said territory, dying intestate, shall descent to, and be distributed among their children, and the descendants of a deceased child, in equal parts; the descendants of a deceased child or grandchild to take the share of their deceased parent in equal parts among them: And where there shall be no children or descendants, then in equal parts to the next of kin in equal degree; and among collaterals, the children of a deceased brother or sister of the intestate shall have, in equal parts among them, their deceased parents' share; and there shall in no case be a distinction between kindred of the whole and half blood; saving, in all cases, to the widow of the intestate her third part of the real estate for life, and one third part of the personal estate; and this law relative to descents and dower, shall remain in full force until altered by the legislature of the district. And until the governor and judges shall adopt laws as hereinafter mentioned, estates in the said territory may be devised or bequeathed by wills in writing, signed and sealed by him or her in whom the estate may be (being of full age), and attested by three witnesses; and real estates may be conveyed by lease and release, or bargain and sale, signed, sealed and delivered by the person being of full age, in whom the estate may be, and attested by two witnesses, provided such wills be duly proved, and such conveyances be acknowledged, or the execution thereof duly proved, and be recorded within one year after proper magistrates, courts, and registers shall be appointed for that purpose; and personal property may be transferred by delivery; saving, however to the French and Canadian inhabitants, and other settlers of the Kaskaskies, St. Vincents and the neighboring villages who have heretofore professed themselves citizens of Virginia, their laws and customs now in force among them, relative to the descent and conveyance, of property.

Sec. 3. *Be it ordained by the authority aforesaid,* That there shall be appointed from time to time by Congress, a governor, whose commission shall continue in force for the term of three years, unless sooner revoked by Congress; he shall reside in the district, and have a freehold estate therein in 1,000 acres of land, while in the exercise of his office.

Sec. 4. There shall be appointed from time to time by Congress, a secretary, whose commission shall continue in force for four years unless sooner revoked; he shall reside in the district, and have a freehold estate therein in 500 acres of land, while in the exercise of his office. It shall be his duty to keep and preserve the acts and laws passed by the legislature, and the public records of the district, and the proceedings of the governor in his executive department, and transmit authentic copies of such acts and proceedings, every six months, to the Secretary of Congress: There shall also be appointed a court to consist of three judges, any two of whom to form a court, who shall have a common law jurisdiction, and reside in the district, and have each therein a freehold estate in 500 acres of land while in the exercise of their offices; and their commissions shall continue in force during good behavior.

Sec. 5. The governor and judges, or a majority of them, shall adopt and publish in the district such laws of the original States, criminal and civil, as may be necessary and best suited to the circumstances of the district, and report them to Congress from time to time: which laws shall be in force in the district until the organization of the General Assembly therein, unless disapproved of by Congress; but afterwards the Legislature shall have authority to alter them as they shall think fit.

Sec. 6. The governor, for the time being, shall be commander in chief of the militia, appoint and commission all officers in the same below the rank of general officers; all general officers shall be appointed and commissioned by Congress.

Sec. 7. Previous to the organization of the general assembly, the governor shall appoint such magistrates and other civil officers in each county or township, as he shall find necessary for the preservation of the peace and good order in the same: After the general assembly shall be organized, the powers and duties of the magistrates and other civil officers shall be regulated and defined by the said assembly; but all magistrates and other civil officers not herein otherwise directed, shall during the continuance of this temporary government, be appointed by the governor.

Sec. 8. For the prevention of crimes and injuries, the laws to be adopted or made shall have force in all parts of the district, and for the execution of process, criminal and civil, the governor shall make proper divisions thereof; and he shall proceed from time to time as circumstances may require, to lay out the parts of the district in which the Indian titles shall have been extinguished, into counties and townships, subject, however, to such alterations as may thereafter be made by the legislature.

Sec. 9. So soon as there shall be five thousand free male inhabitants of full age in the district, upon giving proof thereof to the governor, they shall receive authority, with time and place, to elect a representative from their counties or townships to represent them in the general assembly: Provided, That, for every five hundred free male inhabitants, there shall be one representative, and so on progressively with the number of free male inhabitants shall the right of representation increase, until the number of representatives shall amount to twenty five; after which, the number and proportion of representatives shall be regulated by the legislature: Provided, That no person be eligible or qualified to act as a representative unless he shall have been a citizen of one of the United States three years, and be a resident in the district, or unless he shall have resided in the district three years; and, in either case, shall likewise hold in his own right, in fee simple, two hundred acres of land within the same; Provided, also, That a freehold in fifty acres of land in the district, having been a citizen of one of the states, and being resident in the district, or the like freehold and two years residence in the district, shall be necessary to qualify a man as an elector of a representative.

Sec. 10. The representatives thus elected, shall serve for the term of two years; and, in case of the death of a representative, or removal from office, the governor shall issue a writ to the county or township for which he was a member, to elect another in his stead, to serve for the residue of the term.

Sec. 11. The general assembly or legislature shall consist of the governor, legislative council, and a house of representatives. The Legislative Council shall consist of five members, to continue in office five years, unless sooner removed by Congress; any three of whom to be a quorum: and the members of the Council shall be nominated and appointed in the following manner, to wit: As soon as representatives shall be elected, the Governor shall appoint a time and place for them to meet together; and, when met, they shall nominate ten persons, residents in the district, and each possessed of a freehold in five hundred acres of land, and return their names to Congress; five of whom Congress shall appoint and commission to serve as aforesaid; and, whenever a vacancy shall happen in the council, by death or removal from office, the house of representatives shall nominate two persons, qualified as aforesaid, for each vacancy, and return their names to Congress; one of whom congress shall appoint and commission for the residue of the term. And every five years, four months at least before the expiration of the time of service of the members of council, the said house shall nominate ten persons, qualified as aforesaid, and return their names to Congress; five of whom Congress shall appoint and commission to serve as members of the council five years, unless sooner removed. And the governor, legislative council, and house of representatives, shall have authority to make laws in all cases, for the good government of the district, not repugnant to the principles and articles in this ordinance established and declared. And all bills, having passed by a majority in the house, and by a majority in the council, shall be referred to the governor for his assent; but no bill, or legislative act whatever, shall be of any force without his assent. The governor shall have power to convene, prorogue, and dissolve the general assembly, when, in his opinion, it shall be expedient.

Sec. 12. The governor, judges, legislative council, secretary, and such other officers as Congress shall appoint in the district, shall take an oath or affirmation of fidelity and of office; the governor before the president of congress, and all other officers before the Governor. As soon as a legislature shall be formed in the district, the council and house assembled in one room, shall have authority, by joint ballot, to elect a delegate to Congress, who shall have a seat in Congress, with a right of debating but not voting during this temporary government.

Sec. 13. And, for extending the fundamental principles of civil and religious liberty, which form the basis whereon these republics, their laws and constitutions are erected; to fix and establish those principles as the basis of all laws, constitutions, and governments, which forever hereafter shall be formed in the said territory: to provide also for the establishment of States, and permanent government therein, and for their admission to a share in the federal councils on an equal footing with the original States, at as early periods as may be consistent with the general interest:

Sec. 14. It is hereby ordained and declared by the authority aforesaid, That the following articles shall be considered as articles of compact between the original States and the people and States in the said territory and forever remain unalterable, unless by common consent, to wit:

Art. 1. No person, demeaning himself in a peaceable and orderly manner, shall ever be molested on account of his mode of worship or religious sentiments, in the said territory.

Art. 2. The inhabitants of the said territory shall always be entitled to the benefits of the writ of habeas corpus, and of the trial by jury; of a proportionate representation of the people in the legislature; and of judicial proceedings according to the course of the common law. All persons shall be bailable, unless for capital offenses, where the proof shall be evident or the presumption great. All fines shall be moderate; and no cruel or unusual punishments shall be inflicted. No man shall be deprived of his liberty or property, but by the judgment of his peers or the law of the land; and, should the public exigencies make it necessary, for the common preservation, to take any person's property, or to demand his particular services, full compensation shall be made for the same. And, in the just preservation of rights and property, it is understood and declared, that no law ought ever to be made, or have force in the said territory, that shall, in any manner whatever, interfere with or affect private contracts or engagements, bona fide, and without fraud, previously formed.

Art. 3. Religion, morality, and knowledge, being necessary to good government and the happiness of mankind, schools and the means of education shall forever be encouraged. The utmost good faith shall always be observed towards the Indians; their lands and property shall never be taken from them without their consent; and, in their property, rights, and liberty, they shall never be invaded or disturbed, unless in just and lawful wars authorized by Congress; but laws founded in justice and humanity, shall from time to time be made for preventing wrongs being done to them, and for preserving peace and friendship with them.

Art. 4. The said territory, and the States which may be formed therein, shall forever remain a part of this Confederacy of the United States of America, subject to the Articles of Confederation, and to such alterations therein as shall be constitutionally made; and to all the acts and ordinances of the United States in Congress assembled, conformable thereto. The inhabitants and settlers in the said territory shall be subject to pay a part of the federal debts contracted or to be contracted, and a proportional part of the expenses of government, to be apportioned on them by Congress according to the same common rule and measure by which apportionments thereof shall be made on the other States; and the taxes for paying their proportion shall be laid and levied by the authority and direction of the legislatures of the district or districts, or new States, as in the original States, within the time agreed upon by the United States in Congress assembled. The legislatures of those districts or new States, shall never interfere with the primary disposal of the soil by the United States in Congress assembled, nor with any regulations Congress may find necessary for securing the title in such soil to the bona fide purchasers. No tax shall be imposed on lands the property of the United States; and, in no case, shall nonresident proprietors be taxed higher than residents. The navigable waters leading into the Mississippi and St. Lawrence, and the carrying places between the same, shall be common highways and forever free, as well to the inhabitants of the said territory as to the citizens of the United States, and those of any other States that may be admitted into the confederacy, without any tax, impost, or duty therefore.

Art. 5. There shall be formed in the said territory, not less than three nor more than five States; and the boundaries of the States, as soon as Virginia shall alter her act of cession, and consent to the same, shall become fixed and established as follows, to wit: The western State in the said territory, shall be bounded by the Mississippi, the Ohio, and Wabash Rivers; a direct line drawn from the Wabash and Post Vincents, due North, to the territorial line between the United States and Canada; and, by the said territorial line, to the Lake of the Woods and Mississippi. The middle State shall be bounded by the said direct line, the Wabash from Post Vincents to the Ohio, by the Ohio, by a direct line, drawn due north from the mouth of the Great Miami, to the said territorial line, and by the said territorial line. The eastern State shall be bounded by the last mentioned direct line, the Ohio, Pennsylvania, and the said territorial line: Provided, however, and it is further understood and declared, that the boundaries of these three States shall be subject so far to be altered, that, if Congress shall hereafter find it expedient, they shall have authority to form one or two States in that part of the said territory which lies north of an east and west line drawn through the southerly bend or extreme of Lake Michigan. And, whenever any of the said States shall have sixty thousand free inhabitants therein, such State shall be admitted, by its delegates, into the Congress of the United States, on an equal footing with the original States in all respects whatever, and shall be at liberty to form a permanent constitution and State government: Provided, the constitution and government so to be formed, shall be republican, and in conformity to the principles contained in these articles; and, so far as it can be consistent with the general interest of the confederacy, such admission shall be allowed at an earlier period, and when there may be a less number of free inhabitants in the State than sixty thousand.

Art. 6. There shall be neither slavery nor involuntary servitude in the said territory, otherwise than in the punishment of crimes whereof the party shall have been duly convicted: *Provided, always,* That any person escaping into the same, from whom labor or service is lawfully claimed in any one of the original States, such fugitive may be lawfully reclaimed and conveyed to the person claiming his or her labor or service as aforesaid.

Be it ordained by the authority aforesaid, That the resolutions of the 23rd of April, 1784, relative to the subject of this ordinance, be, and the same are hereby repealed and declared null and void.

Done by the United States, in Congress assembled, the 13th day of July, in the year of our Lord 1787, and of their soveriegnty and independence the twelfth.

OF THE PRINCIPLE OF THE COMMERCIAL OR MERCANTILE SYSTEM

SOURCE *Adam Smith,* The Wealth of Nations, *[1776], edited with noted and marginal summary by Edwin Cannan in the 1904 Edition (New York: Bantam Classic, 2003), pp. 561-563.*

INTRODUCTION *The eighteenth-century Scottish economist Adam Smith coined the term* mercantile system, *which he used derisively. Smith contended that the fundamental error of the mercantilists was their confusion of wealth with money. Since they believed, mistakenly, that a favorable balance of trade was the primary means of acquiring wealth and money, they had been unable to conceive of the advantages to be derived from foreign trade. In this passage from* The Wealth of Nations *(1776), Smith comments on the mercantile system in a description of the trade relationship between Europe and the Americas.*

The importation of gold and silver is not the principle, much less the sole benefit which a nation derives from its foreign trade. Between whatever place foreign trade is carried on, they all of them derive two distinct benefits from it. It carries out that surplus part of the produce of their land and labour for which there is no demand among them, and brings back in return for it something else for which there is there is a demand. It gives a value to their superfluities, by exchanging them for something else, which may satisfy a part of their wants, and increase their enjoyments. By means of it, the narrowness of the home market does not hinder the division of labor in any particular branch of art or manufacture from being carried to the highest perfection. By opening a more extensive market for whatever part of the produce of their labour may exceed the home consumption, it encourages them to improve its productive powers, and to augment its annual produce to the utmost, and thereby to increase the real revenue and wealth of the society. These great and important services foreign trade is continually occupied in performing, to all the different countries between which it is carried on. They all derive great benefit from it, though that in which the merchant resides generally derives the greatest, as he is generally more employed in supplying the wants, and carrying out the superfluities of his own, than of any other particular country....

It is not by the importation of gold and silver, that the discovery of America has enriched Europe. By the abundance of the American mines, those metals have become cheaper The discovery of America, however, certainly made a most essential [change in the state of Europe]. By opening a new and inexhaustible market to all the commodities of Europe, it gave occasion to new divisions of labour and improvements of art, which, in the narrow circle of the ancient commerce, could never have taken place for want of a market to take off the greater part of their produce. The productive powers of the market were improved, and its produce increased in all the different countries of Europe, and together with it the real revenue and wealth of the inhabitants. The commodities of Europe were almost all new to America, and many of those of America were new to Europe. A new set of exchanges, therefore, began to take place which had never been thought of before, and which should naturally have proved as advantageous to the new, as it certainly did to the old continent. The savage injustice of the Europeans rendered an event, which ought to have been beneficial to all, ruinous and destructive to several of these unfortunate countries.

OF THE SILVER OF THE INDIES, 1590

SOURCE *José de Acosta,* Natural and Moral History of the Indies, *Edited by Jane E. Mangan, Translated by Frances López-Morillas (Durham: Duke University Press, 2002), pp. 172-73, 174, 179-80.*

INTRODUCTION *José de Acosta, a sixteenth-century Jesuit missionary in South America, was a forceful critic of the violent Spanish conquests of Mexico and Peru and the inhumane treatment inflicted on the colonized peoples. Acosta arrived in Peru in 1569 and traveled widely throughout the Andean region, gaining firsthand knowledge of the many difficulties faced by an indigenous population continually confronted with ambitious colonial administrators and often ignorant and unsympathetic missionaries. In his* Natural and Moral History of the Indies, *a treatise on the lives and customs of the region's indigenous peoples, Acosta provided this account of the backbreaking work performed by slaves and native laborers at the silver mines in Potosí.*

The famous mountain of Potosí is located in the province of Los Charcas, in the kingdom of Peru; it is twenty-one and two-thirds degrees distant from the southern or Antarctic Pole, so that it lies within the Tropics near the edge of the Torrid Zone. And yet it is extremely cold, more than Old Castile and more than Flanders, although it ought to be warm or hot considering the distance from the pole at which it lies. What makes it cold is that it is so high and steep and all bathed in very cold and intemperate winds, especially the one they call tomahaui there, which is gusty and very cold and prevails in May, June, July, and August. Its surroundings are dry, cold, and very bleak and completely barren, for it neither engenders nor produces fruit or grain or grass and thus is by nature uninhabitable owing to the unfavorable weather and the great barrenness of the earth.

But the power of silver, desire for which draws all other things to itself, has populated that mountain with the largest number of inhabitants in all those realms; and silver has made it so rich in every sort of foodstuff and luxury that nothing can be desired that is not found there in abundance. And, although everything has to be brought in by wagon, its marketplaces are full of fruit, preserves, luxuries, marvelous wines, silks, and adornments, as much as in any other place. The color of this mountain is a sort of dark red; it is very beautiful to look upon, resembling a well-shaped tent in the form of a sugar-loaf....

This is the way in which Potosí was discovered, Divine Providence decreeing, for the good of Spain, that the greatest treasure known to exist in the world was hidden and came to light at the time when the Emperor Charles V, of glorious name, held the reins of empire and the realm of Spain and seigniory of the Indies. Once the discovery of Potosí became known in the kingdom of Peru many Spaniards went there, along with most of the citizens of the city of La Plata, which is eighteen leagues from Potosí, to establish mining claims; a large number of Indians also came from different provinces, especially those who owned smelting ovens in Porco, and in a short time it became the largest town in the realm....

As I have said, the mountain of Potosí has four chief lodes, namely the Rich, Centeno, Tin, and Mendieta.... Each lode has different mines that form part of it, and these have been taken over and divided among various owners, whose names they usually bear.... There are seventy-eight mines in the lode called Rich;... There are twenty-four mines in the Centeno lode....

The miners always work by candlelight, dividing their labor in such a way that some work by day and the rest by night, and others work at night and the rest by day. The ore is usually very hard and is loosened by blows of a mattock, which is like breaking stone. Then they carry the ore on their backs up ladders made of three strands of leather plaited into thick ropes, with sticks placed between one strand and another as steps, so that one man can be descending while another is climbing. These ladders are 60 feet long, and at the end of each is another ladder of the same length, which starts from a ledge or shelf where there are wooden landings resembling scaffolding, for there are many ladders to climb. Each man has a fifty-pound load in a blanket tied over his breast, with the ore it contains at his back; three men make the climb at one time. The first carries a candle tied to his thumb so that they can see, for, as I have said, no daylight comes from above. They climb by catching hold with both hands, and in this way ascend the great distances I have described, often more than 150 *estados*, a horrible thing about which it is frightening even to think.

Such is the power of money, for the sake of which men do and suffer so much.

OF THE WAR COMBATS, BOLDNESS, AND ARMS OF THE SAVAGES OF AMERICA

SOURCE *Jean de Lery,* History of a Voyage to the Land of Brazil, Otherwise called America Containing the Navigation and the Remarkable Things Seen on the Sea by the Author; the Behavior of Villegagon in That Country; the Customs and Strange Ways of Life of the American Savages; Together with the Description of Various Animals, Trees, Plants, and Other Singular Things Completely Unknown over Here, 1578. *Translation and introduction by Janet*

Whatley (Berkeley: University of California Press, 1990), pp. 112-120.

INTRODUCTION *Jean de Léry was a French Calvinist who traveled in 1556 with a small group of French Protestants to Brazil, where they hoped to establish a colony. The colony was not a success, and the group took refuge among Brazil's Tupinamba Indians until they could return to Europe. Léry later wrote about his experiences in* History of a Voyage to the Land of Brazil, Otherwise Called America, *published in 1578. In this passage from that work, Léry describes the Indians' method of warfare.*

Our Tupinikin Tupinaba follow the custom of all the other savages who live in that fourth part of the world, which includes more than two thousand leagues of latitude from the Strait of Magellan, lying fifty degrees toward the Antarctic Pole, to Newfoundland, at about sixty degrees on the Arctic side: that is, they wage deadly warfare against a number of nations of their region. However, their closest and principle enemies are those whom they call *Margaia,* and their allies the Portuguese, whom they call *Pero,* reciprocally, the Margaia are hostile not only to the Tupinamba, but also to the French, their confederates.

But these barbarians do not wage war to win countries and lands from each other, for each has more than he needs; even less do the conquerors aim to get rich from the spoils, ransoms, and arms of the vanquished: that is not what drives them. For, as they themselves confess, they are impelled by no other passion than that of avenging, each for his side, his own kinsmen and friends who in the past have been seized and eaten, in the manner that I will describe in the next chapter; and they pursue each other so relentlessly that whoever falls into the hands of his enemy must expect to be treated, without any compromise, in the same manner that is, to be slain and eaten. Furthermore, from the time that war has been declared among any of these nations, everyone claims that since an enemy who has received an injury will resent it forever, one would be remiss to let him escape when he is at one's mercy; their hatred is so inveterate that they can never be reconciled. On this point one can say that Machiavelli and his disciples (with whom France, to her great misfortune, in how filled) are true imitators of barbarian cruelties; for since these atheists teach and practice, against Christian doctrine, that new services must never cause old injuries to be forgotten- that is, that men, participating in the devil's nature, must not pardon each other - do they not show their hearts to be more cruel and malign than those of tigers? . . . .

So they are assembled, by the means described to you, in the number of sometimes eight or ten thousand men; there are many women along as well, not to fight, but only to carry the cotton beds and the flour and other foodstuffs. The old men who have killed and eaten the greatest number of enemies are ordained as chiefs and leaders by the others, and everyone sets forth under their guidance. Although they keep no rank or order while marching, when they go by land they are in serried troops with the most valiant in the lead; and it is a wonder how that whole multitude, without field-marshall or quarter-master, can so conjoin that, without any confusion, you will always see them ready to march at the first signal . . . .

They ordinarily go twenty-five or thirty leagues to seek out their enemies; when they approach their territory, here are the first ruses and stratagems of war that they use to capture them. The most skillful and valiant, leaving the others with the women one or two days' journel behind them, approach as stealthily as they can to lie in ambush in the woods; they are so determined to surprise their enemies that they will sometimes lie hidden there more than twenty-four hours. If. the enemy is taken unawares, all who are seized, be they men, women or children, will be led away; and when the attackers are back in their own territory all the prisoners will be slain, put in pieces on the boucan, and finally eaten. Such surprise attacks are all the easier to spring in that the villages - there are no cities - cannot be closed, and they have no doors in their houses (which are mostly eighty to a hundred feet long, with openings in several places) unless they block the entrances with branches of palm, or of that big plant called pindo. However, around some villages on the enemy frontier, those most skilled at warfare plant stakes of palm five or six feet high, and on the approaches to the paths they go around and stick sharpened wooden pegs into the earth, with their points just above ground level . . . .

If the enemies are warned of each others' approach, and the two armies come to confront each other, the combat is cruel and terrible beyond belief – which I can vouch for, having myself been a spectator. For another Frenchman and I, out of curiosity, taking our chances of being captured and either killed on the spot or eaten by the Margaia, once went to accompany about four thousand of our savages in a battle .that took place on the seashore; we saw these barbarians fight with such a fury that madmen could do no worse. First, when our Tupinamba had caught sight of their enemies from something less than a half mile away, they broke out into such howls (our wolf-hunters over here make nothing like such a noise), and their clamor so rent the air that if the heavens had thundered we would not have heard it. As they approached, redoubling their cries, sounding their trumpets, brandishing the bones of prisoners who had been eaten, and even showing off the victims' teeth strung in rows - some had more than ten feet of them hanging from their necks - their demeanor was terrifying to behold. But when they came to join battle it was still worse: for as soon as they were within two or three hundred feet of each other, they saluted each other with great volleys of arrows, and you would have seen an infinity of them soar through the air as thick as flies. If some were hit, as several were, they tore the arrows out of their bodies with a marvelous courage, breaking them and like mad dogs biting the pieces; all wounded as they were, they would not be kept from returning to the combat. It must be noted here that these Americans are so relentless in their wars that as long as they can move arms and legs, they fight on unceasingly, neither retreating nor turning their backs. When they finally met in hand-to-hand combat, it was with their wooden swords and clubs, charging each other with great two-handed blows; whoever hit the head of his enemy not only knocked him to the ground but struck him dead, as our butchers fell oxen.... After this battle had gone on for about three hours, and on both sides there were many dead and wounded lying on the field, our Tupinamba finally carried the victory. They captured more than thirty Margaia, men and women, whom they took off into their own territory. Although we two Frenchmen had done nothing (as I have said) except hold our drawn swords in our hands, and sometimes fire a few pistol shots into the air to give courage to our side, still, since there was nothing we could have done to give them greater pleasure than to go with them to war, they continued to hold us in such high esteem that, since that time, the elders of the villages we visited always showed us the greatest affection.

SECOND TREATISE ON GOVERNMENT-JOHN LOCKE, 1690

INTRODUCTION *By the seventeenth century, the most persuasive and frequently cited argument favoring appropriation of aboriginal lands in America was the theory of property derived from the Roman law of res nullius (no thing) and perpetuated most effectually by the English philosopher John Locke (1632-1704) in his* Two Treatises of Government *(1690). Res nullius held that all lands that were "unoccupied" remained common property until they were put to use, usually agriculturally. Locke's influential views on property, slavery, and war, described in this excerpt from the* Second Treatise, *powerfully legitimated colonial acquisition of indigenous territory through the*

authority of natural law rather than legislative decree. Only the preface and sections 16-39 are included here.

PREFACE

Reader, thou hast here the beginning and end of a discourse concerning government; what fate has otherwise disposed of the papers that should have filled up the middle, and were more than all the rest, it is not worth while to tell thee. These, which remain, I hope are sufficient to establish the throne of our great restorer, our present King William; to make good his title, in the consent of the people, which being the only one of all lawful governments, he has more fully and clearly, than any prince in Christendom; and to justify to the world the people of England, whose love of their just and natural rights, with their resolution to preserve them, saved the nation when it was on the very brink of slavery and ruin. If these papers have that evidence, I flatter myself is to be found in them, there will be no great miss of those which are lost, and my reader may be satisfied without them: for I imagine, I shall have neither the time, nor inclination to repeat my pains, and fill up the wanting part of my answer, by tracing Sir Robert again, through all the windings and obscurities, which are to be met with in the several branches of his wonderful system. The king, and body of the nation, have since so thoroughly confuted his Hypothesis, that I suppose no body hereafter will have either the confidence to appear against our common safety, and be again an advocate for slavery; or the weakness to be deceived with contradictions dressed up in a popular stile, and well-turned periods: for if any one will be at the pains, himself, in those parts, which are here untouched, to strip Sir Robert's discourses of the flourish of doubtful expressions, and endeavour to reduce his words to direct, positive, intelligible propositions, and then compare them one with another, he will quickly be satisfied, there was never so much glib nonsense put together in well-sounding English. If he think it not worth while to examine his works all thro', let him make an experiment in that part, where he treats of usurpation; and let him try, whether he can, with all his skill, make Sir Robert intelligible, and consistent with himself, or common sense. I should not speak so plainly of a gentleman, long since past answering, had not the pulpit, of late years, publicly owned his doctrine, and made it the current divinity of the times. It is necessary those men, who taking on them to be teachers, have so dangerously misled others, should be openly shewed of what authority this their Patriarch is, whom they have so blindly followed, that so they may either retract what upon so ill grounds they have vented, and cannot be maintained; or else justify those principles which they preached up for gospel; though they had no better an author than an

English courtier: for I should not have writ against Sir Robert, or taken the pains to shew his mistakes, inconsistencies, and want of (what he so much boasts of, and pretends wholly to build on) scripture-proofs, were there not men amongst us, who, by crying up his books, and espousing his doctrine, save me from the reproach of writing against a dead adversary. They have been so zealous in this point, that, if I have done him any wrong, I cannot hope they should spare me. I wish, where they have done the truth and the public wrong, they would be as ready to redress it, and allow its just weight to this reflection, viz. that there cannot be done a greater mischief to prince and people, than the propagating wrong notions concerning government; that so at last all times might not have reason to complain of the Drum Ecclesiastic. If any one, concerned really for truth, undertake the confutation of my Hypothesis, I promise him either to recant my mistake, upon fair conviction; or to answer his difficulties. But he must remember two things.

First, That cavilling here and there, at some expression, or little incident of my discourse, is not an answer to my book.

Secondly, That I shall not take railing for arguments, nor think either of these worth my notice, though I shall always look on myself as bound to give satisfaction to any one, who shall appear to be conscientiously scrupulous in the point, and shall shew any just grounds for his scruples.

I have nothing more, but to advertise the reader, that Observations stands for Observations on Hobbs, Milton, and that a bare quotation of pages always means pages of his Patriarcha, Edition 1680.

Of the State of War.

Sec. 16. The state of war is a state of enmity and destruction: and therefore declaring by word or action, not a passionate and hasty, but a sedate settled design upon another man's life, puts him in a state of war with him against whom he has declared such an intention, and so has exposed his life to the other's power to be taken away by him, or any one that joins with him in his defence, and espouses his quarrel; it being reasonable and just, I should have a right to destroy that which threatens me with destruction: for, by the fundamental law of nature, man being to be preserved as much as possible, when all cannot be preserved, the safety of the innocent is to be preferred: and one may destroy a man who makes war upon him, or has discovered an enmity to his being, for the same reason that he may kill a wolf or a lion; because such men are not under the ties of the common law of reason, have no other rule, but that of force and violence, and so may be treated as beasts of prey, those dangerous and noxious creatures, that will be sure to destroy him whenever he falls into their power.

Sect. 17. And hence it is, that he who attempts to get another man into his absolute power, does thereby put himself into a state of war with him; it being to be understood as a declaration of a design upon his life: for I have reason to conclude, that he who would get me into his power without my consent, would use me as he pleased when he had got me there, and destroy me too when he had a fancy to it; for no body can desire to have me in his absolute power, unless it be to compel me by force to that which is against the right of my freedom, i.e. make me a slave. To be free from such force is the only security of my preservation; and reason bids me look on him, as an enemy to my preservation, who would take away that freedom which is the fence to it; so that he who makes an attempt to enslave me, thereby puts himself into a state of war with me. He that, in the state of nature, would take away the freedom that belongs to any one in that state, must necessarily be supposed to have a foundation to f eall athevrest; hasghelthat, hin theestateeofgsociety, would take away the freedom belonging to those of that society or commonwealth, must be supposed to design to take away from them every thing else, and so be looked on as in a state of war.

Sec. 18. This makes it lawful for a man to kill a thief, who has not in the least hurt him, nor declared any design upon his life, any farther than, by the use of force, so to get him in his power, as to take away his money, or what he pleases, from him; because using force, where he has no right, to get me into his power, let his pretence be what it will, I have no reason to suppose, that he, who would take away my liberty, would not, when he had me in his power, take away every thing else. And therefore it is lawful for me to treat him as one who has put himself into a state of war with me, i.e. kill him if I can; for to that hazard does he justly expose himself, whoever introduces a state of war, and is aggressor in it.

Sec. 19. And here we have the plain difference between the state of nature and the state of war, which however some men have confounded, are as far distant, as a state of peace, good will, mutual assistance and preservation, and a state of enmity, malice, violence and mutual destruction, are one from another. Men living together according to reason, without a common superior on earth, with authority to judge between them, is properly the state of nature. But force, or a declared design of force, upon the person of another, where there is no common superior on earth to appeal to for relief, is the state of war: and it is the want of such an appeal gives a man the right of war even against an aggressor, tho' he be in society and a fellow subject. Thus a thief, whom I cannot harm, but by appeal to the law, for having stolen all that I am worth, I may kill, when he sets on me to rob me but of my horse or coat; because the law, which was made for my preservation, where it cannot interpose to secure my life from present force, which, if lost, is capable of no reparation, permits me my own defence, and the right of war, a liberty to kill the aggressor, because the aggressor allows not time to appeal to our common judge, nor the decision of the law, for remedy in a case where the mischief may be irreparable. Want of a common judge with authority, puts all men in a state of nature: force without right, upon a man's person, makes a state of war, both where there is, and is not, a common judge.

Sec. 20. But when the actual force is over, the state of war ceases between those that are in society, and are equally on both sides subjected to the fair determination of the law; because then there lies open the remedy of appeal for the past injury, and to prevent future harm: but where no such appeal is, as in the state of nature, for want of positive laws, and judges with authority to appeal to, the state of war once begun, continues, with a right to the innocent party to destroy the other whenever he can, until the aggressor offers peace, and desires reconciliation on such terms as may repair any wrongs he has already done, and secure the innocent for the future; nay, where an appeal to the law, and constituted judges, lies open, but the remedy is denied by a manifest perverting of justice, and a barefaced wresting of the laws to protect or indemnify the violence or injuries of some men, or party of men, there it is hard to imagine any thing but a state of war: for wherever violence is used, and injury done, though by hands appointed to administer justice, it is still violence and injury, however coloured with the name, pretences, or forms of law, the end whereof being to protect and redress the innocent, by an unbiassed application of it, to all who are under it; wherever that is not bona fide done, war is made upon the sufferers, who having no appeal on earth to right them, they are left to the only remedy in such cases, an appeal to heaven.

Sec. 21. To avoid this state of war (wherein there is no appeal but to heaven, and wherein every the least difference is apt to end, where there is no authority to decide between the contenders) is one great reason of men's putting themselves into society, and quitting the state of nature: for where there is an authority, a power on earth, from which relief can be had by appeal, there the continuance of the state of war is excluded, and the controversy is decided by that power. Had there been any such court, any superior jurisdiction on earth, to determine the right between Jephtha and the Ammonites, they had never come to a state of war: but we see he was forced to appeal to heaven. The Lord the Judge (says he) be judge this day between the children of Israel and the children of Ammon, Judg. xi. 27. and then prosecuting, and relying on his appeal, he leads out his army to battle: and therefore in such controversies, where the question is put, who shall be judge? It cannot be meant, who shall decide the controversy; every one knows what Jephtha here tells us, that the Lord the Judge shall judge. Where there is no judge on earth, the appeal lies to God in heaven. That question then cannot mean, who shall judge, whether another hath put himself in a state of war with me, and whether I may, as Jephtha did, appeal to heaven in it? of that I myself can only be judge in my own conscience, as I will answer it, at the great day, to the supreme judge of all men.

Of Slavery.

Sec. 22. The natural liberty of man is to be free from any superior power on earth, and not to be under the will or legislative authority of man, but to have only the law of nature for his rule. The liberty of man, in society, is to be under no other legislative power, but that established, by consent, in the commonwealth; nor under the dominion of any will, or restraint of any law, but what that legislative shall enact, according to the trust put in it. Freedom then is not what Sir Robert Filmer tells us, Observations, A. 55. a liberty for every one to do what he lists, to live as he pleases, and not to be tied by any laws: but freedom of men under government is, to have a standing rule to live by, common to every one of that society, and made by the legislative power erected in it; a liberty to follow my own will in all things, where the rule prescribes not; and not to be subject to the inconstant, uncertain, unknown, arbitrary will of another man: as freedom of nature is, to be under no other restraint but the law of nature.

Sec. 23. This freedom from absolute, arbitrary power, is so necessary to, and closely joined with a man's preservation, that he cannot part with it, but by what forfeits his preservation and life together: for a man, not having the power of his own life, cannot, by compact, or his own consent, enslave himself to any one, nor put himself under the absolute, arbitrary power of another, to take away his life, when he pleases. No body can give more power than he has himself; and he that cannot take away his own life, cannot give another power over it. Indeed, having by his fault forfeited his own life, by some act that deserves death; he, to whom he has forfeited it, may (when he has him in his power) delay to take it, and make use of him to his own service, and he does him no injury by it: for, whenever he finds the hardship of his slavery outweigh the value of his life, it is in his power, by resisting the will of his master, to draw on himself the death he desires.

Sec. 24. This is the perfect condition of slavery, which is nothing else, but the state of war continued, between a lawful conqueror and a captive: for, if once compact enter between them, and make an agreement for a limited power on the one side, and obedience on the other, the state of war and slavery ceases, as long as the compact endures: for, as has been said, no man can, by agreement, pass over to another that which he hath not in himself, a power over his own life.

I confess, we find among the Jews, as well as other nations, that men did sell themselves; but, it is plain, this was only to drudgery, not to slavery: for, it is evident, the person sold was not under an absolute, arbitrary, despotical power: for the master could not have power to kill him, at any time, whom, at a certain time, he was obliged to let go free out of his service; and the master of such a servant was so far from having an arbitrary power over his life, that he could not, at pleasure, so much as maim him, but the loss of an eye, or tooth, set him free, Exod. xxi.

Of Property.

Sec. 25. Whether we consider natural reason, which tells us, that men, being once born, have a right to their preservation, and consequently to meat and drink, and such other things as nature affords for their subsistence: or revelation, which gives us an account of those grants God made of the world to Adam, and to Noah, and his sons, it is very clear, that God, as king David says, Psal. cxv. 16. has given the earth to the children of men; given it to mankind in common. But this being supposed, it seems to some a very great difficulty, how any one should ever come to have a property in any thing: I will not content myself to answer, that if it be difficult to make out property, upon a supposition that God gave the world to Adam, and his posterity in common, it is impossible that any man, but one universal monarch, should have any property upon a supposition, that God gave the world to Adam, and his heirs in succession, exclusive of all the rest of his posterity. But I shall endeavour to shew, how men might come to have a property in several parts of that which God gave to mankind in common, and that without any express compact of all the commoners.

Sec. 26. God, who hath given the world to men in common, hath also given them reason to make use of it to the best advantage of life, and convenience. The earth, and all that is therein, is given to men for the support and comfort of their being. And tho' all the fruits it naturally produces, and beasts it feeds, belong to mankind in common, as they are produced by the spontaneous hand of nature; and no body has originally a private dominion, exclusive of the rest of mankind, in any of them, as they are thus in their natural state: yet being given for the use of men, there must of necessity be a means to appropriate them some way or other, before they can be of any use, or at all beneficial to any particular man. The fruit, or venison, which nourishes the wild Indian, who knows

no enclosure, and is still a tenant in common, must be his, and so his, i.e. a part of him, that another can no longer have any right to it, before it can do him any good for the support of his life.

Sec. 27. Though the earth, and all inferior creatures, be common to all men, yet every man has a property in his own person: this no body has any right to but himself. The labour of his body, and the work of his hands, we may say, are properly his. Whatsoever then he removes out of the state that nature hath provided, and left it in, he hath mixed his labour with, and joined to it something that is his own, and thereby makes it his property. It being by him removed from the common state nature hath placed it in, it hath by this labour something annexed to it, that excludes the common right of other men: for this labour being the unquestionable property of the labourer, no man but he can have a right to what that is once joined to, at least where there is enough, and as good, left in common for others.

Sec. 28. He that is nourished by the acorns he picked up under an oak, or the apples he gathered from the trees in the wood, has certainly appropriated them to himself. No body can deny but the nourishment is his. I ask then, when did they begin to be his? when he digested? or when he eat? or when he boiled? or when he brought them home? or when he picked them up? and it is plain, if the first gathering made them not his, nothing else could. That labour put a distinction between them and common: that added something to them more than nature, the common mother of all, had done; and so they became his private right. And will any one say, he had no right to those acorns or apples, he thus appropriated, because he had not the consent of all mankind to make them his? Was it a robbery thus to assume to himself what belonged to all in common? If such a consent as that was necessary, man had starved, notwithstanding the plenty God had given him. We see in commons, which remain so by compact, that it is the taking any part of what is common, and removing it out of the state nature leaves it in, which begins the property; without which the common is of no use. And the taking of this or that part, does not depend on the express consent of all the commoners. Thus the grass my horse has bit; the turfs my servant has cut; and the ore I have digged in any place, where I have a right to them in common with others, become my property, without the assignation or consent of any body. The labour that was mine, removing them out of that common state they were in, hath fixed my property in them.

Sec. 29. By making an explicit consent of every commoner, necessary to any one's appropriating to himself any part of what is given in common, children or servants could not cut the meat, which their father or master had provided for them in common, without assigning to every one his peculiar part. Though the water running in the fountain be every one's, yet who can doubt, but that in the pitcher is his only who drew it out? His labour hath taken it out of the hands of nature, where it was common, and belonged equally to all her children, and hath thereby appropriated it to himself.

Sec. 30. Thus this law of reason makes the deer that Indian's who hath killed it; it is allowed to be his goods, who hath bestowed his labour upon it, though before it was the common right of every one. And amongst those who are counted the civilized part of mankind, who have made and multiplied positive laws to determine property, this original law of nature, for the beginning of property, in what was before common, still takes place; and by virtue thereof, what fish any one catches in the ocean, that great and still remaining common of mankind; or what ambergrise any one takes up here, is by the labour that removes it out of that common state nature left it in, made his property, who takes that pains about it. And even amongst us, the hare that any one is hunting, is thought his who pursues her during the chase: for being a beast that is still looked upon as common, and no man's private possession; whoever has employed so much labour about any of that kind, as to find and pursue her, has thereby removed her from the state of nature, wherein she was common, and hath begun a property.

Sec. 31. It will perhaps be objected to this, that if gathering the acorns, or other fruits of the earth, &. makes a right to them, then any one may ingross as much as he will. To which I answer, Not so. The same law of nature, that does by this means give us property, does also bound that property too. God has given us all things richly, 1 Tim. vi. 12. is the voice of reason confirmed by inspiration. But how far has he given it us? To enjoy. As much as any one can make use of to any advantage of life before it spoils, so much he may by his Tabour fix a property in: whatever is beyond this, is more than his share, and belongs to others. Nothing was made by God for man to spoil or destroy. And thus, considering the plenty of natural provisions there was a long time in the world, and the few spenders; and to how small a part of that provision the industry of one man could extend itself, and ingross it to the prejudice of others; especially keeping within the bounds, set by reason, of what might serve for his use; there could be then little room for quarrels or contentions about property so established.

Sec. 32. But the chief matter of property being now not the fruits of the earth, and the beasts that subsist on it, but the earth itself; as that which takes in and carries with it all the rest; I think it is plain, that property in that too is acquired as the former. As much land as a man tills, plants, improves, cultivates, and can use the product

of, so much is his property. He by his labour does, as it were, inclose it from the common. Nor will it invalidate his right, to say every body else has an equal title to it; and therefore he cannot appropriate, he cannot inclose, without the consent of all his fellow-commoners, all mankind. God, when he gave the world in common to all mankind, commanded man also to labour, and the penury of his condition required it of him. God and his reason commanded him to subdue the earth, i.e. improve it for the benefit of life, and therein lay out something upon it that was his own, his labour. He that in obedience to this command of God, subdued, tilled and sowed any part of it, thereby annexed to it something that was his property, which another had no title to, nor could without injury take from him.

Sec. 33. Nor was this appropriation of any parcel of land, by improving it, any prejudice to any other man, since there was still enough, and as good left; and more than the yet unprovided could use. So that, in effect, there was never the less left for others because of his enclosure for himself: for he that leaves as much as another can make use of, does as good as take nothing at all. No body could think himself injured by the drinking of another man, though he took a good draught, who had a whole river of the same water left him to quench his thirst: and the case of land and water, where there is enough of both, is perfectly the same.

Sec. 34. God gave the world to men in common; but since he gave it them for their benefit, and the greatest conveniencies of life they were capable to draw from it, it cannot be supposed he meant it should always remain common and uncultivated. He gave it to the use of the industrious and rational, (and labour was to be his title to it;) not to the fancy or covetousness of the quarrelsome and contentious. He that had as good left for his improvement, as was already taken up, needed not complain, ought not to meddle with what was already improved by another's labour: if he did, it is plain he desired the benefit of another's pains, which he had no right to, and not the ground which God had given him in common with others to labour on, and whereof there was as good left, as that already possessed, and more than he knew what to do with, or his industry could reach to.

Sec. 35. It is true, in land that is common in England, or any other country, where there is plenty of people under government, who have money and commerce, no one can inclose or appropriate any part, without the consent of all his fellow-commoners; because this is left common by compact, i.e. by the law of the land, which is not to be violated. And though it be common, in respect of some men, it is not so to all mankind; but is the joint property of this country, or this parish. Besides, the remainder, after such enclosure, would not be as good to the rest of the commoners, as the whole was when they could all make use of the whole; whereas in the beginning and first peopling of the great common of the world, it was quite otherwise. The law man was under, was rather for appropriating. God commanded, and his wants forced him to labour. That was his property which could not be taken from him where-ever he had fixed it. And hence subduing or cultivating the earth, and having dominion, we see are joined together. The one gave title to the other. So that God, by commanding to subdue, gave authority so far to appropriate: and the condition of human life, which requires labour and materials to work on, necessarily introduces private possessions.

Sec. 36. The measure of property nature has well set by the extent of men's labour and the conveniencies of life: no man's labour could subdue, or appropriate all; nor could his enjoyment consume more than a small part; so that it was impossible for any man, this way, to intrench upon the right of another, or acquire to himself a property, to the prejudice of his neighbour, who would still have room for as good, and as large a possession (after the other had taken out his) as before it was appropriated. This measure did confine every man's possession to a very moderate proportion, and such as he might appropriate to himself, without injury to any body, in the first ages of the world, when men were more in danger to be lost, by wandering from their company, in the then vast wilderness of the earth, than to be straitened for want of room to plant in. And the same measure may be allowed still without prejudice to any body, as full as the world seems: for supposing a man, or family, in the state they were at first peopling of the world by the children of Adam, or Noah; let him plant in some inland, vacant places of America, we shall find that the possessions he could make himself, upon the measures we have given, would not be very large, nor, even to this day, prejudice the rest of mankind, or give them reason to complain, or think themselves injured by this man's incroachment, though the race of men have now spread themselves to all the corners of the world, and do infinitely exceed the small number was at the beginning. Nay, the extent of ground is of so little value, without labour, that I have heard it affirmed, that in Spain itself a man may be permitted to plough, sow and reap, without being disturbed, upon land he has no other title to, but only his making use of it. But, on the contrary, the inhabitants think themselves beholden to him, who, by his industry on neglected, and consequently waste land, has increased the stock of corn, which they wanted. But be this as it will, which I lay no stress on; this I dare boldly affirm, that the same rule of propriety, (viz.) that every man should have as much as he could make use of, would hold still in the world, without straitening any body; since there is land enough

in the world to suffice double the inhabitants, had not the invention of money, and the tacit agreement of men to put a value on it, introduced (by consent) larger possessions, and a right to them; which, how it has done, I shall by and by shew more at large.

Sec. 37. This is certain, that in the beginning, before the desire of having more than man needed had altered the intrinsic value of things, which depends only on their usefulness to the life of man; or had agreed, that a little piece of yellow metal, which would keep without wasting or decay, should be worth a great piece of flesh, or a whole heap of corn; though men had a right to appropriate, by their labour, each one of himself, as much of the things of nature, as he could use: yet this could not be much, nor to the prejudice of others, where the same plenty was still left to those who would use the same industry. To which let me add, that he who appropriates land to himself by his labour, does not lessen, but increase the common stock of mankind: for the provisions serving to the support of human life, produced by one acre of inclosed and cultivated land, are (to speak much within compass) ten times more than those which are yielded by an acre of land of an equal richness lying waste in common. And therefore he that incloses land, and has a greater plenty of the conveniencies of life from ten acres, than he could have from an hundred left to nature, may truly be said to give ninety acres to mankind: for his labour now supplies him with provisions out of ten acres, which were but the product of an hundred lying in common. I have here rated the improved land very low, in making its product but as ten to one, when it is much nearer an hundred to one: for I ask, whether in the wild woods and uncultivated waste of America, left to nature, without any improvement, tillage or husbandry, a thousand acres yield the needy and wretched inhabitants as many conveniencies of life, as ten acres of equally fertile land do in Devonshire, where they are well cultivated?

Before the appropriation of land, he who gathered as much of the wild fruit, killed, caught, or tamed, as many of the beasts, as he could; he that so imployed his pains about any of the spontaneous products of nature, as any way to alter them from the state which nature put them in, by placing any of his labour on them, did thereby acquire a propriety in them: but if they perished, in his possession, without their due use; if the fruits rotted, or the venison putrified, before he could spend it, he offended against the common law of nature, and was liable to be punished; he invaded his neighbour's share, for he had no right, farther than his use called for any of them, and they might serve to afford him conveniencies of life.

Sec. 38. The same measures governed the possession of land too: whatsoever he tilled and reaped, laid up and made use of, before it spoiled, that was his peculiar right;

whatsoever he enclosed, and could feed, and make use of, the cattle and product was also his. But if either the grass of his enclosure rotted on the ground, or the fruit of his planting perished without gathering, and laying up, this part of the earth, notwithstanding his enclosure, was still to be looked on as waste, and might be the possession of any other. Thus, at the beginning, Cain might take as much ground as he could till, and make it his own land, and yet leave enough to Abel's sheep to feed on; a few acres would serve for both their possessions. But as families increased, and industry inlarged their stocks, their possessions inlarged with the need of them; but yet it was commonly without any fixed property in the ground they made use of, till they incorporated, settled themselves together, and built cities; and then, by consent, they came in time, to set out the bounds of their distinct territories, and agree on limits between them and their neighbours; and by laws within themselves, settled the properties of those of the same society: for we see, that in that part of the world which was first inhabited, and therefore like to be best peopled, even as low down as Abraham's time, they wandered with their flocks, and their herds, which was their substance, freely up and down; and this Abraham did, in a country where he was a stranger. Whence it is plain, that at least a great part of the land lay in common; that the inhabitants valued it not, nor claimed property in any more than they made use of. But when there was not room enough in the same place, for their herds to feed together, they by consent, as Abraham and Lot did, Gen. xiii. 5. separated and inlarged their pasture, where it best liked them. And for the same reason Esau went from his father, and his brother, and planted in mount Seir, Gen. xxxvi. 6.

Sec. 39. And thus, without supposing any private dominion, and property in Adam, over all the world, exclusive of all other men, which can no way be proved, nor any one's property be made out from it; but supposing the world given, as it was, to the children of men in common, we see how labour could make men distinct titles to several parcels of it, for their private uses; wherein there could be no doubt of right, no room for quarrel.

SPANISH COLONIAL OFFICIAL'S ACCOUNT OF TRIANGULAR TRADE WITH ENGLAND (c. 1726)

INTRODUCTION *By the late seventeenth century, the countries of Atlantic Europe and their colonies to the west were connected by an elaborate network of commerce known as* triangular trade. *Ships from Europe were loaded with slaves captured in Africa. The slaves were carried across the Atlantic, then sold in the Caribbean, where the ships were loaded with sugar and other goods in exchange. These goods were carried back to Europe, where they were exchanged for rum and other processed goods, which were finally sold in Africa, thus completing the triangle. The following account of the triangular trade system as it was practiced in the early eighteenth century was written by Alsedo y Herrera, an Spanish colonial official and governor of Panama from 1741 to 1749.*

On June 21 of the same year (1721) the Southern Fleet of galleons left Cadiz under the command of Lieutenant General Baltasar de Guevara. Upon its arrival at Porto Bello in time for the annual Fair it encountered the Royal George, the first of the English license ships. Though allowed no more than 650 tons of cargo by the treaty of 1716, the vessel actually carried 975. General de Guevara forthwith intrusted to three license masters of the fleet the duty of measuring the hold of the English ship, but they could not prove the excess. Their failure was due in part to a confusion of the measurement in geometric feet, by which the dimensions of vessels are gauged, with the cubic handbreadths by which the tonnage is determined.

In part, also, another circumstance is responsible for the failure of the Spanish officers to detect any evidence of fraud, assuming, of course, the absence of collusion on their side. Apparently the vessel had no greater carrying capacity than 650 tons, but persons who are expert in the rules of naval construction know very well that the steerage, commonly called "between-decks," equals in capacity a third of the hold, and the cabin a sixth of it; so when all three have been filled,—hold, steerage, and cabin,—the gross tonnage will be 975. The English ship always carried a cargo of this size. Indeed it was laden so heavily that its very gunwales were awash. Bundles and packages filled the hold, the steerage space was crowded with huge chests, and the cabin bulged with boxes and bales.

The English claimed that the materials stored in the steerage and cabin were furniture for the use of their trading houses, cloth goods for their agents and employees, and medicines and drugs for accidents and cures, but all of it was salable merchandise. Some things they could not conceal from the commander and the commercial representatives of the galleons. For example, many of the bales and bundles had not been pressed, the stitches in their seams were recent, and the ink of their lettering was still fresh. Hundreds of items, also, were lacking in the order of enumeration, which, if they had not been thrown overboard to lighten the ship during the course of the voyage, must have been put ashore somewhere.

The proof soon appeared when the Spanish commissioner of trade asked to see the original bill of lading so that he might know by this means whether the cargo was in excess of the amount permitted. On the ground that the treaty had authorized no such procedure, the request was denied.

During the course of the Fair the agents of the Royal George sold their goods to the colonial tradesmen thirty percent cheaper than the Spanish merchants of the galleons could do. This advantage came from the fact that they had been able to bring the commodities directly from the place of manufacture, exempt from Spanish customs duties, convoy charges, transportation expenses, commissions, and the like. Even after the original contents of the ship had been disposed of, the supply was kept up by secret consignments of goods of English and European manufacture received from the packet boats and sloops engaged ostensibly in the slave trade.

Instead of bringing the negroes in the slave hulks directly from Africa to the ports specified in the Asiento, the English cunningly devised the plan of landing them first at their colony of Jamaica. Here the slaves were packed, along with divers kinds of merchandise, into small boats that made frequent sailings. Not only was the cargo of the Royal George thus replenished as rapidly as it was exhausted, but trade could be surreptitiously carried on at times when the Fair was not in progress, and the treasure of the Spanish colonies duly gathered into English hands.

Nor was this all of their duplicity. On the pretext that a number of bales and boxes stored in the warehouse at Porto Bello were an unsold residue of the cargo, the governor of Panama was asked for the privilege of bringing them to that city. In this fashion the English could legitimize goods that had already been smuggled into the warehouses at Panama and then proceed to sell them to the merchants of New Granada and to the traders on the vessels that plied along the Pacific coast. On one occasion in 1723, at the instance of the Spanish commissary, ten loads of twenty bales each of the supposed residue of the cargo of the Royal George were opened on the way from Porto Bello to Panama and found to contain nothing but stones, sticks, and straw.

A knavish trick connected with the slave trade should now be described. Having brought the negroes in a number of small boats to out-of-the-way places not authorized for the purpose in the Asiento, the English traders sold them for a third less than the prices at the regular trading stations. But since the treaty empowered them to seize, as smuggled goods, slaves brought in by individuals of other nations, they posted guards and sentinels in the outskirts of the spot where the sale had just taken place, and had the purchasers arrested. Many a

thrifty-minded Spaniard who relished the thought of buying slaves at cheap rates fell into a snare from which he could not escape until he had paid the regular price in addition to what he had already given.

In order to obscure the facts of these fraudulent transactions as thoroughly as possible, the English contrived a scheme craftier than any hitherto related. It seems that the Asiento had allowed them to appoint "judges-conservators" whose business it should be to defend their privileges against unlawful interference. In the exercise of this right they appointed to the office the local governors of the ports where the traffic was carried on, and gave them a salary of two thousand dollars a year, supplemented by special gratifications in the shape of European furniture, jewels, and delicacies. Thus were the officials pledged to connivance and silence. If any of the governors should decline to be bribed, he was threatened with political destruction by the letters and complaints which the English minister at the Spanish court would surely present to the home authorities. Few there were under such circumstances who were able to resist the frauds, preserve their honor, and uphold their good name.

THE STAMP ACT

INTRODUCTION *The Stamp Act, passed by the British Parliament in 1765, imposed a tax on the issuing of all legal documents in the American colonies. Although Britain had taken control of French possessions in America after the French and Indian War ended in 1763, the war had been a costly enterprise, and London tried to recover its war expenses by increasing the financial burden of the colonies. The Stamp Act was one component of this effort. The colonists regarded the stamp tax as extremely unjust and staged protests and an embargo of British goods throughout the colonies. The tax soon proved to be uncollectible, and the Stamp Act had to be repealed in 1766. The colonists' response to the Stamp Act was an early sign of growing American resistance to British authority.*

March 22, 1765

AN ACT for granting and applying certain stamp duties, and other duties, in the British colonies and plantations in America, towards further defraying the expenses of defending, protecting, and securing the same; and for amending such parts of the several acts of parliament relating to the trade and revenues of the said colonies and plantations, as direct the manner of determining and recovering the penalties and forfeitures therein mentioned.

WHEREAS, by an act made in the last session of Parliament several duties were granted, continued, and appropriated toward defraying the expenses of defending, protecting, and securing the British colonies and plantations in America; and whereas it is just and necessary that provision be made for raising a further revenue within your majesty's dominions in America toward defraying the said expenses; we, your majesty's most dutiful and loyal subjects, the Commons of Great Britain, *in Parliament assembled, have therefore resolved to give and grant unto your majesty the several rates and duties hereinafter mentioned; and do humbly beseech your majesty that it may be enacted, and be it enacted by the king's most excellent majesty, by and with the advice and consent of the lords spiritual and temporal, and commons, in this present Parliament assembled, and by the authority of the same, that from and after the first day of November, one thousand seven hundred and sixty five, there shall be raised, levied, collected, and paid unto his majesty, his heirs, and successors, throughout the colonies and plantations in America, which now are, or hereafter may be, under the dominion of his majesty, his heirs and successors:*

1. For every skin or piece of vellum or parchment, or sheet or piece of paper, on which shall be engrossed, written, or printed, any declaration, plea, replication, rejoinder, demurrer or other pleading, or any copy thereof; in any court of law within the British colonies and plantations in America, a stamp duty of three pence.

2. For every skin or piece of vellum or parchment, or sheet or piece of paper, on which shall be engrossed, written, or printed, any special bail, and appearance upon such bail in any such court, a stamp duty of two shillings.

3. For every skin or piece of vellum or parchment, or sheet or piece of paper, on which may be engrossed, written, or printed, any petition, bill, answer, claim, plea, replication, rejoinder, demurrer, or other pleading, in any court of chancery or equity within the said colonies and plantations, a stamp duty of one shilling and six pence.

4. For every skin or piece of vellum or parchment, or sheet or piece of paper, on which shall be engrossed, written, or printed, any copy of any position, bill, answer, claim, plea, replication, rejoinder, demurrer, or other pleading in any such court, a stamp duty of three pence.

5. For every skin or piece of vellum or parchment, or sheet or piece of paper, on which shall be engrossed, written, or printed, any monition, libel, answer,

allegation, inventory, or renunciation in ecclesiastical matters, in any court of probate court of the ordinary, or other court exercising ecclesiastical jurisdiction within the said colonies and plantations, a stamp duty of one shilling.

6. For every skin or piece of vellum or parchment, or sheet or piece of paper, on which shall be engrossed, written, or printed, any copy of any will (other than the probate thereof) monition, libel, answer, allegation, inventory, or renunciation in ecclesiastical matters, in any such court, a stamp duty of six pence.

7. For every skin or piece of vellum or parchment, or sheet or piece of paper, on which shall be engrossed, written, or printed, any donation, presentation, collation or institution, of or to any benefice, or any writ or instrument for the like purpose, or any register, entry, testimonial, or certificate of any degree taken in any university, academy, college, or seminary of learning within the said colonies and plantations, a stamp duty of two pounds.

8. For every skin or piece of vellum or parchment, or sheet or piece of paper, on which shall be engrossed, written, or printed, any monition, libel, claim, answer, allegation, information, letter of request, execution, renunciation, inventory, or other pleading, in any admiralty court, within the said colonies and plantations, a stamp duty of one shilling.

9. For every skin or piece of vellum or parchment, or sheet or piece of paper, on which any copy of any such monition, libel, claim, answer, allegation, information, letter of request, execution, renunciation, inventory, or other pleading shall be engrossed, written, or printed, a stamp duty of six pence.

10. For every skin or piece of vellum or parchment, or sheet or piece of paper, on which shall be engrossed, written, or printed, any appeal, writ of error, writ of dower, ad quod damnum, certiorari, statute merchant, statute staple, attestation, or certificate, by any officer, or exemplification of any record or proceeding, in any court whatsoever, within the said colonies and plantations (except appeals, writs of error, certiorari attestations, certificates, and exemplifications, for, or relating to the removal of any proceedings from before a single justice of the peace), a stamp duty of ten shillings.

11. For every skin or piece of vellum or parchment, or sheet or piece of paper, on which shall be engrossed, written, or printed, any writ of covenant for levying fines, writ of entry for suffering a common recovery, or attachment issuing out of, or returnable into, any court within the said colonies and plantations, a stamp duty of five shillings.

12. For every skin or piece of vellum or parchment, or sheet or piece of paper, on which shall be engrossed, written, or printed, any judgment, decree, sentence, or dismission or any record of nisi prius or postea, in any court within the said colonies and plantations, a stamp duty of four shillings.

13. For every skin or piece of vellum or parchment, or sheet or piece of paper, on which shall be engrossed, written, or printed, any affidavit, common bail, or appearance, interrogatory, deposition, rule, order or warrant of any court, or any dedimus potestatem, capias subpoena, summons, compulsory citation, commission, recognizance, or any other writ, process, or mandate, issuing out of, or returnable into, any court, or any office belonging thereto, or any other proceeding therein whatsoever, or any copy thereof, or of any record not herein before charged, within the said colonies and plantations (except warrants relating to criminal matters, and proceedings thereon, or relating thereto), a stamp duty of one shilling.

14. For every skin or piece of vellum or parchment, or sheet or piece of paper, on which shall be engrossed, written, or printed, any note or bill of lading, which shall be signed for any kind of goods, wares, or merchandise, to be exported from, or any cocket or clearance granted within the said colonies and plantations, a stamp duty of four pence.

15. For every skin or piece of vellum or parchment, or sheet or piece of paper, on which shall be engrossed, written, or printed, letters of mart or commission for private ships of war, within the said colonies and plantations, a stamp duty of twenty shillings.

16. For every skin or piece of vellum or parchment, or sheet or piece of paper, on which shall be engrossed, written, or printed, any grant, appointment, or admission of, or to, any public beneficial office or employment, for the space of one year, or any lesser time, of or above twenty pounds per annum sterling money, in salary, fees, and perquisites, within the said colonies and plantations (except commissions and appointments of officers of the army, navy, ordnance, or militia, of judges, and of justices of the peace), a stamp duty of ten shillings.

17. For every skin or piece of vellum or parchment, or sheet or piece of paper, on which any grant, of any liberty, privilege, or franchise, under the seal or sign manual of any governor, proprietor, or public officer, alone, or in conjunction with any other person or persons, or with any council, or any council and assembly, or any exemplification of the same, shall be engrossed, written, or printed, within the said colonies and plantations, a stamp duty of six pounds.

18. For every skin or piece of vellum or parchment, or sheet or piece of paper, on which shall be engrossed, written, or printed, any license for retailing of spirituous liquors, to be granted to any person who shall take out the same, within the said colonies and plantations, a stamp duty of twenty shillings.

19. For every skin or piece of vellum or parchment, or sheet or piece of paper, on which shall be engrossed, written, or printed, any license for retailing of wine, to be granted to any person who shall not take out a license for retailing of spirituous liquors, within the said colonies and plantations, a stamp duty of four pounds.

20. For every skin or piece of vellum or parchment, or sheet or piece of paper, on which shall be engrossed, written, or printed, any license for retailing of wine, to be granted to any person who shall take out a license for retailing of spirituous liquors, within the said colonies and plantations, a stamp duty of three pounds.

21. For every skin or piece of vellum or parchment, or sheet or piece of paper, on which shall be engrossed, written, or printed, any probate of will, letters of administration, or of guardianship for any estate above the value of twenty pounds sterling money, within the British colonies and plantations upon the continent of America, the islands belonging thereto and the Bermuda and Bahama islands, a stamp duty of five shillings.

22. For every skin or piece of vellum or parchment, or sheet or piece of paper, on which shall be engrossed, written, or printed, any such probate, letters of administration or of guardianship, within all other parts of the British dominions in America, a stamp duty of ten shillings.

23. For every skin or piece of vellum or parchment, or sheet or piece of paper, on which shall be engrossed, written, or printed, any bond for securing the payment of any sum of money, not exceeding the sum of ten pounds sterling money within the British colonies and plantations upon the continent of America, the islands belonging thereto, and the Bermuda and Bahama islands, a stamp duty of six pence.

24. For every skin or piece of vellum or parchment, or sheet or piece of paper, on which shall be engrossed, written, or printed, any bond for securing the payment of any sum of money above ten pounds, and not exceeding twenty pounds sterling money, within

such colonies, plantations, and islands a stamp duty of one shilling.

25. For every skin or piece of vellum or parchment, or sheet or piece of paper, on which shall be engrossed, written, or printed, any bond for securing the payment of any sum of money above twenty pounds, arid not exceeding forty pounds sterling money, within such colonies, plantations, and islands, a stamp duty of one shilling and six pence.

26. For every skin or piece of vellum or parchment, or sheet or piece of paper, on which shall be engrossed, written, or printed, any order or warrant for surveying or setting out any quantity of land, not exceeding one hundred acres, issued by any governor, proprietor, or any public officer, alone, or in conjunction with any other person or persons, or with any council, or any council and assembly, within the British colonies and plantations in America, a stamp duty of six pence.

27. For every skin or piece of vellum or parchment, or sheet or piece of paper, on which shall be engrossed, written, or printed, any such order or warrant for surveying or setting out any quantity of land above one hundred and not exceeding two hundred acres, within the said colonies and plantations, a stamp duty of one shilling.

28. For every skin or piece of vellum or parchment, or sheet or piece of paper, on which shall be engrossed, written, or printed, any such order or warrant for surveying or setting out any quantity of land above two hundred, and not exceeding three hundred and twenty acres, and in proportion for every such order or warrant for surveying or setting out every other three hundred and twenty acres, within the said colonies and plantations, a stamp duty of one shilling and six pence.

29. For every skin or piece of vellum or parchment, or sheet or piece of paper, on which shall be engrossed, written, or printed, any original grant, or any deed, mesne conveyance, or other instrument whatsoever, by which any quantity of land, not exceeding one hundred acres, shall be granted, conveyed, or assigned, within the British colonies and plantations upon the continent of America, the islands belonging thereto, and the Bermuda and Bahama islands (except leases for any term not exceeding the term of twenty one years), a stamp duty of one shilling and six pence.

30. For every skin or piece of vellum or parchment, or sheet or piece of paper, on which shall be engrossed, written, or printed, any such original grant, or any such deed, mesne conveyance, or other instrument

whatsoever, by which any quantify of land above one hundred, and not exceeding two hundred acres, shall be granted, conveyed, or assigned, within such colonies, plantations, and islands, a stamp duty of two shillings.

31. For every skin or piece of vellum or parchment, or sheet or piece of paper, on which shall be engrossed, written, or printed, any such original grant, or any such deed, mesne conveyance, or other instrument whatsoever, by which any quantity of land above two hundred, and not exceeding three hundred and twenty acres, shall be granted, conveyed, or assigned, and in proportion for every such grant, deed, mesne conveyance, or other instrument, granting, conveying, or assigning, every other three hundred and twenty acres, within such colonies, plantations, and islands, a stamp duty of two shillings and six pence.

32. For every skin or piece of vellum or parchment, or sheet or piece of paper, on which shall be engrossed, written, or printed, any such original grant, or any such deed, mesne conveyance, or other instrument whatsoever, by which any quantity of land, not exceeding one hundred acres, stall be granted, conveyed, or assigned, within all other parts of the British dominions in America, a stamp duty of three shillings.

33. For every skin or piece of vellum or parchment, or sheet or piece of paper, on which shall be engrossed, written, or printed, any such original grant, or any such deed, mesne conveyance, or other instrument whatsoever, by which any quantity of land above one hundred, and not exceeding two hundred acres, shall be granted, conveyed, or assigned, within the same parts of the said dominions, a stamp duty of four shillings.

34. For every skin or piece of vellum or parchment, or sheet or piece of paper, on which shall be engrossed, written, or printed, any such original grant, or any such deed, mesne conveyance, or other instrument whatsoever, by which any quantity of land above two hundred, and not exceeding three hundred twenty acres, shall he granted, conveyed, or assigned, and in proportion for every such grant, deed, mesne conveyance, or other instrument, granting, conveying, or assigning every other three hundred and twenty acres, within the same parts of the said dominions, a stamp duty of five shillings.

35. For every skin or piece of vellum or parchment, or sheet or piece of paper, on which shall be engrossed, written, or printed, any grant, appointment, or admission, of or to any beneficial office or employment, not herein before charged, above the value of

twenty pounds per annum sterling money in salary, fees, and perquisites, or any exemplification of the same, within the British colonies and plantations upon the continent of America, the islands belonging thereto, and the Bermuda and Bahama islands (except commissions of officers of the army, navy, ordnance, or militia, and of justices of the pence), a stamp duty of four pounds.

36. For every skin or piece of vellum or parchment, or sheet or piece of paper, on which shall be engrossed, written, or printed, any such grant, appointment, or admission, of or to any such public beneficial office or employments or any exemplification of the same, within all other parts of the British dominions in America, a stamp duty of six pounds.

37. For every skin or piece of vellum or parchment, or sheet or piece of paper, on which shall be engrossed, written, or printed, any indenture, lease, conveyance, contract, stipulation, bill of sale, charter party, protest, articles of apprenticeship or covenant (except for the hire of servants not apprentices, and also except such other matters as herein before charged) within the British colonies and plantations in America, a stamp duty of two shillings and six pence.

38. For every skin or piece of vellum or parchment, or sheet or piece of paper, on which any warrant or order for auditing any public accounts, beneficial warrant, order grant, or certificate, under any public seal, or under the send or sign manual of any governor, proprietor, or public officer, alone, or in conjunction with any person or persons, or with any council, or any council and assembly, not herein before charged, or any passport or let pass, surrender of office, or policy of assurance, shall be engrossed, written, or printed, within the said colonies and plantations (except warrants or orders for the service of the army, navy, ordnance, or militia, and grants of offices under twenty pounds per annum, in salary, fees, and perquisites), a stamp duty of five shillings.

39. For every skin or piece of vellum or parchment, or sheet or piece of paper, on which shall be engrossed, written or printed, any notarial net, bond, deed, letter of attorney, procuration, mortgage, release, or other obligatory instrument, not herein before charged, within the said colonies and plantations, a stamp duty of two shillings and three pence.

40. For every skin or piece of vellum or parchment, or sheet or piece of paper, on which shall be engrossed, written, or printed, any register, entry, or enrollment of any grant, deed or other instrument whatsoever, herein before charged, within the said colonies and plantations, a stamp duty of three pence.

41. For every skin or piece of vellum or parchment, or sheet or piece of paper, on which shall be engrossed, written, or printed, any register, entry, or enrollment of any grant, deed, or other instrument whatsoever, not herein before charged, within the said colonies and plantations, a stamp duty of two shillings.

42. And for and upon every pack of playing cards, and all dice, which shall be sold or used within the said colonies and plantations, the several stamp duties following (that is to say):

43. For every pack of such cards, one shilling.

44. And for every pair of such dice, ten shillings.

45. And for and every paper called a pamphlet, and upon every newspaper, containing public news or occurrences, which shall be printed, dispersed, and made public, within any of the said colonies and plantations, and for and upon such advertisements as are hereinafter mentioned, the respective duties following (that is to say):

46. For every such pamphlet and paper contained in a half sheet, or any lesser piece of paper, which shall be so printed, a stamp duty of one half penny for every printed copy thereof.

47. For every such pamphlet and paper (being larger than half a sheet, and not exceeding one whole sheet), which shall be printed, a stamp duty of one penny for every printed copy thereof.

48. For every pamphlet and paper, being larger than one whole sheet, and not exceeding six sheets in octavo, or in a lesser page, or not exceeding twelve sheets in quarto, or twenty sheets in folio, which shall be so printed, a duty after the rate of one shilling for every sheet of any kind of paper which shall be contained in one printed copy thereof.

49. For every advertisement to be contained in any gazette newspaper, or other paper, or any pamphlet which shall be so printed, a duty of two shillings.

50. For every almanac, or calendar, for any one particular year, or for any time less than a year, which shall be written or printed on one side only of any one sheet, skin, or piece of paper, parchment, or vellum, within the said colonies and plantations, a stamp duty of two pence.

51. For every other almanac or calendar, for any one particular year, which shall be written or printed within the said colonies and plantations, a stamp duty of four pence.

52. And for every almanac or calendar, written or printed in the said colonies and plantations, to serve

for several years, duties to the same amount respectively shall be paid for every such year.

53. For every skin or piece of vellum or parchment, or sheet or piece of paper, on which any instrument, proceeding, or other matter or thing aforesaid, shall be engrossed, written, or printed, within the said colonies and plantations, in any other than the English language, a stamp duty of double the amount of the respective duties before charged thereon.

54. And there shall be also paid, in the said colonies and plantations, a duty of six pence for every twenty shillings, in any sum not exceeding fifty pounds sterling money, which shall be given, paid, contracted, or agreed for, with, or in relation to, any clerk or apprentice, which shall be put or placed to or with any master or mistress, to learn any profession, trade, or employment.

II

And also a duty of one shilling for every twenty shillings, in any sum exceeding fifty pounds, which shall be given, paid, contracted, or agreed for, with, or in relation to, any such clerk or apprentice...

V

And be it further enacted..., That all books and pamphlets serving chiefly for the purpose of an almanack, by whatsoever name or names intituled or described, are and shall be charged with the duty imposed by this act on almanacks, but not with any of the duties charged by this act on pamphlets, or other printed papers...

VI

Provided always, that this act shall not extend to charge any bills of exchange, accompts, bills of parcels, bills of fees, or any bills or notes not sealed for payment of money at sight, or upon demand, or at the end of certain days of payment....

XII

And be it further enacted..., That the said several duties shall be under the management of the commissioners, for the time being, of the duties charged on stamped vellum, parchment, and paper, in Great Britain: and the said commissioners are hereby impowered and required to employ such officers under them, for that purpose, as they shall think proper....

XVI

And be it further enacted... That no matter or thing whatsoever, by this act charged with the payment of a duty, shall be pleaded or given in evidence, or admitted in any court within the said colonies and plantations, to be good, useful, or available in law or equity, unless the same shall be marked or stamped, in pursuance of this act, with the respective duty hereby charged thereon, or with an higher duty....

LIV

And be it further enacted ... That all the monies which shall arise by the several rates and duties hereby granted (except the necessary charges of raising, collecting, recovering, answering, paying, and accounting for the same and the necessary charges from time to time incurred in relation to this act, and the execution thereof) shall be paid into the receipt of his Majesty's exchequer, and shall be entered separate and apart from all other monies, and shall be there reserved to be from time to time disposed of by parliament, towards further defraying the necessary expenses of defending, protecting, and securing, the said colonies and plantations....

LVII

... offenses committed against any other act or acts of Parliament relating to the trade or revenues of the said colonies or plantations; shall and may be prosecuted, sued for, and recovered, in any court of record, or in any court of admiralty, in the respective colony or plantation where the offense shall be committed, or in any court of vice admiralty appointed or to be appointed, and which shall have jurisdiction within such colony, plantation, or place, (which courts of admiralty or vice admiralty are hereby respectively authorized and required to proceed, hear, and determine the same) at the election of the informer or prosecutor....

THE STATUTE OF WESTMINSTER, 1931

SOURCE *22 George V, c. 4 (U.K.)*

INTRODUCTION *The Statute of Westminster, passed by the British Parliament in December 1931, formally declared the autonomy of dominion governments within the British Empire. By the early twentieth century, the settler colonies of the British Empire had achieved self-rule as dominions, although they were still largely dependent on Britain for defense and financial assistance. Following their participation in World War I (1914-1918), the dominions moved for clarification of their status relative to Britain. The result was the Statute of Westminster, which established the independence of much of the British Empire, including*

Canada, Australia, New Zealand, South Africa, the Irish Free State, and Newfoundland.

An Act to give effect to certain resolutions passed by Imperial Conferences held in the years 1926 and 1930.

[11th December, 1931]

WHEREAS the delegates to His Majesty's Governments in the United Kingdom, the Dominion of Canada, the Commonwealth of Australia, the Dominion of New Zealand, the Union of South Africa, the Irish Free State and Newfoundland, at Imperial Conferences holden at Westminster in the years of our Lord nineteen hundred and twenty-six and nineteen hundred and thirty did concur in making the declarations and resolutions set forth in the Reports of the said Conferences:

And whereas it is meet and proper to set out by way of preamble to this Act that, inasmuch as the Crown is the symbol of the free association of the members of the British Commonwealth of Nations, and as they are united by a common allegiance to the Crown, it would be in accord with the established constitutional position of all the members of the Commonwealth in relation to one another that any alteration in the law touching the Succession to the Throne or the Royal Style and Titles shall hereafter require the assent as well of the Parliaments of all the Dominions as of the Parliament of the United Kingdom:

And whereas it is in accord with the established constitutional position that no law hereafter made by the Parliament of the United Kingdom shall extend to any of the said Dominions as part of the law of that Dominion otherwise than at the request and with the consent of that Dominion:

And whereas it is necessary for the ratifying, confirming and establishing of certain of the said declarations and resolutions of the said Conferences that a law be made and enacted in due form by authority of the Parliament of the United Kingdom:

And whereas the Dominion of Canada, the Commonwealth of Australia, the Dominion of New Zealand, the Union of South Africa, the Irish Free State and Newfoundland have severally requested and consented to the submission of a measure to the Parliament of the United Kingdom for making such provision with regard to the matters aforesaid as is hereafter in this Act contained:

NOW, THEREFORE, BE IT ENACTED by the King's Most Excellent Majesty, by and with the advice and consent of the Lords Spiritual and Temporal, and Commons, in this present Parliament assembled, and by the authority of the same, as follows:—

1. In this Act the expression "Dominion" means any of the following Dominions, that is to say, the Dominion of Canada, the Commonwealth of Australia, the Dominion of New Zealand, the Union of South Africa, the Irish Free State and Newfoundland.

2. (1) The Colonial Laws Validity Act, 1865, shall not apply to any law made after the commencement of this Act by the Parliament of a Dominion.

(2) No law and no provision of any law made after the commencement of this Act by the Parliament of a Dominion shall be void or inoperative on the ground that it is repugnant to the law of England, or to the provisions of any existing or future Act of Parliament of the United Kingdom, or to any order, rule, or regulation made under any such Act, and the powers of the Parliament of a Dominion shall include the power to repeal or amend any such Act, order, rule or regulation in so far as the same is part of the law of the Dominion.

3. It is hereby declared and enacted that the Parliament of a Dominion has full power to make laws having extra-territorial operation.

4. *No Act of Parliament of the United Kingdom passed after the commencement of this Act shall extend or be deemed to extend, to a Dominion as part of the law of that Dominion, unless it is expressly declared in that Act that that Dominion has requested, and consented to, the enactment thereof.*

5. Without prejudice to the generality of the foregoing provisions of this Act, section seven hundred and thirty-five and seven hundred and thirty-six of the Merchant Shipping Act, 1894, shall be construed as though reference therein to the Legislature of a British possession did not include reference to the Parliament of a Dominion.

6. Without prejudice to the generality of the foregoing provisions of this Act, section four of the Colonial Courts of Admiralty Act, 1890 (which requires certain laws to be reserved for the signification of His Majesty's pleasure or to contain a suspending clause), and so much of section seven of that Act as requires the approval of His Majesty in Council to any rules of Court for regulating the practice and procedure of a Colonial Court of Admiralty, shall cease to have effect in any Dominion as from the commencement of this Act.

7. (1) Nothing in this Act shall be deemed to apply to the repeal, amendment or alteration of the British North America Acts, 1867 to 1930, or any order, rule or regulation made thereunder.

(2) The provisions of section two of this Act shall extend to laws made by any of the Provinces of Canada and to the powers of the legislatures of such Provinces.

(3) The powers conferred by this Act upon the Parliament of Canada or upon the legislatures of the Provinces shall be restricted to the enactment of laws in relation to matters within the competence of the Parliament of Canada or of any of the legislatures of the Provinces respectively.

8. Nothing in this Act shall be deemed to confer any power to repeal or alter the Constitution or the Constitution Act of the Commonwealth of Australia or the Constitution Act of the Dominion of New Zealand otherwise than in accordance with the law existing before the commencement of this Act.

9. (1) Nothing in this Act shall be deemed to authorize the Parliament of the Commonwealth of Australia to make laws on any matter within the authority of the States of Australia, not being a matter within the authority of the Parliament or Government of the Commonwealth of Australia.

(2) Nothing in this Act shall be deemed to require the concurrence of the Parliament or Government of the Commonwealth of Australia, in any law made by the Parliament of the United Kingdom with respect to any matter within the authority of the States of Australia, not being a matter within the authority of the Parliament or Government of the Commonwealth of Australia, in any case where it would have been in accordance with the constitutional practice existing before the commencement of this Act that the Parliament of the United Kingdom should make that law without such concurrence.

(3) In the application of this Act to the Commonwealth of Australia the request and consent referred to in section four shall mean the request and consent of the Parliament and government of the Commonwealth.

10. (1) None of the following sections of this Act, that is to say, sections two, three, four, five, and six, shall extend to a Dominion to which this section applies as part of the law of that Dominion unless that section is adopted by the Parliament of the Dominion, and any Act of that Parliament adopting any section of this Act may provide that the adoption shall have effect either from the commencement of this Act or from such later date as is specified in the adopting Act.

(2) The Parliament of any such Dominion as aforesaid may at any time revoke the adoption of any section referred to in sub-section (1) of this section.

(3) The Dominions to which this section applies are the Commonwealth of Australia, the Dominion of New Zealand, and Newfoundland.

11. Notwithstanding anything in the Interpretation Act, 1889, the expression "Colony" shall not, in any Act of the Parliament of the United Kingdom passed after the commencement of this Act, include a Dominion or any Province or State forming part of a Dominion.

12. This Act may be cited as the Statute of Westminster, 1931.

SYKES-PICOT AGREEMENT, 1916

INTRODUCTION *The Sykes-Picot Agreement (1916) was a secret wartime treaty between Britain and France. It was named after its chief negotiators, Mark Sykes of Britain and Georges Picot of France. Based on the premise that the Allied Powers would win World War I, the Sykes-Picot Agreement reflected an effort to divide the Arab Middle East into spheres of influence that would come into effect after the war. The treaty recognized the region now corresponding to Syria and Lebanon, where France had longstanding economic and cultural interests, as part of a future French sphere, and the region of Mesopotamia (now Iraq) as part of a future British sphere. The agreement also provided for the international administration of Palestine and a limited degree of independent Arab control over parts of Syria, Arabia, and Transjordan. The Sykes-Picot Agreement, along with the postwar peace settlement, effectively drew much of the Middle East into the imperial embrace of Great Britain and France.*

It is accordingly understood between the French and British governments:

That France and great Britain are prepared to recognize and protect an independent Arab states or a confederation of Arab states (a) and (b) marked on the annexed map, under the suzerainty of an Arab chief. That in area (a) France, and in area (b) great Britain, shall have priority of right of enterprise and local loans. That in area (a) France, and in area (b) great Britain, shall alone supply advisers or foreign functionaries at the request of the Arab state or confederation of Arab states.

That in the blue area France, and in the red area great Britain, shall be allowed to establish such direct or indirect administration or control as they desire and as they may think fit to arrange with the Arab state or confederation of Arab states.

That in the brown area there shall be established an international administration, the form of which is to be decided upon after consultation with Russia, and subsequently in consultation with the other allies, and the representatives of the sheriff of mecca.

That great Britain be accorded (1) the ports of Haifa and acre, (2) guarantee of a given supply of water from the tigres and euphrates in area (a) for area (b). His majesty's government, on their part, undertake that they will at no time enter into negotiations for the cession of Cyprus to any third power without the previous consent of the French government.

That Alexandretta shall be a free port as regards the trade of the British empire, and that there shall be no discrimination in port charges or facilities as regards British shipping and British goods; that there shall be freedom of transit for British goods through Alexandretta and by railway through the blue area, or (b) area, or area (a); and there shall be no discrimination, direct or indirect, against British goods on any railway or against British goods or ships at any port serving the areas mentioned.

That Haifa shall be a free port as regards the trade of France, her dominions and protectorates, and there shall be no discrimination in port charges or facilities as regards French shipping and French goods. There shall be freedom of transit for French goods through Haifa and by the British railway through the brown area, whether those goods are intended for or originate in the blue area, area (a), or area (b), and there shall be no discrimination, direct or indirect, against French goods on any railway, or against French goods or ships at any port serving the areas mentioned.

That in area (a) the Baghdad railway shall not be extended southwards beyond Mosul, and in area (b) northwards beyond Samarra, until a railway connecting Baghdad and aleppo via the euphrates valley has been completed, and then only with the concurrence of the two governments.

That great Britain has the right to build, administer, and be sole owner of a railway connecting Haifa with area (b), and shall have a perpetual right to transport troops along such a line at all times. It is to be understood by both governments that this railway is to facilitate the connection of Baghdad with Haifa by rail, and it is further understood that, if the engineering difficulties and expense entailed by keeping this connecting line in the brown area only make the project unfeasible, that the French government shall be prepared to consider that the line in question may also traverse the Polgon Banias Keis Marib Salkhad tell Otsda Mesmie before reaching area (b).

For a period of twenty years the existing Turkish customs tariff shall remain in force throughout the whole of the blue and red areas, as well as in areas (a) and (b), and no increase in the rates of duty or conversions from ad valorem to specific rates shall be made except by agreement between the two powers. There shall be no interior customs barriers between any of the above mentioned areas. The customs duties leviable on goods destined for the interior shall be collected at the port of entry and handed over to the administration of the area of destination.

It shall be agreed that the French government will at no time enter into any negotiations for the cession of their rights and will not cede such rights in the blue area to any third power, except the Arab state or confederation of Arab states, without the previous agreement of his majesty's government, who, on their part, will give a similar undertaking to the French government regarding the red area. The British and French government, as the protectors of the Arab state, shall agree that they will not themselves acquire and will not consent to a third power acquiring territorial possessions in the Arabian peninsula, nor consent to a third power installing a naval base either on the east coast, or on the islands, of the red sea. This, however, shall not prevent such adjustment of the Aden frontier as may be necessary in consequence of recent Turkish aggression.

The negotiations with the Arabs as to the boundaries of the Arab states shall be continued through the same channel as heretofore on behalf of the two powers.

It is agreed that measures to control the importation of arms into the Arab territories will be considered by the two governments.

I have further the honor to state that, in order to make the agreement complete, his majesty's government are proposing to the Russian government to exchange notes analogous to those exchanged by the latter and your excellency's government on the 26th April last. Copies of these notes will be communicated to your excellency as soon as exchanged. I would also venture to remind your excellency that the conclusion of the present agreement raises, for practical consideration, the question of claims of Italy to a share in any partition or rearrangement of turkey in Asia, as formulated in article 9 of the agreement of the 26th April, 1915, between Italy and the allies.

His majesty's government further consider that the Japanese government should be informed of the arrangements now concluded.

TREATY OF PARIS 1763

INTRODUCTION *The Treaty of Paris of 1763 ended the French and Indian War, the last great imperial war fought in America. The war began in 1754 in the Ohio Valley, and would determine whether the French settlements in Canada and Louisiana would link up to prevent the westward expansion of English colonies.*

Despite initial setbacks, British victories at the Plains of Abraham in 1759 and Montreal in 1760 effectively destroyed French Canada. The Treaty of Paris saw that all of North America west of the Mississippi was ceded to Britain, along with Grenada, Tobago, and Saint Vincent.

The definitive Treaty of Peace and Friendship between his Britannick Majesty, the Most Christian King, and the King of Spain. Concluded at Paris the 10th day of February, 1763. To which the King of Portugal acceded on the same day.

In the Name of the Most Holy and Undivided Trinity, Father, Son, and Holy Ghost. So be it.

Be it known to all those whom it shall, or may, in any manner, belong,

It has pleased the Most High to diffuse the spirit of union and concord among the Princes, whose divisions had spread troubles in the four parts of the world, and to inspire them with the inclination to cause the comforts of peace to succeed to the misfortunes of a long and bloody war, which having arisen between England and France during the reign of the Most Serene and Most Potent Prince, George the Second, by the grace of God, King of Great Britain, of glorious memory, continued under the reign of the Most Serene and Most Potent Prince, George the Third, his successor, and, in its progress, communicated itself to Spain and Portugal: Consequently, the Most Serene and Most Potent Prince, George the Third, by the grace of God, King of Great Britain, France, and Ireland, Duke of Brunswick and Lunenbourg, Arch Treasurer and Elector of the Holy Roman Empire; the Most Serene and Most Potent Prince, Lewis the Fifteenth, by the grace of God, Most Christian King; and the Most Serene and Most Potent Prince, Charles the Third, by the grace of God, King of Spain and of the Indies, after having laid the foundations of peace in the preliminaries signed at Fontainebleau the third of November last; and the Most Serene and Most Potent Prince, Don Joseph the First, by the grace of God, King of Portugal and of the Algarves, after having acceded thereto, determined to compleat, without delay, this great and important work. For this purpose, the high contracting parties have named and appointed their respective Ambassadors Extraordinary and Ministers Plenipotentiary, viz. his Sacred Majesty the King of Great Britain, the Most Illustrious and Most Excellent Lord, John Duke and Earl of Bedford, Marquis of Tavistock, c. his Minister of State, Lieutenant General of his Armies, Keeper of his Privy Seal, Knight of the Most Noble Order of the Garter, and his Ambassador Extraordinary and Minister Plenipotentiary to his Most

Christian Majesty; his Sacred Majesty the Most Christian King, the Most Illustrious and Most Excellent Lord, Csar Gabriel de Choiseul, Duke of Praslin, Peer of France, Knight of his Orders, Lieutenant General of his Armies and of the province of Britanny, Counsellor of all his Counsils, and Minister and Secretary of State, and of his Commands and Finances: his Sacred Majesty the Catholick King, the Most Illustrious and Most Excellent Lord, Don Jerome Grimaldi, Marquis de Grimaldi, Knight of the Most Christian King's Orders, Gentleman of his Catholick Majesty's Bedchamber in Employment, and his Ambassador Extraordinary to his Most Christian Majesty; his Sacred Majesty the Most Faithful King, the Most Illustrious and Most Excellent Lord, Martin de Mello and Castro, Knight professed of the Order of Christ, of his Most Faithful Majesty's Council, and his Ambassador and Minister Plenipotentiary to his Most Christian Majesty.

Who, after having duly communicated to each other their full powers, in good form, copies whereof are transcribed at the end of the present treaty of peace, have agreed upon the articles, the tenor of which is as follows:

Article I. There shall be a Christian, universal, and perpetual peace, as well by sea as by land, and a sincere and constant friendship shall be re established between their Britannick, Most Christian, Catholick, and Most Faithful Majesties, and between their heirs and successors, kingdoms, dominions, provinces, countries, subjects, and vassals, of what quality or condition soever they be, without exception of places or of persons: So that the high contracting parties shall give the greatest attention to maintain between themselves and their said dominions and subjects this reciprocal friendship and correspondence, without permitting, on either side, any kind of hostilities, by sea or by land, to be committed from henceforth, for any cause, or under any pretence whatsoever, and every thing shall be carefully avoided which might hereafter prejudice the union happily reestablished, applying themselves, on the contrary, on every occasion, to procure for each other whatever may contribute to their mutual glory, interests, and advantages, without giving any assistance or protection, directly or indirectly, to those who would cause any prejudice to either of the high contracting parties: there shall be a general oblivion of every thing that may have been done or committed before or since the commencement of the war which is just ended.

II. The treaties of Westphalia of 1648; those of Madrid between the Crowns of Great Britain and Spain of 1661, and 1670; the treaties of peace of Nimeguen of 1678, and 1679; of Ryswick of 1697; those of peace and of commerce of Utrecht of 1713; that of Baden of 1714; the treaty of the triple alliance of the Hague of 1717; that of the quadruple alliance of London of 1118; the treaty of peace of Vienna of 1738; the definitive treaty of Aix la Chapelle of 1748; and that of Madrid, between the Crowns of Great Britain and Spain of 1750: as well as the treaties between the Crowns of Spain and Portugal of the 13th of February, 1668; of the 6th of February, 1715; and of the 12th of February, 1761; and that of the 11th of April, 1713, between France and Portugal with the guaranties of Great Britain, serve as a basis and foundation to the peace, and to the present treaty: and for this purpose they are all renewed and confirmed in the best form, as well as all the general, which subsisted between the high contracting parties before the war, as if they were inserted here word for word, so that they are to be exactly observed, for the future, in their whole tenor, and religiously executed on all sides, in all their points, which shall not be derogated from by the present treaty, notwithstanding all that may have been stipulated to the contrary by any of the high contracting parties: and all the said parties declare, that they will not suffer any privilege, favour, or indulgence to subsist, contrary to the treaties above confirmed, except what shall have been agreed and stipulated by the present treaty.

III. All the prisoners made, on all sides, as well by land as by sea, and the hostages carried away or given during the war, and to this day, shall be restored, without ransom, six weeks, at least, to be computed from the day of the exchange of the ratification of the present treaty, each crown respectively paying the advances which shall have been made for the subsistance and maintenance of their prisoners by the Sovereign of the country where they shall have been detained, according to the attested receipts and estimates and other authentic vouchers which shall be furnished on one side and the other. And securities shall be reciprocally given for the payment of the debts which the prisoners shall have contracted in the countries where they have been detained until their entire liberty. And all the ships of war and merchant vessels Which shall have been taken since the expiration of the terms agreed upon for the cessation of hostilities by sea shall likewise be restored, bon fide, with all their crews and cargoes: and the execution of this article shall be proceeded upon immediately after the exchange of the ratifications of this treaty.

IV. His Most Christian Majesty renounces all pretensions which he has heretofore formed or might have formed to Nova Scotia or Acadia in all its parts, and guaranties the whole of it, and with all its dependencies, to the King of Great Britain: Moreover, his Most Christian Majesty cedes and guaranties to his said Britannick Majesty, in full right, Canada, with all its dependencies, as well as the island of Cape Breton, and all the other islands and coasts in the gulph and river of St. Lawrence, and in general, every thing that depends on the said countries, lands, islands, and coasts, with the sovereignty, property, possession, and all rights acquired by treaty, or otherwise, which the Most Christian King and the Crown of France have had till now over the said countries, lands, islands, places, coasts, and their inhabitants, so that the Most Christian King cedes and makes over the whole to the said King, and to the Crown of Great Britain, and that in the most ample manner and form, without restriction, and without any liberty to depart from the said cession and guaranty under any pretence, or to disturb Great Britain in the possessions above mentioned. His Britannick Majesty, on his side, agrees to grant the liberty of the Catholick religion to the inhabitants of Canada: he will, in consequence, give the most precise and most effectual orders, that his new Roman Catholic subjects may profess the worship of their religion according to the rites of the Romish church, as far as the laws of Great Britain permit. His Britannick Majesty farther agrees, that the French inhabitants, or others who had been subjects of the Most Christian King in Canada, may retire with all safety and freedom wherever they shall think proper, and may sell their estates, provided it be to the subjects of his Britannick Majesty, and bring away their effects as well as their persons, without being restrained in their emigration, under any pretence whatsoever, except that of debts or of criminal prosecutions: The term limited for this emigration shall be fixed to the space of eighteen months, to be computed from the day of the exchange of the ratification of the present treaty.

V. The subjects of France shall have the liberty of fishing and drying on a part of the coasts of the island of Newfoundland, such as it is specified in the XIIIth article of the treaty of Utrecht; which article is renewed and confirmed by the present treaty, (except what relates to the island of Cape Breton, as well as to the other islands and coasts in the mouth and in the gulph of St. Lawrence:) And his Britannick Majesty consents to leave to the subjects of the Most Christian King the liberty of fishing in the gulph of St. Lawrence, on condition that the subjects of France do not exercise the said fishery but at the distance of three leagues from all the coasts belonging to Great Britain, as well those of the continent as those of the islands situated in the said gulph of St. Lawrence. And as to what relates to the fishery on the coasts of the island of Cape Breton, out of the said gulph, the subjects of the Most Christian King shall not be permitted to exercise the said fishery but at the distance of fifteen leagues from the coasts of the island of Cape Breton; and the fishery on the coasts of Nova Scotia or Acadia, and every where else out of the said gulph, shall remain on the foot of former treaties.

VI. The King of Great Britain cedes the islands of St. Pierre and Macquelon, in full right, to his Most

Christian Majesty, to serve as a shelter to the French fishermen; and his said Most Christian Majesty engages not to fortify the said islands; to erect no buildings upon them but merely for the conveniency of the fishery; and to keep upon them a guard of fifty men only for the police.

VII. In order to reestablish peace on solid and durable foundations, and to remove for ever all subject of dispute with regard to the limits of the British and French territories on the continent of America; it is agreed, that, for the future, the confines between the dominions of his Britannick Majesty and those of his Most Christian Majesty, in that part of the world, shall be fixed irrevocably by a line drawn along the middle of the River Mississippi, from its source to the river Iberville, and from thence, by a line drawn along the middle of this river, and the lakes Maurepas and Pontchartrain to the sea; and for this purpose, the Most Christian King cedes in full right, and guaranties to his Britannick Majesty the river and port of the Mobile, and every thing which he possesses, or ought to possess, on the left side of the river Mississippi, except the town of New Orleans and the island in which it is situated, which shall remain to France, provided that the navigation of the river Mississippi shall be equally free, as well to the subjects of Great Britain as to those of France, in its whole breadth and length, from its source to the sea, and expressly that part which is between the said island of New Orleans and the right bank of that river, as well as the passage both in and out of its mouth: It is farther stipulated, that the vessels belonging to the subjects of either nation shall not be stopped, visited, or subjected to the payment of any duty whatsoever. The stipulations inserted in the IVth article, in favour of the inhabitants of Canada shall also take place with regard to the inhabitants of the countries ceded by this article.

VIII. The King of Great Britain shall restore to France the islands of Guadeloupe, of Mariegalante, of Desirade, of Martinico, and of Belleisle; and the fortresses of these islands shall be restored in the same condition they were in when they were conquered by the British arms, provided that his Britannick Majesty's subjects, who shall have settled in the said islands, or those who shall have any commercial affairs to settle there or in other places restored to France by the present treaty, shall have liberty to sell their lands and their estates, to settle their affairs, to recover their debts, and to bring away their effects as well as their persons, on board vessels, which they shall be permitted to send to the said islands and other places restored as above, and which shall serve for this use only, without being restrained on account of their religion, or under any other pretence whatsoever, except that of debts or of criminal prosecutions: and for this purpose, the term of eighteen months

is allowed to his Britannick Majesty's subjects, to be computed from the day of the exchange of the ratifications of the present treaty; but, as the liberty granted to his Britannick Majesty's subjects, to bring away their persons and their effects, in vessels of their nation, may be liable to abuses if precautions were not taken to prevent them; it has been expressly agreed between his Britannick Majesty and his Most Christian Majesty, that the number of English vessels which have leave to go to the said islands and places restored to France, shall be limited, as well as the number of tons of each one; that they shall go in ballast; shall set sail at a fixed time; and shall make one voyage only; all the effects belonging to the English being to be embarked at the same time. It has been farther agreed, that his Most Christian Majesty shall cause the necessary passports to be given to the said vessels; that, for the greater security, it shall be allowed to place two French clerks or guards in each of the said vessels, which shall be visited in the landing places and ports of the said islands and places restored to France, and that the merchandize which shall be found t herein shall be confiscated.

IX. The Most Christian King cedes and guaranties to his Britannick Majesty, in full right, the islands of Grenada, and the Grenadines, with the same stipulations in favour of the inhabitants of this colony, inserted in the IVth article for those of Canada: And the partition of the islands called neutral, is agreed and fixed, so that those of St. Vincent, Dominico, and Tobago, shall remain in full right to Great Britain, and that of St. Lucia shall be delivered to France, to enjoy the same likewise in full right, and the high contracting parties guaranty the partition so stipulated.

X. His Britannick Majesty shall restore to France the island of Goree in the condition it was in when conquered: and his Most Christian Majesty cedes, in full right, and guaranties to the King of Great Britain the river Senegal, with the forts and factories of St. Lewis, Podor, and Galam, and with all the rights and dependencies of the said river Senegal.

XI. In the East Indies Great Britain shall restore to France, in the condition they are now in, the different factories which that Crown possessed, as well as on the coast of Coromandel and Orixa as on that of Malabar, as also in Bengal, at the beginning of the year 1749. And his Most Christian Majesty renounces all pretension to the acquisitions which he has made on the coast of Coromandel and Orixa since the said beginning of the year 1749. His Most Christian Majesty shall restore, on his side, all that he may have conquered from Great Britain in the East Indies during the present war; and will expressly cause Nattal and Tapanoully, in the island of Sumatra, to be restored; he engages farther, not to erect fortifications, or to keep troops in any part of the dominions of the Subah of Bengal. And in order to preserve future peace on the coast of Coromandel and Orixa, the English and French shall acknowledge Mahomet Ally Khan for lawful Nabob of the Carnatick, and Salabat Jing for lawful Subah of the Decan; and both parties shall renounce all demands and pretensions of satisfaction with which they might charge each other, or their Indian allies, for the depredations or pillage committed on the one side or on the other during the war.

XII. The island of Minorca shall be restored to his Britannick Majesty, as well as Fort St. Philip, in the same condition they were in when conquered by the arms of the Most Christian King; and with the artillery which was there when the said island and the said fort were taken.

XIII. The town and port of Dunkirk shall be put into the state fixed by the last treaty of Aix la Chapelle, and by former treaties. The Cunette shall be destroyed immediately after the exchange of the ratifications of the present treaty, as well as the forts and batteries which defend the entrance on the side of the sea; and provision shall be made at the same time for the wholesomeness of the air, and for the health of the inhabitants, by some other means, to the satisfaction of the King of Great Britain.

XIV. France shall restore all the countries belonging to the Electorate of Hanover, to the Landgrave of Hesse, to the Duke of Brunswick, and to the Count of La Lippe Buckebourg, which are or shall be occupied by his Most Christian Majesty's arms: the fortresses of these different countries shall be restored in the same condition they were in when conquered by the French arms; and the pieces of artillery, which shall have been carried elsewhere, shall be replaced by the same number, of the same bore, weight and metal.

XV. In case the stipulations contained in the XIIIth article of the preliminaries should not be compleated at the time of the signature of the present treaty, as well with regard to the evacuations to be made by the armies of France of the fortresses of Cleves, Wezel, Guelders, and of all the countries belonging to the King of Prussia, as with regard to the evacuations to be made by the British and French armies of the countries which they occupy in Westphalia, Lower Saxony, on the Lower Rhine, the Upper Rhine, and in all the empire; and to the retreat of the troops into the dominions of their respective Sovereigns: their Britannick and Most Christian Majesties promise to proceed, bon fide, with all the dispatch the case will permit of to the said evacuations, the entire completion whereof they stipulate before the 15th of March next, or sooner if it can be

done; and their Britannick and Most Christian Majesties farther engage and promise to each other, not to furnish any succours of any kind to their respective allies who shall continue engaged in the war in Germany.

XVI. The decision of the prizes made in time of peace by the subjects of Great Britain, on the Spaniards, shall be referred to the Courts of Justice of the Admiralty of Great Britain, conformably to the rules established among all nations, so that the validity of the said prizes, between the British and Spanish nations, shall be decided and judged, according to the law of nations, and according to treaties, in the Courts of Justice of the nation who shall have made the capture.

XVII. His Britannick Majesty shall cause to be demolished all the fortifications which his subjects shall have erected in the bay of Honduras, and other places of the territory of Spain in that part of the world, four months after the ratification of the present treaty; and his Catholick Majesty shall not permit his Britannick Majesty's subjects, or their workmen, to be disturbed or molested under any pretence whatsoever in the said places, in their occupation of cutting, loading, and carrying away logwood; and for this purpose, they may build, without hindrance, and occupy, without interruption, the houses and magazines necessary for them, for their families, and for their effects; and his Catholick Majesty assures to them, by this article, the full enjoyment of those advantages and powers on the Spanish coasts and territories, as above stipulated, immediately after the ratification of the present treaty.

XVIII. His Catholick Majesty desists, as well for himself as for his successors, from all pretension which he may have formed in favour of the Guipuscoans, and other his subjects, to the right of fishing in the neighbourhood of the island of Newfoundland.

XIX. The King of Great Britain shall restore to Spain all the territory which he has conquered in the island of Cuba, with the fortress of the Havannah; and this fortress, as well as all the other fortresses of the said island, shall be restored in the same condition they were in when conquered by his Britannick Majesty's arms, provided that his Britannick Majesty's subjects who shall have settled in the said island, restored to Spain by the present treaty, or those who shall have any commercial affairs to settle there, shall have liberty to sell their lands and their estates, to settle their affairs, recover their debts, and to bring away their effects, as well as their persons, on board vessels which they shall be permitted to send to the said island restored as above, and which shall serve for that use only, without being restrained on account of their religion, or under any other pretence whatsoever, except that of debts or of criminal prosecutions: And for this purpose, the term of eighteen months is allowed to his Britannick Majesty's subjects, to be computed from the day of the exchange of the ratifications of the present treaty: but as the liberty granted to his Britannick Majesty's subjects, to bring away their persons and their effects, in vessels of their nation, may be liable to abuses if precautions were not taken to prevent them; it has been expressly agreed between his Britannick Majesty and his Catholick Majesty, that the number of English vessels which shall have leave to go to the said island restored to Spain shall be limited, as well as the number of tons of each one; that they shall go in ballast; shall set sail at a fixed time; and shall make one voyage only; all the effects belonging to the English being to be embarked at the same time: it has been farther agreed, that his Catholick Majesty shall cause the necessary passports to be given to the said vessels; that for the greater security, it shall be allowed to place two Spanish clerks or guards in each of the said vessels, which shall be visited in the landing places and ports of the said island restored to Spain, and that the merchandize which shall be found therein shall be confiscated.

XX. In consequence of the restitution stipulated in the preceding article, his Catholick Majesty cedes and guaranties, in full right, to his Britannick Majesty, Florida, with Fort St. Augustin, and the Bay of Pensacola, as well as all that Spain possesses on the continent of North America, to the East or to the South East of the river Mississippi. And, in general, every thing that depends on the said countries and lands, with the sovereignty, property, possession, and all rights, acquired by treaties or otherwise, which the Catholick King and the Crown of Spain have had till now over the said countries, lands, places, and their inhabitants; so that the Catholick King cedes and makes over the whole to the said King and to the Crown of Great Britain, and that in the most ample manner and form. His Britannick Majesty agrees, on his side, to grant to the inhabitants of the countries above ceded, the liberty of the Catholick religion; he will, consequently, give the most express and the most effectual orders that his new Roman Catholic subjects may profess the worship of their religion according to the rites of the Romish church, as far as the laws of Great Britain permit. His Britannick Majesty farther agrees, that the Spanish inhabitants, or others who had been subjects of the Catholick King in the said countries, may retire, with all safety and freedom, wherever they think proper; and may sell their estates, provided it be to his Britannick Majesty's subjects, and bring away their effects, as well as their persons without being restrained in their emigration, under any pretence whatsoever, except that of debts, or of criminal prosecutions: the term limited for this emigration being fixed to the space of eighteen months, to be computed from the day of the exchange of the ratifications of the present treaty. It is

moreover stipulated, that his Catholick Majesty shall have power to cause all the effects that may belong to him, to be brought away, whether it be artillery or other things.

XXI. The French and Spanish troops shall evacuate all the territories, lands, towns, places, and castles, of his Most faithful Majesty in Europe, without any reserve, which shall have been conquered by the armies of France and Spain, and shall restore them in the same condition they were in when conquered, with the same artillery and ammunition, which were found there: And with regard to the Portuguese Colonies in America, Africa, or in the East Indies, if any change shall have happened there, all things shall be restored on the same footing they were in, and conformably to the preceding treaties which subsisted between the Courts of France, Spain, and Portugal, before the present war.

XXII. All the papers, letters, documents, and archives, which were found in the countries, territories, towns and places that are restored, and those belonging to the countries ceded, shall be, respectively and bon fide, delivered, or furnished at the same time, if possible, that possession is taken, or, at latest, four months after the exchange of the ratifications of the present treaty, in whatever places the said papers or documents may be found.

XXIII. All the countries and territories, which may have been conquered, in whatsoever part of the world, by the arms of their Britannick and Most Faithful Majesties, as well as by those of their Most Christian and Catholick Majesties, which are not included in the present treaty, either under the title of cessions, or under the title of restitutions, shall be restored without difficulty, and without requiring any compensations.

XXIV. As it is necessary to assign a fixed epoch for the restitutions and the evacuations, to be made by each of the high contracting parties, it is agreed, that the British and French troops shall compleat, before the 15th of March next, all that shall remain to be executed of the XIIth and XIIIth articles of the preliminaries, signed the 3d day of November last, with regard to the evacuation to be made in the Empire, or elsewhere. The island of Belleisle shall be evacuated six weeks after the exchange of the ratifications of the present treaty, or sooner if it can be done. Guadeloupe, Desirade, Mariegalante Martinico, and St. Lucia, three months after the exchange of the ratifications of the present treaty, or sooner if it can be done. Great Britain shall likewise, at the end of three months after the exchange of the ratifications of the present treaty, or sooner if it can be done, enter into possession of the river and port of the Mobile, and of all that is to form the limits of the territory of Great Britain, on the side of the river

Mississippi, as they are specified in the VIIth article. The island of Goree shall be evacuated by Great Britain, three months after the exchange of the ratifications of the present treaty; and the island of Minorca by France, at the same epoch, or sooner if it can be done: And according to the conditions of the VIth article, France shall likewise enter into possession of the islands of St Peter, and of Miquelon, at the end of three months after the exchange of the ratifications of the present treaty. The Factories in the East Indies shall be restored six months after the exchange of the ratifications of the present treaty, or sooner if it can be done. The fortress of the Havannah, with all that has been conquered in the island of Cuba, shall be restored three months after the exchange of the ratifications of the present treaty, or sooner if it can be done: And, at the same time, Great Britain shall enter into possession of the country ceded by Spain according to the XXth article. All the places and countries of his most Faithful Majesty, in Europe, shall be restored immediately after the exchange of the ratification of the present treaty: And the Portuguese colonies, which may have been conquered, shall be restored in the space of three months in the West Indies, and of six months in the East Indies, after the exchange of the ratifications of the present treaty, or sooner if it can be done. All the fortresses, the restitution whereof is stipulated above, shall be restored with the artillery and ammunition, which were found there at the time of the conquest. In consequence whereof, the necessary orders shall be sent by each of the high contracting parties, with reciprocal passports for the ships that shall carry them, immediately after the exchange of the ratifications of the present treaty.

XXV. His Britannick Majesty, as Elector of Brunswick Lunenbourg, as well for himself as for his heirs and successors, and all the dominions and possessions of his said Majesty in Germany, are included and guarantied by the present treaty of peace.

XXVI. Their sacred Britannick, Most Christian, Catholick, and Most Faithful Majesties, promise to observe sincerely and bon fide, all the articles contained and settled in the present treaty; and they will not suffer the same to be infringed, directly or indirectly, by their respective subjects; and the said high contracting parties, generally and reciprocally, guaranty to each other all the stipulations of the present treaty.

XXVII. The solemn ratifications of the present treaty, expedited in good and due form, shall be exchanged in this city of Paris, between the high contracting parties, in the space of a month, or sooner if possible, to be computed from the day of the signature of the present treaty.

In witness whereof, we the underwritten their Ambassadors Extraordinary, and Ministers Plenipotentiary,

have signed with our hand, in their name, and in virtue of our full powers, have signed the present definitive treaty, and have caused the seal of our arms to be put thereto. Done at Paris the tenth day of February, 1763.

Bedford, C.P.S. Choiseul, Duc de Praslin. El Marq. de Grimaldi.

(L.S.) (L.S.) (LS)

SEPARATE ARTICLES

I. Some of the titles made use of by the contracting powers, either in the full powers, and other acts, during the course of the negociation, or in the preamble of the present treaty, not being generally acknowledged; it has been agreed, that no prejudice shall ever result therefrom to any of the said contracting parties, and that the titles, taken or omitted on either side, on occasion of the said negociation, and of the present treaty, shall not be cited or quoted as a precedent.

II. It has been agreed and determined, that the French language made use of in all the copies of the present treaty, shall not become an example which may be alledged, or made a precedent of, or prejudice, in any manner, any of the contracting powers; and that they shall conform themselves, for the future, to what has been observed, and ought to be observed, with regard to, and on the part of powers, who are used, and have a right, to give and to receive copies of like treaties in another language than French; the present treaty having still the same force and effect, as if the aforesaid custom had been therein observed.

III. Though the King of Portugal has not signed the present definitive treaty, their Britannick, Most Christian, and Catholick Majesties, acknowledge, nevertheless, that his Most Faithful Majesty is formally included therein as a contracting party, and as if he had expressly signed the said treaty: Consequently, their Britannick, Most Christian, and Catholick Majesties, respectively and conjointly, promise to his Most Faithful Majesty, in the most express and most binding manner, the execution of all and every the clauses, contained in the said treaty, on his act of accession.

The present Separate Articles shall have the same force as if they were inserted in the treaty.

In witness whereof, We the underwritten Ambassadors Extraordinary, and Ministers Plenipotentiary of their Britannick, Most Christian and Catholick Majesties, have signed the present separate Articles, and have caused the seal of our arms to be put thereto.

Done at Paris, the 10th of February, 1763.

Bedford, C.P.S. Choiseul, Duc El Marq. de

(L.S.) de Praslin. Grimaldi.

(L.S.) (L.S.)

His Britannick Majesty's full Power.

GEORGE R.

GEORGE the Third, by the grace of God, King of Great Britain, France and Ireland, Defender of the Faith, Duke of Brunswick and Lunenbourg, ArchTreasurer, and Prince Elector of the Holy Roman Empire, c. To all and singular to whom these presents shall come, greeting. Whereas, in order to perfect the peace between Us and our good Brother the Most Faithful King, on the one part, and our good Brothers the Most Christian and Catholick Kings, on the other, which has been happily begun by the Preliminary Articles already signed at Fontainebleau the third of this month; and to bring the same to the desired end, We have thought proper to invest some fit person with full authority, on our part; Know ye, that We, having most entire confidence in the fidelity, judgment, skill, and ability in managing affairs of the greatest consequence, of our right trusty, and right entirely beloved Cousin and Counsellor, John Duke and Earl of Bedford, Marquis of Tavistock, Baron Russel of Cheneys, Baron Russel of Thornhaugh, and Baron Howland of Streatham, Lieutenantgeneral of our forces, Keeper of our Privy Seal, Lieutenant and Custos Rotulorum of the counties of Bedford and Devon, Knight of our most noble order of the Garter, and our Ambassador Extraordinary and Plenipotentiary to our good Brother the Most Christian King, have nominated, made, constituted and appointed, as by these presents, we do nominate, make, constitute, and appoint him, our true, certain, and undoubted Minister, Commissary, Deputy, Procurator and Plenipotentiary, giving to him all and all manner of power, faculty and authority, as well as our general and special command (yet so as that the general do not derogate from the special, or on the contrary) for Us and in our name, to meet and confer, as well singly and separately, as jointly, and in a body, with the Ambassadors, Commissaries, Deputies, and Plenipotentiaries of the Princes, whom it may concern, vested with sufficient power and authority for that purpose, and with them to agree upon, treat, consult and conclude, concerning the reestablishing, as soon as may be, a firm and lasting peace, and sincere friendship and concord; and whatever shall be so agreed and concluded, for Us and in our name, to sign, and to make a treaty or treaties, on what shall have been so agreed and concluded, and to transact every thing else that may belong to the happy completion of the aforesaid work, in as ample a manner and form, and with the same force and effect, as We ourselves, if we were present, could do and perform; engaging and promising, on our royal word, that We will approve, ratify and accept, in the best manner, whatever shall happen to be transacted and concluded by our said Plenipotentiary, and that We will never suffer any person to infringe or act contrary to the same, either in the whole or in part. In witness and confirmation whereof We have caused our great Seal of Great Britain to be affixed to these presents, signed with our royal hand. Given at our Palace at St. James's, the 12th day of November, 1762, in the third year of our reign.

His Most Christian Majesty's Full Power.

LEWIS, by the grace of God, King of France and Navarre, To all who shall see these presents, Greeting. Whereas the Preliminaries, signed at Fontainebleau the third of November of the last year, laid the foundation of the peace reestablished between us and our most dear and most beloved good Brother and Cousin the King of Spain, on the one part, and our most dear and most beloved good Brother the King of Great Britain, and our most dear and most beloved good Brother and Cousin the King of Portugal on the other, We have had nothing more at heart since that happy epoch, than to consolidate and strengthen in the most lasting manner, so salutary and so important a work, by a solemn and definitive treaty between Us and the said powers. For these causes, and other good considerations, Us thereunto moving, We, trusting entirely in the capacity and experience, zeal and fidelity for our service, of our most dear and well-beloved Cousin, Csar Gabriel de Choiseul, Duke of Praslin, Peer of France, Knight of our Orders, Lieutenant General of our Forces and of the province of Britany, Counsellor in all our Councils, Minister and Secretary of State, and of our Commands and Finances, We have named, appointed, and deputed him, and by these presents, signed with our hand, do name, appoint, and depute him our Minister Plenipotentiary, giving him full and absolute power to act in that quality, and to confer, negociate, treat and agree jointly with the Minister Plenipotentiary of our most dear and most beloved good Brother the King of Great Britain, the Minister Plenipotentiary of our most dear and most beloved good Brother and Cousin the King of Spain and the Minister Plenipotentiary of our most dear and most beloved good Brother and Cousin the King of Portugal, vested with full powers, in good form, to agree, conclude and sign such articles, conditions, conventions, declarations, definitive treaty, accessions, and other acts whatsoever, that he shall judge proper for securing and strengthening the great work of peace, the whole with the same latitude and authority that We ourselves might do, if We were there in person, even though there should be something which might require a more special order than what is contained in these presents, promising on the faith and word of a King, to approve, keep firm and stable for ever, to fulfil and execute punctually, all that our said Cousin, the Duke of Praslin, shall have stipulated, promised and signed, in virtue of the present full power, without ever acting contrary thereto, or permitting any thing contrary thereto, for any cause, or under any pretence whatsoever, as also to cause our letters of ratification to be expedited in good form, and to cause them to be delivered, in order to be exchanged within the time that shall be agreed upon. For such is our pleasure. In witness whereof, we have caused our Seal to be put to these presents. Given at Versailles the 7th day of the month of February, in the year of Grace 1763, and of our reign the fortyeighth. Signed Lewis, and on the fold, by the King, the Duke of Choiseul. Sealed with the great Seal of yellow Wax.

His Catholick Majesty's full Power.

DON CARLOS, by the grace of God, King of Castille, of Leon, of Arragon, of the two Sicilies, of Jerusalem, of Navarre, of Granada, of Toledo, of Valencia, of Galicia, of Majorca, of Seville, of Sardinia, of Cordova, of Corsica, of Murcia, of Jaen, of the Algarves. of Algecira. of Gibraltar. of the Canary Islands, of the East and West Indies, Islands and Continent, of the Ocean, Arch Duke of Austria, Duke of Burgundy, of Brabant and Milan, Count of Hapsburg, of Flanders, of Tirol and Barcelona, Lord of Biscay and of Molino, c. Whereas preliminaries of a solid and lasting peace between this Crown, and that of France on the one part, and that of England and Portugal on the other, were concluded and signed in the Royal Residence of Fontainbleau, the 3rd of November of the present year, and the respective ratifications thereof exchanged on the 22d of the same month, by Ministers authorised for that purpose, wherein it is promised, that a definitive treaty should be forthwith entered upon, having established and regulated the chief points upon which it is to turn: and whereas in the same manner as I granted to you, Don Jerome Grimaldi, Marquis de Grimaldi, Knight of the Order of the Holy Ghost, Gentleman of my Bedchamber with employment, and my Ambassador Extraordinary to the Most Christian King, my full power to treat, adjust, and sign the beforementioned preliminaries, it is necessary to grant the same to you, or to some other, to treat, adjust, and sign the promised definitive treaty of peace as aforesaid: therefore, as you the said Don Jerome Grimaldi, Marquis de Grimaldi, are at the convenient place, and as I have every day fresh motives, from your approved fidelity and zeal, capacity and prudence, to entrust to you this, and otherlike concerns of my Crown, I have appointed you my Minister Plenipotentiary, and granted to you my full power, to the end, that, in my name, and representing my person, you may treat, regulate, settle, and sign the said definitive treaty of peace between my Crown and that of France on the one part, that of England and that of

Portugal on the other, with the Ministers who shall be equally and specially authorised by their respective Sovereigns for the same purpose; acknowledging, as I do from this time acknowledge, as accepted and ratified, whatever you shall so treat, conclude, and sign; promising, on my Royal Word, that I will observe and fulfil the same, will cause it to be observed and fulfilled, as if it had been treated, concluded, and signed by myself. In witness whereof, I have caused these presents to be dispatched, signed by my hand, sealed with my privy seal, and countersigned by my underwritten Counsellor of State, and first Secretary for the department of State and of War. Buen Retiro, the 10th day of December, 1762.

(Signed) I THE KING.

(And lower) Richard Wall

TREATY OF UTRECHT

INTRODUCTION *The Treaty of Utrecht of 1713 ended the War of the Spanish Succession, a conflict that began in Spain with the death in 1700 of King Charles II, who had no children and no clear successor. By 1702 the conflict had spilled into North America, where it was called Queen Anne's War, after the queen of England. The settlement of Utrecht encompassed two other treaties, the Treaty of Rastatt and the Treaty of Baden, which together restored the balance of power in Europe. The terms of the Treaty of Utrecht suggested the ascendancy of Britain's colonial endeavors relative to France and Spain, as England obtained from France what is today much of eastern Canada, as well as access to the slave trade dominated by the Spanish.*

ARTICLE X JULY 13, 1713

The Catholic King does hereby, for himself, his heirs and successors, yield to the Crown of Great Britain the full and entire propriety of the town and castle of Gibraltar, together with the port, fortifications, and forts thereunto belonging; and he gives up the said propriety to be held and enjoyed absolutely with all manner of right for ever, without any exception or impediment whatsoever.

But that abuses and frauds may be avoided by importing any kind of goods, the Catholic King wills, and takes it to be understood, that the above-named propriety be yielded to Great Britain without any territorial jurisdiction and without any open communication by land with the country round about.

Yet whereas the communication by sea with the coast of Spain may not at all times be safe or open, and thereby it may happen that the garrison and other inhabitants of Gibraltar may be brought to great straits; and as it is the intention of the Catholic King, only that fraudulent importations of goods should, as is above said, be hindered by an inland communications. it is therefore provided that in such cases it may be lawful to purchase, for ready money, in the neighbouring territories of Spain, provisions and other things necessary for the use of the garrison, the inhabitants, and the ships which lie in the harbour.

But if any goods be found imported by Gibraltar, either by way of barter for purchasing provisions, or under any other pretence, the same shall be confiscated, and complaint being made thereof, those persons who have acted contrary to the faith of this treaty, shall be severely punished.

And Her Britannic Majesty, at the request of the Catholic King, does consent and agree, that no leave shall be given under any pretence whatsoever, either to Jews or Moors, to reside or have their dwellings in the said town of Gibraltar; and that no refuge or shelter shall be allowed to any Moorish ships of war in the harbour of the said town, whereby the communication between Spain and Ceuta may be obstructed, or the coasts of Spain be infested by the excursions of the Moors.

But whereas treaties of friendship and a liberty and intercourse of commerce are between the British and certain territories situated on the coast of Africa, it is always to be understood, that the British subjects cannot refuse the Moors and their ships entry into the port of Gibraltar purely upon the account of merchandising. Her Majesty the Queen of Great Britain does further promise, that the free exercise of their religion shall be indulged to the Roman Catholic inhabitants of the aforesaid town.

And in case it shall hereafter seem meet to the Crown of Great Britain to grant , sell or by any means to alienate therefrom the propriety of the said town of Gibraltar, it is hereby agreed and concluded that the preference of having the sale shall always be given to the Crown of Spain before any others.

THE TWO MIDDLE PASSAGES TO BRAZIL, 1793

SOURCE *Luiz Antonio de Oliveria Mendes,* Discurso academico ao programa: determinar com todos os seus symptomas as doencas agudas, e chronicas, que mail frequentemente accometem os pretos recem tirados da Africa *(Lisbom: Real Academia, 1812), pp. 8,18-32. Translated and published by Robert Edgar Conrad in* Children of God's Fire: A Documentary History of Black Slavery in Brazil *(University Park: The Pennsylvania State University Press, 1994), pp. 16-23.*

INTRODUCTION *This account of the Middle Passage, the shipboard journey of enslaved Africans from ports in West Africa to the Americas, was written by Luiz António de Oliveira Mendes in 1793. Millions of Africans were forcibly shipped to the Caribbean, Jamaica being the chief trading center, and then transshipped to Brazil, British North America, and other Caribbean islands. Many did not survive the Middle Passage, a horrific experience marked by inhuman conditions of transport, overcrowding, insufficient food, and disease. Mortality rates incurred from the point of capture in the African interior to transfer to a slave ship along the coast may have been even higher, suggesting the tremendous toll on human lives that slave trafficking exacted.*

Having been reduced to slavery in Africa, either because he was so condemned, or as a result of piracy and treachery, this once free black human being is the most unhappy person imaginable; because he is immediately placed in irons, and in this condition he eats only what the tyrants, the worst enemies of humanity, wish to give him.

In that moment in which he loses his freedom, he also loses everything which for him was good, pleasant, and enjoyable. In the presence of everything which he must suffer, how could we compare even the suffering of Adam when hewas banished from Paradise.

Since all those fortified places are spread inland at a distance of a hundred, two hundred, three hundred and more leagues, such as Ambaque and others, and since it is always expected that there will be slaves there who have been condemne and imprisoned in order to be bartered, there are backlanders, who in some places are called *funidores* and in other places *tumbeiros,* who are always journeying through those interior areas for the purpose of acquiring slaves condemned to captivity through the exchange of the merchandise . . . which they most prefer, including glass beads, coral, tobacco, rum, some iron instruments which they use, and muskets, powder, and lead.

After the deal has been concluded and the purchased article delivered over, there is a cruel scene, -because the *furidores* or *tumbeiros* carry in their *manpas* or baggage the needed libambo, [an iron chain used to bind the slaves together]. And the slaves leave the stocks or shackles or any other sort of confinement for the *libambo.* Each of the slaves is attached to this iron chain at regular intervals in the following manner; the backlanders and those persons who accompany the convoy pass a piece of iron through the ring of the chain in the proper place, and out of this piece of iron the pound out another .ring, -placing the iron -points one above the other so that the slave's hand is imprisoned in this new iron ring . . . .

The backlanders or *funidores* pass from fortress to fortress, taking with them in the convoy the slaves they have purchased. Each slave carries on his back a provision sack, which the backlanders have brought for them to feed themselves until they arrive at another settlement, where they are resupplied . . . .

This brutal and laborious trek lasts from one to six, seven, or eight months. On the way they do not drink water whenever they wish, -but only when they reach some pool or pond. They camp whenever the *funidor* decides. Their bed is the earth, their roof the sky, and the blanket they cover themselves with the leaves of the trees, which do not cover them completely. The morning dew falls upon them. Their pillows are the trunks of the trees and the bodies of their companions. After the camping place has been selected, the slaves are arranged in a circle, and a bonfire is lit to provide heat and light. This lasts until dawn, when having warmed the earth with their bodies, their journey is resumed.

The night is passed in a state of half sleep and watchfulness, because even during the hours intended for rest and sleep, they are constantly aroused by their black guards, who, fearing an uprising, scream at them and frighten them, when in fact the exhausted and mistreated travelers are more disposed to sleep and to die than to resist. All this results from the unreasonable fear that, with so many slaves together, some might open the iron ring that attaches them to the *libambo*. And because of an even greater prejudice, and this is common to all, that the captive slaves know of a plant that causes iron to soften and break . . . .

When the slaves coming from many different parts of the interior reach the maritime ports of Africa, they are there once more traded for goods and merchandise to the many agents or merchants who have their houses established there for that purpose. Acquiring the slaves by means of such trading, they keep them for a time in the same libambo, and if they are not kept this way they are closed up in a secure ground-level compound surrounded by high walls, from which they cannot escape.

Here takes place the second round of hardships that these unlucky people are forced to suffer. By these new tyrants they are terribly handled and most scantily provided for, and for them they are like mere animals, their human nature entirely overlooked. The dwelling place of the slave is simply the dirt floor of the compound, and he remains there exposed to harsh conditions and bad weather, and at night there are only a lean-to and some sheds or warehouses, also on the ground level, which they are herded into like cattle. . . .

They suffer in other ways. When they are first traded, they are made to bear the brand mark of the backlander who enslaved them, so that they can be recognized in case they run away. And when they reach a port-they are branded on the right breast with the coat of arms of the king and nation, of whom they have become vassals and under whom they will live subject to slavery, This mark is made with a hot silver instrument in the act of paying the king's duties, and this brand mark is called a *carimbo.*

They are made to bear one more brand mark. This one is ordered by their private master, under whose name they are transported to Brazil, and it is put either on the left breast or on the arm, also so that they may be recognized if they should run away . . . .

In this miserable and deprived condition the terrified slaves remain for weeks and months, and the great number of them who die is unspeakable. With some ten or twelve thousand arriving at Luanda each year, it often happens that only six or seven thousand are finally transported to Brazil . . . .

Shackled in the holds of ships, the black slaves reveal as never before their robust and powerful qualities, for in these new circumstances they are far more deprived than when on land. First of all, with two or three hundred slaves placed under the deck, there is hardly room enough to draw a breath. No air can reach them, except through the hatch gratings and through some square skylights so tiny that not even a head could pass through them . . . .

The captains, aware of their own interests, recognize the seriousness of the problem, and try to remedy it to some extent. Twice a week they order the deck washed, and, using sponges, the hold is scoured down with vinegar. Convinced that they are doing something useful, each day they order a certain number of slaves brought on deck in chains to get some fresh air, not allowing more because of their fear of rebellion. However, very little is accomplished in this way, because the slaves must go down again into the hold to breathe the same pestilent air . . . .

This contemporary watercolor shows crowded and emaciated slaves on the slave deck of the Albanez. It was painted by Francis Meynell, a lieutenant on a British anti-slavery vessel. "The Slave Deck of the Albanez," c. 1860, is today located at the National Maritime Museum, England.

Second, the slaves are afflicted with a very short ration of water, of poor quality and lukewarm because of the climate - hardly enough to water their mouths. The suffering that this causes is extraordinary, and their dryness and thirst cause epidemics which, beginning with one person, soon spread to many others. Thus, after only a few days at sea, they start to throw the slaves into the ocean.

Third, they are kept in a state of constant hunger. Their small ration of food, brought over from Brazil on the outward voyage, is spoiled and damaged, and consists of nothing more than beans, corn, and manioc flour, all badly prepared and unspiced. They add to each ration a small portion of noxious fish from the African coast, which decays during the voyage....

With good reason, then, we may speak of these black Africans, who resist so much and survive so many afflictions, as men of stone and of iron.

VERSAILLES TREATY: ARTICLES 1–26

INTRODUCTION *The first twenty-six articles of the Treaty of Versailles (1919), which established the terms of peace after World War I, constitute the Covenant of the League of Nations, an international body formed to promote cooperation, prevent war, and achieve lasting peace around the world. Article 22 of the Covenant created a new form of political supervision, called a* mandate, *under which the former colonies of the defeated countries were entrusted to "advanced nations" among the victorious Allies. These nations were to govern only until the mandated states were sufficiently developed to "stand by themselves," but because the assignment of mandates indulged the self-interests of the imperial powers, many mandates became a cover for colonial ambitions. All of the mandated territories, with the exception of Palestine, eventually gained independence.*

THE COVENANT OF THE LEAGUE OF NATIONS

THE HIGH CONTRACTING PARTIES, In order to promote international co-operation and to achieve international peace and security by the acceptance of obligations not to resort to war by the prescription of open, just and honourable relations between nations by the firm establishment of the understandings of international law as the actual rule of conduct among Governments, and by the maintenance of justice and a scrupulous respect for all treaty obligations in the dealings of organised peoples with one another Agree to this Covenant of the League of Nations.

ARTICLE I

The original Members of the League of Nations shall be those of the Signatories which are named in the Annex to this Covenant and also such of those other States named in the Annex as shall accede without reservation to this Covenant. Such accession shall be effected by a Declaration deposited with the Secretariat within two months of the coming into force of the Covenant Notice thereof shall be sent to all other Members of the League. Any fully self-governing State, Dominion, or Colony not named in the Annex may become a Member of the League if its admission is agreed to by two-thirds of the Assembly provided that it shall give effective guarantees of its sincere intention to observe its international obligations, and shall accept such regulations as may be prescribed by the League in regard to its military, naval, and air forces and armaments. Any Member of the League may, after two years notice of its intention so to do, withdraw from the League, provided that all its international obligations and all its obligations under this Covenant shall have been fulfilled at the time of its withdrawal.

ARTICLE 2

The action of the League under this Covenant shall be effected through the instrumentality of an Assembly and of a Council, with a permanent Secretariat.

ARTICLE 3

The Assembly shall consist of Representatives of the Members of the League. The Assembly shall meet at stated intervals and from time to time as occasion may require at the Seat of the League or at such other place as may be decided upon. The Assembly may deal at its meetings with any matter within the sphere of action of the League or affecting the peace of the world. At meetings of the Assembly each Member of the League shall have one vote, and may not have more than three Representatives.

ARTICLE 4

The Council shall consist of Representatives of the Principal Allied and Associated Powers, together with Representatives of four other Members of the League. These four Members of the League shall be selected by the Assembly from time to time in its discretion. Until the appointment of the Representatives of the four Members of the League first selected by the Assembly, Representatives of Belgium, Brazil, Spain, and Greece shall be members of the Council. With the approval of the majority of the Assembly, the Council may name additional Members of the League whose Representatives shall always be members of the Council; the Council with like approval may increase the number of Members of the League to be selected by the Assembly for representation on the Council. The Council shall meet from time to time as occasion may require, and at least once a year, at the Seat of the League, or at such other place as may be decided upon. The Council may deal at its meetings with any matter within the sphere of action of the League or affecting the peace of the world. Any Member of the League not represented on the Council shall be invited to send a Representative to sit as a member at any meeting of the Council during the consideration of matters specially affecting the interests of that Member of the League. At meetings of the Council, each Member of the League represented on the Council shall have one vote, and may have not more than one Representative.

ARTICLE 5

Except where otherwise expressly provided in this Covenant or by the terms of the present Treaty, decisions at any meeting of the Assembly or of the Council shall require the agreement of all the Members of the League represented at the meeting. All matters of procedure at meetings of the Assembly or of the Council, including the appointment of Committees to investigate particular matters, shall be regulated by the Assembly or by the Council and may be decided by a majority of the Members of the League represented at the meeting. The first meeting of the Assembly and the first meeting of the Council shall be summoned by the President of the United States of America.

ARTICLE 6

The permanent Secretariat shall be established at the Seat of the League. The Secretariat shall comprise a Secretary General and such secretaries and staff as may be required. The first Secretary General shall be the person named in the Annex; thereafter the Secretary General shall be appointed by the Council with the approval of the majority of the Assembly. The secretaries and staff of the Secretariat shall be appointed by the Secretary General with the approval of the Council. The Secretary General shall act in that capacity at all meetings of the Assembly and of the Council. The expenses of the Secretariat shall be borne by the Members of the League in accordance with the apportionment of the expenses of the International Bureau of the Universal Postal Union.

ARTICLE 7

The Seat of the League is established at Geneva. The Council may at any time decide that the Seat of the League shall be established elsewhere. All positions under or in connection with the League, including he Secretariat, shall be open equally to men and women. Representatives of the Members of the League and offi-

cials of he League when engaged on the business of the League shall enjoy diplomatic privileges and immunities. The buildings and other property occupied by the League or its officials or by Representatives attending its meetings sha11 be inviolable.

ARTICLE 8

The Members of the League recognise that the maintenance of peace requires the reduction of national armaments to the lowest point consistent with national safety and the enforcement by common action of international obligations. The Council, taking account of the geographical situation and circumstances of each State, shall formulate plans for such reduction for the consideration and action of the several Governments. Such plans shall be subject to reconsideration and revision at least every ten years. After these plans shall have been adopted by the several Governments, the limits of armaments therein fixed shall not be exceeded without the concurrence of the Council. The Members of the League agree that the manufacture by private enterprise of munitions and implements of war is open to grave objections. The Council shall advise how the evil effects attendant upon such manufacture can be prevented, due regard being had to the necessities of those Members of the League which are not able to manufacture the munitions and implements of war necessary for their safety. The Members of the League undertake to interchange full and frank information as to the scale of their armaments, their military, naval, and air programmes and the condition of such of their industries as are adaptable to war-like purposes.

ARTICLE 9

A permanent Commission shall be constituted to advise the Council on the execution of the provisions of Articles 1 and 8 and on military, naval, and air questions generally.

ARTICLE 10

The Members of the League undertake to respect and preserve as against external aggression the territorial integrity and existing political independence of all Members of the League. In case of any such aggression or in case of any threat or danger of such aggression the Council shall advise upon the means by which this obligation shall be fulfilled.

ARTICLE 11

Any war or threat of war, whether immediately affecting any of the Members of the League or not, is hereby declared a matter of concern to the whole League, and the League shall take any action tnat may be deemed wise and effectual to safeguard the peace of nations. In case any such emergency should arise the Secretary General shall on the request of any Member of the League forthwith summon a meeting of the Council. It is also declared to be the friendly right of each Member of the League to bring to the attention of the Assembly or of the Council any circumstance whatever affecting international relations which threatens to disturb international peace or the good understanding between nations upon which peace depends.

ARTICLE 12

The Members of the League agree that if there should arise between them any dispute likely to lead to a rupture, they will submit the matter either to arbitration or to inquiry by the Council, and they agree in no case to resort to war until three months after the award by the arbitrators or the report by the Council. In any case under this Article the award of the arbitrators shall be made within a reasonable time, and the report of the Council shall be made within six months after the submission of the dispute.

ARTICLE 13

The Members of the League agree that whenever any dispute shall arise between them which they recognise to be suitable for submission to arbitration and which cannot be satisfactorily settled by diplomacy, they will submit the whole subject-matter to arbitration. Disputes as to the interpretation of a treaty, as to any question of international law, as to the existence of any fact which if established would constitute a breach of any international obligation, or as to the extent and nature of the reparation to be made or any such breach, are declared to be among those which are generally suitable for submission to arbitration. For the consideration of any such dispute the court of arbitraion to which the case is referred shall be the Court agreed on by the parties to the dispute or stipulated in any convention existing between them. The Members of the League agree that they will carry out in full good faith any award that may be rendered, and that they will not resort to war against a Member of the League which complies therewith. In the event of any failure to carry out such an award, the Council shall propose what steps should be taken to give effect thereto.

ARTICLE 14

The Council shall formulate and submit to the Members of the League for adoption plans for the establishment of a Permanent Court of International Justice. The Court shall be competent to hear and determine any dispute of an international character which the parties thereto submit to it. The Court may also give an advisory opinion upon any dispute or question referred to it by the Council or by the Assembly.

ARTICLE 15

If there should arise between Members of the League any dispute likely to lead to a rupture, which is not submitted to arbitration in accordance with Article 13, the Members of the League agree that they will submit the matter to the Council. Any party to the dispute may effect such submission by giving notice of the existence of the dispute to the Secretary General, who will make all necessary arrangements for a full investigation and conside ation thereof. For this purpose the parties to the dispute will communicate to the Secretary General, as promptly as possible, statements of their case with all the relevant facts and papers, and the Council may forthwith direct the publication thereof. The Council shall endeavour to effect a settlement of the dispute, and if such efforts are successful, a statement shall be made public giving such facts and explanations regarding the dispute and the terms of settlement thereof as the Council may deem appropriate. If the dispute is not thus settled, the Council either unanimously or by a majority vote shall make and publish a report containing a statement of the facts of the dispute and the recommendations which are deemed just and proper in regard thereto Any Member of the League represented on the Council may make public a statement of the facts of the dispute and of its conclusions regarding the same. If a report by the Council is unanimously agreed to by the members thereof other than the Representatives of one or more of the parties to the dispute, the Members of the League agree that they will not go to war with any party to the dispute which complies with the recommendations of the report. If the Council fails to reach a report which is unanimously agreed to by the members thereof, other than the Representatives of one or more of the parties to the dispute, the Members of the League reserve to themselves the right to take such action as they shall consider necessary for the maintenance of right and justice. If the dispute between the parties is claimed by one of them, and is found by the Council, to arise out of a matter which by international law is solely within the domestic jurisdiction of that party, the Council shall so report, and shall make no recommendation as to its settlement. The Council may in any case under this Article refer the dispute to the Assembly. The dispute shall be so referred at the request of either party to the dispute, provided that such request be made within fourteen days after the submission of the dispute to the Council. In any case referred to the Assembly, all the provisions of this Article and of Article 12 relating to the action and powers of the Council shall apply to the action and powers of the Assembly, provided that a report made by the Assembly, if concurred in by the Representatives of those Members of the League represented on the Council and of a majority of the other Members of the League, exclusive in each case of the Rpresentatives of the parties to the dispute shall have the same force as a report by the Council concurred in by all the members thereof other than the Representatives of one or more of the parties to the dispute.

ARTICLE 16

Should any Member of the League resort to war in disregard of its covenants under Articles 12, 13, or 15, it shall ipso facto be deemed to have committed an act of war against all other Members of the League, which hereby undertake immediately to subject it to the severance of all trade or financial relations, the prohibition of all intercourse between their nationals and the nationals of the covenant-breaking State, and the prevention of all financial, commercial, or personal intercourse between the nationals of the covenant-breaking State and the nationals of any other State, whether a Member of the League or not. It shall be the duty of the Council in such case to recommend to the several Governments concerned what effective military, naval, or air force the Members of the League shall severally contribute to the armed forces to be used to protect the covenants of the League. The Members of the League agree, further, that they will mutually support one another in the financial and economic measures which are taken under this Article, in order to minimise the loss and inconvenience resulting from the above measures, and that they will mutually support one another in resisting any special measures aimed at one of their number by the covenant-breaking State, and that they will take the necessary steps to afford passage through their territory to the forces of any of the Members of the League which are co-operating to protect the covenants of the League. Any Member of the League which has violated any covenant of the League may be declared to be no longer a Member of the League by a vote of the Council concurred in by the Representatives of all the other Members of the League represented thereon.

ARTICLE 17

In the event of a dispute between a Member of the League and a State which is not a Member of the League, or between States not Members of the League, the State or States, not Members of the League shall be invited to accept the obligations of membership in the League for the purposes of such dispute, upon such conditions as the Council may deem just. If such invitation is accepted, the provisions of Articles 12 to 16 inclusive shall be applied with such modifications as

may be deemed necessary by the Council. Upon such invitation being given the Council shall immediately institute an inquiry into the circumstances of the dispute and recommend such action as may seem best and most effectual in the circumstances. If a State so invited shall refuse to accept the obligations of membership in the League for the purposes of such dispute, and shall resort to war against a Member of the League, the provisions of Article 16 shall be applicable as against the State taking such action. If both parties to the dispute when so invited refuse to accept the obligations of membership in the League for the purpose of such dispute, the Council may take such measures and make such recommendations as will prevent hostilities and will result in the settlement of the dispute.

ARTICLE 18

Every treaty or international engagement entered into hereafter by any Member of the League shall be forthwith registered with the Secretariat and shall as soon as possible be published by it. No such treaty or international engagement shall be binding until so registered.

ARTICLE 19

The Assembly may from time to time advise the reconsideration by Members of the League of treaties which have become inapplicable and the consideration of international conditions whose continuance might endanger the peace of the world.

ARTICLE 20

The Members of the League severally agree that this Covenant is accepted as abrogating all obligations or understandings inter se which are inconsistent with the terms thereof, and solemnly undertake that they will not hereafter enter into any engagements inconsistent with the terms thereof. In case any Member of the League shall, before becoming a Member of the League, have undertaken any obligations inconsistent with the terms of this Covenant, it shall be the duty of such Member to take immediate steps to procure its release from such obligations.

ARTICLE 21

Nothing in this Covenant shall be deemed to affect the validity of international engagements, such as treaties of arbitration or regional understandings like the Monroe doctrine, for securing the maintenance of peace.

ARTICLE 22

To those colonies and territories which as a consequence of the late war have ceased to be under the sovereignty of the States which formerly governed them and which are inhabited by peoples not yet able to stand by themselves under the strenuous conditions of the modern world, there should be applied the principle that the well-being and development of such peoples form a sacred trust of civilisation and that securities for the performance of this trust should be embodied in this Covenant. The best method of giving practical effect to this principle is that the tutelage of such peoples should be entrusted to advanced nations who by reason of their resources, their experience or their geographical position can best undertake this responsibility, and who are willing to accept it, and that this tutelage should be exercised by them as Mandatories on behalf of the League. The character of the mandate must differ according to the stage of the development of the people, the geographical situation of the territory, its economic conditions, and other similar circumstances. Certain communities formerly belonging to the Turkish Empire have reached a stage of development where their existence as independent nations can be provisionally recognised subject to the rendering of administrative advice and assistance by a Mandatory until such time as they are able to stand alone. The wishes of these communities must be a principal consideration in the selection of the Mandatory. Other peoples, especially those of Central Africa, are at such a stage that the Mandatory must be responsible for the administration of the territory under conditions which will guarantee freedom of conscience and religion, subject only to the maintenance of public order and morals, the prohibition of abuses such as the slave trade, the arms traffic, and the liquor traffic, and the prevention of the establishment of fortifications or military and naval bases and of military training of the natives for other than police purposes and the defence of territory, and will also secure equal opportunities for the trade and commerce of other Members of the League. There are territories, such as South-West Africa and certain of the South Pacific Islands, which, owing to the sparseness of their population, or their small size, or their remoteness from the centres of civilisation, or their geographical contiguity to the territory of the Mandatory, and other circumstances, can be best administered under the laws of the Mandatory as integral portions of its territory, subject to the safeguards above mentioned in the interests of the indigenous population. In every case of mandate, the Mandatory shall render to the Council an annual report in reference to the territory committed to its charge. The degree of authority, control, or administration to be exercised by the Mandatory shall, if not previously agreed upon by the Members of the League, be explicitly defined in each case by the Council. A permanent Commission shall be constituted to receive and examine the annual reports of the Mandatories and to advise the Council on all matters relating to the observance of the mandates.

ARTICLE 23

Subject to and in accordance with the provisions of international conventions existing or hereafter to be agreed upon, the Members of the League: (a) will endeavour to secure and maintain fair and humane conditions of labour for men, women, and children, both in their own countries and in all countries to which their commercial and industrial relations extend, and for that purpose will establish and maintain the necessary international organisations; (b) undertake to secure just treatment of the native inhabitants of territories under their control; (c) will entrust the League with the general supervision over the execution of agreements with regard to the traffic in women and children, and the traffic in opium and other dangerous drugs; (d) will entrust the League with the general supervision of the trade in arms and ammunition with the countries in which the control of this traffic is necessary in the common interest; (e) will make provision to secure and maintain freedom of communications and of transit and equitable treatment for the commerce of all Members of the League. In this connection, the special necessities of the regions devastated during the war of 1914-1918 shall be borne in mind; (f) will endeavour to take steps in matters of international concern for the prevention and control of disease.

ARTICLE 24

There shall be placed under the direction of the League all international bureaux already established by general treaties if the parties to such treaties consent. All such international bureaux and all commissions for the regulation of matters of international interest hereafter constituted shall be placed under the direction of the League. In all matters of international interest which are regulated by general conventions but which are not placed under the control of international bureaux or commissions, the Secretariat of the League shall, subject to the consent of the Council and if desired by the parties, collect and distribute all relevant information and shall render any other assistance which may be necessary or desirable. The Council may include as part of the expenses of the Secretariat the expenses of any bureau or commission which is placed under the direction of the League.

ARTICLE 25

The Members of the League agree to encourage and promote the establishment and co-operation of duly authorised voluntary national Red Cross organisations having as purposes the improvement of health, the prevention of disease, and the mitigation of suffering throughout the world.

ARTICLE 26

Amendments to this Covenant will take effect when ratified by the Members of the League whose representatives compose the Council and by a majority of the Members of the League whose Representatives compose the Assembly. No such amendment shall bind any Member of the League which signifies its dissent therefrom, but in that case it shall cease to be a Member of the League.

Text Acknowledgements

Index

Acapulco, Mexico, **8**

Accomodationism, 1146

Accords of Evian, 543

Accountability Law (Netherlands), 984

An Account of the European Settlements in America (Burke), 449

Accra, 248

Accumulation of Capital (Luxemburg), 593

Aceh

    Dutch United East India Company, 315

    ethical policy, 452

    Snouck Hurgronje, Christiaan, 1042–1043

Aceh War, **8–10**, 984–985

Achebe, Chinua, *10*, **10–11**, 349, 919

The Achenese (Snouck Hurgronje), 1042

Acosta, José de

    anticolonialism, 61

    Enlightenment thought, influence on, 448

    ethnography, 961

    just war, 949

    postcolonialism, 920

Act for the Kingly Title, 647

Action Group (Nigeria), 118

L'Action Tunisienne (newspaper), 859

Act of Algeciras, 856

Act of Piracy (Britain), 167

Act of Union (Britain), 649

Adams, Abigail, 701

Adams, John Quincy, 430, 807, 1098–1099

Adams, Samuel, 143

Adams, William, 472

Adat, 712, 713

Aden

    British annexation, 68, 152

    British maritime dominance, 162

    British rule, 86

    economy, 87

    Edward, Prince of Wales, visit of, *153*

Adikusumo, Pangeran, 673

Adil Shah, 521

Adisoerjo, Tirto, 202

Adivar, Adnan, 336

Administration of justice

    Japanese colonial law, 715

    Portuguese colonialism, 705

    slavery, 1040

    slave trade, 1035

    See also Law

Administrative elite slavery, 1030–1031

Administrative reform

    German colonialism, 748

    Middle Eastern, 565–566

    Spanish Americas, 532

Aerssen, Cornelis, 373

al-Afghani, Jamal ad-Din, **13–14**

    Iranian renewalists, 639

    Islamic modernism, 658

    Islamic reformism, 566

    religious reform, 1127

    tobacco protest, 1080–1081

Afghanistan

    Afghan Wars, 14–16

    Anglo-Russian rivalry, 51–53

    British attempt to control, 205

    British India, 162–163

    Islamic modernism, 659

    Islamist fighters, 568

    mass migration to, 164

    opium, 877

    Russian Empire, 427

    Soviet invasion, 1106

Afghan-Russian Treaty of 1921, 53

Afghan Wars, **14–17**, *15, 16*

    Anglo-Russian rivalry, 52

    British India, 162–163

    Disraeli, Benjamin, 578

    Indian Army, 613

'Aflaq, Michel, 1129

Afonso, Martim, 521

Afonso V, 719, 903

Africa

    abolitionism, 560

    alcohol, 29

    American crops, 38–41, 335

    anticolonial movements, **74–81**

    art, 93–96

    assimilation, **102–103**

    association, **105–106**

    Belgian colonies, **126–130**

    British colonies, **147–150**, *149*

    British recognition of new colonies, 580

    cartography, 189–190

    censorship, 202

    chartered companies in, **212–215**

    Christian clergy, 349

    Christian missionaries, **782–787**

    cities and towns in, **245–249**

    civilizing mission, 788–789

    civil wars, 596

    coffee cultivation, 242

    commodity trade, **270–272**

    cultural imperialism, 574

    decolonization, 367

    diamond production, 301–304

    diseases, 475

    dual mandate, **310–311**, 1136

    Dutch Empire, 372–374

    European colonies, *996*

    exports, 477

    French colonies in, **490–493**, *492*

    German colonies, **517–520**, *519*

    human rights, 561

    independence movements, 865, 881

    indirect rule, **629–631**

    Maji Maji Revolt, 747–748

    manioc cultivation, 39

    manumission, 761

    Marxist theory of neocolonialism, 834

    Mau Mau movement, 766, *767*

    Middle East, slavery in the, 1029

    nationalism, 75–76, **816–824**, 1141

    Organization of African Unity, 880–882

    papal bulls, 902–903

    Portuguese colonies, **916–919**, *917*

    Portuguese Empire, 416–417

    Portuguese exploration, *918*

    race, 929, 931

    racial segregation, *1001*, **1001–1002**

    railroads, 943–944

    rubber, **986–988**, *987*

    Second British Empire, 366–368

    slavery in, 1033

    slaves and race, 934

    slave trade, 2–5, 212, 214, 558, 1035–1038

    trade routes, 634

    trading posts, 705

    traditional religions, 955–956

    trusteeships, 1091–1092

    warrant chiefs, **1123–1125**, *1124*

    Western education, 345–353

    Western religious presence, **963–966**

    World War I, **1134–1136**, *1135*

    World War II, 1140, **1140–1143**

    Zulu Wars, **1150–1151**, *1151*

    See also Pan-African Congress; Pan-Africanism; Scramble for Africa; Specific regions

Africa, scramble for. *See* Scramble for Africa

African Americans

    American Colonization Society, 37–38

    anticolonialism, 59

    Pan-African Congress, 896–898

African Association. *See* Pan-African Association

African Common Market, 901

African culture

    education, 346, 351–352

    mezzonationalism, 819–820

    mission schools, 349

Nkrumah, Kwame, 853
African diaspora
    meganationalism, 823
    Middle East, 1029
    Negritude, 830
    Pan-African Congress, 897–898
    Pan-Africanism, 898–901, 1141
African Economic Community, 882
African International Association, 129,
    997
Africanists, 18
African Morning Post (newspaper), 118
African National Congress, **17–19**
    anticolonialism, 64
    apartheid, 84–85
    ban, lifting of the, 1060
    electoral victory, 27
    Machel, Samore, 745
    Mandela, Nelson, 758–759
    Nyerere, Julius, 865
African National Congress Youth
    League, 758
African Party for Independence and
    Union of Guinea and Cape Verde,
    172
Africans
    Boer Wars, 140
    Middle East slavery, 1030–1031
African slavery in the Americas, **19–25**
African Slave Trade and Its Remedy
    (Buxton), 1020
African soldiers, *1142*
    Sub-Saharan Africa, 1058
    World War I, 1135–1136
    World War II, 1140–1143
African Times (newspaper), 77
African Union
    continental nationalism, 822–823
    micronationalism, 818
    See also Organization of African
        Unity
Afrika Korps, 404, 517
Afrikaner Resistance Movement.
    See Afrikanerweerstandbeweging
Afrikaners, **25–27**
    apartheid, 83–85
    Boer Wars, 138–141
    British expansion, resistance to, 148
    Great Trek, 533–534
    Kruger, Paul, 693–694
    nationalism, 818, 820
    racial segregation, 1001–1002
    Rhodes, Cecil, support of, 982
    South Africa, 1057
    See also Boers
Afrikanerweerstandbeweging, 534
Afro-Caribbean culture, 182

Afshars, 637
After the Empire (Todd), 57
Agbebi, Mojola, 349, 785
Ageng, Kanjeng Ratu, 672
"Age of Discovery," 447–448
Aggrey, James Emmanuel, 118
Agha Khan, 655
Agha Mohammad, 637
Aglipay, Gergorio, 973
Aglipayan Church. *See* Philippine
    Independence Church
Agnese, Battista, 747
Agressi militer Belanda, 313
Agriculture
    alcohol, 31
    American crops in Africa, 38–41,
        335
    Belgian Congo, 127
    Central Asia, 205
    Ceylon, 210, 211
    coffee, 241–245
    Columbian Exchange, 330–335
    cultivation system, 670
    Egypt, 123
    ethical policy, 453
    forced cultivation, 76
    freeburghers, 82
    Goa, 524, 525
    haciendas, 537–538
    Middle East economies, 624,
        625–626
    Middle East slavery, 1030
    New Spain, 847
    Philippines, 1097
    physiocrats, 591
    plantations in the Americas,
        912–915
    protectionist laws, 577
    Roman imperialism, 309
    Soviet collectivization, 207
    Spanish Americas, 109–110
Aguinaldo, Emilio, 1095
Ahelepola, 685
Ahmad, Aijaz, 592
Ahmad, Ait, 70
Ahmad Bey
    debt, 496
    education, 341
    modernization, 70
    resistance, 496
Ahmad Khan, Sir Sayyid, 657–658
Ahmad Shah, 639–640
Ahmed, Jamal, 305
Ahmed I, 410
Ahmed II, 411
Ahmed III, 412
Ahuitzotl, 122

AIC. *See* Association Internationale du
    Congo
Aida (Verdi), 1063
"Aid the King" movement, 505
Ainu, 717
Airborne Warning and Command
    Systems, 1106
Aix-les-Bains Conference, 861
Ajayi, J. F. Ade, 352
Ajman, 86
Akaka, Daniel J., 548
Akbar, 159
Akhundzadeh, Fath 'Ali, 639
Alam Ara (movie), 252
Alaribe, Njoku, 570
Alaska, 473
al-Atrash, 72
Alawi, 500
Al-Azhar *madrasa,* 337, 341
Alberti, Leandro, 189
Albuquerque, Afonso de, **27–29**
    Goa, 520
    India, Portuguese expansion in, 418
    Malacca, 215
    Moluccas, 799
    Thailand, 976
d'Albuquerque, João, 521
Alcock, Rutherford, 227
Alcohol, **29–33,** *30,* 509
Aldeamento system, 720
Al-e Ahmad, Jalal, 1130
Aleijadinho, 94
d'Alembert, Jean le Rond, 448
Alexander I, 48
Alexander II, 50
Alexander VI, Pope, *1088*
    Americas, policy towards the, 195
    Native Americans, status of, 825
    New World, division of the, 704
    papal bull, 573
    papal donations, 904, 905, 947, 948
    Spanish Crown, authority given to
        the, 721
    Spanish sovereignty, 20
    Treaty of Tordesillas, 229, 1088–1089
Alfonso, 903
Algeria, **33–37,** *72*
    anticolonialism, 60, 67, 69–70, 74
    armed resistance, 80
    The Battle of Algiers (movie), 200,
        250, 256
    cafe, *35*
    decolonization, 298
    education, 343–344
    European presence in, 858–859
    French capture of, 854–855

VOLUME 1: 1–480; VOLUME 2: 481–888; VOLUME 3: 889–1316

English East India Company,
438–441
factories, 481–482
French trade, 502
Indian Ocean slave trade,
1039–1040
indigenous religions, 961–962
Italian missionaries, 950
manumission, 761
Ottoman support of Muslim coun-
tries, 410
Portuguese trade, 419–421
silk, 1021–1024
sugar, 1064
trading posts, law and, 705
Xavier, Francis, 1145–1146
See also Specific regions
Asian immigrants
Australia, 116
Pacific Islands, migration to the,
889
Asia-Pacific Economic Cooperation,
890
Asiatic mode of production, 795
Asiatic Society, 175
Asquith, Herbert, 679
Assassinations
Abdullah, Emir, 605
Agha Mohammad, 637
Cabral, Amílcar Lopes, 172
Egypt, 357
Hashdad, Farhat, 859
McKinley, William, 1101
Nadir Shah, 637
Naser od-Din, 639
al-Nuqrashi, Mahmud Fahmi, 811–
812
Rodney, Walter, 901
al-Sadat, Anwar, 358, 603, 812
Assimilation
Africa, **102–103**
art, 90
Central Asia, 208
East Asia and the Pacific, **103–105**
education, 350, 351
French African colonies, 491–492
French colonialism, 1142
French colonial law, 714
French Empire, 384
Inca Empire, 597–598
Japanese Empire, 405
language, 695, 700
Muslim Africans, 654–655
North Africa, 855–856
Association
Africa, **105–106**
education, 350
French Empire, 384

Morocco, 498
Muslim Africans, 655
North Africa, 855–856
vs. assimilation, 103
Association Internationale du Congo,
126, 129, 1052
Association of Francophone Muslims,
343
Association of Islamic Education, 345
Association of the Algerian Muslim,
343
Association of Ulama, 70
Associations. *See* Societies, clubs and
associations
Atahualpa, *599*
execution of, 908
Old World diseases, 134134
Pizarro, Francisco, 108, 826, 912
ransom, 804
sculpture, 90
Spaniards, alliances with, 278
succession, war of, 277
Atatürk, Mustafa Kemal, **106–108,**
107
abolition of slavery, 1029
dress reform, 237, 238
financial dependence, 489
resistance movement, 416
secularism, 567
secular nationalism, 999
Turkish decolonization, 608
Turkish nationalism, 1129
World War I, 1136, 1138
Ath-Thani family, 607
De Atjehers (Snouck Hurgronje), 1042
Atlantic Charter
African anticolonial movements, 80
anticolonialism, 64, 295–296
British failure to honor, 1142
mezzonationalism, 818–819
Wilsonianism, 1132
Atlantic colonial commerce, **108–112**
Atlantic exploration, 552
Atlantic fisheries, 109, **112–114**
Atlantic slave trade, **1033–1039,** *1034,*
1036, 1037, 1038
abolition, 2–4
colonial commerce and, 109,
110–111
human rights, 557–558
race, 931
statistics, 23
Attenborough, Richard, 255
Attlee, Clement, 367
Auckland, Lord. *See* Eden, George
Audiencia, 530, 722, 910
Augustine of Hippo, 948–949, 961

Augustinians
American missions, 229
Goa, 521, 522
Mexico, 195
Tlayacapan, Mexico, convent in, 93
Augustus I, 308
Aungier, Gerald, 141
Aurangzeb, 160
Austin, Stephen F., 1099
Australia, **114–117,** *115, 116*
aboriginal art, 98
British Empire, 371
censorship, 199
dominion status, 579
Eyre, Edward John, 1084
Fiji, anticolonial sentiment in, 67
Mabo and Others v. State of
Queensland, 199, 702
New Guinea, madate over, 137
occupation by, 869
Pacific exploration, 472
Pacific Islands, presence in the,
893–894
Pacific Islands decolonization, 293
Papua New Guinea, 906–907
Second British Empire, 365–366,
367
Western religion, 979
Australian Aborigines, **117–118**
"History Wars," 199
legal rights, 116–117
society, 114
Western religion, 979
Australian and New Zealand Army
Corps, 1137
Austral Islands, 293, 508
Austria
Austrian Revolution, 49
fez industry, 237
Russia, relations with, 47
Austria-Hungary
Andrássy Note, 50
Bosnia and Herzegovina, annexation
of, 50
Ottoman Empire, 51, **883–887**
Austrian Revolution, 49
Authority, papal, 904–905, 946, 1089
Autos, acuerdos, y decretos del gobierno
real y supremo consejo de Indias
(Pinelo), 723
Averroës. *See* Ibn Rushd
Avery, Henry, 160, 440
AWACS. *See* Airborne Warning and
Command Systems
Awooner Renner, P., 7
Axayácatl, 122
Ayres, Eli, 38

Ayutthaya, 1017–1018
Azad, Abu al-Kalam, 658
Azerbaijan, 427
Azikiwe, Nnamdi, **118–119**, 296, 822, *822*, 1058
Azov, 424–425
Aztec Empire, **119–122**, *121*
    archives, destruction of, 197
    conquest and colonization, 20, 277–278
    Cortés, Hernán, 108, 281, 825–826
    cultural imperialism, 573
    Old World diseases, 134
    religion, 962
    Spanish Empire, 398
    Spanish suppression of, 572
    tributary system, 475
Azuzara, Gomes Eannes de, 700

B

Ba Ahmad, 69
Ba'ath Party (Iraq)
    decolonization, 605
    United States support of, 1102
    Western thought, 1129
Babalola, Joseph, 785
Bab El Hadid (movie), 256
Babi movement
    Qajars and, 369, 638
    Shi'i modernism, 660
Babu, A. M., 901
Bacan, 316
Backbay Reclamation, 143
Backhuysen, Ludolf, 91
"Back to Africa" movement, 899
Bacon, Francis, 457
Bacon, Roger, 188
Badan Penjeledik Oesaha-Oesaha
    Persiapan Kemerdekaan, 631
Baden-Powell, Robert, 140
Badran, Margot, 1014, 1015
Baganda, 148
Bagehot, Walter, 679, 1045
Baghdad-Bahn project, 641
Baghdad Pact, 357, 644–645, 1102, 1103
Baguna, Gapi, 800
Bagyidaw, 45
Baha'i movement
    Qajars, 638, 639
    Shi'i modernism, 660
Baha'ullah, 660
Bahrain
    British treaty with, 154
    decolonization, 602
    independence, 158

oil concessions, 88
    Trucial System, 86
    United States military presence, 88–89
Bahrain Petrol Company, 88
Baikie, William Balfour, 1056–1057
Bakhtiar, Shahpur, 896
Bakht Khan, 622
Bakongo, 918
al-Bakr, Ahmad Hassan, 1102
Baku, 427
Balance of power
    hegemony, 550–551
    Ottoman Empire, 412, 886–887
    world-system theory, 796
Balboa, Vasco Núñez de, 465, 911
Balewa, Abubakar Tafawa, 881
Balfour, Arthur James, 155, 273, 939
Balfour Declaration
    Anglo-Arab connection, 1138
    Arabs, 416, 601–602
    British colonialism, 155–156
    Middle East, 1102
    Palestine, 73
    World War I, 1139
Bali, 958
Balkans
    Bismarck, Otto von, 514
    education, 340
    ethnic conflict, 428
    nationalism, 423
    Ottoman Empire, 408–409, 414–415, 885–886
    Russian Empire, 426
    trade, 635
    Treaty of Sevres, 887
Balkan Wars, 51
Ballard Estate, 143
Ballet Rehearsal (Adagio) (Degas), 97
Ballmer, Steve, *87*
Balokole Revival, 786
Baltimore, Lord. *See* Calvert, Cecil
Banda, Hastings, 852, 882, 1141
Banda Aceh, 9
Banda Islands, 240, 315, 316, 798–803
Bandars, 672
Bandeirantes, 22
Banditry Act (Philippines), 1095
Bandung Conference, 357, 814
Banerjea, Surendranath, 175
Bani, John, 1114
Bankruptcy
    Egypt, 154, 162, 487–489, 626
    Ottoman Empire, 414, 499

Tunisisa, 496
    Turkey, 485–487
Banks, 623
Banks, Joseph, 445, 1059, 1072
Ban Me Thoot, *506*
al-Banna', Hasan, 811, *811*
Bantu, 26
Bantu Education Act (South Africa), 84, 759
Bantustans, 84
Banyoro, 817–818
Bao Dai, 506
Baptist Missionary Society of England, 978
Baran, Paul, 596, 834
Baratieri, Oreste, 402
Barbados
    government, 526
    labor, 933
    settlement, 362
"Barbarians," 961
Barbarossa. *See* Khayr ad-Din
Barber, Margaret, 968
Barbot, Jean, 29
Barbour, Violet, 166
Barcelona Company, 267
Baring, Evelyn, **123–124**
    Dinshaway incident, 304–305
    Egypt, 354–355, 1108
Baring, Thomas George, *611*
Barisan Sosialis, 1028
Barnato, Barney, 302
Barnato Diamond Mining Company, 302
Barth, Heinrich, 1056
Barthelemy, Jean Jacques, 92
Bartman, Sara, 1009
Basel Mission, 970, 972
Basic Law of the Hong Kong Special
    Administrative Region, 556
Bassein, 523
Bassey, Magnus, 346
La bataille d'Alger (movie), 200, 254, 256
Batavia, **124–126**, *125*
    Chinese immigrants, 258
    Coen, Jan Pietersz, 240–241
    Dutch United East India Company, 262, 314, 316, *318*
    factories, 481
    freeburghers, 494
    governance, 258
    intermarriage, 259
    religion, 318

British informal imperialism, 832
  Pacific Islands, 371
  territorial expansion, 370
British South Africa Company, 268,
  303, 982
Britons
  American Revolution, 41–42
  extraterritoriality, 479
Broken Arrow (movie), 251
Broken Spears, 700
Bronze Sentries. See Sentinelle di bronzo
  (movie)
Brooke, James, 370, 578, 752
Brooshooft, Pieter, 452
Brown, J. P., 6
Browne, E. G., 640
Bruce, James, 1056
Brunei, 971
Brussels Conference, 31
Brussels Geographical Conference, 129
Bryan, William Jennings, 431
Brzezinski, Zbigniew, 53
Buccaneers, **165–168,** *166*
  Caribbean, 181
  Cartagena de Indias, 184
Büchner, Georg, 1128
Buddhism
  Burma, 170
  Ceylon, 210
  Tibetan, 805–806, 957–958,
    1076–1077
Buenos Aires, 1050
Buffalo, 510
Buffon, Georges-Louis Leclerc de, 286,
  448
Buganda, 148
Bukei Khan, 204
Bukhara, 205
Buller, Redvers, 140
Bullion trade, **168–169**
  Americas, 778–782, 804–805
  bullionism, 111
  exports, 476, 478
  Mexico City, 775–776
  New Spain, 847–848
Bull of Demarcation, *905*
Bulls. *See* Papal bulls
Bulls of donation. *See* Papal donations
Bullt, Jeannot, 539
Bulmer-Thomas, Victor, 834
Bunche, Ralph J., 350
Bunyoro, 148
Buondelmonti, Christophe, 189
Burgerzaal, 90
Burgevine, Henry Andrea, 775

Burgoyne, John, 1122
Burke, Edmund
  abolition, 3
  Enlightenment thought, 449
  "great map of mankind," 445
  Hastings, Warren, impeachment of,
    441, 446
  mercantilism, 772
  trusteeship, empire as a, 677
Burma, **169–170**
  Anglo-Burmese Wars, 45–47
  British East India Company, 365
  British occupation of, 367
  decolonization, 367
  drug trafficking, 877–878
  religion, 977–978
  Singapore, trade through, 1027
  World War II, 1141, 1142
Burmah Oil Company, 872
Burmese Days (Orwell), 1082
Burney Treaty, 1018
Bursa, 407
Burton, Richard, 1082
Burujerdî, Ayatollah, 344–345
Burundi, 129
Bush, George H. W.
  Kaho'olawe Island, 548
  Middle East policy, 1104
  Wilsonianism, 1132
Bush, George W., *1107*
  foreign policy, 1134
  international law, 726
  Middle East policy, 1105–1106
Bush Doctrine, 436
Busia, K. A., 19, 817
Business
  Middle East, 623–624
  tobacco, 150–151
Bustamante, Carlos María de, 286
al-Bustani, Butrus, 1127
Butler, Elizabeth, 96
Buvanekabahu, 683
Buxton, Thomas Fowell, 348, 1020
Byron, Lord, 92, 154
Byzantium
  Constantinople, conquest of, 883
  Ottoman Empire, 407–408
  silk, 1022

C

Cabeza de Vaca, Alvar Núñez, 467
Cabildos, 530–531
Cable telegraphy, 993
Cabot, John, 109, 384, 462
Caboto, Giovanni. *See* Cabot, John
Cabral, Amílcar Lopes, 65, **171–172**

Cabral, Luis, 172
Cabral, Pedro Álvares
  Brazil, 512
  brazilwood, 394
  India, 28
  Portuguese Empire, 417, 418
  sources about, 695–696
  South America, 465
Cabrelli, Alfronso Fernández, 201
Cacao, **172–174,** *173*
  Africa, 272
  Europe, 335
  exports, 477
  West Africa, 40
Cádiz, Las Cortes de, 793
Caetano, Marcello, 298, 1059
Cairo Conference, 643
Cairo Station. See Bab El Hadid (movie)
Cairo trilogy, 735
Caisse de la Dette Publique, 488, 489
Cajamarca, 804
Cakobau, 484
Calcutta, **174–176**
  governance, 258–259
  growth of, 262
  nationalism, 261
  port of, 131
Calcutta Madrasa, 175
Calendar Stone, 119
Calico Jack. *See* Rackman, John
California missions, 232
Caliphate, 159, 164
Callet, Antoine-François, 95
Callistus III, Pope, 903
Calonne, Charles-Alexandre de, 502
Calvert, Cecil, 231, 526, 1075, 1121
Calvinists. *See* Puritans
Cambodia
  French colonialism, 502–507
  independence, 61
  Mekong River exploration, 769–770
  Western religion, 975–976
Cambon, Paul, 856
Cameron, Donald, 630
Cameroon
  anticolonialism, 74
  censorship, 203
  rubber gatherers, *987*
  strikes, 79
Cameroon's National Problem
  (Mbembe), 203
Caminha, Pero Vaz de, 695
Camões, Luís Vaz de
  Goa, 522
  The Lusíads, 416, 511, 513
  tomb, 90

Chiefs *continued*
    Moluccas, 801, 803
Child, John, 430
Child, Josiah, 440, 771
Children
    child removal, 117
    sacrifice of, 121
    slavery, 40
Chilembwe, John, 77, 349, 1136
Chilies, 477
Chimurenga revolt, 199
China, **215–216, 216–220, 220–221**
    Anglo-Dutch Treaty, 1025–1027
    art, 94
    Boxer Uprising, 144–145
    British free trade, 577
    British informal imperialism, 833
    bullion trade, 168
    Burma, 47
    Central Asia, 205
    cigarette production, 150
    coins, 804
    compradorial system, 275
    concessions, scramble for, 998–999
    copper trade, 279
    decolonization, 292
    Dutch trade with, 240
    Dutch United East India Company, 315
    English East India Company, 442
    European presence in, 325–329
    extraterritoriality, 479
    foreign trade, **224–226**
    French missionary school, *967*
    Guangzhou, 534–536
    Hong Kong, 552–554, 554–556
    Imperial Maritime Customs, **227–228**
    indigenous response to colonialism, 627–628
    Japan, trade with, 667
    Japanese demands after World War I, 939–940
    Japanese Empire, 405–407
    Japanese occupation of Southeast Asia, 1047
    Jardine, Matheson & Company, 669
    Korea and the tributary system, 690
    Li Hongzhang, 730–731
    Macao, trade in, 743
    maize, 335
    Mao Zedong, 761–763
    Marxist theories of imperialism, 594–595
    mercenaries, 775
    missions in, **789–791**
    Mongolia, 805–806
    Nagasaki, trade in, 813
    navigation and shipping, 991–992
    occupation, 867
    open door policy, 324–325, 431, 627, 874
    opium, 874–877, *876*
    Opium Wars, **878–880**, *879*
    Pacific exploration, 472
    Portuguese trade, 420
    Qing dynasty, 925–926
    railroads, 943
    religion, 966–968
    revolutions, **221–224**
    Roman Catholic missions, 952
    Russo-Japanese War, 989–990
    self-strengthening movements, 1003–1004
    Shandong Province, 1011
    Shanghai, 1011–1014
    shipping, 1015, 1016, 1026
    silk, 1021–1024, *1022*
    silver, 476
    Soviet relations with, 221
    Taiping Rebellion, **1071–1072**
    tea, 1072–1073
    Tibet, 1076–1077
    trading networks, 258
    treaty port system, 1089–1090
    Unequal Treaties, 1086–1087
    United States, 323–325, 431
    Viet Minh, aid to the, 506
    Western religion, 966
    Xinjiang, 209
    Zongli Yamen, 1149–1150
"China fleet," 8
China Inland Mission, 790
China Maritime Customs Service, 998
China Merchants Steam Navigation Company, **226**, 1016
Chinaware, 94
Chinese Catholic Patriotic Association, 968
Chinese Communist Party
    anticolonialism, 66
    Boxer Uprising, view of the, 145
    decolonization, 292
    Guangzhou, 536
    Hong Kong, 555–556
    Mao Zedong, 761–763
    Marxist theories of imperialism, 594, 595
    Nationalist Party, conflict with, 218–220, 222–223
    Xinjiang, 209
Chinese diaspora, **226–227**, 258
Chinese Eastern Railway, 998
Chinese exclusion laws, 227
Chinese immigrants
    Batavia, 124
    Japan, 664

Malaysia, 752–753
Pacific Islands, 629, 892
port cities and towns, 258
religion, 971, 972
Singapore, 1027
trade, 225
Chinese rites controversy, 215
Chinggis Khan. *See* Genghis Khan
Chissano, Joaquim, 745
Chocolate, 172–174
Choctaws, 827
Choiseul, Duc de, 796
Chongzhen, 925
Chorographic maps, 191
Christianity
    abolitionism, 3, 558
    Acosta, José de, 11–13
    African missions, **782–787**
    African mission schools, 346–349
    American colonial expansion, **228–233**
    anticolonialism, 59
    Boxer Uprising, 144, 328
    Caribbean, 180–181
    cartography, 187
    China, missions in, 789–791
    cultural imperialism, 573–575
    Dinshaway incident, 305
    East Asian missions, 325–329
    European history *vs.* Christian history, 946
    French missionaries, 379
    holy sites, 49
    invincible *vs.* evincible ignorance, 960–961
    Japan, 667
    justifications for empire, 674, *675*
    law, 704–705
    League of Nine, 799–800
    London Missionary Society, 736–738
    Moluccas, 803
    Nagasaki missions, 813–814
    Ottoman Empire, 68
    persecution, 974
    sex and sexuality, 1008
    Sierra Leone, 1021
    slavery and, 20
    syncretic art, 93–94
    treaties, 1086
    women in missions, 584
    See also Syncretism; Specific religions
Christian Maronite community, 1125
Christiansborg, 347
Christian socialism, 1071
Christophe, Henri, 540, 541
Chronology

VOLUME 1: 1–480; VOLUME 2: 481–888; VOLUME 3: 889–1316

VOLUME 1: 1–480; VOLUME 2: 481–888; VOLUME 3: 889–1316

VOLUME 1: 1–480; VOLUME 2: 481–888; VOLUME 3: 889–1316

decolonization, 297–298
Muslim Association Party, alliance
with the, 655
Nkrumah, Kwame, 852
post World War II era, 1142
Convents
Lima, 732
Santa Monica, 521, *522, 523*
Conversation Between the Author and a
Savage of Sound Common Sense
(Lahontan), 450
Conversion. *See* Religious conversion
Coohong, 925
Cook, James
art, 93
Australia, 114, 117, 365
Australia and New Zealand, 371
cartography, 187
Enlightenment, 445, 448
Fiji, 484
Hawai'i, 546
Melanesia, 771
New Caledonia, 844
New Zealand, 850
Nootka Sound, 510
Northwest Passage, search for a, 863
overview, 473
Pacific exploration, 472, 507, 891
Polynesia, 915
travelogues, 1082
Cook Islands, 293
Coolie labor
Aceh War, 8
China, 226–227
Hong Kong, 554
Coordinating Committee for the
Liberation of Africa, 881
Copper trade, **279**, 316
Coppolani, Xavier, 491
Coprosperity Sphere, 1047
Copts, 356
Córdoba, Francisco Hernández de,
134, 911
Core nations, 794, 796
Cornwallis, Charles, 388, 441
Cornwallis Reforms, 561
Coromandel, **279–281**
Dutch United East India Company,
315, 316
Malabar trade, 750
Portuguese Empire, 419
Coronado, Francisco Vásquez de, 108,
192, 467, 826
Coronelli, Marco Vincenzo, 193
Coronil, Fernando, 920
Corpus Christi Procession with the
Parishioners, 94, 95

Cortés, Hernán, **281**
Atlantic commerce, 108
cacao, 335
conquest and colonization, 277–
278
gold, 778
just war, 949
La Malinche and, 699–700
Mexico City, 775
Native Americans, conquest of the,
825–826
requerimiento, 948
South American exploration, 466,
467
Spanish Empire, 398
Tenochtitlán, conquest of, 134
travelogues, 1082
wars of conquest, 1121
Cortesão, Armando, 198
Cosa, Juan de la, 192, 1114, 1115
Cosmographia (Münster), 191
Cosmopolitanism, 257–258
Cossacks, 204, 424
Costa, Cláudio Manoel da, 777
Costner, Kevin, 254, 255
Costs and benefits of colonialism
free trade, 578
liberal theories, 587
world system theory, 797
Cotton, *282,* **282–285,** *284*
Bombay, 142
British East India Company, 364
commodity trade, 270
Egypt, 271, 355–356, 1030
plantations, 914
slave labor, 5
Tanzania, 747
Cotton gin, 282, 283
Council for Oversea Affairs.
See Conselho Ultramarino
Council for the Indies, 697
Council of China, 442
Council of Guardians, 689
Council of Regency, 145
Council of the Indies, 234, 721
A Counterblaste to Tobacco (James I),
1078
Country traders, 438, 619
Court cases
Mabo and Others v. State of
Queensland, 117, 199, 702
Rice v. Cayetano, 548
Courteen, William, 439
Courteen Association, 439
Court of Committees, 438
Courts
Black Circuit, 83

consular, 178
Portuguese Empire, 719
Coussey, Henley, 852
Couto, Diogo do, 523
Covenant of the League of Nations,
1092
Covert operations, 434
Cox, Howard, 151
CPKI. *See* Committee for the
Preparation of Korean Independence
(CPKI)
Craftsmen and artisans
Middle East, 623, 625
Spanish America, 93–94
Creasy, Gerald, 852
Cree, 995
Creek Indians, 1009
Creoles
Angola, 918
anticolonialism, 59
nationalism, **285–287**
New Spain, 849
Peru, 910
postcolonialism, 919, 921
race, 931, 937
slavery, 23
Spaniards, conflict with the,
196–197
Spanish American government,
531–532
Spanish American independence,
1049–1051
Sub-Saharan Africa, 1055, 1058
Crete, 411
Crijnssen, Abraham, 373
Crime, 249
Crimea
Ottoman Empire, 412
Russian Empire, 424–425
Crimean War
Austria, 49–50
France and Austria, 886
French alliance with the Ottomans,
499
Ottoman Empire, 413
Russian Empire, 426
Crispi, Francesco, 402
Cromer, Lord. *See* Baring, Evelyn
Cromwell, John, 250
Cromwell, Oliver
colonial administration, 387
English East India Company, 439
Massachusetts Bay Company, 765
Cromwell, Thomas, 646
Cron, Ferdinand, 521
Crown Colonies, **288,** 365–367
Crowther, Bowley, 254

Crowther, Samuel Adjai, 348, 784
CRUA. *See* Comité Révolutionnaire
   d'Unité et d'Action (Algeria)
Crusader mentality, 228–229
Crusades
   Middle East economy, impact on
     the, 625
   "others," 961
   Ottoman Empire, 408
   silk, 1022, 1023
   Western thought, 1125
Cruz, Apolinario de la, 973
Cuba, *183*
   American imperialism, 836
   Haitian refugees, 541
   Havana, 545–546
   independence leaders, 201
   plantations, 914
   reforms, 532
   slavery, 24, 183
   smallpox, 134
   sugar, 1069–1070
   tobacco, 267, 1080
   United States policy, 1100–1101
Cuffee, Paul, 37, 783
Cugoano, Ottabah, 783, 1020
Cuisinier françois (La Varenne), 113
Cultivation
   sugar, **1067–1070**
   tobacco, **1077–1080**
Cultivation system, **669–671**
   abolition of, 562
   Batavia, 125
Cultural anthropology, 590
Cultural exchange
   East Asian/European, 329
   Japan/western, 714
   religion, 965
Cultural imperialism, 430–431, 436,
   572–576
Cultural nationalism, 650
Cultural reform, 206
Cultural Revolution
   Boxer Uprising, view of the, 145
   China, 221
   Mao Zedong, 762–763
   Tibet, 1077
Cultural Revolutionary Council, 661
Culture
   African cities and towns, 245,
     248–249
   African education, 346, 349,
     351–352
   African worldviews, 964–965
   Afrikaners, 83
   Afro-Caribbean, 182
   American cities and towns, 235

apartheid, 82
British East India Company, 365
British Empire, influence of the,
   368–369
British informal imperialism, 832
Calcutta, 175
Catholic Church, 950
Dutch Empire, 376
Dutch United East India Company,
   317–318
East Asia, 627
education, 346, 350, 351–352
Enlightenment, 445, 446
ethnocentrism, 460
as export, 478
French Indochina, 504, 505
French influence in Egypt, 495
French Middle Eastern colonies,
   501
gender, 581
Goa, 521, 525
human rights, 561
Igbo Women's War, 569–571
Inca Empire, 597–598
Incan cultural revival, 1094
Indian National Movement, 614
Indian Revolt of 1857, 610, 613,
   621–622
Indochina, French influence on,
   507
Japan, 666
justification for empire, 676
law, 706–708
mezzonationalism, 819–820, 820
Middle East slavery, 1031
mission schools, 349
Morocco, 498
Native American, 379
Negritude, 830
Netherlands Missionary Society,
   attitude of the, 843
Nkrumah, Kwame, 853
Ottoman Empire, 410
Pacific Islands, 892
Philippines, 1097
port cities and towns, 261
positivism, 725
postcolonialism, 921
self-determination, 1003
self-strengthening movements,
   1003–1004
slavery and African culture, 23
Snouck Hurgronje, Christiaan,
   1042–1043
syncretism, 77
Tunisian education, 342
Vietnam, 974
Xavier, Francis, 1146
See also Identity; Western culture

Cultuurstelsel, 562
Cumberland Sound, 863
Cunliffe-Owen, Hugo, 150
Curaçao
   Dutch Empire, 377, 390
   Dutch West India Company, 321
Currency. *See* Money
Currey, John Blades, 981
Curtin, Philip, 23, 1037
Curtis, William, 905
Curtiz, Michael, 250, 254
Curzon, George Nathaniel, 163,
   288–289
Customary law
   Dutch colonialism, 712
   Morocco, 498
Customs
   China, 227–228
   Goa, 522
   Shanghai, 1013
Cuzco
   anticolonialism, 59
   sack of, 778–779
   Túpac Amaru, rebellion of,
     1092–1093
Cuzco Revolution, 287
Cyprus
   British control, 154
   ethnic conflict, 307

D

Dadié, Bernard, 1085
Dagomba, 518
Dahlan, Ahmad, 660
Dahomey, 1037
   See also Benin
Daigne, Blaise, 103
Dáil éireann, 652
Daily Comet (newspaper), 118
Dakar, 248, 249
Dakar-Saint Louis railway strike, 79
Dalai Lama, 958, 1076–1077
Dalhousie, James Ramsay, 46, 610
Damas, Léon, 1004
Damascus
   French presence in, 499
   Islamic modernism, 659
Dana, James Dwight, 889
Dana, Richard Henry, 1082
Dancaerts, Sebastianus, 318
Dance of the Tapuya Indians (Eckhout),
   93
Dances with Wolves (movie), 254, 255
Dandi March, 617
Daniell, Thomas, 95

Daniell, William, 95
Danish colonialism, 347
Danqah, . B., 852
Danube, 49–50
Danureja IV, 671
Danurejo, Patih, 672
Daoguang, 926
Dar al-Fonun, 344
D'Arcy, William Knox, 155, 871–872
Dardanelles, 48, 52, 416
Dardanelles campaign, 1137
Dar es Salaam, 248, 619
Darwin, Charles, 938
Darwinism, 1128
Darwith, Mahmud, 736
Daum, Paulus Adrianus, **291–292**
Davenant, Charles, 679, 771
David-Néel, Alexandra, 1082
Davidson, Basil, 198, 1036, 1037
Dávila, Pedrarias, 465
Davis, Clarence, 943
Davis, John, 463, 863
Davitt, Michael, 649
d'Avity, Pierre, 905
Dawson, Owen, 443
Day, Clive, 670
Day, Francis, 439
Deane, William, 702
Dearden, Basil, 254
*The Death of General Gordon,
   Khartoum, 26 January 1885* (Joy), 91
The Death of General Wolf (West), 91
Death of Nelson (Devis), 91
The Death of Sardanapalus (Delacroix),
   96
De Beauvoir, Simone, 56
De Beers Consolidated Mining
   Company, 268, 302–303, 981–982
De Bono, General, 861
De Brazza, Pierre Savorgnan, 1056
DeBrum, Anton, 763
De Bry, Theodore, 92, 1081
Debt, **484–490**
   anticolonialism, 70–71
   Egypt, 162, 354, 355, 495, 626
   Iranian tobacco concessions, 1081
   Ottoman debt to Germany, 515
   Ottoman Empire, 179, 414, 499,
      887
   'Urabi Rebellion, 1108
   World War I, 1138–1139
*Decades of the Newe Worlde or West
   India* (Eden), 448
Decamps, Alexandre, 97
Decentralized administration, 148

Declaration of Human Rights (France),
   562, 714
Declaration of Independence (Mexico),
   285
Declaration of Independence (United
   States), 63, 701
Declaration of the Rights of Man, 539
Declaration on Liberated Europe, 1132
Decolonization
   American Revolution, 43
   Belgian Congo, 127–128
   British African colonies, 150
   British colonies, 367–369
   East Asia and Pacific, **292–294**
   education, 351–352
   Eurocentric view of, 456–457
   French colonies, 381–382
   Indian independence and, 164–165
   Indonesia, 313
   international law, 726
   language of, 701
   Middle East, 157–158, **600–609**
   Moluccas, 803
   Nkrumah, Kwame, 852–853
   Pacific Island missions, 792
   Pacific Islands, 67
   race, 938
   Sub-Saharan Africa, **294–299**
   Sudan, 1062
   trade unions, 79
   United Nations list, 44
   United States support of, 433
   Wilsonianism, 1132–1134
Decree of Muharram, 486, 487
Dee, John, **299–300**, 359
Defamation case, 200
The Defence of Rorke's Drift (Butler), 96
Defiance Campaign, 17, 758–759
Definitions
   mandate, 754
   postcolonialism, 919
   treaty, 1086
   world-system, 793
Defoe, Daniel, 450, 1082
Degas, Edgar, 97
De Gaulle, Charles
   Accords of Evian, 543
   Algeria, 35
   Algeria, reforms in, 858, 860
   Algerian independence, 563
   Algerian nationalists and, 821
   decolonization, 294, 298
   Free France movement, 1141
   French African colonies, 493
   Sub-Saharan Africa, 1059
Degeneration and anti-Americanism,
   53–57
De Goeje, M. J., 1041, 1044

De Graft Johnson, J. W., 6
De Jong, Loe, 200
De Jonge, B. C., 453
Dekker, Eduard Douwes. *See* Multatuli
De Klerk, F. W., 84
Delacroix, Eugène, 96–97
De Lagree, Ernest Doudart, 770
Delany, Martin, 830
Delaporte, Louis, 770
De la Rey, Jacobus Hercules, 140
Delaware, Lord, 1116
De Lesseps, Ferdinand, 487
Delisle, Guillaume, 193
Delle navigationi et viaggi (Ramusio),
   1084
*De l'origine des loix, des arts, et des
   sciences, et de leurs progrès chez les
   anciens peuples* (Goguet), 450
Demarcation, Bull of, *905*
Democracy
   French identity, 380–382, 384
   imperialism and, 432
   Iran, 639
   Wilsonianism, 1130–1132
Democratic Party (United States), 1096
Democratic People's Republic of
   Korea, 692–693
Democratic Republic of Vietnam,
   506–507
Democratic revolution, 594
Democratic Union for the
   Independence of Algeria. *See* Union
   Démocratique du Manifeste Algérien
Democratization, 556
Demographics
   Brazil, *419*
   Caribbean, 182
   English colonies, 232
   French Indochina, 503–504
   French Middle Eastern colonies,
      496–497
   justification for empire, 678
   slavery, 23
   slave trade, 1037–1038
   sugar, 1066
   World War II, 1141, 1143
Les Demoiselles d'Avignon (Picasso), 97
Demolition, 523, 524
Deneuve, Catherine, 255
Deng Xiaoping, 221, 223, 595
Denmark
   abolition, 4
   Coromandel trade, 280
De Pauw, Cornelius, 54, 448, 676
Dependencies, free trade and, 579–580
Dependency theory

E

Eagle of American Imperialism, *436*

Eannes, Gil, 552, 903

Earl, George Windsor, 1024

Early Companies, 314

East Africa
    armed resistance, 75
    commodity trade, 271
    Gama, Vasco da, 511–512
    German colonialism, 518
    Goan emigration, 525
    Indian Ocean trade, 619–620
    mission schools, 348–349

East Asia
    American presence, **323–325**
    anticolonialism, **65–67**
    assimilation, **103–105**
    compradorial system, 275
    decolonization, **292–294**
    European presence, **325–330**
    extraterritoriality, 479
    indigenous responses, **626–628**
    mercenaries, 775
    occupations of, **867–869**
    Portuguese commerce, 719
    Portuguese trade, 420
    railroads, **941–943**
    self-determination, **1002–1003**
    self-strengthening movements, **1003–1004**
    shipping, **1015–1016**
    silk, 1021–1024
    treaties, **1086–1088**
    Western religious presence, **966–968**

East Bengal, 611

The Eastern Nigerian Guardian (newspaper), 118

Eastern question
    British interests, 152–153, 154
    Germany, 514–517
    Ottoman Empire, 412–413
    Ottoman relations with France and Austria-Hungary, 886–887

Easter Rising, 651

East India companies
    companies and colonization, 267
    port cities and towns, 258–263
    Roman prototype, 308–309

East Indies
    Dutch Empire, 374–376
    Multatuli, 809–811
    Royal Dutch-Indisch Army, 984

East Jerusalem, 1105

East Timor, **330**, 1002–1003

East-west trade, 634

Eboué, Ginette, 1004

Ebrahimnejad, Hormoz, 768

Ecclesiastical administration, 521

Eckhout, Albert, 93

E-commerce, 89

Economic development
    Algeria, 36
    Arabia, 89
    Bombay, 142
    British Malaysia, 751–752
    Kuwait, 606
    Micronesia, 483
    Nkrumah, Kwame, 853

Economic expansion in Arabia, **85–89**, 624, 625

Economic exploitation, 934

Economic growth
    British informal imperialism, 833
    Japan, 666
    North Africa, 857
    Papua New Guinea, 137

Economic imperialism, 627

Economic independence, 147

Economic issues
    Africa, scramble for, 996
    anticolonialism, 69, 70–71, 79
    Arabian oil, 87–89
    Asante Wars, 100
    Atlantic colonial commerce, 108–112
    Australia, 115
    Brazil, 145, 146–147
    British African colonies, 149
    bullion trade, 168–169
    Central Asia, 206–207, 209
    Ceylon, 210
    China, 221, 223
    colonialism and capitalism, compatability of, 558–559
    compradorial system, 275
    cultural imperialism, 572, 573, 575
    dependency theory, 834–835
    East Asian modernization, 329
    Egypt, 355–356, 603
    Enlightenment thought, 449–450
    ethical policy, 453
    European capitalism and the Middle East, 425
    financing and debt, 484–489
    French Indochina, 504
    German influence in the Ottoman Empire, 515
    Goa, 525
    hegemony, 550
    Hong Kong, 554
    Igbo Women's War, 571
    Indonesia, 377
    informal imperialism, 831–834

Jordan, 606

justification for empire, 678–679

Korea, 693

Latin America, neocolonialism in, 839–841

liberal theories, 585–591

mandate rule, 757

Marxist theories, 834

mercantilism, 771–774

mezzonationalism, 819

Opium Wars, 879

Organization of African Unity, 882

Pacific Islands, 892

Peru, 909

Philippines, 1097

precious metals exports, 476

railroads, 942–943, 993

Roman imperialism, 308–309

silk, 1023

slavery, 2, 1033

slaves, treatment of, 24

sugar, 1066

transatlantic slave trade, 1035–1037

Túpac Amaru, rebellion of, 1093

Turkey, 608

United States imperialism, 434

wage labor *vs.* slave labor, 3, 4–5

world-system theory, 793–798

World War II, Africa, 1143

Economic nationalism, 142

Economic reform
    Abdülhamid II, 1
    Algeria, 36
    decolonization and, 297
    Egypt, 487
    Korea, 66

Economic subsidies, 88

Eden, Anthony, 1063, 1064

Eden, George, 14

Eden, Richard, 448, 697–698

Eden Commission, 613

Edib, Halide, **336–337**, 736

Education
    Africa, **345–353**
    African Muslims, 653
    anticolonialism, 296
    Belgian Congo, 127
    British African colonies, 148–149
    British Malaysia, 752–753
    Calcutta, 175
    Central Asia, 207–208
    cultural imperialism, 574–575
    Egypt, 495, 1127
    French African colonies, 103, 105–106, 491
    French Indochina, 504

English colonialism. *See* British colonialism

English East India Company, **438–442**
  abolition of, 267
  Arabia, 86
  Bengal exports, 130, 131
  Bombay, 141
  British colonial law, 710
  British Empire, 369
  calcutta, 174–175
  China, **442–443**
  Chinese-English trade, 216
  copper, 279
  Coromandel trade, 280
  Dutch United East India Company, competition with, 316
  East Asian presence, 327
  factories, 481–482
  free trade, 577
  Guangzhou, 536
  hegemony, 797
  human rights, 561
  Indian Army, 612
  Indian Revolt of 1857, 621–622
  Kandy, 685
  Malabar, *749, 750*
  Middle East, 160–162
  Mill, James, criticism by, 588–589
  Pacific exploration, 472
  Qing dynasty, 925–926
  Raffles, Thomas Stamford, 940
  Second British Empire, 364–365
  sepoys, 1005–1007
  shipping, 1015
  Siam, 1017
  silk, 1023
  Singapore, 1024
  Straits Settlements, 1054
  tea, 1072–1073
  transfer of power from, 609–610
  Virginia Company, as model for, 1115

English indentured servants, **443–444**, *444*

English Levant Company, 160

English Russia Company, 265

English soldier, *647*

Engravings, 92

Enlightenment, **447–452**
  abolitionists, influence on the, 3, 4
  African culture, 964–965
  America and the ideals of, 54
  anticolonialism, 61, 63–64, 679–680
  art, 90, 92
  cartography, 194
  empire, **444–447**
  Eurocentrism, 459
  human rights, 562

Indian religions, 956
liberal economics, 586
liberal theories of imperialism, 588, 589
Pacific Islanders, depictions of, 891
race, 937
Spanish American independence movements, 1051

Entente Cordiale, 71

Entertainment, 575

Entrepreneurship, 142

Enver Pasa
  Atatürk, Mustafa Kemal, rivalry with, 106
  Basmachis, 206
  German influence on, 516
  World War I, 1137

Environmental issues, 596–597

Epidemics. *See* Diseases

Epistemological Eurocentrism, 457

Equality and economics, 586

Equatorial Africa
  French colonialism, 490–491

Equiano, Olaudah, 701, 783, 1020, 1035, 1085

Erasmus, Desiderius, 61

Eratosthenes, 187

Eriksson, Leif, 191

Eritrea, 401–403, 455

Escaped slaves, 24

El Escorial, 91

Esheick, Joseph, 144

Esma'il
  rule of, 637
  Safavids, 636
  trade, 635

Espionage, cartographic, 192

L'Esprit des lois (Secondat), 3, 449, 700

Essai sur l'administration de St. Dominque (Raynal), 451

Essai sur les moeurs et l'esprit des nations (Voltaire), 450

Essay on the Administration of St. Dominque. See Essai sur l'administration de St. Dominque (Raynal)

An Essay on the History of Civil Society (Ferguson), 450

Essay on the Manner and Spirit of Nations. See Essai sur les moeurs et l'esprit des nations (Voltaire)

Essentialism, 459

The Essential Wallerstein, 797

Estado Novo, 199

Estates
  Africa, 653
  haciendas, 537–538

Middle East, 623
plans, 189

The Ethical Direction in Colonial Policy. See De Ethische koers in de koloniale politiek (Brooshooft)

Ethical Eurocentrism, 458

Ethical policy, **452–454**
  Dutch Empire, 376, 377
  human rights, 562
  Kartini, Raden Ajeng, 687
  Snouck Hurgronje, Christiaan, 1044

Ethics
  Middle Eastern medicine, 768
  Second Opium War, British opposition to, 577
  slavery, 3

Ethiopia, **454–456**, *455*
  armed reistance, 75–76
  Battle of Adwa, 998
  Italian Empire, 401–404
  mezzonationalism, 818
  World War II, 1140

Ethiopian Church, 77

Ethiopianism. *See* Millennial movements

De Ethische koers in de koloniale politiek (Brooshooft), 452

Ethnicity
  Africa, Berlin Conference's division of, 132
  Balkans, 428
  Bombay, 142
  civilizing mission, 788
  cultural imperialism, 573
  Cyprus, 307
  Eurocentrism, 457
  French Middle Eastern colonies, 496–497
  Guangzhou, 535
  intermarriage, 259
  law, 708
  Lebanon, 499
  Malaysia, 752–753
  mandate rule, 754–755
  micronationalism, 817–818
  Middle Eastern nationalism, 567
  port cities and towns, 261
  Rwanda, 129
  self-determination, 1003
  Syria, 500

Ethnocultural discrimination, 934

Ethnography
  ethnographic present, 457
  indigenous religions, 961
  Snouck Hurgronje, Christiaan, 1041–1044
  travelogues, 1082–1085

étoile Nord-Africaine, 34, 70
Etsi cuncti, 903
L'Etudiant noir (journal), 830, 1004
Eugenics, 1046
Eugénie, 1063
Eugenius IV, Pope, 903
Eunuchs, 1030
Eurocentrism, **456–461**, 919–920
Europe
    African colonies, *996*
    alcohol, 29, 30
    Algerian trade, 33–34
    American crops, introduction of,
        335
    anti-Americanism, 54–56, 57
    art, **89–99**
    Asian cultural influence, 318
    Berlin Conference, 132–133
    biological impact of expansion,
        133–137
    cacao, 174
    capitulations, 177–180
    commodity trade, 474–478
    East Asian indigenous response,
        627–628
    Egyptian debt, 162
    Enlightenment thought, 448
    exports, 477
    gender, 581
    indigenous peoples, representations
        of the, 697
    international law, 724–728
    Middle East, influence on the, 425,
        1125–1130
    Middle East literature, influence on,
        735
    Middle East trade, 634–635
    North African relations with, 857
    North America exploration,
        462–465
    Ottoman support of Protestant
        countries, 410
    Ottoman withdrawal from, 411
    philhellenism, 92
    race, 939
    religion, 960
    Roman law, influence of, 704
    Singapore, trade through,
        1025–1027
    South America exploration,
        465–468
    Southeast Asian importation of
        metals, impact of, 618
    sugar, 1065, 1069
    tariffs, reinstatement of, 578
    tobacco, 1078
    trade boycotts, 79
    Wilsonianism, 1132
    World War II, 1140, 1141

Europeans
    American colonies, migration to,
        468–472, *469, 471*
    in East Asia, **325–330**
    East Asian indigenous responses to,
        626
    factories, 481–482
    health and medicine, 994
    Indian Ocean slave trade,
        1039–1041
    Malabar maritime trade, **748–751**
    nationals, 479
    Native Americans and, *825,*
        825–829
    in North Africa, **857–863**
    in the Pacific Islands, **891–894**
    port towns, 257–260
    sex and sexuality, 1007–1010
    slaveholders, 760–761
    in Sub-Saharan Africa, **1054–1060**
    superiority, attitudes of, 448, 457
    wars with Native Americans, *827*
European Union, 608, 1134
Eusebius, 948
Evangelical Church of Vietnam, 975
Evangelical Fellowship of Cambodia,
    976
Evangelical Fellowship of Thailand,
    977
Evangelicalism, 584
Evangelization
    justification for empire, 674, *675*
    Roman Catholic Church, 950
    See also Missions and missionaries
Evening News (newspaper), 852
Ever-Victorious Army, 1072
Évian Agreements, 35, 859, 860
"Evincible ignorance," 960–961
Exceptionalism, 458, 474
Exchange, modes of, 1026
Exile
    Edib, Halide, 337
    Khomeini, Ayatollah Ruhollah, 689
    Mohammad Reza Shah, 896
    Nkrumah, Kwame, 853, 900
Expeditions. *See* Exploration
Exploration
    Acapulco, 8
    Americas, 192–193
    art of, 93
    cartography, 185–191
    Mekong River, 769
    narratives, 696, 698
    North America, **462–465**
    Northwest Passage, 863–864
    Pacific, **472–474**
    Pacific Islands, 889, 891
    Portuguese, 394, *918*

South America, **465–468**
Sub-Saharan Africa, 1056
travelogues, 1082
Export commodities, **474–479**
Exports
    British, 485
    British free trade, 577
    British informal imperialism,
        833–834
    Ceylon, 210
    coffee, 243–244, 245
    cultivation system, 670
    European railways, 487
    Latin America, 840
    oil, 88
    Philippines, 1097
    rubber, 986–988
    Singapore, 1026
Extirpation of idolatry campaigns, 910,
    961
Extraterritoriality, **479–480**
    British traders, 577
    China, 998
    East Asia, 328
    Japan, 664
    Korea, 691
    Nagasaki, 814
    Ottoman Empire, 884
    Shanghai, 1013
    Siam, 1018
    treaties, 1086
    Treaty of the Bogue, 878–879
Eyre, Edward, 1082, 1084
Ezra, Elizabeth, 384

F

Fa'asamoa, 44
Fabian, Johannes, 1083
Fabian Society, 1128
Factories
    British colonial law, 710
    Egypt, 487
    South and Southeast Asia,
        481–482
Fage, J. D., 350, 1035, 1037, 1038
Fahd bin Abd al-Az al-Saud, 608
Fahmy, Khaled, 768
Faidherbe, Léon César, 102
Faidherbe, Louis, 490, *491*
Fairbank, John K., 926
Faisal
    Arab Revolt, 155
    Iraqi independence, 60
    mandate rule, 156, 755–756
    Syria, 71
    World War I, 1138
Faisal II, 644

VOLUME 1: 1–480; VOLUME 2: 481–888; VOLUME 3: 889–1316

Iraq Petroleum Company
  British interest in the, 756
  formation, 1102
  Gulbenkian, Calouste, 872
  oil concessions, 87
Iraq War, 57, 837, 1106, 1134
Ireland, English colonization of,
  646–649, *647, 674*
Irish Citizens Army, 651
Irish Civil War, 652
Irish Free State, 652
Irish Nationalism Movement, **649–652**
Irish Republican Army, 652
Irish Republican Brotherhood,
  649–651
Irish Volunteers, 651
Iroquois, 184, 508, 509, 845
Irrigation, 333
Isaaco, 1059
Isabella
  Columbus, Christopher, support of,
    269
  currency regulations, 804
  Native American slavery, 195, 930
  South American exploration, 465
  Treaty of Tordesillas, 1089, 1120
  tribute, 1091
'Isa ibn Salman Al Khalifa, 602
Iselin, Isaak, 450
Islam
  Abdülhamid II, religious propa-
    ganda program of, 1
  Acehnese resistance, 9
  al-Afghani, Jamal ad-Din, 13–14
  African anticolonialism, 74
  African missionaries, 786
  Algeria, 34, 496, 562
  Algerian population, 497
  anticolonialism and Islamic reform
    movement, 68–70
  Arab-Islamic cultural identity, 36
  art, 96–97
  Atatürk, Mustafa Kemal, 107
  bond of, 159
  Calcutta, 175
  Caucasus region, 426
  Dutch colonial law, 712
  education, 337–345
  Humayun decree, 153–154
  Iberia, 902
  India, 562
  Indian nationalists, 164
  Morocco, 498
  Muslim Brotherhood, 811–812
  Netherlands Missionary Society,
    attitude of the, 842–843
  North Africa, 854–857
  Ottoman Empire, 68

Ottoman support of Muslim
    countries, 410
  papal bulls, 903
  Russian Emprie, 423–424
  science, 1128
  self-determination, 1003
  slavery in the Middle East, 1028–
    1032
  Snouck Hurgronje, Christiaan,
    1041–1044
  Soviet Socialist Republics, 428
  Sub-Saharan Africa, **652–655**
  Syria, 500
  Western thought, 1125–1130
Islamic fundamentalism
  Islamic modernism and, 656
  Rashid Rida, Muhammad, 659
Islamicization, 340, 689
Islamic law
  dual mandate, 311
  Iran, 639
  Islamic modernism, 659
  Middle East economic policies,
    623–626
  Morocco, 498
  Ottoman Empire, 718
  Snouck Hurgronje, Christiaan,
    1041
Islamic-Marxist groups, 896
Islamic modernism, **656–661**
  education, 339
  Malaysia, 753
Islamic reformism, 68, 70, 376, 566
Islamic Republic Party, 689
Islamic Salvation Front. *See Front
  islamique du salut*
Islamic schools, *657*
"Islamic trend," 1015
Islamism
  Algeria, 36, 344
  anti-Western sentiment, 1130
  clubs and associations, 78
  Middle East political ideology,
    568–569
  Sadat, assassination of, 603
"Islands-Under-the-Wind," 508
L'Isle, Brière de, 490
Isma'il I, 409, 883
Ismail Pasha
  education, 341
  Egyptian debt, 162
  financing and debt, 488
  modernization, 354
Isolario, 189
Isolationism, 430
Israel
  1967 War, 358

anti-Americanism, 57
  anticolonialism, 73
  Egypt, invasion of, 815, 862
  Egypt, relations with, 357
  Egyptian stability, 603
  independence, 158
  Palestine War, 1000
  Suez Canal and Suez Crisis, 1063–
    1064
  United States Middle East policy,
    1101–1105, 1107
  United States support for, 89
Istanbul
  al-Afghani, Jamal ad-Din, 14
  Ottoman Empire, 409
  See also Constantinople
Istanbul University, 340
Isthmus of Panama, 398, 400, 465
Istiqlal Party (Morocco), 73, 79, 860
Ita, Eyo, 349
Italian colonialism, 251
Italian Communist Party, 595
Italian Empire, **401–404**
Italian missionaries, 950
Italo-Abyssinian War, 402
Italo-Turkish War, 402
Italy
  armed resistance to, 75–76
  Battle of Adwa, 998
  China, merchant colonies in, 325
  Ethiopia, occupation of, 454–455,
    818
  Japan, alliance with, 1047
  Libya, presence in, 856, 861
  Ottoman relations, 415
  silk, 1022
  World War II, 1140
Itinerario (Linschoten), 523
Itto (movie), 250
Iturbide, Agustin de, 1051
Itzcoatl, 119, 120, 122
Ius gentium, 705
Iustum bellum. See Just war
Ivan grozny (movie), 251
Ivan III, 424
Ivan IV
  expansion, 424
  Kazan khanate, 204
  Pacific exploration, 472
Ivory, 271, *271*
Ivory, James, 255
Ivory Coast
  armed resistance, 74
  French colonialism, 491, 493
  mass migration, 76
  religious syncretism, 77
  rubber, 986

J

al-Jabarti, 'Abd al-Rahman, 1126
Jabavu, John Tengo, 77, 304
Jackson, Andrew, 43
Jacobson, J. I. L. L., 1073
Jadidism, 659
Jahangir, 438
Jahan Shah, 315
al-Jahiz, 734
Jailolo, 799
Jaja, King, 77
Jakarta
    anticolonial slogans, *893*
    Dutch United East India Company,
        314
    See also Batavia
Jaluit Company, 763
Jamaica
    buccaneers, 166
    post-emancipation revolt, 559
    settlement, 362
Jamaica Act, 166
James, C. L. R.
    mezzonationalism, 818
    Padmore, George and, 900
    Pan-Africanism, 901
James, Duke of York, 526
James I
    Jamestown, 464
    North America settlements, 385
    tobacco, 1078–1079
    Virginia Company, 1115–1116
James II, *527*
    English East India Company, 439
    government in the American colo-
        nies, 526
    Massachusetts Bay Company, 765
    thirteen colonies, British North
        America, 1076
Jameson, Leander Starr, 139, 982
Jameson Raid, 982–983
Jamestown, *1116*
    colonization, 1121
    evangelization, lack of, 232
    Native Americans, 828
    settlement, 360, 463–464, 1074
Jâmia al-Khaldûniyya, 342
Jangali movement, 640
Janissaries, 409, 410, 413
Janssens, émile, 199
Jansz, Willem, 114
Japan, **665–667**
    Americanization, *551*
    anticolonialism, 65–66
    art, 97
    Batavia, occupation of, 125–126

Bengal exports, 130
bullion trade, 168
China, colonization of, 225
China, occupation of, 220
colonized, **663–665**
compradorial system, 275
decolonization, 292–293
East Asian indigenous responses to,
    627
European presence in, 326–329
European standards, 725
extraterritoriality, 479
indigenous religions, 961–962
Indonesia, occupation of, 377,
    631–632, 985
Korea, relations with, 690–691
Malaysia, attack of, 753
Marshall Islands, occupation of the,
    763
Micronesia, relations with, 483
Nagasaki, 813–814
occupation by, 868, 869–870
opening of, **667–669**
opium, 877
Pacific exploration, 472–473
Pacific Islands, 629, 893
Perry, Matthew, 907
Philppines, invasion of the, 1097
Portuguese missionaries, 420, 421
Racial Equality Amendment,
    939–940
railroads, *942,* 942–943
"rape of Nanjing," 223
religion, 966
Russo-Japanese War, 988–990
self-strengthening movements,
    1003–1004
Shandong Province, 1011
shipping, 1016
silk, 1023, 1024
Singapore, occupation of, 1027
Sino-Japanese War of 1894-1895,
    218, 222
Treaty of Shimonoseki, 218
treaty port system, 1090
Twenty-one Demands, 219
United States and, 323–324, 431
Wilsonianism, 1132
World War II, 554–555, 1140
Xavier, Francis, 1145, 1146
Japanese colonialism
    assimilation, 104–105
    Micronesia, 776
    Southeast Asia, **1046–1048**
Japanese Empire, **404–407**
    law, **714–717**
    Southeast Asia, 1046–1048
Japanese immigrants, 1012
Jardine, Matheson & Company, **669**

Jardine, William, 669
Jarvis, Thomas, 443
Java
    coffee, 241
    cultivation system, **669–671**
    Dutch colonial law, 712
    Dutch Empire, 376
    Dutch-Indonesian Wars, 312–313
    Dutch United East India Company,
        314, 316–317
    ethical policy, 453
    independence, struggle for,
        631–633
    Kartini, Raden Ajeng, 686–687
    Linggadjati Agreement, 733
    Multatuli, 810
    peranakan society, 259
    port cities and towns, 260–261, 262
    Raffles, Thomas Stamford,
        940–941
    religious syncretism, 958
    Second British Empire, 366
    tea, 1073
    Western religion, 969–970
Java War, 376, **671–673**, 984
al-Jaza'iri, Tahir, 659
Jeejeebhoy, Jamsetjee, 142
Jefferson, Thomas
    American Revolution, 41
    anticolonialism, 63
    cartography, 193–194
    Cuba, 1100
    Enlightenment, 446
    Haitian Revolution, 542
    Latin America, 1099
    Notes on the State of Virginia, 448, 450
Jefferys, Thomas, 193
Jemal Pasa, 1137, 1139
Jerónimos Monastery, 90
Jerusalem
    holy sites, 49
    trusteeship, 1092
    World War I, 1138
Jesuits
    Acosta, José de, 11–12
    aldeamento system, 720
    Americas, 196, 230, 231, 532
    Brazil, 395, 396, 467, 528
    China, 215, 789–790
    Company of New France, 274
    Confucianism, 966
    East Asian missions, 326–327
    Goa, 521, 524
    indigenous religions, 961–962
    Indonesia, 970
    Japan, 420
    Nagasaki, 813
    Roman Catholic Church, 951–952

Ku'e petition, 546
Kul servitude, 1030–1031
Kunaev, Dinmukhamed, 208
Kundera, Milan, 460
Kunwar Singh, 621
Kuomintang, 594
Kurds, 60, 1102
Kuril Islands, 472
Kusumasana Devi, 683
Kutuzov, Mikhail, 251
Kutuzov (movie), 251
Kuwait
   British treaty with, 154
   decolonization, 606
   independence, 158
   Iraq, invasion by, 1106
   oil, 87, 873, *873*
   Trucial System, 86
   United States, relations with, 1104
   United States military presence, 89
Kuwait National Petroleum Company, 88
Kuyper, Abraham, 453
Kuyucu Murad Pasa, 410
Kwaku Dua II, 101
Kyrgyzstan, 206, 207

L

Labor
   alcohol, 30–31, 32
   apartheid, 81–82
   Belgian Congo, 127
   Chinese Customs Service, 228
   coffee cultivation, 242, 243
   Congo, 126, 129
   diamond production, 303, 981–982
   Dutch plantations, 376
   education for, 351
   English indentured servants, 443–444
   European immigrants, 469–470
   Goa, 525
   Iberian colonialism, 333–334
   indentured system, 366
   international division of, 588–589
   Marxist theories of imperialism, 593
   mining, 334, 399–400, 779, *780,* 780–781
   mita system, 780–781, 792–793, 910, 923, 1093
   Papua New Guinea, 906
   plantations, 914–915
   race, 929–933
   racial segregation, 1001–1002
   reform, 79
   rubber industry, 986–988
   silver production, 476, 1093

   sugar industry, **1064–1067,** *1065,* 1067–1069
   tea, 1073–1074
   textile industry, 280
   tribute, 1091
   World War II, Africa, 1143
   See also Forced labor; Indian labor; Indigenous labor
Labor migration
   blackbird labor trade, 137–138, 771
   British Empire, 368
   Central Asia, 206–207
   China, 226–227
   diamond production, 303
   Fiji, 484
   mita system, 793
   Pacific Islands, 629, 889, 892
   Philippines, 1097
   plantations, 914–915, *915*
   port cities and towns, 258, 260–261
   racial segregation, 1001–1002
Labor strikes. *See* Strikes
Lagaan: Once Upon a Time in India (movie), 256
Lagos, 248
The Lagos Weekly Record (newspaper), 77
Lahontan, Louis-Armand de Lom d'Arce, 450
Laissez-faire economics
   liberal theories of imperialism, 586
   mercantilism *vs.,* 772–773
   physiocrats, 591
Lake Texcoco, 119
Lakota Ghost Dance, 955, *957*
"Lal Paltan," 1006
La Malinche, *696, 699*
Lamarck, Jean-Baptiste, 1045
Lampson, Miles, 356, 357
Lancaster, James, 438
Land Act (South Africa), 17
Lander, Richard, 1056
Land-filling projects, 143
Land grants, 394, 528
Landholding elite
   haciendas, 537–538
   Hong Kong, 554
   Spanish Americas, 109–110
Land League (Ireland), 649
Land policy
   Aborigines, Australian, 117
   American Revolution, 43
   anticolonialism, 69, 78
   armed resistance, 80
   Australian Aborigines, 117
   Brazil, 528
   British African colonies, 150

   Central Asia, 207
   Egypt, 626
   French colonial law, 714
   French Middle Eastern colonies, 496–497
   Goa, 524
   haciendas, 537–538
   Hong Kong, 554
   Iberian colonialism, 333
   Iran, 345
   Ireland, 647, 649–650
   Middle East, 623
   New Zealand, 851
   North Africa, 858
   Ottoman Empire, 718–719
   Steppe Governate, 204
Land Regulations (China), 1013
Lands Bill (Gold Coast), 6, 7, 78, 83
Landscapes, 93, 97
Land taxes
   Java, 672
   Middle East, 623, 625
   physiocrats, 591
Land War (Ireland), 649
Language
   Africa, Berlin Conference's division of, 132
   Algerian education, 343–344
   British African colonies, 148–149, 150
   Central Asia, 208
   Dutch missionaries, 318–319
   education, 350
   English as an international language, 368
   European, **695–703**
   French Middle Eastern colonies, 501
   Inca Empire, 599
   Latin, 306
   law, 706
   literature, colonial *vs.* indigenous languages, 11
   Marshall Islands, 763
   Middle Eastern education, 340, 342, 343
   Middle Eastern nationalism, 567
   Netherlands Missionary Society, 843
   Peru, 910
   Philippines, 1097
   Roman Catholic Church, 948–949
   Snouck Hurgronje, Christiaan, 1043
   Valentijn, François, 1111–1112
   Vanuatu, 1113
   Zongli Yamen, 1149
Laos
   French colonialism, 502–507
   independence, 61

VOLUME 1: 1–480; VOLUME 2: 481–888; VOLUME 3: 889–1316

temperance, 31
warrant chiefs, 1123
Lumière Brothers, 250
Lumumba, Patrice, 203, *740,*
740–741, 900
Luque, Hernando de, 911–912
The Lusíads (Camões), 416, 511, 513,
522
Luso-Africans, 1054
Lutfi al-Sayyid, Ahmed, 305, 356, 567,
1129
Lutherans, 972
Luxemburg, Rosa, 64, 593
Lyautey, Louis-Herbert-Gonzalve, *497*
association, 856
medicine, 768
Morocco, 498
Lynch, John, 1049, 1051

M

Ma'al-Aynayn, 69
Mabo, Eddie, 702
Mabo and Others v. State of Queensland,
117, 199, 702
Macao, **743–744**
China, return to, 329
Portuguese presence, 326
silk, 1023
MacArthur, Douglas, 665, *666*
Macaulay, Herbert, 118, 295
Macaulay, Thomas Babington, 561
Macaulay, Zachary, 346
MacCarthy, Charles, 100
MacCartney, George, 216, 472, 926
Macedo, João Rodrigues de, 777
Mace industsry, 798–803
Maceo, Antonio, 201
Machel, Samore, *744,* **744–745**
Machines, 593
Maciel, Mosé Alvares, 777
Mackay, Alexander, 349
Maclean, George, 100
Macleod, Iain, 297
Macmillan, Harold, 701, 1059
Madagascar
manioc cultivation, *40*
peasant revolts, 76
vanilla, 39–40
Madama Butterfly (Puccini), 814
Madinka Empire, 75
Madison, James, 38, 1098
Madras army, 612
Madras (city)
English East India Company, 439
governance, 258–259

growth, 262
merchants, efforts to attract, 258
nationalism, emergence of, 261
trade, 280
Madras (education), 337–345
Madre de Dios (ship), 438
Madrid, Miguel de la, 201
Magdoff, Harry, 831, 834
Magellan, Ferdinand, **745–747**
in art, 90
cartography, 190
Micronesia, 776
Pacific exploration, 472
Portuguese Empire, 419
South American exploration, 467
Maghreb Unity Party (Morocco), 860
Maghrib Muslims, 653–654
Magiciens de la terre (exhibition), 98
Magnetic lodestone, 185
Mahabanula, 45
Mahan, Alfred Thayer, 432, 890, 1017,
1101
Mahdi, 67, 76, 133, 148, 1060–1061
Mahfouz, Naguib, 735
Mahir, Ahmad, 357
Mahir, 'Ali, 357
Mahmud I, 412
Mahmud II
capitulations, 178
education, 340
military dress, 237
reforms, 565
reign of, 413
Russian interference in Greece, 48
Mahmud Shaltut, 659
Mahmud Syah, 9
Mahu, Jacob, 472
Mail, 993
Maina wa Kinyatti, 203
Maine (battleship), 1100
Mainstream principle, 456–457,
459–460
Maize, 39, 335, 477
Majeke, Nosipho, 201
Maji Maji Revolt, 76, 518, **747–748,**
1136
Majlesi, Mohammad Baqer, 636
Majumdar, Romesh Chandra, 201
Makarov, Stepan Osipovich, 989
Makassar
factories, 482
governance, 258
intermarriage, 259
Malabar, **748–751,** *749*
Malacca
Albuquerque, Afonso de, 28

Dutch United East India Company,
315
Penang and Singapore, displace-
ment by, 262
Portuguese Empire, 421
Portuguese trade, 215
silk, 1023
Straits Settlements, 1053–1054
Malan, Daniel François, 26, 83, *84*
Malaria
Batavia, 124
quinine, 995
Sub-Saharan Africa, 1056–1057
Malawi
British control, 148
mass migration, 76
North Nyasa Native Association, 78
religious syncretism, 77
West Nyasa Native Association, 78
Malay
grammar and language studies,
318–319
Netherlands Missionary Society,
843
Malaya
Singapore and, 1028
trade, 1026
Malayan Chinese Association, 1027
Malayan Chinese Party, 753
Malayan Emergency, 753
Malayan Indian Congress, 753
Malay Bible, 318–319
Malaysia
British colonialism, **751–754**
Catholicism, 968
formation of, 1028
silk, 1023
Western religion, 971–972
Malaysian Constitutional Conference,
752
Malcolm, John, 1005
Malcolm X, 853
Malick, Terrence, 255
Malikite legal school, 338
Malinowski, bronislaw, 958
Malkam Khan, 639
Mallaby, A. W. S., 632
Mallon, Florencia E., 835
Malthus, Thomas, 678
Maluku, 968–969
Mamluks
Middle East economy, 624
Ottoman Empire, 409
Manao Tupapao (Gauguin),
97, *98*
Manchester Congress, 297

VOLUME 1: 1–480; VOLUME 2: 481–888; VOLUME 3: 889–1316

Marxism
  decolonization period, 580
  Machel, Samore, 745
  Middle East, 568, 1102, 1128
  neocolonialism, theories of, 834, 835
  theories of imperialism, **592–597**
Mary, Queen, 765
Maryland, 1075, 1121
Masai, 148
Mason, A. E. W., 250
Massachusetts, 143, 526, 527
Massachusetts Bay Company, 235, 265–266, 360, 526, **764–766**
Massacres
  Bavaria, 124
  Boston Massacre, 143
  Gayo Expedition, 9
  Harkis, 543–544
  Rwanda, 129
  Sharpeville, 18, 759
Massasoit, 828
Massawa, 402
Mass migration
  anticolonialism, as form of, 76–77
  British India, from, 164
  French colonial administration, 105
Mass production, 477
Mataram, 262
Mataungan Association, 137
Mathematics, 194
Mather, Increase, 765
Matheson, James, 669
Matiri, Mahmud, 859
Matrilineal societies, 1008
Matulesia, Thomas, 375–376
Maude, Frederick, 1138
Maugham, Somerset, 892
Maulama Abul Kalam Azad, 659
Mau Mau movement, **766–767**
  archives, destruction of, 198
  armed resistance, 80
  British colonialism, 1059
  decolonization, 298
  Kenyatta, Jomo, 688
  Ngugi wa Thiongo, writing of, 203
  political parties, 296
Mauras, Charles, 54
Maurice, Prince, 1017
Mauritania, 491
Maurits, Johan, 321, 373, 422
Mauro, Fra, 185
Max Havelaar of de koffieveilingen der Nederlandsche Handel-Maatschappij (Multatuli), 291, 562, 809–810

Max Havelaar or the Coffee Auctions of the Dutch Trading Company. See Max Havelaar of de koffieveilingen der Nederlandsche Handel-Maatschappij (Multatuli)
Maxim, Hiram S., 995
Maxim guns, *994,* 995
Maximilian, Ferdinand, 393
Maximilian I, 189
Maxwell, Kenneth, 778
Maya
  archives, destruction of, 197
  cacao, 172
  conquest of, 466, 826
  smallpox, 134
Mayadunne, 683
Maya uprising, 59
May Fourth Movement
  anti-Christian sentiment, 967
  anticolonialism, 66
  Japanese militarism, as response to, 627
  nationalism, 218, 222
Mbeki, Thabo, *18,* 19
Mbembe, Achille, 203
Mboya, Tom, 900
Mbundi, 918
McCarthy, Charles, 348
McCartney, Samuel Halliday, 775
McCauley, Herbert, 78
McClintock, Anne, 921
McClure, Robert, 864
McCormick, Thomas J., 795
McCullough, David, 91
McGillivray, Alexander, 1009
McIntyre, W. David, 101
McKay, Claude, 830
McKinley, William, 836, 1100–1101
McMahon, Henry, 155, 163, 1138
Mead, Margaret, 1082
Measles, 134
Mecca, 1041–1042
Media representations, 89
Mediators, Chinese, 664
Medicine and health
  Africa during World War I, 1135
  Belgian Congo, 127
  Middle East, **767–769**
  opium, use of, 875
  overview, 993–995
  segregation of cities and towns, 246–247
Médicis, Hippolyte de, 904
Medina, Bartolomé de, 334
Mediterranean region
  sugar production, 913
  trade, 634

Medjidiah Company, 488
Megantionalism, 821–823
Mehmed Ali. *See* Muhammad 'Ali
Mehmed I, 408–409
Mehmed II, 409, 883, 1125
Mehmed III, 410
Mehmed IV, 411
Mehmed V
  German relations with, 516
  reforms, 50
Meiji government
  foreign relations, 664
  treaty port system, 1090
Meiji Restoration
  Japanese colonial law, 715
  modernization, 323, 328
  Western presence, as response to, 627
Meillassoux, Claude, 1033
Meirs, Suzanne, 1033
Mekong River, **769–770**
Melanesia, 67, 137–138, **770–771**
Melford, George, 250
Melville, Herman, 889, 1081
Memoirs, 736
Memoirs (Forbes), 142
Memoirs of Halide Edib (Edib), 337
Mencius, 952
Mendaña de Neira, álvaro, 507, 770, 915
Menelik II
  First Italo-Abyssinian War, 402
  modernization of Ethiopia, 454
  resistance movement, 75–76
Menezes, Dom Alexis de, 521
Mensa Bonsu, 101
Mensah Sarbah, John, 6, 7
Menshikov, Aleksandr, 49
Mercantilism, **771–774**
  Atlantic commerce, 111
  chartered companies, 214
  coffee, 241
  cultural imperialism, 572
  economic liberalism as challenge to, 585–586
  First British Empire, 362
  free trade, replacement by, 576–577
  justification for empire, 678–679
  New Spain, 847–848
  Ottoman Empire, effect on the, 412
Mercator, Gerardus, 190–191, 192, 299
Mercedarians, 229
Mercenaries, **775**, 1072
Merchant capital *vs.* industrial capital, 593

Moumouni, Abdou, 346

Mountbatten, Louis, 617, 632

Mouvement National Congolais, 740–741

Mouvement pour le Triomphe des Libertés Démocratiques, 858

Movement for the Triumph of Democratic Liberties. *See* Mouvement pour le Triomphe des Libertés Démocratiques

Movies, 143, **250–257**

Mozaffar od-Din Shah, 639

Mozambican Liberation Front, 744–745, 918

Mozambique
   architecture, 93
   armed resistance, 80
   decolonization, 298
   Machel, Samore, 744–745
   Portuguese colonialism, 918
   strikes, 79

Mozambique National Resistance, 745

Mphahlele, Ezekiel, 830

MPLA. *See* Popular Movement for the Liberation of Angola

MTLD. *See* Mouvement pour le Triomphe des Libertés Démocratiques

Mua'allaqat, 734

Mubarak, Hosni, 358, 603

Mudros Armistice, 1138

Mugabe, Robert, 298, 853

Mughal Empire
   anticolonialism, 61
   Bengal, 130, 131
   British influence, 610
   Calcutta, 175
   English East India Company, 439–440
   India, 159

Mughals
   Indian Army, 622
   Portuguese Empire, 421

Muhammad 'Abduh
   al-Afghani, Jamal ad-din and, 13, 14
   Dahlan, Ahmad, influence on, 660
   Islamic modernism, 658–659
   Islamic reformism, 566
   Western thought, 1127, 1128

Muhammad Ahmad
   anticolonialism, 68
   Khartoum (movie), 254
   Sudan, 1060–1061
   Twelver Shi'ism, 636

Muhammad 'Ali, **808–809,** *809*
   anticolonialism, 70
   British relations with, 154

capitulations, 178
   cotton, 282–283
   economic reform, 626
   education, 341
   French influence, 495
   French support of, 886
   governship, 353–354
   immigration, 356
   nationalism, 999
   Ottoman Empire, 413
   peace of Kutahya, 48
   reforms, 487, 565
   Russian reaction to, 425
   Sudan, 1060
   Western thought, 1126–1127

Muhammad al-Mahdi al-Sanusi. *See* Muhammad Ahmad

Muhammad al-Nasir Bey, 496

Muhammad al-Sadiq Bey, 70

Muhammad Nadir Shah, 53

Muhammad Shahrur, 661

Muhammad V, 73, 501

Muhi al-Din, 69

Muiguithania (newspaper), 687

Mujahideen, 877, 1106

Mukden Incident, 324

al-Mukhtar, Umar, 861

Mulattos, 539–541

Muller, Friedrich Max, 957, 962

Multatuli, 291, 562, **809–811**

Multiculturalism
   discourse of, 702
   United Arab Emirates, 609

Multiethnicity
   British Empire, legacy of the, 368–369
   Ceylon, 211
   Egypt, 356
   port cities and towns, 258
   Suriname, 377

Multilateralism, 436

Multinational corporations
   British American Tobacco Company, 151
   United States imperialism, 434

Muncipal government
   Spanish Americas, 530

Mundus Novus, 186

Municipal government. *See* Local government

Munif, Abdelrahman, 735

Muñoz, Juan Bautista, 676

Munsif Bey, 859

Münster, Sebastian, 191

Murad I, 408

Murad II, 409

Murad III, 177, 410

Murad IV, 410–411

Murad V, 50, 414

Murals, 93–94, 97–98

Murphey, Rhoads, 257–258

Murray, Archibald, 1137–1138

Murray, David, 1083

Murshid Quli Khan, 175

Muryam, Raden Ajeng, 686

Mus, Paul, 504

Musaddiq, Muhammad, 873, 895, 1000, 1102

"Musa Rebellion," 66

Muscat Arabs
   British treaty with, 154
   piracy, 160

Muscovy Company, 299

Museums, 95

Musgrove, Mary, 1009

Music, 249

Musif Bey, 496

Muskets, 995

Muslim Association Party, 655

Muslim Brotherhood, **811–812**
   Egyptian nationalism, 862
   formation, 357
   government treatment of, 358
   Islamism, 568
   al-Nasir, Gamal abd, 603
   secularism, criticism of, 999

Muslim dynasties, 963

Muslim India, 658

Muslims
   Albuquerque's defeat of, 28
   Bengal, partition of, 611
   Ceylon, 211
   clothing and fashion, 235–239
   Copts, tension with the, 356
   Coromandel, 280
   Dinshaway incident, 305
   Iberia, 194
   India, 612
   Indian National MOvement, 616
   "invincible ignorance," 960
   League of Five, 799–800
   Pakistan, creation of, 617
   race, 929
   Reconquista, 228, 229
   Sudan, 1060–1061
   Tatars, 205

Mussolini, Benito
   Ethiopia, occupation of, 75–76, 403–404, 454–455
   films, 251
   World War II, 1140

Mustafa al-Maraghi, 659

Mustafa Fahmi Pasha, 354

Mustafa I, 410

Mustafa IV, 413

Mustafa Kemal. *See* Atatürk, Mustafa Kemal

Mustafa Khaznadar, 70

Mutsuhito, 715

Muzaffar al-Din Shah, 344

Mwanga, Kabaka, 738

Myanmar. *See* Burma

Myths and legends
    Canadian folk-identity, 582
    exploration, as motivation for, 467–468
    Great Trek, 533–534
    Mexico, 119

My Travels Around the World (al-Saadawi), 1085

Mzilikazi, 533, 694

N

NAACP. *See* National Association for the Advancement of Colored People

Nadir Shah, 51, 159, 636, 637

Nagara Vatta (newspaper), 505

Nagasaki, **813–814**
    Dutch United East India Company, 327
    Portuguese presence, 326
    trade, 663, 667

Nagriamel, 1114

Naguib, Muhammad, 73, 357, 814, 862

Nahas Pasha, 862

Nahuas, 122

Naipaul, V. S., 919, 1085

Nairobi, 248

Nallino, Carlo Alfonso, 1129

Namibia
    diamond production, 302
    South West Africa People's Organization, 203

Namibia—The Wall of Silence: The Dark Days of the Liberation Struggle (Groth), 203

Nana Sahib, 621

Nandi, 148

Nanjing, 223

Naoroji, Dadabhai, 142

Napier, Charles, 163

Napoleon, Louis, 562

Napoléon I, *1126*
    art, 95
    British India, as threat to, 161
    cartography, 189
    Egypt, 151, 353, 495, 1126

French Empire, 381
    human rights, 562
    India, 51–52
    liberal criticism of, 589–590
    Napoleonic Wars, 1123
    New Spain, 849
    Ottoman Empire, impact on the, 412
    Portugal, invasion of, 396–397
    slavery, 937
    Spain, invasion of, 532
    St. Domingue, invasion of, 540
    Treaty of Tilsit, 48

Napoleonic Wars
    British Empire, expansion of the, 366
    French colonialism, 1123
    French territorial losses, 392

Napoléon III
    Egypt, arbitration terms with, 488
    French Empire, 392–393
    Ottoman Empire, 50

Narai, 976, 1017, 1018

Narasimha, 520

Narrative of a Five Years Expedition against the Revolted Negroes of Surinam (Stedman), 95

Narratives, 696, 1081

Narrizzano, Silvio, 255

Narváez, Pánfilo, 134

Naser od-Din, 344, 638–639

Naser ul-Mulk, 289

al-Nasir, Gamal abd, **814–816**, *815*
    anticolonialism, 73
    Arab nationalism, 568, 1129
    Arab world, as idol of the, 644
    assassination attempt on, 812
    coup, 809
    Egypt as Middle Eastern vs African country, 823
    Europe, relations with, 862
    Organization of African Unity, 881
    overthrow attempt of, 495
    reforms, 341, 603
    rule of, 357–358
    Suez Canal and Suez Crisis, 158, 165, 1063–1064, 1103

Nasserist Party, 816

Natal
    racial segregation, 1001
    Rhodes, Cecil, 981

Natchez, 827

Nationaal Instituut Nederlands Slavernijverleden, 378

National African Company, 997

National Association for the Advancement of Colored People, 897

National Bloc (Syria), 999–1000

National Charter (Egypt), 358

National Conference of the ANC, 18

National Congress of British West Africa, 7, 64, 78, 820

National Council of Nigerians and the Cameroons, 79, 118, 296

National Council of Sierra Leone, 296

National Democratic Party (Nigeria), 78

National economists, 590

National Front for the Liberation of Angola, 918

National Front (Iran), 1000

Nationalism, **816–824**
    Aborigines' Rights Protection Society, 7
    Aceh War, 10
    Africa, 75–76, **816–824**, 1141
    African missionaries, 786
    Afrikaners, 26, 534, 694
    alcohol, 32
    Algeria, 34, 563, 858
    anticolonialism, 60–61, 64
    association, 106
    Atatürk, Mustafa Kemal, 107
    Azikiwe, Nnamdi, 118
    Balkans, 423
    Baring, Egyptian opposition to, 123
    Brazil, 146
    Cambodia, 505
    Ceylon, 211
    China, 66, 218–219
    Communist peasant movements, 628
    Congo, 127–128, 740–741
    Creole, **285–287**
    East Asia, 324
    economic dependence, 489
    Edib, Halide, 336–337
    education, 352
    Egypt, 356–358, 603, 861–862
    Enlightenment, influence of the, 446
    Ethopia, Italian occupation of, 75–76
    French Indochina, 506
    Guangzhou, 536
    India, 164
    Indian Revolt of 1857 as, 622
    Indian soldiers, 611
    indigenous elites, 561–562
    Indonesia, 376–377
    Ireland, 649–652
    Japan, 406

Naval power, United States, 1017, 1101
Naval warfare, 989
Navigation Acts
    Atlantic commerce, 111
    Boston, 143
    British Empire, 387
    Massachusetts Bay Colony, 765
    mercantilism, 362, 771
Navigational maps, 185
Navy, Chinese, 1149
Navy, U.S.
    American Samoa, 44
    Guantánamo Bay, 1101
    imperialism, 432
    Middle Eastern presence, 1106
    naval strategy, 1017
    Pacific Islands, 890
    Perry, Matthew, 907
Nayakkars, 685
Nazi Germany
    race, 938
    Social Darwinism, 1046
NCBWA. *See* National Congress of British West Africa
NCNC. *See* National Council of Nigerians and the Cameroons
Ndebele, 148
Nduka, Otonti, 349
Nebrija, Elio Antonio de, 695, 700
Nederlands Zendeling Genootschap. *See* Netherlands Missionary Society
Negritude, 819, **830–831**, 1004
Nehru, Jawaharlal
    The Discovery of India, 198
    election of, 612
    Indian National Congress, 615, 616
Nehru, Motilal, 616, 617
Nelson, Horatio, 52
Nelson, Ralph, 254
Neocolonialism, **831–839**
    anticolonialism, 80
    international law, 726
    Latin America, **839–841**
    Marxist thought, 580
    postcolonialism *vs.,* 702, 921
    world-system theory, 797–798
Neo-Destour Party (Algeria), 856
Neo-Destour Party (Tunisia), 79, 859
Neo-imperialism, 433
Neoliberal globalizaton, 597
Neo-Wilsonianism, 1134
Neptune Resigning the Empire of the Seas to Britannia (Dyce), 91
Nestlé brothers, 174
Netherlands

abolition, 4
Aceh War, 8–10
Afrikaners, 25–26
art, 90–91
Brazil, attacks on, 528
buccaneers, 166–167
Cape of Good Hope, 176
censorship, 200
China, trade with, 215
chocolate, 174
cinnamon trade, 233–234
commerce, 111
Coromandel trade, 280
Dutch-Indonesian Wars, 312–313
East Asian presence, 327
East Timor, presence in, 330
English East India Company, competition with the, 439
French occupation, 371, 374
French trade competition, 502
Indian Ocean trade, 619
Indonesia independence, 631–634, *633*
Middle East trade, 635
Portugal, colonial conflicts with, 395
Siam, trade in, 1017
slavery, 22, 1040, *1040*
Netherlands East Indies Constitution, 712
Netherlands Indies
    ethical policy, **452–454**
    Snouck Hurgronje, Christiaan, 1042–1043
Netherlands Indies Army, 8–9
Netherlands Missionary Society, **841–842**
    Indonesia, 970
    Thailand, 977
Netherlands Trading Company, 670
Neu-Guinea Kompagnie, 137
Nevsehirli Ibrahim Pasa, 412
New Amsterdam. *See* New York
New British Revenue Settlements, 613
Newby, Eric, 1084
New Caledonia, **844**
    anticolonialism, 67
    Blackbird labor trade, 137–138
    France, 293
    French colonialism, 892–894
New Conquests, 524, 525
New Culture Movement, 145, 218
New England
    British colonization, 385
    cotton mills, 284
    Eliot, John, 699
    Massachusetts Bay Company, 764–766

Native Americans, 828
    settlement, 1074, 1076
New English, 647
Newfoundland
    fisheries, 109, 112–114
    Gilbert, Humphrey, 463
    settlement, 360
New France, *393,* **844–846,** *845*
    colonization, 1121
    French Empire, 391
    Quebec City, 927
New Granada
    gold, 779
    rebellions, 532
    tobacco, 1080
New Guinea
    Australia and, 116
    Bismarck Archipelago, 137
    decolonization, 293
New Harbour, 1026
New Hebrides
    Blackbird labor trade, 138
    decolonization, 293
New History, 201, 336
New Indian Cinema, 252
New International Economic Order, 726
New Jewel Movement, 901
"New Land," 113–114
Newlands Resolution, 547
New Laws, 20, 195, 437, 722, 908
New Netherland, 374, 389
New Orleans, 541–542
New Peruvian Empire, 287
New South Wales, 365, 708
New Spain, **846–850**
    Acupulco *vs.,* 8
    Mexico City, 775–776
Newspapers
    Aborigines' Rights Protection Society campaigns, 6–7
    Algeria, 343
    anticolonialism, 77–78
    Azikiwe, Nnamdi, 118
    Cambodia, 505
    censorship, 200
    Daum, Paulus Adrianus, 291
    yellow journalism, 432
New Statutes of Batavia, 712
The New World (movie), 255
New York, **850**
    British acquisition, 235
    Dutch Empire, 374
    tobacco merchants, *389*
New York Daily Tribune (newspaper), 592

Production, economic, 623–624
Production quotas, oil, 88
"Programme of Action" (African
    National Congress), 758
Prohibition, 30–31, 875, 876–877
Promiscuity, 1008
Propaganda, 251, 1140
Property
    language, 702
    laws, 705–706, 707, 714
Proprietory colonies, 526
Prostitution, 1009
Protection acts, Aborigines, 117
Protectionism, 586
Protection treaties, 579
Protectorates, 579
Protestantism
    China, missions in, 790
    Dutch United East India Company,
      318
    Florida, 391
    Philippines, 973–974
    slavery, 24
    Süleyman's support, 884
    traditional religions, 956–958
Protestant missions
    Cambodia, 975–976
    East Asia, 966–967
    expansion, 231, 232
    Indonesia, 970
    Laos, 976
    Malaya and Singapore, 972
    Myanmar, 977–978
    Pacific Islands, 979–980
    Sub-Saharan Africa, 1056
    Thailand, 977
    traditional religions, 955
    Vanuatu, 1114
    Vietnam, 975
Protests
    Algeria, 858
    anticolonialism and, 60
    anti-home rule demonstration
      (IReland) 651
    Ghana, 852
    Gold Coast, 6–8
    Igbo Women's War, 569–571
    Iraq, 644
    Khomeini, Ayatollah Ruhollah, 689
    Tunisia, 859
    World War I, Africa, 1136
Providence Industrial Mission, 77
Providence Island, 165–166
Prussia, 514
Pseudogovernmental corporations,
    308–309

Ptolemy, Claudius, 185–186, 188, 192,
    1125
Puaux, General, 860
Public art, 97
Public Debt Fund. *See* Caisse de la
    Dette Publique
Public education, 340–345, 350
Public health, 994
Public Law 103-150 (United States),
    548
Public loans, 488
Public works projects, 487
Puccini, Giacomo, 814
Puerto Rico
    Spanish Empire, 398
    Treaty of Paris, 1101
Puga, Vasco de, 722
Pulitzer, Joseph, 1100–1101
Punjab
    British annexation of, 163
    British East India Company, 365
Punjabi, 614
Purchas, Samuel, 543, 696, 905
Purchas His Pilgrimes (Purchas), 543
Puritans
    Boston, 143
    Massachusetts Bay Company, 764
    Native Americans, relationship
      with, 231, 232
    New England, 1074
    North American colonization, 385
    Plymouth Colony, 360
    South Africa, 82
    traditional religions, 955
"Purity of blood," 931, 934–935
Puyi, 926

Q

Qabbani, Nizar, 736
Qaboos bin Said Al bu Said, 607
al-Qaeda, 1106
Qajar dynasty
    Anglo-Russian competition, 152–153
    education, 344
    overview, 637–640
    Pahlavi dynasty, replacement by the,
      894
Qanun (newspaper), 639
Qasa Amin, 1128–1129
Qasim, 'Abd al-Karim, 73
Qatar
    decolonization, 607
    independence, 158
    oil, 88, 873
    Trucial System, 86
    United States military presence, 89

Qianlong, 926
Qingdao, 219, 1011
Qing dynasty, **925–927**
    anticolonialism, 61
    Boxer Uprising, 144
    compradorial system, 275
    concessions, 998–999
    Hong Kong, 553
    religion, 966–967
    revolutions, 222
    self-strengthening movements,
      1004
    shipping, 1016
    silk, 1023
    Taiping Rebellion, 1071–1072
    Tibet, 1076–1077
    trade, 216, 217, 536
    treaties, 1086
    Zongli Yamen, 1149–1150
Quadrants, *188*
Quakers, 3
Quaque, Philip, 348
Quebec City, *845,* **927**
    Company of New France,
      273–274
    founding of, 1121
    French Empire, 391
Quechua, 599
Queen Anne's War, 1121
Quesnay, François, 591
Quezon, Manuel, 1096, 1097
Quincey, Thomas de, 875
Quinine, 995, 1057
Quirós, Pedro Fernandez de, 507
"Quit India" campaign, 617
Quotas, oil production, 88
Quranic medicine, 768
Quranic schools, 338–343
Qutb, Sayyid, 812

R

Rabelais, François, 1127
Raboisson, Pierre, 679
Race and racism, **933–939**
    Afrikaners, 26–27
    alcohol policy, 31, 32
    Americas, **929–933,** *932*
    Boxer, Charles, writing of, 198
    British Empire, legacy of the,
      368–369
    Cape Town, 1055
    classification, 398–399
    cultural imperialism, 574
    diamond production, 303–304
    Dutch United East India Company,
      81–82
    Enlightenment thought, 450

Russia *continued*
    Russo-Japanese War, 988–990
    World War I, 1136–1139
Russian-Anglo relations. *See* Anglo-
    Russian relations
Russian Empire
    Iran, wars with, 638
    Islamic modernism, 659
    Middle East, **423–428**, *427*
Russian immigrants, 1013
Russian Revolution, 51, 416, 1138
Russification, 208
Russo-Japanese War, 405, **988–990**, *989*
Russo-Turkish War, 47, 426
Rwanda, 129

S

Sá, Mem de, 395
al-Saadawi, Nawal, 735, 1085
Saadi, Yacef, 256
SACPO. *See* South Africa Colored
    Peoples' Organization
Sacred Congregation for the
    Propagation of the Faith, 789
Sacred Hearts of Jesus and Mary, 980
Sacrifice, human, 121–122
Sacrifice of a Hindoo Widow on the
    Funeral Pile of Her Husband
    (Zoffany), 95
SACTU. *See* South African Congress of
    Trade Unions
al-Sadat, Anwar, *1105*
    assassination, 812
    modernization, 603
    al-Nasir, Gamal abd and, 816
    overview, 358
    United States, relations with the,
        1104
Saddam Hussein
    Iran, invasion of, 605, 1105
    Iraqi decolonization, 605
    Soviet Union, treaty with, 1102
    United States Middle East policy,
        1106
Sadrach, Kiai, 970
Safavid dynasty
    education, 338
    Mesopotamia, 641
    Ottoman Empire, 409
    overview, 636
    Portuguese, expulsion of the, 86
    trade agreements, 635
Safi al-Din, 636
Sahagún, Bernardino de
    ethnography, 961
    indigenous culture, 229

religious *vs.* civil leaders, 121
    translation, 700
Sahlins, Marshall, 457, 1083
Said, Edward, 919–920, 1083
Said ibn Sultan, 246, 271
Sa'id Pasha
    modernization, 354
    public works projects, 487
    Suez Canal, 1062–1063
Saija dan Adinda (movie), 200
Sailing, 991–992
Sailor cults, 980
Saint Augustine, Florida, 24, *531*
Saint Croix, *1069*
Saint Domingue. *See* Haiti; Haitian
    Revolution
Saint Joseph University, 501
Saint Kitts, 362
Saint Lawrence River
    exploration of, 1121
    French exploration, 464
    fur trade, 508
    New France, 844
Saint Lawrence Valley, 391
Saint Louis, 248
Saint-Simonianism, 855
Sakoku policy, 663, 667
Saladin, 624
Salafiyya, 656
Salama Musa, 1128
Salazar, António, 198, 524, 918
Salazar, Domingo de, 973
Salem settlement, 360
Salisbury, Lord. *See* Talbot, Robert
    Arthur
Salkow, Sidney, 253
Salt production, 87, 617
Samaan, Ghada, 735
Samoa
    anticolonialism, 67
    Blackbird labor trade, 137
    division of, 44
San
    Cape of Good Hope, 176
    Dutch United East India Company,
        316
Sanctions
    Commonwealth of Nations, 273
    South Africa, 84
Sanctuary of Bon Jesus do Matozinho,
    94
Sandalwood, 889
Sanders, Otto Liman von, 516
Sanders of the River (movie), 250
Sandys, Edwin, 1117

Sane Charissumus, 902
San Francisco Peace Treaty, 666
Le Sang d'Allah (movie), 250
"Sanitation syndrome," 246–247
San Lorenzo Church, 94
San Martín, José de
    Creole nationalism, 287
    independence movements, 1050,
        1051, 1123
    Peru, invasion of, 732, 910
San Remo Conference, 156, 1139
Sanson, Nicolas, 193
San Stefano, Hieronimo de, 696
Santa Ana, Antonio López, 1099
Santeria, 956
Santiago Liniers, 1050
Santillana, David, 1129
Santo Domingo, 234, *400*
Sanudo, Marino, 187
Sanusi jihad, 68
Sanusiyya brotherhood, 861
São Paulo, 243
São Tomé
    anticolonialism, 59
    Dutch West India Company, 321
    Portuguese colonialism, 918
Sapa Inca, 597–598
Sapeto, Guissepe, 401
al-Saq 'ala al-Saq (al-Shidyaq), 1127
Sarekat Islam, 376
Sarmiento, Domingo Faustino, 1085
Sartre, Jean-Paul, 56, 830, 1130
Sasanov, Sergei, 1137
Sassetti, Filippo, 521
Satha, 974
Sati, 95, 561
Satrapi, Marjane, 735
Sa'ud family, 86–87
Saudi Arabia
    clothing and fashion, 236
    decolonization, 607
    economic subsidies, United States,
        88
    oil, 88, 873
    United States, relations with, 1104
    United States military presence, 89,
        1106
Saudi General Petroleum and Mineral
    Organization, 88
Savage, Akinwade, 820
Savchenko, Igor, 251
Savigny, Friedrich Karl von, 712
Scenes from the Massacres at Chios
    (Delacroix), 96
Schall von Bell, Johann Adam, 215

Schedel, Hartmann, 189

Schermerhorn, Wim, 733

Schlegel, August Wilhelm, 957

Schnapps, 30

Schnizer, Eduard. *See* Emin Pasa

Schoendoerffer, Pierre, 255

School of Midwifery, Cairo, 768

School of Mines, 781

School of Salamanca, 949

School of Translation, 1127

Schoonover, Thomas, 795

Science, **991–996**
  Dutch United East India Company, 319
  Islamic modernism, 656–661

Scientific racism, 937–938

Scipione l'Africano (movie), 251

Scipio the African. See Scipione l'Africano (movie)

Scorched earth policy
  Boer Wars, 140
  Germany, 518
  World War I, 1135

Scotland, 440, 737

Scott, James C., 61

Scott, Ridley, 255

Scottish Enlightenment, 445, 449, 676

Scottish explorers, 1059

Scramble for Africa, **996–998**
  Berlin Conference, 132–133
  British occupation of Egypt as trigger for, 154
  chartered companies, 214
  exports, 477
  free trade imperialism, 578
  French Empire, 381
  Italy, 401
  Second British Empire, 366–367
  Sub-Saharan Africa, 1057

Scramble for concessions, **998–999**

Sea Island cotton, 283

The Searchers (movie), 251

Sea salt, 87

Sea transportation, 477

Sebastian, 521, 916, 984

Se Cathedral, 522

Secondat, Charles-Louis de
  Enlightenment, 446, 449
  L'Esprit des lois, 700
  liberal economics, 586
  Middle East, influence on the, 1127

Second British Empire, 364–369

Second Congress of the Comintern, 594

Second Police Action, 312–313

Second Treatise of Government (Locke), 445

Second United Front, 220

Secota, *828*

Secret Organization (Algeria).
  See Organisation Secrète (Algeria)

Secularism
  Atatürk, Mustafa Kemal, 107–108
  dress, 237–239
  education, 339–345
  Middle East view of, 568
  Qutb, Sayyid, 812
  Turkey, 608
  Western thought, 1128–1129

Secular modernism
  'Abd al-Raziq, 'Ali, 659
  Islamic modernism and, 656

Secular nationalism in the Middle East, **999–1001**

Sedition Act (Philippines), 1095

Segalen, Victor, 891

Segregation
  Africa, *1001,* **1001–1002**
  cities and towns, 246–247, 498
  diamond production, 303
  Japanese colonial administration, 104–105
  Morocco, 498
  port cities and towns, 258
  United States, 938
  See also Apartheid

Seigneurial tenure, 274

Sekyi, Kobina, 899

Selander, Lesley, 253–254

Selassie, Haile
  Organization of African Unity, 880, 881
  Pan-Africanism, 900
  resistance movement, 403–404

Self and other, 919

Self-determination
  East Asia and the Pacific, **1002–1003**
  Wilsonianism, 1130–1134

Self-government, 579

Self-strengthening movements, **1003–1004**
  reform, 217–218
  Taiping Rebellion, 1072

Selim I, 33, 409–410, 883

Selim II, 410

Selim III
  capitulations, 178
  military reforms, 412
  Nizam-i Cedid reforms, 340
  reforms, 565, 1125

Selkirk, Alexander, 450, 510

Semarang, 258, 261

Seminar for Oriental Languages, 515

Semiperipheral nations, 794

Sen, Mrinal, 252

Senegal
  Diagne, Blaise, 300–301
  French colonies, 490–492
  Senghor, Léopold Sédar, 1005
  settlements, 1055
  strikes, 79
  Young Senegalese Club, 78

Senghor, Léopold Sédar, 830, **1004–1005**

Sentinelle di bronzo (movie), 251

Separate but equal theory, 83–84

The Sepoy Mutiny and the Revolt of 1857 (Majumdar), 201

Sepoy Rebellion. *See* Indian Revolt of 1857

Sepoys, 612–614, **1005–1007,** *1006*
  See also Indian Revolt of 1857

September 11th attacks, 57

Sepúlveda, Juan Ginés de, 697, 949

Sericulture, 1021–1024

Servants, 470

Seton-Watson, Hugh, 286

Settlements
  Ireland, 646–648
  Sub-Saharan Africa, 1055–1058

Settler colonies
  African anticolonialism, 74
  armed resistance, 80
  British African colonies, 149–150
  British colonial law, 710
  cities and towns, 245–248
  commonwealth system, 272–273
  decolonization, 298
  law, 706
  New Netherland, 374

Settlers
  Company of New France, 274
  cultural imperialism, 575
  French Middle Eastern colonies, 496
  Libya, 861
  mezzonationalism, 818, 820–821
  Sub-Saharan Africa, 1057–1058
  thirteen colonies, British North America, 1074–1076
  Tunisia, 859

Seven Essays of Interpretation of Peruvian Reality (Mariátegui), 595

Seven Parts. *See* Siete Partidas

Seventh-Day Adventists, 976

Seven Years' War, *1122*
  Atlantic commerce, 109
  British Empire, 387
  British territorial gains, 362

British Empire, 387
cacao production, 40
Cape of Good Hope, 26
Caribbean Islands, 109, 182, 1122
coffee cultivation, 243
cotton production, 283, 284–285
Dutch Empire, 376, 378
Dutch United East India Company,
316
Enlightenment, 446, 450
exports, slaves as, 475, 478
French African colonies, 491
French Empire, 380, 392
human rights, 557–561
Latin America, 333
liberty, 700
manumission, 759–761
Middle East, **1028–1033**
Montesinos, Antonio de, 195
mortality, 993
Pacific Islands, 889
papal donations, 904
papal views, 905
plantations, *913,* 913–914
Portuguese Empire, 420
race, 929–933, 934–937
Roman Catholic Church, 952
Spanish Americas, 398
sugar plantations, 1064, 1068
thirteen colonies, British North
American, 1075–1076
United States, 43
Slaves, *936*
Cape Town, 176
clove plantations, 271
diseases, 134, 135
language, 696
Liberia, 728–729
Minas Gerais, conspiracy of, 777
Moluccas, 799, 801
St. Domingue, 538–541
United States, importation into the,
542
Slave trade
abolition, 2–4, 3*t*
alcohol, 29–30
American crops in Africa, 39
Atlantic, *1033,* **1033–1039,** *1034,*
1036, 1037, 1038
Batavia, 124
Berlin Conference, 132
Brazil, 395
British abolition, 346
British informal imperialism, 832
Caribbean Islands, 182, 1122
Cartagena de Indias, 183–184
chartered companies, 212–214
Christianity, 964
cities and towns, 245

colonial commerce, 109, 110–111
Columbian Exchange, 331
commodity trade, 270
companies and colonization, 266
Congo, 988
Dutch Empire, 373, 374
Dutch West India Company, 321–
322
Enlightenment, 446
exports, slaves as, 475, 478
First British Empire, 362
free trade and abolition, 576–577
guns, 995
human rights, 557–561
Indian Ocean, 620, **1039–1041,**
1040
Industrial Revolution, 477
language, 700–701
Old World diseases, 134–135
Ottoman Empire, 1028–1032
plantations, 913–914, *914*
Portuguese colonial law, 719
Portuguese Empire, 420
Protestant missions, 956
race, 931
Roman Catholic Church, 952
Sierra Leone, 1019–1021
Spanish Americas, 1049
statistics, 23
Sub-Saharan Africa, 1054–1055
sugar plantations, 1065
world-system theory, 796
Slave Trade Abolition Act, 1021
Slavin, David Henry, 250
Sloane, Hans, 93
A Small Place (Kincaid), 1085
Smallpox, 135, *136,* 599, 994
Smeatham, Henry, 1020
Smissaert, 672
Smith, Adam, *587*
abolition, 3, 4
companies and monopolies, 267
Enlightenment thought, 449
free trade, 366, 576
history, stages of, 1044
laissez-faire economics, 586–587
mercantilism, 679, 772
Turgot, influence of, 591
Smith, Ian, 820–821
Smith, John, 464
Smith, John Hope, 100
Smith, Thomas, 674, 704, 1115
Smuts, Jan, 83, 140, 1091
Snaats, Cornelia, 1111
Snouck Hurgronje, Christiaan, 9, 10,
1041–1044
Soares de Albergaria, Lopo, 419, 521
Soarez de Mello, Diogo, 974

Sobel, Dava, 191
Sobieski, Jan, 885
Social change, 211
Social class
clothing and fashion, 236
codfish, 113
coffee cultivation, 242
piracy, 167
The Social Contract and Discourses
(Rousseau), 103
Social Darwinism, **1044–1046**
Africa, scramble for, 997
Algeria, 496
assimilation, 104
cultural imperialism, 572–576, 575
Eurocentrism, 459
justification for empire, 676, 679
race, 937–938
United States, 431
Social Democrats (Iran), 640
Social evolution. *See* Social Darwinism
Social Gospel Movement, 790, 967
Socialism
anti-Americanism, 54
Arab world, 1128
Hong Kong, 556
Mao Zedong, 762–763
Middle East, 1102
Nkrumah, Kwame, 851–852
Nyerere, Julius, 865
Pan-African Congress, 897, 898
Pan-Africanism, 901
social revolution as precondition
for, 593
Socialism and Colonial Policy (Kautsky),
593
Socialist Party (Iran), 640
Socialist Republic of Vietnam, 507
Social patronage, 1032
Social policy and religion, 230
Social revolution, 594
Social status
opium, 875
race, 931
sex and sexuality, 1007–1008
Social structure
African Muslims, 653–654
cultural imperialism, 572–573
Dutch United East India Company,
317
education, 341
freeburghers, 493
Inca Empire, 598
Indian Army, 613–614
Indian National Movement, 614
Korea, 690
labor systems, 333–334

Vedanta, 956

Vega, Garcilaso de la, 448, 731, 1094

Vegetable oil industry, 270, 1056

Veiled Protectorate, 1108

Veiling, 236, 237–238

Velasco, Luis de, 722

Velázquez, Diego de, 281, 466, 545

Velázquz Chávez, Agustín, 98

Velho, Álvaro, 511

Vellore mutiny, 1007

Venezuela, 174, 267–268

Venice, 410–412, 635, 1023

Venkatappa, Damarla, 439

Verbiest, Ferdinand, 215

Verdi, Giuseppe Fortunino Francisco, 1063

Verenigde Oost-Indische Compagnie. *See* Dutch United East India Company

Vernacular medicine, 768

Verrazano, Giovanni da, 390, 508, 844

Verres, Gaius, 308–309

Versailles palace, 91–92

Versailles Peace Conference, 1019

Vertical archipelagos, 598

Verwoerd, H. F., 26, 84

Vesconte, Pietro, 187

Vespucci, Amerigo, *466,* **1114–1115**
    Brazil, 394, 398
    cartography, 187, 192
    South American exploration, 465

Veyre, Gabriel, 250

Viajes por Europa, Africa, y América (Sarmiento), 1085

Viceroyalties, 400, 530, 721–722

Victoria I
    art, 91
    Indian sovereignty, 621, 622
    India policy, 365, 609, 610

Videla, Jorge, 201

Vieira da Silva, Luís, 777

Vienna, siege of, 885, *885*

La Vie Scélérate (Condé), 1085

Viet Minh independence movement, 506

Vietnam
    anticolonialism, 60–61
    French colonialism, 502–507
    French Empire, 382
    Japanese occupation, 1047
    movies, 255
    occupation, 868–869
    Western religion, 974–975

Vietnam War
    anti-Americanism, 56

Nixon, Richard, 837
    self-determination, 1003

Vijayanagara, 520

Villagization, 865

Villegagnon, Nicolas Durand de, 391, 983–984

Vincent, David, 785

Virginia
    colonization, 1121
    cultural imperialism, 574
    English-Native American relations, 232
    government, 526, 527
    Native Americans, 828, *828*
    representative government, 526, 527
    settlement, 385, 1074–1075
    tobacco, 1078–1079

Virginia Company, **1115–1117**
    charter, 385
    Jamestown, 526, *1116*
    settlement, 1075
    tobacco, 1079

Virginia Company of London, 463–464

Virginia Company of Plymouth, 463

"Virgin Lands scheme," 207

Virgin of Guadelupe, 1050

The Virgin of the Navigators (Fernañdez), 90

Vitoria, Francisco de
    Enlightenment, 446, 448
    justifications for empire, 674, 677
    language, 700
    natural rights, 705, 724
    papal donations, 905
    Sepúlveda, criticism of, 949

Vivekananda, 958

VOC. *See* Dutch United East India Company

Vodou, 956

Vohor, Serge, 1114

Voice of the Arabs radio, 1103

Voltaire
    anticolonialism, 61, 450
    commerce, 586
    Enlightenment, 446
    Indian religions, 956
    Middle East, influence on the, 1127
    slavery and freedom, 700

Von der Goltz, Colmar, 1137

Von Haller, Albrecht, 450–451

Von Humboldt, Alexander, 286, 1082

Von Kotzebue, Otto, 763

Von Lettow-Vorbeck, Paul, 1135

Von Sanders, Otto Liman, 1137

Von Trotha, Genera, 351

Voor-Compangieën, 314

Voortrekker Monument, *27*

Voortrekkers, 26

Vorontsov-Dashkov, Count, 428

Vorster, B. J., 26

Voting rights, 139

Voyage autour du monde (Bougainville), 448

A Voyage Round the World. See Voyage autour du monde (Bougainville)

W

Wafd
    Egyptian nationalism, 356–357, 603
    secular nationalism, 999
    Sha'rawi, Huda, 1014

Wafdist Women's Central Committee, 1014

Wages, 593, 1007

Wahhabi movement, 68, 86

Waitangi, **1119**

Walcott, Derek, 919

Waldseemüller, Martin, *186, 187,* 192, 1115

Walker, William, 1099

Wallace-Johnson, Isaac, 900

Wallachia, 49–50

Wallerstein, Immanuel, 596, 793–798

Wallis, Samuel, 507, 915

Walvin, James, 1065

Wangenheim, Hans von, 515

Waqfs, 623

War captives. *See* Prisoners of war

War crimes
    Dutch Army, 985
    Japan, 665

Ward, Frederick T., 775, 1072

Warfare
    arms, 95–996
    communication, 993
    slave trade, 1035, 1037
    Spain and Britain, 1049

Wargnier, Régis, 255

Warlords, 218–219, 223, 877

War of Independence, Algerian, 34–35, 860

War of Spanish Succession, 167, 360, 387, 903

War of the Knives, 540

"War on terror," 436, 726, 1106

Warrant chiefs, Africa, **1123–1125,** *1124*
    dual mandate, 311
    Igbo Women's War, 570, 571
    Lugard, Frederick, 738
    Nigeria, 630

"Warring States" period, 667
Wars and empires, **1119–1123**
Washington, Bushrod, 37
Washington, George, 41, 430, *1122*
Washington Naval Conference, 324, 867, 874, 940
Watchman Nee. *See* Ni Duosheng
Watchtower movement, 1136
Water diversion projects, 754
Wa Thiong'o, Ngugi, 351
Watson, A. K., 852
Watson, Charles, 175
Watt, Harry, 254
Wauter, Father, 348
al-Wazzani, Hassan, 860
Wealth
    Enlightenment thought, 449
    Marxist theories, 593
The Wealth and Benefits of the Spanish Monarchy under Charles III (Tiepolo), 90
The Wealth of Nations (Smith), 3, 267, 366, 449, 586–587, 772, 774
Weapons, *994*
    technology, 75, 995–996
    United States-Israeli alliance, 1104
    See also Guns
Weapons of mass destruction, 1106
Weaving industry, 280
Weber, Max, 958
Weimar Republic, 517
Wellesley, Marquis, 162, 175
Wellesley, Richard, *440*
Wellman, William, 250
Wells, H. G., 1128
Werndly, George Hendrik, 318
West, Benjamin, 91
West Africa
    Aborigines' Rights Protection Society, 6–7
    alcohol, 29, 30, 31
    anticolonialism, 60
    armed resistance, 74, 75
    Asante Wars, 100–102
    assimilation, 103
    association, 105–106
    British presence in, 147–148
    cacao cultivation, 40
    commodity trade, 270
    decolonization, 298
    Dutch Empire, 372
    Dutch West India Company, 322
    French colonies, 490–493

Islam, 652–654
    Kingsley, Mary, 1084
    maize, 335
    mass political parties, 296
    mission schools, 347–348
    Portuguese colonialism, 918
    settlements, 1055
    slave trade, 19, 362, 1122
    strikes, 79
    Sumatra Treaty, 8
    transatlantic slave trade, effects of the, 1035–1037
West African Pilot (newspaper), 118
West African Youth League, 78
West Bank, 1104, 1105
Westerling, Raymond, 985
Western areas removal scheme, 759
Western culture
    Japan, 329, 664
    Marxist theories of imperialism, 595
    mezzonationalism, 819–820
    Middle East, 1125–1130
    Muslim Africans, 654–655
    self-strengthening movements, 1004
Western economic expansion in Arabia, **85–89**
Western education
    cultural imperialism, 574–575
    indigenous elites, 478, 561–562, 567
    Snouck Hurgronje, Christiaan, 1044
Western Education and the Nigerian Cultural Background (Nduka), 349
Western education in Africa, **345–353**
Western European anti-Americanism, 55–56
Western hemisphere, 187
Western historiography, 816
Westernization
    dress, 237–238
    Egypt, 626
    Iran, 604
    Islamic modernism, 656
    self-strengthening movements, 1003–1004
    Siam, 1018–1019
Western medicine, 768–769
Western perceptions
    of traditional religions, **954–959**
    of world religions, **959–963**
Western religion
    Africa, **963–966**
    East Asia, **966–968**

Pacific Islands, **979–981**
    Southeast Asia, **968–979**
Westerns, 251, 254–255
Western Samoa, 293
Western thought, Middle East, **1125–1130**
Westervolt Treaty, 683
West Germany Society for Colonization and Export, 517
West India Company
    Dutch Empire, 371, 372–374, 388–390
    Netherlands Missionary Society and, 842
West Indies
    Britain, relationship with, 527
    British Empire, 386–387, 387, 388
    coolie labor, 8
    decolonization, 367–368
    Dutch Empire, 372, 373
    English colonization of, 648
    English indentured servants, 443
    European immigrants, 469, 470
    race, 932–933
    Second British Empire, 367–368
    sugar, 914, 1064–1066, 1068–1069
West Indies Federation, 367–368
West of Zanzibar (movie), 254
West Papua, 1002–1003
West Timor, 330
Westward expansion, U.S., 429
Whaling, 889
Wheatley, Phillis, 701
Wheaton, Henry, 1149
Whipping, 987–988
White, John, 92, 93
White, Luise, 248
"White Australia" policy, 115–116
Whitefield, George, 1076
White Lotus Rebellion, 217
"The White Man's Burden" (Kipling), 938
White Revolution, 345, 604–605, 895–896
White Skin, Black Masks (Fanon), 920
White Squadron. See Squadrone bianco (movie)
White supremacy, 819–820
White Women's Protection Ordinance, 906
Whitney, Eli, 282
Wijayabahu IV, 683
Wilberforce, William, 3, 346, 1020
Wilhelm II, 515
Wilhelmina, 452
Wilkes, Charles, 889

Xenophobia
    Boxer Uprising, 790
    China, 328, 967
    racism *vs.,* 934
Ximenes brothers, 521
Xinjiang, 209

Y

Yaa Asantewaa, 77, 102
Yakub Beg, 205
Yandabo Treaty, 45
Yanqui Years, 836
Yaquis, 829
Years of the Century (television series), 199
Yellow fever, 135–136
Yellow journalism, 432
Yogyakarta, 672
Yokohama, 329
Yom Kippur/Ramadan War, 358, 1104
Yoruba
    armed resistance, 75
    dual mandate, 311
    slave trade, 1035
Yorubaland, 311
Young Algerians, 856
Young Egypt, 357
Younghusband, Francis, 1077
Young Kikuyu Association, 1136
Young Men's Christian Association, 790
Young Ottomans
    Islamic Modernism, 658
    Islamic reformism, 566
Young Senegalese, 78, 300–301
Young Turks

Abdülhamid II, opposition to, 1–2, 50
    Atatürk, Mustafa Kemal, 106
    capitulations, 179
    education, 341
    German relations with, 516
    Ottoman Empire, 414–416
Yuan Shikai, 218, 222, 999
Yusuf Adil Shah, 520
Yusuf Gurgi, 520

Z

Zacatecas, 779, 781
Zaghlul, Sa'ad
    anticolonialism, 861
    deportation, 356
    nationalism, 603
    secular nationalism, 999
Zahiriyya library, 659
Zambia, 148, 1058
Zand tribe, 637
Zanzibar
    clove plantations, 271
    Indian Ocean trade, 619–620
    Omar's separation from, 86
    overview, 245–246
Zapolyai, John, 884
Zayed bin al-Nahyan, 609
Zeehandelaar, Stella, 86
Zeki, Salih, 336
Zeng Guofan, 730, 1071–1072
Zhang Zhidong, 1003
Zheng Boshao, 151
Zheng Chenggong, 215, 315, 472
Zheng Guanying, 275
Zheng He, 224, 617

Zhu Dachun, 275
Ziamet system, 625
Zikist Movement, 118
Zimbabwe
    archives, destruction of, 197–198
    armed resistance, 80
    British control of, 148
    decolonization, 298
    Machel, Samore, 745
    mass migration, 76
    Rhodes, Cecil, 303
    sanctions, 273
    settlers, 1057
Zinn, Howard, 837
Zionism
    anticolonialism, 73
    Arab nationalism, 1000
    Balfour Declaration, 155–156
    German foreign policy, 517
    Iraq, 645
    nationalism, 567
    United States foreign policy, 1101–1105
    World War I, 1139
Zoffany, Johann, 95
Zola, Émile, 291
Zongli Yamen, **1149–1150**
Zoological Society in London, 941
Zorita, Alonzo de, 61, 722
Zulu
    anticolonialism, 59
    Boers, attack on the, 533
Zulu Dawn (movie), 254
Zululand, 1150
Zulu (movie), 254
Zulu Wars, 96, **1150–1151**, *1151*

The Natior

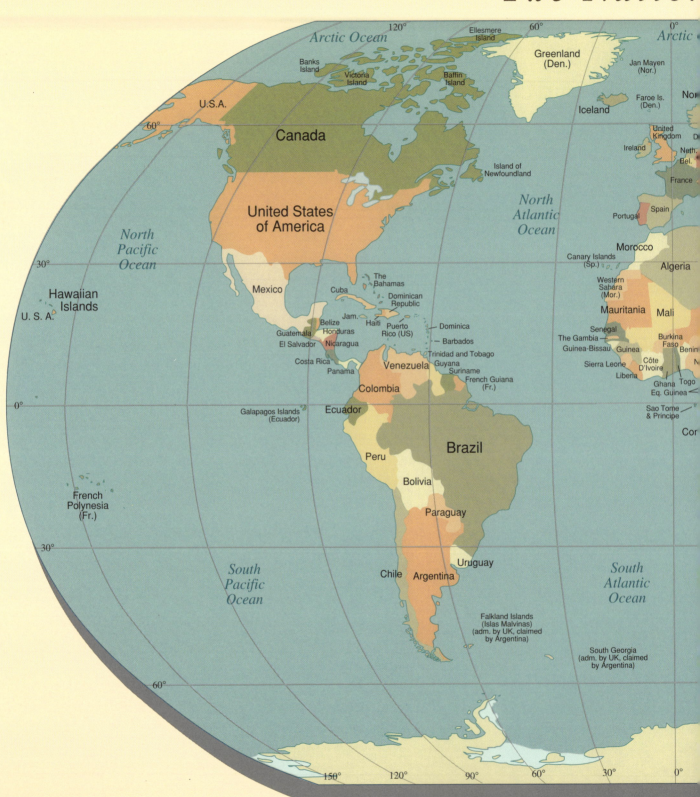

Arctic Ocean

120°

Ellesmere Island

60°

Greenland (Den.)

0°

Arctic

Banks Island

Jan Mayen (Nor.)

Victoria Island

Baffin Island

Faroe Is. (Den.)

Nor

U.S.A.

60°

Iceland

Canada

United Kingdom

D

Ireland

Neth.

Bel.

Island of Newfoundland

North Atlantic Ocean

France

Portugal

Spain

North Pacific Ocean

30°

Morocco

Canary Islands (Sp.)

Algeria

United States of America

Mexico

The Bahamas

Western Sahara (Mor.)

Hawaiian Islands

U. S. A.

Cuba

Dominican Republic

Mauritania

Mali

Jam.

Haiti

Belize

Guatemala

Honduras

Puerto Rico (US)

Dominica

Senegal

Burkina Faso

Benin

El Salvador

Nicaragua

Barbados

The Gambia

Guinea-Bissau

Guinea

N

Costa Rica

Venezuela

Trinidad and Tobago

Sierra Leone

Côte D'Ivoire

Panama

Guyana

Liberia

Galapagos Islands (Ecuador)

Colombia

Suriname

French Guiana (Fr.)

Ghana

Togo

Eq. Guinea

0°

Ecuador

Sao Tome & Principe

Cor

Peru

Brazil

French Polynesia (Fr.)

Bolivia

30°

Paraguay

Uruguay

South Atlantic Ocean

Chile

Argentina

South Pacific Ocean

Falkland Islands (Islas Malvinas) (adm. by UK, claimed by Argentina)

South Georgia (adm. by UK, claimed by Argentina)

60°

150°

120°

90°

60°

30°

0°

© MAGELLAN Geographix℠ Santa Barbara, CA (800) 929-4MAP